THE NATURAL ADVANTAGE OF NATIONS

Business Opportunities, Innovation and Governance in the 21st Century

Edited by

Karlson 'Charlie' Hargroves and Michael H. Smith

EARTHSCAN

London • Sterling, VA

First published by Earthscan in the UK and USA in hardback in 2005 and
in paperback in 2006
Hardback edition reprinted 2005, 2006
Paperback edition reprinted 2006

ISBN-10: 1-84407-121-9 (hardback)
  1-84407-340-8 (paperback)
ISBN-13: 978-1-84407-121-0 (hardback)
  978-1-84407-340-5 (paperback)

Typesetting by MapSet Ltd, Gateshead, UK
Printed and bound in the UK by The Bath Press
Cover design by Andrew Corbett

This publication was developed by The Natural Edge Project (TNEP) in collaboration
with a range of international partners, co-authors, reviewers and supporters. For more
information on TNEP please refer to **www.naturaledgeproject.net**

For a full list of publications please contact:
Earthscan
8–12 Camden High Street
London, NW1 0JH, UK
Tel: +44 (0)20 7387 8558
Fax: +44 (0)20 7387 8998
Email: earthinfo@earthscan.co.uk
Web: **www.earthscan.co.uk**

22883 Quicksilver Drive, Sterling, VA 20166-2012, USA

Earthscan is an imprint of James & James (Science Publishers) Ltd and publishes in
association with the International Institute for Environment and Development

A catalogue record for this book is available from the British Library

Library of Congress Cataloging-in-Publication Data

The natural advantage of nations : business opportunities, innovation, and governance
in the 21st century / edited by Karlson 'Charlie' Hargroves and Michael H. Smith.
    p. cm.
  Includes bibliographical references and index.
  ISBN 1-84407-121-9 (hardback)
  1. Sustainable development. 2. Economic development—Environmental aspects.
3. Technological innovations—Environmental aspects. 4. Business enterprises—
Environmental aspects. 5. Environmental policy—International cooperation.
6. Environmental protection—International cooperation. 7. Sustainable
development—International cooperation. I. Hargroves, Karlson, 1974- II. Smith,
Michael H., 1969-

HC79.E5N3546 2004
338.9'27—dc22

2004019814

This book is printed on elemental chlorine free paper

Until one is committed, there is hesitancy, the chance to draw back. Concerning all acts of initiative (and creation), there is one elementary truth the ignorance of which kills countless ideas and splendid plans: that the moment one definitely commits oneself, then Providence moves too. All sorts of things occur to help one that would never otherwise have occurred. A whole stream of events issues from the decision, raising in one's favor all manner of unforeseen incidents and meetings and material assistance, which no man could have dreamed would have come his way. Whatever you can do, or dream you can do, begin it. Boldness has genius, power, and magic in it. Begin it now.

William H. Murray, The Scottish Himalayan Expedition (1951), incorporating the words of Johann Wolfgang von Goethe

CONTENTS

SECTION 1: THE NEED FOR A NEW PARADIGM

SECTION 3: ACHIEVING A NATURAL ADVANTAGE OF NATIONS

SECTION 5: A NATIONAL COLLABORATIVE APPROACH: THE BIGGER PICTURE – BUILDING RESILIENCE

LIST OF FIGURES AND TABLES

Figures

Tables

FOREWORD BY ALAN ATKISSON

To-do List for a Sustainable Civilization

The challenge of sustainability places greater demands on us than is commonly understood. People often speak of 'balancing' economic, social and environmental needs – as though performing a mere tight-rope act, a skilful stroll above the crowd and the safety-net, was all that was required. But there is no safety-net; to fail is to crash. The crowd cannot just watch; all must participate. And we need far more than balance: we need *transformation*, a wave of social, technical and economic innovation that will touch every person, community, company, institution and nation on the Earth. The irony is that this transformation is still viewed as an economic 'cost', when it is in fact an enormous economic *opportunity* – an opportunity that we are increasingly being forced to recognize. Consider the widening abyss between how we run our economies and what Nature's systems can tolerate. Consider the rising levels of international tension as gaps widen between the have-a-lots and the have-not-at-alls, the techno-rich and the food-and-water-poor. Consider that we are rapidly losing whole peoples, whole species, whole ecosystems. Technology is, of course, an enormous blessing. Bhutanese villages celebrate the arrival of electricity as though it were 'the coming of the sun'. Few alive today understand the horror of smallpox and other diseases that have been all but eradicated (even though other diseases, like AIDS and malaria, continue to haunt us). Who wants to turn back the clock on dental care, or withhold it from those who do not yet have it?

The developed world's quality of life represents success in the human struggle of a hundred thousand years – the struggle for survival, health, longer life, safety from Nature's unpredictable rages, comfort, happiness. Those living in the world's richer demographic groups can now expect their children to grow up healthy, to see grandchildren do the same and to watch all this from the vantage point of technology-based personal satisfaction. But this amazing accomplishment has come to us via catastrophically destructive methods. It is physically impossible to spread such wonders to the whole world, doing things the way we do them now. It is very likely impossible even to maintain this quality of life for those who already have it, without enormous changes. In the industrialized world, we do not need 'sustainable development'. We need sustainable *re*-development, a set of transformations in the direction of sustainability, in virtually every sector. Here are just a few of the challenges we actually face, challenges that we inherited from our recent ancestors and that we will almost certainly pass on to our descendants:

The complete redevelopment of our energy systems. Energy is the life-blood of our economies but producing it is destroying our climate, damaging our health and degrading nature. We must make our energy sources and systems climate-neutral, or better yet climate-restorative. This transformation involves much more than just energy efficiency or hybrid engines. We must either put fossil-carbon-based energy systems essentially to rest in our cars, planes and power plants; or we must find a way to permanently sequester the carbon and manage the Earth's atmosphere, permanently.

The complete redevelopment of chemical, material and building technologies. While we have begun a transformation in all these areas, the work remains far from finished. We still release dizzying amounts of poisonous substances into nature, where they accumulate in living bodies. We still build incredibly wasteful, toxic and inefficient products and buildings. We are now adding the wild cards of nanotechnology and biotechnology to this strange brew. How we make things, and how we *think* about how we make things, must change radically.

The complete redevelopment of industrial agriculture. If we are to feed the world and coming generations, we need farming and food production systems that do not depend on fossil fuel, fossil water, chemical pesticides, ever-increasing nitrogen fertilizers and the like. Despite many wonderful experiments with change, most people's very lives still depend on one or all these things – all of which are known to be dangerous, devastating, or deadly. This is perhaps the transformation nearest to our survival needs.

The preservation of the world's remaining species and ecosystems. I say 'remaining' to remind us that much is already lost. The cost of that loss is immeasurable, even in gross economic, human-centred terms. Cures for cancer, models for chemical production and farmable sources of food have all certainly disappeared, without our knowing it. Gone already are many sources of inspiration, joy and – think of the dodo – even laughter. 'Nature' as we have known it for millennia is disappearing. And yet there is no more precious inheritance to preserve for future generations than the richness of life itself.

Stable and long-lasting international peace. We must never forget that human beings have created the means to destroy whole cities at the press of a button. We have created garbage with the power to poison us and other creatures for thousands of years. We are, as I have written elsewhere, 'doomed to a high-technology future', because we must forever maintain our technical capacity to deal with the results of opening Pandora's Box. For this and so many other reasons, striving for basic peace, stability and security is not an ideal; it is a precondition for the maintenance of civilization.

Given the scale of these challenges, perhaps our greatest need is a drastic increase in the number of people who understand them, accept them and dedicate their efforts to addressing them. This book is meant to support just such an increase in committed engagement. And fortunately, the increase is well under way, as the number of people working directly on 'sustainability', or incorporating it into their existing work, continues to grow exponentially. In part, this increase is driven by moral concerns and idealistic feelings, as well it should be. The development of morality and the ability to envision better futures are fundamental to the human animal. Love and vision are our 'better angels'.

But one need not be an impassioned visionary to understand the profound economic advantages of embracing sustainable (re)development. In the transition from horse-drawn carriages to cars, from firewood to fossil fuel, from typewriters to the Internet, tremendous fortunes have been made. The transformation to next-generation energy, transport, agriculture and industry – indeed the rebuilding of the 20th century's ageing and increasingly dangerous infrastructure – will make greater fortunes still. And the past century's best examples have already given us plenty of case study proof that morality and profit can be easily combined to conserve habitat, reduce poverty and build peace. The continuing explosion of creative and determined efforts to build a world that is environmentally, economically, socially and humanly healthy is hope-giving. But it is not so hard to understand. If this book's 'to-do list for a sustainable civilization' is not worth the dedication of a life's work, what is?

Stockholm, Sweden
26 March 2004

FOREWORD BY AMORY B. LOVINS

'To be truly radical', said critic Raymond Williams, 'is to make hope possible, rather than despair convincing.' That is the charge of anyone who thinks it's better to avoid problems than solve them, and better to solve them than whinge about them. It is also the purpose of this book and the opportunity of all who read it. I recently taught a college class where a young lady bleakly explained how she'd lost hope. Every step forward was offset by two steps back; politics was irreparably corrupted; community was eroding; destruction had gained the upper hand. She felt she could never bring children into such a world. Yet as further discussion revealed, she had not actually lost hope. She knew exactly where she'd left it. So do we all. If we've set down this precious bundle somewhere on the path, it's time to pick it up again, strengthened in our common purpose by the many signs of renewal glimmering all around us, even in the darkest times and the most unexpected places. Many big changes in the world are now converging to help those whose hearts are guided by hope, brains by invention (which Edwin Land called 'a sudden cessation of stupidity') and hands by the discipline of the severely practical.

Today the foci of power and action in the world are tripolar: business, civil society and government (all too often in order of decreasing effectiveness). More than perhaps any other institution, business has the leadership, management, resources, skill, speed, innovation, integration and motivation to solve tough problems quickly. Such a dynamic force in a tripolar world creates many new ways to get things done. No longer need one wait for new public policies to emerge from the legislative sausage-works. To do what government should do but often can't or won't, business is increasingly teaming up with civil society – whether in outright collaboration, in predator–prey coevolution, in response to customers' market preferences, or in the certain knowledge that sustaining one's public franchise or 'licence to operate' depends on public approbation that is hard to earn and easy to forfeit. Business leaders increasingly realize that green innovations can make money and make sense, simultaneously and without compromise. Business can evolve, as Interface Inc's Chairman Ray C. Anderson puts it, to take nothing, waste nothing, do no harm – and do very, very well by doing good.

Another revolution comes from demographics. Brains (as Libba Pinchot reminds us) are evenly distributed, one per person. Most of the brains are therefore in the developing world, and half are in the heads of women. As women, the poor and the oppressed gain a greater voice, they become better able to contribute their ideas to the global conversation and spread them through the new global nervous system so solutions emerge faster. Teaching and technology transfer are starting to flow ever faster from poor to rich – if the rich gain the humble and receptive spirit to learn. So far as we know, there is nothing in the Universe so powerful as 6 billion minds wrapping round a problem. And the problems we have, from the village to the planet, suffice to concentrate those minds wonderfully.

Another powerfully emerging force for good is the revolution in design – in the translation of intention into action. Turning depletion into pollution, resources into wastes, is a problem we needn't have, and it's cheaper not to. Radical resource productivity, far from costing more, typically costs *less up front*. In recent months, my colleagues and I have helped major firms worldwide to redesign over US$10 billion worth of major facilities – from a giant LNG plant in Australia to a microchip fabrication plant in Texas, from a hydrocarbon synthesis plant in the Middle East to the world's largest platinum mine a kilometre beneath South Africa. Without exception, we find enormous scope for saving energy, water, pollution and money while reducing capital expenditure in new installations, or with paybacks of a few years or less in retrofits. Whether it's saving 92–98 per cent of the energy in a pumping loop, 89 per cent in a data centre, 50–70 per cent in a supermarket or 90+ per cent in a home or office, the bar has been reset far higher than we dared to leap before – yet surpassing it is easier than ever. The bigger the savings get nowadays, the *cheaper* they get – turning diminishing returns into expanding returns through the new kind of design described in *Natural Capitalism* and here.

This wouldn't be possible, of course, if those facilities had been properly designed in the first place. Typically their designers had optimized isolated components for single benefits, thereby 'pessimizing' the system. Designing instead to optimize whole systems for multiple benefits yields multiple forms of value from single expenditures. Expertly practised, this can often cut energy and resource use by fourfold, tenfold, even a hundredfold, whilst reducing capital expenditure, slashing operational expenditure and improving performance. Few if any engineering schools yet teach this rediscovered Victorian systems engineering: we need a fundamental shift in how design is taught and done. Rocky Mountain Institute's 10XE (Factor Ten Engineering) project, which The Natural Edge Project is supporting, therefore aims to create a compelling casebook of such designs, ranging across all the engineering applications and their main applications, to serve as a fulcrum to leverage the non-violent overthrow of bad engineering. Meanwhile, the word is spreading among business leaders that what was considered impossible is now not just possible but deliciously profitable, and that many of today's inefficient technologies are worth so much more dead than alive that we should pay bounty-hunters to find and scrap them.

A fruitful question as we choose technologies is how to make them the right size for the job. The hallmarks of advanced industrial economies are gigantic, vulnerable, highly centralized infrastructures: power plants and grids, potable-water plants, sewerage and wastewater treatment plants, wireline telecoms, hub airports, car-centric land use, vast farms. Yet *Small Is Profitable* found ample evidence that the lowest-cost size is often orders of magnitude smaller than today's norms. Rather than connecting all our new buildings to remote infrastructure via pipes and wires, we may find that all the purposes so served can now be better served by autonomous services at the scale of the building itself.

Another key part of the design revolution comes from Janine Benyus's synthesis in *Biomimicry: Innovation Inspired by Nature*. For the past 3.8 billion years, nature's design genius has been learning what works. From zany experimentation and rigorous testing came roughly 99 per cent successful failures (designs that didn't work, all long recalled by the Manufacturer) and 1 per cent successes – the life around us. With nature as model, mentor and measure, we can imitate how life makes things, how they work and how they fit to achieve succession and resilience. The biomimetic revolution – every bit as important as nanotechnology but a lot less double-edged – is only just beginning, but it will change everything. Whether you want to dissipate heat, show colour, glue things underwater, extract water from air, whatever – somewhere in the world is an organism that can teach you how to do it with brilliant innovation, benign insouciance and elegant frugality. The Zero Emissions Research Initiative (ZERI) applies its own flavour of bio-innovation to remarkably effective practical solutions for development challenges. The 'biophilic' design of buildings that embracing nature can also make people healthier, happier and more productive. The knock-on benefits of better thermal, visual and acoustic comfort can be immensely valuable: 6–16 per cent higher labour productivity,

40 per cent higher retail sales. In Curitiba, Brazil, my team recently installed simple lightshelves in a primary schoolroom. The 75 per cent electricity saving let the school afford books. Students also learn approximately 10–26 per cent faster in well-daylit classrooms. Those sheets of white wood or plastic, guiding the light up on the ceiling where it belongs, become really important when you remember the multiplier from education to democracy and prosperity. And such multi-purpose investments may soon become financeable through Hank Patton's institutional innovation of 'intergenerational commerce' – a partnership that enables our descendents, despite not having been born yet, to buy in today's marketplace the goods and services, or the abated bads and nuisance, that best serve their interests as well as ours.

Even the world's biggest problems are falling before the power of a vision across boundaries. Those who believe, for example, that protecting the climate will be dreadfully costly have got the amount perhaps about right but the sign wrong, for a simple reason: saving fuel costs far less than buying it, so climate protection is profitable even if climate is valued at zero. DuPont set out to raise its energy productivity in this decade by at least 6 per cent a year (the same rate IBM has sustained) whilst shifting a fourth of its raw materials and a tenth of its energy to renewable sources and cutting its 2010 greenhouse gas emissions by 65 per cent below the 1990 level. Through 2003, DuPont had cut those emissions by 67 per cent and saved US$1.5 billion. STMicroelectronics, one of the world's largest chip makers, has similarly cut electricity use per chip by 6 per cent per year with a 2.5-year average payback just by retrofitting its plants. (New plants offer manyfold efficiency gains at reduced capital expenditure.) BP bashfully announced in 2003 that its 2010 goal for operational carbon reductions (10 per cent below 1990 emissions) had been achieved seven years early at no net cost. Actually the firm's net *profit* from this accomplishment was US$0.65 billion, because efficiency is that much cheaper than fuel.

These and many other private-sector examples of profitable climate protection are but the tip of a vast world of integrative benefits just coming into view. In July 2004, my team at RMI will publish *Winning the Oil Endgame: American Innovation for Profits, Jobs, and Security*. Co-sponsored by the Pentagon, for all the right reasons, this study shows how to get the US – and any other society so inclined – *completely* off oil, attractively, rather rapidly and profitably even for oil companies. No magic is required – just methodical application of modern techniques for using oil very efficiently, displacing some with saved natural gas, and replacing the rest with a least-cost mixture of biofuels and hydrogen. The efficiency opportunities alone, if fully used in 2025, could save half the projected oil use at half its price, but with none of its hidden costs or nasty side-effects.

Oddly, nobody seems to have added this up before. It's a bit like the mid-1850s, when American whalers ran out of customers before they ran out of whales: whale oil's high price had already elicited fatal competitors (kerosene and manufactured gas, both made from coal) even before whale stocks crashed or Drake struck oil in Pennsylvania. The whalers were surprised, because they hadn't paid enough attention to what was on the market or emerging from the lab (ultimately including electric lighting). Now history may be about to repeat itself with petroleum as private enterprise discovers the compelling case for providing oil's services more cheaply without it. Innovative public policies can help, but fundamentally the transition to the post-oil economy will be led by business for profit. This will be good for the world, and all the more so if other countries seize their own opportunities – most of all if China fulfils its potential to leapfrog the West.

Consider, for example, a single compact fluorescent globe (lamp), of which nearly a billion are made each year (mostly in China). It yields the same light as an incandescent globe whilst using 75–80 per cent less electricity and lasting 5–13 times longer. Over its life it will make its owner about US$30–70 richer and will keep a tonne of CO_2 out of the air. Such globes, deployed in numbers, can cut by a fifth the evening peak load that crashes the Mumbai grid, or raise an American chicken-grower's profits by a fourth, or boost a Haitian family's disposable income by as much as a third. Making the globe needs about 10,000 times less capital than supplying additional electricity to produce the same light from incandescent globes. Such savings could turn the power sector, now devouring a fourth of the world's development capital, into a net *exporter* of capital to fund other development needs. Compact fluorescents are also the key to affordable solar power for the homes of 2 billion poor people without electricity, so girls can learn to read at night, greatly advancing the role of women. Compact fluorescents are cheaper for an electricity company to give away than just to *operate* its existing thermal power stations. You can buy such a globe and install it yourself. One globe at a time, we can make the whole globe fairer and safer. Sometimes, as Churchill reminded us, one must do what is necessary.

As summarized in *Natural Capitalism*, that task and opportunity are arrestingly simple. The first Industrial Revolution made people 100 times more productive because people were relatively scarce while nature seemed boundless. The next industrial revolution faces the opposite challenge – abundant people and scarce nature. Therefore it uses nature 10–100 times more productively, with integrative design that makes very large resource savings cost *less* than small or no savings. It produces in closed loops with no waste and no toxicity. In its 'solutions economy' business model, service providers and customers both profit from doing more and better with less for longer. Their increased profits support reinvestment in natural capital. These four interlinked ways of behaving as if natural capital were properly valued are called 'natural capitalism' because they productively use and reinvest in the natural capital that supports all life. Even today, when nature is valued at approximately zero, natural capitalist firms are achieving higher profits, lower risks, more innovative and excited workers, happier customers and strong competitive advantage. This approach appears to offer important potential benefits for development, and is receiving encouraging attention in China. That nation's 5000 years of experience teaches that societies whose human wisdom follows the way of nature and nurtures nature's fecundity will outlast societies whose human cleverness liquidates natural capital. So arises the natural advantage of nations.

Striving to become much higher primates is a risky business with an uncertain outcome in a dangerous world. The bold evolutionary experiment of combining a large forebrain with opposable thumbs clearly has its dangers and drawbacks; the jury is still out on whether it was ultimately a good idea. But it has equipped us to avoid or solve the problems we've created, and already the search for intelligent life on earth is turning up promising specimens. We are all starting to realize that 'We are the people we have been waiting for'.

There is much hard work to do, much suffering in the Universe, much to be fixed and healed. Making the world better and more life-sustaining, its beings healthy and whole, its people free from fear from privation or attack, is an endless task in progress, but one worthy of our species' promise and potential. We need good tools and provisions for our common journey. *The Natural Advantage of Nations* will help guide that long passage from here to hope.

Rocky Mountain Institute
Old Snowmass, Colorado
14 May 2004

FOREWORD BY WILLIAM MCDONOUGH

Imagine a world in which all the things we make, use and consume provide nutrition for nature and industry, a world in which everything is so intelligently designed that human activity generates a delightful, restorative ecological footprint. Imagine having the choice, in every sphere of life – at home, on the job, travelling from place to place – to use goods and services that enhance the well-being of your community. Imagine those goods designed with only safe, healthful materials that can be either returned to the earth to replenish the soil or recovered by their manufacturers to be *upcycled* into products of higher value, virtually eliminating the concept of waste. Think of packaging becoming food for the pea patch, automobiles designed for disassembly, and cost effective factories powered by the energy of the sun. Imagine high-tech buildings so in tune with the biosphere that they inhabit the landscape like native trees, making oxygen, sequestering carbon, fixing nitrogen, purifying water, providing habitat for thousands of species, accruing solar energy, building soil and changing with the seasons – while also generating remarkable productivity and providing beauty, comfort and delight. And then consider the many ways in which these changes, this rediscovery of our connection to life, could revitalize our cities, our economies and our nations, remaking the way we make things and transforming humanity's relation to the Earth.

Such changes are not only in our grasp, they are emerging with such energy one could say that we have reached a 'tipping point', a moment in history when we have begun to understand, as Albert Einstein said, that 'the world will not evolve past its current state of crisis by using the same thinking that created the situation'. But there is still much to do and much to learn. That is why *The Natural Advantage of Nations* is an important contribution to our common future. A veritable encyclopedia of inspiring case studies, it shows how whole systems thinking, effectively applied by cooperative stakeholders, can achieve real, lasting change in the design of our world. Indeed, the range of stakeholders involved in the book parallels a larger, global shift in which the principles of ecologically intelligent design are being adopted by businesses, communities, non-governmental organizations (NGOs), universities and entire nations. This book captures the remarkable scope of this current shift.

In addition to the exciting revolution in product and facility design we can see new thinking in many realms. We see the City of Chicago adopting sustainable design principles to guide decision-making for generations of civic leaders. We see business competitors in major industries, such as packaging and electronics, working together to develop business-to-business communities devoted to creating new, ecologically intelligent standards that will transform conventional manufacturing. We see one of the world's top business schools, Spain's Instituto de Empresa, establishing a new Centre for Eco-Intelligent Management to foster innovative thinking among business leaders. In so many respects we have already 'tipped' towards a new world.

But the old ways of thinking die hard, even among those working towards sustainable development. The conventional wisdom would have us believe, for example, that the ecological crisis is the inevitable outcome of economic activity, or, on the other hand, that we need only reduce the negative impacts of industry to move safely and prosperously into the future. But both views are simplifications. Both assume an inherent conflict between nature and commerce, and so each fails to see that economic, social and environmental concerns are synergistic and can propel effective innovation. As well, such thinking obscures the fact that the destructive qualities of today's industrial system are the result of a fundamental design problem, a problem that neither regulation nor timid reforms can ever hope to address. And so the conventional wisdom fails to get to the heart of the matter – which is simply this: an industrial system powered by fossil fuels and nuclear energy that puts billions of tons of toxic material into the air, water and soil every year; requires thousands of complex regulations to keep people and natural systems from being poisoned too quickly; and which erodes the diversity of species and cultural practices is not only unsustainable in any form, but is a miserably unsatisfying way to do business – and to live. The alternative is thorough reinvention, addressing design problems at their source, rather than tinkering with the flawed engines of conventional industry. That's why understanding design's central role in transforming manufacturing and commerce is so crucial. And that's why *cradle-to-cradle* design offers hope for an entirely different world.

Cradle-to-cradle design begins with the proposition that the effective, regenerative cycles of nature – the cyclical flows of energy, water and nutrients that support life – provide an unmatched model for wholly positive human designs. In the natural world, one organism's 'waste' cycles through an ecosystem to provide nourishment for other living things; its productivity is beneficial and regenerative – waste equals food. Just so, cradle-to-cradle products are designed to circulate in closed-loop cycles that virtually eliminate waste and provide 'nutrients' for nature and industry. The cradle-to-cradle framework developed by my colleague Michael Braungart and myself recognizes two metabolisms within which materials flow as healthy nutrients. First, nature's nutrient cycles constitute the *biological metabolism*. Materials designed to flow optimally in the biological metabolism are *biological nutrients*. Products conceived as these nutrients, such as biodegradeable fabrics, are designed to be used and safely returned to the environment to nourish living systems. Second, the *technical metabolism*, designed to mirror earth's cradle-to-cradle cycles, is a closed-loop system in which valuable, high-tech synthetics and mineral resources – *technical nutrients* – circulate in perpetual cycles of production, recovery and remanufacture. Ideally, all the human artefacts that make up the technical metabolism, from buildings to manufacturing systems, are powered by renewable energy. Working within this framework we can, by design, enhance humanity's positive impact on the world. Rather than limiting growth or reducing emissions or using brute force to overcome the rules of the natural world, we can create economies worldwide that purify air, land and water; that rely on current solar income and generate no waste; that support energy-effectiveness, healthy productivity and social well-being. In short, sound, regenerative economies that enhance all life.

A brief look at some of the innovative work inspired by cradle-to-cradle thinking strongly suggests that we can achieve a healthy, sustaining economy in this century. Products designed as biological and technical nutrients, for example, have already successfully entered the marketplace. The upholstery fabric Climatex Lifecycle is a blend of pesticide-residue-free wool and organically grown ramie, dyed and processed entirely with non-toxic chemicals. All of its product and process inputs were defined and selected for their human and ecological safety within the biological metabolism. The result: after the end of its useful commercial life the fabric can be used as garden mulch for growing fruits and vegetables, returning the textile's biological nutrients to the soil. Honeywell, meanwhile, is marketing a textile for the technical metabolism, a high-quality carpet yarn called Zeftron Savant, which is made of perpetually recyclable nylon 6 fibre. Zeftron Savant is designed to be reclaimed and repolymerized – taken back to its constituent resins – to become new material for new carpets. In fact, Honeywell can retrieve old, conventional nylon 6 and transform it into Zeftron Savant, upcycling rather than downcycling an industrial material. The nylon is rematerialized, not dematerialized – a true cradle-to-cradle product. Shaw Industries, the world's largest commercial carpet maker, is going a step further, developing a safe, technical nutrient carpet tile *and* a system for its recovery and remanufacture – a technical metabolism. Responding to widespread scientific and consumer concern about PVC in carpet backing, Shaw developed a safe, polyolefin-based backing system with all the performance benefits of PVC, which it guarantees it will take back along with its high quality nylon 6 carpet facing. All the materials that go into the carpet will continually circulate in technical nutrient cycles. Raw material to raw material. Waste equals food.

This cradle-to-cradle cycle is altogether different from typical eco-efficient recycling, which tends to mix carpets' face fibre and PVC backing, yielding a hybrid material of lesser value. In effect, the materials are not recycled at all but *downcycled* – and they are still on a one way, cradle-to-grave trip to the landfill or incinerator. There, the PVC content of the material makes recycled carpet hazardous waste. Shaw's ground-breaking work, however, shows how the material flows of an entire industry can be transformed by adopting the cradle-to-cradle paradigm. Indeed, Shaw has changed its corporate mission to reflect its new direction. As Shaw's Steve Bradfield says, 'Sustainability is our goal; cradle-to-cradle is our path'. After a decade in which cradle-to-cradle thinking emerged, business by business as companies such as Shaw, Nike, Ford and Herman Miller integrated eco-effective thinking into everyday operations, we are now seeing a new wave of innovation that is carrying cradle-to-cradle principles beyond company boundaries into cooperative inter-business communities and the wider world.

Consider, for example, how competitors in the packaging industry are using cradle-to-cradle design as a catalyst for industry-wide change. Currently, the life cycle of most packaging is a one-way, cradle-to-grave stream of materials. In the US alone, 45 million tons of containers and packaging are discarded annually, creating a host of unintended environmental problems. But what if packaging flowed in cradle-to-cradle cycles, generating only positive effects? What if it provided nutrition for soil and created no waste? Those were the questions that came to the fore in March 2003 when the EPA-sponsored Cradle-to-Cradle Design Challenge invited the industry to re-design e-commerce packaging. The purpose of the challenge was to stimulate creativity and offer the industry positive alternatives to regulation.

'Regulations will always be a part of the picture', said EPA Office of Solid Waste Project Director Claire Lindsay. 'But we are also trying to find ways to encourage "beyond compliance", and cradle-to-cradle design is totally beyond compliance. That resonates with industry. Industry wants maximum freedom to innovate, and going beyond compliance by means of this new paradigm generates innovative thinking.'

Indeed it does. Not only did the design challenge encourage the packaging industry to consider the ecological and human health characteristics of materials, it laid the foundation for an industry working group devoted to implementing cradle-to-cradle principles. After a pair of meetings arranged by GreenBlue, the non-profit established to shepherd cradle-to-cradle design into the public domain, industry giants such as Cargill Dow, Dow Chemical, Estee Lauder/Aveda, Mead/Westvaco, Nike, Starbucks, Tropicana/Pepsi and Unilever organized to pursue 'a positive, robust environmental vision for packaging' which includes developing cyclical material flows and 'increasing demand for environmentally intelligent, cradle-to-cradle materials'. The resulting Sustainable Packaging Coalition, officially launched in March 2004, represents a promising, replicable model in which cooperation, quality and innovation drive mutually beneficial, industry-wide change.

EPA Office of Solid Waste has also partnered with GreenBlue on the eDesign Idea Competition to develop cradle-to-cradle standards for the electronics industry. Like packaging waste flows, the electronics solid waste stream is formidable and far-flung. But as electronics designers work with and internalize cradle-to-cradle principles, they will be able to apply them to the design of products, production processes, distribution logistics and delivery systems. Cradle-to-cradle principles also provide a platform for shared leadership and collaboration among a range of stakeholders – suppliers, manufacturers, dismantlers, government agencies, academia and NGOs – involved in realizing integrated systems of design, manufacturing and material recovery.

The design competitions also marked the beginning of a promising new relationship between government and industry. Commenting on the new industry groups sparked by the competitions, EPA Policy Analyst Angie Leith noted: 'Looking into the future, we see that we have to look upstream. We have to look at material flow management and not waste management. We have to think of cradle-to-cradle rather than cradle-to-grave. That's the direction we want to go.'

Cities, too, want to go in that direction. In Chicago, for example, cradle-to-cradle principles are serving as a reference point for long-term urban planning as the city strives to become the greenest in America. And the work is well underway. Along with a host of traditional beautification efforts, such as the planting of some 300,000 trees, Mayor Richard Daley's administration is also working to make the city a model of how industry and ecology, city and nature, can flourish side-by-side. To that end, the City has installed a green roof on City Hall and undertaken the largest brownfield redevelopment effort in the US. It has begun to restore the Lake Michigan shoreline and is committed to buying 20 per cent of its electricity from renewable sources by 2006. Meanwhile, renewable energy companies, such as the solar panel manufacturer Spire, have moved their headquarters to the Chicago Center for Green Technology, a new ecologically intelligent facility built on a restored industrial site. Spire is already supplying Chicago with locally manufactured solar panels, which the City has installed on the roofs of the Field Museum, the Mexican Fine Arts Museum and the Art Institute of Chicago. Chicago's successful application of an ecologically intelligent, technologically advanced urban planning strategy suggests a bright future for cradle-to-cradle cities. As cradle-to-cradle material and energy flows become an integral part of industry, re-industrialization will become a clean, safe, option for healthy urban growth. The 21st century city will not only fit elegantly into the natural landscape, it will become a revitalizing force in its region.

In this new regional metropolis, biological and technical nutrition flow back and forth between city and countryside, enriching both. The city receives food, water and energy from a broad nexus of solar-powered, biologically-based, photosynthetic systems. The energy of the sun is harvested on rooftops; rural windmills power city buildings; water falls on a network of rooftop gardens and interconnected greenways, flowing safely into the soil, into the watershed, into the air. In the countryside, farmers grow food using implements manufactured in the city – technical nutrients – and the city receives this nourishment, digests it and excretes it back to its source, returning biological nutrients to the rural soil. The windmills on the farm, a new cash crop, are forged in the city, produce power for the region in the countryside, and then are returned to the city every 20 years to be refurbished and returned to the farm. Everything moves in regenerative cycles, from city to country, country to city, all the polymers, metals and synthetic fibres flowing safely in the technical metabolism, all the photosynthetic nutrients – food, wood, natural fibres – flowing in the biological metabolism. These flows of nutrients are the twin metabolisms of the living city that allow human settlements and the natural world to thrive together. Building the infrastructure to support them is a key challenge for the 21st century city.

From the borders of the regional metropolis we can begin to imagine the cradle-to-cradle national economy. A national economic strategy developed around biological and technical nutrient flows inherently supports national industry. In the US, for example, making quality, innovation and environmental health the hallmarks of industry would give a whole range of businesses a competitive edge and create new markets for American products. Perhaps more importantly, it would lay the foundation for the re-vitalization of on-shore manufacturing as companies move their operations close to home to optimize the value of their technical nutrient cycles, which are most beneficial when materials are recovered and re-used with a minimum of transportation. As we have seen in Chicago, this kind of deeply considered, ecologically intelligent re-industrialization would make manufacturing a safe, beneficial addition to community life. This does not mean an end to trade between regions or nations. On the contrary, it simply suggests that, as in politics, all sustainability is local and that a nation of cradle-to-cradle economies would be an economically vibrant nation as well as a good trading partner.

Consider the relationship between China and the US. Currently, the two nations can be seen as suffering from the commercial exchange of toxic products that ultimately damage the economic, social and environmental health of both nations. While China becomes the world's low-cost supplier of environmentally questionable products, the US brings those products to market with one of the world's most 'efficient' distribution systems, moving goods in a rapid, one-way trip from retailer to consumer to landfill. In many cases, the US sends the most contaminated products back to China, where lead and copper are unsafely recycled from computers and televisions. This is trade as mutually assured destruction.

Yet it offers an unparalleled arena for innovation. China has recognized that the cradle-to-cradle strategy can be applied on a large scale and in 2002 Madame Deng Nan, China's Vice Minister of Science and Technology, put forward that it will begin to develop industries and products based on cradle-to-cradle principles. Working with the China–US Center for Sustainable Development, China is already applying cradle-to-cradle thinking to urban and rural planning and developing a variety of solar and wind powered enterprises. These are the kinds of projects that could transform the relationship between China and the US, and indeed the foundations of world trade. The two powers represent critical dimensions of the human enterprise that clearly have a profound influence on the future of the planet. The combined impact of their industrial practices alone calls forth both great responsibilities and great opportunities. As the cradle-to-cradle infrastructure grows in China, as it is growing in the US, the two nations could well become cradle-to-cradle industrial partners, developing products and enterprises that support the life and health of both. This cooperative relationship, at its best, will be a competitive one. Rather than competing to destroy each other, however, China and the US could compete in the classic sense of the word, which in Latin means 'to strive together' like great athletes in training – like the Williams sisters working out together to become more polished players. Imagine, then, the two nations – or a coalition of nations – working vigorously towards a common goal: not an end game in which one player wins, but a field of endeavour in which China and the US get fit together as each nation strives to create enterprises that generate commercial productivity, ecological intelligence and cultural wealth.

That will only be a beginning. The birth of truly regenerative industry and commerce calls for global action. It requires energy, genius, creativity and commitment from all sectors of society from all nations. It asks that communities, governments, NGOs, educators and business leaders from Beijing to Buenos Aries apply cradle-to-cradle design and development to the pursuit of a prosperous, equitable future for all. We must, all of us, reach for nothing less.

The Natural Advantage of Nations is one of the first books to bring together examples of leadership in all these sectors of society. Its breathtaking scope, supported by an extensive online resource, outlines inspiring case studies from all over the world. It shows that what many people saw as impossible just 15 years ago is now already happening. Within these pages you will see that there is reason for robust hope, and as you read, we hope you will be inspired to contribute to this magnificent re-evolution of human enterprise, a moment in our history when the things we make and build and grow can become a truly regenerative force.

Charlottesville, Virginia
12 August 2004

FOREWORD BY L. HUNTER LOVINS[1]

Young people often ask what gives me hope. Many things make me hopeful, but the best answer, just now, is this book: *The Natural Advantage of Nations* (NAON). The team of young engineers, scientists and policy-makers who bring this to you are representative of the young people who are the future not only of Australia, but also the world. It is particularly pleasing that this book has emerged not from the US or Europe, but from a Southern nation. The numerous examples given here of profitable ways to improve the environment, human well-being *and* the bottom line come not from the familiar poster children of the sustainability movement, but from communities across Australia and Asia. It proves a belief that has grown in me for several years that while the tipping point of environmental devastation may be frighteningly close, the people with the commitment to implement the solutions we already know can solve the problems are also at hand. This book presents a robust business case for sustainability. It cites the sorts of examples that I am now teaching to my MBA students at Presidio World College. Studying for the first accredited MBA in Sustainable Management, these students are reading material like *Natural Capitalism* that gave rise to this book. NAON will be required reading next semester.

Business as usual is not a safe place to stay

Corporate leadership desperately needs to internalize the message of this book. Companies today reside on the edge of a crumbling precipice. Beneath the feet of the world's major corporations, the edges of the earth that they have taken for granted are disintegrating. Farseeing business leaders realize that change is inevitable and have identified a realm of stability across the chasm. They know that a migration strategy is necessary, but even these business leaders are struggling to manage it. Less innovative companies seek to shore up the ground as it erodes and haven't yet even realized that they need an exit route. As NAON describes, one example of the challenges that face every company is how to limit its emissions of climate changing gases like carbon dioxide.

In March 2004, Reuters reported that:

> The world's second largest re-insurer, Swiss Re, warned that the costs of natural disasters, aggravated by global warming, threatened to spiral out of control, forcing the human race into a catastrophe of its own making. In a report revealing how climate change is rising on the corporate agenda, Swiss Re said the economic costs of such disasters threatened to double to $150 billion (82 billion pounds) a year in 10 years, hitting insurers with $30–40 billion in claims, or the equivalent of one World Trade Centre attack annually.[2]

Environmental challenges are only part of the erosion. As NAON describes, the whole basis of what makes a company competitive is shifting. Companies are increasingly realizing that shareholder value is not only created by the physical product that they produce, their cash profits, or next quarter's share price, but by ideas, reputation, brand equity and especially by their ability to attract and retain the best talent.

These 'intangibles' are now a greater component of businesses' value than the physical assets that used to be considered the basis of core business value. Tom Peters in his book *Re-imagine!* states:

> We are in the midst of redefining our basic ideas about what enterprise and organization and even being human are – about how value is created and how careers are pursued. Welcome to a world where 'value' (damn near all value!) is based on intangibles – not lumpy objects, but weightless figments of the Economic Imagination. We are in 'a brawl with no rules'. What can we do? Relish the Mess! Enjoy the Fray!… We have entered an Age of Talent. People (their creativity, their intellectual capital, their entrepreneurial drive) is all there is. Enterprises that master the market for talent will do better than ever. But to attract and retain the Awesome Talent, an organization must offer up an Awesome Place to Work.[3]

The penalty for failure? Over 40 per cent of the businesses listed in the 1985 Fortune 500 are not in business today. Companies like Enron and WorldCom that demonstrated a lack of integrity risk the entirety of shareholder value. In an Internet empowered world, a small group of determined citizens can deligitimize any company.

Talk about a crumbling cliff.

Peter Drucker writing in *The Economist* stated: 'In the next society, the biggest challenge for the large company – especially for the multinational – may be its social legitimacy: its values, its missions, its visions.'[4]

Business leaders must manage all assets of a corporation seamlessly, tangible and intangible, and do this successfully in a time in which the legitimacy of such institutions as large corporations is being questioned. Many companies are finding that the only way to do this is to begin finding their way across the bridge to a more sustainable world.

What's wrong with where we are?

In 1995 Royal Dutch Shell came under worldwide criticism for its complicity in the hanging of African activist Ken Saro Wiwa and its proposals to scuttle the Brent spar oil drill rig in the North Sea. The confrontation escalated to the point that activists in Europe firebombed Shell gas stations. In the words of the *New Statesman*:

> Shell found itself forced rapidly to reassess its intentions. Public identification with the campaign was threatening to have a runaway impact on its competitive position in the petrol forecourts of Europe. Better to cut its losses, whatever the short-term loss of face. At the 11th hour, on 20 June 1995, Shell backed down. For Greenpeace it was an historic victory; for the Prime Minister, John Major, who had put the weight of the British government behind the dumping plan, it was a humiliation.[5]

In 1997, Sir Mark Moody-Stuart took over the helm of a battered Royal Dutch Shell group of companies as Chair of the Managing Directors. Among his early actions was the announcement of a commitment to transform Shell into a more sustainable company. This included creating a department of sustainability in the company, public apologies and in 2000, the release of a Shell Sustainability Report that admitted to a variety of mistakes and committed Shell to transparency and a transition to becoming a sustainable company. Shell acknowledged mistakes and identified needed areas for reform. It acceded to Greenpeace's demands and dismantled Brent Spar on land. It is actively engaged in conversations with the local tribespeople in Nigeria to try to re-establish the company's legitimacy and regain its franchise to do business there. During Sir Mark's reign, Shell invested in a variety of renewable energy and energy efficiency technologies. Shell Hydrogen was founded. Its Chair Don Huberts remarked: 'The stone-age did not end because we ran out of stones, the oil age will not end because we run out of oil – hydrogen will be a better business to be in'.

In an interview in the UK newspaper the *Independent*, Sir Mark stated that:

> *Shell was investing heavily in developing renewable sources out of self-interest, 'to be seen' as an energy company to be serving the needs of society not damaging it. People want somebody to do something about global warming, and we need to look at new sources of energy. The role of energy companies is changing from an enabler of mobility to the developer of innovative, clean technologies, says Sir Mark Moody-Stuart, and within that role there is a huge and commercially viable scope for improvement.[6]*

In 2000, *Business Wire* reported:

> *Responding to new, higher expectations of stakeholders, Shell not only has implemented company-wide guidelines for ethical behavior, but plans to invest millions of dollars in programs and projects that reflect the company's commitment. In an article for World Energy(R) magazine, Shell's chairman, Sir Mark Moody-Stuart, said, 'Successful companies will need to develop new approaches for addressing key ethical, social and environment concerns, "but" good intentions are meaningless without real action to put ethical principles into practice'. Shell plans investments of half a billion dollars in commercial renewable energy resources and $30 million for the new Shell Foundation, which will focus primarily on sustainable energy. Already, 20 projects to bring energy to poor communities in developing nations have been announced.[7]*

During Sir Mark's tenure revenues rose and Shell was hailed by many former critics as a company that merited investment.

Fast forward to 2001. Sir Mark left Royal Dutch Shell in the company's usual rotation of Chairs. He took a far larger role on the world stage, headlining the World Summit on Sustainable Development (WSSD) in Johannesburg, and assumed the Chair of Anglo-American. Meanwhile, back at Shell his successor, Phil Watts, began a quiet campaign to dismantle Sir Mark's commitments. Watts ordered the removal of the section of the Shell website that invited criticism. He oversaw a move to promote exploration and extraction technologies in the American West that would be extremely environmentally damaging. He fired Anita Burke, the prior head of Shell's sustainability operations in The Hague. These acts enabled BP to eclipse Shell in the seriousness of its commitments to transition to renewables and environmentally responsible behaviour. Shell also began making efforts to regain its operations in Oginiland in Nigeria, eliciting a return of tribal activism.

Three years later, it turns out that Watts cooked the books. Despite his rhetoric about sustainability, Watts was really an old-line oil-man. A *New York Times* story describes his enthusiasm about oil:

> *Arriving on stage in a spaceship and an astronaut suit, Philip Watts, then the senior executive in charge of exploration and production for the Royal Dutch/Shell Group, glowed as he delivered a message of optimism to a conference of 600 company executives in June 1998.*

> 'I have seen the future and it was great', he declared.
> He was talking about the success of a special management program that had recently addressed a fundamental problem of the company – that it was pumping oil and gas out of the ground faster than it was finding new supplies. Internal documents show, however, that the program allowed Royal Dutch/Shell to increase its oil and gas reserves not by discovering major new sources, but by changing its accounting to add reserves that it was not sure could ever be tapped.[8]

Not everyone was enthusiastic about Watts' manipulations. *The New York Times* story went on to state that:

> A July 2002 memorandum to the Royal Dutch/Shell Group's committee of managing directors from Walter van de Vijver, the head of exploration and production at the time. It indicates that the company's senior executives had concerns about shortfalls in its proven reserves of oil and natural gas. Most of the misstated reserves were recorded from 1997 to 2000, when Sir Philip was in charge of exploration and production. Last year [2003] executives began to grow increasingly concerned about the way the company was accounting for its reserves, and they commissioned a review that led to the revisions made in January.[9]

In March 2004 Watts and the two other top managers were forced to resign. The annual general meeting of shareholders was held two months late because of the turmoil. Shareholders were livid that managing directors be absolved of responsibility for their management for the year 2003, and that Watts was paid a lump sum of over £1 million. Shell stock took a pounding and various lawsuits are pending.

Is a commitment to sustainability the hallmark of good corporate governance and a guarantor of shareholder value?

But wait!? How can a company be committed to sustainable behaviour and a transition to greater corporate responsibility and at the same time be hiding vital information that indicates the company's core business value from investors?

If your business model is a transition away from oil to a company that produces an array of energy products and services, then falling reserves are less of a worry. But if your mental model is to mine oil until the day you die, it's a serious problem. Shell under Sir Mark's management was undertaking a strategic redefinition of its future. He understood that to survive Shell had to capture the high ground of brand equity. A Shell official chastened by the Nigerian and Brent Spar disasters privately said, 'We're not so worried about regulation, because through the World Trade Organization we can get round anything we don't like. But we're absolutely terrified of the way these citizen networks can instantly delegitimize our company and destroy our franchise. It's terribly difficult to get all our people worldwide to appreciate the risks of this new accountability'. Shell's then Vice President of sustainability Tom Delfgauuw stated that the challenges Shell had faced were 'the best thing that ever happened to us, first because we've come out of it much stronger as a company and second because it accelerated a great many needed corporate developments'.[10]

The issue is management integrity: integrity of vision, and integrity of performance. Sir Mark captained Shell's essential turning of the corner, its embarkation across a 50-year bridge away from the business that had built the company to its future. Phil Watts, perhaps lacking that integrity, tried to turn back, and fell into the abyss, wreaking havoc on shareholder value. Watts's return to Shell's former direction, forced him to hide from investors the news that this about face was bad business for a variety of reasons.

From a purely capitalist point of view, either strategy can be viable. This book argues, however, that business-as-usual is no longer a safe bet, and that only a sustainability strategy can protect shareholder value in the long run. It argues that even the most doctrinaire capitalists should reassess their assumptions about whether what is happening to the environment, how external stakeholders perceive their company, and how a company's definition of its responsibility to the rest of the world affects its own employees should become a core part of their planning for the future. My belief is that companies that realize the seriousness of these challenges, and commit to a transition to more sustainable behaviour *and* that deliver on that commitment, will be the companies that succeed in the coming decades. Corporate commitment to and follow-through on sustainability will come to be the hallmark of corporate integrity and management capacity. The investment community will see the absence of such a commitment, or any backsliding on one, as a real red flag.

Building a bridge to tomorrow

Milton Friedman once queried, 'If businessmen do have a social responsibility other than making maximum profits for stockholders, how are they to know what it is?' The leading companies, some of them profiled in this book, are showing how to construct a bridge across the gulf that now confronts us all, from business-as-usual to the greater profitability, lowered risk, enhanced brand equity, and stronger shareholder value that sustainability can confer. No business, even an imperiled one, will embark on a course of action that would compromise profitability. But as companies shift their behaviour, taking the first steps across the bridge, they are also realizing that this can make them more profitable. They are realizing that they live in a very different world from the one in which Milton Freedman wrote.

In April 2000, British Petroleum announced a commitment to reduce its carbon emissions 10 per cent below its 1990 levels by 2010. It only took it two years to achieve this. Doing it is now saving them US$650 million. The results, and the thinking that led to the commitment in the first place also convinced BP to announce a rebranding to 'Beyond Petroleum', and to regular corporate announcements that its efforts to become a more sustainable company are 'a start'. BP sees that it cannot remain on the cliff's edge. It has begun to build a bridge to the other side. Rodney Chase, Deputy Group Chief Executive of BP recently stated that even if BP's climate abatement programme cost them money, it would be worth doing because it makes them the sort of company that the best talent wants to work for.

Nike was attacked by social activists because it had erroneously thought that it could draw the boundary within which it had to concern itself with social responsibility at its American plant gates. This forced them to seriously consider eliminating the 'Swoosh', its multi-billion dollar brand symbol, when citizen's groups protested the labour practices in the companies overseas from which Nike purchased its products. In response, Nike recommitted itself to sustainability, implementing third party verification of its human rights policies, undertaking a major effort to increase its environmental performance and hiring the sustainability consulting group, The Natural Step, to guide its efforts.

A 2004 survey of some of the world's leading CEOs, undertaken by the World Economic Forum at Davos, found that the responding leaders feel that corporate reputation is now a more important measure of success than stock market performance, profitability and return on investment. Only the quality of products and services edged out reputation as the leading measure of corporate success. Fifty-nine per cent of the respondents estimated that corporate brand or reputation represents more than 40 per cent of a company's market capitalization. Perhaps it should not come as a surprise that essentially all of the world's top 150 companies now have a sustainability officer at the vice president level or higher.[11]

Whole organizations such as the World Business Council for Sustainable Development now exist to help their members, including 160 other major corporations, capture such opportunities. In the book, *Walking the Talk*, WBCSD's prime movers, the CEOs of DuPont, Anova and Royal Dutch Shell, state:

> *sustainability's business case is strengthened by the ways in which thinking of sustainable human progress encourages us toward innovation. It offers business opportunity, and it pushes companies toward thinking about more 'sustaining' forms of energy, agriculture, construction, mobility, and forestry. The relatively straightforward concept of eco-efficiency has already encouraged some companies to make radical shifts from sales to selling nothing at all – and being cleaner and more profitable in the process... Taking eco-efficiency and environment seriously can, and should, lead to strategic corporate innovation... By capitalizing on these assets a company stands to gain customer success, brand strength, first mover advantage, motivated employees and potentially more profits.[12]*

Former IBM executive, Bob Willard, was one of the first to quantify the business case for behaving more socially and environmentally responsibly. He listed seven categories in which a commitment to greater sustainability will enhance doing business. These include: easier hiring of the best talent, higher retention of top talent, higher employee productivity, reduced expenses in manufacturing, reduced expenses at commercial sites, increased revenue/market share, reduced risk and easier financing.[13]

Of these, perhaps the most significant first step that companies can take is to increase the efficiency with which they use resources. Such 'eco-efficiency can result in enormous cost reductions, while improving the company's reputation, brand equity and reducing its environmental footprint'. The book *Factor Four* and its successor, *Natural Capitalism*, detail the massive savings possible to companies that enhance their sustainability. For example over a 12-year period, Dow's Louisiana plant was able to save enough energy implementing worker-suggested savings measures to amount to an addition of US$110 million each year to the bottom line. Each measure also reduced Dow's carbon footprint.[14]

This book takes that work, updates it by four years and presents an even more compelling case.

The challenge for strategists is to create a culture in which the journey across the bridge can unfold without undue cost and disruption. It means confronting such common business problems as how systematically to create a culture and adopt a set of processes that continually identify key intangibles for investment (new ideas, reputation, opportunities) while keeping an eye on tangibles (aligned customers = brand equity, eco-efficiency = reduced costs, revenues = market share = brand equity = reduced costs, etc.). How do you assess new trends and determine which priorities should rise to the top? And how do you ensure that innovation and market leadership will emerge from these investments?

This book is an important plank that will enable business leaders, elected officials, and citizen activists together to construct the bridge across the chasm.

Natural Capitalism Inc
Eldorado Springs, Colorado
20 September 2004

FOREWORD BY MICHAEL FAIRBANKS

'The Latest Best Chance': Prosperity, Competitiveness and Natural Capitalism – the Ultimate Integration

Last year I received a call from the authors of this book. We had mutual friends in Amory Lovins, Hunter Lovins and William McDonough. These 'new' authors from Australia (most innovation comes from the periphery!) impressed me with their earnest commitment to integrate the concepts of Natural Capitalism and competitiveness. They knew all the literature; they had a vision; and the vision was correct, something that I dreamed of myself for some time, but had precious little to show for it. By the second or third phone conversation between Australia and my home in Massachusetts, I knew that I was speaking to people who had the energy, insight and commitment to begin the discussion of what I call 'the ultimate integration'; that is, integration of the concepts of competitiveness and Natural Capitalism.

This new book teaches us to think that there are four constituents to any business model: purchasers, shareholders, employees and *future generations*.[1] All business models serve the purchasers, or the business model wouldn't exist. Most serve the shareholders or the business model wouldn't exist, for long. Fewer still serve the workers of the world; and in fact, there are only a handful of countries where workers participate in the value created in a business model; and even in these few countries there is precious little thought to future generations. That is what this book is about. How can we create business models that serve all the constituents that we think of in the present; but how do we make sure we leave the world better off; how do we think intergenerationally when it comes to business models; indeed, how do we create value for future generations? My view is that we need to consider two upgraded concepts that come before Natural Capitalism, in order to get the most out of it: 'What is Prosperity?' and 'What is Competitiveness?'

What is prosperity?

Prosperity is the ability of an individual, group or nation to provide shelter, nutrition and other material goods that enable people to live a good life,[2] according to their own definition. Prosperity helps to create the space in peoples' hearts and minds so that, unfettered by the everyday concern of the material goods they require to survive, they might develop a healthy emotional and spiritual life, according to their preferences. We can think of prosperity as a flow and a stock. Many economists view it as a *flow* of income; the ability of a person to purchase a set of goods, or capture value created by someone else. We use an improved notion of income called purchasing power.[3] Prosperity is also the enabling environment that improves productivity. We can therefore look at prosperity as a set of *stocks*.[4]

There are seven kinds of stock, or *Seven Forms of Capital*, the last four of which constitute social capital.[5] In this conceptualization we see all forms of prosperity falling into the following categories: *natural endowments* such as location, sub-soil assets, forests, beaches and climate; *financial* resources of a nation like savings and international reserves; *man-made* capital which includes buildings, bridges, roads and telecommunications assets; *institutional* capital such as legal protections of tangible and intangible property, government departments that work with little hidden costs to the economy, and firms that maximize value to shareholders, and compensate and train workers; *knowledge* resources such as international patents and university and think-tank capacities; *human* capital which represents skills, insights, capabilities; and *culture* capital which means not only the explicit articulations of culture like music, language and ritualistic tradition; but also attitudes and values that are linked to innovation.

Moving away from a conceptualization of prosperity as simply a flow of per capital income, enables us to consider a broader system, and the decisions for investment in an enriched and enabling, 'high-productive' environment.[6] Nobel laureate Amartya Sen suggests that: 'The advantage of a stock view would be to give us a better idea of a nation's ability to produce things in the future'.[7]

Why does prosperity matter?

We know that individuals around the world have vastly different purchasing powers and countries possess stocks of wealth in different proportions. According to Thomas Sowell, 'We need to confront the most blatant fact that has persisted across centuries of social history – vast differences in productivity among peoples, and the economic and other consequences of such differences'.[8] Recent reports by the World Bank indicate that the standard of living in many regions in Africa, Latin America and Asia are being threatened because of declining productivity. There are intimate connections between poverty and malnutrition: muscle wastage, stunting of growth, increased susceptibility to infections, and the destruction of cognitive capacity in children; but poverty is more insidious than statistics can indicate. Poverty destroys aspirations, hope and happiness. This is the poverty you can't measure, but you can feel. There is a rich literature on correlation between incomes and such progressive human values as: productive attitudes toward authority, tolerance of others and support of civil liberties, openness toward foreigners, positive relationships with subordinates, self-esteem, sense of personal competence, the disposition to participate in community and national affairs, interpersonal trust and satisfaction with one's own life.[9] Ronald Inglehart writes that higher rates of self-reporting of both objective and subjective well-being are correlated with the levels of national prosperity.[10]

What is competitiveness?

Nations that don't create wealth for its citizens share much in common. Our evidence, and that of others,[11] suggests that they are over-reliant on natural resources, including cheap labour; and that they believe in the simple advantages of climate, location and government favour. Because of this they often do not build the capacity to produce differentiated goods and services that create greater value for demanding consumers who are willing to pay more money for these goods. By focusing on these *easily imitated advantages*, on these lower forms of capital, they compete solely on the basis of price and, therefore, tend to suppress wages. Keeping wages low is what I call competing to see: 'which country can stay the poorest, the longest'. It is exports based on poverty, not exports based on wealth creation; and the only competition they are in is to see which country can stay the poorest the longest until its society disintegrates. A nation's ability to create *both* price and non-price value for consumers inside and outside the country is what determines its productivity and, therefore, its prosperity.[12]

One can categorize the many competitiveness choices available to firms and governments as follows:

The micro choices of competitiveness focus business strategy on an integrated set of choices designed to achieve a specific set of objectives in an informed and timely manner. We see few strategies of companies in developing nations that are informed by good research, made explicit, and shared by the firms' leaders. We have found seven patterns of uncompetitive behaviour at the microeconomic level: overdependence on natural resources and cheap labour, poor understanding of foreign customers' buying preferences, lack of knowledge of competitor activities, poor inter-firm cooperation, lack of forward integration into global markets, a paternalistic relationship between government and the private sector, and a high amount of defensiveness among government, private sector, the unions and the press. These seven patterns are the norm of companies in countries where the average citizen does not have a high and rising standard of living.[13] The results of these seven patterns are simple exports which compete on price and, therefore, low wages, in an increasingly demanding marketplace which provides fewer returns. Mitigating patterns of uncompetitive behaviour requires a set of firm-level choices around structuring new learning and decision-making. For inside each of these patterns lies a hidden opportunity for creating prosperity.

The macro choices of competitiveness are the extent to which the government supports the private sector. Some say that government needs to do more for the private sector, and some say government needs to get out of the way. If we characterize government choices around its level of intervention in the economy we can see a broad range of choice between *classic socialism* and *monetarism*.[14] In Cuba, the government has become overresponsible for the welfare of the average citizen; supplying housing, health care, education, jobs, food and even entertainment and news. Ownership is by the state and accomplished through collectives and accompanied by centralized planning which uses quantitative targets and administrative prices. Income distribution tends to be even, and growth tends to be low. The monetarist approach is a sparse but rigid social contract between government and the private sector that says: government will create a stable macroeconomic environment and the emerging private sector entrepreneurs will create growth. This strategy emphasizes stabilizing markets, freeing wages and the currency exchange rates, and allowing markets to develop. This strategy appears to create, especially in the near term, more poverty and greater gaps in income. It fails to acknowledge that the government has a role in the innovation process. In my view, it is an overreaction to the failed policies of government intervention, such as import substitution which was so popular in Africa and Latin America in the 1970s and 1980s.

My view is that the government needs to do *everything* it can to help the private sector succeed, except to impede competition. This means investing, or helping the private sector to invest, in the higher forms of capital. In poorer countries, government will have to do more than in richer countries. The relationship has to be customized, based on a nation's stage of growth, and the innate capacities of each sector to contribute. I believe that if these competitiveness choices, these *micro* and *macro* choices, are informed and bounded by the principles of Natural Capitalism, we produce the best chance to build business models that create value for all four constituents: purchasers, shareholders, workers; and perhaps most important, future generations. I also believe that The Natural Edge Project, this group on the periphery, has produced the latest, best effort for learning how to do it.

OTF *Group*
Boston, Massachusetts
September 2004

PREFACE

Let us keep in mind that we are the generation for which previous generations committed themselves to save the environment. We are the generation for which the commitment was made to restore the balance. In 1972 the first global inter-governmental meeting on the environment was held in Stockholm, Sweden. Progress since then has been widely regarded as being insufficient. It is now our generation's responsibility to take on this challenge as a central motivating principle and use the lessons from the last 30 years to do all we can to ensure the next 30 are different. It is essential that we learn from, acknowledge and work with those who have gone before, in order for us to build on their great work as we are at a critical juncture in the Earth's history. In another 30 years, if things do not change, it will be too late: the impacts of global warming will be truly felt across the globe and the development paths of fast growing economies like China will be well and truly decided.

What is most concerning, however, are the uncertainties regarding the environment's response to human development: and increasingly, the responses being monitored are non-linear. There is real cause for concern that scientific models have overestimated the resilience of ecosystems, owing to an inadequate understanding of their complexity, and that these models are being used as the basis for political decision-making. What is clear is that, even if a decision is made tomorrow to truly adopt appropriate strategic approaches to the problems outlined herein, they will still require significant lead-time to implement. For 300 years we have built infrastructure and chosen technological paths (e.g., fossil fuels) without consideration of their long-term environmental impacts. Consequently, there is over 300 years worth of accumulated and often highly inefficient infrastructure that will need to be addressed. The good news, and the main point of this book, is that there are proven examples of practical, profitable and sustainable solutions available now. Studies of these examples clearly demonstrate that, with the right policy balance phased in over time, shifting to a sustainable economy can actually lower costs. This is partly because externalities, such as environmental degradation, are themselves adding significant costs to the economy if we do not act. It is also because new enabling technologies and new methods of design are bringing costs down significantly, thus enabling such a transition despite constant bottom line pressures.

This publication will show that this new form of development, sustainable development, is far from being in conflict with economic goals and actually builds on the traditional central goal of economics that seeks to improve the well-being of all. Sustainable development simply seeks to do that whilst also seeking to ensure non-declining well-being for future generations. What is reassuring, is that this is no longer a walk into unknown territory; rather, as this book will demonstrate, in many cases the solutions already exist and are being implemented by companies, governments, civil society groups, churches, trade unions, universities, schools and professional bodies around the world. So, if we are humble and willing to learn from the best around the world and apply it to our own context, many of the answers are already there; all we need is a unifying sense of urgency and the will to change. There are now significant national and global networks within many sectors throughout the whole of society that are working on these challenges. Hence, this book is a collection of possible ways to address the systemic problems we will face in the coming century. It provides demonstrably relevant and successful solutions, already being applied, of which its co-authors have first hand experience. These are people who are working at the coalface (or should we say solar face) of change, having been either a part of these processes of reform within significant institutions or advisers to them.

What we need now in every nation are processes, partnerships and collaborations that pool this collective wisdom of the best in academia, government, research and development bodies, the community, business and government. Imagine if, as in the Netherlands, every government initiated a programme to work out how they could achieve a 90 percent plus reduction of their environmental load over the next 50 years? Imagine if, as in Western Australia, every state or regional government worked with business, universities and civil society in a spirit of partnership to develop a sustainability strategy? Imagine if every state or regional government committed to halving its ecological footprint over the next 20 years? Imagine if, as in Goa, a state in India, every nation's experts tackled the challenge of how to create sustainable cities cost effectively in 30 years? Every nation and regional government can and should. Those involved with these and many other significant projects have given their time and effort to this book because they want to share what they have learnt. They want to share the good news that sustainable development is achievable in our lifetimes. They want to share the joy and excitement of working on projects that provide real solutions and genuine hope because they are grounded in rigorous science, engineering and economics. They want to pass on the truth that it is possible to combine idealism with bottom line reality if we are wise. Finally, they want to pass on an honest account of their experiences and lessons learnt. The challenges facing us are great. However, by being realistic about them and by working together, we are confident that we can achieve sustainable development this century.

The Natural Advantage of Nations has been developed as an initiative of The Natural Edge Project (TNEP). TNEP having been founded by volunteers, is now driven by an growing number of active and dynamic young professionals and researchers committed to working towards meeting the major challenges of the 21st century. The team receives mentoring from a range of professionals, public servants, business leaders and academics internationally. TNEP is supported by partnerships with a range of groups, bodies, companies, government agencies and institutions and operates on a not-for-profit model with donations, sponsorship, royalties and revenue being invested in further projects and initiatives. Our work over the past three years started as an attempt to draw together some of the best case studies in sustainability and to communicate them to businesses in a way which would show them that the days of trade-offs between the environment, society and business were over. Through this experience we found that there was a need to improve the communication generally of how science, engineering, business and institutions can together play a constructive role in meeting the global challenges. This publication will take you on a journey through many areas of society, touching on the various roles of the key players, and showing how we, as a society, can move towards a sustainable future by working together. We are confident that this book has something for everyone. This work is part of a larger conversation that is needed to examine the key issues of sustainable development and identify ways forward from a business, innovation and governance perspective. The material in this publication has been peer reviewed by a range of groups, institutions, corporations and bodies. This book seeks to build on and integrate a range of the best and most important journal papers, reports and books in the field. It is a major overview, designed to save you significant time.

There are several seminal works upon which this book builds. These include:

- The title for this book is inspired by both Michael Porter's *Competitive Advantage of Nations* and the Australian Conservation Foundation's *Natural Advantage: Blueprint for a Sustainable Australia* by Mike Krockenberger* et al (2000).
- The work of leading advocates of the so-called 'next industrial revolution' such as Amory Lovins*, Hunter Lovins*, Paul Hawken, Ernst von Weizsäcker, William McDonough* and Michael Branguart, Alan AtKisson*, James Womack and Daniel Jones, David Suzuki* and Peter Senge.
- The work of Professor Michael Porter in *Competitive Advantage: Creating and Sustaining Superior Performance* together with works such as *Green and Competitive: Ending the Stalemate* and *Toward a New Conception of the Environment–Competitiveness Relationship* with Claas van der Linde.
- The groundbreaking work of Rocky Mountain Institute*, Natural Capitalism Inc*, the German Wuppertal Institute for Climate, Environment and Energy*, The AtKisson Group* and the On the Frontier Group*.
- Key publications such as *Sustainable Technology Development* by Paul Weaver et al, *Global Business Regulation* by John Braithwaite* and Peter Drahos* (2000), *Ploughing the Sea, Nurturing Hidden Sources of Growth in the Developing World* by Michael Fairbanks* and S Lindsey (1997), *The Natural Wealth of Nations: Harnessing the Market and the Environment*, by David Roodman (1999), *Sustainability and Cities: Overcoming Automobile Dependence*, by Peter Newman* and Jeff Kenworthy* (1999), *Design for Sustainability: A Sourcebook of Integrated Ecological Solutions*, by Janis Birkeland* et al (2002).

Whilst this book deals with contentious issues, such as the Kyoto Protocol, we seek to stick to the facts and avoid hyperbole. In Australia we have a saying in sporting circles, that one should 'play the ball and not the person'. So for instance, on the Kyoto issue we present the facts, the latest reports and scientific studies and let you draw your own conclusions. We have also made every effort to report the leading case studies and examples of best practice from all over the world. It is too easy to criticize business and governments. We live in an imperfect world where things could always be better. Most acknowledge that we face serious challenges. What is so heartening is that recent developments in information technology are allowing easy communication amongst the thousands who wish to work together to constructively address these issues. This book is an example of that. We have consciously done our best to build upon the major reports and forums of the last few years to build a strong resource for the coming decade. Even more encouraging is the fact that increasingly, business, government and civil society are adopting integrated approaches to strive for a future that does not leave successive generations to clean up the mess. In this book, rather than focusing on the negative, we seek to learn from the success stories in these sectors from all over the world. Sometimes people tend to deny problems when they cannot see any solutions to them. We believe that what little remaining opposition to sustainable development exists, remains because people still do not realize that we now have most of the solutions and working models we need to achieve sustainable development. This is no longer a leap into the unknown or a political risk if approached wisely. Through sharing these solutions and inspiring institutional reforms in this book, we hope to inspire greater cooperation and progress towards a sustainable future for this world.

---

* Denotes that this individual or group has made direct contributions towards the development of this publication either through endorsement, mentoring, peer review or through the contribution of material, content and research.

Many have asked us for more Australian case studies. We ask you to understand that, despite the fact we come from the land 'Down Under', this is a truly global book. Our task was to seek best practice internationally and in many cases we have found just that in Australia. For those specifically interested in Australian case studies and research, we recommend the online document *Natural Advantage: Blueprint For A Sustainable Australia* containing detailed online case study folders. We hope that this book, *The Natural Advantage of Nations*, inspires all nations to develop similar detailed online blueprints for a sustainable future such as that which Australian Conservation Foundation has provided for Australia. We trust you will understand that above all we have tried to be honest and balanced. We have conducted many interviews and consulted with many experts to ensure that many varied views have been considered. At all times we have asked what is true, and tried to communicate it simply whilst doing justice to the complexity of the real world. The Earth is the only planet we have. Our generation simply must work together this century to restore the balance before it is too late. This book and the online companion resource is a step towards showing how we can realistically do this.

Where otherwise not attibuted in the Contents, the text has been researched, compiled, written and proofed equally by the editors in consultation with TNEP's advisory, steering, working group and editorial committees. Michael H. Smith, TNEP Content Coordinator, is the point of contact for enquiries regarding the material presented and can be contacted at mike@naturaledgeproject.net. Karlson 'Charlie' Hargroves, TNEP Project Coordinator, is the point of contact for further information on collaborations, training, speaking and education material based on the material presented and can be contacted at charlie@naturaledgeproject.net.

Karlson 'Charlie' Hargroves and Michael H. Smith
October 2004

ACKNOWLEDGEMENTS

The secretariat of The Natural Edge Project – Karlson 'Charlie' Hargroves, Michael H. Smith, Cheryl Paten and Nick Palousis – would like to thank the following groups and individuals for making the development of this publication possible. First a special thank you must go to our families; in particular Stacey Hargroves, Tim and Angela Smith, Scott Paten, Theo and Maria Palousis, Elizabeth Sutton, Dianne James, Judy and Bhaskar Desha, Sarah Chapman, Margaret Talbot, Rupert and Christine Balint-Smith, Nikki Smith, Roger Dennis and Angela Groves.

Thanks must go to our closest supporters: Martin Dwyer, Geoff McAlpine, Steve Williamson, Michael Collins, Peter May, Doug Jones, Elizabeth Heij, Fiona Wain, Rob West, Ron Clark, Philip Sutton and TNEP co-founder James Bradfield Moody. A multi-disciplinary book like this was only possible through the generous time given by the following foreword writers, chapter co-authors, contributors and advisers and peer reviewers.

The secretariat would also like to say a special thank you to Amory Lovins, Alan AtKisson, Hunter Lovins, Michael Fairbanks and William McDonough for taking the time to mentor our project and write forewords for our publication. A thank you must also go to The Institution of Engineers Australia for offering to host our project as a form of in-kind support. Thank you also to the Nature and Society Forum for its continued mentoring and support.

- **Authors**: Alan AtKisson, Alan Pears, Bruce Paton, Cheryl Paten, Chika Saka, Chris Ryan, Jeff Kenworthy, Karlson Hargroves, Michael Fairbanks and Andrew Smith, Michael Smith, Paul Weaver, Peter Newman, Philip Sutton, Rob McLean, Roger Burritt, Stefan Schaltegger, Stephen Dovers, Tobias Hahn and Valerie Brown.
- **Contributors**: Anna McKenzie, Charles Berger, Craig Townsend, Colin Butler, David Dumaresq, Deb Lange, Elizabeth Heij, Fiona Waterhouse, Hugh Forde, Hunter Lovins, Janis Birkeland, Jayarethanam Sinniah Pillai, Jenni Goricanec, Jim McColl, John Braithwaite, John Cronin, Mark Diesendorf, Martin Brennan, Mike Young, Nick Palousis, Peter Drahos, Raimund Bleishwitz, Rob Coombs, Rob Hunt, Rob Murray-Leach, Roger Hadgraft, Steve Morriss, Walter Link, Wayne Wescott and Yolande Strengers.

Thank you to TNEP copy editors and proof-readers Roger Dennis, Stacey Hargroves, Michael Deves and Tim Smith.

Thanks must also be extended to the following representatives from these organizations who kindly agreed to join TNEP's Advisory Board, Steering Committee, Editorial Support Team and the young professionals Working Group. These teams have been working on a number of TNEP initiatives and provide valuable mentoring and contributions. Thank you to:

- **TNEP *Advisory Committee* members**: Alan Tate, Barry Grear, Brian Walker, Brendan Mackey, Dexter Dunphy, Frank Fenner, Fiona Wain, Graeme Barden, Greg Bourne, Hunter Lovins, John Cole, Molly Harris Olsen, Paul Perkins, Ron Clarke, Phillip Toyne, Shaun Mays, Tricia Caswell, Valerie Brown and Gerry Te Kapa Coates.
- **TNEP *Steering Committee* members**: Mike Krockenberger, Andrew Higham, Cameron Hoffmann, Geoff McAlpine, Joanne Kildea, Tim Macoun, Stephan Kaufman, Bryan Furness, Joan Cornish and Daniella Tilbury.
- **TNEP *Editorial Support* Team**: Hunter Lovins, Philip Sutton, Dexter Dunphy, Alan Pears, Michael Krockenberger, Peter Brain, Greg Bourne and Shaun Mays.
- **TNEP *Working Group* members**: Alex Green, Bolle Borkowsky, Craig Butterworth, Christina Foo, David Hobbs, David Marsden Ballard, Debbie Maher, Jayarethanam Sinniah Pillai, Jenni Goricanec, Kate Clark, Kate West, Kerry Dawborn, Nicky Brennan, Peta Lindsay, Peter Stasinopoulos, Rob Murray-Leach, Rory Eames, Simon Nash, Steve Szyndler, Mia Kelly, Victoria Hart and Viet Duong.

Without Engineers Australia's support and the support of the following partners, the creation of this publication would not have been possible. The secretariat of The Natural Edge Project formally wishes to thank its:

Foundation partners

- Engineers Australia, in particular Peter Greenwood, Doug Jones, John Boshier, Barry Greer, Tim Macoun, Bill Rourke, Julie Armstrong, Martine Griffiths and Bolle Borkowsky.
- CSIRO, in particular Geoff McAlpine, Elizabeth Heij, Grant Farrell, Steve Morton, Brian Walker, Graeme Pearman, Geoff Clark and the CEO of CSIRO Geoff Garrett.
- RMIT Global Sustainability Institute, in particular Tricia Caswell, Donna Stephenson, Caroline Bayliss, Sarah Holdsworth and Helen Scott.
- Environment Business Australia, in particular Fiona Wain, Joanne Kildea and Paul Perkins.
- The Barton Group, including Collex, SA Water and Coffey, in particular Bill Leane and Jill Grant.
- Chris Johnson and the team at Izilla for developing our amazing website as a form of in-kind support for our project.

Principle partners

- The Centre for the Encouragement of Philanthropy in Australia – Ron Clarke
- The Australian National University National Institute for the Environment, in particular Colin Butler, Valerie Brown, Sasha Courville, Bob Wasson.
- The Environmental Engineering Society (Australia) and the Engineers Australia Environment College, in particular Gary Codner and Tim Macoun.

Project partners

- ARUP, in particular David Singleton and Cathy Crawley.
- HATCH, in particular Stephen Gale and Philip Bangerter.
- Queensland Environment Protection Agency – Sustainable Industries Division, in particular John Cole.

Project supporters (in alphabetical order)

AtKisson Inc,
Australian Association of Environmental Education (AAEE),
Australian Conservation Foundation (ACF),
Australian Green Development Forum (AGDF),
Australian Virtual Engineering Library (AVEL) – Sustainability Knowledge Network,
Asia-Pacific Forum for Environment and Development (APFED),
Business Council for Sustainable Energy (BCSE),
Commonwealth Engineers Council,
Design Inc,
Eco-Industrial Development Council of North America,
EcoFutures,
Environs Australia,
Environment Institute of Australia and New Zealand (EIANZ),
Green Innovations,
Griffith University,
Forum for the Future (UK),
Institute of Professional Engineers of New Zealand (IPENZ),
International Council for Local Environmental Initiatives Australia and New Zealand
    (ICLEI),
International Young Professionals Foundation (IYPF),
Monash University Centre for Green Chemistry,
Natural Capitalism Solutions (NCS),
Nature and Society Forum,
New Zealand Business Council for Sustainable Development,
OzGreen,
(The Council of) Professions Australia,
Rocky Mountain Institute (RMI),
The Australian Collaboration,
Triple Bottom Line Australia,
University Leaders for a Sustainable Future (ULSF),
UN International Environment Technology Centre (IETC),
Waalitj Environmental Technology Centre, Murdoch University,
World Federation of Engineering Organisations (WFEO) – ComTech,
Young Engineers Australia (YEA)

Numerous individuals formally support TNEP, many of whom have offered invaluable advice, peer review and assistance. Thank you to the following people:

Alex Fearnside	Bruce Thomas	David Singleton
Alexandra de Blas	Cameron Burns	David Suzuki
Alexis Karolides	Cameron Hoffmann	David Yencken
Andrew Donovan	Cameron Neil	Dennis O'Neill
Andrew Thiele	Cameron Tonkinwise	Dick Smith
Anne Harvey	Catherine Greener	Don Henry
Barbara Hardy	Cathy Zoi	Fiona Waterhouse
Barry Jones	Cecilia Hilder	Gary Codner
Bernard Amadei	Chris Page	Graeme Pearman
Bob and Chris Cameron	Chris Strauss	Greg Bourne
Bolle Borkowsky	Christine Loh	Heather Lloyd
Brendan Smyth	David Kemp	Heather Tallent
Bruce Roff	David Kimber	Ian Lowe

Istemi Demirag
James Porteous
Jane Moran Alspach
Janis Birkeland
Jenny Boshier
Jim McKnoulty
Jo Baker
Jo Hume
Joe Herbertson
John Gardiner
John White
Jonathan Sinclair Wilson
Josephine Lang
Julia Birch
Julie Johnson
Junko Edahiro
Karen Alexander
Karen Cameron
Kasey Arnold-Ince
Kate MacMasters
Kathryn Smith
Katherine Wells
Keith Daniel
Maggie Hine
Maria Simonelli

Margaret Metz
Mark Coffey
Mark Mills
Martine Griffiths
Masayoshi Takahashi
Mathis Wackernagel
Mei Ng
Michael Buxton
Michael Lunn
Michael Mobbs
Mike Young
Monica Vandenberg
Moss Cass
Nathan Fabian
Nathan Malin
Neal A. Donahue
Nick Moraitis
Nicolette Boele
Odd-Even Bustnes
Peter Brain
Peter David Pederson
Peter Greenwood
Peter Lowitt
Peter May
Peter Ottesen

Ric Brazzale
Rick Belt
Roger and Jean Venables
Ronnie Harding
Rupert Posner
Sara Parkin
Sasha Courville
Simon Molesworth
Steve Halls
Steven Boyden
Steven Dilli
Sue Lennox
Suzanne Benn
Takashi Matsumura
Terry Hills
Thomas Brinsmead
Thorsten Schuetze
Tony Marjoram
Tony Ridley
Trevor Daniell
Tricia Caswell
Walter Leal Filho
Wayne Smith
William Scully-Power

LIST OF ACRONYMS AND ABBREVIATIONS

10XE	Factor Ten Engineering (RMI)
AU$	Australian dollar
AAA	Australian Automobile Association
AAEE	Australian Association of Environmental Education
ABARE	Australian Bureau of Agricultural and Resource Economics
ABGR	Australian Building Greenhouse Rating
ABS	Australian Bureau of Statistics
ACA	Australian Consumers' Association
Acc	accounting
ACCA	Association of Chartered Certified Accountants (UK)
ACF	Australian Conservation Foundation
ACT	Autralian Capital Territory
ACTU	Australian Council of Trade Unions
AGDF	Australian Green Development Forum
AGO	Australian Greenhouse Office
AIRP-SD	Adaptive Integration of Research and Policy for Sustainable Development
AMA	American Management Association
ANCID	Australian National Committee on Irrigation and Drainage
ANU	Australian National University
ANZ	Australian/New Zealand
APFED	Asia-Pacific Forum for Environment and Development
AU	Australian
AVEL	Australian Virtual Engineering Library
BCSE	Business Council for Sustainable Energy
BedZED	Beddington Zero (fossil) Energy Development (UK)
BSI	British Standards Institute
CCT	Café Cooperativa Timor
CERES/GRI	Coalition of Environmentally Responsible Economies/Global Reporting Initiative
CICA	Canadian Institute of Chartered Accountants
CO_2	carbon dioxide
COAG	Council of Australian Governments
COM	Commission of the European Union
CPI	consumer price index
CSIRO	Commonwealth Scientific and Industrial Research Organisation
DfE	Design for Environment
DOE	Department of Ecology
DTC	developing and transition countries
DTIE	Division of Technology, Industry and Environment (UNEP)
Ecol	ecological
EET	Economy, Ecology, Technology (the Netherlands)
EFFAS	European Federation of Financial Analysts Societies

EI	ethical investment
EIANZ	Environment Institute of Australia and New Zealand
EIS	Environmental Impact Statement
EITI	Extractive Industry Transparency Initiative
EMA	environmental management accounting
EMS	Environmental Management Statement
Env	environmental
EPA	Environmental Protection Agency
ESD	ecologically sustainable development
ESDI	Environment and Sustainable Development Indicators (Canada)
ESI	Environmental Sustainability Index
Ext	external
FEE	Fédération des Experts Comptables Européens
Fin	financial
FSC	Forest Stewardship Council
GCC	Global Consumer Class
GDP	gross domestic product
GHG	greenhouse gas
GIS	geographic information systems
GJ	gigajoule
GMO	genetically modified organism
GNP	gross national product
GPI	genuine progress indicators
GPS	global positioning satellite
GRI	Global Reporting Initiative
IASC	International Accounting Standards Committee
ICC	International Chamber of Commerce
ICLEI	International Council for Local Environmental Initiatives (Australia and New Zealand)
ICT	information and communications technology
IETC	UN International Environment Technology Centre
IMF	International Monetary Fund
IPCC	Intergovernmental Panel on Climate Change
IPENZ	Institute of Professional Engineers of New Zealand
IRN	International Rivers Network
ISO	International Organization for Standardization
IT	information technology
ITDP	Institute for Transportation and Development Policy
IYPF	International Young Professionals Foundation
Man	management
MDG	Millennium Development Goals
MEMA	monetary environmental management accounting
MJ	megajoule
MSC	Marine Stewardship Council
MSP	multi-stakeholder process
NCSD	National Councils for Sustainable Development
NGO	non-governmental organization
NMP3	third National Environmental Policy Plan (the Netherlands)
NMP4	fourth National Environmental Policy Plan (the Netherlands)
nrg4SD	Network of Regional Governments for Sustainabel Development
NSW	New South Wales
OECD	Organisation for Economic Co-operation and Development
OPEC	Organization of Petroleum Exporting Countries

OTF	On The Frontier
PEMA	physical environmental management accounting
PG&E	Pacific Gas and Electric Company
Prod	product
PV	photovoltaic
R&D	research and development
RMI	Rocky Mountain Institute
RMIT	Royal Melbourne Institute of Technology (now RMIT University)
RTD	research and technology development
SD	sustainable development
SEA	strategic environmental assessment
SEC	Securities and Exchange Commission (US)
SEI	Social and Economic Integration (Australia)
SRI	socially responsible investment
STD	Sustainable Technology Development (the Netherlands)
STEP	Sustainable Transport Environment in Penang (Malaysia)
SudVEL-SKN	Sudan Virtual Engineering Library's Sustainability Knowledge Network
TBL	triple bottom line
TNC	transnational corporation
TNEP	The Natural Edge Project
UK	United Kingdom
ULSF	University Leaders for a Sustainable Future
UN	United Nations
UN CSD	United Nations Commission on Sustainable Development
UN DESA	United Nations Department of Economic and Social Affairs
UN-HABITAT	United Nations Human Settlements Programme
UN ISAR	United Nations Intergovernmental Working Group of Experts on International Standards of Accounting and Reporting
UNCED	United Nations Conference on Environment and Development (Rio de Janeiro, 1992, also known as the Earth Summit)
UNCTAD	United Nations Conference on Trade and Development
UNDP	United Nations Development Programme
UNEP	United Nations Environment Programme
UNESCO	United Nations Educational, Scientific and Cultural Organization
US	United States
US$	United States dollar
USAID	United States Agency for International Development
USGCRP	US Global Change Research Program
VOC	volatile organic compound
WA	Western Australia
WBCSD	World Business Council for Sustainable Development
WCD	World Commission on Dams
WFEO	World Federation of Engineering Organisations
WHO	World Health Organization
WRI	World Resources Institute
WSSD	World Summit on Sustainable Development (Johannesburg, 2002)
WTO	World Trade Organization
WWF	*formerly known as* World Wide Fund For Nature and World Wildlife Fund
YEA	Young Engineers Australia
ZERI	Zero Emissions Research Initiative (Japan)

INTRODUCTION:
INSURMOUNTABLE OPPORTUNITIES

The next 50 years could see a fourfold increase in the size of the global economy and significant reductions in poverty, but only if governments act now to avert a growing risk of severe damage to the environment and profound social unrest. Without better policies and institutions, social and environmental strains may derail development progress, leading to higher poverty levels and a decline in the quality of life for everybody. Misguided policies and weak governance in past decades have contributed to environmental disasters, income inequality, and social upheaval in some countries, often resulting in deep deprivation, riots, or refugees fleeing famine or civil wars. Today, many poor people depend on fragile natural resources to survive. Similarly, trust between individuals, which can be eroded or destroyed by civic unrest, is a social asset with important economic benefits, since it enables people to make agreements and undertake transactions that would otherwise not be possible. Development polices need to be more sharply focused on protecting these natural and social assets... New alliances are needed at the local, national and global levels to better address these problems.

World Bank, *World Development Report 2003: Sustainable Development in a Dynamic World*

At the heart of Western culture is the optimistic faith and belief in progress. The belief that life will get better is embedded in our psyche. We have a unique ability, as a species, to learn, reflect and analyse as individuals, and also to communicate and work together as a community. We have the capacity to gain wisdom and seek the truth, with hope in a better future. Faith that we can better ourselves, our community and our society, is at the core of who we are. Despite this, there has been significant loss of trust in our ability to improve our society and meet the pressing challenges of our time. These major challenges now faced by our civilization include poverty, pestilence and disease, unemployment and an increasing dependence on non-renewable energy sources.

So serious is this decline in trust that it was the theme of the World Economic Forum's 2003 meeting. Figure I.1 shows the results of a recent global public opinion survey of 36,000 people, released by the World Economic Forum in early 2003. It shows that 48 per cent of people express little or no trust in global companies, with 52 per cent expressing similar scepticism about large national businesses. But trust has been eroded far beyond the corporate sector. Two-thirds of those surveyed were of the opinion that their country was 'not governed by the will of the people'.

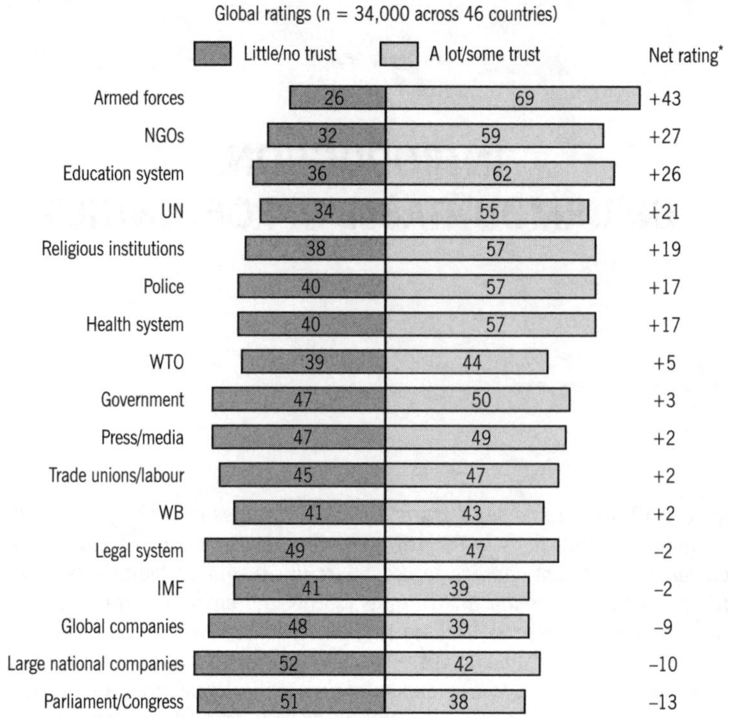

Global ratings (n = 34,000 across 46 countries)

	Little/no trust	A lot/some trust	Net rating*
Armed forces	26	69	+43
NGOs	32	59	+27
Education system	36	62	+26
UN	34	55	+21
Religious institutions	38	57	+19
Police	40	57	+17
Health system	40	57	+17
WTO	39	44	+5
Government	47	50	+3
Press/media	47	49	+2
Trade unions/labour	45	47	+2
WB	41	43	+2
Legal system	49	47	-2
IMF	41	39	-2
Global companies	48	39	-9
Large national companies	52	42	-10
Parliament/Congress	51	38	-13

* % trust minus % distrust = net rating

Source: Gallup International and Environics International 'Voice of the People' Survey.

Figure I.1 *Trust in institutions to operate in society's best interests*

As Australia's former Minister for the Environment and current Defence Minister, Senator Robert Hill, has stated:

> It is more than three decades since man first walked on the moon. The Apollo 11 mission captured the imagination of the general public and was viewed at the time as an example of how far we had progressed as a people. In the following years, however, it also became a defining contrast: we were clever enough to put a man on the moon but we couldn't come up with the answers to our problems here on earth – poverty, hunger, disease, cross-border violence and so on. This requires a commitment from governments, industry and the community.
> Australian Senator Robert Hill, in his address to The International Society of Ecological Economists, Australian National University, Canberra, 6 July, 2000.

Our generation can little afford to ignore the lessons of the last 30 years. Fundamental to our future, now as never before, will be the answers to questions such as those posed at the founding of the United Nations, and again at the 1972 United Nations Conference on the Human Environment in Stockholm:

- What future do we want?
- What sort of life, community and society do we want?

- What legacy will we leave our children and grandchildren?
- What sort of quality of life do we value?
- What sort of institutional frameworks, incentives and structures do we need, in order to be true to those values and meet people's real needs?

How effectively we can bring to bear the ingenuity, creativity, passion and motivation in our societies, to achieve this preferred future we so desire, will dictate the quality of life for our children and their children. We all want to leave the best legacy possible. Nobody would argue against reducing poverty or unemployment, and you are unlikely to find anyone saying the destruction of the rainforests, coral reefs and indigenous culture is a good thing. There is consensus on what we do not want and what the problems are and the world has become increasingly united on what it does want. There is a growing consensus that the threat of irreversible decline of our natural ecosystems, together with the failure to make significant progress on global inequality, means that we need a new paradigm of development: a new way forward that improves the well-being of this generation whilst ensuring the non-declining well-being of future generations as argued by Nobel Laureates of Economics like Solow and Stiglitz.[1]

> *Today, there is a need to reinvent development. A new paradigm can only be achieved by many stakeholders working together and tackling economic, as well as social and environmental issues with equal results.*

Jose Maria Figueres, Senior Managing, Director of the World Economic Forum

There are signs of change as shown in a worldwide survey by the UN that identified 15 global issues that will dominate the future; the foremost of these was achieving sustainable development. The UN commented that: 'Never before has world opinion been so united on a single goal as it is on achieving sustainable development'.[2] At the United Nations' Millennium Summit in September 2000, world leaders from 189 nations placed sustainable development at the heart of the global agenda by adopting the Millennium Development Goals (MDGs). These goals set clear targets for the reduction of poverty, hunger, disease, illiteracy, environmental degradation and discrimination against women by 2015. Therefore, 189 nations have committed to the UN Millennium Goals to reduce world poverty by 50 per cent by 2015. The UN Millennium Goals Committee has made it clear in the 2003 UNDP Human Development Report that meeting the environmental MDGs is vital for the achievement of the other goals of poverty reduction and improved health outcomes.

The speed with which we shift to a sustainable economy will depend on whether we adopt truly integrated and holistic approaches. Fundamentally, the challenge of sustainable development is complex; as such, it requires integrated systems approaches and whole of society engagement. The situation is further complicated by the fact that there is both a local and global dimension to sustainable development. Hence, our rate of progress will depend on achieving the correct mix and balance between the state and the market, between competitive and cooperative action at the local, national and global levels, and between government and non-governmental organizations (NGOs).

This is no easy task, and it is why we devote chapters of this book to focus on the role various sections of society can play: in order that we can adopt better, more holistic and systemic approaches to addressing the challenges of the coming century. It is also why we have chosen to provide not only overviews of inspiring local success stories, but also a discussion of how global progress has been achieved in the past, and hence provide leadership on how it can be achieved in the future. Section 1 of the book provides a detailed overview of the core thesis. Sections 2 and 3 outline the role played by business and government respectively in partnership with other actors in society. Section 4 outlines how business, government and civil society can work together most effectively to address major issues like urbanization, global warming, energy and water. Section 5 offers a blueprint of integrated sustainable production and consumption and details how, for instance, leading educational institutions are already playing their part in the lead up to the UN Decade of Education in Sustainable Development and how individuals can and are making a difference.

Table I.1 *Why reaching the environmental goals is so important for achieving the Millennium Goals*

1 Eradicate extreme poverty and hunger	Poor people's livelihoods and food security often depend on ecosystem goods and services. The poor often have insecure rights to environmental resources, inadequate access to markets, a lack of decision-making and environmental information which limits their ability to protect the environment and improve their livelihoods and well-being.
2 Achieve universal primary education	Time spent by children collecting water and fuelwood reduces the time available for schooling. In addition, the lack of energy, water and sanitation services in rural areas discourages qualified teachers from working in poor villages.
3 Promote gender equality	Women and girls are especially burdened by water and fuel collection, reducing their time and opportunities for education, literacy and income-generating activities.
4 Reduce child mortality	Diseases (such as diarrhoea) tied to unclean water and inadequate sanitation, and respiratory infections related to pollution are among the leading killers of children under five. Lack of fuel for boiling water also contributes to preventable waterborne diseases.
5 Improve maternal health	Inhaling polluted indoor air and carrying heavy loads of water and fuel wood impacts significantly on women's health. This can make them less fit to bear children and place them at greater risk of complications during pregnancy.
6 Combat major diseases	Up to 20% of the disease burden in developing countries may be due to environmental risk factors (as with malaria and parasitic infections).
7 Develop a global partnership	Many global environmental problems, such as climate change, loss of species diversity and depletion of global fisheries can be solved only through partnerships between rich and poor countries.

Source: Selection of the United Nations Millennium Development Goals

SECTION 1

THE NEED FOR A NEW PARADIGM

CHAPTER 1

NATURAL ADVANTAGE OF NATIONS

Progress, competitiveness and sustainability

M. Scott Peck, respected psychiatrist and bestselling author of *The Road Less Travelled*, writes in *The Road Less Travelled and Beyond* (1997) that one of the biggest problems in the world today is people not thinking well:

> *One of the major dilemmas we face both as individuals and as a society is simplistic thinking – or the failure to think at all. It isn't just a problem, it is the problem... Thinking well is more urgent now – perhaps more urgent than anything else – because it is the means by which we consider, decide and act upon everything in our increasingly complex world... If we are to think well, we must be on guard against simplistic thinking in our approach to analysing crucial issues and solving the problems of life.*

He continues:

> *In Ireland, the Middle East, Somalia, Sri Lanka and countless other war torn areas around the world prejudice, religious intolerance, greed and fear have erupted into violence that has taken the lives of millions. In America the damage caused by institutionalized racism is perhaps more subtle but no less devastating to the social fabric. Rich vs. poor, black vs. white, straight vs. gay – all are social, political and economic conflicts found under the banner of some ideology or deeply held belief. But given the divisive and destructive results, are these ideologies and beliefs rational or mere rationalizations for otherwise unreasonable acts? How often in fact do we stop to think about what we believe?*

According to Peck, so many of these logjams and stalemates could be overcome if only we took more time to think through the assumptions underpinning our beliefs, and made the effort to understand the other point of view; take the time to see the world from someone else's perspective. If people did that, they would see that the points on which they agree by far outweighed the points on which they don't.

In the mind of the public, another eternal conflict is that between business and the environmentalists. In the public mind most assume that environmentalists and developers do not agree on much. But until the 1980s, most did agree on one thing: that the more you do for the environment the worse off the economy will be, or the more you promote development and growth the worse off the environment will be. In other words, major trade-offs are required between the two objectives and there is little possibility of significant win–win outcomes. Since no one book can cover all these areas of genuine disagreement and conflict, this latter area of seeming conflict is primarily what this book focuses on. We will show that, unless this conflict between development and the environment is resolved, our generation will leave a grim legacy to future generations. Significant concern for this was given expression in the 1980s when a range of major initiatives to find common ground were started. One outcome of this process was the Bruntland Report, *Our Common Future*, published in 1987 by the United Nations' World Commission on Environment and Development. This landmark report proposed that it was possible to reconcile the concerns of developers and ecologists through better balancing of short- and long-term needs and government leadership. It coined the new phrase 'sustainable development' to sum up this new paradigm of development. It defined Sustainable Development as 'development that meets the needs of the present without compromising the ability of future generations to meet their own needs'. This report was and remains instrumental in achieving the acceptance of the emerging paradigm of sustainable development in mainstream governmental structures, departments and programmes. Support for this new form of development was demonstrated by the attendance at the first world summit on sustainable development (known as the Earth Summit) in Rio de Janeiro in 1992 of more than 100 world leaders and representatives from 167 countries.

However, despite the groundbreaking work presented in *Our Common Future* and the optimism displayed at Rio in 1992, there was sharp disappointment that no binding agreement had been reached at the summit.[1] In addition, there was great concern regarding potential areas of conflict arising from the interaction of the emerging principles of 'sustainable development' with the short-term pressures on businesses' financial bottom line. Since the mid-1990s, business corporations have constituted the majority of the 100 largest 'economies' in the world.[2] Today, the largest business corporations have higher incomes than the GDP of many developing countries. It will be impossible, therefore, to achieve sustainable development without their involvement. In the 2000 publication, *Global Business Regulation*, Braithwaite and Drahos highlight that until the 1980s the dominant attitude amongst business leaders regarding environmental regulation was that globalization will provide ways to 'get around it': that globalization would make it easier to move to countries, with the lowest regulatory costs, known as 'pollution havens'.[3] If the majority of companies in a sector were doing this, then to be competitive many business people wondered if they would have a real choice not to move to pollution havens as well. There are those within government who still assume that if OECD (Organisation for Economic Co-operation and Development) nations tighten their environmental regulation, then companies will be compelled to move operations to countries with the lowest regulatory costs. Furthermore, if developing nations were 'burdened' with environmental regulation, this would hinder their development and remove opportunities for achieving competitive advantage. This perceived dilemma is emerging as the crux of the debate regarding sustainable development: namely, can businesses be both competitive and achieve sustainable development in an increasingly globalized, competitive world? The answer to this question is a qualified 'YES'. This book will outline how many business and political leaders, researchers, practitioners and public servants are turning their attention, insight and creativity towards how to achieve this synergy. The assumption, namely that it is inevitable that business will have to relocate to lowest regulatory cost havens, is disputed by mounting evidence to the contrary.[4] Since the 1980s, there has been a rapidly growing body of work showing that win–win outcomes are not just possible, but are already happening. Evidence is also mounting that demonstrates that companies and nations which wisely pursue best practice in sustainable development, far from reducing the productivity and competitive advantage of their firms, can in fact improve it.[5] As Michael Porter wrote:

> [Countries should] establish norms exceeding the toughest regulatory hurdles or product standards. Some localities (or user industries) will lead in terms of the stringency of product standards, pollution limits, noise standards and the like. Tough regulatory standards are not a hindrance but an opportunity to move early to upgrade products and processes. [And that firms should] find the localities whose regulations foreshadow those elsewhere. Some regions and cities will typically lead others in terms of their concern with social problems such as safety, environmental quality and the like. Instead of avoiding such areas, as some companies do, they should be sought out. A firm should define its internal goals as meeting, or exceeding, their standards. An advantage will result as other regions and ultimately other nations modify regulations to follow suit. Firms like governments are often prone to see the short-term cost of dealing with tough standards and not their long-term benefits in terms of innovation. Firms point to foreign rivals without such standards having a cost advantage. Such thinking is based on an incomplete view of how competitive advantage is created and sustained.

Michael Porter, Harvard Business School, *The Competitive Advantage of Nations*[6]

The most elegant example of this is the story of the Montreal Protocol, and how it significantly progressed the phasing out of ozone destroying chemicals internationally. Early adoption, in the US, of regulations to reduce the emissions of ozone depleting chemicals, had given American-based firms a head start on the rest of the world in innovating alternative chemicals. Rather than resisting the US regulations, companies harnessed their innovation to develop alternative chemicals to those that destroy the ozone layer. Dupont and other leading US companies then successfully lobbied the Reagan administration literally to take the lead in establishing the Montreal Protocol. The Reagan administration could see the moral, scientific and economic benefits for the US in the globalization of their legislation, and played a significant role in generating the political will for the Montreal Protocol's establishment. Sixty US embassies were instructed to lobby for a strong ozone Protocol, first by issuing information and media kits to convince other nations of the validity of the science and the risks.[7] At the 1987 G-7 Summit in Venice, President Reagan successfully influenced the meeting to make protection of the ozone layer the highest priority environmental issue. History shows that, through the adoption of the Montreal Protocol, Dupont achieved a significant increase in global market share for its alternative ozone friendly chemicals.[8]

There are numerous other examples from around the world. For instance, Porter wrote about how Japanese Energy Conservation Laws in 1979 set demanding energy efficiency standards for refrigerators, air-conditioning and automobiles, stimulating product improvements that strengthened the international position of Japanese firms in these markets.[9] Analyses by the German Environment Ministry have found that its higher environmental standards have been not only an environmental asset to the country, but an economic one as well.[10] Pollution control accounts for roughly 700,000 jobs in the German economy. Growth trends in employment in this area are similar across the OECD nations.[11]

> As other nations have pushed ahead, US trade has suffered. Germany has had perhaps the world's tightest regulations in stationary air-pollution control, and

> *German companies appear to hold a wide lead in patenting and exporting air-pollution and other environmental technologies. As much as 70 per cent of the air pollution-control equipment sold in the US today is produced by foreign companies. Britain is another case in point. As its environmental standards have lagged, Britain's ratio of exports to imports in environmental technology has fallen from 8:1 to 1:1 over the past decade. In contrast, the US leads in those areas in which its regulations have been the strictest, such as pesticides and the remediation of environmental damage. Such leads should be treasured and extended. Environmental protection is a universal need, an area of growing expenditure in all the major national economies and a major export industry. The strongest proof that environmental protection does not hamper competitiveness is the economic performance of nations with the strictest laws.*

> Professor Michael Porter, excerpt from April 1991 *Scientific American*

Such a shift towards 'ecological modernization' amongst policy élites in government, NGOs and international bodies was identified in 1992 by Albert Weale in the publication, *New Politics of Pollution* where Weale stated that 'Instead of seeing environmental protection as a burden upon the economy, the ecological modernist sees it as a potential source of growth. Since environmental amenity is a superior good, the demand for pollution control is likely to increase and there is, therefore, a considerable advantage to an economy to have the technical and production capacity to produce low-polluting goods or pollution control technology'.[12]

In 1993, the US Secretaries of Commerce and Energy, together with the Environmental Protection Agency (EPA) Administrator, produced a *Strategic Framework for US Leadership*[13] in environmental exports. It made the admission that US companies have operated in a laissez-faire climate which did not recognize the positive connection between environmental stewardship and economic competitiveness, especially when compared to foreign competitors. The report stated: 'Environmental technologies play a central role in our drive to move beyond the outdated notion that jobs must be traded off against sound environmental policies. Indeed, environmental technologies are a powerful engine for the creation of national wealth and high paying jobs.' The experience of sustainable development related research and consultancy bodies, like Rocky Mountain Institute in Colorado, is that the right strategies can result in large resource productivity improvements often more cheaply than incremental change.[14] Such new strategies are opening up new ways to achieve further competitive advantage for firms. While these new methods assist firms' competitiveness, there are also multiple benefits for the nations within which they do business. For example, designing production processes to eliminate the generation of pollutants is often much cheaper for governments, who frequently have to clean up the impact. There are phenomenal business opportunities for innovation in the development of sustainable solutions that can assist companies to gain an increase in market share.

Examples of Eco-Innovation in Australia enabling gains in market share include:

- Chemical giant Dupont and CSIRO (Commonwealth Scientific and Industrial Research Organisation) have pioneered a new range of coatings that are cheaper to make, cleaner, 'greener' and more durable than today's car paints. CSIRO sold a US$40 million patent to Dupont, who in turn have won the contract with the lucrative US auto paints market.
- Rockcote, Australia's foremost manufacturer of Architectural coatings, inspired by books such as *Natural Capitalism* have developed the 'Eco Style' range of non-toxic paint, a scientific breakthrough that means healthier conditions for builders, tradespersons and consumers.

- Caroma is a Brisbane-based Australian-owned subsidiary of GWA International Limited, and is regarded as the leader in the Australasian sanitary ware industry. Caroma products, including the 6/3 litre dual flush toilet system, which it developed, are shipped to over 30 countries.

This new paradigm is bringing environmental improvement and competitiveness together. As the previous US President Bill Clinton[15] stated in 1997, 'The lesson here is simple: Environmental initiatives, if sensibly designed and flexibly implemented, cost less than expected and provide unforeseen economic opportunities... If we do it right, protecting (the climate) will yield not costs, but profits; not burdens, but benefits; not sacrifice, but a higher standard of living. There is a huge body of business evidence now showing that energy savings give better service at lower cost with higher profits.' More recently Yale University, Columbia University and the World Economic Forum have undertaken a project to rank nations according to a Environmental Sustainability Index (ESI).[16] The ESI provides a basis for addressing a number of pressing policy questions, such as: does good environmental performance come at a price in terms of economic success? The ESI suggests it does not. Finland and Belgium, for example, have similar GDP (gross domestic product) per capita, but are ranked widely apart by the ESI. Interestingly, Finland, as of October 2003, is at the top of both the World Economic Forum's Competitiveness Index and the new Environmental Sustainability Index showing that, if done correctly, there is not an inevitable trade-off. Finland's place at the top of the ESI 2002 ranking is due particularly to its strength in three keys areas of environmental protection: success in minimizing air and water pollution, high institutional capacity to handle environmental problems and comparatively low levels of greenhouse gas emissions.

Thus, if enacted wisely, it is possible for the paradigms of sustainable development and competitiveness to merge. There does not have to be an inevitable trade-off. This merger is being motivated by the following six facts (please note that this list is not intended to be exhaustive, but rather to set a structure for further discussion of the topics):

1   Throughout the economy there are widespread untapped potential resource productivity improvements to be made to be coupled with effective design.
2   There has been a significant shift in understanding over the last three decades of what creates lasting competitiveness of the firm.
3   There is now a critical mass of enabling technologies in eco-innovations that make integrated approaches to sustainable development economically viable.
4   Since many of the costs of what economists call 'environmental externalities' are passed on to governments, in the long-term sustainable development strategies can provide multiple benefits to the tax payer.
5   There is a growing understanding of the multiple benefits of valuing social and natural capital, for both moral and economic reasons, and including them in measures of national well-being.
6   There is mounting evidence to show that a transition to a sustainable economy, if done wisely, may not harm economic growth significantly, in fact it could even help it. Recent research by ex-Wuppertal Institute member Joachim Spangenberg, working with neo-classical economists, shows that the transition, if focussed on improving resource productivity, will lead to higher economic growth than business as usual, while at the same time reducing pressures on the environment and enhancing employment.

Significant potential for resource productivity improvements

There are numerous methods for combining sustainable development and competitiveness that are profitable, backed up by numerous case studies of cost effective, resource efficient production, and numerous examples of product eco-design that are convincing to even the most sceptical.[17]

> *Our central message is that the environment–competitiveness debate has been framed incorrectly. The notion of inevitable struggle between ecology and the economy grows out of a static view of environment regulation, in which technology, products, processes and customer needs are all fixed. In this static world, where firms have already made their cost-minimizing choices, environmental regulation inevitably raises costs and will tend to reduce the market share of domestic companies on global markets. Managers must start to recognise environmental improvement as an economic and competitive opportunity, not as an annoying cost or an inevitable threat. Environmental progress demands that companies innovate to raise resource productivity, precisely the new challenge of global competition. It is time to build on the underlying economic logic that links the environment, resource productivity, innovation, and competitiveness.*
>
> Professor Michael Porter, Harvard Business School[18]

Porter's line of argument is consistent with the literature covering issues of levels of inefficiency, which has produced convincing empirical evidence of widespread and significant inefficiencies within firms in the modern economy.[19] This area of writing is known as X-inefficiency literature. Empirical research in the approach to measuring X-inefficiency has shown that the actual performance of firms in many industries falls significantly below that of the observed efficiencies of the most efficient firms in those industries, typically 65–97 per cent. For example, one of the significant sources of gains still poorly understood is the improved level of resource productivity possible through whole system design. Whole system design is showing that companies can often achieve bigger resource productivity gains for less cost than incremental change.[20]

> *I believe we can accomplish great and profitable things within a new conceptual framework: one that values our legacy, honours diversity, and feeds ecosystems and societies… It is time for designs that are creative, abundant, prosperous, and intelligent from the start.*
>
> William McDonough, *Time Magazine* Hero of the Planet, 1999[21]

Consider the case of Jan Schilham's famous work on pipes and pumps for Interface Ltd. In 1997, while Interface was building a factory in Shanghai: 'One of its industrial processes required 14 pumps. In optimizing the design, the top Western specialist firm sized the pump motors to total 95 horsepower. But by applying methods learned from Singaporean efficiency expert Eng Lock Lee (and focusing on reducing waste in the form of friction), it cut the design's pumping power to only 7 horsepower – a 92 per cent or 12-fold energy saving – while reducing its capital cost and improving its performance in every respect.'[22] Why is this significant? As Amory Lovins writes: 'Pumping is the biggest use of motors, motors use 3/5 of all electricity. Saving one unit of friction in the pipe saves 10 units of fuel. And, because of all the large amount of losses of electricity in its transmission from the power plant to the end use, saving one unit of energy for the pump/pipe system saves upwards of ten units of fuel at the power plant.'

This case study highlights a key reason why these new methods offer such benefits to any company and/or nation that implements them. Such approaches offer multiple

Table 1.1 *Emerging solutions and rewards: pioneers who are 'walking the talk'*

Mining	BioHeap, is a climate positive leaching process, (the process actually absorbs carbon dioxide out of the atmosphere) for treating nickel and copper ores. Developed by Titan Resources in Western Australia, the process eliminates the need to grind ore finely and leaves behind an inert residue. BioHeap has reduced the cost of producing nickel to less than half its value on the world market.
Climate neutral buildings	The Beddington 'zero (fossil) energy development', involving a range of bodies such as Arup, is Britain's first urban carbon-neutral development. BedZED's zero-carbon 'total energy strategy' is achieved via energy-efficient design of the buildings, use of renewable energy sources and a green transport plan.
Mining wastes or mining resources?	Hatch Engineering has developed a revolutionary method of reusing slag waste in concrete, significantly reducing the greenhouse emissions whilst also achieving zero waste outcomes and increasing productivity. They are now applying the Cemstar Process technology with clients globally as part of a major international programme.
Desalination	A London-based group has recently developed a revolutionary design to dramatically reduce the costs of desalination. The ingenious building for desalination operates at a fraction of the cost of traditional desalination plants. The first seawater greenhouse has been built on Tenerife, partly with European Commission funds. A second is under development in Oman and there are plans for many others.
Oil companies	BP Australia are offering petrol at slightly higher cost with the promise that the money will be used to begin to off-set the carbon emissions, in an attempt to achieve an overall climate neutral outcome. If successful, this programme to internalize the real costs to the environment of petrol use will be rolled out by BP internationally.
Win–win options for waste and forestry	The 1999 Gold Medal for CSIRO research was awarded to a team that worked for ten years on how best to re-use treated effluent. Urgent research was commissioned into the disposal of town effluent, partly as a response to toxic blue green algae outbreaks in the Murray Darling system. CSIRO Land and Water and CSIRO Forestry and Forest Products have used their experience over ten years to produce environmental guidelines for councils, irrigators and foresters on the sustainable use of effluent in forestry.
Filtration of industrial processes	The University of Melbourne together with the CSIRO have developed a totally new form of industrial pressurized filtration. Industrial pressurized filtration is responsible for over one-third of all the energy used in filtration globally. This completely new methodology and design provides at least 30–40% efficiency gains for existing plants, and significantly more for new plants.

Source: Adapted from Porter (1990)

benefits because as much as 70 per cent of their resource usage is locked into the design: by then, much of the environmental impact, that may be designed away, is already inevitable.[23] Change the design and there are numerous flow on benefits. In the famous case study above additional benefits included a reduction in friction loss from pipes; theses changes led to reduced noise and maintenance, whilst providing a longer life for the pipes.

When properly understood, the sustainable development paradigm offers significant productivity gains through such proven methodologies as lean thinking. These improve *resource and labour* productivity whilst *simultaneously* reducing inventory and capital costs and the risk of exposure to excess stock in an economic downturn.[24] The growing understanding of this by many companies is illustrated by the fact that of the 150 global corporate members of the World Business Council for Sustainable Development (WBCSD),[25] 92 have Vice Presidents for Sustainable Development. Wise firms are now integrating sustainable development orientated reforms as part of their strategic lean thinking programmes. The ideas behind lean thinking have resulted from a re-examination of global manufacturing systems and supply chains. World-renowned industrial economists James Womack and Daniel Jones[26] have found that, far from being beneficial, the globalization of production often creates enormous unnecessary waste in global inventories. Apart from demonstrating the wisdom of re-examining the nuts and bolts of companies and their supply chains, they also found that an alternative closed-loop economy involving more recycling was much more cost effective than transporting materials from all over the world.

Creating competitive advantage of the firm

There has been a significant change in understanding, over the past three decades of what creates lasting competitiveness of the firm. Professor Michael Porter showed, in *The Competitive Advantage of Nations*, that globalization, the shortening timeframe of technical innovation and the rise of the multinational corporation mean that the ability to innovate processes in advance of one's competitors is the key to increasing productivity gains and competitive advantage today. Porter writes: 'competitiveness is not merely greater efficiency based on working harder or even working smarter. It is not merely doing things better but doing better things. It requires firms with the know-how to capture greater value in the market place not just by being more efficient at what they do, but also in choosing where to compete. The new paradigm of international competitiveness is a dynamic one, based on innovation. Competitiveness at the industry level arises from superior productivity; either in terms of lower costs than rivals or the ability to offer products with superior value[27] (value adding)[28] that justifies a premium price. Detailed case studies of hundreds of industries, based in dozens of countries, reveal that internationally competitive companies are not those with the cheapest inputs or the largest scale, but those with the capacity to improve and innovate continually. Competitive advantage, then, rests not on static efficiency or on optimizing within fixed constraints, but on the capacity for innovation and improvement that shift the constraints.'

Traditionally, nations have sought to assist their firms to achieve competitive advantage on the basis that you need to reduce labour and resource costs, run a lower exchange rate and so on. Countries that, for instance, had abundant and cheap natural resources were seen to have a 'natural advantage' over those nations that did not. However, as Porter demonstrated in *The Competitive Advantage of Nations*, there are firms that have succeeded in achieving international competitive advantage whilst doing the exact opposite of these standard assumptions.

Increasingly then, companies that are most competitive, achieving the greatest productivity gains, are not those with access to the lowest cost inputs. Rather, they are those firms which constantly innovate to become the best in the world. A study undertaken by Collins and Porras[29] compared the stock price of visionary companies, especially those companies with a socially conscious vision, with their major competitors. What they found was staggering: visionary companies were up to 15 times more profitable than the market average, even though the bottom line was not their major concern. Such companies, which include 3M, Boeing and General Electric, all outperformed their major competitors in stock price, often by a factor of ten or more.

Because technology is constantly changing, the new paradigm of global competitiveness requires the ability to innovate rapidly for new emerging markets. This is evidenced by the fact that the most competitive companies are those that employ the

Table 1.2 *Traditional assumptions of what creates competitiveness are not always true*

Cheap and abundant labour	Germany, Switzerland and Scandinavian countries have done well for decades with high wages and shortages of labour.
Interest rates, government deficits, and exchange rates	There are many nations that have enjoyed rising living standards with budget deficits (Korea, Italy and Japan), appreciating currencies (Germany and Switzerland), and high interest rates (Italy and Korea) over the last 30 years.
Possessing abundant, cheap raw resources	From the 1970s to the 1990s, resource poor nations like Singapore, Japan, Korea, Switzerland and Germany prospered. Singapore achieved a rise in per capita GDP, in the 15 years from 1980 to 1995, that resource rich US needed 50 years to accomplish.
Labour-management relations	It is not easy to generalize here, as unions are very strong, for instance, in Germany and Sweden with representation by law in management (Germany) and on boards of directors (Sweden). Both nations over the last 30 years have prospered, contradicting the view that strong unions will lead to loss of competitiveness.

Source: Adapted from Porter (1990)

most advanced technology and methods in using their inputs. A major study by McKinsey & Co of over 1000 companies in 15 sectors over 36 years, found that innovating to become the best in new emerging markets was a key element of success.[30] Companies simply sticking to 'business as usual' automatically under-performed. For example, faced with the threat of the Personal Computer, IBM continued to insist on picturing tomorrow as an extrapolation of today and assumed the demand for the PC would not be great enough to warrant a change in strategy. In doing so, the companies missed market opportunities worth an estimated US$70 billion.[31] The McKinsey & Co report added: 'As capital markets become less forgiving of long-term under-performance, so corporate life-spans shrink. The average life of companies on the Standard & Poor's index fell from over 65 years in the 1920s and 1930s to around ten years by 1998. Too often, corporations are slowed down by their fears about cannibalizing their own markets, potential customer channel conflicts, or the dilution of earnings. Markets, by contrast, have "no lingering memories or remorse", creating more surprise, more innovation.'[32]

The fastest growing new emerging markets are increasingly in the area of sustainable solutions. In addition, Porter and van der Linde[33] demonstrated that firms can achieve further competitive advantage through greater resource productivity, the eco-design of products (reducing process costs) and the production of 'clean and green' goods and services (product differentiation).

A broader shift is starting to occur. There are many examples of unilateral initiatives that have helped firms differentiate their products and gain market share based on environmental attributes of their products and processes. For example, BP has exploited its marketing and technology management capabilities, developed through the fossil fuel businesses, to build a market leading position in renewable energy technologies, particularly solar cells. BP's differentiation has been heightened by: (i) the decisions by all the other major American energy companies except Amoco to divest their alternative energy businesses, and (ii) the decision by many of the oil companies to play a visible role in resisting the adoption of effective climate change policies. Similarly, two carpet companies, Interface, Inc[34] and Collins and Aikman[35] have chosen to differentiate their products by investing in materials that can be almost completely recycled into new

Table 1.3 Benefits of eco-efficiencies, whole system design and industrial ecology to a company's competitive advantage

Process benefits	Product benefits
• Material savings from better whole system design.	• Higher quality, more consistent products.
• Increases in process yields and less downtime through designing out waste and designing the plant and process to minimize maintenance and parts.	• Lower product costs (for instance, from material substitution, new improved plant efficiencies).
	• Lower packaging costs.
• Better design to ensure that by-products and waste can be converted into valuable forms.	• More efficient resource use by-products.
	• Safer products.
• Greater resource productivity of inputs, energy, water and raw materials to reduce costs.	• Lower net costs of product disposal to customers.
• Reduced material storage and handling costs through 'just in time' management.	• Higher product resale and scrap value.
• Improved occupational heath and safety.	• Products that meet new consumer demands for environmental benefits.
• Improvements in the quality of product or service.	

Source: Adapted from Porter and van der Linde (1995a)

carpets. Ford Motor Company has developed a commanding lead over its domestic competitors in the design and manufacturing of low emission vehicles selling nearly 95 per cent of all such vehicles in the US.[36]

These are not isolated case studies, nor do they apply only to billion-dollar companies. As we will show, actual experiences reported in many studies and reports have consistently shown that eco-efficiencies, eco-innovation and cleaner production provide numerous ways to improve the triple bottom line, and thereby begin the journey to genuine sustainable development. Section 2 will present the emerging consensus of how firms can achieve sustainable competitive advantage.

A critical mass of enabling technologies

> Innovation is the central issue in economic prosperity.
> Michael Porter, Harvard Business School

> Innovation is a central driver of economic growth and social development. The evidence for this relationship is compelling and now widely recognised: innovation is a major determinant of the success of firms and of economies. The development and commercialisation of new products, processes and services are key drivers of economic growth. Innovation depends on research and ready access and receptiveness to new technology and ideas. It propels productivity, spawns new industries and transforms existing industries. Economies which can effectively foster and commercialise innovations will grow faster and will generate more jobs and higher living standards.
> Investing for Growth, Commonwealth of Australia, 1997[37]

Nations and firms are increasingly aware of the importance of being ahead of the next so called 'wave' of innovation and are asking 'What will give rise to the new areas of innovation?' In order for a wave of innovation to occur, there needs to be a significant

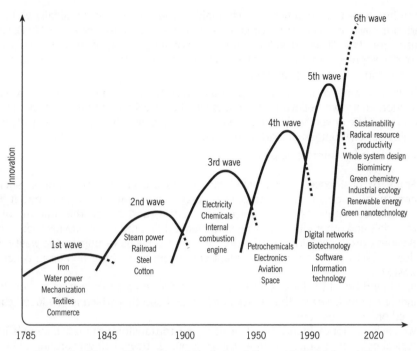

Figure 1.1 *Waves of innovation of the first and the next industrial revolution*

array of relatively new and emerging technologies and a recognized genuine need in the market that is leading to a market expansion. As *Natural Capitalism* discussed, the first Industrial Revolution began with the steam engine and new machines to increase the labour productivity of cotton-spinning and the production of steel. This was followed by further industrial shifts with the engineering that evolved out of advances in the understanding of, for instance, electro-magnetism. This was followed by a focus on mass production of the automobile and electrification of cities, a wave which lasted until the 1940s. The rise of semiconductors and electronics provided just some of the enabling technologies that helped create new business opportunities throughout the 1950s and 1960s. In the case of the Information and Communications Technology (ICT) wave of innovation, it is easy to identify the technologies that were driving the growth of capacity in the industry. Innovations in computer processing power, network bandwidth and data storage have all helped achieve the predictions of Gordon Moore in the 1970s that 'computing power will continue to double every 18 months, while costs hold constant.'[38] This last wave of industrial activity was largely based on semiconductors, fibre optics, networks and software.

Many of the applications in the previous IT wave of innovation were based on the idea of reducing transaction costs.[39] In the book, *Unleashing the Killer App*, Downes and Mui suggest that the market for the many Internet applications was in the reduction of 'transaction costs'.[40] For instance, email is a cheap and fast means of communication, finding information is now much faster and cheaper online, together with Internet booking, purchasing and banking significantly reducing the costs of customer transactions.[41] The ICT revolution is just one in a series of long waves of industrial innovation first noted in the 1940s by Joseph Schumpeter, an Austrian-born economist. In his work, Schumpeter tracked the rise and flow of economies with respect to technology. We submit that there is now a critical mass of enabling eco-innovations making integrated approaches to sustainable development economically viable. As reported in *Small is Profitable*,[42] voted as one of the three best books by *The Economist* magazine for 2002: 'These developments form not simply a list of separate items, but a web of developments that all reinforce each other. Their effect is thus both individually important and collectively profound.'

If the last wave of innovation, ICT, was driven by market needs such as reducing transaction costs, we believe that there is significant evidence that the next waves of innovation will be driven by the twin needs simultaneously to improve productivity whilst lightening our environmental load on the planet.

Consider a few interesting points:

- Some of businesses' most significant costs are capital and inputs, such as construction costs, raw materials, energy, water and transportation. It is in businesses' interests to minimize these costs, and hence the amount of raw materials and other inputs they need to create their product or provide their service. Business produces either useful products and services or unsaleable waste. How does it assist a business to have plant equipment and labour tied up in generating waste?
- It is in individual business's interests to find markets for this 'waste' and/or design industrial processes so that waste is minimized and that which is produced can be used or sold elsewhere.
- Womack and Jones found that it takes a year to transform the raw materials into a typical cola can. During this time, these resources travel half way around the world. *Lean Thinking* analysis shows that recycling cola cans would create numerous win–win benefits and dramatically reduce costs through the supply chain.[43]

But the fundamental reason why the pure scale of the challenge of sustainability will drive innovation is best illustrated through the five years of work of the Netherlands Government's Sustainable Technology Development project. The study found that, given projected increases in global population and the trends of the spread of western consumerism, humanity needs to reduce its negative environmental load by at least 90 per cent[44] or there will, over time, be a significant decline of ecosystem resilience.

> *In setting a time-horizon of 50 years – two generations into the future – it was found that ten- to twenty-fold eco-efficiency improvements will be needed to achieve meaningful reductions in environmental stress. It was also found that the benefits of incremental technological development could not provide such improvements.*
>
> Leo Jensen, Chairman, Dutch Inter-ministerial, Sustainable Technology Development Program 2000[45]

This view may seem extreme, but it comes from a detailed understanding of trends in resource usage globally and how, despite the apparent success of eco-efficiencies, energy and material flows are still increasing globally. This is the dilemma marring the apparent success of eco-efficiency and de-materialization in that consumption outpaces the system-wide gains in production, total resource use grows and so does the GDP. In Japan, total energy consumption has continued to rise, despite significant efforts in eco-efficiencies. This trend is found in many OECD nations and industry sectors.

We now possess both the technological innovations and design know-how to tackle many environmental problems cost effectively and in some areas very profitably. Specifically, this involves everything from green buildings, hybrid cars, wind power, resource processing, transport systems, a wide array of recycling and other enabling technologies that will be covered in Section 4. However this is just the start, still more

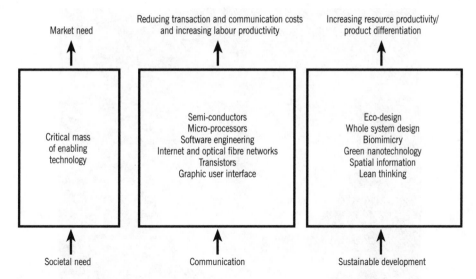

Figure 1.2 *Critical mass of innovations meeting real market needs creates new waves of innovation*

innovations are emerging from the fields of materials science, green chemistry, green nanotechnology and from simply having the humility to learn from nature. One of the best books on this is by Janine Benyus called *Biomimicry*.[46] Her book asks how does nature do business? How does nature work? Nature manufactures an amazing array of products and yet it does it very differently than our present industrial system. Nature manufactures with low energy flows, near body conditions, no persistent toxics. Everything that is an output of a process is food for some other process. The loops are closed. If you look at our manufacturing it's very different. Benyus uses the example of an abalone. It manufactures in seawater at ambient temperature immediately next to the creature's body an inner lining, stronger than our best ceramic. How does it do it? It turns out you can find out. Scientists at Sandia Laboratory in New Mexico in the States realized that the abalone was inducing calcium ions from surrounding seawater to fit exactly into its ionic blueprint. They found that if they take silicon wafers and electrically charge them and dip them into alternating baths of calcium carbonate and polymer they can to create a similar material as it self-assembles at the molecular level. The same way nature does it. So you can make scratchless eyeglasses and breakless windshields and even a nose cone for space shuttles. Researchers and business people can learn from nature to create better products. Nature has evolved over billions of years. Hence, there is much we can learn from the way nature designs things.

For instance, the rotor technology – fan blades, mixers, propellers – developed by PAX Scientific, Inc, of San Rafael, California is modelled on streamlined shapes found in nature. Using these shapes, the company's biomimetic inventions demonstrate remarkable improvements in energy efficiency and productivity with significant reductions in noise. One example is the PAX mixer. The company was approached by an engineering firm to help improve problems of stratification and stagnation in municipal water storage tanks. Water held in these tanks, which can contain more than 1 million gallons, stratifies according to weather conditions, with each depth maintaining a different temperature. This stratification allows bacteria to grow more rapidly in the upper, hotter layers of the tank. Additionally, the tank's single inlet/outlet pipe does not support effective mixing, creating pockets of stagnation throughout the water. Perth-born Jay Harman, PAX's CEO, found a solution in the shape of swirling seaweeds from

Figure 1.3 *Mixer/impeller inspired by kelp* (Rotor 7-03)

which he developed a mixer/impeller. The PAX team then installed this mixer inside a 1 million gallon reservoir/holding tank. Twenty hours later, the entire reservoir had been completely and effectively mixed by the impeller, which used only 24 watts of power to achieve this effect.

Harman attributes the mixer's success to the unique design geometries PAX employs. Harman bases all PAX designs on classic geometric ratios found in nature; the resulting shapes cause fluids to flow in a streamlined, centripetal pathway (towards the centre axis). In contrast, most conventional rotors use a centrifugal model, forcing the fluid outward and bouncing it off a boundary wall to force movement in a desired direction. This less direct and less controllable method also causes turbulence. By accelerating the fluid centripetally with very little turbulence, PAX's rotors diminish vibration and reduce heat gain while delivering more directional thrust with virtually no cavitation. (Cavitation is turbulence that causes destructive bubbles to form.) The mixer's performance is representative of similar successes with fan blades and boat propellers. PAX fans, for example, produce up to 75 per cent less noise while using up to 45 per cent less electricity. Amory Lovins, a strong supporter of the PAX technology, remarks that 'Not only are rotors of this shape potentially far more efficient, they are remarkably quiet, and gentle on anything that goes through them like, for example, fish through a hydroelectric turbine. This technology has great potential and many obvious applications. If this invention, or rather, rediscovery of nature's genius, fulfils its promise, it could be one of the greatest technical breakthroughs in energy efficiency in a long time.'

Essentially, science shows very clearly that we, as a species, need to reduce our environmental load on the planet and achieve long-term sustainable development. The past neglect of the importance of resource productivity offers significant opportunities to innovate and gain competitive advantage for those firms and nations that lead. The resource productivity gains, and product differentiation possibilities for firms through sustainable development, will complement and drive the next cycle of innovation. But in the end the greatest challenge of achieving sustainable development is to design industry and the built environment to also be truly regenerative and restorative. This is probably where the greatest amount of research is needed as we have so much to learn from nature.

Table 1.4 *New enabling technologies tunnelling through the cost barrier*[47]

Spatial data	The new wave of IT innovation in Spatial Data analysis and micro-satellites now allows any nation to have extremely cheap access to information about many aspects of their natural resource management, urban design and planning. This even includes the ability to measure precisely underground salinity pathways from satellites. This will be a powerful driver for business and government to embrace sustainability as Spatial Data now allows governments, firms and farmers to make use of as much additional information as they wish in undertaking better sustainability assessment and planning.
Greenhouse technologies	CSIRO innovation in industrial mixing will reduce energy usage by 80%. Australian scientists at CSIRO have developed a revolutionary new mixer for everything from explosives to cosmetics. This new method can mix twice as well as an equivalent commonly used static mixer, consumes five times less energy and has very low shear. (Numerous other case studies like this will be covered in Section 4.)
Novel materials: bamboo	Bamboo absorbs over 40 times as much CO_2 as plantation forests whilst also growing to maturity three times as fast. This is faster than any other harvestable timber. Treated appropriately, bamboo can last for over 100 years. The Costa Rican Government is committed to building over 3000 bamboo homes every year. Bamboo is being used as it excels at coping with and surviving earthquakes and can be built extremely cost effectively. Architects and engineers are showing increasing interest in adopting these modern applications of bamboo as used, for example, in Balinese resorts. Bamboo is also being used in numerous products. (Birkeland 2002)
Cars	Another application of whole-system design is the re-design of cars. There is US$10 billion per annum being invested in eco-car research. Hybrid cars are now available in Japan, Europe and the US. Australia's CSIRO has developed one of the best hybrid car designs in the world, which led to over AU$700 million in additional exports of Australian light car components. Demonstration hydrogen fuel-cell cars are already here.
Climate neutral buildings	In Melbourne, Australia, the 60L Green Building demonstrates the commercial viability of a building designed to operate with minimized impact on the environment. Built at roughly the same cost as a conventional building, it uses over 65% less energy and over 90% less water than a conventional commercial building. It features many innovations, using the latest in stylish office amenities and is completely made from recycled materials.
Mining wastes or mining resources	Ausmelt is a new smelting process for base metals that increases the capacity of metal producers to recycle repeatedly the planet's finite mineral resources. The technology has since been further developed to reprocess toxic wastes, such as the cyanide and fluorine-contaminated pot-lining from aluminium smelters. The Sirosmelt/Ausmelt/Isasmelt technologies have become the system of choice as smelting companies slowly modernize.

> *We do believe that the efficiency revolution is to a large extent profitable for a country. It (will) provide competitive advantage to those countries pioneering it. And for the other countries it would be dangerous to miss the boat. We also (demonstrated) that some elements of the efficiency revolution are profitable now at the company level. But we emphasised that the state can do much to expand dramatically the range of profitability for both producers and consumers.*
>
> Ernst von Weizsäcker, Amory Lovins and Hunter Lovins, *Factor Four*[48]

Externalities: who pays?

Current industrial technologies are incredibly wasteful and this not only adds to the costs of doing business, it has an direct impact on the environment and our communities. The famous British economist, Arthur Cecil Pigou, pointed out the hidden costs of externalities[49] in his 1920 classic, *The Economics of Welfare*. He described, for instance, how the externality of smoke pouring from factories and fireplaces in Manchester, England, had many hidden costs for the economy. Such costs, including extra laundry cleaning, repair of corroded buildings and the need for additional artificial lighting due to this smoke, were assessed at £290,000 annually. Through this basic estimation of costs, not even including health, Pigou showed that for every £100 steel makers earned, they were doing £200 worth of damage. In effect, pollution victims (tax-payers) were subsidizing pollution causers, whilst making society poorer as a whole. The bottom line is that presently tax-payers in most OECD countries are being charged twice: initially through the subsidization of industries that directly or indirectly harm the environment, and then for cleaning up the damage once it has been done. Nations can no longer ignore the costs of these externalities. *The Economist* magazine argued recently that the increased costs from the externalities, such as the damage to the environment and health, resulting from the US's oil addiction simply no longer add up. The last ten years have marked a turning point where the US is now spending more money to protect its oil reserves than it is gaining from doing so. This is reminiscent of the Roman Empire's last days when the cost of maintaining its energy flow was becoming more expensive than the net value of the energy being secured. Almost all of Rome's energy needs were met by burning trees, forests, biomass and fossil fuels. It cost Rome more to maintain certain colonies, for example Spain and England, than it gained from the revenue generated by those colonies.[50]

> *The only long-term solution to this connected set of problems is to reduce the world's reliance on oil. Achieving this once seemed pie in the sky, but now hydrogen fuel cells are at last becoming a viable alternative... Every big car maker now has a fuel cell program, and every big oil firm is busy investigating how best to feed new cars their hydrogen... The best way to curb the demand for oil and promote innovation in oil alternatives is to tell the world's energy markets that the 'externalities' of oil consumption, such as security considerations and environmental issues alike, will influence policy from now on. And the way to do that is to impose a gradually rising gasoline tax.*
>
> *The Economist*, 'The End of the Oil Age', 25–31 October, 2003

It is always difficult to place a figure on the costs of externalities due to their very nature; however, one industry is acutely aware of such costs. The insurance industry is in the business of assessing risk and the cost of insurance is one way to put a dollar figure on what may previously have been an unknown risk. Additional money spent by governments on disaster relief, or measures to mitigate risk such as flood control, provide a figure for

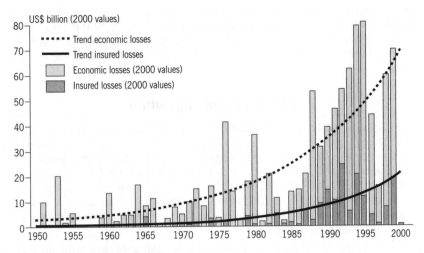

US$ billion (2000 values)

- - - - - Trend economic losses
——— Trend insured losses
Economic losses (2000 values)
Insured losses (2000 values)

Source: Munich Re Annual Review (2002)

Figure 1.4 *Economic insured and uninsured losses with trends*

the effects of externalities such as greenhouse gas emissions and global warming. Even in a highly insured country like Australia, individuals and governments bear the majority of the loss from natural disasters. In 2000, the Reinsurance Association of America pointed out that 50 per cent of the insured losses throughout the world, over the previous 40 years, that were due to natural catastrophes, had occurred since 1990. The Red Cross have warned that annual weather-induced disasters increased sharply worldwide in the late 1990s, from 200 before 1996 to 392 in 2000.

The increased risk posed by climate change may lead to insurance companies assessing some areas as un-insurable as they believe the risks are too great. In certain high risk (US) states, insurance companies are being forced to consider reducing clients or even leaving the state because of concern about hurricanes. In Florida one insurance company announced it intended to cancel 300,000 policies. Florida's Insurance Commissioner, Bill Nelson said to the *New York Times* on 25 April, 1996 that 'There are limits to what the state can cover, and they warn of difficulties if a hurricane hits a large metropolitan area and causes residential losses of US$25 billion to US$50 billion. If we have another big hurricane, all bets are off.' In 1998 alone, weather-related catastrophes claimed 50,000 lives and cost an estimated US$93 billion. Of these losses, only US$15 billion were insured. The United Nations Environment Programme (UNEP) and reinsurer Munich Re calculate that, by 2050, the negative effects of global warming will cost the global economy US$300 billion/annum.[51]

The uncertainties of climate responses to rising greenhouse gas levels are multiplied by the non-proportional response of human systems to weather phenomena. Extreme weather events are causing exponentially increasing damage to human property as small increases in intensity are causing disproportional damage to infrastructure. This puts the costs of preventing global warming into perspective. As will be shown in Section 4, even some of the Kyoto Protocol's harshest economic critics now acknowledge that if business and government work together, with a sound policy mix, ratifying Kyoto will only amount to a minimal negative impact on GDP per annum.

Clearly, there are numerous benefits in better attaching value to externalities so that the market signals better reflect the real environmental load of services and goods. In a market economy, prices are determined largely by supply and demand. But 'What price does one put on a stable climate?' What price do you put on things essential for life but for which we have no price because they are not traded in the market place? It is questionable whether we will ever find a method for measuring the value of natural capital upon which all agree. But we all agree that nature is valuable. In fact, arguably, the ecosystems of the world are priceless and it is clearly wrong to continue to assume they have no value.

Benefits of valuing nature

Many scientists have attempted to value nature or natural capital and significant efforts have been undertaken to work out ways to create markets for ecosystem services. CSIRO, Australia's major scientific and industry research body, has a major programme to do just this in conjunction with other major peak bodies such as the Australian Productivity Commission.[52] When world experts calculated the value of nature's ecosystem services, they found it was worth at least US$36 trillion annually.[53] That figure is close to the annual gross world product of approximately US$39 trillion: a striking measure of the value of natural capital to the economy.

Since 1992, the World Business Council for Sustainable Development has made formal recommendations for the proper valuation of natural services. It has called on governments to progress towards full-cost pricing; to use economic instruments and tradeable permits instead of command-and-control regulations; to phase out subsidies that harm the environment directly or indirectly and, finally, to change the standard national accounts (such as GDP) to reflect environmental scarcity.[54]

The failure to assign any value at all to natural capital until now, has clearly meant that numerous win–win opportunities have been missed. Take the case of Napa in California's famous Napa Valley, described by Gretchen Daily in her book *The New Economy of Nature* in 2003.[55] Over the past 30–40 years the Napa river has caused half a billion dollars in flood damage, during peak rainy periods, when it has burst its banks and inundated the town. The town was faced with two options to stop the flooding. It could invest in an enhanced system of dikes and levies building on what had been constructed by the army corps of engineers, or alternatively, it could invest in nature and restore the

Table 1.5 *Examples of cost benefits to the economy of ecosystem services*

Pollination services	Economists calculate the annual cost to American agriculture of the decrease in pollination services at around US$5 billion. In the mid-US, the single biggest cost to alfalfa growers is the provision of beehives for crop pollination.
Forest services for clean water	The Thomson River catchment in central Gippsland Australia provides water for Melbourne. Using a discount rate of 4% and water valued at AU$530 per mega litre, the study showed that the present policy of 80 year logging rotations does not maximize the total value of the timber and water outputs. The very long rotation option (200 years), or no logging at all, produced the maximum cost benefit overall and this result held for water prices as low as AU$200 per Ml. It is now accepted everywhere throughout Victoria, Australia, that forests in catchment areas need to be protected in order to keep the water in the catchments and the dams as pure as possible.
Costs of non-native species	Scientists warn that poorly funded control programmes are losing the battle against 50,000 non-native species in the US, resulting in US$137 billion in costs each year in ecosystem destruction, endangered species, increased disease and crop damage.[56]

wetlands that once safely absorbed the energies of the river. On the one hand, the physical capital approach would cost an estimated US$200 million, whereas restoring nature would cost an estimated US$250 million. Despite this cost differential, residents fought hard and voted to adopt the approach of restoring nature. The community had the wisdom to ask themselves, what sort of future do we want? What sort of legacy do we want to leave? Do we want to be living in a system of dikes and levies, or do we want to be living in a beautiful town on a beautiful river that's more likely to attract tourists and other economic activity? Having chosen the approach of restoring nature, they removed over a hundred buildings, removed or moved nine different bridges and restored these wetlands of 650 acres, with beautiful bird and fishing opportunities. The residents have no regrets at all. It has rejuvenated the town and brought many other benefits in addition to the security from flooding.

Daily also describes how Costa Rica has heeded these general principles and is now, for instance, providing incentives to farmers to maintain or increase forest cover on their land. In 1997, the Costa Rican Government began a programme which encourages individuals to sign a contract with the government pledging to protect the environment on the land they own. In exchange for this pledge, they are paid US$20 per acre annually for the ecosystem services derived from their private property: a payment that is now protected under Costa Rican law. In Costa Rica, most of the services come from forested land and the government is paying anybody who presently has forest on their property, or who agrees to regrow forest on their property in the future. These payments are being made for four different ecosystem services:

1 watershed protection, both for maintaining drinking water quality and for hydroelectric power production;
2 biodiversity protection for pharmaceutical prospecting – there are many companies that are looking for new drugs in Costa Rican rain forests;
3 to mitigate global warming, by sequestering carbon;
4 scenic beauty and the attraction their country represents for eco-tourism and tourists in general.

The policy is working. Since the enactment of these policies, Costa Rica has gone from having the highest deforestation rates in the world to achieving a net increase in forest cover and, essentially, one of the lowest deforestation rates in the world. They are still clearing some primary forest, but overall people are planting more forest than ever before.

Implications and benefits for global development

There has also been a significant shift in our understanding of how sustainable development which seeks to improve resource productivity can also help sustain economic growth, and thus assist global development this century. It is physically impossible for all developing nations to achieve Western material living standards with previous modes of development, as the global 'ecological footprint'[57] (the equivalent land and water area required to produce a given population's material standard, including resources appropriated from other places) is already greater than the carrying capacity of our planet.

> *If China were to consume seafood at the per capita rate of Japan, it would need 100 million tonnes, more than today's total catch. If China's beef consumption was to match the USA's per capita consumption and if that beef was produced mainly in feedlot, this would take grain equivalent to the entire US harvest.*
>
> Sustainable Consumption – A UNEP Global Status Report, 2002

Achieving a high level of resource productivity and efficiency will also assist in positive global economic development, as at present approximately 25 per cent of global development aid capital is spent on energy.[58] Governments, such as China's, are increasingly focusing on efficient energy use in future development models:

> *When Chinese authorities decided to make refrigerators more accessible, they imported numerous assembly lines. The saturation of refrigerators in Beijing households rose from 2 per cent to 62 per cent in six years, but the refrigerators' inefficient design created $500 million in unintended shortages of power and of capital to generate it. A cabinet member said that this error must not be repeated: energy and resource efficiency must be the cornerstone of the development process. Otherwise resource waste will require supply side investment of the capital meant to buy the devices that were supposed to use those resources. This realisation contributed to China's emphasis on energy efficiency (halving primary energy/GDP elasticity in the 1980s and nearly re-halving it since), laying the foundation for the 1996 shift from coal to gas, renewables, and efficiency – the greatest contribution of any nation so far to reducing greenhouse emissions.*[59]
>
> Amory Lovins (2004)

Many countries, including China, are now focused on water efficiency strategies to forestall the need for additional dams. One of the key findings of a landmark report from the World Commission on Dams (WCD), headed by Nelson Mandela, was that few dams have ever been analysed to see if the benefits outweighed the real costs. It reported that the construction of dams has been the biggest single drain on aid budgets for the past 50 years, costing US$4 billion annually, for instance, in the 1980s.[60] The report also found that dam building has driven up to 80 million people from their homes; that shallow dams in the tropics are significant greenhouse gas emitters due to rotting vegetation, and, surprisingly, some dams were found to be larger greenhouse emitters than coal-fired power stations.[61]

Whilst there is growing awareness of the need to change and of the multiple benefits of sustainable development, there is still 'business as usual' inertia from governments and some business sectors because many continue to believe, incorrectly, that sustainable development will significantly harm economic growth. This debate matters because the result of the current belief that sustainable development will hurt economic growth is that governments, research and development (R&D) institutions and companies have not been encouraged as much as they could have been to explore economically feasible and desirable paths to an ecologically sustainable economy.

It used to be assumed that economic growth entailed parallel growth in resource consumption and, to a certain extent, environmental degradation. However, the experience of the last few decades indicates that economic growth and resource consumption and environmental degradation can be decoupled to a considerable extent. As Philip Sutton, founder and Director of Strategy, Green Innovations Inc, explains, the traditional assumption arises from a simple semantic confusion:[62]

> *When businesses and governments talk about growth they generally mean economic growth. They mean (assuming the expenditure model of measuring GDP) the amount of monetary transactions as measured by the GDP. When environmentalists talk about growth they mean physical growth, resource consumption with concurrent environmental degradation. But economic and physical growth are not the same thing. Economic growth is an acceleration in the production of economic value. Physical growth of the economy means it spreads over*

more area or has a larger material and energy throughput or has a larger stock of physical products or buildings or infrastructure.

Certainly for most of the last 200 years these two forms of growth have moved in lock-step. So it is not surprising that the iron law 'economic growth = physical growth' has lodged itself firmly people's minds.

However there is now both significant evidence of a decoupling of economic growth from physical growth and greater knowledge of how to achieve this through much of the economy. In the US, for seven years after the OPEC oil price shock of 1979, the economy grew by 19 per cent while energy use fell by 6 per cent. Over the last 30 years the UK's GDP has doubled yet CO_2 emissions and energy use have increased marginally. The UK has achieved a significant decoupling of GDP growth, energy use and CO_2 emissions. In the US between 1980 and 1995 the amount of fresh water withdrawn per American fell by 21 per cent and water withdrawn per dollar of real GDP fell by 38 per cent. This empirical experience challenges the iron law.

In fact, recent research is showing that a transition to a sustainable economy, if focused on improving resource productivity, will lead to higher economic growth than business as usual, while at the same time reducing pressures on the environment and enhancing employment. This has been shown by economic modelling in Europe by ex-Wuppertal Institute member Joachim Spangenberg working with neo-classical economists. The project was called Labour and Environment, and Joachim is currently working in a team to demonstrate this fact with global economic scenario models used in several EU funded projects, including one called Modelling Opportunities and Limits for Restructuring Europe Towards Sustainability (MOSUS). Some of the factors that allow higher than expected economic growth from sustainable development are described here.

First, as we have shown, there exist great opportunities for increased resource productivity, and large radical resource productivity gains often cost less than smaller resource productivity gains. Second, obviously many of the direct and indirect costs of large-scale environmental damage and resource depletion will be avoided at significantly less cost and the economy will be protected from environmentally induced destabilization. Third, during the transition to a fully operational ecologically sustainable economy, which would be a period of several decades at least, the economy would have a strong structural tendency to higher levels of employment. The structural tendency to favour higher employment is caused by three things: (i) the recycling of revenues from eco-taxes to reduce payroll taxes or other costs of employing labour; (ii) the greater labour intensity of new ways of doing things where the technology and the manufacturing and operational techniques are not yet highly refined; and (iii) the pump-priming effect of investments brought forward to replace scrapped capital.

Fourth, a strongly green economy will enhance the dynamics of the economy to favour the greatest source of productivity improvement in the modern economy – the information sector. To create economic wealth with significantly lower physical resource inputs and environmental impact is going to require clever development; and clever development depends on a strong information economy. Skilled labour, sophisticated machinery and technology, and lots of top quality information will be needed. Fifth, contrary to the intuition of many economists and the ideology of many politicians, wise social spending has contributed to, rather than inhibited, economic growth. This is one of the conclusions of a recently published respected historical study by Peter Lindert called *Growing Public: Social Spending and Economic Growth Since the Eighteenth Century*. This extensive study on whether social policies that redistribute income impose constraints on economic growth concluded that, contrary to traditional beliefs, the net national costs of government social programmes are virtually zero.

Sixth, corruption around the world is widely regarded as one of the biggest impediments to sustainable development. Removing corruption will not just help to create a more just and sustainable world but would also assist economic growth. *The World Bank Development Report* summed it up well in 1997 when it discussed how corruption also harms economic growth especially over the long-term because it leads to sub-optimal decision-making by governments. Seventh, properly designed eco-taxes can be used to increase firm level productivity and economic growth. Many papers including OECD reports have shown how revenues raised from eco-taxes are expected to create virtually fully offsetting output and productivity gains in other parts of the economy provided they are channelled back into the economy in the most effective ways. There are many other significant reasons and we consider some of them now in more detail.

Eighth, new design for sustainability ideas on how to design the built environment, well summarized in books such as *Green Development: Integrating Ecology and Real Estate*,[63] can have remarkably positive effects on a nation's GNP, because construction and the built environment make up a very large fraction of GNP – for instance 9 per cent in the US and 18 per cent in Japan. Therefore, even small improvements in construction techniques can have effects on national income that are large compared with more exciting basic science discoveries. The lesson from the remarkable growth rates of Japan over a significant part of the last 40 years is clear: seemingly mundane forms of applied research, such as design work or product and process engineering, can have large cumulative benefits for the firm that undertakes them and even larger benefits for society as a whole.

There is increasing interest in the link between urban development and economic growth. Mainstream concern about these issues is such that the US *Newsweek* magazine dedicated an entire special issue on Asia's urban explosion. *Newsweek* wrote: 'Rome was the first settlement to reach 1 million people in 5 BC and only in 1800 did London become the second. By 2015 Asia alone will have 267 cities with 1 million or more residents. Urbanization will either make or break the Asian miracle economies. The growth of many cities in Asia is astounding. In 25 years from now most Asians will live in cities and towns.'[64] Dhaka, Mumbai and Delhi will number among the world's five largest cities[65] and Asia, as a whole, will account for 12 of the world's largest 21 cities by 2015. Today's largest metropolis is Tokyo, which has an estimated 27 million residents. By 2050, trends suggest there will be over 50 mega-cities globally, with most of them in Asia.[66]

In Section 4 we will show in detail that, if cities adopt sustainable development, it will help them foresee and overcome many of the problems of rapid urbanization. For example, one of the biggest influences on the economic costs of cities are the transport choices made by urban designers. It has long been believed that building roads is good for the economy of cities while public transport is a financial drain. A report to the World Bank (published in *Sustainability and Cities*[67]) prepared by researchers at Murdoch University is turning this way of thinking on its head.

Professor Peter Newman says: 'they have found that cities that emphasize walking, cycling and public transport are healthier financially and spend less of their wealth on transport costs. The six cities that came out the best were cities like Zurich, Copenhagen, Stockholm – very wealthy cities now, which spend only 4 or 5 per cent of their wealth on transport, and yet they are the cities that are putting their money into public transport. And the cities still pouring money into freeways use up to 17 per cent of their wealth. Australian and US cities like Perth and Phoenix are wasting far more of their valuable wealth on just getting around. Our data would really question that freeway building has any economic rationale; unless you are building up the rail system (as in Perth) you are not going to help it economically. As soon as you put in big roads, you create a market for city sprawl and this is very expensive. If you build railways, particularly light rail, it

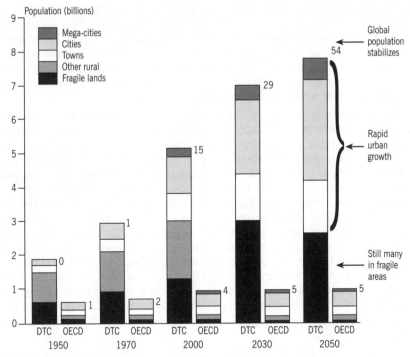

Source: World Bank (2003)

Figure 1.5 *Historic and future trends for urbanization of developing and transition countries*
(DTC) and OECD countries

concentrates a city as developers like building around it, thus helping to stop the sprawl. Then you get a whole lot of flow ons.' The study also found that the mechanisms driving this additional cost include the following:

*   The land required to build the infrastructure and its subsequent requirements for parking; a single lane of railway can carry up to 50,000 persons per hour, a bus way can carry 7000 persons per hour and a highway lane just 2500 persons per hour.[68]
*   The direct cost to households of owning a car are considerable, especially if it is a second or third car. A study in Australia showed that a household could save AU$750,000 over a lifetime if a second car could be avoided.
*   The opportunity cost of such capital and land can be considerable if seen on a whole city basis. The difference between the most competitive cities, in terms of their transportation costs as a proportion of city wealth, and the least competitive (5–8 per cent compared to 12–18 per cent) can be equivalent to an extra day a week of work in car dependent cities.[69]

A still more recent study of 84 cities undertaken by Kenworthy and Laube,[70] has shown that cities with well designed public transport systems have significantly less total transport costs, as a proportion of their city wealth, than those which have built in a heavy reliance on freeways and cars.[71] There is still further evidence that a transition to sustainable transport need not harm economic growth. In fact, an important new study provides significant evidence to support the notion that it would be highly profitable for major nations to make the transition to get off oil. Rocky Mountain Institute (RMI) has released *Winning the Oil Endgame: Innovation for Profits, Jobs, and Security*,[72] a Pentagon-cofunded blueprint for making the US oil-free. *Winning the Oil Endgame* proves viable ways exist through which, by 2015, the US can save more oil than it gets from the Persian Gulf; by 2025, use less oil than in 1970; by 2040, import no oil; and by 2050, use no oil at all. 'For the first time, RMI's report adds up the new ways to provide all the services now obtained from oil, but without using oil – which will save us $70 billion a year', concludes Amory Lovins the lead author of this new study.

Ninth, the potential benefits of energy efficiency to the environment productivity and economic growth are well documented. Numerous government programmes demonstrate that significant energy efficiency savings still exist in all OECD modern economies and even more so in developing or rapidly emerging economies. In their publication *Energy Security Facts: Details and Documentation*, Rocky Mountain Institute (RMI) argues that there are still US$300 billion of available savings through better energy efficiency in the US economy. The recent White Paper on energy for Australia estimated that there are still close to a billion dollars that could be added to the nation's GDP through energy efficiency in the commercial sector alone. But this ignores significant gains to the economy possible in the residential sector. In Section 4 we discuss how the economic benefits of more energy efficient homes have been demonstrated by a recent economic study by Allen Consulting (see Chapter 17). They showed remarkably that 5-star energy efficient homes would be better for the economy than 4-star homes, leading to the adoption of 5-star standards for new homes by the State Government of Victoria in Australia. Section 4 features many more studies and evidence to support this line of argument.

Another significant work by Fairbanks and Lindsey[73] provides further insights to the benefits of sustainable development for countries' standards of living and economic growth. Their work shows that significant economic benefits exist for developing countries from diversifying their economies rather than relying on exports of natural resources for their income (often at considerable environmental and social cost).

Fairbanks and his colleagues, at the On the Frontier Group, work with 'emerging economies' to assist in identifying and acting upon opportunities to achieve international competitive advantage with their firms. Their work has shown that emerging economies can find additional opportunities to add value and help break the poverty cycle and point out that: 'The challenge that business and political leaders of those countries face is twofold: (i) to develop more sophisticated sources of advantage that are not so easily imitated, and (ii) to realize that depleting natural resources and suppressing wages will not lead to sustainable, long-term wealth creation. It is critical for leaders to develop the capacity to think about the future and to move out of such unattractive 'factor-based' industries.

Fairbanks and Lindsay argue that emerging economies that simply rely on their input conditions (raw or natural resources) not only increase the risk of reinforcing existing poverty traps, but they can simultaneously miss opportunities to improve the competitive advantage of and opportunities for their firms. In addition, countries dependent on key natural resources, and lacking diversity in their economy are vulnerable to commodity price shocks. Jeffrey Sachs and fellow economists at the Harvard Institute for International Development found, through statistical analysis, that the more a developing country's economy depended on resource exports in 1971 the less it grew in per capita terms between 1965 and 1990. Overall, among the countries sampled, a 10 per cent point increase in resource exports, as a share of GDP in 1971, corresponded to a half-percentage point fall in average growth over the 1965–1990 period.[74]

Ironically, overwhelming evidence indicates that countries seemingly blessed with massive reserves of oil and minerals and other natural resources are, on average, not outperforming less resource rich nations. Previously, having such natural resources was believed to contribute to a nations 'natural advantage' over others. However, this is no longer the case. This reality has led to these same resource rich countries attempting to remedy their overall poor economic progress by liquidating their natural assets (forests, mineral wealth or oil) even faster. Over the past 50 years there has been a consistent increase in the volume of natural resources being extracted by developing countries. Today, resource rich developing countries now mine five times the copper they mined in 1955, pump six times the oil and fell seven times the timber for paper and lumber production.[75] This has occurred because it is relatively easy for companies in resource rich developing nations to imitate OTHER companies based on resource extraction. Firms competing on low labour and resource costs also leave themselves exposed if there are changes in other countries that result in even lower labour and resource costs. For instance, a rival firm may be granted subsidies by the government of another country which enables them to beat your price in the marketplace, no matter how efficient you are. Second, technology has delivered greater options to firms in the developed world for reducing the relative advantage of cheap labour and resource conditions in the 'developing world'. This paradox is commonly known as the 'Resource Curse' and it has generated much debate amongst experts globally. Other factors that contribute to poor economic performance from the 'resource curse' may include:[76]

- pressure on government by interests associated with large scale resource companies;
- strong revenues flowing to government from the resource sector;
- declining terms of trade (meaning that imports outweigh exports);
- skills of workers not being easily transferable to other industries; and
- lower multiplier effects for resource industries than would exist for the same dollar utilized in manufacturing, particularly export oriented manufacturing.

Rather, as we will show in detail in Section 2, there is another way. The latest studies show that it is the firms that are innovating for new emerging markets and value adding that are the most profitable. Fundamentally a firm can increase its productivity by innovating to offer new services to more attractive customers (product differentiation) or by creating the same value with fewer inputs (operational efficiency).

New ideas like the pipes and pumps case study above are increasingly being understood to help both operational efficiency and product differentiation through helping firms to create 'greener' products that command higher prices in the marketplace. Intuitively one would expect this to also assist economic growth as well as assisting firms' competitiveness. New developments in economics now show that such new ideas and innovations at the micro-economic level do also assist economic growth. Significant advances in economics are showing that new designs, new ideas and innovations are very important to achieving lasting economic growth. One of the chief architects of this 'New Growth Theory', Stanford economics Professor Paul Romer, shows that economic growth does not arise just from accumulating more capital. His work shows that is also arises from new and better ideas expressed as technological progress. Before New Growth Theory, economists recognized that technology contributed substantially to growth, but they couldn't figure out how to incorporate rigorously and completely that insight internally into their economic models. Romer's innovation, expressed in technical articles with titles such as 'Increasing Returns and Long-Run Growth' and 'Endogenous Technological Change', has been to find ways to describe rigorously and exactly how technological progress brings about economic growth. In the old growth models, the rate of technological progress was assumed to be a given and was not modelled explicitly. Rather it was simply set at a constant rate of productivity growth. New growth theorists make technological progress internal to their economic growth model including modelling of R&D and technological changes in production explicitly. In new growth models, the rate of technological progress is determined by aspects of the model itself rather than simply been set at a constant rate of progress as it was in the old growth models. This provides at least a start to building economic models that link how positive changes in the productivity at the firm level influence economic growth at the macro-economic level. This at least provides a start of the theoretical foundation needed to model rigorously how improvements in design, technological processes at the firm level (outlined in detail in Section 2) can positively effect macro-economic growth. Paul Romer writes:[77]

> *We now know that the classical economic suggestion that we can grow rich by accumulating more and more pieces of physical capital is simply wrong. The problem an economy faces is what economists call "diminishing returns". In handling heavy objects a forklift is a really useful piece of equipment. When there were few fork lifts in the economy, the return on an investment in an additional lift is significant. But eventually buying additional forklifts would have no value and become a nuisance (to the firm). The return on investment in an additional fork lift diminishes and eventually becomes negative. As a result an economy cannot grow merely by accumulating more and more of the same kind of capital goods.*

Romer continues:[78]

> *Economic growth occurs whenever people take resources and rearrange them in ways that are more valuable. A useful metaphor for production in an economy comes from the kitchen. To create valuable products, we mix inexpensive ingredients together according to a recipe. The cooking one can do is only limited by the supply of ingredients, and most cooking in the economy produces undesirable side-effects. If economic growth could be achieved only by doing more and more of the same kind of cooking, we would run out of raw materials and suffer from unacceptable levels of pollution and nuisance. Human history teaches us however that economic growth springs from better recipes, not just from more cooking. New recipes generally produce fewer unpleasant side-effects and generate more economic value per unit of raw material.*

As we have stated (see the section on 'A critical mass of enabling technologies' earlier in this chapter), the scale of the challenge of achieving sustainability plus the remarkable array of potential resource productivity gains that exist in the economy provide a significant stimulus for innovation this century. We propose then that a transition to an ecologically sustainable economy will help further drive the development of new designs, methods and mechanisms to meet the needs of society and, wisely done, could also stimulate economic growth greater than business as usual.

To conclude, as well as all the benefits outlined so far, this new development paradigm of sustainability if pursued on a global scale, will offer still more significant benefits for governments, society and business. As the book will show, these benefits include many indirect benefits such as benefits to health,[79] reduced numbers of environmental refugees, increased resilience to infrastructure failure or terrorist attack, plus many other benefits to national security.[80] In Section 4 these benefits are discussed in detail. Also security experts are now predicting that, unless current unsustainable resource useage patterns change to become sustainable, access to key raw resources, such as oil and water, could be a potential source of conflict this century.[81] Today, the US imports 50 per cent of their oil, Europe 70 per cent and it is estimated that China will import 50 per cent of its oil within ten years. On the economic front, key studies by experts in the field report that the world is close to the midpoint of world oil supplies,[82] which has significant implications for balance of payments. For instance, the forecasts for Australia are that the AU$1.2 billion surplus in petroleum products in 2000 will be a AU$7.6 billion deficit in trade of liquid hydrocarbons by 2010.[83] Therefore the choices urban designers and planners make also have implications for national security and the economy. Section 4 of the book will cover these issues in detail. Finally pursuing sustainable development will ensure that nations and their firms who practise it will not face direct or indirect trade sanctions from significant trading blocks such as Europe on the grounds of environmental performance.

Hence this publication will show that *wisely applied sustainable development will lead in multiple ways to a Natural Advantage of Nations*.

CHAPTER 2

RISKS OF INACTION ON SUSTAINABLE DEVELOPMENT

A great transition

It is important to discuss here the dangers of inaction as we are truly at a critical juncture in the relationship between *Homo sapiens* and planet earth. Our relationship with nature has forever changed over the last three centuries due to our technological might as a species. Rerouting entire river systems, levelling huge areas of forest, changing the composition of the global climate, pollution of land and waterways will leave a terrible legacy to future generations if present trajectories and trends are not altered. This publication provides the supporting argument to show that we can actually achieve a transition to a society based on sustainable development principles and completely bypass the nightmarish scenarios of 'barbarism' and 'fortress world' as described in the Global Scenario Group Report 'Great Transition'.[1] Figure 2.1 summarizes some of the potential visions of the future and the likely effects on six areas (Population, Economy, Environment, Equity, Technology, Conflict) of such scenarios.

According to an analysis of the world's ecosystems prepared by the United Nations, the World Bank and the World Resources Institute in 2000, 'There are considerable signs that the capacity of ecosystems, the biological engines of the planet, to produce many of the goods and services we depend on is rapidly declining.[2] Hence, before continuing, it is worth pausing to consider the real measurable risk of 'business as usual'. The risks are now recognized as being significant – as reflected by World Bank dedicating its 2003 *World Development Report* to these issues.

> *Some problems of sustainability are already urgent and require immediate action; Another category of issues unfolds over a longer time horizon. These problems may not be urgent, but the direction of change is unmistakable. For these it is essential to get ahead of the curve and prevent a worsening crisis before it becomes too costly. Biodiversity loss and climate change are in this category... What is clear is that almost all of the challenges of sustainable development require that action be initiated in the near term.*
>
> World Bank (2003)

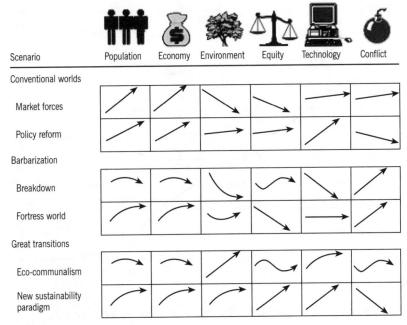

Source: Stockholm Environment Institute

Figure 2.1 *Potential future scenarios*

Clearly throughout the first Industrial Revolution not enough attention was paid to the impact of development on the ecosystems that are required to underpin the survival of the planet's biodiversity. Bill McDonough puts it like this, 'If someone were to present the Industrial Revolution as a retroactive design assignment, it might sound like this: Design a system of production that:

- puts billions of kilograms of toxic material into the air, water and soil every year;
- measures prosperity by activity, not legacy;
- requires thousands of complex regulations to keep people and natural systems from being poisoned too quickly;
- produces materials so dangerous that they will require constant vigilance from future generations;
- results in gigantic amounts of waste;
- puts valuable materials in holes all over the planet, where they can never be retrieved; and
- erodes the diversity of biological species and cultural practices.

Obviously, we are not going to be able to sustain this approach forever. The critical point of this chapter is that no matter how determined a company or a nation is to change, these changes will take time to implement; hence we have no time to waste. Very simply, the sooner we start, the longer we have to phase changes in, the less disruptive and more beneficial this will be to business and society and the best chance we have of long-term success. For instance, it has taken Australia almost two decades since the government mandated that all new cars purchased from 1 January 1986 run on unleaded petrol to achieve a shift in the dominant fuel source for vehicles.

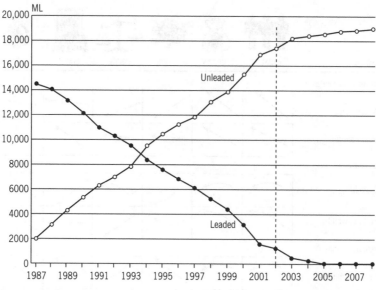

Source: Robinson (2002)

Figure 2.2 *Australian petrol sales: 1987–2008, leaded vs. unleaded*

A sense of urgency

There is real concern in the science community that due to significant uncertainties inherent in modelling complex ecosystems we have overestimated their resilience and now face the risk of unknown consequences. Let us consider a high profile issue like global warming, a case where climate modelling now has enough data to begin to make predictions about how fast we need to change to reduce such risks. The International Panel on Climate Change (IPCC) points out that the effects on climate due to pollution, land clearing and the industrial economy are now very apparent. The majority of the world's scientists have repeatedly warned, whether through the IPCC or other committees, that we do not have time to waste on the greenhouse issue. Dr Graeme Pearman, former chief of the CSIRO's (Commonwealth Scientific and Industrial Research Organisation's) atmospheric physics division and Australia's representative on the IPCC, said that the panel's report in 2001 had concluded that at whatever level global warming was stopped, it would take a 70 per cent cut in global emissions to stop it. 'We don't have that much longer', he said.

Dr Pearman's comments come from a detailed understanding of atmospheric science and the global future trends in development, and material and energy flow. According to the IPCC, stabilizing concentrations at double the pre-industrial levels will require deep cuts in annual global emissions, eventually by 60 per cent or more. Dr Pearman qualifies this by pointing out that, given the wide variation in national levels of emissions per capita and income per capita, it would be infeasible and unfair to require all nations to cut their emissions by 60 per cent of their current levels by 2050. Developing countries might expect to reduce their emissions by less than this amount and wealthy countries, with high per capita emissions, by more than this amount. As a sign of international commitment more than 160 nations met in Kyoto, Japan in December 1997, to negotiate binding limitations on greenhouse gases for the developed nations, pursuant to the objectives of the Framework Convention on Climate Change of 1992. The outcome of the meeting was the Kyoto Protocol, in which the developed nations agreed to limit their greenhouse gas emissions, relative to the levels emitted in 1990. Clearly we need change soon, but we cannot replace 300 years of fossil-fuel-based industrial infrastructure overnight. Recent studies by the UK Government[3] and The Australia Institute[4] show that deep cuts to greenhouse emissions of 60 per cent in principle are possible by 2050 using a combination of energy efficiency, demand management and green energy. The good news is that, if phased in over fifty years, such changes will not overburden the economy as the total life cycle costs of delivering energy related services will often be reduced together with other benefits such as increased employment.[5]

> *If renewable fuels, for instance, cost three times as much as present fossil fuel prices, the impact of Britain switching to a primarily renewable basis by 2050 would be to reduce national income in that year by just 4 per cent. This would cut annual growth from now till then by only one-tenth of one per cent – implying that we would reach in 2052 the standard of living otherwise attained in 2050. This is a choice we can afford to make, and a trade off we have no right to reject at the expense of vulnerable people elsewhere in the world.*
>
> Quoting from Cambridge Econometrics. Adair Turner, former director general of the Confederation of British Industry

The costs of inaction on this issue will lead to such visible impacts as increased health problems (tropical diseases spreading) and insurance costs, (increased occurrence of natural disasters), loss of land (with sea level rises), and a less stable climate. To put the issue of global warming from the greenhouse effect in perspective it is important to understand 3 key factors:

1   Detailed data in Figure 2.3, based on air extracted from ice cores drilled in the Antarctic ice cap, shows that we are actually adding man-made greenhouse gases to a peaking of the natural cycle.

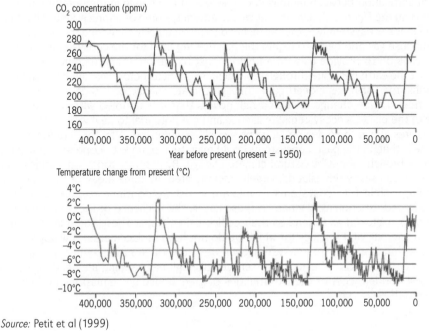

Source: Petit et al (1999)

Figure 2.3 *Plot of CO_2 concentrations and temperature from 400,000 years ago to 1950*

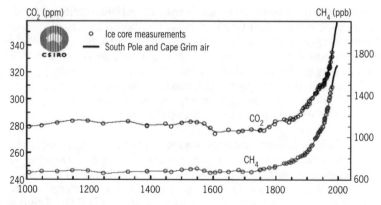

Source: Etheridge et al (1998)

Figure 2.4 *Changes in atmospheric CO_2 and methane in the last millennium*

2   Figure 2.4 shows that the CO_2 levels in the atmosphere are over 360 parts per million. They have not been above 300 parts per million for at least 400,000 years. Further, data based on isotope ratios in marine micro fossils suggests strongly that CO_2 levels have not in fact been above, or much above, 300 parts per million for about 23 million years.

3   CO_2 pumped into the atmosphere will remain there for 80–100 years and so will influence temperature and contribute to the greenhouse effect for a long time after its release. This means that that even if new emissions of CO_2 are reduced, the overall concentration of CO_2 will continue to increase as the continuing emissions combine with background levels.

The high correlation between increased CO_2 levels and a change in temperature, as can be seen from the Figure 2.3, means that we are entering a time of unprecedented heating of the planet's ecosystem. We, therefore, need to move quickly to reduce the production of greenhouse gas and begin to regain the balance required for the ecosystems that our planet relies on to provide us with a healthy host to live on. Climate change sceptics argue that the earth has gone through rapid climate changes before. As can be seen from the graphs, the Earth has indeed gone through climate change of 1–6 degrees. But the reason that climate change is such a risk now is that it is coupled with a significant decline of the planet's ecosystems' resilience and the potential to deal with increases in temperatures above the 6 degree range previously experienced. A factor in reducing the resilience is that, in the past, ecosystems could migrate and move to cope with changing conditions brought about by natural climate change. By contrast today our 'wilderness areas' are increasingly tiny islands, largely unconnected. In some areas of the planet it will be impossible for ecosystems to migrate whilst we continue to undertake this unprecedented experiment.[6] Hence, in these cases, the resilience of these ecosystems could be so stretched as to lead to their ecological collapse. These same ecosystems provide numerous vital services for which we do not have replacements. Few appreciate the stress that the planet's ecosystems will be under once more significant climate change occurs. The loss of ecosystem services from global warming may end up being the largest 'hidden' cost of the externalities of greenhouse gas emissions and global warming to the economy.

Declining ecosystems: a new limiting factor for growth?

Different pressures on the world's ecosystems from different sources have a compound effect on each other. 'When one problem combines with another problem, the outcome may be not a double problem, but a super-problem.' This is the assessment of Professor Norman Myers, an Oxford University ecologist who is one of the most active pioneers in the field of 'environmental surprise'[7] (see Table 2.1). He believes that we have hardly begun to identify those potential super-problems, but in the planet's increasingly stressed natural ecosystems, the possibility of rapid, unexpected change is pervasive and growing.[8] When different phenomena feedback on each other, scientists call these 'coupling effects'. The impacts of the greenhouse effect alone may be significantly mitigated, but when these are combined with deforestation and biodiversity loss, the conversion of vast land mass to freshwater intensive modern agriculture, increasing urban waste streams, then the stress on our remaining natural ecosystems can no longer be ignored. The combination of these impacts can prove deadly, as experienced in the year 1998, which set a new record for economic losses from weather-related disasters.[9]

In most cases, the cost of destroying ecosystem services becomes apparent only when the services start to break down. The Worldwatch Institute cites the following examples.[10]

- Bangladesh suffered its most extensive flood of the century in the summer of 1998. Two-thirds of this low-lying nation at the mouth of the Ganges and Brahmaputra rivers was inundated for months with 30 million left temporarily homeless; 10,000 miles of roads were heavily damaged, and the rice harvest was reduced by 2 million tons. Damage estimates exceed US$3.4 billion. Logging upriver in the Himalayas of north India and Nepal exacerbated the disaster, as did the fact that the region's rivers and floodplains have been filled with silt and constricted by development. Climate change and rising sea levels are projected to make Bangladesh even more vulnerable to flooding in the future.
- In China's Yangtze basin in 1998, heavy rainfall plus upstream deforestation triggered flooding that killed 3700 people, dislocated 223 million and inundated 60 million acres of cropland. That US$30 billion disaster forced a logging moratorium and a US$12 billion crash programme of reforestation. The damage was caused not just by heavy rain but also by deforestation and extremely dense settlement on the floodplain. The Yangtze had lost over 85 per cent of its forest cover.

In 2003, a report by the World Bank listed the risks of environmental damage and social unrest as major factors that, if not addressed and significant progress made, will limit the extent to which the world economy can grow.

> *The next 50 years could see a fourfold increase in the size of the global economy and significant reductions in poverty but only if governments act now to avert a growing risk of severe damage to the environment and profound social unrest. Without better policies and institutions, social and environmental strains may derail development progress, leading to higher poverty levels and a decline in the quality of life for everybody.*
>
> World Bank (2003)

Herman Daly, a leading academic ecological economist, previously working at the World Bank, advanced similar arguments over ten years ago. Daly argued that we are facing a form of 'limiting factor' today, unlike anything our economies have faced before. He wrote that: 'soon it will be forests not mills, fisheries not boats, that which will be the limiting factor for economic growth'. As CSIRO's David Priestly states: 'If we [Australia]

Table 2.1 *Examples of environmental surprise*

Land degradation	Globally, the area of arable land has been declining, with a loss of greater than 12 million hectares over the past decade, due to land degradation.[11] In Australia alone salinity already affects 2.5 million hectares (5% of cultivated land) and this could rise to 12 million hectares (25% of cultivated land).
The Aleutian Islands, Alaska	One would have thought that off the coast of Alaska, hundreds of miles from civilization, nature would be relatively safe from human influence. But throughout the Gulf of Alaska and the Bering Sea, the ecosystem has collapsed. Waters once brimming with seals, otters and king crab are now dominated by sharks, pollock and urchins. Long-term research has documented the extensive decline of Aleutian sea otters, 70% since 1992 and 95% or more throughout much of the Aleutian Islands since the 1980s. Scientists discovered that the collapse was driven by increased killer whale predation of sea otters caused by a complex string of effects such as whaling removing the primary food source and the death of the phyto-plankton food source resulting from an ocean temperature increase through global warming.
Impacts on ocean currents	The findings of a Pentagon report into the rapid climate change event that occurred 8200 years ago came to a disturbing conclusion. Following an ongoing period of global warming, similar to the one we have been experiencing, a sudden period of cooling ensued. This cooling was, in all likelihood, a consequence of the collapse of the conveyer current due to reduced salinity resulting from a gradual warming that melted the glaciers. Over the last 130 years, there has been a similar overall reduction in the salinity concentrations in the conveyor current. The report highlights that there is scientific research showing that gradual global warming could possibly lead to a relatively abrupt slowing of the ocean's thermohaline conveyor, which could lead to harsher winter weather conditions and more intense winds in certain regions. With inadequate preparation, the result could be a significant drop in the human carrying capacity of the Earth's environment. The research suggests that once temperatures rise above a certain threshold, adverse weather conditions could develop relatively abruptly, with persistent changes in the atmospheric circulation causing drops in some regions of degrees in a single decade. (Refer to Chapter 17 for more detail.)
The Amazon	The Amazon will become drier in the future, potentially even becoming a desert in centuries to come unless deforestation and its causes are more seriously addressed. The reasons are firstly El Niño, which is forecast to become more common with global warming. In 1997–1998, during an El Niño event, there was a drought throughout the Amazon. Secondly, deforestation and the accompanying burning off in the Brazilian Amazon increased 40% between August 2001 and August 2002 compared to the previous 12 months due to a range of factors.[12] And thirdly, the predictions for the future temperature of the tropics in places like the Amazon are getting higher and higher, so even if rainfall stays the same and temperatures are getting higher, there is going to be more water evaporating from the Amazon and droughts are going to be more severe.

Fall of the Roman Empire[13]	Historically the fall of civilizations has been heavily influenced by environmental surprise. For instance during the later period of the Roman Empire, agriculture provided more than 90% of the government's revenue. By the fifth century the government and military bureaucracy had more than doubled. The taxes on farmers from Rome were beyond what farmers could afford, so they had to go into debt and constantly work their land. Poor incentive structures to farmers, and massive deforestation required to fuel the Roman War Machine led to rapid soil degradation. By the 3rd century AD over farming the land had got to the point that in some parts of North Africa and through the Mediterranean, up to one half of the arable land had to be abandoned. Depopulation of the countryside had other repercussions. The un-stewarded land further degraded leading to the spreading of swampland which became breeding grounds for disease. Malaria outbreaks were common in the last days of Rome, further weakening the already impoverished population. Plagues broke out in the 2nd and 3rd centuries AD, killing a third of the population in some regions of Italy.[14] It took Europe 600 years to recover.

continue to waste water as we do now, water will be the limiting factor in Australia's economic development'.[15]

Australia's Deputy Leader, and leader of the National Party, John Anderson has alluded to this sentiment whilst talking about the significant salinity problem for Australian soils and agriculture. He says: 'Salinity is bigger than tax reform. You can always fix a broken policy, but you can't fix a ruined food-bowl country'.[16] The mounting evidence of ecosystem collapse with its limiting effects on growth, and the great uncertainties that inherently exist when trying to understand the complex systems of nature and society and the biosphere, suggest that we would be wise to use an anticipatory precautionary approach that leads the economy away from areas of risk and towards areas where human endeavours can be carried out with a low level of inherent risk. Fundamentally, sustainability is wise from a risk management perspective for nations, businesses, governments and communities.

Can we replicate nature's services?

Whenever the economy has faced factors limiting development in the past, industrial nations sought to optimize the productivity and increase the supply of the limiting factor. In the past, economic development has periodically faced one or more limiting factors, including the availability of workers, energy resources and financial capital. Engineers and scientists found new energy sources and created new enabling technologies that helped make global transportation and communication possible. Financial capital became universally available through central banks, credit, stock exchanges and currency exchange mechanisms. Human ingenuity has accomplished remarkable things over the last 300 years. But can we really hope to find substitutes for all natural ecosystem services? The complexity and diversity of natural ecosystems is very hard to replace. Nobel laureate, and world famous physicist, Richard Feynman once said that attempting to understand nature is like trying to learn how to play chess by watching a game while being able to see only two squares at a time. The ecosystem services listed below that nature provides for free are not cost effectively replaceable or substitutable by technological innovation. These services complement and are depended on by life on our planet.

Ecosystem services include (adapted from *Natural Capitalism*):

- production of atmospheric gases;
- supporting evolutionary processes, and biodiversity;
- purification of soil, water and air;
- storage and cycling of fresh water and nutrients;
- regulation of the chemistry of the atmosphere and oceans;
- maintenance of habitats for wildlife;
- disposing of organic wastes;
- sequestration and treatment of waste;
- pest and disease control by insects, birds and other organisms;
- production of the variety of species for food, fibres, pharmaceuticals and materials;
- conversion of solar energy into natural materials;
- prevention of soil erosion and sediment loss;
- alleviating floods and managing runoff;
- protection against UV radiation;
- regulation of the local and global climate;
- development of topsoil and maintenance of soil fertility;
- production of grasslands, fertilizers and food.

CHAPTER 3

ASKING THE RIGHT QUESTIONS

Asking the right questions is critical to achieving a better future. What do we truly need? We need paper, not paper mills; mobility and access, not more gas guzzling cars. We need energy, not necessarily from fossil fuel power stations. Wouldn't it be great, for instance, if we could simply re-use our paper by de-inking it in our printers? That technology is not far away.[1] Significant resource efficiency gains are possible if we think backward from a service or product that we genuinely need, and discover ways to redesign the process to provide just as good or better a service with improved resource productivity. In this chapter we look at a series of questions regarding measuring growth, defining sustainability, trade-offs, measuring progress, legacy and designing industry. Through the exploration of these questions we seek to show that many practical answers are available that can yield tangible benefits both in the short and longer terms.

How should we measure growth?

Asking the right questions is also vital in economics. Many politicians today use the gross domestic product (GDP) measure as though it is the indicator of national well-being and progress. Nevertheless, many economists have adhered to the warning made by the creators of the GDP not to mistake it for a measure of national well-being.[2] Most economists use a raft of additional data to supplement the GDP to better inform judgements and predictions, data such as unemployment figures, terms of trade and so on. Most first year economics textbooks discuss the limitations of the GDP measure. Some quote Robert Kennedy when he said in 1968:[3]

> The Gross National Product includes air pollution and advertising for cigarettes, and ambulances to clear our highways of carnage. It counts special locks for our doors, and jails for the people who break them. GNP includes the destruction of the redwoods and the death of Lake Superior. It grows with the production of napalm and missiles and nuclear warheads. And if GNP includes all this, there is much that it does not comprehend. It does not allow for the health of our families, the quality of their education, or the joy of their play. It is indifferent to the decency of our factories and the safety of our streets alike. It does not include the beauty of our poetry or the strength of our marriages, or the intelligence of our public debate or the integrity of our public officials... GNP measures neither our wit nor our courage, neither our wisdom nor our learning, neither our compassion nor our

devotion to our country. It measures everything, in short, except that which makes life worthwhile; and it can tell us everything about America – except whether we are proud to be Americans.

Robert Kennedy, 1968 (Attorney General of the USA 1961–1964,
US Senator 1964–1968)

Thus it is recognized by many professional economists that GDP is not a good indicator of welfare because:

- the same level of economic output can produce wildly different levels of well-being depending on what types of products and services are offered, how well these products match human and environmental need and how these goods and services are distributed throughout the community;
- GDP measures production of both defensive expenditures that are needed to correct or compensate for avoidable problems as well as expenditures that cause a boost in welfare; and
- many additions (e.g., volunteer activities) to or subtractions (declines in the state of the environment or the vitality of communities) from welfare are not part of the monetized economy and so do not register in the GDP figures at all.

It is often assumed that if economic growth is occurring (i.e. the size of the monetized economy is growing over time) welfare will increase even if society has to bear the cost of some defensive expenditures. This might be misleading if defensive expenditures are having to expand faster than the overall economic growth rate or if non-monetized declines in the environment or society are growing faster than the gains from an expanded monetized economy. Genuine Progress studies have shown that this has indeed been the trend in quite a few countries, especially since the 1970s.

This explains why it is that many people have formed a view that economic growth (e.g. expansion in the size of the monetized economy) is a generally bad thing. But it should not be assumed that growth, development and progress are in themselves automatically bad. If damaging production processes are used and damaging products are produced then growth in the economy driven by those production processes and products will be bad. But if the economy radically changes its production processes and products so that they are benign or even restorative, then growth in the economy caused by an expansion of the beneficial production process and products would be a blessing. Presently, slowing growth is not going to help achieve sustainability, as it indicates to business and government not to invest, which in turn leads to job losses, and reductions in all the good aspects captured by the GDP indicator.[4] As Steve Dodds wrote in the publication *Human Ecology, Human Economy*, 'Discouraging economic growth would do little to encourage a more sustainable society. Indeed, engineering a recession is likely to have perverse consequences, increasing unemployment, reducing the willingness of consumers and firms to adopt improved social and environmental practices, and encouraging farmers and resource based industries to eat into our natural capital to maintain cash flows and living standards.'[5]

The important point is that we must be clear on what the economic growth is physically made up of. We must work very hard on the task of decoupling growth from negative environmental and social impacts.

It is important to acquire good measures that enable us to track this decoupling. Over the last five years significant efforts have gone into developing genuine progress indicators (GPI), that take into account social and environmental costs more accurately. The Canadian Government for instance has started the Environment and Sustainable Development Indicators (ESDI) initiative to create a set of authoritative and understandable indicators to track whether Canada's current economic activities are sustainable. This initiative was announced in the Finance Minister's 2000 Budget Speech. To better track Canada's ecosystem services and human capital, the Round Table has proposed six new measurements – or indicators. These indicators augment familiar economic data, such as the gross domestic product (GDP) and the consumer price index (CPI). The six indicators, released in May 2003, include five natural capital and one human capital indicator. The indicators are: forest cover, freshwater quality, air quality, greenhouse gas (GHG) emissions, extent of wetlands, and educational attainment. In the February 2004 Speech from the Throne outlining the general direction of the Canadian Government, the federal government made a commitment to begin using several of the recommended indicators.

What is meant when we speak of 'sustainability' and 'sustainable development'?

Currently, a very large number of people use the terms 'sustainability' and 'sustainable development' interchangeably; and this mixed usage is found in this book also. However, a debate is beginning over the way that our language shapes what we do at a practical level,[6] and we need to begin to grapple with this issue. It is now clear from the work that has been done on Genuine Progress Indicators that welfare for people and nature is enhanced through:

- sustaining (maintaining) the things that we love and that we depend on; and
- improving the condition of people for the first time in some new way.

So we want change in society in certain areas and we want continuity in some other areas. No society is ever completely static, nor would we want it to be, but equally there are some critical things that we want to maintain despite all the other changes (e.g., life support systems or human life or the existence of the other species on the planet). Both ethical and utilitarian concerns drive our efforts for sustainability.

Concepts that clearly bring together the idea of sustaining some things and changing other things for the better are sustainable development and sustainable genuine progress. Although the term sustainability is often now used as a shorthand for sustainable development, its meaning is probably most powerful when it is thought of as meaning simply 'the ability to sustain'. We can gain great clarity in our actions if we begin any sustainability programme with the question: 'What are we trying to sustain?' The next question to ask is: 'What needs to be done to ensure that those things are indeed sustained?'

The sustainability programmes of individual organizations could legitimately concentrate on environmental issues, or social questions or economic questions. But for society as a whole there are things or outcomes to be sustained in all three areas. Also, sustainability programmes to ensure the survival or maintenance of ecosystems services and biodiversity and to maintain human potential in areas currently afflicted with poverty and violence will require massive levels of innovation (i.e. strategic change) and will in many cases also require massive restorative programmes.

So, continuity and change and means and ends combine in interesting but practical ways to achieve sustainability of the things that society values. To sustain things that we value ethically ('ends' or highest order goals) we need massive innovation (so change in other parts of society is a 'means' to achieve the sustainability goal). If sustaining the things that we value is really important then, logically, it is vital that we achieve sustainability, otherwise the things that we have said we want to sustain will not be sustained. They will be degraded or made extinct. We need to approach sustainability goals with a very practical mindset, that is, sustainability goals are goals to be achieved, with no major trade-offs.

Ecological	Social	Economic	
Survival sustainability			Global
Protection of life support systems Prevention of species extinction	Capacity to solve serious problems	Subsistence	↕
			Local
Maintaining quality of life			Global
Maintenance of decent environmental quality	Maintenance of decent social quality (e.g. vibrant community life)	Maintenance of decent standard of living	↕
			Local
Improving quality of life			Global
Improving environmental quality	Improving social quality	Improving standard of living	↕
			Local

Source: Philip Sutton, Green Innovations

Figure 3.1 *Dimensions and levels of sustainability/sustainable development*

Sustainable Genuine Progress =   *progress that genuinely sustains and improves economic, social and environmental well-being with no major trade-offs, locally and globally, now and in the future.*

Natural Advantage of Nations =   *the multiple advantages a nation can achieve through a whole-of-society approach to the pursuit of sustainable genuine progress.*

Figure 3.1 communicates the main ideas and concepts involved in sustainable development and attempts to show the integrated nature of the key aspects.

Achieving sustainable genuine progress or sustainable development

Despite differences, a number of common principles are embedded in most charters or action programmes to achieve sustainable development or sustainable genuine progress. These include:

- dealing cautiously with risk, uncertainty and irreversibility;
- ensuring appropriate valuation, appreciation and restoration of nature;
- integration of environmental, social and economic goals in policies and activities;
- equal opportunity and community participation;
- conservation of biodiversity and ecological integrity;
- ensuring inter-generational equity;
- recognizing the global dimension;
- a commitment to best practice;
- no net loss of human or natural capital (*Hunter Lovins's working definition of sustainability*);
- the principle of continuous improvement; and
- the need for good governance.

At their core, the principles of sustainable development summarized in Table 3.1 are simply common sense articulated. This is because they have a solid basis in science. Not surprisingly these principles overlap with some of the best of the wise practical principles that also underpin world religions, the law and medicine that have assisted societies to live together harmoniously over thousands of years. Similarly, the stretch goals summarized in Table 3.2 are widely seen as critical to achieving sustainable genuine progress. They are becoming recognized more and more as important by both sides of politics. As Australian Senator Robert Hill states, 'We need to develop decision-making processes which take into account, not only the financial costs and benefits of our actions, but also the social and environmental consequences. Those processes will need to shift the focus away from short-term economic gain towards long-term economic, social and environmental impacts – the triple bottom line.'[7]

Can we achieve no major trade-offs and win–win opportunities?

One of the critically important implications to the triple bottom line decision-making process where society wants to pursue a range of goals simultaneously is that it must be based on the principle of 'no-major-trade-offs'. Logically, if society is committed to sustaining something, it cannot trade-off the continued existence of that thing or attribute in order to meet other goals. Similarly, in a triple bottom line approach, it is desirable for actions taken in the pursuit of one goal to also contribute to the achievement of other goals: 'win–win–win' outcomes.

In the past, following a rather simplistic application of optimization theory, it has been assumed that the pursuit of multiple goals means that no one goal can be maximized; there must be major trade-offs. But, in complex systems such as economies, societies and ecosystems, we are still so far from a theoretical perfect optimum that there is a huge potential to find solutions that can deliver multiple goals through 'no-major-trade-offs' and 'win–win outcomes'. To deliver such outcomes does require a major commitment to foster innovation and to increase greatly the capability of long-term thinking and the handling of complex issues. Take for instance the award-winning, AU\$3 billion project to tackle salinity in south-western Western Australia. The company, Woodside Petroleum, is the partner for this biomass/activated charcoal/eucalyptus oil project, which will involve the planting of millions of mallee eucalyptus trees to lower the water table and thus mitigate the effects of salinity in Western Australia. The activated charcoal from plantations will take the pressure off the native forests that are presently being used for activated charcoal all over the world, as it is in high demand as a reductant in mineral refining.[8] Finally, it will also act as a carbon sink whilst creating new jobs. This book will show, through such case studies, that genuine win–win–win opportunities exist and are economically profitable.

Figure 3.2 suggests some key questions to be raised as part of both strategic planning within governments and government–business, government–civil society partnerships when considering the impacts of future developments to ensure that all future development does provide multiple benefits for all.

> *For many years we pursued economic, environmental and social goals in isolation from each other. We have come to recognise that our long-term well-being depends as much on the promotion of a strong, vibrant society and the ongoing repair of our environment as it does on the pursuit of economic development. Indeed, it is becoming obvious that these issues cannot be separated. The challenge is to find new approaches to development that contribute to our environment and society now without degrading them over the longer term.*

West Australian Premier, Dr Geoff Gallop

Table 3.1 *Summary of emerging principles to guide activities into the 21st century*[9]

Source document	Item number
Respect for life and intrinsic right of all species to exist now and in the future	
Earth Charter	(1) (2) (3) (4) (11) (12) (15) (16)
Hannover Principles, William McDonough	(1)
1992 Rio Declaration on Environment and Development	(1) (3) (21) (22) (25)
First do no harm	
CERES Principles	(1) (6)
Earth Charter	(6)
Hannover Principles, William McDonough	(5)
Natural Step Principles	(1) (2) (3)
UN Global Compact	(7)
1992 Rio Declaration on Environment and Development	(2) (7) (15)
Waste not want not	
CERES Principles	(3)
Earth Charter	(7)
Hannover Principles, William McDonough	(6)
Natural Capitalism Principles, Amory Lovins, Hunter Lovins and Paul Hawken	(2)
Next Industrial Revolution Principles, William McDonough	(1)
1992 Rio Declaration on Environment and Development	(8) (13)
Efficient use of energy and resources	
CERES Principles	(2) (4)
Hannover Principles, William McDonough	(7)
Natural Capitalism Principles, Amory Lovins, Hunter Lovins and Paul Hawken	(1)
Natural Step Principles	(4)
Next Industrial Revolution Principles, William McDonough	(2)
We reap what we sow (We are responsible)	
Earth Charter	(10)
Hannover Principles, William McDonough	(4)
UN Global Compact	(1) (2) (3) (4) (5) (6) (8)
1992 Rio Declaration on Environment and Development	(4)
Learn from Nature: Design for sustainability	
Hannover Principles, William McDonough	(2) (8)
Natural Capitalism Principles, Amory Lovins, Hunter Lovins and Paul Hawken	(3)
Next Industrial Revolution Principles, William McDonough	(3)
Clean up after yourself	
CERES Principles	(7)
Earth Charter	(5)
Natural Capitalism Principles, Amory Lovins, Hunter Lovins and Paul Hawken	(4)

Note: Summarized by the editors.

Table 3.2 *Stretch goals to achieve sustainable genuine progress*

Achieve radical resource productivity – Beyond Factor 10	The key idea behind resource productivity is to maintain or increase the service flow while radically cutting the physical resource requirements of the physical delivery platform. It is argued by organizations such as the German Wuppertal Institute and the Dutch Sustainable Technology Development programme that resource intensity per unit of economic output needs to and can be cut by a Factor 10 or more (i.e. by 90 percent or more).
Develop closed-loop and zero waste systems	Radical resource productivity in part depends on the creation of a closed-loop economy whilst allowing for economic growth. The work of lean thinking experts shows the real benefits to the economy of increasing recycling, helping to make the economy a more closed-loop economy. Womak and Jones, two eminent industrial economists, stated in their book *Lean Thinking* that: 'Currently, only 16% of aluminium cans in the UK are recycled… If the percentage of cans recycled moved towards 100%, interesting possibilities would emerge for the whole value stream. Mini-smelters with integrated mini-rolling mills might be located near the can makers in England, eliminating in a flash most of the time, storage and distances involved today in the steps taken by most cola can makers.' They argue further that: 'the slow acceptance of recycling is surely due in part to the failure to analyse costs in the whole system rather than just for the recycling step in isolation'.
Ensure non-toxic products and production	Design for the environment and green chemistry programmes open up the possibility that our economy can innovate towards very close to zero toxicity. Argonne National Laboratory in the US has developed a process based on selective membranes that permits low-cost synthesis of high-purity ethyl lactate and other lactate esters from carbohydrate feedstock. The process requires little energy input, is highly efficient and eliminates the large volumes of salt waste produced by conventional processes. The innovation enables the replacement of toxic solvents – potentially over 80% of 3.8 million tons used in the US each year.
Economy based on renewable resources	Highlighted by the Natural Step from Sweden, the continued economic dependence on resources extracted from the earth's crust will cause systematic increases in concentrations of materials in the biosphere, which will eventually cause serious environmental problems.
Protect and enhance a rich biodiversity	Biodiversity needs to be sustained not only in order to maintain essential ecosystem services, but also because we have a moral responsibility to ensure that other species of life have a chance to survive, flourish and continue their evolutionary development in the wild.
Reduce major risks	Cost effectively restructure the economy to reduce major threats and risks. Some issues that are known to have huge implications for the scale and speed of change required to achieve an ecological sustainability are: greenhouse impact, decline of cheap/high net energy oil, biodiversity loss, scarcity of useable water, decline of soil, salinity.

Source: Adapted from the work of Philip Sutton, Green Innovations

	Environment	Society	Economy
Sustainability (maintaining)	What would it take for the aspects of the environment/society/economy that we value to be sustainable?		
Genuine progress (improving)	What would it take for everyone to have a worthwhile life? How can we improve the status quo?		
No major trade-offs (essential)	What would it take for specific initiatives in pursuit of sustainability/improvement not to undermine sustainability and the achievement of a decent life in general?		
Win–win (desirable)	What would it take for specific initiatives in pursuit of sustainability/improvement to contribute simultaneously to sustainability and the achievement of a decent life in general?		
Sustainable genuine progress	How can development and progress of all projects/activities add up to a desirable outcome of sustaining what is good and ensuring genuine progress?		

Source: Adapted from the work of Philip Sutton, Green Innovations

Figure 3.2 *Five layer planning approach*

How do nations measure progress?

Until a nation state does show a lead by solving the technical problems and putting a persuasive model of environmentally adjusted national accounts on the table, sustainable development will probably remain a rhetorical rather than an institutional principle.

Braithwaite and Drahos (2000, p284)

Measurement matters, because, unless we can develop reliable methods and good indicators to measure the sustainability process, it will be impossible for governments, businesses and communities to be accountable. As we have said, the point is not to be working endlessly towards sustainability but to achieve it. It is important, therefore, that we have adequate measurement frameworks for nations to assess if they are achieving progress that is truly genuine and sustainable. Many economists supplement macroeconomic measures such as GDP by various indicators, data sources and reports on environmental issues in assessing progress, and making predictions and planning. Progressing beyond the limitations of these established tools are measures such as the Genuine Progress Indicators, various 'Green GDP' or 'Green Net Product' measures, and now the World Bank measures of Genuine Savings, or Genuine Investment, which link the use of natural resources to human well-being.[10]

A significant project is underway in Australia, led by the CSIRO, focused on applying the recently developed 'inclusive wealth framework', a new methodology developed by Arrow, Dasgupta and Maler.[11] The framework measures an economy's capital stocks, using weights from the estimation of market value for each capital component, using shadow prices for non-market goods (human, natural and manufactured capital). The framework interprets non-declining net (weighted) capital stocks as an indication that the current set of development activities is sustainable. In the inclusive wealth framework, the well-being of a nation is defined as being the sum of the traditional forms of capital, namely financial, manufactured, human, natural and social. Other forms of capital that are difficult to measure – that we all know are important for our sense of well-being – are also included.

Table 3.3 *Key indicators of sustainable genuine progress*

Name or proposed indicator	Measurement of sustainable genuine progress
Green GNP/Green GDP[12]	Measures national income or output adjusted for the depletion of natural resources and degradation of the environment. A larger number signifies greater sustainability.
Genuine Investment/Savings[13]	Measures the net change in national assets including natural and human capital. A larger number signifies greater sustainability.
Genuine Progress Indicator[14]	Measures the change in social well-being, through 25 indicators, covering consumption (broader than GDP) and value of capital stocks. A larger number signifies greater sustainability.

Source: Pearson et al (2003)

> *The definition of inclusive wealth developed in Arrow et al is where a nation can be seen as achieving sustainable development if social welfare (intergenerational well-being) is at least maintained. Social welfare is the present value aggregation of all humans' well-being, current and future (including soil, water, biodiversity, buildings, education, etc.). The best available proxy for measuring social welfare is the measurement of the 'value' of all capital stocks (human, manufactured and natural). The sum of an economy's capital stocks, weighted by their shadow prices for each capital component, is a measure of the country's inclusive wealth. Therefore, a country is achieving sustainable development if its measure of inclusive wealth is non-declining.*
>
> Brian Walker, CSIRO, Executive Summary, MMSD Project Description[15]

Hence, non-declining well-being for future generations can be initially measured in terms of the overall stock of capital. The inclusive wealth framework also seeks to measure to what extent different forms are actually substitutable.[16] There are two main lines of thought on the ability to both aggregate different forms of capital and in turn substitute them. One is the 'Weak' or 'Narrow' definition, which assumes that all forms of capital are substitutable. The other is the 'Strong' or 'Broad' definition, where the ability to transform one form of capital into another is not assumed; rather great efforts are made to determine whether substitutability is in fact possible. The limitation of the Weak definition is that both human and manufactured capital are complemented by nature and will struggle to find cost effective substitutes for many of its services. Also nature has an intrinsic right to exist. As we described earlier, there is mounting evidence that our ecosystems are more fragile than first thought, suggesting that nature (natural capital) is to be cherished and restored and not converted into other forms of capital. Hence, the inclusive wealth framework brings in the best of the Strong or Broad definition by placing more restrictive conditions on the ability to substitute particular forms of capital. Pearson, Harris and Walker suggest that an 'ideal' national measure of sustainable development would incorporate the most useful aspects of both the Weak and Strong definitions and have something like the following properties:[17]

- The measure would allow for the quantification of the total capital stock, thus allowing analysis of the overall trend.
- The measure would allow the substitutability of each form of capital within the measure to be governed by an assigned relative weighting.

- The limitations effecting substitutability of each form of capital would be clearly understood and accounted for. In particular, any critical thresholds such as ecological limits or the inability to be further substituted would be taken into account, together with the level of difficulty in reversing the substitution of different types of capital (irreversibility).

How do we design for legacy?

Achieving sustainable genuine progress requires, in part, tracking and measuring the negative impacts on the environment. However, at the same time, we need to work on designing systems and industry that will eliminate waste and pollution. If our time is spent measuring negative impacts on the environment, it leaves little time to develop solutions and focus on those areas we can change. The difficulty of the task should not be underestimated. Michael Braungart, cofounder of the McDonough Braungart Design Chemistry Group (MBDC) found it very hard in the early days to discover any other chemists who were interested in designing for sustainability at all, let alone had any experience of doing so. He writes in the book *Cradle to Cradle*: 'The scientific community is usually paid to study problems, not solutions'.

But it is vital that we do put significant effort into re-thinking through these serious problems because as Albert Einstein wrote: 'The world will not evolve past its current state of crisis by using the same thinking that created the situation.' Many of the best examples to date of this out-of-the-box thinking have been featured in books like *Natural Capitalism*,[18] *Factor Four*,[19] *Cradle to Cradle*,[20] *Design for Sustainability*[21] and *Believing Cassandra*.[22] These books show that much of the re-thinking has already been done. They show that globally numerous pioneers have been developing the much needed knowledge of how to shift to an ecologically sustainable economy, and they show there is significant progress already towards a new wave of innovation for sustainability. They have also helped to communicate the multiple benefits to business of increasing resource productivity and operational efficiency using biologically inspired production models (i.e. closed-loop production systems), developing new business models based on value and service and reinvesting in natural capital to allow both business and nature to be productive. These authors have called this shift the 'next industrial revolution'. McDonough and Braungart point out that even if eco-efficiency is a 'valuable and laudable tool, and a prelude to what should come next'[23] it, too, fails to move us beyond the first revolution. It is time for effective designs that are in harmony with nature and based in biomimetic principles. Their concept of eco-effectiveness leads to human industry that is regenerative rather than depletive. It involves the design of things that celebrate interdependence with other living systems. From an industrial-design perspective, it means products that work within cradle-to-cradle life cycles rather than cradle-to-grave cycles. It means systems innovation rather than innovation of parts of the whole.

McDonough tells the following story as an example:

> In 1993, we helped to conceive and create a compostable upholstery fabric, a biological nutrient. We were initially asked by Design Tex to create an aesthetically unique fabric that was also ecologically intelligent, although the client did not quite know at that point what this would (tangibly) mean. The challenge helped to clarify, both for us and for the company we were working with, the difference between superficial responses such as recycling and reduction and the more significant changes required by the Next Industrial Revolution. For example, when the company first sought to meet our desire for an environmentally safe fabric, it presented what it thought was a wholesome option: cotton, which is natural,

combined with PET (Polyethylene Terephthalate) fibres from recycled beverage bottles. Since the proposed hybrid could be described with two important eco-buzzwords, 'natural' and 'recycled,' it appeared to be environmentally ideal. The materials were readily available, market-tested, durable, and cheap. But when the project team looked carefully at what the manifestations of such a hybrid might be in the long run, we discovered some disturbing facts. When a person sits in an office chair and shifts around, the fabric beneath him or her abrades; tiny particles of it are inhaled or swallowed by the user and other people nearby. PET was not designed to be inhaled. Furthermore, PET would prevent the proposed hybrid from going back into the soil safely, and the cotton would prevent it from re-entering an industrial cycle. The hybrid would still add junk to landfills, and it might also be dangerous.

The team decided to design a fabric so safe that one could literally eat it. The European textile mill chosen to produce the fabric was quite 'clean' environmentally, and yet it had an interesting problem: although the mill's director had been diligent about reducing levels of dangerous emissions, government regulators had recently defined the trimmings of his fabric as hazardous waste. We sought a different end for our trimmings: mulch for the local garden club. When removed from the frame after the chair's useful life and tossed onto the ground to mingle with sun, water and hungry micro-organisms, both the fabric and its trimmings would decompose naturally. The team decided on a mixture of safe, pesticide-free plant and animal fibres for the fabric (ramie and wool) and began working on perhaps the most difficult aspect: the finishes, dyes, and other processing chemicals. If the fabric was to go back into the soil safely, it had to be free of mutagens, carcinogens, heavy metals, endocrine disrupters, persistent toxic substances and bio-accumulative substances. Sixty chemical companies were approached about joining the project, and all declined, uncomfortable with the idea of exposing their chemistry to the kind of scrutiny necessary. Finally one European company, Ciba-Geigy, agreed to join. With that company's help the project team considered more than 8000 chemicals used in the textile industry and eliminated 7962. The fabric – in fact, an entire line of fabrics – was created using only 38 chemicals. The resulting fabric has garnered gold medals and design awards and has proved to be tremendously successful in the marketplace. The non-toxic fabric, Climatex®Lifecycle™, is so safe that the fabric's trimmings can indeed be used as a mulch by local garden clubs. The director of the mill told a surprising story after the fabrics were in production. When regulators came to test the effluent, they thought their instruments were broken. After testing the influent as well, they realized that the equipment was fine – the water coming out of the factory was as clean as the water going in. The manufacturing process itself was filtering the water. The new design not only bypassed the traditional three-R responses to environmental problems but also eliminated the need for regulation.

McDonough and Braungart (2001)

This example is one of creativity and applied science combined with a commitment to genuinely find a sustainable solution by reassessing the entire process and seeking out any and all opportunities to improve. This process is crucial as, when most designs are done, as much as 80 per cent of their resource usage is locked into the design and much of the environmental impact, that may be designed away, is already inevitable.[24] Whole systems thinking is a process through which the inter-connections between systems are actively considered and solutions are sought to address multiple problems at the same time. Some refer to this process as the search for 'solution multipliers'. For example, most energy-using technologies are sub-optimally designed in two ways so pervasively that they often go unnoticed:

1   components are optimized in isolation (thus pessimizing the systems of which they are a part); and
2   optimization typically considers single rather than multiple benefits.

Amory Lovins, CEO of Rocky Mountain Institute (RMI), writes that whole system redesigns, such as the example of Schilham's 'Big Pipes/Small Pumps' in Chapter 1 can be achieved for air-handling, cleanroom, lighting, drivepower, chillers, insulating, heat-exchanging, buildings and other technical systems in a wide range of sizes, programmes, and climates, commonly yielding empirical energy savings of an order of magnitude, usually with reduced capital cost.[25]

Can we turn 'vicious cycles' into 'virtuous circles'?

The answer to this question is clearly 'yes'. To illustrate how, let us consider a region's energy market. Intuitively, one would assume factors such as increasing populations, increased use of electrical appliances and equipment and increased industrialization would dictate energy use in society and be driving energy production. But the main driver to build new power stations typically comes from the seasonal peak energy demands for cooling and heating. This means that the entire system is designed to meet these peaks and then carries a redundancy during the predominant non-peak periods. Amazing but true. This presents a unique design challenge; if homes and commercial buildings were properly designed, and properly insulated, the need for heating and cooling would be reduced. So why is this a vicious cycle? Let us consider the situation in the state of Victoria, Australia.[26] To meet summer peak energy demands in the 1970s and 1980s, the Victorian Government invested in more power stations. Once these new power stations were built to meet peak energy demand, there was little incentive for governments to encourage passive cooling design, demand management and energy efficiency for the rest of the year as, with the new power stations, there was excess capacity that could be sold to the market. The government's regulatory framework at the time meant that the more energy the state sold the more money it made. This created a vicious cycle.

Hence, the Victorian Government kept building more power stations and, in the end, incurred a debt of over AU$9 billion by the late 1980s – a scale of debt completely unnecessary if it had targeted incentives for energy efficiency and retrofitting buildings to reduce the need for air-conditioning. This debt, from capital expenditure for building the new power stations, was the chief justification given by a newly elected Victorian Government for the privatization of the sector in the 1990s. The rules set under the new privatized market give energy companies little incentive to conserve energy or to encourage energy efficiency in the community and the vicious cycle continues. The fact is that the Victorian energy grid is 20 per cent larger than it needs to be and every energy bill is higher than it needs to be as Victorians pay for the grid to be bigger and bigger – all because of the heavy use of air-conditioning during seasonal extremes.[27] The legacy of inefficient, poorly insulated Victorian homes built over the last 100 years is, therefore, profound. In addition to the design options chosen by engineers, architects, urban planners, farmers, etc., the actions of governments in setting the regulatory frameworks, subsidies, market signals and incentives have a wide reaching influence on development.

We, as a community, have a choice. We do not have to continue moving in these vicious cycles. We now know how to design the home differently and often more cost effectively. On the regulation front, governments, like that of Sacramento in the US, have adopted relatively enlightened regulatory frameworks for their energy sector. In Sacramento the regulatory frameworks reward the energy utility for encouraging energy efficiency and conservation. At the regional level the choice is truly that of the voters. Never doubt for a second that we, as individuals, can make a difference through the choices we make.[28] As Ken Henry, the Secretary Head of Treasury, Australia stated (in referring to what he has learnt as an economist): 'I learned about the importance of prices in guiding resource allocation. And I came to the view that people's behaviours had a lot to do with their pursuit of self interest, and that a lot of what I might have found objectionable about the things humans did could have had something to do with the opportunities and incentives established by governments.'[29]

Professor Alan Pears, Adjunct Professor and Senior Lecturer in Environment and Planning at RMIT University, advises on some of the ways that the right incentives can be put in place for the energy sector. First we must realize that in order to provide appropriate incentives for energy companies, each decision they take must make more money and support the company's growth. If you introduce higher pricing at peak times to reduce the peak demand, this will send a signal to users to avoid using energy at critical times. But the high price also sends a perverse message to energy suppliers that they can make windfall profits during peak periods. Alternatively, in this case, the revenue from higher prices at times of peak demand could go into a government fund to be used as an incentive for the electricity industry in ways that are consistent with long-term societal objectives. It is clear that the solution lies in finding a way for the energy supply industry to maintain revenues while reducing consumer demand. This may be achieved through a combination of increased mandatory requirements to pursue energy efficiency and incentives to encouraged demand-side action by offering suppliers trade-offs, or higher rates of return or payments from a government levy. (This topic will be greatly expanded in Chapter 17.) These sorts of positive feedback loops can create virtuous circles. This is the 'Catch 22'.

Whilst seminal books like *Natural Capitalism* show that there is much that any nation and business can do now with no change to existing government subsidies and incentives (as the same authors alluded to in *Factor Four: Doubling Wealth, Halving Resource Use*), progress would be much faster if government incentives and framework conditions were to be adjusted. This would greatly encourage the uptake of, and help kick start greater market penetration of, sustainable technologies, best available technologies and whole system design. Many governments[30] have acknowledged that these issues are critical and are addressing their incentives and frameworks. But, despite all the evidence and references we have outlined so far, there is significant inertia for change. We highlighted one of the reasons in Chapter 1: the current mistaken belief that a transition to sustainability will harm economic growth. The result of this belief is that governments, R&D institutions and firms have not been encouraged as much as they could have been to explore economically feasible and desirable paths to an ecologically sustainable economy. However, as we have already shown in the later part of Chapter 1, significant new studies show these assumptions to be incorrect. We showed that in fact the opposite could more than likely be the case. The inertia also comes from the fact that the growing environmental crisis has also occurred during a time when the political climate has been to roll back the role of government. There are some who believe that this should all be left to the market. They argue, broadly speaking, that the invisible hand of the market is the best way to ensure scarce resources are allocated efficiently. But as we will now show, over the last 30 years in economics a far more sophisticated understanding of markets and market failure has evolved that can be used by governments to determine when it may be appropriate to act, and how. These developments in economics are theoretical but they inform all the discussion about the role of government in this book. The economists who developed this new field of the economics of information were awarded the Nobel Prize for Economics in 2001 for this work. Hence these exciting developments in economics are summarized in Chapter 4 and discussed in greater detail in Section 3, Chapter 12.

CHAPTER 4

A DYNAMIC 'PLATFORM FOR CHANGE'

Economic policy: the broader context

Up until the 1970s, Keynsian economics[1] had proved remarkably successful at helping economies to grow and smooth out the extremes of the traditional boom–bust cycle. But in the 1970s, through a range of factors including the Organization of Petroleum Exporting Countries (OPEC) oil crisis,[2] Western economies were faced with a serious challenge. By the late 1970s and early 1980s, many economies were faced with both a stagnant economy but high inflation, what economists call stagflation. Many saw this simplistically as a failure of Keynesian economics. The crisis of stagflation in the 1970s and the fall of the Soviet Empire in 1989 have led economic policy to shift to more laissez-faire approaches which have idealized the market whilst belittling the role of government and the need for regulation. This sentiment was summed up by Bill Clinton in 1996 in his 27 January radio address on CNN, when he said that: 'The era of big government is over'. The most ardent free market proponents believe that the market is the best way to address environmental degradation, unemployment and issues of social inequity, arguing that the market and innovation on their own will solve these problems and that governments would best get out of the way as much as possible. Behind this is a belief in unfettered or unregulated markets. Adam Smith, the author of *Wealth of Nations*, in 1776, was credited with supporting this belief on the basis that he wrote about an invisible hand that works through the markets. No idea has had more power than that of Adam Smith's invisible hand. It is said that free markets, as if by an invisible hand, lead to the most efficient, and fair, allocation of scarce resources and that each individual in pursuing his or her own self-interests, advances the greater good. The relevant passage is probably the most famous (and selectively cited) passage in Smith's classic *The Wealth of Nations*.

> But the annual revenue of every society is always precisely equal to the exchangeable value of the whole annual produce of its industry, or rather is precisely the same thing with that exchangeable value. As every individual, therefore, endeavours as much as he can both to employ his capital in the support of domestic industry, and so to direct that industry that its produce may be of the greatest value; every individual necessarily labours to rend the annual revenue of the society as great as he can. He generally indeed, neither intends to promote the public interest, nor knows how much he is promoting it. By preferring the support of domestic to that of foreign industry, he intends only his own security, and by

directing that industry in such a manner as its produce may be of the greatest value, he intends only his own gain, and he is in this, as in many other cases, led by an invisible hand to promote an end which was no part of his intention. Nor is it always the worse for the society that it was no part of it. By promoting his own interest he frequently promotes that of the society more effectually than when he really intends to promote it.

Adam Smith, *An Inquiry into the Nature and Causes of the Wealth of Nations*, p572 (First published in 1776 and republished in 1999)

Thus, what he in fact said was that each individual pursuing his or her own self-interest, led by an invisible hand, frequently promotes the interests of society. Markets do bring enormous benefits. They have been responsible for lifting more people out of poverty faster than any other economic mechanism in history. In a well-functioning market, prices provide information about the demand and supply conditions in that market, both buyers and sellers can observe and act upon the information embodied in the price. The economist Friedrich Hayek described the interconnectedness of markets as follows:

Suppose that someone has found a new use for tin, so that the demand for tin increases and its price rises. Then the effect will rapidly spread throughout the whole economic system and influence not only all the uses of tin but also its substitutes and the substitute of these substitutes, the supply of all things made of tin, and their substitutes and so on; and all this without the great majority of those instrumental in bringing about these substitutions knowing anything about the original causes of these changes. The whole acts as one market, not because any of its members survey the whole field, but because their limited individual fields overlap so that through many intermediaries the relevant information is communicated to all.

Economist Friedrich Hayek (1949)

The invisible hand

It would be foolish in the extreme, therefore, for any government to seek to even attempt to replace this role of the market. Actually, it is extreme folly to suggest that even the most benevolent of centrally-planned states could acquire the amount of information necessary to replace the market. We saw in Russia the disastrous results of such a policy. But one of the great intellectual achievements of the mid-20th century (by Gerard Debreu of the University of California at Berkeley and Kenneth Arrow of Stanford, both of whom received Nobel prizes for this achievement) was to establish the conditions under which Adam Smith's 'invisible hand' did in fact work.

The results showed that, for the 'invisible hand' to work:

- information had to be either perfect, or at least not affected by anything going on in the economy;
- whatever information anybody had, others had the same information; and
- competition was perfect and, for instance, one could buy insurance against any possible risk.

Arrow and Debreu's Nobel prize-winning work also showed that for Smith's invisible hand to apply, it implicitly assumed that information is fixed, costless and perfect. We know that information is not fixed, costless or perfect. The amount, nature and distribution of knowledge within a society change over time. Individuals and organizations must invest time and money in order to acquire new information. Even though everyone recognized that these assumptions were unrealistic, it was hoped that the real world did not depart too much from such assumptions and that Adam Smith's invisible hand theory would still provide a good description of the economy. Subsequent Nobel prize-winning work has shown that this was a hope based on faith not science. Sometimes, knowledge lies with parties who have an incentive to conceal it, so that information is unevenly or 'asymmetrically distributed' between buyers and sellers. Economists such as George Akerlof, Joseph Stiglitz and Carl Shapiro have emphasized that the kinds of assumptions economists make about information is important, because changing these assumptions results in significantly different economic models. In the 1970s and 1980s, these and other pioneering economists set about including information distribution in their models. Rather than producing more complicated models making essentially the same predictions, the explicit inclusion of information distribution resulted in models capable of predicting and explaining behaviour in many different markets.

Importantly, in these and other new models, the market mechanism was shown to be inefficient in the face of imperfect information. Bruce Greenwald and Joseph Stiglitz[3] analytically demonstrated in 1986 that this conclusion is a general one. Differences in the levels of access to information within the market will affect the distribution of resources, and better information may actually lead to a more efficient distribution. Greenwald and Stiglitz found that these asymmetries of information are pervasive throughout the economy and found them to be endemic, especially in developing economies, where the market for information does not work as well. In fact, these advances in economics show that the invisible hand of Adam Smith may well be 'invisible' because it may not exist in the real world, especially in these cases where asymmetric information is significant. Moreover, in simple situations involving a market with a single informational problem, there is in many cases a government intervention which could make everybody in the market better off. In more complicated settings involving complex multiple informational problems, it may be the case that clear opportunities for government interventions to improve welfare will not necessarily exist.

In addition to providing us with a better picture of the economy, the work of Greenwald and Stiglitz has also recast the old debate about whether or not there is a role for government in a market economy in a new light. The theorem shows us that there is indeed a role and that the relevant debate is not the existence of this role but its precise nature.[4] For instance, in Section 3 we show that national governments have a role to address externalities as the market tends to produce too little of positive externalities like education and research and development (R&D) whilst producing too much of negative externalities like pollution. We will show that whether firms can successfully lead new waves of innovation can be affected by government policy and actions because success often requires integration of innovation across many fronts. Governments can greatly assist firms through their unique position in society to help coordinate the multiple initiatives needed, often over decades, to lead the next waves of innovation. Government sponsored research and innovations have been responsible for many of the successes of the US economy in the 19th and 20th centuries. Advancements such as building the first telegraph line between Baltimore and Washington in 1844 and contributions to much of the R&D for the Internet were supported by the US Government. The German Government played a pivotal role in Germany catching up and in certain areas overtaking Britain in the late 19th century. Likewise, governments played a critical role in the Asian tiger economies catching up to the technological frontier so quickly in the last half of the 20th century. This will be discussed in detail in the context of governments' role to assist a shift towards achieving sustainable genuine progress in Section 3 of this book.

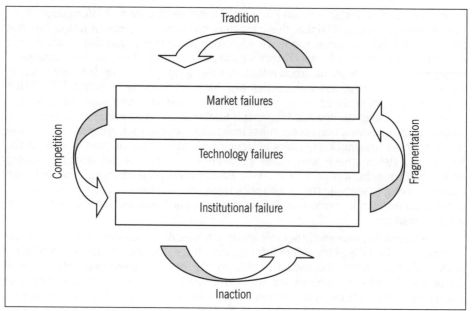

Source: The Natural Edge Project

Figure 4.1 *Drivers restricting sustainable outcomes*

Collaborative approaches

Governments, even well-intentioned ones, are not perfect either. Politically powerful interest groups can exert undue influence over policy processes and regulatory agencies can be 'captured' by the groups that they were designed to monitor. As the *World Bank Development Report* 1997 states: 'Market failure and the concern for equity provide the economic rationale for government intervention. But there is no guarantee that any such intervention will benefit society. Government failure may be as common as market failure.' The overall trend of declining ecosystem resilience can be understood as an example of a market failure due to externalities and the challenges in managing public goods summed up in 1968 by Hardin in 'The Tragedy of the Commons' paper. A better understanding, therefore, of recent analytic, non-ideological breakthroughs in economics will help us to build a consensus on new ways forward to improve the well-being for all. There is growing consensus within modern economics that market, information and institutional (such as government) failures, are amongst the key drivers of unsustainable development (see Figure 4.1).[5]

As stated earlier, one of the fundamental information failures comes from our inability to value non-market goods such as ecosystem services. What is clean air worth? The air has no economic value, as it is not bought and sold. As Hunter Lovins asked the delegates to the recent Network of Regional Government for Sustainable Development (nrg4SD) conference in Perth,[6] 'What price does one put on a stable climate?' It is questionable whether we will ever find a method for measuring the value of natural capital upon which all agree. But all agree that nature is valuable. In the past, failure to assign any value at all to natural capital clearly was an information failure, which then led to both market and institutional decisions being made with insufficient information. As the Australian Treasury states:[7] 'Inappropriate behaviour can also arise where government policies fail to provide appropriate incentives. For example, pricing water below the full cost (i.e. including the environmental cost) will lead to overuse, with a resultant increase in salinity and decline in river quality.' But herein lies part of the

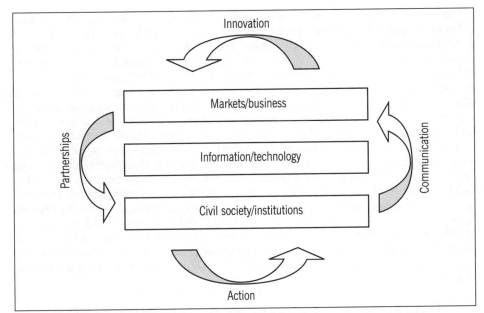

Source: The Natural Edge Project

Figure 4.2 *Platform for change diagram*

solution. By addressing informational, market and institutional failures, we can turn them around to be drivers for sustainability. This will be discussed in detail in Section 3.

So endemic in our market system are information failures that there are significant business opportunities in providing the information that people need. Consider these examples:

- **Information technology**: In Australia, salinity threatens half of the Australian food bowl. Salinity pathways underground can now be accurately detected by satellites for less cost than previous methods and spatial data technologies can now analyse and present the information in a highly-useable interface. These new enabling technologies are the basis of a new wave of innovation in the IT sector creating exciting new ways to tackle complex systems problems through improved real-time information.
- **Mining**: Many accidents are avoidable, and are caused by a lack of simple prevention measures such as knowing the potency of chemicals at a mine site, or having quick access to a database. For instance, for BHP Billiton, compensation and lost time through injury are estimated to cost AU$78 million a year. To address this, BHP is now a client of Risk Management Technology (RMT). The founder and chief executive of RMT, Dean Apostolou, says: 'When we set up the business, we found that most employers – and employees – had no idea what chemicals they had on site, or what damage they could do. Warning notices from chemical companies were more like a sales pitch, which did not cover all the hazards or warn of potential side-effects.'

In addition, information for civil society through independent, trustworthy eco- and fair trade labelling, certification schemes and education, is needed to achieve more systemic change by addressing the fundamental information failure impeding sustainable development. In particular, the consumer presently has little to no idea about the environmental load and social costs of the product or service they are purchasing relative to another product or service.

Information can also be indirect and businesses can also create product differentiation and improve market share by correctly reading changes in regulatory and institutional frameworks within any nation. The Bendigo Bank, the major community bank network in Australia, offers lower mortgage interest rates for a 5-star energy efficient home. Such action to promote energy efficiency in the home is supported by the fact that in 2003 the Victorian Government began to phase in regulation encouraging all new homes to have 5-star energy efficiency. The Victorian Government has done this with the full support of Treasury. Treasury was impressed with the economic study undertaken by Allen's Consulting showing 5-star homes would help the economy more than 4-star homes and hence backed this change in the Victorian Government's Cabinet meetings. These types of reforms are translated industry wide through National Building Codes or equivalent regulating documents that outline minimum standards required in building projects. This type of collaboration is at the base of sustainability with business and institutions working together to improve standards continuously where possible on a firm foundation of good engineering, design and economics and community/ stakeholder engagement. An example of such reform can be seen in the Building Code of Australia (BCA) adding new requirements for improved energy efficiency standards within design and construction; such standards will be required to be adhered to throughout Australia.

> *Following wide consultation between the Australian Government and the building industry, the Australian Ministerial Council on Greenhouse announced on 24 March 1999 that it had reached agreement on a comprehensive strategy aimed at making homes and commercial buildings more energy efficient. This agreement featured a two pronged strategy: (a) the introduction of mandatory minimum energy performance requirements through the Building Code of Australia while (b) encouraging voluntary best-practice initiatives.*

Building Code of Australia (BCA)[8]

This action has established a very positive shift in the thinking of practising architects towards giving attention to sustainability and its principles and, most importantly, towards the methods of implementation which can be adopted within practice. Although the execution of the new principles is in its early stages, and is suffering from some problems, mostly generated from the complexity of the issue, the direction is encouraging and the possibilities heartening.[9]

In many countries, however, there are, at present, contrary drivers such as the following:

*   Materialistic, instant gratification values and culture that promotes and rewards consumption in a throw away society. In OECD countries children from a very young age are exposed to thousands of exciting advertisements carefully designed to encourage a perception of false needs (for unnecessary luxuries) as real. Until recently in Australia, some States even allowed gambling to be advertised to children.
*   Lack of communication between the silos and within civil society: The findings of the 2001 CSIRO (Commonwealth Scientific and Industrial Research Organisation) Futurecorp Forum – Shaping Australian Business for 21st Century Conditions, held in the Australian Parliament House in 2001 stated that 'Massive "silo busting" is required to establish effective dialog within and across the institutions of government, education, science, business and the community – including the removal of competition (among the States) on key areas of sustainability. The issue for government is that current structures and accountabilities support and reinforce silos. Greater career mobility across sectors needs to be encouraged with

appropriate training, recognition, reward, and superannuation structures.' These findings apply to many nations.

- Lack of market incentives and fair regulatory frameworks to drive commercialization of eco-innovation. Environmental technology regulation that promotes the best available technology potentially could have a profound influence on whether progress is made on the environment nationally and globally this century. Professor Michael Porter has demonstrated since 1991 that there is much evidence to support the notion that environmental regulation, wisely administered, can help a nation's economy through rewarding and inspiring the pursuit of resource efficiency and innovation. In addition, when this is coupled with regulation requiring continuous environmental improvement and auditing standards under EU regulation 1836/93. Europe has given itself significant potential long-term competitive advantage in the field of environmental technologies.
- Lack of meaningful partnerships between various groups actively seeking sustainable outcomes.

Tripartite world

Hunter Lovins writes: 'We now live in interesting times. Of the 100 biggest economic entities over 50 are companies, not nation states. And at the same time thanks to the Internet, civil society has the capacity to de-legitimize any company or country. So who is in charge here? Clearly government, the private sector, and civil society all have power and responsibility here. In this tripartite world, they all therefore have a part to play in solving the challenges of sustainable development.'

The World Business Council for Sustainable Development[10] put forward a preferred scenario for development that addresses the tripartite nature of our world. They likened their preferred development process to Jazz music in the sense that everyone is playing in the same song with various leaders at particular times, and innovation and trials are constantly being attempted.[11] The 'Jazz' scenario requires that we recognize the essential value in all three sectors – the private sector, government and community. When all three sectors work together, the synergy is unbounded in its potential. Sustainability experts and governments are realizing that partnerships are essential for lasting progress. Put simply, for government environmental programmes to work, there have to be partnerships and understanding within the community. For business eco-innovation to succeed in the marketplace, civil society needs to be an active and willing partner. For example, in Australia farmers and the environment movement had been at loggerheads until the landmark Landcare agreement in the 1980s between the National Farmers Federation, represented by Rick Farley, and the Australian Conservation Foundation, represented by Phillip Toyne. The process of reaching and then implementing this agreement created the strong collaboration and consensus needed between key business and civil society groups for Australian institutions to significantly fund land rehabilitation programmes in rural Australia. This has led over the last decade to significant cultural change as the traditional business vs. environment prejudices were broken down.

As Peter Newman writes:

> There are many heroic stories of farmers creating more sustainable land uses. The WA government were taking a political risk when they announced clearing bans for agriculture in 2002, but the Landcare movement in Australia is now so broad and engages so many in the bush, it was almost a non-issue. Recently the Federal Government of Australia and the Queensland government announced that all land clearing would cease in Queensland by 2006.

Newman (2003)

This publication focuses on how such partnerships, networks, and collaborations can bring about the necessary building of trust, and political will to minimize the political risk of the process, thereby allowing the key stakeholders to work together to create the new regulatory frameworks needed to achieve a sustainable future.

Whole of society approach

Whole of government approaches are growing in application worldwide. We argue that new broader partnerships are now possible between government and the rest of society as an increasing number of sectors of society are supportive of sustainable development. We call this more than just a whole of government approach to sustainable development, but a whole of society approach (see Figure 4.3). As reported in Chapter 1, it is now being widely understood that to achieve systematic change we need systems, that is holistic, approaches.

The 1992 Earth Summit's Agenda 21 document was one of the major attempts to address sustainability holistically. It outlines in detail how each sector of society can play its part to achieve sustainable development. By 2002 a wide array of societies' institutions, professional bodies, churches, universities, schools, and businesses were represented at the World Summit on Sustainable Development (WSSD) with a greater understanding of the role they can play to help. Hence in 2002, the WSSD rightly emphasized how we can achieve much through partnerships for sustainability. New partnerships are now possible given the range of bodies and organizations committed to sustainability. Institutions within a society are the biggest allies or barriers to operationalizing sustainable development. But now, increasingly, societies' institutions understand these issues, change is cost effectively possible. Governments can significantly help these processes by creating National Councils for Sustainable Development or equivalent councils at the regional government level to bring together representatives from key stakeholder/institutional groups. This is covered in detail in Chapter 12.

What is particularly significant is that businesses are now understanding that they too need the partnerships, as much of society is involved in creating markets for eco-innovation and ecologically sound products. Fiona Wain, CEO of Environment Business Australia asked exactly this question at the major biennial conference for the environmental industries of Australia in 2002. She asked: 'How can we encourage the whole of society to be involved? How can we encourage this shift so as to create increased markets for environmentally sound products?' One avenue is public procurement. For instance, the European Commission reports that as public procurement amounts to over €1000 billion every year across the European Union (14 per cent of EU GDP), 'greening' these purchases could contribute substantially to a sustainable future.[12]

Partnerships are essential to achieve reforms to make markets work better and to get the market signals right so that they reflect the real costs to present and future generations. Partnerships for sustainability are at the core of the landmark Western Australian State Sustainability Strategy released in 2003, after lengthy public consultation. Remarkably, in the first three days of release of the consultation draft over 17,000 copies were downloaded from the website, with a third of the downloads coming from the US. In Section 3, the architect of the strategy, Professor Peter Newman will discuss how the WA Government has taken a whole of society approach to sustainable development. The reality of sustainability is that an innovation can now occur anywhere in the world and be of value almost everywhere. For example, after the Irish Government took steps to reduce the use of plastic bags, much of the rest of the world has followed suit. The political risk taken in Ireland proved to be worthwhile as massive numbers of

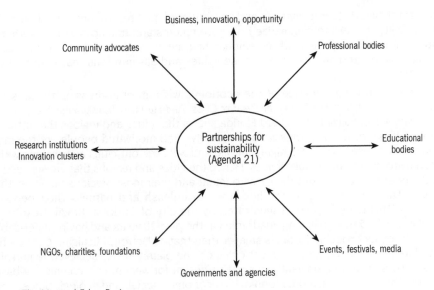

Source: The Natural Edge Project

Figure 4.3 *Whole of society approach to sustainable development*

plastic bags disappeared from the system once a levy was imposed at the counter to consumers. The challenge is to ensure that the political process and institutional structures get the incentives right, so that their interventions actually improve the well-being of nations whilst ensuring the non-declining well-being of future generations.[13] As both governments and markets can fail, a consideration of the strengths and weaknesses of both should help inform a sophisticated dialogue about their appropriate roles as we address the challenges of achieving sustainable development this century. At present, addressing the challenge can involve political risks for government.

For example, consider the political risk taken by Ken Livingstone in introducing the congestion eco-tax[14] in London. For most, traffic is one of the few areas of politics that remains untouchable. Although economists could see that charging people directly for driving in certain areas of a city would make traffic more manageable, especially if linked to an hypothecated long-term improvement of public transport, no politician would take on the powerful car lobby. The political risks were very high. Ken Livingstone, Mayor of London, faced them in 2002. An expensive, though non-invasive, system of monitoring cars has been established. Payment is easily made if a driver has to cross through inner London. In the first few weeks a 20–25 per cent reduction in traffic was observed (and was greatly appreciated by communities and by business). The £130 million per year collected is already being channelled into improved public transport. There have been few substantial complaints. Cities around the world are now preparing to copy the London experiment. A long-term project to tackle what was seen as an insurmountable problem has begun to work. The political risk has paid off – vision worked.[15] There are many great efforts and remarkable individual achievements to report, but to ensure that over the next 30 years we achieve more than the last 30, more integrated approaches are needed.

In order to highlight the various factors and clearly demonstrate how they interact between all the key stakeholders, we have developed our platform for change diagram (Figure 4.2). It attempts to illustrate simply the otherwise complex nature of the relationships, interaction and dynamic need to turn failures into drivers to achieve sustainable genuine progress. This diagram seeks to summarize how we can together turn around market, information and institutional failures to become drivers for sustainability. It seeks to summarize how governments and firms can work together to innovate for new emerging markets, emphasizing the importance of partnerships, good communication and an awareness of the values and assumptions that underpin our decisions.

There is growing evidence of the economic wisdom of addressing these issues creatively. In his book *The Rise of the Creative Class: And How It is Transforming Work, Leisure, Community and Everyday Life*, Richard Florida shows that cities and regions that attract a 'creative class' of highly professional, innovative and motivated people are the most prosperous. These people are highly mobile and will seek out cities and regions with a good environment and social services. Hence the cities and regions that are succeeding are the ones that care about their environment and their most precious resource, their people. They are the cities who find ways to unleash and harness their people's creativity. This is perhaps best illustrated by the city of Curitiba, Brazil. Despite its population of 2.5 million having quadrupled in the past 20 years and having a per-capita municipal budget roughly 15 times smaller than that of Detroit, Michigan, Curitiba has solved its problems better than most cities on the planet. It has achieved remarkable success by substituting brilliantly integrative design for wealth. In a community-based process, the city has treated its formidable economic, social, and ecological needs not as competing priorities to be traded-off, but as interlinked design elements with synergies to be captured. Hydrology was integrated with physiography, nutrient flows with waste flows, transport with land use, education with health, participation with dignity. As described in Chapter 14 of *Natural Capitalism*, Curitiba has built one of the world's great cities – by design.

Most of the biggest tasks in Curitiba's development were carried out by private companies, often in partnership with their communities, and working under simple rules that rewarded the desired results. For example, the city has probably the world's best public transport system, based on a safe, fast, clean, cheap and radically redesigned bus service. It carries three-quarters of all commuters and serves all neighbourhoods fairly, because the ten competing private bus companies are rewarded not for how many people they carry but for how many kilometres of route they serve. Neal R. Peirce from the Washington Post Writers Group writes:

> Downtown has delightful pedestrian-only streets. To foster equity, small-scale, low-income dwellings (rather than high-rise housing ghettoes) have been spotted across the city. An extensive new park and lake system covers 18 per cent of the city's land area, doubling as a much-needed flood protection scheme (so that the ducks, it's quipped, just float a metre higher after rains). Over 1100 tax-relieved private woodlands allow rain to soak in where it falls. Volunteer citizens, since the 1970s, have planted over 1.5 million trees along streets and avenues. Curitiba invented 'Lighthouses of Knowledge' – 50 of them, brightly coloured, glassy lighthouse-shaped towers, are spotted through the neighbourhoods, providing thousands of books and now Internet connections for citizens aged 3 to 80. Another innovation: 'Citizenship Streets' – two-storied pedestrian malls, located beside the heavily-used bus terminals, offering clusters of city services from job training to day care, gyms to small claims courts.

Jaime Lerner, who has had several terms as Mayor of Curitiba and Governor of Parana, Curitiba's state, reminds visitors that Curitiba has the problems of all Latin American cities, tough slums included. The apparent difference: the fundamental respect for all citizens, the poorest included, that he and his team of architect-planner associates have sought to build over three decades. Citizens who are shown respect with health clinics, good buses, decent schools, insists Lerner, accept 'co-responsibility'. They're willing to build their own simple housing, especially with a little architectural counsel and utility connections. They volunteer for environmental projects. They start cottage industries. Civic society flourishes. Most families and firms now pre-sort their trash and 70 per cent is recycled or composted. In the slums, or favelas, where refuse vehicles can't negotiate unpaved alleys, small trucks fan out in a massive 'Green Exchange'. For bags of sorted trash, tens of thousands of the city's poorest receive bags of rice, beans, eggs, bananas, carrots that the city buys inexpensively from the area's surplus production. The result is both better public health (less litter, rats and disease) and better nutrition. Lerner explains that Green Exchange exemplifies his distaste for 'creativity killers'; a type of person 'you can smell in meetings', who insists on having all the answers before any project can start. That's wrong, he insists: 'Creativity means certain risks. It's important to start, then make changes. The ideal can easily be the enemy of the possible'. So does it matter if a city has imaginative leadership over years? One shred of evidence – surveys show 99 per cent of Curitibans (as opposed, for example, to 60 per cent of New Yorkers) wouldn't want to live elsewhere. Lerner recounts a 1990s meeting with Renault officials at his jungle office. Parana wasn't even on their list for a Brazilian expansion site. Suddenly, a hummingbird flew in and alighted on the table. 'We had no contract with that bird', says Lerner. But clearly Curitiba's quality of life, its spirit and imagination, was key in drawing Renault, and then equally coveted Chrysler and Volkswagen/Audi plants, to the province.

It was argued in Chapter 1 that making the transition to an ecologically sustainable economy need not harm economic growth. In fact recent studies suggest it may even help economic growth. Curitiba is a great example of this. Curitiba began its journey of holistic development with roughly the same level of gross national product (GNP) per capita as any other Brazilian city. In 1980 its per capita gross domestic product (GDP) was just 10 per cent above the national average. By 1996 its per capita GDP was 65 per cent above the national average, a remarkable increase in just 16 years. Sustainable development is the big challenge of the 21st century and, if we are to meet this challenge, all need to be encouraged to play their part. As Curitiba has shown, involving the people, building community, respecting and valuing people and valuing the human dimension are key to enabling more profound constructive changes to occur. Critical to empowering people to play their part is providing capacity building opportunities.

Importance of capacity building

There is greater awareness now that, since many decisions affecting society are made by corporate boards of accountants, lawyers, engineers and economists, they all need professional development in the critical literacies related to sustainable development. Already steps are being taken. For instance, Toyota Australia has engaged sustainability consultants to provide professional development for its staff. While programmes to inform and educate Boards and staff are important and must continue, more is needed. What is required as a matter of urgency, and for the long term, is the inclusion of education in sustainability issues and principles for all students in all schools and tertiary institutions. Also required is the development of professional certification programmes by professional bodies, trainers of the world's decision-makers, designers, teachers. There is a great shift in understanding in society of the need for change. It has manifested itself in the formation of significant new global sectoral networks almost every year. For instance, UNESCO has responded to the massive shift globally in the university sectors by forming the Global Higher Education Partnership for Sustainability. This already involves over 1000 universities internationally including Harvard and Cambridge Universities. Now that universities are shifting, this makes partnerships for sustainability in OECD countries possible that the world genuinely has never seen before. Sustainable development is the big challenge of the 21st century and, if we are to meet this challenge, all need to be encouraged to play their part.

CHAPTER 5

THINKING LOCALLY, ACTING GLOBALLY

Whilst there is much we can do locally, action is also needed at the global level. We all share the same planet, the same atmosphere, so emissions from one country can affect sea levels in other countries like Bangladesh and the Pacific Islands. Hence, there is an inevitable need for nations to collaborate to solve common problems. Many of our institutional structures are nationally based and are struggling to address these issues on the scale required, a global scale, to make a lasting difference.[1] But what decisions should be made at the global level? Clearly global public goods and externalities need to be addressed at the global level with cooperation amongst nations. The Montreal Protocol that governs the phasing out of ozone depleting chemicals, as discussed earlier, is a great successful example of global cooperation. But new forms of governance from both government and business together and reform of institutions will be needed. But more than just economics and environmental externalities are at play in the real world.

The globalization of firms, markets and regulation has meant that the countries of the world are more closely integrated economically and culturally than ever before. The rules of the game of global commerce are being written to create greater globalization that will have profound effects for future generations. At the same time, there are calls for greater decentralization of government, to take government back closer to the communities. These two trends, and the actors involved, are often at odds with each other but both are simultaneously undermining the traditional focus of political power, the nation-state. How has globalization affected businesses and business regulation? What does this mean for nation-states? What of democratic sovereignty in a globalized age? These are significant topics in their own right and are covered in detail in many books including Braithwaite and Drahos's recent award-winning seminal book *Global Business Regulation*.[2] The central question is: will we raise standards in accordance with the principle of best practice or will we lower them? Do we want a race to the top based on the principles of world's best practice, continuous improvement, wise economics and adoption of best available technologies? Or will the principles of lowest-cost location and reluctant compliance (multinationals investing in regions with the lowest standards) dominate and lead to a race to the bottom?

Braithwaite and Drahos show that the most important contest is between the principles of Lowest Cost Location (including regulatory costs) vs. World's Best Practice. If firms and nations adopt the principle of lowest cost location, firms in relocating to these lowest cost States set in motion a race to the bottom. Nations reduce standards in the hope of attracting investment and a vicious cycle ensues. Alternatively, we can pursue best practice. As we discussed, the US Reagan administration through diplomacy helped to tighten world standards for phasing out ozone depleting chemicals because it understood the competitive advantage for US firms of pursuing world's best practice. Another important contest Braithwaite and Drahos identify is that between 'Rule Compliance' and 'Continuous Improvement'. In a globalized world where nations and firms are seeking lowest cost locations and regulation, companies who simply comply with that lowest common denominator regulation, reinforce the race to the bottom. On the other hand, in a world where firms and nations recognize the competitive advantage benefits of being ahead of the next waves of innovation and seek best practice, a philosophy of continuous improvement leads to standards rising, not falling. Companies like Dupont, for instance, are committed to building plants in developing countries to at least the same standard as that in the US, whether the developing country requires this high standard or not. Overall the work of Braithwaite and Drahos shows that, contrary to what some would assume with globalization, the principle of best practice is more prevalent than the principle of lowest cost location.[3] Braithwaite and Drahos's book also outlines in detail strategies for non-governmental organizations (NGOs) to help improve wise regulation and standards globally.

Whether sustainable development is given a real chance to restore and nourish the essential ecosystem services for future generations will in no small part depend on the form of globalization the global institutions adopt. Significant new global institutions have been created like the World Trade Organization, whose trade principles are presently in conflict with the principles of sustainable development agreed to at the Earth Summit in Rio in 1992.[4] As CSIRO (Commonwealth Scientific and Industrial Research Organisation) FutureCorp Forum stated, 'WTO and national policies need to address the issue of sustainability criteria being challenged as non-tariff trade barriers. It is in the long-term interest of both Australia and the global community to ensure strong cross-border support for sustainable industry practices. Currently, Australia's import policies do not discriminate between good and bad triple bottom line (TBL) performers, leading to price disadvantages for organizations attempting to support sustainable practices in their own Australian-based operations.'[5]

So far there have been several cases where a country's efforts to ensure better environmental outcomes have been challenged. The WTO has ruled against the environment in all but one case. In several cases, Mexico and Venezuela won against the US in the WTO courts leading to the US having to reduce environmental standards that had existed for decades. For example, on behalf of its oil industry, the Venezuela Government challenged the US Clean Air Act regulation that required gas refineries to produce cleaner gas. Venezuela claimed that the rule was biased against foreign refineries and took the case to the WTO. The WTO ruled against USA law. In 1997, the US EPA was forced to lower its baseline minimum requirement allowing Venezuela to sell dirtier gasoline in the US which deteriorates air quality and public health.[6] Global issues like environment and trade are some of the most complex. If the OECD (Organisation for Economic Co-operation and Development) countries do want to have higher environmental standards as part of trade deals, then it clearly is incumbent on the OECD to further assist developing countries to have access to cleaner technologies. Hunter Lovins, a long time leader in sustainability, strongly believes that the trade of old industrial technology to the developing world is as insidious as the drug trade.

The CSIRO FutureCorp Forum pointed this out. The forum's findings concluded that 'Developed countries have a responsibility to ensure that developing nations have immediate access to the latest clean technologies and are not forced to go through earlier, heavily polluting and resource inefficient stages of industrialization.'[7] The report cites the example of six of the world's smoggiest cities benefiting from the introduction

Table 5.1 *Do we want a race to the top based on best practice or a race to the bottom?*

RACE TO THE BOTTOM **Principle of lowest-cost location**	RACE TO THE TOP **Principle of world best practice**
Government response	
Protect uncompetitive industry	Set a level playing field
Leave it to the market	Provide information to address asymmetric information failures
Leave costs of negative externalities to future generations	Tax shift from taxing labour ('societal goods'), such as payroll tax to taxing waste ('societal bads'). Utilize feebates
De-regulatory strategy	Strategic Trade Strategy
Total Faith in the 'Invisible Hand'	Improving National Systems of Innovation
De-legitimizes NGOs	Consult with legitimate NGOs
Corporate response	
Reluctant compliance	Energetic continuous improvement based on best available technology and world's best practice
Threat of capital strike/flight	Innovating to improve competitive advantage
Divide and conquer/rent seeking	Strategic alliances with government and leading NGOs
Relocate to lowest-cost regulatory zones	Work with government to innovate to create genuine wealth
Downsizing	Pursue the triple bottom line
Civil Society Response	
Always oppositional	Creating independent certification schemes (eco-/Fair Trade labelling)
Few links with industry or government	Building strategic alliances between business, government, and R&D bodies to ratchet up standards nationally and globally
Re-active: focused on stopping development	Pro-active: setting the agenda by providing new models to tighten standards nationally and internationally by linking Porter's *Competitive Advantage of Nations* analysis to best available technology and best available practice standards

Source: Adapted from Braithwaite and Drahos (2000, Table 12.1 by Robyn Eckersley)

of 46 buses powered by fuel cells for Mexico City, Sao Paulo, Cairo, New Delhi, Shanghai and Beijing. Introducing fuel-cell transport technology to these cities, which have some of the worst urban air pollution in the world, is aimed at spurring the development of fuel-cell industries whilst pioneering new ways to reduce greenhouse emissions and urban pollution. United Nations Development Programme (UNDP) studies indicate that if all the diesel buses in developing countries were replaced with fuel-cell buses operating on hydrogen produced from natural gas, 440 million tons of carbon dioxide emissions would be cut each year, and up to 40 per cent of potentially dangerous airborne particulate matter would be eliminated.

To conclude, this book will outline many of the ways business (Section 2), government (Section 3) and civil society and educators (Section 5) can work together to play their part to achieve a race to the top. The book will show how, in working together, they can solve significant challenges and create greater opportunities for future generations (Section 4). In working together, they will help markets to work in the way in which they were always intended, namely, to ensure freedom and equality of opportunity whilst improving well-being for all of this and future generations. There is now a clear understanding from numerous fields of how we can achieve these goals. We believe that the discussion of how to achieve these goals is the debate of our times, a debate that we need to have before it is too late.

SECTION 2

NATURAL ADVANTAGE: A BUSINESS IMPERATIVE

CHAPTER 6

NATURAL ADVANTAGE AND THE FIRM

In Section 1 we argued that no one part of society can address the scale of the sustainability challenge on its own. In a world where business, government and civil society all have significant roles to play, we need to find the best ways to move forward together. This section will focus on the role business can play in this process.

The changing nature of competition

This section cannot emphasize enough the importance in business of seizing new opportunities, encouraging creativity and the ability to work effectively in teams to achieve innovation. Running a business requires skill and frequently demands long hours and significant personal sacrifice. If there was an easy way always to stay ahead of the competition, we would all be millionaires. But there isn't. Successful business people seek to remain up to date with the shifting market for their products and services and will come to see that sustainability provides numerous opportunities for unleashing creativity and innovation. Whilst this chapter, and the online databases it references, is designed to assist any business to do its homework faster, improve its strategic position, and unleash the creativity of its staff, this is not enough. Genuinely innovative and highly competitive businesses are always on the look out for new opportunities and ways to improve business. The frameworks and guides that follow will, we believe, help but at the end of the day someone has to have good ideas and be willing to take risks. In the end, success comes down to the determination and united purpose of those people involved. Is the risk worth the effort? Many companies, such as Close the Loop® and Interface, believe it is.

The story of the Australia based company Close the Loop® provides an insight into the sort of lateral thinking and risk taking that innovative firms need in order to truly succeed. Close the Loop® has achieved zero waste to landfill through technological innovation. They are the only company in the world that can recover all material and resource value from toner and inkjet cartridges. When they began, there was no machinery in existence to completely re-process the complex mix of metals, plastics, toner powder, electronics and inks. A team of Australian engineering companies, and Australian recycling experts like Dr John Scheirs formed with the goal of achieving zero waste to landfill from this complex and potentially hazardous waste stream, and ultimately returning the raw material output streams back to the manufacturer for reuse in new printers and cartridges, effectively closing the loop. They designed and built their now famous 'Green Machine' to process all-in-one toner cartridges, drum units, fuser assemblies, and more. Close the Loop® have continuously improved the machine based on hands-on experience, and will continue to learn and upgrade their processes through research and development (R&D) and continuous improvement. The inkjet cartridge processing line, built with the same philosophy, has just been completely rebuilt with consideration given to fast up scaling capacity again in the near future. 'Around 30 per cent of our current business is export – earning export dollars by processing cartridge waste from manufacturing plants in other countries', says founder and CEO Steve Morriss. Close the Loop® is now ready to offer their service of recycling all inkjet and toner cartridge waste with zero waste to landfill to cartridge manufacturers worldwide.

Close the Loop® started as a thought, an idea I had in the shower one day. I find the shower a great place for dreaming: water is so cleansing, it's possible to wash away the clutter and expose moments of clarity. I'm sure most people have authentic thoughts, not many act on them though. The thought that is the starting point of Close the Loop® is still clear in my mind today and it goes something like this. 'Printer manufacturers will need to get their environmental (sustainability) act together sooner or later. If I can help them, I could make a fortune and feel good about myself at the same time.' As the owner of a toner and inkjet cartridge remanufacturing company, the manufacturers of original equipment (OEMs) and their distributors were my biggest competition. I would win business because our cartridges were cheaper than the original brands, and because I'd use the environmental angle to my advantage. I'd contact prospects – schools, government departments, universities, etc. and offer to collect and recycle their empty imaging consumables for free. They'd usually take up my offer because nobody had ever made such a bold offer before, which would give me the opportunity to build a relationship and eventually sell them my cartridges. This system worked really well but created a problem – how do we recycle the growing stockpile of empty bottles, cartridges and drum units, etc. mounting up in our small factory?

After much analysis of the complex and potentially hazardous stockpile, it became obvious that this was a waste stream that was not commercially viable for a small remanufacturer to recycle. The problem, or opportunity, was that I'd promised it would not go to landfill and I was absolutely resolved not to dump the stuff. How could I do it? It would take machinery not currently in existence to process the complex mix of metals, plastics, toner powder, electronics, and inks. It would cost millions to mechanise the process and how could I finance that? I was lucky to make ends meet for my young family, how could I do it? That's when the idea came, if I offered a cartridge collection and recycling service to the 20 or so multinationals that manufacture printers, copiers, and fax machines, they'd have the money. I did approach them all, numerous times, and several responded quite favourably but guess what? They wanted to see that we could recycle their cartridges before they'd sign any contracts and certainly before any money would be paid for such a service. By this stage that intangible little packet of energy, my idea, had grown in power. The idea had gained momentum by being fed continuous doses of 'can do attitude' and 'never say die determination' so that by now, it was bigger than the constant stream of obstacles that inevitably confront every idea.

On it went. I was constantly talking up the idea with infectious passion and it had the effect of drawing the people I needed to help at just the right time in the idea's life cycle. I met a supplier at a trade show in Las Vegas who'd had recent experience, and contacts, from raising significant money for a medical start-up. From that meeting, and ensuing late night talkfest in my room in Vegas, we are now an unlisted public company with over 350 shareholders who have contributed some 4.5 million dollars to the project called Close the Loop®. The commitment to 'Zero Waste to Landfill' has its origins in my original promise to customers. I look back now and realize that not compromising on that original, somewhat naïve, claim is a crucial part of our success. Our strength lies in the plant and equipment we have developed to recycle every single imaging consumable known to man with zero waste to landfill. With no precedent, and a very big recycling challenge, we set about finding existing technologies, mainly from the mining industry, that we could adapt to our project. A relationship was struck with an Australian engineering company, and with the only real option available to us, trial and error, we designed and built our now famous 'Green Machine' to process all-in-one toner cartridges, drum units, fuser assemblies and more. We've continuously improved the machine based on hands-on experience, and will continue to learn and upgrade our processes because research and development (R&D), and continuous improvement of all systems are now heavily ingrained components of our culture at Close the Loop®. The inkjet cartridge processing line, built with the same philosophy, has just been completely rebuilt with consideration given to fast up scaling capacity again in the near future.

Our customers have confirmed that there is a need for our service but getting the volumes to make it commercially viable was the next problem. By now, the original thought is the size and strength of a freight train and most problems are actually opportunities in disguise, the trick is being open enough to recognize them. Enter Planet Ark. We have co-created 'Cartridges 4 Planet Ark', Australia's leading multi-vendor, extended producer responsibility (EPR), electronics take-back programme. With year 1 coming to an end, the volumes are increasing nicely and combined with our contracts to import and recycle manufacturing scrap from several leading inkjet cartridge manufacturers, we have passed operational breakeven and are charging towards good profits. Today, we are working closely with our customers to plan our future direction in terms of reuse of output streams like ink, toner powder, metals, engineering grade plastics, etc., and even closing the loop in terms of designing with the end (recycling) in mind. The future is very bright for any business that provides sustainable solutions if you have big dreams, the drive to put them into action, and the determination to overcome any obstacle.

Steve Morriss, CEO, Close the Loop®

Interface Ltd[1] is emerging as a well cited example of a company that from the outside appears to have taken significant risks, risks that most companies would not have contemplated. They have replaced petrochemical based carpets with carpets made from renewable biomass, such as corn waste, that can be recycled with little loss of quality. The new carpet is the first certified climate-neutral product in the world, that is, all the climate impact of making and delivering it has been offset before it gets to you. The carpet is so non-toxic you can eat it, if you had a mind to, thus eliminating occupational health and safety (OH&S) concerns. In the first four years of this business model and removing waste from its own operation, Interface more than doubled its revenue, more than tripled its operating profit, and nearly doubled its employment, all at the same time. Overall they have achieved a 97 per cent total reduction in materials used, whilst providing a better service in every respect. They have gone further than the Factor 10 that most sustainable development experts estimate to be required to achieve 'sustainable development'. Interface Ltd is on the way to achieving Factor 100 and, in doing so, is placing itself in the right position to become the first genuinely 'Sustainable Corporation' on the planet.

Whilst such a radical change may seem risky, the strategies that Interface Ltd has adopted to achieve these results are, in fact, standard business strategies based on innovation. The key, in this case, is the company innovating to achieve sustainable development. The organization first identified new areas where they could save money. With strong leadership from their CEO, Ray Anderson, it then identified opportunities for win–win eco-efficiencies, resulting in gains that were quick and effective. As a consequence, Interface Ltd is saving approximately US$200 million per annum through its eco-efficiency initiatives, which is, in turn, financing all the remaining initiatives. Improvements then began affecting the company on a much more fundamental level. They were able use this money to embark on Eco-Design to create product differentiation. This led to the company's development of a new form of non-toxic carpets from renewable feedstocks drawn from agriculture.

> *Our factories and our suppliers consumed around 1.2 billion pounds of material in 1995 – which made me want to throw up; 400 million pounds was relatively benign, 800 million was petro-based, with two-thirds of that valuable stuff burned up-fossil fuel gone for ever, except the CO_2, helping us lose coastal Florida in an instant of geological time. Our company's technology is plundering the earth. Society considers me a captain of industry, but I stand convicted, by myself alone, as a plunderer and legal thief with perverse tax laws as my accomplice in crime. Maybe the 'new industrial revolution' can keep my kind of out of jail, renewable, cynical benign, emulating nature, where there is no waste; we can begin to reinvent civilisation in a quest to become sustainable, then restorative. [In response to a question regarding how real this all is, Anderson responds] Our efforts would be seen through if insincere. Customers are inclined to support us, which helps the top line, efficiency helps the bottom line. It's a positive feedback loop (of doing well by doing good): the more good you do, the better you can do, the more you attract attention, which helps the top line... It's one of the few positive feedback loops that's good for the earth. [When a journalist asked] 'Can a $1 billion company make a difference in a $25 trillion global economy?', [Anderson responded], 'I don't know. But unless somebody leads, nobody will'.*

Ray Anderson, CEO of Interface

This may seem groundbreaking, but in fact there is now great experience in all these areas of sustainability that companies can tap into. There is now even a new academic field of knowledge called 'green chemistry' that is amongst other things developing systematically an understanding of how to make everyday chemicals from crops and biomass waste. As previously stated, there is a now an emerging 'wave' of enabling technologies and innovations in understanding how we can re-design the industrial system in harmony with the environment. The changes that Ray Anderson initiated have also achieved something far greater than any of this. They have improved morale, made Interface a high profile company and, consequently, highly attractive to the top graduates. These changes have significantly altered the culture of the organization, unleashing positive changes throughout their operations globally. It is true, however, that during the period around the year 2000 Interface Ltd profits and stock price fell, but that was true of the whole carpet industry. In that downturn a number of carpet companies went out of business. Ray Anderson, the CEO of Interface, argues that the combination of the cost savings from eco-efficiencies plus the increased profile globally from Interface's genuine sustainability strategy is what kept them in business during this tough period.

Rob Coombs, Asia-Pacific President of Interface, writes of what the experience has been like from the inside of Interface in the Asia Pacific. He summarizes many of the key concerns, relevant to all companies, that have driven these changes within Interface. This testimony also illustrates some of the key points in this section of the book. Namely, that there are significant strategic business opportunities available – through the adoption of sustainable solutions – that multinationals and firms cannot ignore. As with all waves of innovation, however, companies need to be strategic in deciding where to invest. Furthermore, he honestly and openly discusses how a multinational, in this case Interface, can strategically position itself, in the Asia-Pacific region, to lead and consolidate in countries where there are market drivers for sustainable solutions (i.e. Japan and Australia), whilst awaiting the emergence of further market opportunities in Asia.

The business world is slowly coming to the realization that it needs to develop practices sympathetic with the natural environment in which it operates. The slumbering giant is beginning to understand that there are also a range of stakeholders affected by business practices and that there is a social contract that needs to be re-thought and redeveloped. This awakening brings with it many pressures; the need to rethink age old values and approaches to problems, the need to find solutions to previously unapproached technical barriers, and the need to create a new set of decision making criteria. For Interface in the Asia-Pacific region, the evolution of sustainable business practice has created another challenge: How to play an important part in the process of becoming a sustainable business within a large organization at the leading edge of the debate? How to support the position for which the company is known globally and how to live up to the position on a local basis?

Led by Ray Anderson, Interface has created a culture in which the drive to sustainability is an imperative. In doing so, the company has established a position as an early mover, an example to be used when looking for the route map to an environmentally better business model. With a vision to become sustainable and then restorative through the power of its influence by 2020, Interface has already established a clear measure of business success. It is moving towards this goal through the adoption of a strategy on seven fronts: eliminating waste, using only renewable energy sources, creating only benign emissions, closing the product loop, energy efficient transport, energizing people and changing the nature of commerce itself. Asia-Pacific represents 5 per cent of global Interface revenues and although the region is seen as a growth engine for the business, the relatively small scale of the division creates a series of challenges around the move to sustainability. How has Asia-Pacific embraced the philosophy and what has it done to support it? What are the challenges faced by a small division of a leading force in sustainable business development? In answering these questions it is important to note that the culture of sustainability within Interface globally is well developed, with a broad base of leadership created over the past six years. Whilst there are pockets around the company where knowledge and activity are lower than in others, no part of the business could operate without a long-term commitment to the vision for the company – it would simply not fit with the whole.

Let me start with some general observations. First, there is no Asia-Pacific! The size and cultural diversity of the region is such that there is no simple answer to these questions. The response differs by country. Second, we are driven by the corporate goal in many different ways and these ways are influenced by the communities around each site. In some communities the commitment to sustainability is greater than in others and therefore more conducive to active participation by Interface. The focus of the debate is influenced greatly the same way. For example, Japan has embraced, by necessity, the concept of recycling as a noble activity and it is promoted by government and within the business community. Thus, Interface is engaged in a wide range of activity in Japan around this issue, while discussion around renewable energy receives much less attention. A third observation is that the two countries across the region that appear most engaged are Japan and Australia. In most other countries, sustainability remains a very low priority and Interface operates with less external stimulus. As Ray Anderson would say, the stimulus from customers for more sustainable solutions is the greatest driver we have. With this less evident, Interface operates in a vacuum. No less committed but with the need for more self discipline to press forward. This discipline is self imposed by the measurement systems we have in place to monitor progress on quality, waste, sociometrics, ecometrics and environmental procedures and standards. The company's wide visibility of these measures assures that the focus is not lost.

In the Asia-Pacific division the progress across the seven strategic fronts has been in line with its place in the Interface world. That is, it is able to move forward independently in many facets of the effort. Yet there are some developments it is unable to embrace at the same pace as its larger divisional cousins because of the scale of the organization. There are also some areas in which the company actively centralizes investment and activity in order to maximize the speed of projects and the return on investment. Some examples from each of these three categories follows: the region has a strong track record in waste elimination, the cornerstone and enabler of the Interface programme. In both the Australian and Thailand manufacturing facilities, Interface has reduced dramatically all forms of process and material waste. In Australia, for example, waste per unit of production has reduced by 90 per cent since 1996, an achievement that has both funded other sustainability projects and helped to deliver greatly improved business performance. The waste effort has been driven in both facilities by people working in teams at operator level with strong supervisor leadership. It is very much a grass roots programme to reduce the company's environmental footprint. Equally, regional success in reducing harmful emissions has been encouraging. Since 1999 our annual greenhouse gas emissions have reduced from approximately 1650 metric tons of CO_2 to 1450 metric tons, while at the same time we have increased our production throughput by 35 per cent. The source of these emissions is electricity production 63 per cent (indirect contribution) and the burning of natural gas 37 per cent (direct production). We have reduced and rationalized the use of solvents at our production facilities and even gone to the extent of identifying new cleaners with less solvent emissions for our Carpet Spot Cleaning Kits, admittedly a small component, but significant in the message we are trying to put out into the market place. In the short term we are evaluating the sale and use of 'Climate Neutral' products and services.

Interface has invested significantly in the region over the past six years in the education of its own people around the principles of sustainability. This investment has covered training programmes around the scientific basis for the philosophy, programmes of engagement and training around Interface's strategic methodology, communication tools for use with customers and other interested parties and the investment in managers dedicated to leading the Interface Asia Pacific sustainability effort. There has also been a wide ranging programme of engagement with the wider community. Probably most importantly, it has led to activity within the local communities in which we operate, with projects ranging from regeneration of natural habitat to the fostering of sustainable business opportunities within Thai village communities. Interface strives for a situation where the nature of commerce changes, from the linear 'take, make, waste' process based on 'making stuff', to a cyclical process in which the transactions become service based. This will result in the customer leasing the benefits of the product rather than purchasing the physical properties that provide them. In Australia and Japan, Interface has developed leasing programmes involving the leasing of carpet (or the functional benefits of it), where Interface retains ownership of the product, maintains and then reclaims it at the end of its life to ensure landfill is avoided. The success of the programme is growing, but so far has been limited by customer acceptance. Long established procurement methodologies are embedded in many organizations and will take time to change.

These are some areas in which Interface Asia-Pacific has independently engaged in sustainable development. We have also made progress in other ways but at a slower pace. For example, the adoption of renewable energy sources has been less widespread than in other Interface locations, mainly due to the lack of availability of the source. Local infrastructure is not available to the same extent in support of this objective. The company is actively seeking alternatives to fossil fuels, and remains committed but frustrated with the lack of realistic options available. Then there are the areas in which Interface Asia-Pacific has, through necessity, left major development to central bodies within the company. Closing the product loop represents the greatest technical sustainability challenge faced by Interface, a company whose product is founded on numerous petro-chemical based raw materials historically designed not to separate during or even after use. Creating products that use post consumer product as raw materials that can then be recycled (not just down cycled) into their own raw material stream at the end of their life, is a goal that has the undivided attention of many people within the company. Great progress has been made in Asia Pacific with many of the raw materials we use. Locally, Interface has been active in working with outside companies to research ways to reduce and re-use waste streams. Internally, we have developed a process that could recycle backing material and reduce landfill quantities by 80 per cent. Globally, Interface is inching ever closer to the end goal. The resources required to undertake the major technical developments required in this area have been centralized in the United States. Local part-recycling initiatives are underway, but the large scale break through projects will probably be undertaken elsewhere, before results are implemented here.

So, where is the scope for improvement? Well, as staff turns over in a five year period, we have a need to regenerate some knowledge and vigour around the subject and with some new champions in place. Any long-term programme needs regular stimulus and re-growth: there is a need to redevelop tactical activity to support each of the seven fronts, to re-focus leaders and the company as a whole on the importance of the journey the company is undertaking. There are also some strategies which require greater focus, notably the transportation initiative and the drive for renewable energy sources. As the low hanging fruits have been picked we now need to be more innovative. We are a small part of a large company fully engaged in a long journey. We are learning more from mistakes than we are from successes. The region is in the great position of being able to draw on the resources of a larger parent whilst enjoying the freedom to develop its own initiatives as well. Trying to keep pace with the vision and determination of Ray Anderson, to create the world's first sustainable enterprise, is no easy task. But we wouldn't have it any other way.

Achieving competitive advantage through strategic positioning

The case studies of Close the Loop® and Interface demonstrate that competitive advantage and sustainability are not mutually exclusive. Productivity can be improved by

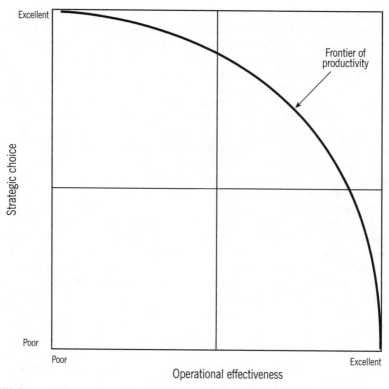

Source: OTF Group

Figure 6.1 *The Frontier of Productivity*

choosing wisely which markets to serve and how to operate most effectively. A firm can increase its productivity by offering new services to more attractive customers (*product differentiation*) or by creating the same value with less inputs (*operational efficiency*). Firms that pursue sustainability have the opportunity to increase productivity in both of these ways. The Frontier of Productivity developed by the OTF Group,[2] shown in Figure 6.1, illustrates the two axes upon which the productivity of a firm is mapped.

Companies positioned near the Frontier of Productivity in the upper left quadrant of Figure 6.1 have poor operational efficiency but pursue customer segments willing to pay premiums for unique products. If we use the example of the food industry, this would be the delicatessen that charges high margins for custom, gourmet sandwiches but moves small volumes of goods relatively inefficiently. Companies in the lower right quadrant produce less differentiated products but have high levels of operational efficiency. Continuing with the food industry example, this would be the fast food hamburger restaurant that captures low margins but effectively distributes and sells large quantities of basic food products like sandwiches and sodas. Companies in the upper right quadrant pursue demanding customer segments and do so effectively. A company in this quadrant would be a gourmet restaurant that has achieved economies of scale through a chain of stores while maintaining a high level of specialization. Firms in the lower left quadrant are in trouble. They have not positioned themselves as a leader in either unique product offerings or operational effectiveness relative to their competitors. A company stuck in this position eventually will go out of business as competition increases.

The semi circle curve in Figure 6.1 highlights the best-practice combination of strategy and operational effectiveness in a given industry. Firm executives must constantly question themselves about how to best position themselves along the Frontier of Productivity or push the Frontier outwards. The remainder of this section provides further examples of businesses that have migrated towards the Frontier of Productivity by focusing on sustainable development. It will explain what companies should learn from these experiences and how sustainable business practices can maximize innovation. Most significantly, this section will explain how companies can migrate towards the Frontier of Productivity most cost effectively.

The companies previously mentioned are succeeding and gaining significant long-term competitive advantage through the application of Porter's ideas of Complementary Activity Systems with sustainable development as the goal.[3] With this goal, these companies have integrated many new eco-effective operational initiatives and other new forms of innovation, that it will take their competitors literally years to catch up on. As Porter states: 'Rarely does sustainable advantage grow out of a single activity in a business. A company doesn't get sustainable advantage simply because it has some unique product design or a unique sales force. Sustainable advantage comes from systems of activities that are complementary.'[4] These 'complementarities' occur when performing one activity gives a company not only an advantage in that activity, but also provides benefits in other activities such as marketing, service, design and customer support. As a result, competitors don't have to match just one component, they have to match the whole system. And until rivals achieve the whole system, they do not get very many of the benefits. Companies that can innovate to achieve Sustainable Development through real eco-design of products, using the most efficient processes and designing out waste, are therefore on the way to achieving sustainable competitive advantage.

These companies are also innovating for emerging markets. As the McKinsey study,[5] *Innovating for New Emerging Markets*, highlighted in Section 1, demonstrated, new market segments are crucial to the success of a firm. Porter showed in *The Competitive Advantage of Nations*,[6] being first or earlier into a new market is one of the best ways to create lasting competitive advantage, both in domestic and international markets. There are numerous examples of this globally. Those companies that first perceived a new opportunity and seized it, have since gone on to be industry leaders. This is true of a remarkable number of organizations and applies to many industries including automotive (Ford), aircraft (Boeing), cosmetics (MaxFactor, Body Shop), men's razors (Gillette), recycling (Visy Industries) and motorcycles (Honda). Early movers reap long-term benefits from having built significant positive brand recognition, loyalty, and having been the first with a product to build relationships with suppliers and distribution chains. By innovating for new and emerging markets, using complementary activity systems, the above companies have strategically positioned themselves to be ahead of the pack.

What will be the major driver of innovation in the 21st century?

Innovation for emerging markets is, by definition, not easy. There is considerable risk and no guarantee that the marketplace will either be ready for the innovation, or see the need for new products to replace those with which it is already familiar. Furthermore, the best laid plans can be ruined by significant boom and bust cycles in the economy, which operate beyond anyone's control. What area, then, will definitely be a part of 21st century innovation? Innovation can occur when science and engineering make significant breakthroughs, such as the steam engine, polymer science, electronics or the laser, to name but a few. These new 'enabling' technologies were a spur for the development of new products and services. A similar revolution is occurring today, with scientific breakthroughs in nanotechnology and genetics, that will allow new products to be developed. The re-design of drugs, chemicals and industrial processes, based on the insights gained from these new areas of science, represent vast opportunities.

Table 6.1 *Sample of some emerging business opportunities*

Innovations in greenhouse technologies[7]	CSIRO's combustion team have developed revolutionary pulsed combustion technologies that promise to double thermal energy conversion rates for numerous domestic, industrial and commercial processes. The business opportunities from this are immense.
Greening the built environment Eco-cements and recycling	Cement accounts for over 6% of global greenhouse emissions and the World Business Council for Sustainable Development has initiated a major programme to address this. Consequently there are now several types of eco-cements (50% or less emissions) available. CSIRO also has a major programme to address the eco-cement issue, and has developed a cement that uses 40% less energy, which was used on the Sydney Olympic Stadium.
Harvesting the urban forests	Cosco Holdings Ltd, is a local 'closed loop' company in Australia. Cosco collect office paper from offices and universities locally, recycles it into tissue products and then sells the 100% post consumer tissue products back to those same offices. They also make the Coles supermarket in house brand tissue product from 100% post consumer office paper waste. Another great innovating company, the Paper Converting Company, sells 24 million SAFE toilet rolls roughly per annum, made from 100% post consumer waste.
Metals recycling	Ten years ago Australia earned little from mining and metallurgical 'know-how'. Australia's mining 'knowledge economy' is now worth over AU$1 billion per annum in overseas consultancy work. Whilst mining a finite resource is clearly not sustainable, numerous innovations have occurred to greatly reduce the impacts of mining. Much is now known about how the mining sector can improve efficiency, waste management and rehabilitation whilst shifting increasingly to metal recycling.
CSIRO innovation-Recycled car tyres: solution to worldwide waste[8]	A technological breakthrough by Australian scientists has produced a solution for the world's mountains of waste truck and car tyres. Every year more than 700 million new car and truck tyres are manufactured and there's not much use for them when they are replaced – most are buried or burned. CSIRO has developed a new technology that can turn old rubber tyres into a range of useful plastic and rubber composites that are suitable for many engineering applications throughout the rubber and plastics industry, The scientific challenge was to discover how to chemically modify the surface of crumb rubber molecules to transform it into a reactive ingredient to effectively grab hold of and combine with rubber or polymers (plastics). Examples of applications include: shoe soles, automotive components, tyres, non-pneumatic tyres, wheels, building products (roofing materials, insulating materials, window gaskets) coatings/sealants, containers for hazardous waste, industrial products (enclosures, conveyor belts, etc.) and many more.

However, as the cliché goes, 'necessity is the mother of invention.' The first section of this book showed that lessening our environmental load on the ecosystems of the planet is one of the most urgent tasks for humanity this century. In the first section we showed that experts and the Netherlands Government, UNEP and the OECD plus numerous other bodies now argue that we need a shift of at least Factor 10. Hence, whilst the biotech revolution, innovative developments in materials science, energy and nanotechnology offer new enabling technologies, the major overarching driver for innovation this century will be the need to achieve sustainable development. Those companies that seek to be the early movers in this area stand the best chance of achieving lasting competitive advantage this century and many business opportunities already exist (see Table 6.1).

The future belongs to those businesses who play a proactive role in devising ways in which we can meet our commercial needs and sustain the world we live in.

Richard Pratt, CEO, Visy Industries, the largest private recycling company in the world.

Many nations and firms have missed these multi-billion dollar opportunities in the past because they imagined the future to be the same as the present. Australia was the third country in the world, after the US and the UK, to develop an electronic programmable computer (CSIRAC, in 1949). CSIRAC's co-inventor, Dr Trevor Pearcey, went on to build a highly advanced transistorized computer, CIRRUS, at the University of Adelaide, in 1963. Both projects lapsed from lack of private and government support, and Australia lost a clear opportunity to join the world leaders in the computer revolution. It has not been a wave of innovation that was 'creatively destructive' of traditional businesses. The IT revolution has largely added to the productivity of traditional sectors. But the scale of change needed to genuinely achieve sustainable development this century will see 'Creative Destruction' in traditional sectors in how they deliver services. We will always need, for instance, energy but how that is delivered will change significantly. Hence firms and nations that miss these next waves of innovation to achieve sustainable development risk losing significant long-term market share and eventually being completely replaced.

Moving early to exploit structural change

Smart companies believe that sustainable development makes them more competitive and more resilient to shocks. It can also make them more at ease with employees, regulators, governments and society.

Björn Stigson, President of the WBCSD

Globally, industries like energy, building, housing, transport, automotive, cement, paper, mining and chemicals are moving early with extensive programmes to create new solutions to environmental problems.[9] Most major companies accept that the future will be carbon-constrained and that will create significant new global markets worth as much as a trillion dollars. Many business people are already aware of niche market opportunities for sustainable solutions. However, what many are unaware of is the phenomenal rate of growth in these market opportunities.

Businesses, governments, and the school and university sectors, have significant purchasing power, and increasingly are joining forces locally, nationally and globally to reduce the risk of shifting to green procurement. Collectively they can share research, information, experience and also pool their purchasing power to further drive down the prices of preferred products. In doing so, they provide businesses with potential buyers with whom to build strategic customer loyalty to help with subsequent strategies to increase market penetration. New markets are also being driven by necessity. Many Asian economies such as Japan, Hong Kong, Singapore, Taiwan and South Korea, import the bulk of their raw materials and have little space for landfill waste. In 10 years Japan will no longer have landfill space in which to store waste materials of any description, according to Japan's Ministry of the Environment. These economies are formally working to both increase their level of recycling and move to green procurement. Singapore, for instance, has a target of 70 per cent recycling within 10 years from a present base of 40 per cent in its 10 year plan. Japan is the first country in the world to bring in a raft of significant legislation under 'The Basic Law for Establishing the Recycling-based Society' that commits Japan to become just that: a recycling based society. The Asian environmental engineering market alone (excluding Japan) is worth at least US$37 billion a year and has the potential to triple to US$105 billion by 2010.[10]

Table 6.2 *Fast growing markets*

Greener building design	In the US, the Green Building market is already worth US$300 billion,[11] and features everything from environmentally sound New York skyscrapers[12] to homes and shopping malls. There is much more to this, however, than simply environmentally sound buildings; namely the lifespan of the built environment as a whole. In 2002 Thomson Prometric and the United States Green Building Council (USGBC) collaborated to promote buildings that are environmentally responsible, profitable and healthy places to live and work. Productivity gains of 6–16%, including decreased absenteeism and improved quality of work, have been reported from energy-efficient design.[13] The US based Leadership in Energy and Environmental Design (LEED) forecast an estimated 30% growth and 4000 new green building certified professionals in 2004. Already in Canberra, Australia, existing homes must be energy rated at the time of sale, and the rating displayed in all advertising.
Wind power	The global market for wind energy has averaged 40% growth annually in cumulative capacity over the last five years.[14] The global turnover of wind generation equipment is estimated at US$1.5 billion per year, and total industry turnover is estimated to reach between US$5 and US$10 billion.[15] The global wind turbine market is expected to grow, driven by improved cost structures and supportive government policies. Both Germany and the UK have renewable energy targets of 10% by 2010, and California has a renewable energy target of 20% by 2017. The annual export market for wind manufacturing products from Asia has been estimated at US$110 million.[16] China's Tenth Five Year Plan (2001–2005) calls for a nearly five-fold increase in wind capacity to 1.5 GW. The Philippines plans to introduce over 3500 MW of renewable capacity by 2012, and New Zealand has introduced a renewable energy target similar in scale to the Mandatory Renewable Energy Target in Australia.
Recycling and remanufacturing	In the US the remanufacturing market is now worth almost US$53 billion dollars. The US recycling sector is worth over US$250 billion per annum. A recent report by the Recycling Coalition Group found that the industry created more than 56,000 public and private sector recycling facilities, with 1.1 million jobs, US$236 billion in gross, annual sales, US$37 billion in annual payroll.
Eco-tourism	Eco-tourism involves responsible travel to natural areas that helps conserve the environment whilst improving the well-being of local people. It is growing at around 30% per annum, which is significantly higher than the annual rate of growth of 4% for tourism as a whole. Also, studies show that tourists are more willing to pay extra for eco-tourism than standard tourist packages.
	In Queensland the Binna Burra Mountain Lodge, often has guest speakers from the local community on environmentally-focused topics. The Black Cat Group of New Zealand, significantly contribute to the preservation of a rare species of dolphin, Hector's Dolphins, which are shown as part of the Group's eco-tours. The Boat Landing Guesthouse in Laos creates awareness among the local population and staff regarding the importance of energy efficiency in environmental conservation

In addition, the uptake of eco-efficiency continues to grow.[17] As Bill McDonough and Michael Braungart point out in their 1998 paper 'The Next Industrial Revolution', Stephan Schmidheiny, the inaugural honorary chairman of the World Business Council for Sustainable Development, said in 1996: 'I predict that within a decade it is going to be next to impossible for a business to be competitive without also being eco-efficient: adding more value to a good or service while using fewer resources and releasing less pollution.' As Schmidheiny predicted, eco-efficiency has been working its way into industry with extraordinary success. The number of corporations committing themselves to it continues to increase. Its famous three R's (Reduce, Reuse, Recycle) are steadily gaining popularity in the home as well as the workplace. The trend stems in part from eco-efficiency's economic benefits, which can be considerable. There are also fast growing niche markets from effective eco-efficiency strategies, including industrial products and know how, which reduce the use of energy, water and other resources in production processes.

> It is extremely profitable to wring out waste, even today when nature is valued at approximately zero, because there is so much waste – quite an astonishing amount after several centuries of market capitalism. In the American economy, the material that we extract from the planet, that we mobilise for economic purposes, and process and move around and ultimately dispose of, totals about 20 times your body weight per person per day. So worldwide this resource flow is in the order of a half-trillion tons per year. And what happens to it? Well, only about 1 per cent of it ends up in durable goods, the system (6 months after a product has been sold) is about 99 per cent waste. That's a business opportunity.

Amory Lovins, CEO, Rocky Mountain Institute[18]

Why integrate sustainable development into corporate strategy?

Interest in the application of new strategies for sustainable development to enhance competitive advantage is growing amongst progressive businesses, business schools, and investment institutions. This is attributable to changes in the nature of competition that have taken place over the last 30 years. The new business paradigm places a premium on innovation and, as we stated earlier, many now recognize that the combination of the need to reduce our impact on the planet plus the potential resulting resource productivity gains will drive innovation over the coming century. As will become clear, there is great interest, amongst members of the OECD and emerging economies, in new strategies that can broaden companies' approaches. The last decade of downsizing has left so little meat on the corporate bone, that there is now tremendous interest in new strategies that will enable businesses to both increase market share and target new markets.

As discussed in Section 1, in the past, companies and nations were considered competitive if they were large scale and had access to the lowest cost inputs – whether they be capital, labour, energy or raw materials. Countries were said to have natural advantages if these 'input conditions' were relatively low cost. Because technology changed slowly, a comparative advantage of a business could be achieved through low cost inputs, cheap resources, wages and so on. This is known as the theory of comparative advantage developed by the famous 19th century economist David Ricardo. In today's increasingly complex world of globalization and the rapid development of new technologies, Ricardo's theories of comparative advantage are no longer sufficient to describe competitive advantage. The globalization of companies, trade, communications and regulations, in conjunction with economic deregulation and tariff reduction, has created intense competition in the marketplace. This has meant that cheap raw materials, components and technology are now available from many sources globally. Since the fall of the iron and bamboo curtains, hundreds of millions of low paid workers have been added to the world's workforce. Hence, competing on low wage and resource costs is a race that no firm based in an OECD country can win. Attempts to compete through downsizing and cost cutting, without broader strategies, have been shown rarely to work.

Downsizing: a strategy that no longer cuts it

In the past two decades, many OECD based companies have become locked in a series of cost-cutting exercises. This downsizing and outsourcing has been adopted to such an extent that, in the past 12 years for example, Australian organizations have retrenched one in two full-time employees. While there is nothing wrong with seeking the best staff, companies need to be in a position to expand and hire, not of being forced to fire. Those responding to falling profit margins by downsizing are often throwing away experienced employees with valuable networks, significant contacts and clients frequently walk out the door with downsized staff. Companies often dismantle teams that took years to build and in many cases thus reduce the resilience of the company to shocks. The time and effort required to rebuild those teams is considerable. Other factors then come into play, such as the emergence of cultures of fear, significantly affecting morale, and leading to risk aversion in the workplace. In its turn this also inadvertently discourages innovation. For these reasons alone, if no others, all companies should be looking for new strategies to achieve growth to help avoid the need to downsize.

Significant research from overseas, particularly the US, demonstrates that downsizing only works within the context of a much broader and detailed strategy of renewal. In the majority of cases, however, downsizing does not work.[19] On the day of the announcement of downsizing, companies' share prices generally increase, but thereafter steadily decline. Research indicates that, after two years, half of the downsized companies were trading up to 48 per cent below their previous market value, and two-thirds were below comparable firms in their industry. There are obviously limits to how far downsizing can go without affecting the core activities of a business. CEOs and managers are realizing that they will need to broaden their strategies if they are to improve their bottom line. As discussed in Section 1, alternative strategies do exist. There is an undisputed body of evidence that demonstrates how the successful visionary companies can avoid unwanted (business cycle permitting) downsizing and achieve lasting competitive advantage through:

- taking advantage of new enabling technologies to design new products;
- having a strong focus on customers' needs, especially new trends;
- innovating to gain increased market share or for new emerging markets; and
- an overall commitment to best practice and continuous improvement.

This is part of the core thesis of Porter's *Competitive Advantage of Nations*, and is supported by studies, such as Collins' and Porras's.[20] They showed that the stock prices of visionary companies were up to 15 times more profitable than the market average when compared with their major competitors. One of the firms featured in the study was 3M, which is recognized as setting a global benchmark for innovation.[21] The results of this focus are impressive. Even though 3M is already a US$15 billion company, it still maintains the following:

- 30 per cent of sales are derived from new products developed within the past four years;

- in 1998 the 35 new technology programmes that 3M had targeted for accelerated investment generated sales of US$1 billion;
- it consistently ranks in the top ten US companies in patents granted, securing 611 patents in 1998;
- it produces multiple products for multiple markets from 30 proprietary 3M technology platforms; it has 41 trade-marked products at the last count;
- it invests in excess of US$1 billion annually in R&D, with 7100 employees engaged full-time in technical R&D;
- 3M continually reinvests in itself, with capital spending in 1998 being US$1.4 billion.

Whilst generalizations are always dangerous, a 2004 article by Yale Management Professor Jeffrey Sonnenfeld, appearing in the MIT *Sloan Management Review*,[22] argues that the CEOs of the US's Fortune 500 companies of the 1990s are being replaced by CEOs who have a renewed focus on creativity, ideas and innovation. In other words, this new generation of CEOs of major US multinationals want to make their companies more vibrant and innovative. Examples of the new focus on ideas and innovation abound, but several prominent CEOs have been particularly outspoken. Saro Lalmisano, CEO of IBM, raised the priority of innovation by dismantling executive structures that filtered out controversial ideas, and by giving talented, visionary computer scientists new prominence in the firm's decision-making structure. At General Electric, CEO Jeff Immelt placed a new emphasis on invention and new products. He has publicly argued that many large US companies have lost their innovative spirit because they have become business traders, rather than business creators.

Focusing on best practice and innovation for sustainability can deliver numerous other previously unseen benefits to business and communities and is often more cost effective in the long term. For instance, it is nonsensical to build plants that are as energy inefficient as the previous generation. A study commissioned by the US Environmental Protection Authority and Department of Energy found that the iron and steel sector in South Korea and Brazil are more energy efficient than in the US, while these sectors in Mexico and India have achieved an efficiency level equal to the US. Nobody builds a new power station, an aluminium smelter with worse energy efficiency and environmental performance than the average stock. For example, the aluminium smelter being built in Mozambique is better than the average smelter in US, Canada, Norway or Sweden. Braithwaite and Drahos explain: 'companies pursue higher standards globally not simply to gain short-term competitive advantage, it is also asset-reputation building'.[23]

There are a range of other important factors that indirectly affect the bottom line, such as reputation, that is crucial in attracting and retaining the best staff. There are many examples emerging of organizations and businesses willing to seek best practice, even at increased cost, if it helps to ensure a good reputation. In the transport sectors, sea, air, and motor vehicles, the principle of world's best practice is becoming stronger. Car companies competing in the lucrative markets of the US, Europe and Japan cannot afford to substantially undercut best practice.

> *The best-run corporations recognise that business ethics and corporate awareness of the environmental and societal interest of the communities in which they operate can have an impact on the reputation and long-term performance of corporations.*
> OECD Principles of Corporate Governance

Boeing is also a supporter of the principle; thereby making life harder for its competitors. In financial regulation, fear of systemic failure increasingly inclines actors like the Basle Committee towards adopting the principle. Other actors, such as the New York Stock Exchange, favour it because they see it serves their economic interests. Likewise, the reputational value of world's best practice is becoming increasingly important to states and regions in the area of financial regulation and practice, as they seek to divert global investment flows into their economies. Companies are also committed to continuous improvement for these same reasons. Many employers have embraced the principle in employment and training opportunities for women and occupational health and safety. In sea transport, improving the safety and environmental management of shipping is not a contested matter of principle.[24]

The shifting nature of competition in emerging economies

What is less well understood is that the nature of competition is also shifting in emerging economies as well. The sole focus on competitive advantage from cheap labour, cost cutting and cheap natural resources does not always lead to lasting competitive advantage of firms in developing countries.

This occurs for several reasons: First, it is relatively easy for other companies in other resource rich developing nations to imitate companies based on resource extraction. Firms competing on low labour and resource costs also leave themselves exposed if there are changes in other countries that result in even lower labour and resource costs. For instance, a rival firm may be granted subsidies by the government of another country that enables them to beat your price in the marketplace, no matter how efficient you are. Second, technology has delivered greater options to firms in the developed world for reducing the relative advantage of cheap labour and resource conditions in the 'developing world'. As Porter explained in detail in *The Competitive Advantage of Nations*, 'in the 1980s, manufacturing firms often moved production to high labour cost locations to be close to markets, not the reverse. The usage of materials, energy and other resource based inputs has been substantially reduced or synthetic substitutes developed. Modern materials such as engineering plastics, ceramics, carbon fibres, and the silicon used in making semiconductors are made from raw materials that are cheap and ubiquitous.'

Additionally, Michael Fairbanks and Stace Lindsey argue in their book, *Plowing the Sea: Nurturing the Hidden Sources of Growth in the Developing World*, that new emerging issues are now critical for firms in merging economies given the reduced protection in their local markets, and the increased difficulty in penetrating export markets due to less favourable exchange rates and government incentives. Previously, due to favourable exchange rates and industry protection, many firms in emerging economies did not need to be so focused on strategically positioning themselves in their local, regional or global marketplace. In comparison to the developed world, competitors from emerging economies did not need to be particularly rigorous in their understanding of customer needs and the market opportunities in which they could increase profits.[25] Now they do. Fairbanks and Lindsey also argue that it is critical for leaders to develop the capacity to think about the future and to move out of such unattractive natural resource-based industries. This will require both business and political leaders in developing countries to understand that the sources of growth for developing nations are hidden behind the abundance of natural resources that so many of them possess. Fairbanks and Lindsey state that: 'Company managers and government bureaucrats (in developing countries) remain imprisoned by old-fashioned thinking: over-reliance on cheap labour and abundant natural resources, and ignorance of the demands of a sophisticated world marketplace.'

As a result, companies in developing countries are often trapped into being suppliers of inexpensive commodities. It's a pattern that is repeated in many poor countries around the world. Because companies compete on price instead of quality and innovation, they pay slim wages and living standards remain low. Meanwhile, they sell natural resources to countries that use them to make higher-margin goods. For all of the

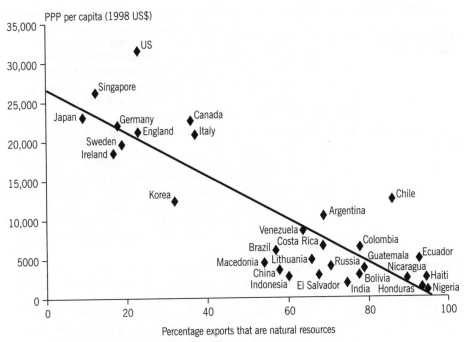

Notes: (a) Basic products include raw materials and processed products based on natural resources and labour, (b) The coefficent of correlation was 0.77.
Sources: IITC – International Trade Center; CIA, *The World Factbook 1999*; OTF Group Analysis, Macedonia 2001 data from OTF Group trade statistics analysis; CIA, *The World Factbook 2002*

Figure 6.2 *Percentage of exports that are basic products vs. purchasing power parity,* 1998

developing countries' brave talk about industrialization, the dependence on exports of natural resources has been rising, not falling, the authors write. *Plowing the Sea* argues that for these developing countries, economists' macro-economic prescriptions for growth are necessary but insufficient. What is needed for businesses to achieve sustainable competitive advantage in the long term, and for these countries to raise standards generally, is a radical change at the micro-economic level of the firm. 'The fundamental dynamic of what it takes to create and sustain wealth ... does not appear to have stuck with the leaders of the developing world.'

It may be considered a high expectation for firms in developing or emerging economies to compete with the OECD. However, as we will demonstrate, firms and governments in developing and emerging economies are realizing that they need to change and are succeeding in competing in the highly competitive markets for innovation such as medical and IT (see Tables 6.3 and 6.4). Technology networks are changing the conventional development pathways, raising people's awareness of what is possible and creating the opportunity to achieve in a decade what would have previously taken generations. The United Nations Development Programme (UNDP) 2001 report stated that: 'In 1995–1997 US scientists collaborated and published research papers with over 173 countries, scientists in Brazil with 114, in Kenya with 81, in Algeria with 59.' Clearly such collaboration can only help R&D and innovation opportunities for companies in developing or emerging economies. Already, by 1999, 52 percent of Malaysia's exports were high-tech, 44 percent of Costa Rica's, 28 percent of Mexico's, and 26 percent of the Philippines.' Consequently, worldwide interest is being generated

Table 6.3 *Sample of case studies of innovation of world importance from 'emerging economies'*

Thailand's drug to fight malaria	Thailand has the world's highest resistance to malaria drugs. However, scientists at Thailand's Clinical Research Management Coordinating Unit are optimistic about a drug they are developing specifically for local conditions. The World Health Organization (WHO) has hailed it as one of the most important developments in the treatment of malaria. The new drug, dihydro-artemisinin (DHA), is in the last stage of approval.
Cuba's meningitis vaccine	In 1985, Franklin Sotolongo injected himself with a vial of experimental liquid. He was the director of a team of Cuban scientists determined to save their nation from an epidemic of group-B meningitis. Hundreds of children were dying, and there was no cure. Thirteen years later, group-B meningitis has been virtually eliminated. The UNDP 2001 Human Development report states that each year meningitis kills 50,000 children worldwide. Cuba and Sotolongo's government institute hold the patent on a group-B meningococcal vaccine which has been licensed to the major international pharmaceutical giant SmithKline Beecham.
Indian Bagasse paper	Indian scientists at Tamil Nadu Newsprint and Papers Limited (TNPL) have developed a cost effective quality photocopy paper made from 75% bagasse (sugar cane waste) and 25% plantation eucalypt fibre. The process uses 90% less chlorine than is used to make normal paper. Such chlorine chemicals are used to separate cellulose fibres which are bound together by lignin. However, bagasse contains much less lignin than wood and the lignin also has a different structure. Most of the energy used by the mill is generated via its own wind-farm. Effluent is reprocessed into water and then used to irrigate the cane-fields, with the sludge also being treated and returned to the land as compost.
Natura, Brazil	Natura is a large cosmetics, personal hygiene and perfume company in Brazil that employs over 3000 people. In 2000, Natura joined the UN Global Compact and is addressing sustainability issues systematically. It has created a new line of hygiene and cosmetic products, based on natural Brazilian floral extracts harvested by local communities, that are certified by the Forest Stewardship Council. Natura has also ensured that the way in which the floral extracts are made is up to standard as well. The company supports the environmental restoration of the 650 acre Fazenda Bulcao and the Pomar project. They are also pro-active in sponsoring documentaries about the biodiversity of Brazil for the public broadcasting station of Sao Paulo.
Micro-credit	Micro-enterprise schemes are emerging all over the world as a successful way to help poor entrepreneurs to help themselves. The idea emerged in the 1970s, when the Grameen Bank in rural Bangladesh began lending small sums of money to the landless poor. Almost everyone repaid the loans and the scheme was so successful that a few years later, it had over a million borrowers. Most of its clients are women who form groups of about 25 to receive small business loans and mentoring. (India also has a Self-Employed Women's Association established in 1975). They co-guarantee each other's loans and, since almost all their businesses succeed, their repayment rates are excellent at over 90%. Micro-enterprise development has become recognized by many international agencies, particularly the World Bank and United Nations as being the most effective form of sustainable poverty alleviation. Simply giving people handouts is not a hand up and it doesn't sustain. The Gareem Bank is now Bangladesh's largest financial institution.

by numerous examples of innovation for sustainable development, together with genuinely world class advances in health, that are emerging from the R&D in 'developing' countries.[26] This is the beginning of a significant shift.

Table 6.4 *Critical mass of enabling technologies helping businesses in the developing world gain access to vital information*

Village payphones: A Gareem innovation	The Gareem Bank began with a focus on micro-credit to assist rural entrepreneurs' various self employed businesses. The scope has since broadened to address the myriad of factors that make poverty cycles so hard to break. One such factor is the lack of access to resources, technology and information as well as credit. To address this the Gareem Bank has established several subsidiaries such as Gareem Telecom (GT), a wholly owned subsidiary. GT has been established to provide cellular village telephone services in urban and rural areas. The new phones are also leading to increased profits and business for those communities that have had them installed.[27]
Cost effective computers In Brazil	Brazilians' access to the Internet has been retarded not by the cost of the Internet, but rather the cost of computers. The goal of OECD-based computer companies has been to increase processing power and speed, not reducing costs. The Brazilian Government hired a group of computer scientists at the Federal University of Minas Gerais to do the reverse: produce a basic computer for around US$300. A prototype was produced within two months with most standard features. The government is providing incentives for its manufacture, with the goal being its provision to millions of Brazilians.
India's wireless Internet access	Most people in the West are used to Internet access being provided through telephone lines. But the cost of this in a country like India means that only 3% of Indians can afford them. New technology, from the Indian Institute of Madras, has created a low-cost Internet access system that doesn't require a modem, eliminates the need for expensive copper lines and is faster and much cheaper than using telephone lines. The basis of the technology is a wireless local system developed by Midas Communication Technologies in Madras in conjunction with US-based Analog Devices. It is currently licensed to manufacturers in India, Brazil, China and France. The technology is a significant advance and has been implemented in many countries.
Cheap Internet access: The Simputer	The Internet and computers are too expensive for the vast majority of people in developing countries. In response to this problem, academics at the Indian Institute of Science collaborated with engineers at the Bangalore-based design company Encore Software Ltd to produce a hand-held device, costing less than US$200, with multiple connectivity options based on free linux software. 'This is a world-class product, ahead of anything being done anywhere else in the world,' says Kenneth Keniston, Director of the India Program at the Massachusetts Institute of Technology. The benefit of this device is that, unlike the Brazil computer, it is portable and can therefore easily be shared within communities. It has since won the inaugural Dewang Mehta Award for innovation in IT.

Additional drivers for sustainable development

There are numerous other drivers, in addition to pressures to innovate, for business to pursue sustainable development,[28] and considered collectively, they leave researchers such as ourselves with little doubt that change is inevitable.

An example of this is the multi-billion dollar reinsurers, such as Swiss Re, are reviewing their provision of CEOs' professional indemnity insurance based on their efforts to reduce greenhouse gas emissions.

> *With all the talk of potential shareholder lawsuits against industrial emitters of greenhouse gases, the second largest re-insurance firm, Swiss Re, has announced that it is considering denying coverage, starting with directors' and officers' liability policies, to companies it decides aren't doing enough to reduce their output of greenhouse gases.*
>
> Jeffrey Ball, Wall Street Journal, 7 May 2003

'Emissions reductions are going to be required. It's pretty clear,' Christopher Walker, Managing Director for a unit of Swiss Re recently told the *Wall Street Journal*. 'So companies that are not looking to develop a strategy for that are potentially exposing themselves and their shareholders.' In addition, numerous companies are adopting sustainable development as part of their strategic planning to improve intangible assets, such as a reputation for adhering to basic standards and basic community expectations. Reputations that have been built over decades can, fairly or unfairly, be ruined in a matter of days through the Internet, email, global communications and media. With the Internet there is nowhere left to hide.

> *Information technology has empowered civil society to be the true guardians of democracy and good governance everywhere. In a sense, [civil society] has been the new superpower – the people determined to promote better standards of life in larger freedom.*
>
> Kofi Annan, United Nations Secretary-General[29]

Table 6.5 *Emerging drivers for sustainable development: global and local*

Economic and business opportunities	• Increase productivity, create product differentiation • Lean thinking, total quality management • Ethically/socially responsible investment • Reduce risk of consumer boycott, NGO activism
People and populations	• Increasing population in developing countries • Decreasing population in the developed world • Urbanization and migration
Enabling technologies	• ICT, ET, spatial data, renewable energy
Environmental crisis	• Need to restore natural capital • Environmental disasters • Climate change, desertification • Toxics, insurance blowouts
Global inequality, deep divide	• Access to clean water, sanitation • Trade barriers, free vs. fair trade • Environmental refugees
Staying ahead of regulation	• Global, national and local

Source: Adapted from a table developed by the RMIT Global Sustainability Institute, Australia

The three-year campaign by the US's Rainforest Action Network against Citibank's policy of loaning to projects that directly or indirectly harm the environment is an example of this.[30] It has led to first 9, now 19, large banks signing onto the new Equator Principles. These principles require potential projects over a prescribed gross project amount to undergo an environmental assessment to produce an Environmental Impact Statement (EIS) and an Environmental Management Plan (EMP) before being approved for a loan. This list of banks includes ABN AMRO Bank, N.V, Bank of America, Barclays plc, CIBC, Citigroup Inc, Credit Suisse Group, ING Group, Royal Bank of Canada, The Royal Bank of Scotland, and the Westpac Banking Corporation. With impressive speed, the Equator Principles have become the new market standard, thus transforming project finance. The Equator banks – based in Europe, North America, Japan and Australia – arranged over 78 per cent of project finance lending for the year through to October 2003, according to *Dealogic ProjectWare*. As more financial institutions adopt the Equator Principles the coverage will be truly global. Meanwhile, some banks that have not formally adopted the principles are following its procedures, knowing that this is the new standard by which they will be evaluated. Project sponsors planning to raise funds in the project finance market are anticipating and preparing to meet the requirements of the Equator Principles. With the current range of coverage, successful loan syndications are likely to depend on the extent to which projects are Equator Principles compliant.

The adoption of the Equator Principles is a sign of a growing awareness amongst business generally that for those businesses willing to embrace this emerging new reality, there is tremendous opportunity to achieve competitive advantage while simultaneously making a positive contribution to the world. Indeed many businesses presented case studies at the 2002 World Summit on Sustainable Development (WSSD) showing how a commitment to sustainability had conferred greater profits, bolstered public goodwill, generated positive publicity, increased brand equity, increased shareholder value and reduced liability. Clearly business is increasingly realizing that it has much to gain from strategically tackling sustainable development.

Despite the economic downturn in parts of the world, many companies are concluding that they cannot afford *not* to invest in being socially responsible. Business-as-usual is becoming a high-risk occupation, due to the potential for:

- consumer boycotts and bad publicity;
- higher insurance premiums or withdrawal of coverage;
- regulatory requirements, fines and penalties;
- competition from more eco-efficient producers;
- class action law suits and legal expenses;
- personal liability for corporate negligence.

Risk managers surveyed in over 800 organizations identified loss of reputation as the risk with the highest direct impact. 'We're facing the greatest demand for our assistance that we've seen in our nine year history', states Bob Dunn, CEO of Business for Social Responsibility (BSR), a US-based not-for-profit advisory organization. Following the collapse of Enron, WorldCom, Andersen Consulting, the fallout from Vivendi and, in Australia, the collapse of HIH and OneTel, there has been a tremendous loss of trust in corporations with poor corporate governance.[31] South Korean electronics company Samsung has also battled to convince investors that its corporate governance is sound. Yet one financial analyst has estimated that poor governance represents a price drag of as much as 50 per cent on Samsung stock. Poor corporate governance and lack of transparency were also critical factors in the Asian economic crisis.

Pressure to improve corporate governance is increasing in most countries, and is frequently leading to increased regulation. The loss of trust resulting from the collapse of companies, such as Enron, has been acknowledged by US President George Bush in 2002 when he stated in his speech on corporate responsibility on 9 July: 'At this moment, America's highest economic need is higher ethical standards – standards enforced by strict laws and upheld by responsible business leaders.' There are many other creative attempts being made globally to raise the standards of corporate governance. In Brazil, for instance, the Sao Paulo Stock Exchange created the Novo Mercado (New Market) in 2000. This is a voluntary strategy aimed at improving corporate governance. Any firm that wishes to list on the Novo Mercado has to comply to higher governance standards. These include equal rights for all shareholders, greater requirements for disclosure, and more accountable procedures for the election of board members. Good corporate governance alone, however, is insufficient to restore trust and good will. There is growing anecdotal evidence that firms that do not have a real commitment to sustainable development are exposing themselves to significant risks in both the short and long term.

Hunter Lovins, as she tours the world, speaks of how the story of Monsanto shows that even a large company can suffer significant loss of reputation if targeted effectively by small groups of people working with the Internet. In the UK, a group of mothers joined together to discuss their concerns about buying baby food made from crops that were genetically modified. Hunter points out that these mothers were not scientists, politicians or experts. But they cared. They shared their concerns, and they educated themselves, talking to academicians, and ultimately involving the Prince of Wales. They started going to their supermarkets and asking that the baby food be labelled whether or not it contained genetically modified organisms (GMOs). They told the markets that they would not buy from that supermarket unless the baby food was labelled. They communicated this concern to Gerber and Heinz, leading baby food producers, who, rather than risk a consumer boycott, removed GMOs from their products. The mothers mounted an Internet campaign demanding that major grocery chains in Great Britain label GMOs. Soon, non-GMO products were trading at a premium, while GMO-content foods were trading at a discount. Monsanto's aggressive approach on Frankenfoods, its patents on the Terminator gene, its attempt to buy out seed companies and monopolize seed stocks, and its persecution of hundreds of North American farmers for the 'crime' of seed-saving, had led to Monsanto's reputation plunging globally. In 1999 the then CEO Robert Shapiro said that his organization had under-estimated the public concerns regarding the safety of genetically modified organisms.[32] 'We have probably irritated and antagonized more people than we have persuaded', he told a conference organized by Greenpeace, the environmental group. 'Our confidence in this technology and our enthusiasm for it has, I think, been widely seen – and understandably so – as condescension or indeed arrogance.' Monsanto went on to record one of the biggest losses in US corporate history, leading to the CEO Hendrik Verfaillie resigning in late 2002, and the company becoming a takeover target.[33]

Now, more than ever, it is imperative that corporations 'walk the talk'. It is not surprising then, that the *Financial Times*/Price Waterhouse Coopers 'Most Respected Companies' survey of 750 CEO's across Europe listed increasing pressure for social responsibility and increased environmental demands as two of their top three concerns. As well as providing companies with strategic insurance against numerous risks, a pro-active sustainable development strategy delivers a range of benefits to business, such as unleashing the creativity of staff. In 1997, for example, British Petroleum (BP) set a target for greenhouse gas reductions of 10 per cent below 1990 levels. At the time they only knew how to achieve 5 per cent of this cut and assumed it would take 10 years to achieve a further 5 per cent. Their solution was to create an internal emissions trading scheme, to provide a clear incentive to the divisions of the company to act. By sending a clear signal to staff, BP found that it had unleashed innovation within the company and achieved its target of 10 per cent in two years. Staff are still coming forward with great ideas of how to be more efficient.[34] Not only do BP's initiatives help the planet and the company's bottom line, they also help to reduce BP's exposure to the risk of rising energy prices.

Initiatives that encourage an organization to reconsider outdated processes can create simultaneous improvements in resource productivity and economic performance. For example, research on corporate decision-making, in relation to energy and the environment, has indicated that these decisions may be determined largely by routines based on old assumptions. A policy intervention that leads firms to re-examine the assumptions underlying long established, and no longer efficient, manufacturing processes may lead firms to discover opportunities for simultaneously reducing costs and pollutant emissions. Many participants in the US voluntary challenge programmes, such as 33/50[35] and Green Lights,[36] reported that the programmes forced them to re-examine their decision-making methods.

Companies are starting to realize that resource inefficiencies in their businesses are often indicators of a much greater waste occurring in areas from product design to overall plant design and operation. Consider the chemical industry. The costs of complying with the regulations that deal with environmental problems through remediation activities (i.e. waste treatment, control and disposal costs) rather than prevention methods, has been estimated to be in the range of US$100–150 billion per year for industry in the US. In addition, the costs of cleaning up the existing hazardous waste sites are also estimated to be in the hundreds of billions of dollars range. In a smaller economy like Australia, during the year 1996–1997, 26.7 million tonnes of solid, sludge and liquid wastes were disposed of into the Australian environment.[37] Many individual chemical companies have budgets for environmental compliance programmes that are as large as their budgets for R&D, and for some of the largest chemical companies, environmental compliance budgets can approach AU$1 billion per year. In smaller chemical companies, the ratio between environmental programme budget and research programme budget is significantly weighted towards environmental programmes because of compliance costs. A realization that is currently occurring throughout the chemical and related industries is that re-designing waste out of the initial process will not only save significant costs but can also result in greater profits. With the challenges of increased global competition facing industry, both domestically and internationally, and increased regulatory requirements, it is clear that every company is redoubling its efforts to find new ways of turning cost centres into profit centres.

Solutions for bypassing the environmental and economic hurdles associated with waste treatment and disposal in the chemicals industry are now an increasingly high priority. The chemicals industry has turned to research institutions for guidance. From this has come new fields such as green chemistry[38] and green engineering[39] – new approaches to industrial chemistry and engineering – which seek to reduce or eliminate the use or generation of hazardous substances in the design, manufacture and application of chemical products. Or, in other words, the objective is to be 'benign by design' when inventing new synthetic pathways, or addressing manufacturing problems associated with 'end-of-pipe' treatment.[40] This marks a significant shift for both chemical research and industry. As Barry Trost, a respected chemist writes, 'In focusing on immediate problems, the implemented solution sometimes ignores the question of what new problems arise as a result of the solution. Making chemical manufacturing more environmentally benign by design must now become an integral part of the product development process.'[41]

Achieving radical resource productivity

Many business leaders will still claim that companies must pay increasing amounts to achieve further resource productivity. However, the fact is that effective whole system design will allow n industry to 'tunnel through the cost barrier'.[42] Overwhelming evidence exists that proves significant resource productivity, of at least 75 per cent or more, can frequently be achieved at a greater profit than is possible from incremental resource productivity improvements.[43] As discussed in Section 1, whole system design means optimizing the entire system, not just the components. The authors of *Natural Capitalism* point out that optimizing components individually often results in the 'pessimizing' of the whole, integration and synergy are lost, resulting in complexity, over-sizing, and inefficiency.[44] The concerns of business managers and economists who associate strict environmental measures with increased costs are founded on a fundamental lack of understanding and awareness of tangible alternatives to 'end of pipe' solutions to pollution. The leaders in the field understand that strategically it is in their long-term interests to design out waste in the first place.

As Amory Lovins, Hunter Lovins and Paul Hawken wrote in *Natural Capitalism*:

> *At the heart of this chapter, and, for that matter, the entire book, is the thesis that 90–95 per cent reductions in material and energy are possible in developed nations without diminishing the quantity or quality of the services that people want. Sometimes such a large saving can come from a single conceptual or technological leap, like Schilham's pumps at Interface in Shanghai, or a state-of-the-art building. More often, however, it comes from systematically combining a series of successive savings. Often the savings come in different parts of the value chain that stretches from the extraction of a raw resource, through every intermediate step of processing and transportation, to the final delivery of the service (and even beyond to the ultimate recovery of leftover energy and materials). The secret to achieving large savings in such a chain of successive steps is to multiply the savings together, capturing the magic of compounding arithmetic. For example, if a process has ten steps, and you can save 20 per cent in each step without interfering with the others, then you will be left using only 11 per cent of what you started with – an 89 per cent saving overall.*

Hawken et al (1999)

Many assume these changes are solely in Europe, the reality is, however, that around the world companies and governments are seeking to improve their competitive advantage through these whole system approaches. A Mexican chemical company, Girsca, has reaped returns in excess of US$30 million dollars from an initial investment of US$20 million in environmental efficiency measures. These include the capture and use of energy generated in its industrial processes. Between 1991 and 1998, wastewater and CO_2 emissions, per tonne of production, were reduced by at least 80 per cent and solid waste, per tonne, by 90 per cent. This has resulted in an improvement in net income as a percentage of sales, and the industrial plant has been transformed from being a significant concern, to being a source of pride for the local community. Girsca has gone on to win numerous awards, including the Mexican Environmental Ministry's National Quality award in 1997 and the National Award for Ecological Merit in 1999.

In Australia, the Federal government has run the Energy Efficiency Best Practice (EEBP) programme, which is based on a whole systems approach to energy efficiency:

Table 6.6 *Achieving the same functions with, in many cases, a 90 per cent reduction in resources by using available technology*

Toxins	Waste dumps are being cleaned up through using a series of microbes, mushrooms and earthworms – and the end products include toxin-free potting soils. Oils spills are being cleaned up with bio-solvents made from vegetable oil. For instance, Vinyl chloride is the third most produced chemical in the world. Recently scientists reported in *Nature* that they have found a microbe that will convert vinyl chloride into an inert substance. Loeffler has already tested the bacterium on vinyl chloride at the contaminated site in Michigan. Its ability to eat the toxic compound – and render it harmless – was hastened in one test by adding plant fertilizer and other nutrients to the soil. In another trial, vinyl chloride was destroyed by injecting the soil with concentrated amounts of BAV1 developed in the lab. 'These organisms can only grow when the contaminants are present,' he said. 'When the material is gone, their numbers decline because they don't have any food. So really it's a perfect system.'
Water	Wastewater is being decontaminated by a series of 'living machines' that contain ecosystems which produce healthy fish or plants at the end of the process.
Air	Indoor air is being cleaned by using carefully selected plants and 'planting walls' (NASA) while roofs are being designed to support gardens to increase usable space, insulation and useful crops.
Pests	Effective non-toxic insecticides are being produced from mushrooms to replace harmful agricultural and domestic poisons.
Energy	Simple cost effective changes to new or existing buildings can reduce the operating energy demands of buildings by up to 90%. (*Natural Capitalism*)
Soil	Nutrients and soil conditions can be increased by farming practices that find a synergistic mix of crops and animals.
Biodiversity	Agricultural systems are being developed that integrate farming and ranching with natural ecosystems.

Source: Table prepared by Dr Janis Birkeland, editor and co-author of *Design for Sustainability* (2002)

Electric motors are used to provide motive power for a vast range of end uses – with crushing, grinding, mixing, fans, pumps, material conveying, air compressors, and refrigeration compressors, together accounting for 81 per cent of industrial motive power. Every year running an electric motor can cost ten times the purchase price. Inefficient and poorly maintained systems can lead to reduced profits, unnecessary downtime, and even safety risks. Achieving best practice means you will improve motor system reliability, minimize energy costs, maximize profits and, ultimately, reduce greenhouse gas emissions. International surveys estimate that a whole-of-system approach to optimizing industrial motor driven applications, when coupled with best practice motor management, can deliver savings of between 30–60 per cent.

Department of Industry, Tourism and Resources, Motor Solutions Online[45]

The RMIT University's National Design School in Australia have been practising whole system design with numerous industry clients for roughly a decade. In the US, leading think tanks, such as Rocky Mountain Institute and the McDonough Braungart Design Chemistry Group (MBDC), have, or are, working with many of the US Fortune 500 companies who already understand this. McDonough's team is striving to put these ideas into practice at the home of the modern industrial production line and one of the largest industrial plants in the world, the Detroit Ford plant, which was first built by Henry Ford's company 100 years ago. They are also presently working with Nike, BASF, Volvo, and the City of Chicago amongst others.

Professor Michael Porter summarizes the key insight that many are still failing to realize as he and Claus van der Linde wrote:

> *Environmental improvement efforts have traditionally overlooked these (whole) systems costs. Instead, they have focused on pollution control through better identification, processing, and disposal of discharges or waste – costly approaches. In recent years, more advanced companies and regulators have embraced the concept of pollution prevention, sometimes called source reduction, which uses such methods as material substitution and closed-loop processes to limit pollution before it occurs. But, although pollution prevention is an important step in the right direction, ultimately companies must learn to frame environmental improvement in terms of resource productivity. Today managers and regulators focus on the actual costs of eliminating or treating pollution. They must shift their attention to include the opportunity costs of pollution – wasted resources, wasted effort, and diminished product value to the customer. At the level of resource productivity, environmental improvement and competitiveness come together. This new view of pollution as resource inefficiency evokes the quality revolution of the 1980s and its most powerful lessons. Today many businesspeople have little trouble grasping the idea that innovation can improve quality while actually lowering cost. But as recently*

Table 6.7 *Competitive advantage through cost savings from whole system design*

Refrigeration	Refrigerators today can save about 98–99% of the energy used by refrigerators in 1972. These massive advances in refrigeration efficiency have come through whole system design. In Australia the average refrigerator being purchased is 50% more efficient than the ones bought in the late 1970s. However, there is the potential for saving at least another 40% through the application of whole system design.
The laptop computer	The laptop computer is a classic case study because it shows what happens when you give engineers a stretch goal. In this case the stretch goal was that computer companies needed laptops to be 80% more efficient than desktop computers so that the computer could run off a battery. With this stretch goal the engineers delivered a solution through a whole system design.
Wastewater treatment	With sewerage, most of the costs are in the piping used to transport it to the treatment plant. Biolytix, a new development resulting from years of research by the University of Queensland, treats the water onsite by optimizing nature's own way of treating and purifying water with no odour. The Biolytix Filter can treat up to ten times the BOD5 (organic) loading of rival technologies. Incredibly, it can treat more wastewater than a septic tank in the same tank volume, and to a much higher secondary standard needed for safe irrigation on site. Biolytix commissioned respected engineering consultants GHD to conduct an independent analysis of the Biowater concept for the Australasian context. Their desk top study, and subsequent actual project costing, clearly demonstrated that Biowater will typically cost as little as half that needed for conventional sewerage infrastructure, even without factoring in the garbage collection cost savings brought by Biolytix Filtrations ability to integrate putrescible waste and wastewater treatment on site. A cheaper way to treat sewerage and the water can then be used on gardens.

as 15 years ago, managers believed there was a fixed trade-off. Improving quality was expensive because it could be achieved only through inspection and rework of the 'inevitable' defects that came off the line. What lay behind the old view was the assumption that both product design and production processes were fixed. As managers have rethought the quality issue, however, they have abandoned that old mind-set. Viewing defects as a sign of inefficient product and process design – not as an inevitable by-product of manufacturing – was a breakthrough. Companies now strive to build quality into the entire process. The new mind-set unleashed the power of innovation to relax or eliminate what companies had previously accepted as fixed trade-offs.

Porter and van der Linde[46]

The wise implementation of resource efficient strategies, therefore, can be cost effective in both the shorter and longer terms. By reducing, remanufacturing, recycling, and reclaiming or on-selling, businesses can realize immediate cost savings. As well as providing new ways to cut costs and improve productivity, the challenge of sustainable development also provides firms with a new opportunity to differentiate their products and gain market share based on the environmental attributes of their products and processes.

New opportunities for product differentiation

As previously highlighted, BP has exploited its marketing and technology management capabilities, developed in its fossil fuel businesses, to build a market leading position in renewable energy technologies, particularly solar cells. BP's differentiation has been heightened by the decisions of all the other major American energy companies except Amoco to divest their alternative energy businesses, and the decision by many oil companies to play a visible role in resisting the adoption of effective climate change policies. Ford Motor Company has developed a commanding lead over its domestic competitors in the design and manufacturing of low and very low emission vehicles, accounting for almost 95 per cent of the market in the US.[47]

Whilst eco-efficiency gains may be significant, it must be understood that simply slowing the rate of usage is not going to solve the problem in the long term but rather a change in direction is needed. William McDonough points out that eco-efficiency seeks to:

- release fewer pounds of toxic material into the air, water, and soil every year;
- measure prosperity by less activity;
- meet or exceed the stipulations of thousands of complex regulations that aim to keep people and natural systems from being poisoned too quickly;
- produce fewer dangerous materials that will require constant vigilance from future generations;
- result in smaller amounts of waste;
- put fewer valuable materials in holes all over the planet, where they can never be retrieved.

As McDonough writes: 'eco-efficiency is valuable and laudable too. But it, too, fails to move us beyond the first (industrial) revolution. Eco-efficiency is an outwardly admirable and certainly well-intended concept, but unfortunately, it is not a strategy for success over the long term because it does not reach deep enough. It works within the same system that caused the problem in the first place, slowing it down. It is time for designs that are creative, abundant, prosperous, and intelligent from the start.'[48] This is why the challenge of achieving a sustainable future will be such a key driver for innovation this

Table 6.8 *Case studies of product/service differentiation through sustainable development*

Tecon Salvador	The adoption of an environmental management system allowed Tecon Salvador, which runs a cargo container facility in North East Brazil, to win a significant contract with a newly established industry plant. The contract helped the company expand their market share by 75%.
Jolyka Bolivia	In the year 2000, Jolyka Bolivia was one of the winners of the business plan competition for firms 'walking the talk' on the TBL run by New Ventures, a World Resources Institute programme. They are the first South American producer of laminate and other tropical hardwood flooring products to be certified by the US. Both the award and the certification have attracted worldwide interest. The award generated significant media interest and also helped to raise capital. In the six months proceeding the award, four investors visited the company; consequently Jolyka Bolivia has negotiated US$2 million in loans. This has helped them to crack the European and US markets where consumer concerns over logging in the Amazonian rainforests is significant.
Eco-tourism, The Conservation Corporation Africa	The Conservation Corporation Africa, is Africa's largest eco-tourism company, employing around 3,000 people. They operate 27 lodges and camps in 6 countries, including Tanzania, Kenya and South Africa. Their eco-credentials have helped raise the foreign capital to allow them to, for instance, build lodges in the southern part of Maputaland in KwaZulu-Natal, one of the most biologically diverse areas of South Africa.
Café Mesa de los Santos	Café Mesa de los Santos is one of the largest makers of organic coffee in Columbia. Its target market is North America, where the demand for organic coffee is growing at 15% annually. In 1999 the company produced more than 2% of all specialty coffee consumed in the US, and has plans to expand into the Japanese and European markets.

century. It is the reason the challenge of sustainability offers industry a totally new way to differentiate their products from their competitors. Furthermore, it offers research organizations new ways to work with business to achieve lasting competitive advantage. As McDonough and Braungart wrote in their seminal paper, 'The Next Industrial Revolution':[49] 'The hope was that eco-efficiency would transform human industry from a system that takes, makes, and wastes, into one that integrates economic, environmental, and ethical concerns. But more is needed to truly achieve sustainability.' Nature can be a source of inspiration of what these next generation designs may look like. It is time for effective designs of products that are in harmony with nature and based in biomimetic principles.[50]

> *This concept of sustainability is best illustrated by natural ecosystems, which consist of nearly closed loops that change slowly. For example, in the food cycle of plants and animals, plants grow in the presence of sunlight, moisture and nutrients and are then consumed by insects and herbivores which, in turn, are eaten by successively larger animals. The resulting natural waste products replenish the nutrients, which allows plants to grow and the cycle to begin again. If humans are to achieve truly sustainable development, we will have to adopt patterns that reflect these natural processes. The role of engineers and scientists in sustainable development can be illustrated by a closed-loop human ecosystem that mimics natural systems.*

World Federation of Engineering Organisations submission to the WSSD[51] (2002)

Table 6.9 *Achieving product differentiation through design for sustainability strategies*

2003 USA Presidential Green Chemistry Award winner	Shaw Industries received a Presidential Green Chemistry Challenge Award from the EPA for the company's EcoWorx carpet tile backing and Eco Solution Q carpet yarn. Shaw was given the award for its use of technology and chemistry to benefit the environment. Having initially developed this backing and yarn combination for its inherent recyclability and other environmental attributes, Shaw then engaged MBDC to assess each ingredient in the products, using the Cradle-to-Cradle Design Protocol, to ensure maximum environmental and human health benefits.
Reln Pty Ltd— creating market share with Design for Sustainability products	Reln Plastics is an Australian company that designs and produces innovative quality plastic products in the waste, wastewater and agricultural products sector for the Australian and international markets. In 1990, the company developed a line of organic waste recycling products including compost bins and worm farms from 100% post consumer plastic. The products allow households to compost their organic waste, reducing their contribution to the waste stream, while producing hygienic, odourless solid and liquid fertilizer. The products themselves can be recycled at the end of their useful lives.
Cheaper, green chemicals to replace toxics	A technology of Argonne National Labs (US) produces non-toxic, environmentally friendly 'green solvents' from renewable carbohydrate feedstocks, such as corn starch. This discovery has the potential to replace about 80% of petroleum-derived cleaners, degreasers and other toxic and hazardous solvents. Overall, the process uses as much as 90% less energy and produces ester lactates at about 50% of the cost of conventional methods. The lactate esters from this process can also be used as platform building blocks for other polymers. The markets for these biodegradable polymers and oxychemicals surpass those of green solvents.

The good news is that, far from inevitability being a burden, companies that embrace this next step and work towards truly meeting the challenge of sustainability can also achieve truly sustainable competitive advantage. This sentiment was eloquently expressed by a previous Australian Minister for Environment, Senator Robert Hill: 'Building construction and motor vehicles are two high profile industry sectors where producers are utilizing Design for Environment (DfE) principles in their product development processes, thereby strategically reducing the environmental impact of a product or service over its entire life cycle, from manufacture to disposal. Companies that are incorporating DfE are at the forefront of innovative business management in Australia. As the link between business success and environmental protection becomes clearer, visionary companies have the opportunity to improve business practices, to be more competitive in a global economy, and increase their longevity.' The competitive advantage value of this is supported by the wealth of practical work and many case studies from many of the largest companies in the world (see Table 6.9).[52]

Although many are pointing our that resource productivity gains available to a company from energy costs, for example, may only be 3–5 per cent of total business costs, these savings can be a significant percentage of a company's profit margin. A wide range of empirical evidence and theoretical argument exists that suggests energy inefficiencies within firms provide a clear indication of other inefficiencies that are quantitatively significant, thus they can help identify where significant gains can be made.[53]

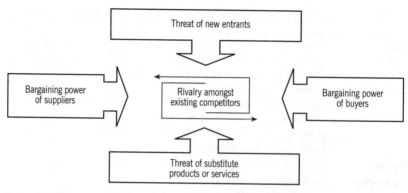

Source: Porter (1985)

Figure 6.3 *The five factors or forces affecting competition in an industry*

Increasing profitability and minimizing risks (Porter's 5 Forces Model)

Given what has been covered in the preceding sections, it should come as no surprise that in a US study covering a 'large and representative' sample of US companies (330 from S&P500) it was found that adopting a more environmentally pro-active approach reduces operating costs together with 'a significant and favourable impact on the firm's perceived riskiness to investors and accordingly its cost of equity capital and value in the marketplace.' The authors suggested this could increase a firm's stock price by as much as 5 per cent.[54] The biggest driver for sustainability in business will be its capacity for improving profit margins, reducing risks and building key assets such as reputation, attracting and retaining staff and access to capital. Students of business strategy will recognize that adopting a strategy of sustainable development will help many firms constructively address the issues and risks for business summarized in Porter's 5 Forces Model. For those not familiar with the 5 Forces Model, it is regarded as one of the leading guides and checklists for the main factors that influence businesses profitability.

The 5 Forces Model focuses on addressing and minimizing risks to business and strategically maximizing positive outcomes (see Figure 6.3).

Due to space restrictions in this book we cannot consider in detail all aspects of the 5 Forces Model and how sustainable development strategies for business help to address them. Instead, we will provide a thumbnail sketch of some of the key issues under the 5 themes.

Threats of new entrants

Unlike previous waves of innovation that affected only specific sectors, innovation for sustainable development will affect all industries, as industry affects the communities and environment within which it operates. Increasingly, threats from many overseas firms are emerging because many national research bodies are increasingly focusing on this challenge of eco-innovation for a sustainable future. This means, therefore, that all sectors will be threatened by businesses, both small and large, that actively commercialize new eco-innovation arising from partnerships with these major research bodies, as well as from internal commercial R&D. Numerous firms are already responding profitably to threats from new products and services. In response to the threat from the fast growing renewable energy market, fossil fuel companies, such as BP and Shell, have undergone major changes in their mindsets and now see themselves as energy providers. Aidan Murphy, Vice President of Shell International, says the Kyoto Treaty has prompted the British-Dutch oil company to shift some of its focus from petroleum towards alternative fuel sources. While the move has helped the company make early strides towards achieving its goal of surpassing treaty requirements and reducing emissions to 10 per cent below 1990 levels, he says Shell is being driven largely by the lure of profits. 'We are now involved in major energy projects involving wind and biomass, but I can assure you this has nothing to do with altruism. We see this as a whole new field in which to develop a thriving business for many years to come. *Capital is not the problem, it's the lack of ideas and imagination.*'[55] Shell's position is indicative of an important shift that has taken place in the mindset of multinationals over the past two decades, which is evidence of a more general shift in thinking amongst business leaders.

Threat of substitute products or services

Firms and nations that ignore the sustainability revolution will be left behind and expose themselves in the long term to serious risks. In order to achieve truly sustainable solutions to the challenges facing our civilization, there is a need for radical technical change to develop new goods or services which offer improved environmental performance at lower prices. New forms of service delivery are enabling companies to achieve this whilst also building greater customer loyalty and long-term competitive advantage. BP realize they are no longer a fossil fuel company: they are providing energy services. Ford understand that they are not simply a car company, but rather providers of mobility services. Dow Chemical doesn't just recycle toxic chemicals: it provides chemical services. Likewise, mining companies are increasingly diversifying into metal recycling, paper companies into paper recycling and so on. Most industrial processes have not been designed for sustainability. Much supposed 'green development' is so far from being that, that there is still significant scope for innovation in order to achieve genuine sustainable development. Increasing percentages of national R&D budgets are being spent on this eco-innovation and on technologies to better manage the environment. This is generating a continual flow of opportunities for firms to commercialize these innovations. Combining the latest in competitive advantage theory with the latest in eco-design, eco-innovation and lean thinking will help firms to target the higher end segment of the market where they can command higher returns for their products and services.

Bargaining power of buyers

Large multinationals are often significant purchasers in their own right. Increased scrutiny of multinational corporations has meant that many of them are committing to sustainable development strategies. Over the past five years, numerous large companies have gone to great lengths to incorporate the language and verbal commitments of sustainable development into their operations. Increasingly, these multinationals realize that a genuine commitment to sustainable development in their own operations is not sufficient as a significant part of their ecological footprint is determined by what they buy from their suppliers. In addition, multinationals are looking for ways to ensure that their suppliers are not acting unethically anywhere in the world and that the quality of product from their suppliers is also guaranteed. This is having a significant effect. Asian businesses are moving to adopt ISO 14001 because transnational corporations (TNCs) like IBM say they will favour ISO 14001-certified suppliers. Companies that have strong supply networks and are intent on implementing and improving ISO 14000 and other standards are already encouraging environmental efficiencies in their suppliers. Ford, Nike and IBM are companies which have demonstrated success in pressuring upstream companies in this way.[56] A further example is General Motors (GM), which requires its supply chain to recognize issues of 'continuous improvement, eco-efficiency, reducing waste in material, energy and resource usage, design for the environment, and recyclability.'[57]

The Warehouse Ltd, New Zealand's largest mixed retailer, has an annual turnover of NZ$1 billion. In 1999 it declared a national corporate goal of zero waste. To minimize the waste generated in stores, the company's buyers have been given a radical packaging reduction target in their 'terms of trade' document. This means that The Warehouse's buyers and suppliers have to work together to address packaging issues.[58] A further example is that of Nike when, about 5 years ago, it began addressing a serious discrepancy between its goals and its practice. Created to encourage health and vitality, Nike realized that it was making products that included potentially harmful chemicals. The company now markets an entire line of organic clothing, made from cotton produced by small farmers around the world, and are revamping their entire chemical supply chain. Their goal is to mass-produce non-toxic organic fibres for all their products. This is creating new markets for organic cotton farmers around the world. In Europe, supermarket chains are increasingly purchasing organic produce in response to increased demand from the public. Despite these changes by progressive supermarkets in many countries, including Australia, supermarket chains have been slow to embrace organic agriculture. One of the biggest obstacles to the mainstreaming of organic agriculture has been building sufficient scale in the industry in order to overcome supermarkets' fears regarding the industry's ability to deliver on promised supply. The scale of an organic industry in its infancy does not compare to the equivalent in mainstream agriculture. Hence, buyers have enormous power to make or break businesses in industries that are still niche markets. Therefore, companies that can find ways to break through these barriers through their own value adding strategies, can achieve real lasting competitive advantage.

An example of this is organic agriculture, as highlighted in a 15-year study by ANU agricultural systems researcher David Dumaresq, who compared an existing organic wheat farm which had been functioning for 40 years with comparable conventional farms.[59] 'While organic yields were lower than conventional crops, costs per hectare were lower and returns were much higher because of the premium for organic produce. If we assume that the farms are run in a similar way, organic wheat is substantially more profitable than conventionally grown wheat'. The organic farm in the study and the historic 'Junee Flour Mill' built in 1934–1935 is currently operated by Green Grove Organics, to target this growing niche market. Dumaresq points out that 'Wheat farmers typically sell their wheat for AU$200/tonne. Organic wheat farmers for AU$400 a tonne but by value adding with their confectionary mill these organic farmers are effectively earning AU$8000 a tonne for the organic wheat is sold now as part of confectionary rather than straight wheat grain. The first export of organic confectionary to the USA was in 2003.' Organic agriculture is established worldwide. Many countries regulate locally based organic production by government and non-government certification. Scotland has a target of an organic sector that makes up 20 per cent of its agriculture sector. The industry's peak international body is IFOAM, the International Federation of Organic Agriculture Movements, established some 25 years ago, and now has 527 member organizations in 92 countries including five in Australia.

One of the most interesting examples of buyers' commitment to sustainability having the potential to influence the rest of the supply chain comes from the lean thinking work of Tesco, a large supermarket in Europe. Working with Tesco, leading 'lean thinking' experts like James Womack, from the Japan Program at MIT, and Professor Daniel Jones, the Head of the Lean Enterprise Research Centre at the Cardiff Business School worked to reduce waste throughout its operations. 'Lean Thinking' defines waste, according to its founder, Tauchi Ohno, famous CEO of Toyota, as 'any human work that uses resources but creates no value.' The six types of waste can be defined as:

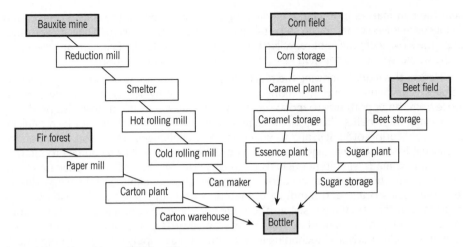

Source: Womack and Jones (1996, p42)

Figure 6.4 *Confluence of cola value streams*

1 Defects (in products).
2 Overproduction of goods not needed.
3 Inventories of goods awaiting further processing or consumption.
4 Unnecessary processing.
5 Unnecessary movement, transport (of people and goods).
6 Waiting (for process equipment to finish its work or on an upstream activity).

With Womack and Jones's team from the Lean Enterprise Institute, Tesco was achieving great progress in making its own operations lean, having dramatically reduced the instances of not stocking a requested product, whilst reducing its inventories by half. Tesco realized, however, that to further reduce its waste it would need to work with its suppliers to help them become more responsive to fluctuations in supply and demand. Womack and Jones claim that 85 per cent of the costs to Tesco are outside its control. Hence, Tesco became very interested in understanding ways to help its suppliers become lean. Womack and Jones considered a particular Tesco product, a generic cola can, as a case study to illustrate this style of thinking. A detailed analysis of the value stream (supply chain) for the cola can (see Figure 6.4) showed that there were four main chains:

1 from the aluminium bauxite mine to the can maker;
2 from the corn field through a process to the plant;
3 from turning beet into sugar, storing it; and finally
4 wood from the fir forest to create cardboard packaging.

By far the biggest source of waste was the process of mining and refining the aluminium: from bauxite ore in Australia to the can maker took over 200 days. This process was the main reason why 319 days elapsed from the start of the process at the bauxite mine to the placing of the can on the Tesco shelf. In addition, their research showed that the can, and the aluminium it is made of, are picked up and put down 30 times. Further, the aluminium and cans are moved through 14 different storage lots and warehouses. This left the two eminent industrial economists with no choice but to state the obvious: 'Currently, only 16 per cent of aluminium cans in the UK are recycled... If the percentage of cans recycled moved towards 100 per cent, interesting possibilities would emerge for the whole value stream. Mini-smelters with integrated mini-rolling mills might be located near the can makers in England, eliminating in a flash most of the time, storage, and distances involved today in the steps taken by most cola can makers.' They argue further that: 'the slow acceptance of recycling is surely due in part to the failure to analyse costs in the whole system rather than just for the recycling step in isolation'.[60]

Hence, this work is showing the real benefits to the economy of increasing recycling, helping to make the economy a more closed-loop economy. The Lean Thinking concept arose from the opportunity to reduce costs by reducing waste. Its success also produced environmental benefits. Professor Jones now sees the next logical step for lean thinking as the application of its lessons to environmental challenges. Their work is important because it is showing that significant labour productivity as well as resource productivity gains can be made simultaneously through this strategy. In addition, reducing global inventories in the long term will allow multinational significant capital savings due to requiting less storage and handling of materials and supplies globally. Their work is important in that they have shown there are significant economic gains obtainable, through lean production, that will offset the short-term costs of adopting new environmentally motivated technologies and continue to supply savings into the future. Professor Jones is currently engaged in a ten-year project to investigate how businesses can best minimize their impact on the environment.[61] He is working with a range of people and bodies, their aim being, as he says: 'Not to dream about high tech solutions. But to find the next steps, the win–win opportunities that we can take together. To think about how we can design our supply chains for the future and to think about efficient consumer response for the next ten years.'[62]

Power of suppliers

The main development that is making industry wake up and take notice of sustainable processes, is the range of products that can be produced, with no increase in cost, and that can actually save you money whilst being better for the environment. The combination of product differentiation and same or less cost will give any firm in any industry competitive advantage. How can traditional paint companies expect to compete with suppliers of paint that has very low to zero volatile organic compounds (VOCs), that has amazing durability, and is cost-competitive with conventional products, such as Oikos in Europe and Rockcote in Australia. Or the Easiwall, a straw-based Australian wall panel that can save AU\$15/m^2 on interior wall construction, is quick to erect, and replaces timber studs and plasterboard together. Or the Interface graphlar-backed (PVC-free) modular carpet system that is now available in Australia under a lease or rental scheme. Interface use a proprietary low-VOC glue and, under the lease scheme, will replace any worn tiles over the life of the contract, ensuring a floor that looks 100 per cent over its entire life. Indeed new products are emerging almost every day. An Australian company has just begun producing a 1.5W light emitting diode exit light with a battery backup. A super-efficient light, it has significant environmental benefits over conventional exit lights, including dramatically reduced power consumption, but at no increase in costs.

CHAPTER 7

INNOVATION AND COMPETITIVENESS THROUGH INDUSTRY CLUSTER DEVELOPMENT

Businesses can join numerous networks[1] that assist their efforts to commercialize eco-innovation and improve resource efficiency. The partnerships and alliances in these networks can promote policies and business practices that result in increased sustainability. Many businesses are already in strategic partnerships with each other or national/sub-regional research and development (R&D) institutions. For example, Australian research bodies like the Commonwealth Scientific and Industrial Research Organisation (CSIRO) helped companies and institutions invest an average of 23 per cent of Australia's R&D spending in the environment industry in 2003. The Australian Government has made achieving an 'Environmentally Sustainable Australia' one of its main research goals. The government is aiming for the Australian Environment Industry to become a AU$40 billion dollar export industry by 2010.

Modern interest in industry clustering is presented in the Harvard Business School Professor Michael E. Porter's classic work, *The Competitive Advantage of Nations*.[2] Using cases from around the world, Porter argues that, in advanced economies today, regional clusters of related industries (rather than individual companies or single industries) are the source of jobs, income, and export growth. An industry cluster is a regional concentration of competing, complementary and interdependent firms that create the wealth of regions through exports. These clusters form 'value chains' that are the fundamental units of competition in the modern, globalized world economy. Clusters form over time and stem from the region's economic foundations, its existing companies and local demand for products and services. They emerge from the fabric of the local community to become the economic champions of the region. Examples are cars around Detroit, films around Los Angeles, leather goods around Milan, financial services around London and aircraft around Seattle. National economies rarely develop evenly. The role of regional government to national competitiveness, therefore, is often crucial in optimizing the success of clusters. Regional policy is most effective when it builds on its strengths, from its industry clusters within the national context. In the last few decades, the concept of industry clustering has come to the forefront of economic development policy.

Clustering is a *knowledge creating process* that provides a democratic environment for power sharing across an industry sector. Clusters are not an economic entity in the same way a firm is; they are a living community sustained by relationships built on mutual trust between individuals and member institutions. They are not necessarily asset rich but they are brain rich, not in the head of the individual, but knowledge on which the cluster as a whole can act as grouping of members (competencies/resources), or of members and their foundations. The success of a cluster depends on the extent to which they create, share and apply knowledge. They are learning communities that develop their own ecology and persona and whose effectiveness evolves over time.[3]

Cocoa beans... and what else?[*]

Michael Fairbanks and Andrew Smith

EDITORS' NOTE: Facilitating cluster development is a challenging task. When asked about whom to approach on this topic, Hunter Lovins replied very quickly – Michael Fairbanks. After some research we learned that, over the past decade, Michael and the On The Frontier (OTF) team have advised business and government leaders in North and South America, Africa, Asia, Europe and the Middle East on making strategic choices in a changing global economy. OTF Group is recognized globally for its business strategy work and has led projects in more than 35 countries and 20 industrial sectors, from petrochemicals in Colombia to defence conversion in the former Soviet Union. As Michael recalls in his Foreword, we invited him to mentor the development of this book and asked that he and his team summarize the key strategic elements and processes involved in cluster development.

A cocoa bean farmer in the Dominican Republic walked into the OTF project office in Santo Domingo and said, 'My grandfather built my family's farm. He became wealthy growing and selling cocoa beans. My father inherited the farm and since then has passed it on to me. Why can't I be like my grandfather and earn a decent wage growing cocoa?'

The answer to this farmer's question was that his grandfather didn't become wealthy because he grew cocoa beans. He became wealthy because he was an astute businessman and an entrepreneur who saw cocoa farming as an opportunity. He became wealthy by building relationships with the suppliers of his raw materials and the distributors of the beans allowing his business, at that specific moment in time, to be competitive. The world has changed. The Dominican cocoa farmer needs new strategies and new networks of relationships to create wealth. The reduced cost of communication, transportation and technology transfer in the global economy demands that the cocoa grower, as well as loggers, textile manufacturers, automobile assemblers, food processors, call-centre operators and software programmers, all figure out what is going to be a little better or a little different about their products and services relative to their competitors around the globe. If they do not learn how to differentiate themselves, they will fall into the 'commodity trap'. Markets will force them to compete based on low prices and low wages. Otherwise, they will lose their business to foreign competitors.

OTF Group[4] has worked at the level of the cluster[5] to help this prototypical Dominican cocoa farmer as well as thousands of other business people to recognize the consequences and opportunities of globalization. OTF has identified a clear set of steps to help industry clusters see new business opportunities and pursue environmentally and socially responsible business development. The focus of this piece is to outline a cluster development process developed by OTF and show how it helps business leaders to:

---

[*] This part was developed by Michael Fairbanks, Chairman of OTF Group, and Andrew Smith, a Senior Manager of OTF Group focused on competitiveness and sustainable business practices.

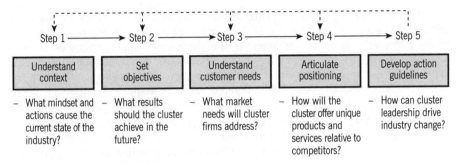

Source: OTF Group Cluster Development Process Framework

Figure 7.1 *Five-step process for cluster mobilization*

- see alternatives to business models that are not creating wealth;
- improve strategic positioning and operational efficiency through environmentally sustainable business practices; and
- develop the complex network of relationships needed to identify and serve attractive market opportunities.

The process we describe takes the theory behind clusters as the 'engines of economic development' and converts it into practical project opportunities for governments, business associations, universities and companies. The process helps the Dominican cocoa farmer, and his counterparts in industries worldwide, create prosperity in an increasingly challenging global business environment.

The cluster development process

The initial step in the active development of any industry cluster is to identify a core group of leaders within the cluster. These leaders serve as the 'early adopters'[6] of new ideas and the key drivers of industry change. In the Serbian furniture industry, cluster leaders range from manufacturers to wood processors, forestry professors to labour union representatives. The Jamaican tourism cluster is led by a diverse group of hotel owners, tour operators, and even the vendors of jerk-chicken. These leadership groups include important decision-makers; however, a commitment to pro-active industry change weighs as heavily as does rank or position. Once a broad-based leadership group is identified, a five-step process creates the tension, receptivity, and insights needed to advance cluster development. The process begins with (i) understanding industry context and follows with (ii) setting objectives, (iii) understanding customer needs, and (iv) articulating strategic positioning. The process concludes with cluster leaders (v) developing action guidelines for the industry. Figure 7.1 is an explanation of these steps and how these steps have influenced change.

Understand context

Cluster leaders must understand what mindsets and actions cause the current state of their industry: the simplest way to understand the context of an industry is to analyse how that industry uses capital. Does the industry invest in cultural, human, knowledge, and institutional capital to create complex competitive advantages, or does it depend on cheap labour, weak environmental regulations, and low energy and material costs?[7] Does an industry reinvest the rents it generates back into education, research and development, or does it degrade the social and environmental welfare of a region in exchange for short-term revenue streams? Leaders of commodity based industries, from the coal mining industry in the US to the food processors in Latin America blame a range of factors, from trade regulations, to government policies, to high interest rates, for failing businesses. The problem, however, is far more fundamental. Their business models depend on the most basic, easily imitated forms of capital. Their products are undifferentiated and must be sold for a price as low as the price of their least-expensive international competitor. Their business strategies lack the complexity required to create wealth in the global economy.

Cluster leadership takes the first step towards building competitive clusters by understanding industry context. Poorly performing companies in commodity industries become receptive to modifying their strategies once they recognize the inevitable impact of globalization on their business models. Companies are willing to change once they realize that investment in people, sustainable business practices, and institutional partnerships yields far greater returns than efforts to secure cheap labour and access to raw materials. By understanding industry context, cluster leaders are eager to start setting new objectives for the future.

Set objectives

Cluster leaders must establish shared objectives for the future so that there is a reason to work together in the present: Gridlock occurs when people debate process, not objectives. Answers to the question, 'Where do you want to be in the future?' are more often compatible than not. People seek economic freedom and quality of life for themselves and their children.

Leaders prepare a country for change by helping diverse parties to rally around a shared set of future objectives. Take the extreme case of Rwanda. Genocide took the lives of 800,000 citizens in the country in 1994. As millions of displaced people returned to the country, Rwandans and the international community wondered how the once-warring factions, the Hutus and the Tutsis, could join together to rebuild the country. However, as peace and increased economic prosperity became widely embraced as national objectives, political parties and ethnic tribes dedicated themselves to looking beyond the tensions of the past. The Rwandan Government set the target of achieving middle-income status by 2020 (US$900 GDP/capita), and retained OTF Group to help it strategize how to get there. With the economy of Rwanda starting at US$2 billion in 2000 and accounting for population growth rates, Rwanda determined that it needed to increase the size of its economy by 8 per cent per year to US$14.4 billion in 2020.[8] This shared objective encouraged leaders to work towards concrete goals. By establishing shared objectives, Rwanda avoided the question 'What should we do?'. Instead, the country's leadership could focus on the question, 'What needs to be true to reach our goals?'.

Understand customer needs

Cluster leaders must understand customer needs and how the cluster can be configured to profitably serve those needs: Rwanda's plan for dramatically growing the size of its economy by 2020 included nothing about increased mineral extraction or attracting manufacturing plants to the region to employ Rwanda's cheap labour. Instead, the country chose to invest in understanding customer needs and how an environmentally sustainable industry could serve those needs. Competition is about convincing customers to purchase your product rather than someone else's. No matter how a firm intends to create value for shareholders, employees, or other stakeholders,[9] no economic development occurs unless the firm meets or exceeds customer needs. Rwanda evaluated the range of customer needs that its private sector could realistically serve; one important industry cluster on which it focused was coffee.

The Rwandan coffee sector illustrates how an industry can create sustainable flows of wealth or, under other circumstances, how it can undermine the future of a country. In the 1980s and early 1990s, Rwanda produced low-grade commodity coffee, maintaining low wages to keep prices competitive with the hundreds of other impoverished coffee-exporting regions around the world. When global prices fluctuated, so did the social stability of rural Rwanda. Transitioning the industry to environmentally friendly specialty coffee production offered an alternative. If farmers employed sustainable irrigation, drying and crop management techniques, Rwanda could produce high-grade specialty coffee for targeted customer segments. Specialty coffee prices fluctuated less than commodity coffee prices, and environmentally sound production techniques saved money by reducing water, energy, and fertilizer costs. Rwanda opened its eyes to the potential for a competitive coffee sector by learning about customer needs. The coffee cluster surveyed 75 specialty coffee importers and roasters worldwide to learn about a market opportunity that was growing at more than 15 per cent per year, capturing 50 per cent or greater premiums by weight than commodity coffee, and in some cases even rewarding farmers who preserved bird habitats with their production techniques. By improving its understanding of customer needs, Rwanda mobilized a depressed industry into one that will generate as much as US$120 million in revenue for the Rwandan economy by 2010 and help significantly to preserve the environmental health of the country.[10]

Specialty coffee, like organic food and eco-tourism, is an obvious product area where environmentally conscious businesses can achieve clear market advantages. Environmentally focused clusters, however, can develop within all industry sectors if entrepreneurial businesses improve how they think about and serve customer needs.[11] When our firm brainstorms new business opportunities with a cluster, we remind our clients that most customers don't want products; they want services. Coffee drinkers don't want coffee beans; they want help feeling good in the morning. Similarly, homeowners don't actually want electricity; they want climate control and lighting. Commuters want ease of mobility and comfort, not automobiles. The more an industry cluster innovates to meet these customer needs (as opposed to increasing the production of existing products), the more competitive it will be. 'Understanding the needs of customers' is another way of saying, 'mapping opportunities'. Market research to support cluster development needs to go beyond analysing what is currently being sold. In the case of Rwanda, it needed to look beyond the global sales figures for low-grade coffee beans. An effective cluster development process will identify new ways for firms to serve customers and differentiate themselves in the market.

Articulate positioning

Individual companies must make choices about where to compete and how to compete. Government and civic organizations in the cluster must make choices about how to guide and encourage competition. After identifying which customer needs to serve, firms must align their activities and assets accordingly. They need to strategically invest in product development, marketing and sales. They need to establish a brand, an appropriate management structure, and a culture of innovation. The responsibility for articulating a cluster strategy, however, falls broadly. In a strong cluster, the strategies of private-sector players are well aligned with the efforts of government and civic organizations. Government and civic organizations play a major role in driving firm-level productivity, because they influence the environment in which firms compete. These organizations accelerate cluster development by establishing policies and infrastructure that support competitiveness and environmental sustainability. The experiences of Costa Rica and Iceland illustrate this point. In recent years, Costa Rica effectively branded itself as the ecological leader of Latin America. This led to significant growth in biology research, tourism, and pharmaceutical development. Iceland, in the meantime, succeeded in spurring environmentally-competitive energy and transportation cluster development by setting the objective of being the world's first hydrogen economy by 2050. These examples

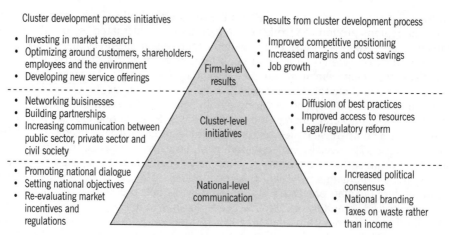

Cluster development process initiatives

- Investing in market research
- Optimizing around customers, shareholders, employees and the environment
- Developing new service offerings

Results from cluster development process

- Improved competitive positioning
- Increased margins and cost savings
- Job growth

Firm-level results

- Networking buisinesses
- Building partnerships
- Increasing communication between public sector, private sector and civil society

- Diffusion of best practices
- Improved access to resources
- Legal/regulatory reform

Cluster-level initiatives

- Promoting national dialogue
- Setting national objectives
- Re-evaluating market incentives and regulations

National-level communication

- Increased political consensus
- National branding
- Taxes on waste rather than income

Source: OTF Group Cluster Development Process Framework

Figure 7.2 *Cluster Development Pyramid*

demonstrate that the more government, civil society, and private companies can articulate a regional strategy, the faster industry clusters are able to take root.

Develop action guidelines

Cluster leaders must develop action guidelines that will stimulate change throughout an entire industry: The Five-Step Process helps cluster leaders establish new strategies for their industries that increase regional economic, environmental, and social prosperity. Implementing these strategies, however, is difficult. Far too many economic development initiatives result in little beyond glossy reports. A cluster development process, therefore, must develop action guidelines that account for the messy reality of how businesses are launched, make money, impact the environment and generate prosperity. The action plans must have the potential to influence hundreds, even thousands of industry players. The Cluster Development Pyramid, outlined in Figure 7.2, helps to organize the many activities required of a cluster leadership group. The three-tier pyramid structure reinforces the concept that cluster development requires results at the firm level, the cluster level and the national level. The Cluster Development Pyramid translates the theoretical concept of a cluster into specific actions for a cluster leadership body to pursue.

Firm-level results: Cluster development requires tangible case studies to show how discontinuous leaps in firm-level business models are possible. Consider the example of the centuries-old sheep industry in Macedonia. The region's sheep farmers have been raising herds and producing milk and meat for generations, even though the geopolitical boundaries for Macedonia were only formed in 1991. The industry has been well-versed in caring for livestock and making cheese, but Macedonian sheep farmers never contemplated selling their products beyond local markets. Neither the quality of the Macedonian cheese nor the price has been competitive with those of neighbouring countries such as Bulgaria and Greece. The result in the last decade has been a 50 per cent decrease in flock size, as well as poverty and social instability in rural Macedonia. Like so many natural resource-based industries globally, the Macedonian lamb and sheep cheese cluster did not have the option of simply making incremental changes to its current business practices. That was a recipe for failure. The industry had to re-invent itself. Working together, it had to identify customer segments willing to pay for branded specialty-food products (for example, Macedonian organic sheep cheese) and to improve resource efficiency at every level of the value chain.

Convincing cheese producers, dairies, food distributors, government regulators and thousands of sheep herders to change their old ways is challenging under any circumstances. In this case, the most critical catalyst was a handful of firm-level case studies: the top of the Cluster Development Pyramid. These examples of firm-level results started the 'snowball rolling down the hill'. Interviews during the summer of 2003 with specialty cheese distributors in New York, Chicago, Boston and San Francisco demonstrated the market potential for unique Macedonian sheep cheeses. Development organizations sponsored visits to the region by specialty cheese experts to help promising firms in the cluster improve their production techniques. Some US$500,000 of cheese exports later, and a small group of leading companies in the cluster has provided the firm-level results needed to convince the entire industry to change.

Cluster-level initiatives: Rapid industry development cannot occur with firms acting alone. For this reason, the cluster development process revolves around a network of leaders who dedicate time and resources to cluster-level initiatives. These initiatives are illustrated in the middle band of the Cluster Development Pyramid. Cluster-level initiatives create networks of businesses, build partnerships, and increase communication so that new ideas and best practices constantly flow within the industry. Cluster initiatives range from regional marketing campaigns, to university/private sector technology partnerships, to market research studies. Cluster-level initiatives are essential for the development of environmentally sustainable clusters. Business models that account for environmental impact often require new networks of partners to become viable. A potential cluster project in the Jamaican energy sector provides an illustration.[12] Energy companies operating in Jamaica are proposing the construction of a new power plant on the island despite substantial concerns about the social, financial and environmental impact of the investment. Case studies demonstrate that simple efficiency measures, such as installing fluorescent light-bulbs and climate control technology, could help the island meet its energy needs inexpensively (at a price of US$0.01–0.02 per kWh of energy saved). This compares quite favourably to the alternative of building a new fossil fuel based power plant that would sell electricity for as much as US$0.12 per kWh.[13] A cluster initiative that brings together local entrepreneurs with international lighting and green design experts could effectively trigger the kind of development needed to re-invent the energy sector. For an impoverished island already suffering from high electricity costs, investments in low-cost/environmentally sound energy technologies are promising. Cluster-level initiatives can build the types of partnerships necessary to make those investments viable.

National-level communication: The third band of the Cluster Development Pyramid refers to the communication that must take place at the national level to encourage cluster development. After a cluster leadership group has set its objectives, understood its target customers and articulated its positioning, it needs to diffuse its strategy as broadly as possible. This diffusion will create national level support for cluster activities. Rather than targeting government handouts or favours, clusters present politicians with opportunities to focus resources on cluster development. Clusters do not have to wait for slow-moving bureaucratic reform. The message is, 'Through increased cooperation and innovation, we are going to overcome the obstacles to doing business, but the government's help would be much appreciated!' This communication also creates a multiplier effect on a cluster's efforts to build firm-level competitiveness. A national-level communications campaign can take what begins as an effort to mobilize one industry cluster and leverage its impact across multiple sectors of the economy. Here it is useful to return to the example of the Macedonian cheese industry: If rural sheep herders can develop strategies to enter US specialty markets, then producers of Macedonian wine or other food products may be able to achieve similar successes. Stories of free-market success are scarce in this former communist country, still suffering from the effects of ethnic tension and stagnant economic growth over the last ten years. Against this backdrop, the cluster, OTF Group and partner organizations developed a national public education campaign to share the cheese industry experience across the nation, encourage new cluster formation, and create optimism for the future.

Government role in promoting cluster competitiveness

Although private sector leadership drives the cluster development process, government can support cluster competitiveness and environmental sustainability through three policy areas: market policy, legal policy and administrative policy. Table 7.1 outlines key principles that should guide government actions in each of these policy areas. The table also lists example instruments that a government should employ to accelerate economic development and environmentally beneficial private sector behaviour.

Table 7.1 *Guiding principles and example instruments*

Direct market policy	
Guiding principles	Government should do everything possible to assist the private sector except impede competitiveness. Government market policy should reward environmentally sustainable innovation.
Example instruments	• Align government procurement policies to reward companies offering environmentally sound products and services. Base government procurement guidelines on environmental factors in combination with cost factors to create sophisticated market demand.
	• Drive 'discontinuous-leaps' in technology development by investing in major R&D efforts in partnership with the private sector.
Legal policy	
Guiding principles	Government should stimulate innovation while protecting the physical and social capital of a region. Laws should have clear phase-in periods, include positive market incentives, and limit negative externalities. Laws should be easy to understand.
Example instruments	• Increase taxes on waste streams/environmentally degrading activities; reduce taxes on income streams.
	• Develop life cycle ownership laws to encourage corporate responsibility for product disposal/re-use.
Administrative policy	
Guiding principles	Government should make the regulatory process as simple, inexpensive and stable as possible. Government should train regulators well and enforce laws consistently and fairly.
Example instruments	• Enforce environmental protection and intellectual property laws to promote private sector innovations.
	• Maintain an appropriate social net to assist workers to make the transition to knowledge-based, environmentally sustainable industries.

Source: Table based on OTF Group analysis; classification of policy instruments draws on OTF Group experience and is inspired by Austin (1990, p89); guiding principles draw on Porter and van der Linde (1995a) and Fuller (1965, p657)

A way forward

OTF Group developed the Five-Step Cluster development process because helping industries to evolve presents enormous challenges. The Cluster Development Process produces results by addressing the realities of the global marketplace and the complexities of the stakeholders involved with industry change. The process encourages industries to focus on environmental and social prosperity in the long term while increasing financial profits in the short term. It allows regional leaders to set ambitious objectives, and accelerate the microeconomic innovation needed to achieve them. What happened to the Dominican cocoa grower introduced at the beginning of this piece? Although we maintain long-term relationships with the majority of our clients, we simply do not know what became of him after he left our office. He may not have changed his business model. He may still be trying to sell cocoa beans to international buyers who have access to over 2.5 million cocoa producers dispersed throughout the equatorial regions of Africa, Asia and the Americas.[14]

Alternatively, the cluster development process may have turned the grower into an innovator of a new, more competitive business strategy. The farmer may have begun selling the husks of the cocoa beans to a Dominican ice cream producer who turned what had been a waste product into fancy, all-natural bowls for gourmet chocolate ice cream exported to target markets in the US. He may have worked with a chocolate factory to develop a regionally branded high-quality Caribbean chocolate bar. He may have converted his farm into a cluster research station for sustainable agriculture techniques. All of these strategies require him to understand the needs of specific customers and build the appropriate relationships to serve them.

The cluster development process does not immediately eliminate the farmer's risk of doing business. The process does not eliminate the pain of poverty or the difficulty of developing a complex new business model. It does, however, present the farmer with a choice. He has a choice to be a cocoa farmer, or a choice to be an entrepreneur like his grandfather who was a successful competitor in cocoa farming generations ago.

CHAPTER 8

THE POLITICAL AND SOCIAL CONTEXT: A SIXTH FORCE ON BUSINESS?

In Chapter 6 we showed that there are many drivers for change for business to embrace sustainability; there are many win–win options for most business. Chapter 6 also showed how Porter's 5 Forces Model provides a framework within which to understand how sustainability strategies could help business. Shaun Mays, in his report *Corporate Sustainability: An Investor Perspective*,[1] points out that 'in assessing the external environment, approaches such as Porter's five forces are used. However, most companies and analysts also look at the political and social environment when looking at the future of the industry in which they operate. Sustainability provides a framework in which to assess this "sixth force";[2] the political and social forces that are also driving a company's external environment.' (See Figure 8.1 for key sustainability principles and characteristics of less and more sustainable companies.) By way of example, Mays refers to the Canadian based CIRANO research centre's industry level study looking into environmental regulation and productivity.[3] Regulatory change is one of these additional political and social drivers that are additional key reasons for business to change. We consider some of these in detail now, starting with changing consumer demands.

Consumer demand change: knowing your market

There is strong evidence to indicate that consumer demand is changing. The 1997 Cone/Roper Cause-Related Marketing Trends Report found that 76 per cent of consumers polled said they would most likely switch to a brand or retail store associated with a good cause. A further 58 per cent said they had a more favourable opinion of companies that helped good causes, with 29 per cent saying they were more likely to buy the company's brand. This is reflected by the views of the companies themselves. A 1998 survey by Saatchi & Saatchi, *Cause Connection of Marketing Directors*, at 170 leading UK companies, found that 34 per cent believed that cause-related marketing could enhance their brands. The environment also provides firms with a credible way to target the youth market. Professor Peter Senge, MIT, author of the highly respected book *The Fifth Discipline* stated, 'Many youth today have grown up acutely aware of the imbalances in the world, especially those living in poverty or in countries with obvious social divisions. They're beginning to network with each other internationally to initiate changes in our social and environmental conditions.' For example, groups such as the International Young

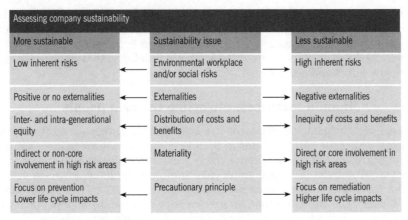

Assessing company sustainability				
More sustainable		Sustainability issue		Less sustainable
Low inherent risks	←	Environmental workplace and/or social risks	→	High inherent risks
Positive or no externalities	←	Externalities	→	Negative externalities
Inter- and intra-generational equity	←	Distribution of costs and benefits	→	Inequity of costs and benefits
Indirect or non-core involvement in high risk areas	←	Materiality	→	Direct or core involvement in high risk areas
Focus on prevention Lower life cycle impacts	←	Precautionary principle	→	Focus on remediation Higher life cycle impacts

Source: AMP Henderson Global Investors[4]

Figure 8.1 *The key sustainability principles and characteristics*

Professionals Foundation, Pioneers of Change and Taking IT Global are emerging online global learning communities of people in their 20s and early 30s involved in significant projects focused on achieving a preferred future around the world. Senge concludes, 'If you talk to these young people, they'll tell you that they're basically trying to figure out how people can live together well.'

In countries such as Germany, the work of civil society groups is leading to significant changes in purchasing choices. The German Government funds consumer organizations to play a significant role in helping to inform the German public. One such organization is the consumer watchdog Stiftung Warentest (SW). As Suzuki and Dressel reported in *Good News for a Change*: 'In Germany, big business and multinational corporations have little choice but to respond to consumer watchdogs. Stiftung Warentest is a consumer watchdog that assesses and rates all aspects of thousands of products annually, including whether the product is environmentally sustainable. The results are published online and in a monthly magazine that is read by 700,000 people. Its director, Peter Sieber, says "A product with a minus or 'unsatisfactory' rating is off the market in a very few months time". SW also releases their findings to the media and TV networks. There are now about 2500 TV spots per annum dealing with their specific findings on products. Polls show that more than 70 per cent of Germans follow SW's advice when making a purchase.'[5]

There are significant organizations working on change internationally. Consumers' International (CI), which has a membership of more than 260 organizations in almost 120 countries, was founded in 1960 as the International Organisation of Consumers' Unions (IOCU) by a group of national consumer organizations. The group recognized that they could build upon their individual strengths by working across national borders. The organization grew rapidly and quickly became established as the voice of the international consumer movement on issues such as product and food standards, health and patients' rights, the environment and sustainable consumption and the regulation of international trade and public utilities. CI has developed a set of policies, available to consumer groups worldwide, that focus particularly on products' environmental impacts. These emphasize the right to a healthy environment, environmentally sound products and the responsibility of consumers to preserve and protect the total environment through sustainable consumption. CI has been responsible for a number of sustainable consumption campaigns since the adoption of Agenda 21. Working through their regional offices, their programme for action by consumer groups mirrors and supports the UN sustainable consumption and production guidelines. The IT revolution provides the potential to directly inform and empower the consumer and investors about the activities of companies. Websites such as the US-based Responsible Shopper[6] provide well-researched details on companies' performance in relation to workplace issues, the environment, ethics and disclosure.

Human resources: attracting the best people

The pursuit of sustainable development strategies has the further advantage of helping companies attract the top graduates in their field. Businesses are acutely aware that human resourcing is the critical determining factor in ensuring success in the long term. A recent study in India of 52,000 employees in more than 200 companies across 15 industries found a correlation between employment practices and financial returns. It found, 'Indian CEOs are more than aware that they now handle a global talent pool. While the labour cost advantage has eroded gradually, the biggest challenge for CEOs is to retain people and manage career aspirations, whether through motivation or training.'[7] A study entitled *Best Employers in India*[8] came to similar conclusions. The CEOs of the top 20 companies rated in this survey emphasized that people were the key to their success, hence attracting and holding onto the most talented employees was critical. These top 20 CEOs believed that employees are attracted to and stay with their companies because of learning and development opportunities, company image and culture and the workplace itself. A recent book by Professor Jeffrey Pfeffer of Stanford University, *The Human Equation*, carefully reviewed the research evidence on the characteristics of high performing organizations and concluded that the most critical factor was human resource practices.[9] He concurred with people like Sir John Brown, CEO of BP, who states: 'At the high end of the employment market, we have to attract more than our fair share of good people, a disproportionate fair share.'[10] Firms need employees who can contribute high levels of customer service and who are motivated to achieve by the long-term philosophy of the firm.[11] This philosophy must be put into action throughout the operations of the company as young professionals are no longer seeking 'socially conscious' employers, but rather 'socially pro-active' ones; not just minimizing the damage and impact but maximizing the positive contribution. In business, one's reputation is priceless and is key to attracting the best people. No public relations campaign by the Pacific Gas and Electric Company (PG&E) can undo the US$333 million worth of damages due to Chromium(VI) exposed by Erin Brockovich and the Hinkley community.

There has been a sea change of attitudes in the mining sector globally, as shown by the 2002 global Mining and Metallurgy for Sustainable Development (MMSD)[12] initiative to address these concerns. The change in attitudes has come from concern that the mining sector is at present not attracting the smartest and best graduates. It has also come from concerns over loss of reputation and public trust from major mining accidents in the past decade. As the Australia chapter of the Global MMSD initiative report stated, 'Minerals development will play an important role in the continuing health of the Australian economy. But it seems likely that the sector is entering an important transitional phase. Mining may take a less prominent role as the industry moves further down the value chain – exploring the economic benefits of reuse, recycling and reprocessing of metals. Such a strategy might offer more efficient management of minerals resources.' In Australia major players in the mining sector and the Australia commitment have committed significant funds to a new Commonwealth Research Centre for Sustainable Resource Processing. An Executive Statement of the centre coordinated by Joe Herbertson states: 'The global goal of Sustainable Development is not achievable without major changes in the way goods and services are delivered and material needs are satisfied, which requires tremendous innovation in the supply chains and life cycles in which minerals and energy processing take part. The ratio of the value of products and services delivered to net environmental impacts will need to improve by a Factor X over the coming decades, where X could be as high as 10 or more; the challenge is to find economically attractive and socially responsible ways to get there.'[13]

The situation was well summed up by Jeoen van der Veer, Vice President of the Shell Committee of Managing Directors in 2001 when talking about the chemical industry when he said, 'If we continue with business as usual, to do the same, our reputation and profitability will suffer. While industry has been successful in terms of products, there has been a rapid and continual loss in public confidence and esteem. Industry reputation lies at the heart of the long-term future of the chemical industry, as does attracting the right people to jobs. Hence if we are to build the right type of company for the 21st century, we have to put people first. Companies that focus on people, innovation, speed and empathy will attract the right sort of people.'[14]

Staying ahead of changes to government regulations

If regulation of the environmental standards of technology does not change, and outcomes remain roughly fixed, pollution will escalate dramatically this century. As more nations' economies develop and the world's population grows, the scale of pollution will increase even though the rate of pollution from each specific technology used remains unchanged. It seems inconceivable, therefore, that regulatory environmental standards for technology will not increase this century. In fact, environmental technology regulation could potentially have a profound influence on whether progress is made on reducing pollution this century. At the same time, we have shown that the challenge of sustainability is so great, and the possible resource productivity gains so significant, that this will inevitably lead to opportunities for increased market share through product differentiation. Consequently, there is also the threat of substitutes from firms in nations who have leading environmental standards.

Can market based mechanisms be designed to assist firms to achieve competitive advantage?

In the paper, *Reinventing the Wheels* by Amory Lovins and Hunter Lovins, the idea of a feebate is described as a potential governance mechanism to encourage the use of more efficient cars. 'Under the feebate system, when you buy a new car, you pay a fee or get a rebate. Which and how big depends on how efficient your new car is. Year by year the fees pay for the rebates. Better still, the rebate for an efficient new car could be based on how much more efficient it is than an old car that's scrapped (not traded in). That would rapidly get efficient, clean cars on the road and inefficient, dirty cars off the road (a fifth of the car fleet produces perhaps three-fifths of its air pollution). The many variants of such 'accelerated-scrappage' incentives would encourage competition, reward the industry for bringing efficient cars to market, and open a market niche in which to sell them. Feebates might even break the political logjam that has long trapped the US in a sterile debate over higher gasoline taxes versus stricter fuel-efficiency standards – as though those were the only policy options and small, slow, incremental improvements were the only possible technical ones.' The idea of feebates can be applied widely to appliances and even homes to reward efficiency and good design.

Additional market-based mechanisms, such as cap and trade, will be covered in Section 3.

Can regulation be designed to assist firms to achieve competitive advantage?

Professor Michael Porter has argued, since 1991, that mounting evidence exists to indicate that environmental regulation, when administered wisely, can help a firm's bottom line through inspiring and rewarding the pursuit of resource efficiency and innovation. One example of such wise regulation is Germany's 'Best Available Technology' legislation. This sets rising standards for industry based on the environmental standards met by the best available technologies globally.

In their seminal book *Global Business Regulation*,[15] Braithwaite and Drahos write that, 'The German Best Available Technology legislation has been the most influential model in the world, and is one of the most significant developments in environmental regulation of technology's environmental standards.' The rest of Europe, including Eastern Europe, have now followed Germany's lead. The legislation does not involve mandating specific technologies; however German law does require firms to implement and apply specific new technologies. Instead, the German Government upwardly adjusts standards that industry has to meet based on the standards met by the best and most cost effective available technologies. In theory, whenever a new and improved technology is created globally, German industry is expected to meet the environmental standard achieved by that technology. Of course, regulatory practice is more flexible, ambiguous and much less instantaneous. However, it is sufficient to provide significant incentive for German firms to develop new technologies that make it cheaper for them to meet the competition from Best Available Technologies globally. When this is coupled with regulation requiring continuous environmental improvement and auditing standards under EU regulation 1836/93, this gives Europe significant potential long-term competitive advantage in the field of environmental technologies. In an interview Braithwaite and Drahos conducted in 1994 with the German Ministry for the Environment, Nature Protection and Nuclear Safety, an official stated, 'We look worldwide for the Best Available Technology. Then we set standards that can be met by this technology. Industry can meet it with this technology or any other ones. This forces innovation. It is becoming more a general view that Best Available Technology can force harmonization upwards.'[16]

Improving on best practice: regulating for continuous improvement

At the end of the day, one of the strongest drivers for change in business is a fear of competitors getting ahead. Consequently, many firms have adopted strategies of continuous improvement of their organization and standards. Frameworks of continuous improvement, like Total Quality Management (TQM), have spread through most multinationals. Firms that comply with TQM for environmental management for instance, have to cause less environmental harm this year than they did the previous year. The results have to be reported to the Board of Directors. This change has been significant enough to gain the attention of major regulatory bodies, such as the EU and the International Organization for Standardization (ISO), who could see the benefits of generalizing the shift. Some governments have enacted legislation requiring companies above a certain size to develop management plans for continuous improvement.

Braithwaite and Drahos write, 'The ISO sought to generalize the trend into a global voluntary standard, knowing that many corporations would pay ISO's intellectual property right in the standard because some states and large corporations would decide not to purchase from firms which did not meet the standard. ISO believed this because of its experience of large purchasers (particularly states) requiring certification of compliance with the TQM standards of ISO 9000 (on product quality). It is easy for a large purchaser, concerned about either legal liability or public criticism for using defective or environmentally destructive products, to protect itself by saying that it has a policy of purchasing only from ISO certified products ... big corporate players and industry associations see the benefits of this, In this way voluntary standards have a cascading effect throughout industry'.[17]

This explains why European businesses, which are subject to rigorous continuous improvement and auditing standards under EU regulations, are working with green constituencies within the ISO for a tougher global voluntary standard that will lift the US and Asia to the Eco-Management and Auditing Scheme (EMAS) standards. ISO standards have also been popular with multinationals who realized the cost of compliance with multiple individual national standards would be far greater with common global standards. Once US and Japanese industry (who thought their standards were high enough already) saw the impact of the ISO 9000 standard in the marketplace, they realized that standard setting could not be ignored. US and European experts now collaborate in the setting of standards, because in the global economy no country can afford to leave the table for fear of its opponents setting standards that disadvantage them. Already Asian business is moving to adopt ISO 14001 due to multinationals such as IBM stating they will favour ISO 14001-certified suppliers.[18] Over 20,000 companies have been certified to ISO 14001, which prescribes corporate environmental management systems, with nearly a fifth of these in developing economies. In a survey of Thailand, for example, 76 per cent of respondents said they achieved cost savings from ISO 14001. More than two-thirds said they also achieved greater efficiency.[19] In Australia, both Lend Lease in the building industry and Ford in the automotive industry are adopting the same standards as IBM with their suppliers. The power of Best Available Technology and Best Available Practice legislation is that it only takes a few international firms to improve their practice significantly for their new standard to become the performance benchmark for all companies that are signatories to ISO 14001. Therefore, the combination of Best Available Practice, Technology and ISO systems can raise standards.

Raising the bar: independent certification schemes

Having said this, increasing numbers of innovative companies are seeking further recognition for their efforts. They are achieving this through paying for their products and services to be certified with specific eco-/fair trade labelling schemes to communicate to the marketplace an even higher standard. The evidence to date shows that there is a strong business case for this move. Companies who have certified their products or services with these labels have gained new contracts, access to new markets or to new sources of investment capital from socially responsible funds. Companies who certify also gain access, usually through the certifying body, to advice and networks that can further assist in their journey towards becoming more sustainable. Importantly, these companies are positioning themselves to also gain access to the top end of the market that is willing to pay a premium for such products.

> *Consumers are increasingly interested in the world that lies behind the product they buy. Apart from price and quality, they want to know how, where and by whom the product has been produced.*
> 1999 Klaus Töpfer, Executive Director, United Nations Environment Programme, (UNEP News Release NR99-90)

New Zealand's Hoki Fishery, certified to the Marine Stewardship Council Standard in March 2001, is a case in point. The goal is to improve the management of the hoki fishery and enable consumers to support the fishery via access to labelled hoki products.

Available evidence shows the fishery to be both sustainable and well managed, as the stocks of hoki are at an acceptable level and strong controls are in place. By signing up to the MSC standard, they have sent clear information to the marketplace, primarily Europe, through 100 labelled hoki products. The market demand for the products is considerable and a notable success is the increasing acceptance of hoki as an alternative to cod, much of which comes from overfished stocks in the North Sea. This increased demand for premium fish will help all those involved to succeed in their efforts to manage the fishery responsibly.

Certification and labelling systems are one of the most sophisticated non-governmental regulatory frameworks for social and environmental corporate responsibility. The best of these schemes are complex, fully integrated regulatory structures. They include widely recognized standards, transparent processes, democratic decision-making processes or widespread consultation on key matters at the very least and separation of powers between standard setting and enforcement. They also offer a range of sanctions and incentives and are open to any interested stakeholders. They are

Table 8.1 *Sample of certification, labelling and accreditation systems available internationally*

Forest Stewardship Council	The FSC is an international body, founded in 1994, that accredits certification organizations in order to guarantee the authenticity of their claims. In all cases, the process of certification is initiated voluntarily by forest managers who request the services of a certification organization. The goal of the FSC is to promote environmentally responsible, socially beneficial and economically viable management of the world's forests by establishing a worldwide standard of recognized and respected Principles of Forest Stewardship.
Eco-tourism certification: Green Globe	GREEN GLOBE 21 is the global benchmarking, certification and improvement system for sustainable travel and tourism. It is based on Agenda 21 and the principles for Sustainable Development endorsed by 182 Heads of State at the United Nations Earth Summit in Rio de Janeiro in 1992. It provides companies, communities and consumers with a path to sustainable travel and tourism. GREEN GLOBE provides a benchmarking and certification product for over 20 business sectors in the travel and tourism industry and has participants in all continents and 48 countries.
Good Environmental Choice	The Good Environmental Choice Label was founded in 2000 and is administered by the Australian Environmental Labelling Association Inc., a non-profit non-governmental organization with a national outreach. The full product life cycle label is product focused with standards in a range of consumer, building and industrial products. The programme is self declared to comply with the requirements of ISO 14 024: International Standard for Third Party Environmental Labelling and Declaration Programs.
Marine Stewardship Council	The MSC's role is to recognize, via a certification programme, well managed fisheries and to harness consumer preference for products bearing the MSC label of approval. The MSC is a non-profit international organization. Australia hosts the first fishery certified to the MSC Standard (West Australian Rock Lobster Fishery) and has some 25 products from certified fisheries available in Australian retail outlets, including products from the New Zealand hoki fishery and the Alaskan salmon fishery.
Mining Certification Trial	This project aims to evaluate whether independent, third-party certification could be applied to mine sites. The project will seek to develop principles and standards for social and environmental performance, and evaluate a model through site trials in Australia.

dynamic and include provisions for revision of standards and change. Some systems, such as Social Accountability International's SA 8000 system, or the Forest Stewardship Council (FSC), also include an accreditation system to ensure quality and consistency of verification. Additionally, a range of certification systems are emerging in many countries, often under the umbrella of the major global certification and labelling systems like the FSC, which is a very fast moving area. For instance, the Australian Environmental Labelling Association ran a major conference in Australia in early 2004, where the certification and labelling schemes shown in Table 8.1 were represented.

In some industries, independent certification labels are helping to return a fair wage to workers. In the case of the coffee industry, for example, many cooperatives gain fair-trade certification in the hopes of obtaining better prices for their members' coffee. The estimated additional benefits for coffee producers through fair trade labelled sales in 2002 were over US$32 billion. Fair trade certified coffee producer groups represent more than 670,000 farmers and their families in 24 countries. There are significant success stories here, for example East Timor's rebuilding after independence has been greatly assisted by initiatives such as the Café Cooperativa Timor (CCT). Founded by East Timorese farmers to fill the void left in cooperatives after gaining independence from Indonesia, the CCT includes 16 affiliated rural cooperatives and provides marketing, processing, transport and export services to its 17,000 smallholder coffee farmer members who depend on coffee for 98 per cent of their income. Fair trade helps to support the work of the CCT, facilitating 600 organized farmer groups with democratically elected leaders and creating job opportunities in East Timor. In 2000/2001, nearly 4000 jobs were created through the CCT. Fair trade coffee standards encourage environmentally friendly coffee production, including the use of integrated pest management and organic agricultural techniques, and CCT has an extensive organic certification programme. 'With the Fair-trade Premium, the co-op has invested in 8 fixed rural health clinics and 24 mobile health clinics, providing services to more than 17,000 coffee farmers and their families.'[20]

The insurance industry: responding to climate change

One of the most significant issues facing business, government, professionals and community groups has been the crisis in the insurance industry. The natural business cycle aspect of this crisis has been compounded by exposure to natural disasters. The emerging evidence that global warming increases the risks of extreme weather events has caught the attention of the insurance industry globally. Even in Australia, the insurance industry is now lobbying for the ratification of the Kyoto Protocol. Bruce Thomas, of Swiss Re Australia, stated at the Enviro 2002 conference in Melbourne, Australia, 'We conclude that climate change represents a real and relevant hazard. The damage may assume dimensions that are beyond control. We must reduce greenhouse gas emissions, develop new concepts for extreme weather protection and develop new efficient strategies to control anticipated damage. Climate change involves methodological, political, social, technical and cultural aspects; it concerns us all and cannot be delegated to single institutions, e.g., research or political bodies.' Figure 8.2 shows the increasing level of natural disasters and man made catastrophes.

A report by members of the United Nations Environment Programme's (UNEP) Financial Services Initiative indicates that annual losses due to more frequent tropical cyclones, loss of land as a result of rising sea levels and damage to fishing stocks, agriculture and water supplies could be around US$304.2 billion[21] by 2050. Insurance companies are retreating from insuring areas prone to natural disasters. The 1990s were the years of record weather-related disasters. In 1998 alone, more than 100 'large-loss' natural disasters caused more than US$90 billion dollars in economic losses, far

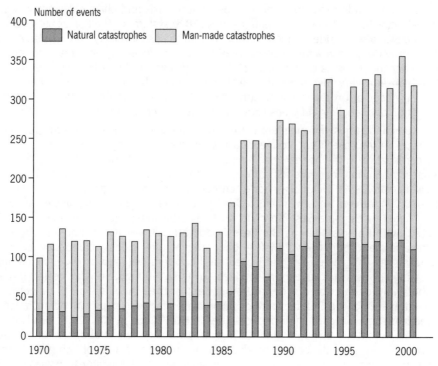

Source: Swiss Re Australia

Figure 8.2 *Number of events, 1970–2001*

outweighing the insured tally, according to reinsurance firm Munich Re. Munich Re issued a report in late 1998 suggesting that large areas of the world, including the south-eastern US and Indonesia, may become virtually uninsurable in the years ahead.

Managers are faced with ensuring that their risk management strategies are sufficient to respond sensitively to environmental issues. Such issues effect not only the obvious greenhouse gas sensitive sectors, but transportation, food, agriculture, tourism and financial services sectors. The January 2003 decision of the Attorneys-General in Maine, Massachusetts and Connecticut to plan to sue the US Environmental Protection Agency (EPA) to force it to regulate carbon dioxide emissions, could have major repercussions.

Jeffrey Ball, of the *Wall Street Journal* (7 May 2003), wrote 'With all the talk of potential shareholder lawsuits against industrial emitters of greenhouse gases, the second largest re-insurance firm Swiss Re has announced that it is considering denying coverage, starting with directors and officers liability policies, to companies it decides aren't doing enough to reduce their output of greenhouse gases. "Emissions reductions are going to be required. It's pretty clear," Christopher Walker, Managing Director for a unit of Swiss Re told the *Wall Street Journal* recently. So companies that are not looking to develop a strategy for that are potentially exposing themselves and their shareholders.'

National insurers rely on, and are influenced by, the activities of the large re-insurance firms; this in turn influences national and regional insurance policies . Results obtained by the Carbon Disclosure Project[22] suggest that few industries will escape this policy shift. In 2002, 35 institutional investors representing assets of more than US$4.5 trillion wrote to the Chairmen of the FT500 Global Index Companies requesting investment relevant information relating to greenhouse gas mitigation; 80 per cent of survey respondents acknowledged the importance of climate change as a business risk, while 35–40 per cent are already taking concrete action. Their work found companies varied widely in their risk exposure. For European electric utilities for instance, the costs of achieving required greenhouse gas emissions reductions could equate to anything from 20 per cent of net income, to 3 per cent or less. Auto manufacturers varied by a factor of 35 in terms of reported GHG emissions per vehicle sold/produced.

The finance industry: a new paradigm in investment*

These are examples of new paradigms in investment that is changing the way we understand capital and, as a result, the way we will do business in the future. Increasingly, the myopic focus on physical and monetary capital is being replaced by a more holistic understanding of the true nature of capital that embraces its physical, monetary, natural, social and human forms. The purveyors of all forms of capital are being increasingly held accountable for its effective use for the benefit of current and future generations. Foremost in this paradigm shift are new investment approaches referred to as either ethical investment (EI) or socially responsible investment (SRI).[23]

> If you had to touch on a single issue that's at the heart of this era, it is whether you can make money and be ethical at the same time. The world is hostage to people who think you've got to make money and everything else is an impediment. On the one hand, there is this broad sense that being ethical will not make you money. On the other hand, most people are deeply uncomfortable with this view and would like to think it's not really like that but don't feel like it's been tested. Now the SRI has tested that and shown you can get equal or better returns than the mainstream.
>
> Francis Grey, Sustainable Asset Management's Research Co-ordinator for Australia & New Zealand (having developed the methodology for the DJSI)

In the debate over the wisdom of investing in ethical funds, the general argument ranges from one of disbelief, that an ethically screened fund could make money, to one which suggests that any ethical fund making money must not be true to its moral beliefs. Those who wish to focus on the negative will suggest that a portfolio constructed on anything other than strict financial risk weighted criteria will affect performance and increase risk. The proponents of EI would point out, on the other hand, that a business taking into consideration these non-financial criteria will outperform and be more sustainable in the long term.

Significant investment houses now recognize sustainability as a 'useful indicator of corporate performance and as being an important indicator of corporate risk'.[24] Shaun Mays, who co-founded the WestPac EcoFund in Australia, the first mainstream banking environmentally ethical fund, has recently published a major report in Australia on the business case for investment houses embracing sustainable development. He writes of one of the responses he received: 'When asked why they were willing to invest time and effort in the pursuit of greater understanding of corporate sustainability, their response was 'because the more I look at these issues, the more I get to see the operation of the company and its management in a way I would not traditionally enjoy. The deeper my knowledge of the company, the better will be my investment decisions'.

---

* The Editors would like to thank John Cronin of TBATI Consulting for his detailed edit of this piece, based on his extensive research in ethical investment related issues and best practice.

Internationally, major investment houses like the European WestLB Panmure have conducted significant studies that support the conclusions of the Mays' report. In their 2002 study, entitled 'More Gain than Pain, SRI: Sustainability Pays Off', leading European analysts showed that 'it can pay to take the "sustainability factor" into account when selecting stocks. There is an additional return even after risk adjustment'. They concluded that, 'One still encounters considerable scepticism when attempting to convince investors of the financial advantages of this new investment style. However, the hard empirical facts show the concern expressed by investors is unfounded.'[25] There are also emerging signs that Superannuation Schemes themselves are looking for new models of how to encourage long-term investment perspectives. A competition, aptly entitled 'Managing pension fund assets as if the long term really did matter', was launched in March 2003 by the UK University Superannuation Scheme (USS) and consultants Hewitt, Bacon and Woodrow, with a view to stimulating new thinking and innovation in the pension fund industry. It did this by inviting individuals or organizations to respond to an imaginary mandate that operated in a 'genuinely long-term and responsible manner'. The competition was won by AMP's London based fund manager, Henderson Global Investors (HGI). Henderson's proposal won out of a field of over 88 entries. The *Australian Financial Review*[26] wrote that, 'Part of Henderson's model had for instance in it a 5 year waiver of their performance fee in return for an agreement with super investors to forgo their right to quarterly results. The British Government then sponsored a leading academic to conduct an independent review of all the ideas generated'.

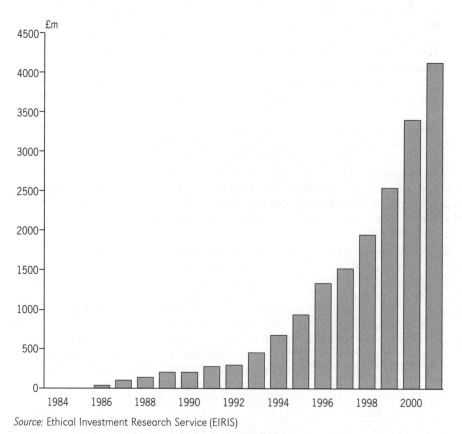

Source: Ethical Investment Research Service (EIRIS)

Figure 8.3 *Total value of retail ethical funds under management*

This form of investment practice has as its central precept that of considering criteria other than the financial return when making investment choices. This emerging investment practice provides significant opportunity for those organizations seeking to conduct business in an ethical and socially responsible manner, giving them unprecedented access to investment capital. EI/SRI is already one of the fastest growing investment markets, and is now worth trillions internationally. This growing trend, clearly evidenced in the case of the UK, is typical of developments globally where EI/SRI investment activities are becoming mainstream (Figure 8.3).

The global increase in the number of investors has led to a massive increase in funds available for investment generally. This is partly the result of global trends towards privatization, whereby government assets have been sold off, and partly from growth in pension or superannuation arrangements. Australia, for example, has on a per capita basis one of the largest rates of share ownership in the world. Government policy has focused on addressing the challenges presented by an increasing age profile and declining birth rate, through compulsory superannuation legislation. Since the introduction of compulsory superannuation in the early 1980s, government policy has targeted superannuation as the primary vehicle for increasing national savings. Through this mechanism, workers are required to become investors and as a result superannuation fund assets have increased significantly over the past 20 years. Australia's gross national savings rate is approximately 20 per cent of GDP. Savings accumulated through the compulsory superannuation system have seen superannuation assets increase by more than 15 per cent per annum since 1985, and they are currently in excess of 70 per cent of gross domestic product (GDP). There is already AU$497 billion in superannuation funds in Australia and the amount invested is growing at 9 per cent annually. The growing voice of pension and superannuation fund members has led to new regulations in the UK and Australia by governing superannuation/pension funds by requiring them to disclose the extent to which they consider the ethical and/or social responsibility criteria. In the UK, this was manifested in the July 2000 amendment to the 1995 Pensions Act requiring all UK occupational pension funds to disclose the extent to which they take into account ethical, social and environmental considerations. A similar amendment to Australia's Financial Services Reform Bill[27] requires all Australian investment fund managers to disclose their policy on labour relations, environmental and social or ethical issues.

> The European Commission is also getting in on the act. As a first step it has helped to fund an umbrella group for national bodies set up in member states including Italy and Holland. The Commission's discussion paper says that in the UK, ethical investment, defined broadly, accounts for around 5 per cent of all investments. In the US however, the equivalent figure is 13 per cent according to a report by merchant bankers UBS Warburg, which says that the amount grew from US$682 billion to US$2160 billion between 1995 and 1999. Meanwhile a fledgling socially responsible investment forum has been formed in Asia to generate interest among investors there.

London based Ethical Investment Research Centre (EIRIS)

Such is the interest and significance of trading activities in stocks of companies deemed to perform in an ethical or socially responsible manner, that a number of stock market indices have been developed to focus specifically on EI/SRI opportunities. These include the Domini 400 Social Index in the US, the NPI Social Index in Britain, the Janizi Social Index in Canada, and the Dow Jones Sustainability Group Index for international shares.

The practice of ethical and socially responsible investment

This substantial and growing class of investors now require not only that their investments be profitable, but that they also meet certain non-financial criteria. These ethical or socially responsible investors are guided by a sense of concern or duty to balance the pursuit of wealth with ethical, environmental and/or community concern. In general, these investors do not wish to forsake or adversely affect financial return, but instead attempt to construct financially balanced investment portfolios while maintaining a commitment to certain personal or global values. In response, many financial institutions now provide investment opportunities that similarly seek to balance financial return with ethical, environmental and/or social concerns.

Throughout its evolution, the EI/SRI industry has used a number of criteria to define an investment as 'ethical' or 'socially responsible', and in turn, various activities have been identified as constituting the practice of ethical or socially responsible investing. The beginning of EI/SRI in a discernable form is generally attributed to religious groups using their resources to invest according to their moral principles rather than financial growth alone. Early efforts in the US by groups such as the Quakers withdrawing from investments involving the slave trade in the 18th century and church prohibitions on investment in liquor, tobacco and gambling in the 1920s were grounded in a specific set of moral beliefs based on religious traditions. In the UK, church funds had some ethical guidelines as far back as 1948, although the growth of this form of investment was severely constrained by the belief that fiduciary responsibility could not be mixed with ethical concern.

EI, as a practice of any significance outside of religious groups, only began to emerge in the early 1960s. This second phase in the evolution of EI/SRI, and for many the birth of modern EI, is seen to have grown primarily out of the social movement surrounding the campaign against apartheid in South Africa. Further impetus was added through students questioning the use of university funds in relation to businesses that had involvement in the Vietnam War during the early 1970s. In the UK, the Animal Rights movements of the mid-1980s, and in more recent years the surge of interest driven by the environmental lobby, have been the primary second wave drivers. A major milestone in the emergence of this as a legitimate form of investment practice was the launch, in 1984, of the UK based Friends Provident Stewardship fund. Although dubbed the 'Brazil' fund, because it was thought to be a 'nutty' idea,[28] the fund gradually gained respect and stature. In the intervening years, this form of investment has grown from a fringe activity, practised by a small group of committed individuals and institutions, to a worldwide phenomenon with investments worth trillions of dollars. In the US, for example, it accounts for around US$2.2 trillion dollars, or 13 per cent of the market, and in the UK US$7.2 billion. The growth rate of funds invested in EI/SRI has been twice that of the general market. In the UK, socially responsible investments grew from US$1.7 billion in 1998 to more than US$7.2 billion in 1999.[29]

The term ethical investment is sometimes used in the context of the first wave of this investment practice, which was primarily faith-based and relied on avoiding so-called sin stocks, such as those issued by companies involved in tobacco, alcohol or armament production. More recently, some market participants appear to use the term socially responsible investment to denote the second wave of this investment practice that claims to incorporate environmental, human, social and more recently sustainability concerns into investment decisions. Although the developing nature of this practice understandably yields some divergence in approach, three distinct strategies have emerged, and are identified in the literature, describing ethical and/or socially responsible investment. These are screening, shareholder activism and community investing. Through these strategies, investors can express their desire to invest in an ethical or socially responsible manner.

Screening

Screening is by far the most notable contributor to the practice and the focus of interest for the large fund managers. It involves the inclusion or exclusion of companies from a portfolio, based on moral, social and/or environmental criteria, resulting in acceptable businesses being labelled Ethical or Socially Responsible. Traditionally, funds have 'screened out' organizations based on criteria such as their involvement with alcohol, tobacco, uranium, armaments and other undesirable activities. Positive screening supports investment in businesses that are involved in new and emerging technologies with an emphasis on the development or protection of social, human and natural capital.

WestLB Panmure refer to numerous empirical studies done over the last 30 years to back this up, including a report from Margolis and Walsh in 2001, focused on the US equity market and covering 95 studies that showed overall a high correlation between CSR and financial performance.[30] Additionally Schafer and Stederoth's 2002 study[31] also provides an overview of this vast literature and came to similar conclusions to the Panmure report that 'Sustainability filters can create added value regardless of whether one is a value investor, a growth investor, or an investor opting for the small, mid or large cap style... We found that the use of sustainability filters can also enhance performance within the context of market timing activities... Sustainability will therefore become increasingly important for the capital markets also for performance reasons. We are, at any rate, convinced that sustainability filters will be used as a matter of course in equities investments in only a few years time. Mainstream investors too, should be aware of this and of the possible 'early bird' benefits.'

Increasingly, ethical investment funds will be asking whether companies are parties to the following:

* International Chamber of Commerce Business Charter for Sustainable Development;
* UNEP Statement by Financial Institutions on the Environment and Sustainable Development;
* UNEP Statement of Environmental Commitment by the Insurance Industry;
* CERES (Valdez) Principles;
* UN Secretary-General's Global Compact;
* OECD Guidelines for Multinational Enterprises;
* Global Sullivan Principles;
* International Council on Metals and the Environment Sustainable Development Charter; and
* Local and National Business Council and Industry Codes and Charters.

Shareholder activism

Through their role as shareholders, EI/SRI advocates the fund managers' attempts to voice their concerns and use their shareholding to further their particular ethical, environmental or social objectives. Whilst all shareholders are, in a sense, active by virtue of the impact of their share purchase decision, EI/SRI promotes more socially oriented activism reminiscent of the social movements of the 1970s and 1980s. For example, a recent UK publication, from authors Hildyard and Mansley[32] provides activists with tips on how they can influence financial markets. The behaviours promoted by this strategy are more active rather than passive, promoting the use of various interventions such as undertaking dialogue with business owners, directors and managers; submitting shareholder resolutions to highlight issues to the management of companies in which they invest; and publicizing the actions of companies to the wider community. This practice has a significant profile in Europe and America, although it is still rare in other markets, such as Australia. The influence of shareholder activism in shaping the direction of a company is a significant force in business.

As reported in the 2002 Spring Edition of *Ethical Investor*, increased shareholder awareness of the environmental and social risks associated with plans to build a controversial dam in Turkey has played a part in persuading the developer to withdraw from the project. Balfour Beatty, the UK-based civil engineering giant had hoped to help build the Ilisu dam on the Tigris River in south-eastern Turkey, 40 miles from the border with Iraq and Syria. But protest groups, led by Friends of the Earth, warned the dam would make more than 78,000 local people homeless and drown dozens of towns and villages, including the world historic site of Hasankeyf. Friends of the Earth bought £30,000 worth of shares in the company so it could submit a resolution on the dam contract at the company's annual general meeting last May. This was an important landmark in the campaign to stop the company becoming involved. The outcome was that the company announced last year that 'after thorough evaluation of the commercial, environmental and social issues it is not in the best interests of our stakeholders to pursue the project further'. 'This is a tremendous win for campaigners against a disastrous dam project', said Friends of the Earth director Charles Secrett. Balfour Beatty's decision to drop out of the project shows the power of shareholder pressure and publicity campaigns.

Community investing

The third and even lesser-used strategy is that of Community Investing, which is sometimes called Socially Directed Investing or Cause-Based Investing. The broad underlying principle in this investment strategy is one of supporting a particular cause or activity through financing it by investment. These investors may, in some cases, accept a lower or zero financial return in order to achieve a social dividend from their investment. However, unlike making a donation, investors require that, at a minimum, the original value of the investment can be returned. Investments may take a number of forms and provide an opportunity for investors to invest in banks and credit unions who provide financing to people in such areas as low-income communities, small business and community projects. A number of 'ethical banks' have grown up around the world that measure their success by social as well as financial results, and provide investors with the opportunity to place their money in accounts where small or large amounts can be used to further their ideals. Another form of investment that is sometimes grouped with these is Alternative Investing: a strategy of investing money in businesses or other investments that promote a vision of an alternative form of economy. These investors often place money in cooperatives, community owned businesses, not-for-profit enterprises or community loan funds, to name but a few.

Community banking case study: Bendigo Bank Group

Testimony, by Rob Hunt, Managing Director Bendigo Bank Group

The world of banking is changing rapidly and more organizations aspire to offer banking services. This continues to blur the business of banking – yet banks themselves are increasingly looking and acting the same. Customers too are changing their expectation of banks. Today it is feasible to bank without ever setting foot inside a branch or coming face-to-face with the service provider. More than ever the customer has the capacity to choose – and will do so. But what is it that customers want from their bank – and do they perceive they are receiving value today? Why will customers in future choose Bendigo Bank as their preferred banker?

Will it be sufficient to have the best staff, quality product, superb customer service, public trust and a commitment to the community in which they live? These things are important, and will be increasingly so, but not for all customers. Certainly if everything is based on price alone it will become increasingly difficult to attract back the capital required to sustain and grow our own community. So it will be important for the community to understand the ramifications of the decisions and the selections they make when purchasing financial products. To secure our unique Australian culture, we will need a special kind of bank and financier – one who understands the importance of linking creation, community, enterprise and success. Banking through history has played a key facilitating role in this development. In the new environment, this will be equally true. Bendigo Bank will be a bank that has the capabilities to play this important role – and a number of the ingredients required stem from our long history, community origins and values. Bendigo Bank began its life in 1858 as a banker to the community. Although fortunes were won on the goldfield, most of the money was exported to the capital cities. A group of citizens therefore formed Bendigo Building Society – now Bendigo Bank – to help create a community infrastructure – our homes, small businesses, churches, public amenities, etc. A city was born. Some of these simple elements are also required in the new environment. Special skills need to be developed within each community, town and suburb, to enable people to understand the impact of capital movement and the importance and opportunity of better managing our capital resources.

Today Bendigo Bank continues to perform similar functions – but in recent times has expanded its role well beyond 'banking' and has developed some sophisticated product and structure to enable this to be built into a strong commercial framework. We believe successful customers and successful community will enable us to be an extremely successful and relevant bank. While other banks were pulling out of country towns, we sat down and designed a purpose-built model – Community Bank – that would work for communities and Bendigo Bank. We are focused on their success first – which in turn creates our success and a unique position in the market which would not be possible were we simply competing on price with the traditional banking methodology. Our early communities either lost, or were about to lose, their traditional banking branch. By devising a new structure (a cooperatively spirited but solidly commercially-based partnership between Bendigo and the community) we are able to achieve improved financial outcomes for the community – and the business volumes generated by the partnership are far greater than we could have achieved on our own. Successful communities create a successful bank – and the partnership helps us become part of the fabric of that community.

We have also taken the view that to create successful communities we need to be involved in more than just banking. We are building a raft of community development projects not normally associated with banking – a range of initiatives with the capacity to help communities retail capital and engage with the new economy now evolving internationally. Services such as telecommunications, e-commerce and energy will be delivered through community owned and operated companies. Through obtaining wide community commitment to buy through these local companies, we will contract with suppliers to provide upgraded services which otherwise would not be available to a fragmented and uncommitted marketplace.

We see community spirit and co-operation becoming more important throughout the Australian population as we move towards the new borderless environment. The basic ingredients for sustainable communities are:

- Mobilize, involve, engage local leadership to create a community that believes in itself.
- Use quality information in our decision-making and assessment.

- Better use the region's entire capital base.
- Reduce the capital drain from our regional centres.
- Produce world quality product and global equivalent efficiency.
- Create environmentally sustainable enterprise and activity.
- Improve the marketing and communication of our region's enterprise.
- Use technology to open up new markets (global or domestic).

Performance of EI/SRI funds

Whilst it would be great to declare that EI/SRI portfolios outperform other less ethical investment strategies, the data currently available is insufficient for claims of superior performance to be substantiated. Numerous studies have been carried out over the years in an attempt to ascertain whether screening does in fact produce better performance. In an excellent summary of a number of these studies Peter Camejo concludes that they indicate no loss of performance, and may indeed show some gain. However, a recent study in the US by Geczy, Stambaugh and Levin,[33] of the Wharton School, failed to confirm any evidence of improved returns. Studies by Angel and Rivoli[34] and others also fail to support a significant impact from shareholder activism. The positive news, however, is that one does not have to overly sacrifice financial reward in pursuit of more responsible business performance. Geczy et al conclude that whilst those allocating 30–100 per cent of their portfolios to such investments may pay a penalty for doing so, those who allocate smaller percentages presumably benefit from a more balanced approach to portfolio management and index hugging. While the jury is still out on the evidence of superior returns on EI/SRI funds, other data shows that in the five years to August 2001, the Dow Jones Sustainable Index (DJSI) outperformed the Dow Jones Global Index with an annualized return of 15.8 per cent, compared with 12.5 per cent.

> *The process of continuous monitoring and reporting of environmental progress is seen by J B Were as positive and necessary… In the future, resource companies that do not respond to community standards and attitudes on environmental issues will have their growth potential severely limited.*
>
> J B Were Report, 1998 (Major mainstream Australian stockbroking firm)

Hugh Morgan, former CEO of mining giant WMC Resources and chair of the Business Council of Australia, commenting on the above said: 'The commentary from J B Were may not be all that surprising to some, but coming from a leading stockbroker, the J B Were report is, to the best of my knowledge, a first. If there was ever any doubt that financial markets viewed environmentalism as a mainstream issue, by which I mean an issue that has the capacity to directly affect shareholder value, then J B Were has dispelled that doubt.' As WestLB Panmure investment analysts write: 'Many companies now regard CSR as an important value driver and are willing to allocate resources to the internal development of this topic. CSR has found its place in management theory. It is now not only regarded as compatible with the idea of shareholder value according to Alfred Rappaport[35] and with Michael Porter's theory of competitive advantage, but also are exemplary implementations of them.'[36]

CHAPTER 9

ACCELERATING THE SUSTAINABILITY REVOLUTION

Overcoming short-termism

Despite the benefits and drivers for change, success stories, and numerous obvious benefits to business outlined in this book, there is a lack of progress overall in the business world.[1] David Suzuki and Holly Dressel lament the lack of progress in their book *Good News for a Change*; 'We now know that we can do it, we can make efficient cars, build green buildings, substitute for toxins, reuse and conserve, save the world's resources for the use of future generations. So the question remains: Why don't we?'[2]

The short answer is that a lot of this is new, this is a historical shift, and a lot of these pressures are relatively new. In addition few engineers, architects and designers are trained at universities in the latest whole system design techniques needed to make green buildings cost effective, for instance. Then there can also be significant institutional, regulatory barriers, disincentives and market failures that can often halt change. For instance, one of the best win–win opportunities for business comes from energy efficiency investment. Significant work has been done since the OPEC (Organization of Petroleum Exporting Countries) oil crisis of the early 1970s in this area, demonstrating the benefits. But even here there can be disincentives for firms adopting energy efficient best practice. For instance, PricewaterhouseCoopers consultants, at the November 2003 Sustainable Energy Authority Victoria (SEAV)/Business Council for Sustainable Energy (BCSE) energy efficiency conference in Melbourne, presented on how the taxation system in Australia discourages investment in energy efficiency. Apparently, if a business maintains old equipment, it can claim 100 per cent of the cost as a tax deduction in that year, but if it improves the equipment (for example by making it more efficient) that's considered to be a capital investment, and the tax deduction can only be claimed over the estimated life of the improved equipment. Even worse, equipment purchased before 1999 is eligible for accelerated depreciation (a higher tax deduction each year) if it is upgraded: but purchase of new equipment is ineligible for accelerated depreciation. So the least attractive option financially for a business is to invest in a new, more efficient plant. Even upgrading efficiency is less attractive than just maintaining equipment. Of course, this doesn't necessarily mean we should change the tax system, because it is designed to take into account many issues. But where are the incentives for energy efficiency to overcome these disincentives?

This is not the only barrier. Amory and Hunter Lovins showed in *Climate: Making Sense and Making Money*[3] that, whilst we have most of the technologies we need to significantly reduce greenhouse gas emissions now, there are up to 80 such barriers preventing the uptake of best practice and wise energy usage. The good news is that this is increasingly understood and, as they reported in 1997, all of these barriers can be overcome. Their report shows, through inspiring case studies, example after example of where in the world leading businesses and governments have significantly addressed and overcome each of these barriers. (Chapter 17 will discuss this further.) In addition to the barriers outlined in *Climate: Making Sense and Making Money* there are three other key drivers for short-termism that have made it harder for longer-term triple bottom line style investments to be taken up by businesses. Specifically:

1   CEOs themselves identify that the constant 'market' pressure to deliver short-term quarterly profit results prevent them from considering the triple bottom line.
2   Superannuation and Pension Fund trustee fiduciary duty requirements by law have prevented them applying socially or environmentally responsible screens to their investments.
3   Business boards have often been making decisions based on accounts that have often not included the environmental risks and impacts of their company. Conventional management accounting has not normally given explicit, separate recognition to company-related environmental impacts.[4] Instead, it is mainly designed to satisfy the needs of managers seeking information about the economic performance of the company as a basis for decision-making. Board members, therefore, have not traditionally been given the information they need to make informed decisions on the sustainability of the firm.

We consider these three issues now. In business, one of the most obvious issues regarding progress on sustainable development is that it will often depend on support from a single person, the CEO. In the case of Interface Ltd, the CEO Ray Anderson truly was more than just supportive of this shift. Hence the pressures on and incentives within which CEOs operate are critical for many businesses on whether they choose to take the sustainable development path or not. We will therefore start the discussion on accelerating sustainability through business here.

Incentives for business leaders

Hunter Lovins and Walter Link write: 'Many companies' CEOs who may wish to do things in a more sustainable way feel that investors will not give them the time to make the conversion from the inefficient, wasteful, polluting processes, to entirely new ways of providing their goods and services. It's a lot to ask of a company to remain profitable in today's competitive economy and to completely reinvent themselves at the same time.'[5] A recent survey of a significant number of CEOs in Australia found that the biggest single reason for lack of progress on implementing more sustainable development practices is the significant short-term pressures some external, some internal, on CEOs and Boards in Australia to deliver quarterly returns from investment houses. Professor Dexter Dunphy, University of Technology Sydney, has conducted a series of interviews with 20 leading CEOs in Australia and in stating his findings he says:

> One of the things that quite a number of them pointed to was the difficulty of them actually running organizations which are sustainable in the longer term when in fact they've got the analyst breathing down their necks constantly asking for short-term returns, and there's an inherent conflict between managing for the short term and managing for the long term. This is one of the things all managers face but the emphasis has been very strongly from economic rationalism to push for the short-term return and to see organization as primarily there for their shareholders. I guess

what I see emerging is a new view that says, shareholders are only one of a variety of stakeholders and we can in fact destroy organizations, quite effective organizations, if we only manage for the short term. So these senior executives were saying, until the financial analysts, the investments funds and so on actually reward us for taking a longer-term and a broader view of what our responsibilities are, whatever our personal views about this, it's very hard for us to achieve this, we're sort of running up a staircase that's moving down faster than we can run up it.

External pressure from investors and analysts is not the only force driving short-termism. The structure of incentive-based executive remuneration is another major force. In Australia in 2001, 45 per cent of an average CEO's remuneration was in the form of variable remuneration, of this, roughly 57 per cent was in the form of bonuses and 43 per cent was in the form of stock options; 67 per cent of Australian CEOs receive stock options.[6] Bonuses are usually annual and usually pegged to short-term performance measures such as annual earnings per share or share price. This approach to remuneration tends to focus CEOs' minds on short-term thinking.[7] Stock options are little better, and are widely regarded as responsible for the unsustainable business practices of Enron. In short, so long as executives are rewarded for short-term performance, they will have a personal incentive to adopt short-term policies and to resist policies that only pay out in the long term (R&D, long-term environmental risk management).

In his book *Corporate Governance & Wealth Creation in New Zealand*, Joseph Healy outlines a number of options, for instance: CEO bonuses can be paid out over rolling terms (three or five years are often proposed, but seldom adopted), with offsets for poor or good performance in intervening years. This approach smooths performance-based remuneration and removes some incentives for short-term approaches.[8] This is just one way remuneration structures can better align executive incentives with the long-term prospects of the company and, thus, encourage better long-term environmental and social behaviour of the firm.

Reform of fiduciary duty for pension and superannuation funds trustees

L. Hunter Lovins and Walter Link

As we have explained, there is a significant shift growing for ethical investment (EI). But it could be growing much faster. Another significant change in the last 20 years in OECD countries has been the widespread rise of superannuation schemes. But there has been a corresponding lack of initiative to invest in the triple bottom line by institutional investors. Most people would be surprised to know that at present there is a significant obstacle for the growth of screened funds, or EI/SRI, in most countries due to fiduciary duty[9] requirements of superannuation trustees.[10] This reflects the common law duty that trustees act in the best financial interests of beneficiaries of the trust. In the absence of a screened investment methodology that can satisfy this trustee duty, superannuation trustees will, understandably, continue to be hesitant in committing funds to screened investments. This helps explain the historical lack of pioneering initiative in this area by institutional investors. Fiduciary duty stipulates the responsibility of the pension fund trustees to take good care of the money that is entrusted to them and invest it so that at the end of the pension fund members' work life there will be money to pay a pension. This term was defined in such a way that it explicitly excluded making socially and environmentally oriented investments. The definition arose because of the pervasive economic belief that such investments were financially less attractive. We have shown in 'The Finance Industry: a new paradigm in investment' that this is not true. Socially responsible funds are performing as well and often better than the market average. A US study,[11] examined the returns of an unscreened equity universe composed of 1300 stocks compared to a socially screened universe of 950 stocks. The study concluded no significant difference between the average monthly returns of the screened and unscreened universes for the period 1987–1994. This was affirmed for the period 1995–1996 in follow-up research.

This allowed Calvert Socially Responsible Investment Funds in the US to file a suit against the old definition of fiduciary responsibility and win in court because it could demonstrate that there is no reason not to invest in companies with a superior social and environmental performance for pension funds. After this court victory, in April 2003, the Global Academy's Natural Capitalism Group lead by Hunter Lovins, in partnership with Progressive Asset Management (Eric Leenson and Peter Camejo) organized a conference, bringing together the trustees and managers of pension funds.[12] At the conference, the chair of the California Public Employees' Retirement System (CalPERS) stated that it really did not matter significantly to him whether he invested in a company that did really well in the next quarter as against another company. CalPERS is so big, US$160 billion in assets, that he's invested in essentially every major company in the US economy. What he cares about is whether the whole of the economy is there, is healthy, 20 years from now, 50 years from now when he has to pay out the pensions. Pension and superannuation funds may be the institution in society with the biggest vested interest in seeing that sustainable development is achieved. American pension funds have assets equivalent to 46 per cent of the US GDP. Pension funds should have been investing in socially and environmentally responsible companies all along. Pension funds represent what should be value driven investors: workers, teachers, the churches. But fiduciary duty regulations for superannuation trustees have been keeping these funds from being a force for social change.

At the pension fund conference, people were saying what a ground-breaking event it was, this bringing together for the first time of the pension fund trustees and managers with people doing socially responsible investing, and that it couldn't have happened five years ago. Obviously the result of the conference was to begin to shift a massive accumulation of capital in the direction of sustainable development. CalPERS has already committed to invest US$200 million in environmental technology companies and projects. Change is occurring around the world in this area. For instance, VicSuper in Victoria, Australia now state on their website that they 'invest 10 per cent of the listed equity portfolio of VicSuper Fund's investment options in large Australian and international companies rated as having the best sustainability business strategies in their industry sector. VicSuper also offers its members the option of investing 100 per cent of their superannuation in projects that meet their sustainability criteria.'

Similar shifts are occurring in the UK, where they are starting to address the obstacle of the way fiduciary duty is currently defined in law. The UK investment market is already seeing strong growth for screened investments. This is partly due to changes in the 1995 Pensions Act that requires all trustees to declare in their Statement of Investment Principles:

- the extent (if at all) to which social, environmental or ethical considerations are taken into account in the selection, retention and realization of investments;
- the policy (if any) directing the exercise of the rights (including voting rights) attaching to investments.

This was laid before the UK Parliament on 1 July 1999 and influenced Prudential's decision to introduce screening on its £140 billion investment portfolio. Surely it is in any nation's interest to address any obstacles to investment in companies walking the talk on the triple bottom line, given the social and environmental benefits to national well-being? The most critical next step to transforming pension funds into the instrument of funding investments in the triple bottom line will be ensuring reliable and accurate information upon which superannuation trustees and investment advisers can make their decisions.

This brings us to Corporate Sustainability Reporting. Currently the leading international initiative to encourage and promote corporate sustainability reporting is the Global Reporting Initiative (GRI), founded in 1997 by the Coalition for Environmentally Responsible Economies in partnership with the United Nations Environment Programme (UNEP). The GRI has been an important catalyst in the drive for environmental reporting and, to date, 70 per cent of the 250 largest global companies published reports that cover the triple bottom line (TBL), up from 35 per cent in 1998. As previously mentioned, France passed legislation in 2003 requiring French companies wanting to be listed on its stock exchange to make information about their social and environmental performance available to investors. Similar legislation, requiring pension funds to publish the percentage of their portfolios that are in socially responsible investments, was passed by Britain in 2000. Almost half of the UK's top 100 companies are now courting the funds with details of their TBL credentials. In Japan, a rapidly increasing percentage of the country's top 100 companies now produce sustainability reports. There are many reasons for nations to legally require the GRI sustainability reporting guidelines that are now widely accepted by the international business community as the best set of indicators for sustainability reporting.[13]

Charles Berger, from the Australian Conservation Foundation, outlined some of the supporting reasons for sustainability reporting in a recent report to the Australian Treasury:[14]

- It would provide more objective information. A standard reporting framework would increase the objectivity and quality of investor and community information sources, such as ratings of corporate responsibility and recommendations by ethical investment advisers.
- It would streamline analyst and community information requests. There is currently a good deal of frustration in the corporate sector regarding multiple, duplicative and sometimes voluminous requests for information. Standardized, universal reporting would lessen the number of these requests considerably.
- It can lead to better business performance. There is a growing body of evidence that public reporting improves financial performance by creating organizational structures to monitor and improve resource efficiency and waste minimization, as well as by suggesting strategic business opportunities and raising environmental awareness overall.

The past decade has seen a marked increase in new sustainability reporting requirements around the world, with comprehensive disclosure laws or rules being enacted in France, Denmark, the Netherlands, Norway, South Africa and Sweden, among others.[15] France, for example, requires detailed disclosure of water, energy and other resource consumption, greenhouse and other emissions, waste management, impacts on biodiversity, management policies and procedures, and compliance issues. Even more notably, the European Commission has issued a recommendation that all member states ensure environmental performance reporting in company annual reports, specifically mentioning quantitative disclosure of emissions and consumption of energy, water and materials.[16]

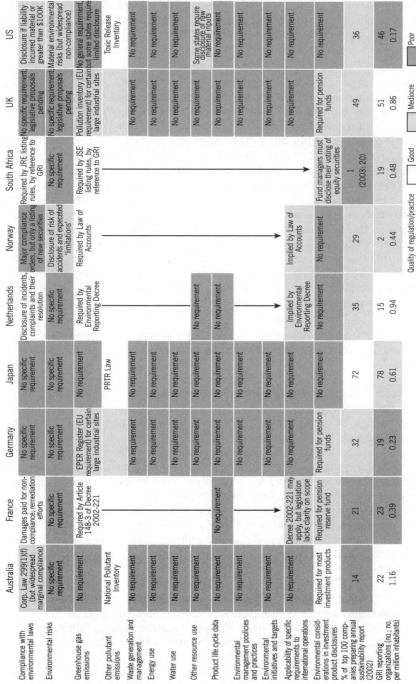

Figure 9.1 *A comparison of corporate environmental disclosure requirements and practice*

Source: Australian Conservation Foundation (ACF) (2004)

Note: The figure compares reporting requirements for publicly listed companies. In some countries, certain requirements apply more broadly. For the Netherlands, statutory reporting requirements apply to approximately 300 companies with serious impacts on the environment.

Under 'Compliance with environmental laws' and 'Environmental risks', the figure addresses the existence of specific environmental requirements in these categories; it does not reflect (i) general securities law requirements to disclose material risks and/or liabilities, or (ii) accounting rules that may result in the disclosure of contingent or incurred environmental liabilities in financial statements.

Environmental management accounting in Japan: trends and current practices of environmental accounting disclosure and environmental management accounting[*]

Chika Saka, Roger Burritt, Stefan Schaltegger and Tobias Hahn

Reporting from companies has traditionally focused on financial reporting. Company reporting is used to predict future performance and, as enterprises are becoming increasingly large and exert greater influence on all aspects of life around the globe, future reporting will need to include other issues, such as environmental information. Accounting for environmental issues and environmental information is important in furthering sustainable development and improving eco-efficiency. It is important, therefore, that environmental accounting and environmental reporting are researched and developed to improve the usefulness of the information supplied to investors.

Stig Enevoldsen, Chairman, International Accounting Standards Committee; Partner, Deloitte & Touche, Copenhagen, 2000

Corporate environmental reporting has taken off in many countries. This is certainly true of Japan. According to the Japanese Ministry of Environment 650 listed and unlisted companies published environmental reports in 2002.[17] In fiscal year 2002, 474 of the 650 companies (73 per cent) that publish environmental reports disclosed environmental accounting information. An increasing trend is observable. Moreover, 251 extra companies signalled their intention to publish environmental reports in 2003, raising the expected number of corporate environmental report publications to about 1000 per annum.

This is occurring because of all the drivers already mentioned in this section. For example, environmental reporting helps firms to gain access to ethical investment funds. In Japan, 11 funds at nine organizations manage a total of more than US$1 billion, as of March 2002. In Japan, there are several environmental rating agencies. The presence of these systems means that the market is in a position to penalize companies that do not disclose environmental information. Mukoyama and Ishikawa have shown that corporate environmental information disclosure contributes to an increase in the value of company share prices.[18] The investor market is increasingly aware that the costs of negative environmental impacts to companies has risen dramatically, and so environmentally related information is now seen as highly relevant to business managers and CEOs. Fines for environmental non-compliance are also much higher than they have been in the past. At the same time, the costs of information management per unit of information have substantially decreased in recent decades. As a result, the relationship between environment related costs and the costs of environmental information management have changed. Take the *Exxon Valdez* oil spill in 1991. Exxon faced a bill of as much as US$16.5 billion in addition to the US$1.1 billion paid in the State of Alaska and federal criminal penalties and the US$2 billion clean-up costs.[19] Hence, from a purely economic perspective over the past ten years, it has become economical for many more companies to introduce environmental management and environmental information management systems.[20] This is certainly the opinion of one of the world's gurus of business competitiveness.

* This part was developed from the paper, 'Trends and Current Practices of Environmental Accounting Disclosure and Environmental Management Accounting in Japan', by Dr Chika Saka, Kwansei Gakuin University and Roger Burritt, School of Business and Information Management, Australian National University.

> *Our research indicates that the act of measurement alone leads to enormous opportunities to improve productivity. Companies that adopt the resource-productivity framework and go beyond currently regulated areas will reap the greatest benefits. Companies should inventory all unused, emitted, or discarded resources or packaging ... so managers can learn to recognize the opportunity cost of underutilized resources. Few companies have analysed the true cost of toxicity, waste, and what they discard, much less the second-order impacts that waste and discharges have on other activities. Many companies do not even track environmental spending carefully, and conventional accounting systems are ill equipped to measure underutilized resources. Companies evaluate environmental projects as discrete, stand-alone investments. Straightforward waste or discharge-reduction investments are screened using high hurdle rates that presume the investments are risky, leaving ten-dollar bills on the ground. Better information and evaluation methods will help managers reduce environmental impact while improving resource productivity.*

Porter and van der Linde (1995a)

There are even now two environmental reporting award systems in Japan: 'Environmental Report Award' sponsored by Global Environmental Forum and 'Green Reporting Award' sponsored by Green Reporting Forum and Toyo Keizai. Most environmental reports have begun to expand their contents to include additional information about the social activities of companies. These practices have been influenced by the Global Reporting Initiative (GRI) Sustainability Reporting Guidelines. Some companies attach reports of discussions with non-governmental organizations. At present, 80 Japanese companies publish their reports based on GRI Guidelines. This trend in Japan has been encouraged by government initiatives and guidelines; two key government initiatives have greatly encouraged the uptake of environmental accounting disclosures, supported by physical environmental accounting information. The first initiative is the Ministry of Environment (MOE) *Environmental Reporting Guidelines (Fiscal year 2000 version)*. This guideline outlines the principles of reporting, the structure, and the contents of environmental reports. In May 2000, MOE released *Developing Environmental Accounting Systems – year 2000 report*, which was a revised version of *the 1999 Draft Guidelines – Disclosing Environmental Accounting Information*. Later, as a result of the rapid progress of practice, MOE revised its guidelines and published *Environmental Accounting Guidelines – 2002 version* and the *Environmental Accounting Guidebook* that includes questions and answers and various case studies to help understanding by companies. Although these guidelines are not mandatory, many companies have chosen to use the MOE environmental accounting format. MOE has also published *the Guidelines for Environmental Performance Indicators for Business – Fiscal Year 2002 version*. MOE uses these guidelines in an integrated manner.

In the concept as developed by MOE, environmental accounting consists of accounting procedures that companies can use to evaluate the costs and effectiveness of environmental conservation activities. MOE seeks standardization of the form of disclosure and contents of environmental accounting, to maximize the usefulness of that information, especially comparability. Environmental accounting for MOE purposes consists of three components: environmental costs (monetary unit), environmental conservation benefits (physical unit), and economic benefits (monetary unit).

These are consistent with the framework for environmental accounting provided by Burritt, Hahn and Schaltegger.[21] The framework allows firms to compliment their present accounting systems with an environmental management accounting system. Conventional management accounting has not normally given explicit, separate recognition to company-related environmental impacts.[22] Instead, it is mainly designed to satisfy the needs of managers seeking information about the economic performance

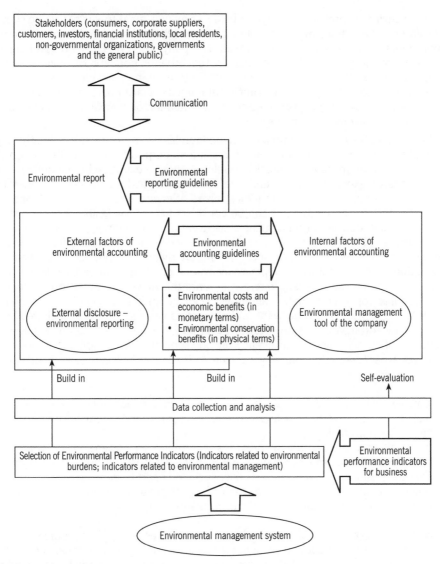

Source: Dr Chika Saka

Figure 9.2 *Cross relationships between environmental accounting, environmental reporting and environmental performance indicators as used by* MOE

of the company as a basis for decision-making. Yet, from a pragmatic perspective, the critical test for any accounting system is whether it produces information, such as environmental information, that is useful to stakeholders (e.g., managers) for evaluating their own ends.[23] For example, top managers are interested in monetary information that shows material effects on shareholder value, including environmentally related impacts on the economic situation of companies. Corporate environment managers, on the other hand, are interested in various waste and pollution figures, expressed in physical units, and generally have no direct interest in, for example, whether the costs of pollution abatement or waste reduction measures are capitalized or considered as expenses in the monetary account.[24]

Using environmental accounting as a business management tool is becoming known as environmental management accounting (EMA). EMA is used by managers, various departments in an organization, and all company personnel. A comprehensive framework of EMA has to be anchored in the broader concept of environmental accounting. In relation to environmental accounting, there is a wide consensus that there are two main groups of environmental impacts related to company activities: environmentally related impacts on the economic situation of companies; and company-related impacts on environmental systems.[25]

Environmentally related impacts on economic systems are reflected through monetary environmental information addressing all corporate related impacts on its past, present or future financial stocks and flows, and are expressed in monetary units (e.g., measures expressed in expenditure on cleaner production; cost of fines for breaching environmental laws; monetary values of environmental assets). Monetary environmental accounting systems can be considered as a broadening of the scope of, or a further development or refinement of, conventional accounting in monetary units, as they are based on the methods of conventional accounting systems. Related impacts of corporate activities on environmental systems are reflected in physical environmental information. At the corporate level, physical environmental information includes all past, present and future material and energy amounts that have an impact on ecological systems. Taken together, monetary and physical environmental accounting form a basis for EMA.[26] It is proposed that EMA be defined as a generic term that includes both monetary EMA (MEMA) and physical EMA (PEMA). This is illustrated in Figure 9.3. Conventional accounting systems already provide separate information about monetary and physical aspects of the company's activities. These systems, expressed in monetary units, include:

- management accounting, designed to satisfy internal needs of corporate decision-makers for short-term cost and revenue, long-term investment information and internal accountability;
- financial accounting, which provides external corporate stakeholders with information about the company's dated financial position and changes in the financial position on a regular basis over specified periods; and
- other accounting systems such as tax or bank regulatory accounting, intended to provide specific information, mostly for regulatory purposes.

Conventional accounting systems with information expressed in physical units include approaches such as production planning systems, inventory and material accounting systems and quality systems. Hence this new environmental accounting system builds on established norms in accounting.

MEMA deals with the environmental aspects of corporate activities expressed in monetary units and generates information for internal management use (e.g., costs of fines for breaking environmental laws; investment in capital projects that improve the environment). In terms of its methods, MEMA is based on conventional management accounting that is extended and adapted for environmental aspects of company activities. It is the central, pervasive tool providing the basis for most internal management decisions, as well as addressing the issue of how to track, trace and treat costs and revenues that are incurred because of the company's impact on the environment.[27] MEMA contributes to strategic and operational planning, provides the main basis for decisions about how to achieve desired goals or targets, and acts as a control and accountability device.[28]

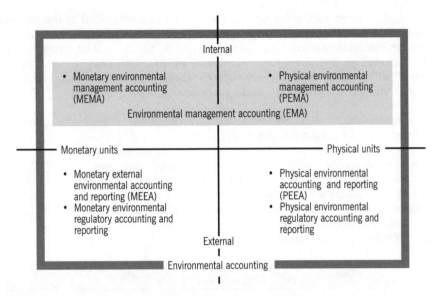

Source: Modified by Burritt et al (2002) from Bartolomeo et al (2000)

Figure 9.3 *Environmental accounting systems*

PEMA also serves as an information tool for internal management decisions. However, in contrast with MEMA, it focuses on a company's impact on the natural environment, expressed in terms of physical units such as kilograms. PEMA tools are designed to collect environmental impact information in physical units for internal use by management.[29]

According to Schaltegger and Burritt, PEMA as an internal environmental accounting approach serves as:[30]

- an analytical tool designed to detect ecological strengths and weaknesses;
- a decision-support technique concerned with highlighting relative environmental quality;
- a measurement tool that is an integral part of other environmental measures such as eco-efficiency;
- a tool for direct and indirect control of environmental consequences;
- an accountability tool providing a neutral and transparent base for internal and, indirectly, external communication; and
- a tool with a close and complementary fit to the set of tools being developed to help promote ecologically sustainable development.

Figure 9.4 categorizes these environmental management accounting systems according to the two dimensions, internal vs. external and monetary vs. physical. Building on these arguments, which support the notions of MEMA and PEMA as core constructs in EMA, additional dimensions can also be seen as being a necessary, important part of environmental management accounting. In particular, three dimensions of environmental management accounting tools are emphasized:

1   timeframe – the period being addressed by different tools (e.g., past, current or future);

2   length of timeframe – the duration of the period being addressed by the tool (e.g., tools addressing the short term vs. those with a focus on the long term); and

3   routineness of information – e.g., ad hoc vs. routine gathering of information. Figure 9.4 includes all five dimensions – internal vs. external, physical vs. monetary classifications, past and future timeframes, short and long terms, and ad hoc vs. routine information gathering – in the proposed framework for EMA.

In September 2002, MOE released an Environmental Report Database. The environmental report database is designed to help:

- compare the contents of the environment reports of companies;
- provide an incentive for improving the reports by disclosing the names and report contents of companies that publish environmental reports;
- encourage equitable treatment between the companies that carry out acceptable environmental activities and those that do not; and
- promote dialogue with various stakeholders.

Environmental management accounting (EMA)				
	Monetary environmental management accounting (MEMA)		Physical environmental management accounting (PEMA)	
	Short-term focus	Long-term focus	Short-term focus	Long-term focus
Past oriented — Routinely generated information	1. Environmental cost accounting (e.g., variable costing, absorption costing, and activity based costing)	2. Environmentally induced capital expenditure and revenues	9. Material and energy flow accounting (short-term impacts on the environment – product, site, division and company levels)	10. Environmental (or natural) capital impact accounting
Past oriented — Ad hoc information	3. Ex post assessment of relevant environmental costing decisions	4. Environmental life cycle (and target) costing Post investment assessment of individual projects	11. Ex post assessment of short-term environmental impacts (e.g., of a site or product)	12. Life cycle inventories Post investment assessment of physical environmental investment appraisal
Future oriented — Routinely generated information	5. Monetary environmental operational budgeting (flows) Monetary environmental capital budgeting (stocks)	6. Environmental long-term financial planning	13. Physical environmental budgeting (flows and stocks) (e.g., material and energy flow activity based budgeting)	14. Long-term physical environmental planning
Future oriented — Ad hoc information	7. Relevant environmental costing (e.g., special orders, product mix with capacity constraint)	8. Monetary environmental project investment appraisal Environmental life cycle budgeting and target pricing	15. Relevant environmental impacts (e.g., given short run constraints on activities)	16. Physical environmental investment appraisal Life cycle analysis of specific project

Source: Schaltegger et al (2000)

Figure 9.4 *Proposed framework for environmental management accounting system*

Table 9.1 *Classification of EMA tools based on applicable object*

Product	Environmental cost planning Life cycle costing	Environmental quality cost accounting	Environmental corporate performance evaluation
Capital investment	Environmental capital investment appraisal		
Production/ distribution process	Material flow cost accounting		

Source: METI's Environmental Management Accounting Tools Workbook, 2002

From this database, it is possible to find out whether companies make the specific disclosures recommended under the MOE Environmental Reporting Guidelines. At first, the database contained data for 180 companies. From October 2002, more data have been included, including environmental performance indicators. In the future, MOE plans to include all corporate environmental reports in the database. The number of third party initiatives is also rising. The number of companies that attach third party reviews to their reports is increasing. With the spread of environmental accounting disclosures as the next stage of environmental accounting, there is a growing interest in making good use of environmental accounting information by management to achieve both a reduction in environmental burdens and increased profits – the classic 'win–win' situation.

The second government initiative of note in Japan is the Ministry of Economy, Trade and Industry (METI) project to develop EMA tools suitable for Japanese companies. Pilot testing was launched in 1998. This project was completed in 2001 and METI published in 2002 the *Environmental Management Accounting Tools Workbook*. In this project, there were five working groups considering different areas of environmental management accounting: environmental capital investment appraisal, environmental cost management, material flow cost accounting, life cycle costing and environmental corporate performance evaluation. Classification of each of the tools, based on applicable cost objects, is shown in Table 9.1.[31]

Environmental capital investment appraisal is used to assess the value of environmental capital investment. Because this kind of investment was evaluated by focusing on cost burden, conventional investment appraisal sometimes leads to unfavourable environmental outcomes. However, this tool presents the concept of considering aspects of potential profit from cost reduction and environmental impact in investment appraisal.

Environmental cost management has two tools, environmental quality cost accounting and environmental cost planning and makes use of budgeting by analysing the effectiveness of environmental expenditures and by providing environmental information to support environmental decision-making in product development and design.

Material flow cost accounting is a tool that captures the material flows and monetary flows in productive processes, and makes clear any inefficiency in productive processes by using physical and monetary information. The environmental costs to be managed include raw material costs and all related overheads charged to waste (non-product) output. Therefore, the scope of the environmental costs is very wide and high environmental costs are often identified, drawn to the attention of managers, and managed once their size is realized.

Life cycle costing adds an economic viewpoint to life cycle assessment. In a recycling-orientated society like Japan, it is important to manufacture products considering not only internal costs but also the costs of exploiting natural resources. Information can be gathered about up- and downstream activities and so life cycle costing is facilitated by the MOE and METI systems of environmental accounting.

Environmental corporate performance evaluation is used to integrate environmental performance information with performance evaluation systems. Putting environmental factors into performance evaluation systems that form the basis of business is thought to be the most effective method of promoting environmental management. Prior use of this evaluation approach appears to have been limited.[32] There have also been a number of surveys to investigate corporate environmental accounting practices in Japan such as the Kokubu and Nashioka[33] and Saio et al[34] surveys. The second of these is a comprehensive survey that examined many aspects including: corporate disclosure practices in relation to environmental costs and benefits, how and to what extent the MOE's guidelines influence environmental accounting practice, the effects of the influences of the METI project, corporate attitudes to introducing environmental accounting, the usefulness for companies, how companies account for investment costs, depreciation, employment cost, research and development costs and environmental conservation effects and cost reduction, third party review, etc. This survey was conducted by a questionnaire producing 159 valid responses from companies that are listed on the First Section of the Tokyo Stock Exchange, and disclose environmental accounting information as at October 2001.

Results about corporate attitudes to environmental accounting are of interest here. First, the types of benefit companies achieve through the introduction of environmental accounting system are shown in Figure 9.5.

A total of 85.5 per cent of responding companies recognize that they could understand the amount of environmental costs incurred by their company. There remains a question, however, whether these categories are independent of each other, as environmental cost information could also be considered a practical use of environmental management. The kinds of benefits these companies obtain from practical uses of environmental accounting for internal management are shown in Figure 9.6.

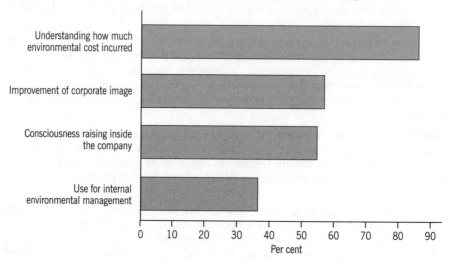

Source: Saio et al (2002)

Figure 9.5 *Benefits through the introduction of an environmental accounting system*

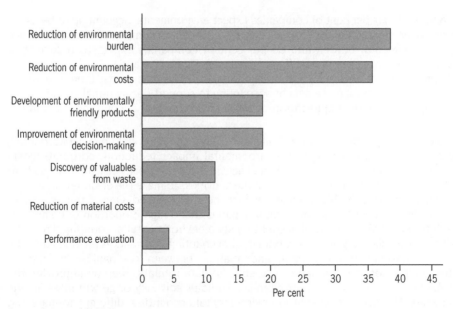

Source: Saio et al (2002)

Figure 9.6 *Benefits from environmental accounting for internal management*

A total of 38.4 per cent of companies answered that they could reduce environmental burden and 35.8 per cent answered that they could reduce environmental costs. In contrast, Figure 9.7 shows the benefits that companies expected to obtain from introducing environmental accounting.

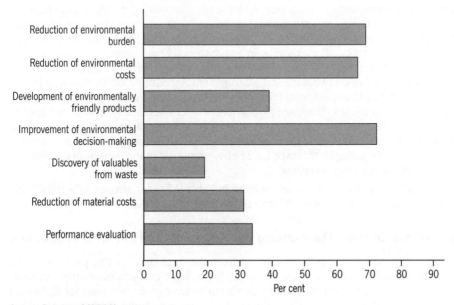

Source: Saio et al (2002)

Figure 9.7 *Potential benefits from environmental accounting that companies expected*

A total of 71.7 per cent of companies expect environmental accounting to be useful to improve environmental decision-making, 67.9 per cent of companies expect to reduce their environmental burden and 66 per cent of companies expect to reduce their environmental costs. A notable difference between Figures 9.6 and 9.7 is the percentage of 'Improvement of environmental decision-making'. This means that there is a strong need for environmental management accounting to support decision-making, which will encourage the practical application of METI environmental accounting tools in the future.

There are a number of future challenges. Under conventional financial accounting rules, when companies invest in environmental impact reduction, corporate costs increase but the benefits of environmental activities are not clearly visible. It is also hard to obtain a picture of the effectiveness of the activities. To make the environmental costs and benefits clearer, the MOE Guidelines have been introduced. One of the features of environmental accounting information in Japan is that a high proportion of companies have introduced MOE-financial accounting style environmental accounting. From the evidence available, corporate environmental accounting information provides a useful basis for stakeholder comparison and analysis between companies. In financial statements, almost all companies use specific data formats, thereby improving the possibilities for comparison of profitability, liquidity, solvency or growth rates among companies. However, at present in environmental accounting, different formats and measures of environmental costs and benefits exist. In addition, many companies measure environmental costs and benefits using the trial-and-error method and caution should be exercised when undertaking comparison and analysis. Also, conventional accounting data consist of articulated flow and stock information. However, so far, environmental accounting information has mainly focused on flows rather than articulation with stock information.

Though 'environmental investment' in Japan is disclosed, this is only in the form of current expenditures, not the capitalized 'stock' amount. This has downside effects because flow information does not make environmental liabilities, accumulated environmental burdens, or environmental assets clear – areas that are of critical importance to management. Such issues are, however, being addressed through international cooperation. For example, in environmental management accounting, the following international networks exist: Environmental Management Accounting Network – Europe (EMAN–Europe), Environmental Management Accounting Network – Asia Pacific (EMAN-AP) and the Environmental Management Accounting Research and Information Center (EMARIC) in the US. These are global networks for the discussion and exchange of information on the international harmonization of environmental accounting. The United Nations Division for Sustainable Development also has an ongoing international experts group designed to promote the take-up of environmental management accounting in developed and developing countries.

Principal stakeholder groups, as outlined in Table 9.2, now also include the Global Reporting Initiative as the foremost attempt to develop sustainability reporting.

Grounds for change: the exciting developments in firm-level economics

Another major barrier for progress arises from the fact that, in the past, business managers and CEOs have been implicitly taught in business and economics schools micro-economics courses that resource productivity savings do not exist (or if they do they are rare). If the business managers of the future are taught that these resource productivity opportunities do not exist then they are not going to spend money on them.

Table 9.2 *Principal stakeholder groups having published standards, regulations, guidelines or recommendations affecting environmental accounting*

Stakeholder group	Affected accounting and chapter	Specifications for accounting	Characteristics
Regulatory bodies			
SEC, USA	Financial Acc.	Very specific	Legal, binding for firms listed on a US stock exchange
DOE Washington	Management Acc.	Very specific	Guideline accompanying a regulation
EU (EMAS/Eco-label)	Site-/Prod.- or Ecol. Acc.	General	Voluntary
Professional accounting and financial analysts' associations			
EFFAS	Fin. Acc./Ext. Ecol. Acc.	Specific	Statement and demand of financial analysts
ACCA	Financial Accounting	Specific	Environmental reporting awards
Australian Society of Certified Practising Accountants	Management Accounting	General	Environmental management
FEE	Financial Accounting	Specific	Framework for environmental reporting, guidelines for external ecological accounting and reporting
Society of Management Accountants of Canada	Management Accounting	Specific	Writing environmental reports
CICA	Conventional Accounting	Specific/general	Statement of professional accountants
Accounting standardization organizations			
IASC	Financial Accounting	Specific	Have not dealt with topic so far
FASB	Financial Accounting	Very specific	Strong influence of SEC
Other standardization organizations			
BSI	Man. Acc.; Ecol. Acc.	General	Focus on environmental management systems
ISO	Man. Acc.; Ecol. Acc.	General	Focus on environmental management systems
Industry			
ICC	Environm. Acc. in general	Very general	Starting point for environmental management
Minerals Industry	Ecological Accounting	Specific	Voluntary code of environmental management
Chemical Industry	Ecolological Acc. in general	Very general	Starting point for environmental management. Responsible Care voluntary codes of conduct

Table 9.2 *continued*

Stakeholder group	Affected accounting and chapter	Specifications for accounting	Characteristics
'Green' organizations			
CERES/GRI	External Ecological Acc.	Very general	Addresses environmental interests of potential investors. Voluntary
SustainAbility	Environmental Reporting	Specific	Provides pro forma categories for assessing environmental reports
WWF	External Ecological Acc.	Specific	Addresses 'green' stakeholders
Scientific certification systems	Product and Ext. Ecol. Acc.	Specific	Addresses 'green' customers
Other international organizations			
UNEP	Environm. Acc. in general	Specific intentions	Addresses corporations in UN-countries
UNCTAD	External Ecological Acc.	General	Environmental performance indicators
UN ISAR	Fin. Acc.; Ext. Ecol. Acc.	Specific	Guidelines for financial and ecological reporting
Tellus Institute	Management Accounting	Specific	Full cost accounting; total cost accounting; green metrics
World Bank	Internal Ecological Acc.	Specific to different sectors (e.g. mining)	Environmental assessment for scenario planning
WRI	Man. Acc.; Ext. Ecol. Acc.,	General	Corporate environmental performance; environmental costs
WBCSD	Goal, Man. Acc.; Ecol. Acc.	General	Eco-efficiency; shareholder value, environmental metrics
OECD	Ecological Accounting	Very general	Addresses multinationals in OECD-countries, eco-efficiency

Source: Schaltegger and Burritt (2000)

Abbreviations
Acc. = Accounting
Ecol. = Ecological
Env. = Environmental
Ext. = External
Fin. = Financial
Man. = Management
Prod. = Product
ACCA = Association of Chartered Certified Accountants (UK)
BSI = British Standards Institute
CERES/GRI = Coalition of Environmentally Responsible Economies/ Global Reporting Initiative
CICA = Canadian Institute of Chartered Accountants
COM = Commission of the European Union
DOE = Department of Ecology
EFFAS = European Federation of Financial Analysts Societies

FEE = Fédération des Experts Comptables Européens
IASC = International Accounting Standards Committee
ICC = International Chamber of Commerce
ISO = International Standards Organization
OECD = Organisation for Economic Co-operation and Development
SEC = Securities and Exchange Commission (US)
UN ISAR = United Nations Intergovernmental Working Group of Experts on International Standards of Accounting and Reporting
UNCTAD = United Nations Conference on Trade and Development
UNEP = United Nations Environment Programme
WBCSD = World Business Council for Sustainable Development
WRI = World Resources Institute
WWF = World Wide Fund For Nature

As late as 1995, economists have argued exactly that, in published peer reviewed journals. The proposition central to this book and many other major works is that there are resource productivity gains, such as energy efficiency, available throughout the economy. In making this assertion we maintain that previously engineers and business managers have either missed these opportunities (through not seeing the whole of system benefits) or they were prevented from implementing best practice due to a lack of time, cost or other regulatory barriers. As Professor Bruce Paton will show, this does not contradict modern micro-economic theory.

Traditional classical micro-economics assumed that the firm maximizes profits by incorporating an optimal mix of labour, capital and other inputs in accordance with a standard production function, using fixed technologies freely available to all industry participants. It assumed that under perfect competition any inefficiencies will be eliminated. Under these assumptions, efforts to reduce pollution would be expected to add costs to an idealized firm which had already maximized its profits through implementing all cost effective cost cutting strategies. The highly stylized picture of the firm in conventional micro-economic analysis denies what may be the most significant motivation for pursuing sustainable development strategies, namely eliminating economic inefficiencies within the firm. Interface Ltd started on its journey to sustainable development through a raft of new eco-efficiencies that are saving the company significant dollars. Thus allowing for research and development (R&D) and innovations in process, cultural change and whole system design.

Classical micro-economic theory that assumes that firms maximize profits and that they operate in perfectly competitive markets cannot explain the success of private initiatives or voluntary government partnership eco-efficiency initiatives. Such has been the success of eco-efficiencies that many governments now have programmes to assist industry to develop eco-efficiency strategies as part of their broad portfolio to assist their respective industries to be internationally competitive. In Australia numerous businesses have reaped the benefits of joining the Australian Greenhouse Office's Greenhouse Challenge, which offers advice and expertise to assist business to identify win–win ways to reduce greenhouse gas emissions. As the Australian Government wrote: 'There is an ever increasing need for industry to address sustainability and energy issues cost effectively to enhance their domestic and international competitiveness.' As a result of this understanding, governments are increasingly providing programmes with online resources to help implement these changes in business, with everything from freely downloadable Environmental Management Systems to databases on eco-efficiency techniques for many industries.

To this end, the Australian Government's Department of Industry, Tourism and Resources has run a five-year programme, in partnership with industry, to implement Energy Efficiency Best Practice. The lessons they learnt, plus significant databases of relevant information are now being reported online so that any company can reproduce similar results themselves. The programme began in partnership with the beverage and packaging sectors. It was so successful that it was applied across other sectors where it re-defined best practice in energy management by providing a fresh approach to this issue. The programme recognized from day one that energy problems and opportunities are often complex and multifaceted. Making progress frequently required the participation of a range of business stakeholders, new thinking to address old problems and, finally, sensitivity to negotiate an organization's cultural characteristics in order to achieve real outcomes.

For large-scale energy projects (see Table 9.3), an organizational development programme called Best Practice People and Processes was conducted, the aim of which was to build capacity within companies, so they can apply and sustain effective energy management programmes. The programme recognized the need to address both

Table 9.3 *Sample of big energy projects under the Energy Efficiency Best Practice government programme*

Site	Core business	Elements of the programme	Key quantifiable outcomes
Barrett Burston Malting (Geelong, Victoria and across sites nationally)	Malt manufacture	BEP (new plant with focus on heating/cooling) BPPP modules: refrigeration compressed air, BEP outcomes workshop	Savings across six sites within the year to December 2001 yielded an improved energy consumption of around 50,000Gj of combined gas and electricity savings, whilst maintaining product quality. Total operational costs bettered budget by 12%, with savings in excess of 20% in one malt house. The improved trend is being continued to this day in all six plants. Significant savings identified for the Geelong site and future Greenfield sites with the potential to reduce greenhouse gas emissions by 43%.
Amcor Packaging Thomastown, Victoria	Bottle closure manufacturing	BPPP modules: energy management team	In the first phase, a 'changeover' project was identified by the team, resulting in a productivity increase with a sales value of AU$330,000 annually.
Amcor Packaging, Dandenong, Victoria	Aluminium can manufacturing	BPPP modules: energy management	Efficiency of one gas fired oven has been improved by 25%, with a saving of 4Gj per hour as well as reliability and productivity benefits. A power factor correction project has been identified that will yield savings of AU$17,000 per year. A compressed air optimization project has identified savings of AU$46,000 per year.
Bakers Delight, Mascot, Sydney	Bakery	BEP: designed a Showcase Bakery	The project achieved 32% savings in annual energy costs and 48% reduction in greenhouse emissions per year compared to a standard Bakers Delight bakery. The project also led to improvements in waste minimization, water conservation and purchasing energy from renewable sources.

Source: Summary of various documents of the Australian Government's Department of Industry, Tourism and Resources

technical and organizational issues in order to achieve practical ways to improve energy efficiency. The programme assisted businesses to develop a process tailored to their needs with 'innovation workshops' and customized training modules. The main outcome of these workshops was the development of a cross-functional, site-based energy management team, that identifies and develops a business implementation plan for potentially energy efficient projects. Again, this involved workshops and tailored training modules with a strong emphasis on both addressing internal communication issues that limit the implementation of energy efficiency initiatives; and encouraging a pro-active response to addressing internal cultural barriers. The department then provided follow-up meetings or assistance through consultation.

The trial of these workshops in the beverage sector involved three brewing companies: Barrett Burston Malting, Carlton & United Breweries and Lion Nathan. The team from Barrett Burston Malting examined ways to more efficiently cool and dry barley during the malting process, leading to realistic energy efficiency options for both existing and Greenfield sites. The Carlton & United team found new ways to make their refrigeration more efficient by identifying that it had previously been operating at a greater capacity than was required. Lion Nathan found ways to make its pasteurization processes more energy efficient with a view to replacing its system at one of its key plants.

> *In a global marketplace, where companies must not just identify, but jump on all opportunities to enhance their international competitiveness, it is impressive to see the level of innovation that has been shown by the companies involved in this project. They are successful examples of how a completely fresh approach can lead to cost savings, lower greenhouse gas emissions and a range of other business benefits.*
>
> Hon Ian MacFarlane, MP, Minister for Industry, Tourism and Resources, Australia

Government eco-efficiency programmes can be especially helpful for small to medium sized businesses, which make up a significant percentage of the business sector in any country. Fields like energy efficiency are moving so fast that if firms have not checked what is best practice within six months they will probably be out of date. Most small businesses do not have the time or resources to source the best information let alone the funds. It makes sense then for governments to address these information and market failures to help them implement resource productivity programmes wisely. Therefore, increasingly, OECD countries are running numerous government programmes, business clusters and online databases to assist any business to improve their present situation.

According to Dr John Cole, Queensland EPA, Sustainable Industries Division Executive Director, the wide variety of good news stories in Queensland demonstrate that 'the means of improving environmental sustainability is often remarkably obvious, remarkably simple and remarkably beneficial to the bottom line of businesses that embrace them' (see Table 9.4).

Table 9.4 *Sample of projects underway in Queensland supported by the* EPA, *Sustainable Industries Division*

Case study	Description
Industry Partnership – Sustainable Urban Development Program (Project information and information on the Sustainable Urban Development Program can be found on the UDIA and EPA website.)	Through a partnership with the EPA, the Urban Development Institute of Australia – Queensland (UDIA) has established the Sustainable Urban Development Program (SUDP) to encourage continued improvements in development projects. The programme advocates a collaborative approach to identify issues and find solutions in a positive, proactive and timely manner, benefiting all stakeholders. Launched in 2002, 25 projects were submitted by the development industry for consideration and champion projects were then chosen on the basis of the range of initiatives they incorporated to deliver triple-bottom-line outcomes. The partnership considers that the selected projects will provide practical demonstrations of the viability of sustainable development and set a high benchmark for future development.
Paddock to Plate – Sustainability in Meat Production	Australian Country Choice (ACC) an integrated livestock producer and meat processor, and one of Queensland's largest privately owned companies. The Queensland EPA , Meat and Livestock Australia and the United Nations Environment Programme (UNEP) are assisting ACC to implement an industry best practice environmental strategy over a ten-year period. Winning the 2002 Queensland Primary Industry Achievement Award for its environmental stewardship, ACC has developed an eco-efficiency programme that aims to decrease operating costs whilst also reducing environmental impacts. Paul Gibson, ACC Manager for Research and Development, explains that 'this strategic programme will eventually measure and monitor environmental impacts over the whole product life cycle, making a direct connection between eco-sustainability and long-term profitability'. ACC is keen to communicate what it has learned with other agribusinesses, so that they can share the benefits and help Australian industry to lead the world in moving towards sustainable meat production. According to Gibson, 'We anticipate others will take what we've done and improve it further still – the benefits are tangible for anyone wishing to implement an environmental management programme'.
Eco-efficiency in the Food Industry	The EPA joined with the UNEP Working Group for Cleaner Production, the Australian Water Association and eight local governments to produce a booklet called *Eco-Efficient Food! Save Money While Saving the Environment*. This guide shows restaurants, cafes, hotels, clubs and fast food outlets how businesses can become more eco-efficient and save money; providing an efficient service to customers while using less energy, less water and producing less waste. With one of the key resources for food-related business being water, the publication provides readers with facts and simple calculations on what savings can be achieved.

Efficiency gains within firms under voluntary environmental initiatives*
Bruce Paton

Porter hypothesis and the energy efficiency gap debate

Conventional economic theory cannot readily explain the success of private initiatives or voluntary public policies to increase eco-efficiency. Under conventional economic assumptions, firms should not be able to improve their environmental performance without lowering their profits.

Two contemporary debates in energy and environmental policy – concerning the 'Porter hypothesis' that we alluded to earlier and the 'energy efficiency gap' – focus on the potential for voluntary environmental initiatives to improve economic efficiency within the firm, and the barriers preventing many companies from addressing these opportunities. The Porter hypothesis, alluded to earlier in the introduction to Section 2, argues that the relationship between environmental improvements (including energy conservation) and economic efficiency has been improperly framed as a conflict.[35] Under the Porter hypothesis, companies acting to improve their environmental performance may, under appropriate circumstances, simultaneously increase profits. Similarly, economic inefficiencies imbedded in organizations provide opportunities for appropriately designed policy interventions to improve economic efficiency, while simultaneously improving environmental performance. Porter and van der Linde detailed evidence from a wide range of industries to indicate that firms often gain competitive advantage from their efforts to improve environmental performance. Since the publication of their papers, there has been extensive evidence published to further back up this hypothesis.[36] The key element of Porter and van der Linde's argument is the concept of product and process offsets. These are product or process innovations, resulting from resource productivity improvements, that provide the firm with positive net returns. Product improvement offsets occur when resource productivity improvements increase revenues through product differentiation or reduce costs either on product inputs or reducing customers' costs – for instance by lowering product-related waste disposal or energy costs. Process offsets occur when environmental improvements reduce costs by raising process yields, reducing machine downtime and maintenance or reducing the cost of process inputs. Porter and van der Linde argue that 'offsets will be common because reducing pollution is often coincident with improving the productivity with which resources are used'.

Palmer et al[37] counter Porter and van der Linde's empirical studies with a model that predicts that such inefficiencies should be relatively rare. Palmer et al's model is a classic example of how the assumptions of an economic model inevitably lead to a certain conclusion. Palmer et al adopt the conventional micro-economic assumptions that firms maximize profits and that they operate in perfectly competitive markets. Under these assumptions, a firm cannot reduce emissions without raising marginal costs. The importance of Palmer et al's work is that it identifies (correctly) a key assumption, that the validity of the Porter hypothesis rests on 'pre-existing opportunities for cost savings or profitable product enhancements that have, for some reason, gone unrealized'. Such unrealized efficiencies should not be significant under the traditional micro-economic assumptions of profit maximization and perfect competition, but, as many have found, they appear to be pervasive in actual practice.

The energy efficiency gap is the second important debate in this area. It focuses on the unrealized opportunities to reduce energy consumption that persist in companies. This debate seeks to understand why many individuals and firms forgo energy-saving investments with potentially high positive rates of return[38] while others undertake energy efficient investments and achieve significant cost savings. This work is important because there should not be a different response to the same economic opportunities if firms' behaviour fit the conventional economic assumptions. The energy efficiency gap literature has focused on barriers to change that inhibit firms from undertaking energy-saving investments with potentially high positive rates of return. This literature identifies behavioural barriers arising from principal–agent problems, other information asymmetries, and bounded rationality.[39]

The debate over the energy efficiency gap is fundamentally important to current debate concerning the potential economic impacts of policies to reduce global greenhouse emissions.[40] Top-down economic modelling estimates, based on conventional micro-economic assumptions, assume that existing energy demand patterns are optimally adjusted to prevailing market prices. As a result, 'reductions in greenhouse gas emissions can only be purchased at the expense of a reduction in the output of other goods and services'. Therefore, under conventional micro-economic assumptions, policy measures to increase energy efficiency must harm the economy. On the other hand, bottom-up technological, engineering approaches recognize barriers that may have inhibited firms from taking advantage of potentially profitable energy-saving opportunities. Bottom-up estimates typically predict that policy initiatives can induce reductions in energy consumption. As a result, bottom-up estimates typically suggest less economic disruption from programmes to reduce global greenhouse gas reductions. The controversies over the Porter hypothesis and the energy efficiency gap illustrate the critical role of underlying assumptions about economic efficiency within firms in the formulation of environmental policy. In recent years, these same assumptions have become the focus of very extensive debates on the economic theory of the firm. Fortunately, we now have far more advanced economic modelling, that does factor in the energy efficiency opportunities, when modelling the impacts of reducing greenhouse emissions on the economy. These will be discussed in detail in Section 4.

New micro-economic perspectives on efficiency within the firm

Mainstream economic theory has evolved significantly in recent years in ways that can accommodate potential inefficiencies, but these changes have not yet been incorporated effectively into environmental policy debates. Updating environmental economics to address these recent advances can greatly enrich the ability of this field to explain current innovations in practice. This will be done in Section 3 of the book. Several different lines of inquiry, in micro-economic theory, technological change and economic modelling, help to explain why firms may fail to maximize profits. We covered some of the issues around technological change and economic modelling in the introduction to this Section, so here we will just cover the line of inquiry from micro-economic theory in detail. Advances in micro-economic theory have begun to relax some basic assumptions of conventional theory, in ways that leave room for inefficiencies within firms. Kreps argues that a 'somewhat revolutionary shift in the economic paradigm has begun', based on a partial abandonment of three 'canonical principles':[41]

1   Farsighted rationality.
2   Purposeful behaviour.
3   Equilibrium.

These principles have allowed economists to build a powerful system of deductive reasoning to predict or explain the behaviour of firms and markets. Modifying or abandoning these 'canonical principles' has become necessary to increase the ability of economic theory to predict or explain commonly observed economic behaviours. In short it provides a richer picture. One result of these recent advances has been to provide potential explanations for inefficiencies within firms that eco-efficiencies, whole system design and lean thinking can exploit.

1 The far-sighted rationality assumption. This requires that each economic actor base his or her actions on a 'detailed probabilistic picture of the future'. Teece argues that this 'rational' behaviour really constitutes super- or hyper-rational thinking.[42] Behavioural arguments suggest that relaxing the far-sighted rationality assumption allows us to incorporate human cognitive limits into calculations concerning decision-making.[43] These limits may include systematic biases, simple errors, and behaviours motivated by political rather than economic rationality. This allows us to take into account the simple fact that business decisions are often made without perfect information. If you do not know how to implement eco-efficient, whole system design or lean thinking approaches, the chances are you won't do it.

2 The purposeful behaviour assumption. This assumption requires that each economic actor 'acts purposefully, to achieve a well-defined goal'. Relaxing this assumption permits the firm to be considered as a collection of partially aligned interests, rather than a single, monolithic actor capable of acting purposefully. The Australian Department of Industry Tourism and Resources Energy Efficiency Best Practice programme found cases in which a lack of communication led to reduced efficiency. For instance, one of the dairy companies was producing a third more steam than needed on average, simply because those in the boiler room thought it was their job to produce at all times enough steam for peak usage periods. Requiring staff to ring the boiler room ahead of time to inform them when they would need extra steam is now saving this firm over 30 per cent of its energy usage.

In other words problems in vertical coordination, excessive hierarchy and the communication problems that go with it, within a firm, may create barriers to change. Leibenstein suggests that hierarchy is effective in adjusting the firm to outside pressures, but only up to a point.[44] Pressure from the top often limits the issues that members of the organization choose to focus on. Directives from top management to focus on issues such as growing market share and nothing else, can prevent an organization from focusing their efforts on potential savings from more efficient consumption of energy or other resources. BP have started to address these issues globally by reducing the number of levels within BP from 30 to four, making BP globally far more responsive to change and opportunities. Problems in *horizontal coordination* within a firm may also limit its ability to achieve its intended purposes. For example, differences in priorities and incentives and competition for budgets among research and development, marketing and manufacturing functions, often inhibit the design of environmentally sound products.[45]

Voluntary initiatives by governments can focus attention on opportunities to improve both economic and environmental performance by helping to overcome these problems in horizontal and vertical coordination. Some initiatives succeed by focusing senior management attention on specific opportunities.[46] Other initiatives, for example ISO 14001, may help to coordinate the actions of different functions within the firm.

3 The equilibrium assumption. This assumes that all parties adopt their best alternatives, given that all actors will do the same. Relaxing this assumption allows researchers to explore industry dynamics that cannot be described adequately by static equilibrium assumptions.[47] This allows economists to create models closer to what actually happens. These models include the following assumptions about the actors:

- First, the management team for each firm must attempt to optimize the mix of technologies, marketing programmes, and production schedules to compete for current business.
- Second, it must choose an appropriate portfolio of investments in research and development, market research, process development, and capacity development to prepare to compete in future time periods. Different firms are likely to hold diverse beliefs about consumer desires and competitor strategies for future time periods.
- Finally, each firm must calculate the appropriate investments in environmental performance improvement and energy efficiencies to meet customer and investor expectations in future time periods.

As a result of these complex requirements, calculating the most efficient mix of current and future product offerings and production schedules is beyond human computational abilities. In response to this challenge, firms experiment and adjust offerings and production schedules iteratively. Firms often choose a better way but not the best way forward, as there will be potentially more efficient solutions outside their experience and beliefs. This applies equally to decisions about organizational structures and processes, research and development opportunities, energy efficiency and environmental performance. Industries that are not aware of the best solutions can be enormously wasteful in other ways.[48] The pressure on each individual firm to move innovations quickly to market reduces the ability of management to focus on many efficiency-improving moves, including efforts to conserve energy or reduce pollutant emissions.

All of these recent advances provide explanations, consistent with modern economic theory, for the persistence of inefficiencies within firms. In this emerging view, firms are incapable of finding the best way to maximize profits for many reasons, and instead tend to find better ways forward. Firms clearly seek profits, but the cognitive limits of their managers, and the massive complexity inherent in developing the optimum configuration prevent them from achieving an optimal outcome. Although many firms fail in such an environment, market competition is not always strong enough to eliminate firms that are significantly less efficient than the industry leaders. Evidence from research on evolutionary game theory suggests that very strong selective pressures may be necessary to eliminate inefficient behaviours.[49] Under these conditions, opportunities for firms to harbour inefficiencies abound. Relaxing the key assumptions of conventional micro-economic theory now allows economists to provide potentially valuable methods for approximating the efficiency frontier against which the efficiency of actual firms could be estimated.

Voluntary environmental initiatives can be powerful tools for focusing management attention on opportunities for simultaneously improving energy efficiency, environmental performance and economic efficiency. Elimination of internal inefficiencies cannot, however, explain all of the successful voluntary environmental initiatives that have emerged over the past decade. Some initiatives, such as European negotiated agreements, appear to have succeeded primarily because they reduced inefficiencies in the interactions between industries and regulators. Others, such as the Energy Star Office Products programme[50] appear to have succeeded by helping to overcome coordination problems within industries. However, the recent advances in economic theory described above suggest that inefficiencies within firms are likely to be common and economically significant. Integrating these recent advances in micro-economic theory into environmental economics can greatly enrich the ability of this field to understand current innovations in practice and to make significant contributions to the design and evaluation of efficiency-enhancing initiatives by public, private and non-government actors.[51]

CHAPTER 10

OPERATIONALIZING NATURAL ADVANTAGE THROUGH THE SUSTAINABILITY HELIX

The business case for sustainability

The last three decades have been difficult for many firms. No sooner do governments set environmental standards than communities demand higher standards. Business leaders believe that there is an inherent trade-off between environmental quality and economic production; that activists do not respect this; and that the goalposts keep shifting. One of the best reasons for a company to commit to increasing its sustainability is that it is the best way to avoid this dilemma. Once firms adopt a sustainability orientation, the shifting challenges become a rationale for continual improvement leading to mutually reinforcing environmental and economic outcomes: that is, to sustainable development.

So far, in this section, we have demonstrated why companies should achieve both pioneering and systemic change, and how many are doing so. The arguments for the adoption of sustainable development practices are becoming increasingly clear to business. A further indication of this commitment is shown by the number of organizations that are members of the International Chamber of Commerce (ICC) (2300 and growing), and have signed the 'Business Charter for Sustainable Development'. ICC members include such corporations as Norsk Hydro, Deloitte & Touche, Akzo Nobel and Xerox.[1] Increasingly, the focus of the international business community is on the challenge of finding genuine solutions to the problems of development. At the core of sustainable development is the concept of resource productivity and ensuring that resources are used to benefit society. We have shown how doing this can lower costs; reduce hazards through designing out toxics and carcinogens; and build brand equity. Firms that adopt sustainable development as a core principle are strategically positioning themselves to achieve lasting competitive advantage by:

- staying ahead of government regulations, broader societal changes and community expectations;
- capitalizing on an increasing number of market-based mechanisms, such as cap and trade schemes for greenhouse gas emissions, i.e. the Chicago Climate Exchange and the European Climate Exchange; and
- foreseeing and avoiding major threats and adapting to major societal changes through applying Porter's 5 Forces Model with the latest consensus on the potential sixth force as outlined in this section.

This section has shown that there is much that business can do in the coming century to increase competitive advantage in ways that are complimentary to the environment and the world's communities. As the understanding of the challenge broadens, so too does the realization that we all have a role to play: both as individuals and as a members of the various teams we are involved with. The work in this section, along with the growing volume of international material on this subject, suggests that, for firms, it is clear that sustainability needs to be implemented under the following activity streams:

- governance and management;
- operations and facilities;
- design and process innovation;
- human resource development and corporate culture;
- marketing and communications; and
- partnerships and stakeholder engagement.

The management helix for the sustainable organization (Sustainability Helix)

In an attempt to both understand and strategically communicate how business can become more sustainable, our team has taken these streams and woven them together to form the management helix for the sustainable organization (Sustainability Helix), shown in Figure 10.1. Unlike a 'roadmap' that is both anthropocentric and in many cases focused on a linear progression, a helix was chosen to show that the interactions between the various streams are complex and interactive. The biological nature of the helix reflects that each stream is important and ongoing, and that each of the streams provides an important platform for increasing competitiveness. Recognizing that changing any process that is set up to turn a profit is going to, in many cases, reduce profit, the helix provides a way forward to achieve systemic changes profitably. For example, capturing opportunities such as the low hanging fruit that is so abundant in our currently wasteful industrial economy can provide an opportunity to run a dual track transition. This means that, as a firm begins to hunt for opportunities to improve efficiency, these gains can be used to invest in the innovation that can enhance the sustainability of the overall process.

The Sustainability Helix is supported at each stage of each of the activity streams by a detailed set of methodologies, frameworks, strategies and tools. The helix process and supporting taxonometric programme matrix combine to provide an operational tool for business that can be implemented from day one through to the process of becoming a sustainable corporation. This process will be the topic of the upcoming publication *Sustainable Business Practice: The Fieldguide to Natural Capitalism*, being developed by a collaboration of international leaders and organizations that are pooling their experience to create a consensus on how best to guide businesses through the challenge of actually implementing sustainable business practice and delivering results to both stakeholders and shareholders. Lead editors of the publication will include this book's lead editors Karlson 'Charlie' Hargroves and Michael H. Smith, along with Hunter Lovins and Christopher Juniper of Natural Capitalism Inc. in collaboration with Walter Link of Global Academy and Fiona Waterhouse and John Cronin from the TBATI Group. The development of the publication will draw on material developed by Natural Capitalism Inc. based on learnings from the process of working with companies to implement natural capitalism. In addition, the development of content will be supported by contributions from the members, partners and mentors of The Natural Edge Project, including Alan AtKisson, Janine Benyus, Roger Burritt, Sasha Courville, Phillip Sutton, Chris Ryan, Professor Masayoshi Takahashi and others.[2]

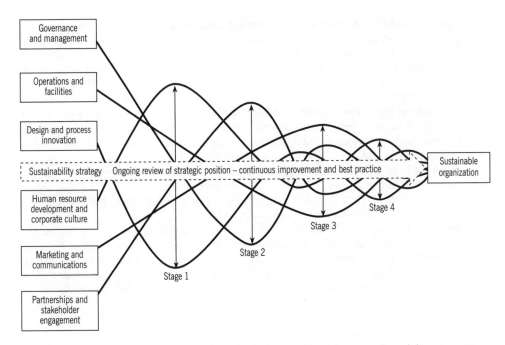

Governance and management

Operations and facilities

Design and process innovation

Sustainability strategy   Ongoing review of strategic position – continuous improvement and best practice

Sustainable organization

Human resource development and corporate culture

Marketing and communications

Partnerships and stakeholder engagement

Stage 1

Stage 2

Stage 3

Stage 4

Note: A mutually reinforcing process to achieve lasting competitive advantage through lowering cost and differentiating products and services while delivering genuinely sustainable progress.
Source: The Natural Edge Project and Natural Capitalism Solutions

Figure 10.1 *Management helix for the sustainable organization* (Sustainability Helix)

The Sustainability Helix has been developed to enable organizations around the world to develop and implement a strategy to enhance their competitive advantage and increase profits through increasing the sustainability of their operations. It will provide the next level of detail for what an organization actually does 'on Monday morning' to implement such principles as those of natural capitalism. Each of the helix's six streams are important and will interact in some way with the others; however, the priority and attention paid to a particular stream may vary over time. This interaction and synergy will be managed through the development of a sustainability strategy to ensure ongoing assessment of strategic positioning and the implementation of best practice and continual improvement.

Sustainable Business Practice: The Fieldguide to Natural Capitalism

The *Fieldguide* presents a whole-system approach, expanding on the ideas presented in this book and other leading books, such as *Natural Capitalism: Creating the Next Industrial Revolution*, together with a wide array of new and emerging material. Although the focus of the publication will be on business development, it will also highlight potential policy implications and identify opportunities for government to underpin and assist business in moving towards sustainability. This will, therefore, making this book a primer for businesses, governments and individuals alike to implement the best sustainable business practices.

The concept for the *Fieldguide* features three main sections:

1   **Achieving Natural Advantage: An Emerging Consensus** will contain a description of how the emerging frameworks and methodologies are building an international consensus. It will include a re-framing of the principles of natural capitalism specifically for a business audience, showing both how the human dimension can be considered and how natural advantage can be achieved through their implementation along with a selection of other leading sustainability frameworks.

2   **Unleashing Your Firm's Natural Advantage** will present the helix as a means for integrating tools, frameworks and principles such as natural capitalism into existing organizational management techniques. Making a transition to sustainability is not a linear process that can be mechanically followed like a roadmap. It requires an integrated whole-systems strategy to capture the synergies. Running throughout the helix is the core activity of strategy: it can be considered an overarching element or even a seventh stream. The purpose of the strategy is to build sustainability into the DNA of a business as its central organizing principle.

3   **What do You do on Monday Morning?** will present a programme to strategically implement the detail behind the helix's activity streams, focusing on specific tools for implementation and how they impact a company's transition to sustainability. The step by step programme matrix will provide a practical tool to guide a company as it follows the helix's six streams, through four levels of increasing commitment to sustainability.

Sustainability strategy

*   *Rationale*: A coherent strategy is necessary to guide a company as it undertakes to explore the opportunities that new sustainable practices and products can offer in enhancing competitive advantage. The development of a sustainability strategy will enable a company to set a clear vision for its future, define what sustainability will mean for it, integrate the human dimensions of sustainability, and set long-term indicators of success.
*   *Actions*: The strategic process will explore future business constraints and opportunities such as access to resources; knowledge management and technology mapping; responsibilities for the life cycle impacts of products and services; and the costs of doing business in a carbon constrained world. It will ensure that measures are in place to exceed compliance with laws, regulations and the business' own operating policies, and to build on existing business planning and auditing activities.
*   *Benefits*: A sustainability strategy helps to protect and enhance business reputation; enables a company to exceed compliance; allocates accountability, capturing of new markets; and providing assurances to shareholders and regulators that the business is being managed effectively.

The six streams

Stream 1: Governance and management
*   *Rationale*: Corporate governance in the 21st century requires a broad set of management tools and processes to ensure that companies not only prosper economically, but are also socially and environmentally responsible. This section will guide management in framing and implementing best practice in management systems to achieve the goals of a sustainability strategy.
*   *Actions*: The stream will describe how to manage: the implementation of the strategy; ethical considerations; systems for environmental management and sustainability accounting; financial issues; project development systems; issues of risk and shareholder value management; compliance issues; legal implications; intellectual property considerations; and corporate relations. It will describe the roles of such

tools as the Global Reporting Initiative, SA 8000, ISO 14001, life cycle assessment and many more.
- *Benefits*: Practitioners will be able to integrate sustainability into existing and emerging management systems, develop sustainability analyses for new projects, account for the benefits and costs of sustainability measures and make transparent public commitments for sustainability performance.

Stream 2: Operations and facilities
- *Rationale*: There is an enormous scope for improving the efficiency and effectiveness of most business practices and operations and in doing so to reduce costs and external impacts. A well recognized suite of tools now exists to offer greater profitability for business through reducing material and energy inputs, waste and pollution, and minimizing health risks to employees and customers.
- *Actions*: The stream will describe how to implement tools associated with activities such as eco-efficiency, lean thinking, waste reduction, dematerialization and biological designs for sustainability. Such tools can improve efficiency, effectiveness and product quality while reducing the costs of manufacturing and production, transportation and facility management and meeting the challenges of a carbon constrained world. Using wastes as productive inputs and providing products as a service, rather than selling the product itself, can offer superior enhancements to a business model. Managing facilities more effectively can increase worker productivity and dramatically improve sustainability and financial performance, whilst reducing impacts on nature and society.
- *Benefits*: This stream will provide a comprehensive guide to capturing the opportunities described above. Reducing the costs and risks associated with materials use, energy, water, toxins, waste and packaging, whilst simultaneously increasing profitability and identifying and capitalizing on new processes, technologies and approaches can enable a company to better meet customer needs and deliver shareholder value.

Stream 3: Design and process innovation
- *Rationale*: The capacity of an organization to innovate has always been a strong source of competitive advantage, and is becoming increasingly important for survival in an information-based global world. Businesses that can rapidly translate customer needs into new or improved products and services, in light of constraints (present or anticipated), reap the benefits of first mover advantage. Whole systems thinking, eco-innovation, green design or design for sustainability based on such elegant frameworks as biomimicry, cradle-to-cradle and lean thinking, can offer new opportunities for businesses to leverage their knowledge and unleash the creativity of their staff. Such innovations can drive the re-design and innovation of new designs and processes to produce new and improved products and services.
- *Actions*: This stream will describe how to create a culture of innovation; catalyse and manage the development of new processes and products; spin-off new technologies or new businesses; increase or augment product life cycles; meet the requirements of eco-labelling schemes; and overcome market barriers through product or systems certification.
- *Benefits*: Practitioners will be able to enhance their capacity for achieving eco-innovation; for increasing the effectiveness of process and activities to increase revenues through charging a premium for first mover differentiated products or services; and for spinning-off new products and services.

Stream 4: Human resource development and corporate culture
- *Rationale*: Sustainability strategies often dramatically improve productivity by creating healthier and more inspiring workplaces; fostering feedback and employee contributions to continuous improvement; encouraging strategic risk-taking cultures; improving knowledge of global developments and technological advances; and aligning corporate goals with long-term societal and personal values.
- *Actions*: This stream will describe how to enhance human resource development systems and shift corporate cultures to support the sustainability success, drawing on best practice internationally including the work of Professor Masayoshi Takahashi and colleagues through the Strategy-Driven Human Productivity Development programme. Positive corporate cultural changes, including whole systems thinking, sustainability-based employee and value chain incentives can enable a company to overcome the short-term mentality that has, in many cases, led to unsustainable behaviour. Achieving this requires a systematic approach to recruitment/retention, diversity, training, reward systems, leadership development and stakeholder partnerships. Tools and frameworks such as self-organizing systems, employee ownership, human productivity improvement tools, strategic choice frameworks, and external engagement tools can all increase the human capital and improve a company's relation to its host community.
- *Benefits*: Practitioners will be able to create a work environment in which people feel engaged, have ownership of the success of the business, and are inspired by tangible attempts to improve sustainability performance (i.e. reduce environmental and social impacts). Companies that have done this find that it is crucial for attracting and retaining the best employees and for creating a platform on which to capitalize upon competitive opportunities and respond quickly to increasing community expectations and tightening government regulations.

Stream 5: Marketing and communications
- *Rationale*: Competitive advantage arises out of the value that a firm continues to provide to its customers. Trust is now an underpinning value between an organization and its consumers, and sustainability offers opportunities for businesses to strengthen their competitive advantage by meeting customer needs to feel good about their consumption choices.
- *Actions*: This stream will show readers how to leverage sustainability activities to achieve a superior corporate relations position. Key strategies include external stakeholder engagement, internal communications and tracking systems, transparency, new market exploration and development, and compliance with emerging reporting standards. This strengthens the market position through responding to Porter's 5 Forces, being the defence against the threat of new entrants, the bargaining power of buyers, rivalry among existing firms, substitute products or services and the bargaining power of suppliers.
- *Tools*: Tools such as brand development and management; business model analysis; Porter's 5 Forces analysis; business reputation management; business life cycle assessment; and product life cycle assessment will be explored.
- *Benefits*: Practitioners will be able to develop strategies for: mitigating the threat of new entrants by changing the basis for competition on sustainability grounds; meeting or getting ahead of distribution channel pressure for improved environmental performance; and positioning themselves as more conscious of, and responsive to, sustainability than their rivals.

Stream 6: Partnerships and stakeholder engagement
- *Rationale*: In order to remain competitive in a market growing in complexity, an organization must take advantage of developing relationships, partnerships and

alliances with a range of other organizations, institutions and groups within society. Through actively building partnerships, businesses can innovate and market themselves in ways not possible on their own, such as through partnering with government programmes; forming active partnerships with 'green', human rights and other community groups; getting products or services independently verified to build credibility; developing incentives for the supply chain; and accessing new markets through flexible networks and other appropriate systems.

- *Actions*: This stream will describe the benefits of companies taking part in a whole of society approach through a range of partnerships and alliances. Many companies have found great value through partnerships with a range of groups and institutions that foster supportive relationships. Specific strategies and techniques to develop and nurture partnerships and alliances are central to sustainability's competitive advantages.
- *Tools*: Tools such as partnership development and community engagement techniques; industry cluster development processes (cross sector and through supply chains); multi-stakeholder engagement processes; systems of innovation (broad and narrow); and methods to deal with individual and multiple groups of partners and stakeholders.
- *Benefits*: Practitioners will be able to develop their own strategies, first for engaging in and benefiting from multi-stakeholder engagement processes including; broad systems of innovation, competitive advantage, risk mitigation management, formation of new institutions, creation of innovative regulation, sustainability capacity building and educational systems and workforce development. And second, in the development of strategy for external stakeholders that can help, or hinder the company such as NGOs and activists, research and innovation resources, suppliers, industry colleagues and competitors, communities, governments and educational systems.

The four stages

Many companies will consider the realm of sustainability and see opportunities that they wish to cherry-pick. They may choose to implement one or another of the programmes outlined in this approach, without initially adopting a comprehensive strategy. This is obviously a valid option, but should not be considered as a sustainability strategy. Some companies that have done this have subsequently reconsidered and undertaken a more comprehensive strategy after seeing that sustainability offers numerous benefits. Similarly, the approach outlined here is not the only possible one. A company can tailor these activities in many combinations with varying levels of interaction between the streams. The flexibility of the model allows the range of activities listed in the programme matrix to have varying levels of importance and activity over time. In short, the sustainabilty helix and programme matrix offer a company the ability to produce a mutually reinforcing process to achieve lasting competitive advantage, lower costs and differentiate its products and services while delivering genuinely sustainable outcomes. The helix will be of great benefit to a company that has decided that the concept of sustainability has something to offer. At Stage 1 the company is interested in exploring the opportunities that sustainability may offer and the business case for making a commitment to it. Implementation is typically limited to the exploration of the potential of sustainability. In Stages 2–4 the commitment goes beyond exploration to pilot projects to the systemic implementation of more sustainable practices in the various business units. In the latter stages, the company takes a public leadership role in its industry and the global business community.

Stage 1: Explore the sustainability opportunity

The willingness to embark on the sustainability journey typically arises when a change agent within the company has determined that this is a process worth exploring. The work of this stage is to develop an understanding of what sustainability is (to the company), and to then explore the value of sustainability to the mission and business model of the company. This includes an exploration of what other companies are doing and how a commitment to sustainability can add core business value to the operation. The tasks listed do not all have to be conducted at once, but are likely to be necessary at the point at which a company is ready to make a commitment to sustainability.

Stage 2: Testing the business case: key initiatives and pilot projects

At this stage, the company becomes willing to make a commitment to operating in more sustainable ways. It frames an internal definition of what sustainability means to it and sets a vision of what operating in a more sustainable manner would look like. The company undertakes to commit resources to set clear indicators of success, assess its social and environmental impacts, and prove through the pilot projects the validity of the business case for sustainability. The stage is characterized by a quiet learning mode of implementation through experimentation, capacity building and development and testing of internal tools and procedures to use resources more efficiently, improve the design of products and processes, and manage the company in more sustainable ways. The goal is to use these pioneering efforts to make the case for committing to a whole systems approach.

Stage 3: Sustainability leadership

At this stage, the company has assured itself that there is a strong business case for sustainability and is ready to make a systemic commitment to behave responsibly towards the planet and society through its operations and influence. In this stage a company implements its sustainability strategy throughout its operations, activities and its value chain. It builds upon its responsibility to enhance shareholder value by taking a public leadership role within its industry and the world at large. Public commitments perpetuate momentum towards minimizing its impacts on natural and human capital, and beginning to behave in ways that reinvest in all forms of capital.

Stage 4: A restorative company

At this stage, a company is in a position to ensure that a high level of competitive advantage has been realized through integration of sustainability concepts, methodologies and processes into business practice. By the end of this level, the goal is for the company to be become a truly sustainable corporation. Through its activities, the company restores human and natural capital, maximizes shareholder value and finds its rightful place in the whole of society in which business, civil society, government and all other stakeholders contribute to achieving genuine progress.

SECTION 3

ACHIEVING A NATURAL ADVANTAGE OF NATIONS

CHAPTER 11

THE ROLE OF GOVERNMENT

Leading governments around the world are already making significant changes in order to address the challenges of sustainable development, seeking to achieve progress that does not penalize future generations. In this section of the book, we will demonstrate that leadership in this area is no longer a political risk and a walk into the unknown for governments. Rather, governments can be inspired to develop a range of new mechanisms and structures to underpin a shift to sustainability, lead by the experience of other leading governments illustrated throughout this section. In Section 1 it was reported that the Netherlands Government has funded a five-year programme to address the challenges of sustainable development. This project, involving hundreds of organizations and scientists, found that a factor of 10 to 20+ improvements in resource productivity are possible over the next 50 years. Better still, they have published an extensive book on their findings that explains in detail this landmark body of work, thus assisting other nations to do the same.[1] This is, however, not an isolated initiative of government. In Germany, for example, there is the Socio-Ecological Programme, in Austria, the Programme on Technologies for Sustainable Development, and in Japan there is the Zero Emissions Research Initiative (ZERI).

The Australian Government funds a significant percentage of the Commonwealth Scientific and Industrial Research Organisation (CSIRO), Australia's peak science and industry research body. CSIRO is carrying out a comprehensive Future Scenarios programme for Australia, analysing the country's material and energy flows to better understand how resource productivity improvements can be made. CSIRO's Flagship programmes have been designed partly to address the need to achieve ecological sustainability under the themes of preventive health, leading the light metals age, water for a healthy country, food futures, wealth from Australia's oceans and energy transformed. CSIRO states that, 'National teamwork, collaboration and partnership are primary ingredients for success in science, technology and innovation. Partnerships provide us with the critical mass to compete with the world's best in areas essential to our future. Every Flagship is a partnership of leading Australian scientists, research institutions and commercial companies. Intense social, economic and environmental forces are shaping Australia's destiny in the 21st Century. These place ever-growing pressures on us to be *globally competitive, ecologically sustainable, socially equitable and progressive.'*

This is just the start of a wide range of government institutional reform that is occurring globally, at all levels of government. In Belgium, they have further empowered

Table 11.1 *International programmes identified as targeting sustainable development*

Country	Sample of SD research programmes
Austria (individual programmes)	Austrian Landscape Research Austrian Programme on Technology for Sustainable Development PFEIL 05 Programme for Research and Development in Agriculture, Forestry, Environment and Water Management
Belgium (umbrella programmes and sub-programmes)	Scientific Support Plan for a Sustainable Development Policy 1 (Sustainable management of the North Sea, global change and sustainable development, Antarctica 4, sustainable mobility, norms for food products, Telsat 4, levers for a sustainable development policy and supporting actions) Scientific Support Plan for a Sustainable Development Policy 2 (Sustainable modes of production and consumption, global change, eco-systems and biodiversity, supporting actions and mixed actions) Scientific Support to an Integration of Notions of Quality and Security of the Production Environments, Processes and Goods in a Context of Sustainable Development
Germany (umbrella programme and sub-programmes)	Research on the Environment (Research on sustainable economic management, regional sustainability, research on global change, socioecological research)
The Netherlands (umbrella programme with structured and coordinated individual programmes)	Economy, Ecology and Technology (EET) Dutch Initiative for Sustainable Development (NIDO) Sustainable Technology Development Project[2] HABIFORM (Expertise network – multiple use of space)
Sweden (individual programmes)	Urban and Regional Planning Infrasystems for Sustainable Cities The Sustainable City Economics for Sustainable Development Sustainable Forestry in Southern Sweden Sustainable Food Production Sustainable Coastal Zone Sustainable Management of the Mountain Region Paths to Sustainable Development – Behaviour, Organizations, Structures (Ways Ahead) Innovation Systems Supporting a Sustainable Growth
UK[3] (individual programmes)	Environmental Strategy Research Programme Towards a Sustainable Urban Environment EPSRC Infrastructure and Environment Programme Environment Agency Sustainable Development R&D Programme Sustainable Development Commission Sustainable Technologies Initiative – LINK Programme

Note: The table shows the three main programme types for organizing research for SD; umbrella programmes, sub-programmes and individual programmes.
Source: Leone et al (2002)

their National Council for Sustainable Development to continue its work to encourage whole of government approaches. However, this is not an isolated example, the International Network for National Councils for Sustainable Development has over 70 member countries all at different stages of the process, and the US had a National Council for Sustainable Development under the Clinton/Gore administration. Today, dictatorships are about the only countries that do not have institutional structures within government to help adopt a whole of government approach to sustainable development. Dr Steve Dovers,[4] one of the world's experts in institutional change for sustainable development, considers the Belgium case study in Chapter 12 on broad trends and lessons of institutional reform to date. Since the challenge of achieving sustainable development is going to be one of the major drivers for innovation this century, we need to consider what this means for national systems of innovation. Paul Weaver, one of the lead authors of the Sustainable Technology Development (STD) project, addresses this in Chapter 13.

An inspiring example of government institutional reform to address the challenge of sustainable development was mentioned briefly in Section 1, the State Sustainability Strategy of the Western Australian Government. There, the state/regional government has passed into law a comprehensive state sustainability strategy.[5] Professor Peter Newman, of Murdoch University, who was tasked with facilitating this process, provides an account of what they have achieved, and some of the lessons of the journey, in Chapter 14. Is the WA example an isolated case? No. Newman and his team have also been heavily involved in assisting the development of the Network of Regional Government for Sustainable Development (nrg4SD). This network is comprised of increasing numbers of state/regional/sub-national governments from around the world, some of which already have comprehensive sustainability strategies. The nrg4SD began at the World Summit on Sustainable Development (WSSD) in 2002, and now holds conferences every six months that are hosted by state governments around the world. This relatively new international network is bound to succeed for many reasons, not the least of which being that local government internationally has beaten them to it. There is already a significant international network of local governments learning together how best to achieve sustainable development known as the International Council for Local Environmental Initiatives (ICLEI). This organization facilitates and helps co-ordinate an international network of local councils globally. (ICLEI Asia-Pacific talk about their experiences in the beginning of Chapter 15.)

For instance, over 300 cities are members of the Cities for Climate Protection (CCP), an international climate change programme developed by ICLEI to empower local governments to reduce greenhouse gas emissions. More than 440 local governments from around the world participate in CCP, with campaigns at different stages in Australia, Canada, Finland, India, Indonesia, Italy, Mexico, the Philippines, South Africa, the UK and the US. As of June 2002, 149 Australian councils, covering more than 60 per cent of the nation's population, were actively pursuing greenhouse gas abatement. The City of Melbourne was the first Australian Council to achieve all of the programme's 'Five Milestones', and has committed to being a climate neutral city by 2020: that is, it plans to eliminate all net emissions across the city by then. The Asia-Pacific Economic Cooperation's (APEC) Energy Working Group has endorsed the preparation of the City of Melbourne's plan. It involves stimulating a significant increase in investment and use of renewable energy and energy efficient power, refurbishing and rebuilding many of the commercial and residential buildings to increase the energy efficiency, and some sequestration through forestry programmes. The plan aims to turn a serious threat to Melbourne's economy and way of life into an opportunity for economic growth, environmental improvements and social cohesion. This will be achieved by influencing the billions of dollars of mainstream business investment that will take place in buildings and plant/power generation over the next two decades, using market mechanisms and appropriate regulations to drive commercial, industrial and residential investment in superior energy efficient design. The net result of such investment will be reduced operating costs and enhancement of city business competitiveness, rather than adding to the cost of doing business in Melbourne. The new CH2 Green Building project is a case in point.

This example is the tip of the iceberg of a comprehensive array of programmes designed to take a truly integrated approach to sustainable development. The City of Melbourne's major planning strategy, City Plan 2010, adopts sustainability as its primary theme. The City Council's operational policies, therefore, take into account their contribution to environmental, social and economic sustainability. Melbourne City Council is committed to a 40 per cent reduction in water usage, and has agreed to buy 30 per cent of its electricity for street lighting from renewable sources, with at least 10 per cent sourced from wind power. Furthermore, the council is buying 20 per cent of electricity for its buildings from Victorian wind-generated sources. The Sustainable Melbourne Fund has been established to finance projects that improve environmental sustainability within the municipality, and aims to provide environmental, financial and social benefits. The fund is unique in that it aims to be self-sustaining economically and invest in developments that promote and implement the principles of sustainability and return a financial gain.

Emeritus Professor Val Brown, who has been very active on local government and sustainability issues for over two decades, writes further on these exciting developments in local government in Chapter 15. These changes are examples of the innovative approaches emerging from governments to address the complex challenge of achieving sustainable development. As Professor Peter Newman writes in his paper *On Climbing Trees*,[6] 'the 'wicked' problems of today that sustainability is attempting to address need more than simply traditional approaches. They need innovation, which comes from different voices being brought together under a common desire for outcomes. Industry and community involvement is then not desirable but essential; it cannot be done without them.' There are essential and innovation-generating processes which need to be established within community, government and industry in order to work out how to implement programmes like sustainability assessment of industry projects, integrated approaches to planning neighbourhoods (how to reduce car dependence, preserve biodiversity, and build community together), integrated approaches to planning regions, for example how to link NRM with economic and social issues, and how to achieve indigenous development that involves better land management and creative 'sense of place' cultural development (for all of us living in this land) simultaneously. These require a lot more consideration by academics, communities, industry and government in partnership.

Whether they be projects like the Netherlands' Sustainable Technology Development Project, National Councils for Sustainable Development, State Sustainability Units, or local governments committed to cities for climate protection, all these particular governments are playing their part in bringing key stakeholders together to creatively and constructively address these complex challenges. As Professor Peter Newman writes, 'Sustainability is powered by synergies to achieve win–win outcomes, and thus it is essential to bring all the relevant parties together for this process. Sustainable development has emerged as a new way forward that tries to find integrated and mutually supportive outcomes.' Sustainability, therefore, is a process that requires partnerships.

There can be no return to a massive, simplistic 'state intervention' strategy, or 'leave-it-to-the-market' strategy. This section of the book, plus the complementary online resources which adds a great deal of detail, seeks to provide an apolitical and bipartisan

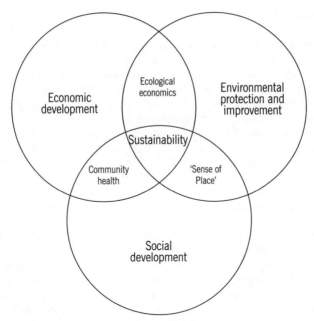

Source: Professor Peter Newman, Murdoch University, Perth

Figure 11.1 *Integrating disciplines of ecological economics*

resource to allow any government at any level to develop both a more operational and effective sustainability strategy based on partnerships. We argue that this is desperately needed now at all levels of government. As the World Bank states:

> *Without better policies and institutions, social and environmental strains may derail development progress, leading to higher poverty levels and a decline in the quality of life for everybody. Misguided policies and weak governance in past decades have contributed to environmental disasters, income inequality, and social upheaval in some countries, often resulting in deep deprivation, riots, or refugees fleeing famine or civil wars.*
>
> World Bank Development Report 2003

There is still a common perception that sustainable development will cost government and taxpayers more and will require significant outlays from government to achieve it. However, as will be shown, this does not need to be the case. In fact, there is much that can be done to turn the tide on the decline of the environment and the rise of global inequity without taxpayers having to pay an extra cent. It is often simply a matter of practising basic good and responsible government, and getting the incentives and market signals right. Implementing incentives that motivate people to do the right thing and to make the right choices is one of the central challenges of economics. Direct or hidden subsidies for activities that harm the environment[7] actually provide incentives to companies to treat the environment as a commodity. Such subsidies from government, at taxpayers' expense, send the wrong signals by pricing environmental resources inappropriately. Sustainability supporting incentives should reflect environmental costs in market prices through pollution charges, feebates schemes, cap and trade markets and other market-based mechanisms and policies that also promote environmentally sound practices and the sustainable use of natural resources.

The World Bank writes:

> Power subsidies in India have resulted in over-pumping of aquifers, reducing the availability of drinking water, and encouraging water intensive crops in areas where water is scarce. In not distinguishing between peak and non-peak tariffs, the implicit subsidy has also increased the incentive to overbuild capacity. In fact, the World Bank estimated in 1991 that various measures to reduce peak power usage could reduce power generation requirements by 12 per cent in 10 years (allowing a reduction in the required system capacity). In addition to facilitating the excess drawdown of aquifers, the subsidy is also costly to the poor (for many reasons). Many subsidies are introduced initially to stimulate the use of a good or service that is underutilised ... but in the absence of sunset clauses and with the creation of a constituency based on perceived acquired rights, these subsidies can persist beyond their economically useful life and be detrimental environmentally.[8]

The United Nations Environment Programme (UNEP) and the Worldwatch Institute have identified at least US$650 billion worth of subsidies globally, per annum, that are either directly or indirectly degrading the environment. Nations globally spend significantly more money on subsidizing activities that harm the environment than we do on looking after it. In some countries as much as ten times more taxpayers' money is spent subsidizing industry behaviour that harms rather than restores the environment.[9] In the past, some governments have failed to impose fair royalty charges for minerals or timber extracted from public lands, leaving another significant area of potential revenue virtually untapped. Economists since Adam Smith have understood the value in properly taxing windfalls generated by natural resources; economists refer to these concessionary windfalls as 'resource rents'. Determining just how much of a person's income is attributable to a lack of political manipulation is often impossible, making windfall taxation impossible. However, when companies make windfall profits on government land, it then provides a case for rent capturing. Just as often, however, governments sell resources at prices high enough to cover their costs, but still far lower than they could. In the past the Philippines, Malaysia, Indonesia and Ghana have sold hardwood concessions for a pittance, earning only a modest profit. Meanwhile, logging companies have obtained timber worth three times what they have paid.[10]

Governments can also incorrectly interfere in the market through subsidizing companies through straight cash handouts, tax breaks, subsidized credit, favourable exchange rates and other market manipulations. In the next chapter we discuss other win–win mechanisms that force governments and nations to address environmental degradation. There are those that oppose such government measures because they see these as interfering with the market. Such is their faith in Adam Smith's 'invisible hand' that they cannot fathom why the government has a role here. However, Adam Smith made it clear that a perfect market requires perfect information and a large role of government is direct information transfer such as education and indirect information transfer through its structures, legislation and involvement in the market. Over the past 30 years, mainstream economics has undergone some quite significant changes. In particular, economists now understand market failure to be widespread. As the World Bank stated in their 1997 report, *The Role of the State in a Changing World*: 'the most economically fundamental justification for the vital role of government is the fact that if uneven or 'asymmetrical information' in a market economy is not addressed, a chain of events will ensue causing market failures and a suboptimal efficiency of distribution of resources'. Hence, Chapter 12 provides a detailed discussion of the fundamental economic justification for the role of government: namely, to address market and information failures, such as externalities. Adam Smith himself acknowledged that markets fail when monopolies form, and hence governments needed to enact anti-trust laws.

One of government's major roles is to correct the inefficiencies resulting from externalities. Externalities are a market failure that arises due to the extra costs and benefits of a transaction (externalities) not being included in the market price. They can be categorized as either positive or negative, depending on whether individuals enjoy benefits they did not pay for, or suffer extra costs they did not incur. Essentially, markets tend to produce too much of negative externalities, such as pollution, but too little of positive externalities, like education and R&D. Research and development is a positive externality, as the majority of profits from most inventions do not go to the inventor but to the company that commercializes the invention. Because R&D and innovation for new emerging markets is inherently risky, the market on its own will often fail to produce the necessary technological innovation needed in a successful economy. Hence, governments need to invest in R&D and their national systems of innovation and ensure that the firms based in their country are as successful as possible. The questions of what the challenge of sustainability means for our national systems of innovation and what countries are doing to address it are the focus of Chapter 13.

As was discussed in the first section of this book, one of the clearest examples of negative externalities are those that harm the environment and lead to excessively rapid losses of our natural resources. For example, part of the fertilizer used to benefit agricultural production tends to end up in streams, causing a change in the balance of the ecosystem resulting in things like algal blooms. It can then go on to affect the health of relatively distant ecosystems such as coral reefs. In this case, the local benefits of fertilizer use would be apparent to the landholder but the external effects would not, due to spatial and temporal separation and the very diffuse nature of non-point source pollution,[11] such as fertilizers, and its effects. Inappropriate behaviour can also arise where government policies fail to provide appropriate incentives and when the costs of these external effects are neither counted nor internalized into actual transaction costs. At the end of the day, we all make decisions based on costs to others and ourselves, and either formally or informally weigh up the cost–benefits of choices in our lives. It is becoming clear that environmental degradation occurs because the current form of our economy makes it cheaper to degrade nature than to care for it.[12] These issues are being widely discussed internationally.[13] They were also the subject of a report by the Australian Treasury[14] in 2001, discussing how, for instance, the failure of individuals to properly consider social costs and benefits can mean that their behaviour, while logical from their own point of view, will not be optimal from a social point of view. As the Head of Treasury in Australia stated recently:

> *We go about our lives making many decisions based on cost. All of us base many decisions on a formal or informal cost benefit analysis. When externalities are present the market price does not reflect the true costs of our decisions. There is much government can do here. Government policies in keeping the price of water for farmers low globally has led to excessive use of water, draining water from underground basins built up over centuries, lowering the water table, and in some cases, leaching out of the soil. For instance, in many countries, much of the timber lies on government lands and the government, in making the land available, has paid less attention to concerns about economic efficiency than it has to the pleading of timber interest groups.*

Ken Henry, Secretary of the Treasury Department, Australia, Speech to the 30th Anniversary of the ANU Economic Masters Program

This report went on to say that 'People generally are unlikely to produce socially optimal environmental outcomes when they do not face the full benefits and costs of their actions'. Under these circumstances, individuals are likely to place greater weight on the costs and benefits they bear themselves, than the costs and benefits their actions impose on others. This is in part because the value of ecosystem services has been unrecognized and unpriced. However, valuing these services is a difficult task. What price is a stable climate worth? How can one put a price on access to drinkable, unpolluted water? This does not mean, however, that these costs are not real.

The tragedy of the commons: 35 years on

Another situation where markets fail to distribute resources efficiently is where it is impossible, or at least very costly, to deny access to an environmental asset. In a situation where many have access to the same limited resource (usually referred to as a common-pool resource), there is an incentive for each consumer to acquire as much of that limited resource as possible, before others do. If all users restrain themselves then the resource has the best chance of being sustained. However, if you limit your extraction of the resource and the others do not, then the resource will still run out and you will have been penalized by not getting your fair share. In these situations there is a tremendous incentive to overuse natural resources. In this case the market has failed to signal the real scarcity of the asset: the invisible hand of the market does not work to provide for the maximum social good for present and future generations. This has been understood for a long time, and was greatly popularized by Garrett Hardin's (1968) article entitled, 'The Tragedy of the Commons'. Hardin asserted that users of a common resource will ultimately destroy the resource on which they depend unless the market failure is addressed.

Hardin's paper is one of the most cited papers of the last 40 years.[15] He described the process of writing the paper as follows:

> With Adam Smith's work as a model, I had assumed that the sum of separate ego-serving decisions would be the best possible one for the population as a whole. But presently I discovered that I agreed much more with William Forster Lloyd's conclusions, as given in his Oxford lectures of 1833. Citing what happened to pasturelands left open to many herds of cattle, Lloyd pointed out that, with a resource available to all, the greediest herdsmen would gain ... for a while. But mutual ruin was just around the corner. As demand grew in step with population (while supply remained fixed), a time would come when the herdsmen, acting as Smithian individuals, would be trapped by their own competitive impulses. The unmanaged commons would be ruined by overgrazing; competitive individualism would be helpless to prevent the social disaster. So must it also be, I realised, with growing human populations when there is a limit to available resources... I scribbled in the changes, most notably the suggestion that the way to avoid disaster in our global world is through a frank policy of 'mutual coercion', [that is] mutually agreed upon. Under conditions of scarcity, ego-centred impulses naturally impose costs on the group, and hence on all its members.

Hardin writes about an example closer to home:

> think of what is happening to the freedom to make withdrawals from the oceanic bank of fishes. In 1625, the Dutch scholar Hugo Grotius said, "The extent of the ocean is in fact so great that it suffices for any possible use on the part of all peoples for drawing water, for fishing, for sailing". Now the once unlimited resources of

marine fishes have become scarce and nations are coming to limit the freedom of their fishers in the commons. From here onward, complete freedom leads to tragedy. (And still the shibboleth, "the freedom of the seas", interferes with rational judgment.) ... Its ['The Tragedy of the Commons'] message is, I think, still true today. Individualism is cherished because it produces freedom, but the gift is conditional: the more the population exceeds the carrying capacity of the environment, the more freedoms must be given up. As cities grow, the freedom to park is restricted by the number of parking meters or fee-charging garages. Traffic is rigidly controlled. On the global scale, nations are abandoning not only the freedom of the seas, but also the freedom of the atmosphere, which acts as a common sink for aerial garbage. Yet to come are many other restrictions as the world's population continues to grow.[16]

The outcome of Hardin's and others' work was a deeper understanding that most market failures with environmental assets can be linked, in one way or another, to the failure or inability of institutions to establish well defined property rights. For example, many people own land and are able to take action to repair any damage done to it. However, people generally do not own the rivers, the oceans, forests or air through which significant pollution can travel. It is our inability to provide clear and well defined property rights for clean air, rivers and oceans that make it difficult for a market to exist, such that people downstream from pollution cannot halt the harm that industry does to them upstream. Hardin's paper was also important because it recognized, for the first time, that nearly all environmental issues have aspects of the commons in them. The difficulty with the tragedy of the commons, in assigning property rights such that a complete set of markets could be created, is that it provides an excuse for governments to intervene, for example, by creating new property rights. The notion that problems of externality can be simply solved by redefining property rights is known as Coase's theorem. Nobel Laureate Ronald Coase, from the Chicago Law School, argues that government should simply reapply property rights. He argues that if property rights are well designed then the market will take care of externalities on its own.

Take the example of fishing. Modern efficient vessels trawl the sea catching significant loads of fish. These highly efficient boats, combined with modern commercial fishing methods, allow trawlers to rapidly catch large numbers of fish. The free market awards companies for the efficiency with which they can catch large volumes of fish. In addition, every trawler knows that the more fish other fishermen catch the less there is for them. Hence, there are real incentives to overfish sites so as to not allow competitors to gain an advantage. However, this can easily go too far, to the point where the fish stocks cannot replace themselves. If the government were to re-design property rights and grant those rights to a single independent body responsible for managing the public commons, such a body could then have every incentive to ensure fishing did not irreversibly damage the ecology for future generations. Such a body could coordinate with other government bodies' research to monitor the health of the ecosystem, and provide licences to respective fishing companies with limits on the amount and types of fish that could be caught. In principle this could be designed to eliminate the externality and to ensure that the long-term health of the marine and ocean ecosystems were looked after as well as the short-term profits of fishing companies. What matters is having well defined property rights.

Simply redesigning property rights, whilst appealing in terms of minimal government intervention, is, in practice, very hard to do; the costs of reaching an agreement can be high, particularly when large numbers of individuals are involved. Consequently, the major policy innovation in many countries, particularly developing ones, has been legislation, more specifically that transferred forests, pasture land, in-shore fisheries, and other natural resources from their previous property rights regimes to government ownership.[17] Extensive research and experience since 1968 shows that these transfers of property rights were sometimes disastrous for the resources they were intended to protect. Instead of creating a single owner with a long term interest in the resource, as a result of corruption in particular, nationalizing common pool resources sometimes led to:

- the poor treatment of indigenous tribes, and even making illegal the actions of these traditional stewards to sustain their resources;
- poor monitoring of resource boundaries and harvesting practices; and
- de facto open access and a race to use the resource.

Thus, in practice, many governments failed to do better than the market.

By the mid 1980s, questions were increasingly being asked. Scholars familiar with the quantitative case study literature in Africa, Latin America, Asia and the US were beginning to point out that the policy reforms that transformed natural resources from governance, as a common property by local communities, into state governance were actually making things worse for the resource, as well as the users. The governments that took these actions frequently did not have enough trained personnel on the ground to monitor the resources. Thus, what had been a de facto common property, with some limitations on access and use patterns because of de jure government property frequently became de facto open access, due to lack of enforcement. Corrupt police officials also turned a blind eye to greed and finite resources. It is often said that in understanding the problem we are half way to solving it. However, in the case of the tragedy of the commons that has not been the case. In practice, in the real world, the problem of externality it is still a very difficult and complex problem to solve.

Having said that, leading writers in the field, such as Elinor Ostrom, are optimistic that after 35 years we do have solutions and answers.[18] Experts are cautiously hopeful, pointing to examples where individuals and groups of Common Pool Resource (CPR) users have come together to forge their own solutions, rather than waiting for governments or other institutions to impose rules and regulations. The authors emphasize that one of the most important lessons learned from empirical studies of sustainable resources is that more solutions exist than those proposed by Hardin. Ostrom stated recently that, 'Hardin's work was originally understood to say that unless you have private ownership of resources, or government control of them, environmental tragedy is inevitable. That was an overstatement. There are situations where that does apply, but it is limited. It applies to situations where there is so much distrust, and communication is so costly, and people see so little benefit to solving environmental problems that they are, effectively, trapped.' Government ownership and privatization are themselves, however, subject to failure in some situations. For instance, experts cite satellite images of northern China, southern Siberia and Mongolia that reveal the effects of different approaches to management of grazing lands. In contrast to the state-owned strategies of Russia and China (the latter having more recently also tried privatization), Mongolia's traditional group-property system has resulted in much less degradation of grasslands. While no single property rights system will be successful in managing every type of common pool resource, the authors agree that it is possible to identify certain 'design principles' that have been employed in the efficient governance of CPRs. Some of the factors that come into play include:

- the variety and proportion of behavioural types among the users of a CPR;
- how well these users are able to communicate with one another;
- the perceived value of the resource and the benefits of preserving it; and

- the extent to which the users are able to monitor the quality of the resource and enforce rules and sanctions.

'There is a huge body of literature that documents where people have overcome these CPR problems,' Ostrom says. 'In the end, building from the lessons of past successes will require forms of communication, information and trust that are broad and deep beyond precedent, but not beyond possibility'.[19] Some of the most important recent case studies of community involvement with the development of regulation are the Florida Everglades,[20] The New York Water crisis[21] and Canada's Coastal Action Program.[22] Also, in Australia recently, significant progress has been made on addressing water rights and trading schemes. This will be discussed in detail in Section 4. In 2002, Ostrom and colleagues completed a major online book, published by the National Academy of Sciences, US, that provides a lay summary of the lessons of the last 35 years of work on the tragedy of the commons.[23] Given that *Science* magazine has also published *Tragedy of the Commons; A Special Issue*, on 12 December 2003, we highly recommend these for those looking for greater detail. Essentially, there is now general agreement that most externalities, such as those concerning the environment, require a wide range of approaches, partnerships and government mechanisms to be employed. As David Roodham wrote in *Natural Wealth of Nations*, 'Achieving a truly sustainable economy involves a variety of approaches.'[24]

Roodham continues to say that 'To achieve a transition to a genuinely environmentally sustainable economy (dramatically reduce these negative externalities) will take nothing less than an eco-industrial revolution, a sweeping and complex process that defies government planning. Unlike today's essentially throwaway economy, a sustainable economy will recycle materials the way a healthy ecosystem does, draw energy from renewable sources, and use all its resources much more efficiently. Bringing resource usage down to environmentally sustainable levels and sharing the quota among a global community of 10 billion affluent people calls for resource productivity improvements of an order of magnitude or more. Averting climate change will require the industrial countries to cut carbon emissions by 90 per cent (A Factor of 10). Environmental progress depends on accelerating the development of new, clean technologies, a process of discovery that is intrinsically unpredictable. No agency can plan it. Markets on the other hand, excel at engineering systemic change. Markets made the industrial and digital revolutions possible. Properly harnessed, they can also guide the next industrial revolution towards environmental sustainability.'

Government mechanisms

Governments have numerous mechanisms to address these externalities and market failures in a general sense. They can, for instance, address information gaps, apply economic measures, and establish clear property rights and other forms of regulatory frameworks. Other forms of government mechanisms that can help markets to work better and help us achieve a transition to a sustainable economy include government and industry partnerships, regulatory measures, economic incentives and penalties, reframing taxes, using marketable permits, and creating a market for externalities. Bridgman and Davis, in *The Australian Policy Handbook*,[25] summarize the policy instruments available to governments as follows, and state that good policy advice relies on choosing the right mix of instruments for the problem at hand:

1 **Advocacy**: arguing a case
   - Education and demonstration projects
   - Reference groups and consultative

- Policy announcements such as the Western Australian State Sustainability Strategy (See Chapter 14).

2 **Economic measures**: using spending and taxing powers
- Fiscal (selling off), taxation and procurement powers
- Grant programmes, incentives, national projects
- Address information failures.

3 **Government actions**: delivering services
- Legislation, creation of new institutions, public service programmes such as hospitals and schools
- Funding for service provision by statutory bodies
- Administrative decisions.

4 **Law**: using legislative power (regulation)
- Legislation (OH&S Act)
- Regulation (applications for refugee status)
- Parliamentary resolution
- Administrative acts.

The point here is that government has numerous mechanisms at their disposal to address and truly solve our environmental problems. As far back as 1997, the World Bank talked about the range of government mechanisms available to solve the environmental crisis:[26] 'Government regulation is not the only answer to pollution (and environmental degradation). An expanding toolkit of innovative and flexible incentives is now available to get polluters to clean up their act. Although there is no substitute for meaningful regulatory frameworks and information about the environment, these new tools, which rely on persuasion, social pressure, and market forces to help push for improved environmental performance, can often succeed where regulation cannot.'

Countries are using some of these tools, with promising results, in areas such as:

- harnessing the power of public opinion (*Advocacy*);
- engaging industry through partnerships (*Money*);
- engaging third parties through mechanisms like green procurement (*Actions*);
- applying self-regulatory mechanisms (*Legislation*);
- choosing effective market-based economic instruments (*Legislation*);
- creating the relevant markets to both optimize the use of scare resources and also reward efforts to use resources wisely (*Legislation*);
- making regulation more flexible to encourage innovation (*Legislation*).

Further explanation and case studies of these mechanisms of government, and how they can be used to achieve genuine sustainable progress, are set out in the following tables. We will consider some of the mechanisms mentioned in Tables 11.2–11.6 in detail.

The regulatory measure response

The strongest response government can make to a negative externality is to outlaw it. For example, the use of chemicals that are not safe at almost any concentration clearly needs to be outlawed, except for strict scientific procedures. In the case of environmental externalities, many governments simply impose regulatory measures that define possible levels of pollution and penalize firms that exceed them. While governments around the world have agreed to the phasing out and banning of all ozone destroying chemicals, simply imposing such standards can backfire. If regulation is seen as demanding changes in business that are perceived as very costly, the government is quite likely to face a backlash as firms decide that paying lobbyists to defeat the

Table 11.2 *Advocacy*

Provide information	Adam Smith's 'Invisible hand' works only under certain criteria that includes the markets having perfect information. But who has perfect information? One of the key roles of government is to supply relevant information to help markets more efficiently allocate resources. There are many creative ways governments can ensure better information is made available to consumers. The Australian Capital Territory (ACT) Government has made it mandatory that at the point of sale, or change over to a new renter, the owner of a property must, by law, inform the buyer or renter of the energy efficiency star rating of that house. This law thus helps to ensure the market has such information to inform choices made. This has led to a significant uptake in the adoption of energy efficient strategies and eco-efficiencies for homes in the ACT.
Education	One of the most cost-effective ways to do that is through funding a good education system that teaches students how to be confident independent learners and encourages them to be active and critical citizens. The amount of information available in the world is growing exponentially. It is vital that the current and next generation know how to research using the latest online databases and find the information they truly need quickly. To help this in the ACT, all Year 9 students through their action-learning, 'Exhibitions Projects' are given real opportunities to embark on problem solving exercises. They have to choose a project with their teachers that will help develop their critical literacy in solving environment problems, community building, whilst understanding sensitive cultural and social aspects of society.[27] More on this exciting educational innovation is covered in Section 5.
Funding demonstration projects: seeing is believing	NSW Government are contributing to funding CSIRO's revolutionary climate neutral Green Building in Newcastle. Local government Melbourne City Council contributed funding for ACF's climate neutral green building in the heart of Melbourne, 60L. Ten years ago the Netherlands Government created Green Building/Sustainable Home demonstration and advisory buildings. Ten years later they are no longer there because they are no longer needed: all buildings in the Netherlands are now built this way.
Reference groups and consultative advisory groups	In 1992, the Philippines were one of the first nations to form a National Council for Sustainable Development.[28] There is now an international network of national councils in over 70 countries including the US.[29] In Australia, when both the South Australian and ACT Government's Office of Sustainability asked for people to nominate to volunteer to be on the South Australian, ACT Sustainability expert reference groups, they were inundated with applications.
Policy announcements	Governments have often used stretch goals. In 1963, J. F. Kennedy announced that by the end of the decade the US would put a man on the moon. Increasingly, governments, as in Western Australia, are committing to stretch goals such as achieving Factor 4 by 2020. The Netherlands and Austria have also publicly committed to achieving Factor 4. These targets allow government time to phase in the necessary changes. Numerous other councils, especially in New Zealand, Europe and Japan, now have similar commitments.

Table 11.3 *Economic measures*

Create a level playing field	*The removal of perverse subsidies:* Strictly speaking economically, subsidies distort the market and are also a drain on the public purse. Globally over there are over US$650 billion in subsidies going to industries that directly or indirectly harm the environment.
Feebates	*Governments at all levels can require a feebate:* For instance those buying a car can either pay a fee or receive a rebate (hence the term 'feebate') depending on a car's energy efficiency and ecological footprint. This does not need to cost the government or taxpayer a cent as the rebates can be paid out of the money raised through the fees on highly energy inefficient cars for instance. Rather it sends a clear market signal to both consumers and manufacturers. Then, over time, as cars become more efficient feebate criteria can be adjusted to ratchet up average environmental outcomes for almost any appliance or car.
Tax shifting and procurement powers	*Tax shifting:* Numerous overseas studies have shown that, by removing them from social goods like employment, in other words reducing payroll tax and instead slightly increasing taxes on environmental negatives, both environmental protection and job creation can be achieved. Sweden has implemented a comprehensive tax shifting package. Overall this has not harmed the competitiveness of its firms. Sweden is ranked third on the world competitiveness index by the World Economic Forum. *Environmental levies:* For example, governments globally are tackling the problem of plastic bags after the Irish Government took it on as an issue. The political risk taken in Ireland proved to be worthwhile, as massive numbers of plastic bags disappeared from the system once a levy was imposed. Now bans or levies on plastic bags have also succeeded in Germany, Denmark, Italy, South Africa, Taiwan, the Northern Mariana Islands and Suffolk County in New York State. *Harnessing third parties: green procurement without picking winners.* Governments can set their purchasing policy to state 'x will purchase products with the highest recycled content … consistent with maintaining a satisfactory level of competition.' The US Clinton administration's policy on the purchasing of energy efficient computers was consistent with this.[30] *Getting the risk/return balance right.* Currently, in many countries, there are many tax disincentives from investing and commercializing new sustainability promoting technologies. This leads to large institutional investors investing in real estate and other ultra low risk investments instead of supporting the commercialization of path breaking eco-innovation.
Create markets for ecosystem services	When one has pollution from point sources, market based trading schemes/mechanisms can work well. The trading scheme for SO2 pollution worked extremely well in the US, and is the model being used for the Kyoto Protocol. Australia projects currently occurring include: the NSW EPA, which has begun load-based licensing schemes;. the Hunter Valley River, whichhas one of the first salinity trading schemes. The NSW EPA is also now licensing emissions trading for a range of pollutants. The Victorian Government's Bush tendering scheme has been very successful. However, as staff from the Australian Productivity Commission have reported, there are limits presently on creating markets for ecosystem services.[31]
Debt for nature swaps	Many third world countries are presently caught in a debt trap where a significant portion of their GDP is paying back debt owed to the OECD countries. At the same time, investments in wilderness in the developing world will often save more than in the developed world. Bilateral debt for nature swaps lead to wilderness in the developing world being protected in return for debt relief from OECD countries. The World Wildlife Fund successfully executed its first swap in Ecuador in 1989. Over the last decade there have been many commercial and bilateral debt for nature swaps.

Table 11.4 *Government actions*

Governments walking the talk	Join government networks to pool resources, learn from, and share experience such as The Network of Regional Government for Sustainable Development (nrg4SD) formed at the World Summit on Sustainable Development in 2002.
Capacity building	Provide Professional Development of public servants, and in partnership with appropriate representative bodies with business, community and institutions
Address the 'human dimension'	No matter how much funding a government department or government initiative has, there is dysfunction at the personal, human level an dmuch time and energy can be wasted
Triple bottom line indicators and budgets	'I can announce the head of my department, Dr Col Gellatly, has established a senior officers' group to look at triple bottom line reporting in the NSW, Australian public sector. TBL indicators could include things such as: • family friendly work practices; • consumer complaint handling and quality improvement processes; • using purchasing power to achieve environmental outcomes; • waste reduction and energy efficiency; and • linking triple bottom line reporting to CEO performance assessment.' Premier of NSW, Australia, Bob Carr, June 2002
Utilizing private–public partnerships	There is now a wealth of experience in how governments can split the costs and risks on needed sustainability infrastructure developments with the private sector through private and public partnerships.
Professional development	Of public servants, and in partnership with appropriate representative bodies with business, community and institutions.
Providing options for superannuation	The Australian 'Vic Superfund', which now invests 10% in sustainability projects, and is largely made up of teachers. Members can choose to allocate up to 100% of their super to be invested in ESD projects.
Add value to existing institutional frameworks, programmes and structures	*ESD compliments many existing programmes within government* National Systems of Innovation and R&D, planning authorities, departments of social services that handle aged care, and numerous areas of government have to take a long-term view and are increasingly seeking to be consistent with ESD. Most governments already have, for instance, teams reviewing school curricula, within which the UN and UNESCO recommendations for all students to have critical literacies in ESD, could be addressed. How ESD can be integrated into national systems of innovation will be considered in more detail below as an example of this general principle and approach.
Require events to meet ESD criteria	The decision by the Sydney Olympic bid to be the 'first Green Games' was critical to the Olympics being awarded to Australia ahead of other competitors. Beijing has committed for 2008 to be a Green Games and is spending significant amounts to achieve it.
Create competitions 'to be the most sustainable'.	Governments can do much to encourage creativity and create interest, excitement in innovative sustainability solutions through creating carefully thought through competitions. These competitions can have as their yardstick that X is 'to be the most ecologically sustainable' for everything from schools to landmark government buildings and green homes.[32]

Note: ESD = ecologically sustainable development.

Table 11.5 *Legislation*

Governments are increasingly are basing operations, regulation and national institutional arrangements for sustainability on the principles of ecologically sustainable development set out in major international documents or specific national legislation.

Reform of regulatory frameworks	The Australian Federal Government is working with state governments on a major overhaul of the regulatory framework governing the use, licensing and trading of water nationally as part of a broad plan to address major environmental problems such as salinity.[33] At present, the trading of water in Australia is complicated by the variety of water 'allocation' and pricing arrangements within and between the states. Inconsistencies in terminology, user expectations, security of supply and trading mechanisms have led to inefficient resource use, over-allocation of rivers and environmental degradation.[34]
Administrative Acts	Western Australian Government is committed to developing a Code of Practise Act that will embed the principles of sustainability in government public servant actions.[35]
Legislate for performance not compliance	Past regulations have often prescribed particular remediation technologies, such as catalysts or scrubbers for air pollution, rather than focusing on setting standards based on outcomes such as 'best available technology' legislation.
Build trust in government	Ensure as much transparency as possible about what the government is trying to do, where funding is coming from. Set clear indicators in line with government goals and report regularly on progress.
Harnessing third parties	*Good Neighbour Agreements* These are common in North America and Europe. For example in the US, a neighbour agreement was struck between a chemical company, local authorities and the community on the condition that representatives from all three form a committee to monitor the performance of the chemical facility. *Community Right to Know Legislation* This stipulates that companies must put on the public record details of, for instance, the environmental impacts of their activities. Positive impacts of this can be seen in the US. *Requiring corporations to report on social and environmental performance* The past decade has seen a spate of new sustainability reporting requirements around the world, with comprehensive disclosure laws or rules being enacted in France, Denmark, the Netherlands, Norway, South Africa and Sweden, among others.[36]

legislation is more cost effective than paying engineers to make a plant more energy efficient. Regulation is then watered down to a point where it simply sets minimum standards that achieve little real progress. Hence, most governments try voluntary approaches for a set period before assessing their success or failure, and whether regulation is needed. If voluntary measures do not work to address a negative externality then government may be justified in bringing in a range of other incentives and binding regulation. In the following, consideration will be given to what the literature says about voluntary initiatives and tools for government to assess their effectiveness.

Table 11.6 *Key role of government community partnership building*

Community involvement, engagement, empowerment and sense of place

Here are a number of key concepts guiding the application of sustainability to community, especially the role of community arts, community services, housing, health and education, in the development of 'sense of place' and social capital. In Western Australia, to assist in the process of focusing the community, an important new organization has been formed, the WA Collaboration, which combines and represents over 300 peak civil society groups from conservation, unions, churches, ethnic affairs, welfare, indigenous, youth and active ageing groups. Funded by the Lotteries Commission, this group has been conducting extensive public consultation to develop a Community Sustainability Agenda. The WA Collaboration is the sister chapter of the National Australian Collaboration similarly formed by national civil society groups that is committed to a Just and Sustainable Australia.

Support third party independent certification of products	The World Economic Forum studies mentioned in Chapter 1 show that there has been a significant loss of trust in corporations and government. This is partly due to corporate green-washing. At the same time, how many people even know if the lemons they buy from the supermarket have travelled half way around the world or are locally grown? How many people even know if the clothes they are wearing are made by sweatshop under-age labour? How many people know if the coffee they are buying is fair trade coffee or not? For both these reasons consumer groups and NGOs globally are increasingly creating third party independent certification schemes to provide reliable information on these matters to the consumer.
Encourage consensus building, respect cultural diversity, and tolerance	In Australia's Cape York Peninsula, farmers, indigenous tribes and environmentalists worked together to map out a plan for the 'Top End ' (of Australia). This unprecedented triumvirate of major groups within society found sufficient agreement amongst themselves to take a unified plan to the Australian Federal Government. The efforts to build consensus and unite around a clear plan were rewarded. They received AU$40 million in Australian Federal Government funding.
Support community sporting, artistic, environmental organizations to build social capital	Robert Putnam from Harvard University studied why particular regions of Italy were more wealthy than others. He was surprised to find that the most powerful association was with the number of soccer clubs and choral societies. Sport and recreation are critical to building social capital, to creating the networks and trust between business, government and community which are totally intermixed and integrated when people join sporting groups and voluntary community associations. As well as helping provide the glue of economic activity, sport and recreation provide the health that enables people to be economically active. Ill health is also a major drain on the economy.[37]
Encourage partnerships, and community initiative	IT provides us with a new opportunity to re-invent democracy, and build networks, share research, and genuinely maintain and build a community from which lasting change can occur. TakingITGlobal, which presently has over 20,000 young professional members globally, is an example of how such IT networks are keen to encourage and support real community and youth initiative.
The value of sectoral networks	Networks that truly meet people's real needs are unstoppable now that civil society, government and business can so easily communicate the Internet, email, phone and teleconferences. These networks help remove the risk from government investment in sustainability initiatives in these sectors by ensuring that every dollar will go as far as humanly possible.
Job creation programmes	National projects: US President Franklin D. Roosevelt, working with Richard St Barb Baker (the Man who Planted Trees) in the 1930s created a green corps, to create jobs during the great depression. As a result, the corps planted millions of trees.

Mental models of voluntary environmental initiatives*

Bruce Paton

Voluntary environmental initiatives are private or public efforts to improve corporate environmental performance beyond legal requirements. Voluntary initiatives have become important instruments for environmental policy and corporate environmental strategy over the past decade. Unlike other policy innovations, voluntary environmental initiatives have been designed and implemented by practitioners with little guidance from formal theory.[38] Over the past several years, theorists have been scrambling to catch up with practice. Theory building has been complex because voluntary initiatives appear to violate long-established principles of conventional economic theory. If firms routinely maximize profits, as conventional economic theory insists they do, then voluntary changes in production processes to reduce environmental damages and energy consumption must reduce their individual economic efficiency. Yet individual and collective voluntary initiatives have become widespread internationally. Useful theory must address this apparent contradiction. In Section 2, Chapter 9 this was addressed. Another critical step in developing theory relevant to voluntary initiatives is identifying the appropriate assumptions and mental models about what they are and what motivates firms to join them. Scholars have taken several conflicting approaches to explaining the essential nature of voluntary environmental initiatives. Differences in assumptions concerning what voluntary initiatives are and how they work have led to very different evaluations of their current effectiveness and future role as instruments of public policy and corporate strategy.

Three distinct models – self regulation, private regulation and civil regulation – have emerged in the literature on voluntary environmental initiatives. Although there is considerable overlap among them, each approach relies on distinct assumptions concerning the fundamental motivations for firms to participate and the likely consequences for the environment and the economy. The similarities and differences among these three models, and the implications for the design of future initiatives, are explored here.

Types of voluntary regulation: self-regulation

The first model, self regulation, has been the dominant framework that researchers have used to understand and reflect upon voluntary initiatives. The phrase 'self regulation' refers to decisions made by firms acting individually, or by industries acting together, to constrain their behaviour in ways that are not required by law. Scholarly evaluations within this perspective have ranged from openly pessimistic to moderately optimistic, concerning the ability of voluntary initiatives to improve social welfare. Andrews points out that two distinct lines of argument motivate the growth of interest in self-regulatory approaches.[39] The first he characterizes as the optimistic literature on the greening of industry, design for environment, industrial ecology and related topics. These approaches emphasize the potential gains to firms from improved environmental management. The second line of argument focuses on criticisms of conventional regulation. It emphasizes the advantages of self-regulation relative to conventional regulation, such as potential increases in flexibility and economic efficiency. Andrews identifies a broad spectrum of self-regulatory schemes, ranging from individual–firm efforts motivated largely by enlightened self interest, to public–private partnerships. He

---

* This piece has been kindly contributed by TNEP mentor Associate Professor Bruce Paton, San Francisco University Business School, and is an excerpt from his unpublished paper 'Mental Models of Voluntary Environmental Initiatives'.

observes that self-regulatory approaches lie on a continuum between legal regulation and complete self regulation, rather than a dichotomy between two distinct alternatives.

The conclusion Andrews draws is that, although self-regulatory approaches can effectively complement traditional approaches, they cannot be considered as a substitute for effective governance regimes. In particular, he finds that self regulation by itself cannot effectively address circumstances in which firms gain significant cost efficiencies by imposing external costs on society. Similarly, he argues that self regulation will not address 'tragedy of the commons' problems, 'in which the cumulative effect of individually small, self interested decisions by multiple users produce environmental destruction'.

King and Lenox expressed pessimism concerning the effectiveness of self regulation in their analysis of a particular example, the chemical industry's Responsible Care programme.[40] They illustrate the adverse consequences of relying on voluntary initiatives without appropriate sanctions to assure that all participants are committed to improving environmental performance. In particular, they point out the strong likelihood of free rider problems. Maxwell and Lyon raise concerns about the likelihood that public policies based on self regulation may result in agency capture by industries that would otherwise be subject to legislation and regulation.[41] To Maxwell and Lyon, voluntary policies are essentially a means for both regulatory agencies and industries to escape scrutiny by legislative bodies and environmental interest groups. Gunningham and Rees reach more optimistic conclusions, considering self regulation from an institutional perspective.[42] They describe self regulation as, 'a special kind of normative institution' with 'variable capacity (or incapacity) to bring the behaviour of industry members within the normative ordering responsive to broader social values.' While they acknowledge that many efforts at self regulation by industries have proven to be self serving, they believe that condemning all such efforts 'throws the baby out with the bathwater.'

According to Gunningham and Rees, either one of two conditions is necessary (though not sufficient) for self regulation to succeed. The first is a strong natural alignment between the public and private interest in establishing self regulation. The second is the existence of sufficient external pressures to align public and private interests. External pressures such as the threat of regulation or effective scrutiny by third parties can make self regulation effective. They conclude that the appropriate question is not whether self regulation is a substitute for conventional regulation, but rather how best to complement self regulation by adapting complementary policy instruments. For them, the challenge is to 'build on the strengths of self regulation while compensating for its weaknesses.'

Private regulation

The second model, private regulation,[43] refers to systems for controlling the behaviour of individual firms or industries through the actions of marketplace actors. Yilmaz describes private regulation as a system for assuring that markets provide safe, high-quality products and services through the certification, rating or approval processes of independent (non-governmental) parties.[44] The concept of private regulation has been offered as a solution to problems as diverse as management of healthcare costs, regulation of financial markets, certification of organic agriculture, control of junk mail, consumer protection in electronic commerce and control over pornography on the Internet.[45] Yilmaz argues that, 'regulations are often desirable because they inform, educate, reduce uncertainty, and help people protect themselves from dubious products. However, it is a mistake to assume that regulation necessarily includes government.' Examples of private regulation include product safety certification by Underwriters Laboratory, certification of Kosher food, hospital certification by the Joint

Commission on Accreditation of Health Care Organisations,[46] and product safety standards administered by the Association of Home Appliance Manufacturers.[47] Each of these examples involves long-standing systems of control, produced and enforced by trade associations or independent third parties.

Yilmaz argues that private regulation offers several advantages over conventional regulation. First, private regulation has been effective in enlisting voluntary participation, developing and maintaining standards, and providing enforcement mechanisms. Second, by relying on private specialized expertise, private regulation has been flexible and responsive to changing requirements. Finally, private mechanisms face more pressures to be cost effective than governmental regulation, because private regulators must charge the full cost of their regulatory processes to the regulated community. Yilmaz acknowledges that private regulation may not be effective in addressing some environmental issues where private property rights are difficult to define and implement. Others raise concerns that self regulation may inappropriately place regulatory functions in the hands of decision-makers who are not sufficiently accountable for their actions. The result may be systems that avoid some of the acknowledged shortcomings of conventional regulation but without the guarantees of procedural fairness provided by legal requirements subject to judicial oversight.

Civil regulation

The third model, civil regulation, refers to systems for controlling the behaviour (through being made accountable for their actions) of individual firms or industries through the actions of non-government organizations, networked together as civil society. Bendell argues that civil regulation is an effective response to the loss of control over corporate behaviour by national governments in the course of globalization.[48] He emphasizes the need to create 'new mechanisms for the democratic control of markets' and increased accountability of market institutions. Further, he argues that networks of civil organizations, linked electronically and acting in support of each other, can be an effective mechanism for regulating behaviour that crosses national boundaries. Civil regulation strategies of NGOs include working collaboratively with firms to improve environmental performance, influencing capital market scrutiny of firm behaviour, and confronting unacceptable behaviour through consumer boycotts and shareholder activism. The distinguishing feature of these activities is that they employ non-market actors to influence the conduct of market activities.

Self regulation, private regulation and civil regulation

The three models just described provide different perspectives for evaluating the goals and effectiveness of voluntary initiatives. Table 11.7 summarizes the key characteristics of each model. The models differ primarily in the source of motivation that they emphasize in explaining firms' decisions to participate. The self regulation model emphasizes the role of self interest in a firms' decision to participate. Firms or industry groups may choose to improve their environmental performance voluntarily in order to reduce costs, increase sales or to avoid external threats such as government imposed regulations or taxes. The improvements in environmental performance may originate within an individual firm, in an industry association or in a government sponsored programme. The private regulation model emphasizes the role of external, non-government actors in regulating firms' behaviour. Private regulation mechanisms enable individual buyers to rely on a third party mechanism to create the desired behaviour in sellers. In some instances, the third party mechanism effectively prevents the sale of products that do not conform to the requirements of the private regulatory mechanism. For example, Underwriters Laboratory certification has become a de facto requirement

Table 11.7 *Characteristics of self regulation, private regulation and civil regulation*

	Key elements	Example	Strengths	Limitations
Self regulation	Regulation of behaviour from within firms or industries	Chemical industry's Responsible Care programme	Can adapt to the capabilities and business circumstances of the regulated	Potential for free rider problems
Private regulation	Direct control or strong influence over decision making by economic actors and processes	Product safety regulation by Underwriters Laboratories	Can revise and update standards quickly; can provide efficient regulatory process	Regulators not sufficiently accountable to avoid abuses
Civil regulation-nodal governance	Indirect control or strong influence over decision-making by civil society	Fair Trade movement scrutiny of coffee production	Rapid response to behaviour not adequately controlled by national governments	Regulators not sufficiently accountable to avoid abuses

Source: Bruce Paton, San Francisco University Business School

to sell electrical goods because certification is required for producers to acquire product liability insurance. The civil regulation model emphasizes the role of pressure from civil society in influencing firm behaviour. This model relies on a firm's concern for their general reputation, risks to their supply chains, risks of customer boycotts, and more recently, pressure from socially responsible investors and shareholder activists.

The three models also offer different strengths and weaknesses as instruments for influencing firm behaviour. The self regulation model can be particularly effective in creating opportunities for firms or industry groups to adapt a set of performance improvements to their particular circumstances. This reduces the chance of the resulting improvements creating economic inefficiencies. On the other hand, the economic literature on the voluntary provision of public goods suggests that firms' and industries' voluntary choices will not provide enough improvement in environmental performance to meet society's needs. In addition, the absence of enforcement mechanisms makes many collective action programmes, such as the chemical industry's Responsible Care programme, vulnerable to free riding problems.[49]

The private regulation model harnesses the power of markets to influence firms' decisions. A private regulation mechanism allows customers and other actors to choose effectively between products that reflect the desired attributes and those that do not. If a private regulation mechanism is effective, it can survive and evolve over long time periods. For example, the product safety certification by Underwriters Laboratory, the certification of Kosher food, hospital certification by the Joint Commission on Accreditation of Health Care Organisations,[50] and product safety standards administered by the Association of Home Appliance Manufacturers[51] have all survived for more than 75 years.

Private regulatory mechanisms may lead to abuses because the private actors may not be sufficiently accountable to outsiders. At one extreme, private regulations may become overly restrictive to the producers of the regulated goods and services. At the other extreme, the private regulation may be 'captured' by the regulated industry. Some critics of the ISO 14000 series of environmental standards have alleged that industry representatives helped create a standard that was not sufficiently stringent to achieve its objectives. Civil regulatory mechanisms can respond very rapidly to unanticipated problems, which may lead to very rapid change in firm behaviour and public attitudes. For example, scrutiny of worker health and safety problems in Nike's Asian supply chain led the firm to much more extensive scrutiny of its suppliers' practices. At the same time, the incident placed other clothing manufacturers on notice, advising that their practices could be subject to similar scrutiny, and helped create additional civil regulation efforts such as the 'No Sweat' campaign against sweat shop conditions in the clothing industry. On the other hand, civil regulatory mechanisms may be very arbitrary in the choice of firms to target. For example, global firms may be singled out for their visibility rather than for the severity of the problems they are creating. The ad hoc character that accounts for the speed and disproportionate influence of civil regulation schemes may also unfairly target some firms relative to competitors with similar practices.

In practice, actual voluntary environmental initiatives may exhibit characteristics of two or three of these perspectives. For example, efforts by large firms such as IBM, Nokia, Ford, Phillips, and Hewlett-Packard to manage the environmental impacts from their supply chains may exhibit characteristics of all three. The firm may be motivated to police its supply chain by self interest in order to improve its own environmental performance and image, potentially to reduce costs, and to reduce the risk of disruptions to the supply of critical parts and components. The firm may simplify its task by relying on a private regulation mechanism such as requiring International Organization for Standardization (ISO) certification of all suppliers. Finally the firm may rely on civil regulation mechanisms to prevent competitors from gaining unfair advantage by engaging in exploitative labour practices or by shifting production to 'pollution havens'.

Initiatives vary in the mix of these three models that they include. That is, voluntary initiatives vary in the degree to which they rely on control from within the firm or organization, from marketplace actors or from civil society. Effective evaluation of existing voluntary initiatives and design of future initiatives will depend on understanding the potential for control of firm behaviour through self interest, market pressures, and external pressures from scrutiny by civil society. Figure 11.2 illustrates a model that incorporates all three of these elements. In this view, each of these pressures may affect firms' decision-making in any initiative.

Any decision by a firm may be influenced potentially by self interest, market pressures and scrutiny by civil society. Evaluation of voluntary environmental initiatives can be improved significantly by a three step analysis of these different pressures. The first step would evaluate the extent to which an initiative takes advantage of self interest, market pressures and scrutiny by civil society. Few initiatives currently harness all three types of pressure effectively. The second step would identify barriers to using each of these pressures. For example, a firm may be motivated by a private perception of risk that is not currently visible to actors in the market place or civil society. Making the underlying information visible outside the firm, for example through a voluntary reporting scheme, might increase external pressures in a way that complements the firm's self interest. The third step would involve designing mechanisms to help harness all three types of pressure. This would require making information available both inside and outside the firm. It would also require mechanisms for putting the information into perspective, for example by collecting comparative information for all firms in an industry or industry segment.

For example, reporting mechanisms such as the Global Reporting Initiative (GRI) may be particularly effective by triggering all three types of mechanism. Some firms preparing GRI reports have identified opportunities to reduce costs and environmental impacts

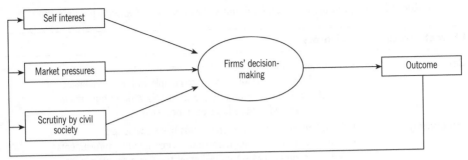

Source: Bruce Paton, San Francisco University Business School

Figure 11.2 *Potential influences on corporate decision-making*

simultaneously, triggering self interest as a pressure to continue. At the same time, the report allows the firm's customers to evaluate the effectiveness of its environmental programmes. Eventually, submitting a GRI report might become an explicit form of private regulation if large firms make preparation of a GRI report a precondition for bidding on large orders. Finally, preparation of a GRI report (or failure to prepare a report) creates opportunities for shareholder activists and other civil society actors to exercise civil regulation by reviewing the individual firm's performance data and by comparing it with other firms in the industry. Design and implementation of voluntary initiatives that harness self interest, market pressures and scrutiny by civil society can create extremely effective new tools for addressing social and environmental problems. Such programmes would be voluntary, but certainly not optional for firms hoping to trade in global markets.

As Bruce Paton's piece has shown, many governments and industry, as a first step, are implementing voluntary schemes to address environmental challenges. But how do governments and industry test the effectiveness of such schemes? Roger Burritt, Australian National University (ANU), has surveyed the major international efforts by Canada, UNEP and Allars to address this in the following section, which provides a comprehensive review of their results.

Voluntary agreements: effectiveness analysis – tools, guidelines and checklists*

Roger Burritt

Allars' characteristics of effective voluntary agreements

Allars defines three main characteristics of voluntary agreements that provide a useful foundation for assessing effectiveness: confining, structuring and checking:[52]

1   **Confining**: Signing an agreement that specifies certain actions will be undertaken which confine organizations who would otherwise be free to follow their own course

---

* This piece is reprinted with permission from Burritt (2002). Dr Roger Burritt is a reader at the ANU School of Business and Information Management, and International Coordinator of the Asia Pacific Centre for Environmental Accountability. Roger has a BA (Jt Hons) (Lancaster), MPhil (Oxford), FCPA, CA, CMA, ACIB, and teaches in management accounting, management control systems, and environmental accounting and reporting. His research areas are environmental accounting and reporting in public and private sectors, environmental cost accounting, mining and environmental accountability – domestic and international, and management accounting and control.

Table 11.8 *Key characteristics and indicators of effectiveness of voluntary agreements*

Characteristics	Indicators
Confining	• Whether a formal agreement has been signed. • What the positive incentives are to comply with an agreement. • What the negative incentives are to comply with an agreement. • Whether agreed actions have been achieved.
Structuring	• Whether an emissions inventory has been developed. • What the baseline is for assessing environmental improvements. • Whether targets are set and whether there is a continuous improvement programme established for targets. • Whether educational and awareness programmes have been introduced.
Checking	• Whether verification is undertaken. • Whether independent verification is undertaken by a third party.

Source: based on Allars (1990)

of action. Governments may adopt mechanisms designed to persuade organizations to sign agreements and comply with them. Allars explains that the organization may be offered a range of positive and negative incentives to sign, one of which is that legislation will not be introduced if the voluntary agreements successfully help the government towards its own goals. The agreement constrains the power of an organization in a voluntary way, while allowing government to reduce its visibility as the wielder of the big stick of legislation, unless the voluntary initiative fails.

2   **Structuring**: Organizations are also constrained by the structure imposed on them in the agreements. When voluntary agreements are signed, organizations accept an obligation to follow certain administrative procedures and processes. For example, these obligations may include development of an appropriate emissions inventory, specific action plans, and an action implementation plan. A voluntary agreement between government and industry may focus on learning and continuous improvement, the educational and innovation aspects.

3   **Checking**: Organizations may be monitored or checked when they claim to have achieved certain targets, or undertaken certain agreed actions. Checking may be by self assessment, internal or independent verification. It provides important 'transparency' and 'participatory' components to an effective accountability process.

In summary, based on Allars' scheme, to the extent that voluntary initiatives exist as part of a responsive regulatory system, consideration needs to be given to the mix of power bases, persuasion, incentives, education, communication and checks that will be included in the system. This mix both reflects and determines the scope of expectations for voluntary initiatives. Key indicators of effectiveness for assessing voluntary agreements are provided in Table 11.8 using the Allars framework.

The generic Canadian pro forma for voluntary initiatives

Experience with voluntary initiatives in Canada, as summarized on the Industry Canada Voluntary Codes Research Forum website, provides additional guidance on how to assess effectiveness.[53] The Office of Consumer Affairs of Industry Canada and the Regulatory Affairs Division of the Canadian Treasury Board Secretariat provided, in a joint initiative, a guide to the successful development and use of voluntary initiatives based on Canadian experience. A pro forma guide outlines an eight-step process-based model for developing voluntary codes. While the Canadian guide recognizes that different codes can be highly diverse in terms of form, content and purpose, it does provide an indication of the characteristics that are associated with effective codes.[54] These characteristics will now be considered in order to examine whether they add to those previously identified using Allars' perspective.

Specific characteristics[55] of 'good' voluntary codes include:

- **Explicit commitment of the leaders who can act as champions for the initiative**: If the leaders of an organization or sector promote the use of voluntary codes, others are more likely to follow. These leaders should be identified early in the process so that they can champion the initiative and be visible during its development and implementation.
- **Rank-and-file buy-in**: It is often the front-line employees (cashiers, factory workers, engineers, supervisors, etc.) and unions who translate the code's provisions into reality. To be able to give their full commitment and support, they must understand the code and its objectives, how it will work, and their role in implementing it. This requires good internal communications, training and, in some cases, fundamental changes in corporate culture.
- **Clear statement of objectives, expectations, obligations and ground rules**: Aims, roles and responsibilities must be clearly articulated early on. This helps to preclude problems such as participant withdrawal.
- **Open, transparent development and implementation**: Codes are more likely to reflect broader socio-economic concerns and be better received if they are developed and implemented openly and with the participation of the larger community (that is, workers, suppliers, competitors, consumers, public-interest groups, governments and neighbours). This enhances the credibility and effectiveness of the code and its proponents and participants. However, where a small number of parties (e.g. government and management) are involved in a voluntary contractual agreement, openness and transparency may be less evident because of the commercial significance of such agreements.
- **Meaningful positive inducements to participate**: If a code makes good business sense and offers meaningful inducements, firms will want to participate. One such inducement might be access to information, technology or marketing tools not available to others. Positive inducements include the use of logos to signify that the member is in good standing and adhering to the code; rating systems to allow the best performers to be recognized; plaques and awards for those who constantly meet or exceed code terms; and seminars, guest speakers, training sessions, publications and other publicity.
- **Negative repercussions for failure to join or comply**: Firms will be more enthusiastic about joining and complying with a code if they discover they could lose business (or receive tighter regulation in a responsive regulatory system) if they do not. For example, they might lose public credibility or customer loyalty. An industry association that publicizes non-compliance and levies fines is an example of negative sanctions that work with voluntary codes. The implication here is that industry associations may have an important part to play in good voluntary codes. Penalties can include negative publicity, fines, suspension or revocation of membership, and withdrawal of certain privileges associated with compliance with the code.
- **Regular flow of information**: Everyone concerned must receive feedback on how the code is working and how others are responding to it. This can be achieved through self-reporting, internal and third party monitoring, compliance verification, public reporting and similar techniques. The importance of a regular flow of information is also recognized in Agenda 21, which adds its weight to the importance of checking

Table 11.9 *Key characteristics and indicators of effectiveness for assessing voluntary agreements extended according to the generic Canadian guide on voluntary codes*

Characteristics	Indicators

Confining	• Explicit commitment of leaders to champion the initiative.[b]
	• Rank and file, union[b] and other stakeholders[d] buy in.[b]
	• Clear statement of objectives[b] set as defined quantitative targets and based on a realistic business as usual benchmark.[d]
	• Clear statement of expectations.[b]
	• Clear statement of obligations.[b]
	• Open, transparent developments.[b]
	• Whether a formal agreement has been signed.[a]
	• What the positive incentives are for the company to comply with a voluntary agreement:
	  – Logos;[b]
	  – Rating system;[b]
	  – Awards or plaques;[b]
	  – Seminars, guest speakers, training sessions, publications and other publicity;[b]
	  – Technical assistance and workshops, best practice information.[d]
	• What the negative incentives are for the company to comply with a voluntary agreement:
	  – Negative publicity;[b]
	  – Fines;[b]
	  – Suspension or revocation of agreement;[b]
	  – Withdrawal of certain privileges associated with code compliance.[b]
	• Regulatory incentives for compliance (e.g., introduction of command and control techniques[b] and advising anti-trust authorities when agreements are signed).[d]
	• Whether agreed actions have been achieved.[a]

Structuring	• Nature of the organization (e.g., company or industry association).[c] • Scope of the agreement.[b] • Size of organizations included in an agreement.[e] • Whether an emissions inventory has been developed.[a] • Whether there is a baseline for emissions reduction and what it is.[a] • Whether targets are set and whether there is a continuous improvement established for targets.[a] • Whether educational and awareness programmes have been introduced.[a]
Checking	• Whether verification is undertaken.[a] • Whether independent verification is undertaken by a third party[a] (e.g., independent verification agency or an industry association).[c] • Reporting of results (internal and external)[b] by organization and sector.[d] • Check that the relevance of the code is maintained.[b]

Sources: Industry Canada and Treasury Board (1998). Updates: *a* suggestions by Allars (1990); *b* additional suggestions made in the generic Canadian code (Industry Canada and Treasury Board 1998); *c* additional suggestions made by UNEP (1998); *d* additional suggestions made by OECD (1999b); *e* pragmatic additions suggested by Professor Roger Burritt

or monitoring, through reporting, as an accountability mechanism for voluntary environmental codes.[56] From the public's perspective, third party verification offers more credibility than does self-reporting. To ensure openness, fairness and honesty, it may be best to have community and NGO representatives involved in compliance verification.

- **An effective, transparent dispute resolution system**: A dispute resolution system that is inexpensive, fair, open, accessible and consistent is often essential to a well-functioning code.

Canada's generic guide for good voluntary codes provides greater detail about the list of characteristics that could be explored when assessing the effectiveness of a voluntary agreement. An amended list of indicators based on the Canadian guide is provided in Table 11.9.

In 2000, Industry Canada provided an evaluative framework for voluntary codes based on their earlier experience.[57] The framework draws attention to the importance of *due process, relevance, success* and *cost effectiveness* when evaluating a voluntary code and a set of performance indicators is drawn up for each of these issues. *Due process* considerations do not appear to add to indicators already evident in the earlier generic guide. *Relevance* is aimed at ensuring the objectives of a code remain important; for example, new policy instruments may reduce or remove the relevance of a code. *Success* issues are directly related to cost effectiveness and, in addition, to previously identified indicators, include the issues of the extent of industry coverage and whether there are regulatory incentives for compliance (e.g., reduced inspection, faster licensing). With a system of responsive regulation in place, behind each of these issues lies the possible threat that other enforcement mechanisms could be used to achieve the government's policy objectives. If industry cannot see any benefit in terms of achieving its own goals (e.g., to introduce actions to abate greenhouse gas emissions only if they improve the financial bottom line) the code may not be effective. Hence, the appropriate incentive structure is critical. If industry coverage is too low; if there is significant non-compliance; if there are inter-jurisdictional overlaps (e.g. between different states in a federal system); if sufficient resources are not voluntarily being devoted to the code; then government may step up the level of enforcement and return to stricter enforcement mechanisms.[58]

The United Nations Environment Programme's (UNEP's) Industry and Environment Technical Report

In 1998, UNEP, in a technical paper entitled *Voluntary Industry Codes of Conduct for the Environment*, added its guidance on how to develop and use voluntary codes. UNEP demonstrates what can be achieved by providing examples from leading voluntary codes based on the experience of industry associations in different countries, with some lessons drawn from international codes. Furthermore, it identifies how voluntary codes can be used as a tool to contribute to sustainable development. Hence, it might be expected that UNEP guidance is likely to be closer to that required for environmental issues, such as agreements to reduce greenhouse gas emissions, than the generic Canadian code. The paper discusses what can and cannot be done, stressing the need for government regulations as a necessary adjunct to voluntary agreements, as well as the importance of industry commitment, continuous support and monitoring.

UNEP's approach is based on the life cycle of a code from the early planning phase, through the development of principles, dissemination and guidance, early implementation and, finally, continuous implementation of the code. Associated with these five phases are 17 key ingredients that are divided into five critical aspects, the five Cs of effective voluntary codes: commitment, content, collaboration, check and communication. Table 11.10 replicates the detail of these five critical aspects and their

Table 11.10 UNEP *guidelines for effective voluntary codes: five critical aspects*

UNEP Critical Aspect	UNEP key ingredient	New indicators raised by UNEP
1 Commitment	• Define a clear sense of purpose that goes beyond improving the public's perception, as a poor environmental performance will still require commitment for improvement, but would encourage 'exit'. • Identify reasons to implement a code (e.g., cost savings, cleaner production, avoiding clean-up costs, improved public image, community confidence, long-term sustainability benefits). • Involve all members (e.g., formal and informal meetings, questionnaires and surveys, working groups). Those making environmental progress can encourage those just starting. • Involve society (e.g., find out what the public expects to reduce, any expectations gaps, focus members on priority issues, involve government authorities, NGOs, citizens).	NO
2 Content	• Cleaner production approach to environmental protection (precautionary strategy from Agenda 21): precautionary and pro-active. • Company management elements. • Target people: top managers, employees, suppliers, etc. • New tools: EMS, internal review and reporting; EIA, risk assessment, life cycle assessment and environmental cost accounting. • Integrate business functions: finance and accounting (e.g., integrate full cost of accounting in the code), marketing, globalize standards. • Social responsibilities. • Public openness and reporting regarding codes. • Interchange with government for responsible laws. • Accept global challenges.	NO
3 Collaboration	Assistance from industry association in implementation of the code: • General dissemination of information about a new code to all members (member involvement in development helps this process), e.g., via press, mailouts, publicize supporting companies, make a public commitment. • Management guidelines and tools to help implementation. • Guidelines: general and technical. • Management tools: EMS, environmental audit and preparation for emergency contingencies. • Case studies to demonstrate implementation. • Education and training. • Peer support and networking (e.g., forums and working groups).	YES

Table 11.10 *continued*

UNEP Critical Aspect	UNEP key ingredient	New indicators raised by UNEP
4 Check	Check if members are aware of a voluntary code, whether is it being implemented, and the environmental results. An industry association can undertake the check. • Review awareness: number of companies or associations signing up, CEO's committed to the code, participation rates at conferences, training sessions, questionnaires, etc. • Monitor implementation: self-assessment agreed and then distributed by industry association, return of self-assessment to the industry association which records results and evaluates industry position. • Check environmental results: measuring real environmental results is the hardest stage in monitoring. Need to agree upon a set of indicators.	YES
5 Communicate	Need to communicate progress to those outside the industry: • Listen to the public, should not just be provision of information about environmental progress, it requires public communication. • Communicate implementation: independent verification of company self-assessments helps demonstrate companies are making progress in implementing the voluntary code. • Communicate environmental results: explain successes and explain delays in achieving targets set.	NO

Source: adapted from UNEP (1998)

key ingredients and indicates where additional indicators might be of use in assessing the effectiveness of voluntary codes. Emphasis on the role of industry associations in collaboration and checking phases provides the main additional contribution to effectiveness identified in the UNEP Guidelines.

The Organisation for Economic Co-operation and Development's (OECD's) approach

The final contribution towards assessing the effectiveness of environmental agreements examined here is that of the OECD. In their 1999 publication, the OECD provided an overview of information available on the assessment of voluntary approaches. Criticism is made through the observation that the approaches are very new and have been created by practitioners.[59] The newness of the approaches is said to constrain empirical investigation and to hinder evaluation because of the lack of availability of theoretical results on the performance of different voluntary approaches. As the OECD approach[60] provides a good review of existing literature on negotiated agreements in Europe and the US, it is not replicated here. Evaluation through the OECD framework is ambitious and considers environmental effectiveness; economic efficiency; administration and compliance costs; competitiveness implications; soft effects (or behavioural changes related to policy instruments); innovation and learning effects; and viability and feasibility.[61] The OECD also makes several recommendations as to how to avoid the main shortcomings of voluntary approaches:

- Set clearly defined targets in quantitative terms.
- Establish business-as-usual trends (assuming normal technical progress) before setting baseline targets.
- Provide negative incentives: a threat of regulation to encourage organizations to go beyond business-as-usual.
- Set and impose penalties for non-compliance through binding commitments and regulatory requirements, and notification of new agreements to anti-trust authorities to avoid anti-competitive agreements.
- Provide positive incentives through technical assistance, technical workshops and provision of information on best practice.
- Monitor progress towards targets at the organizational and sector levels and report the results. Involve other stakeholders in setting the objectives of voluntary approaches and in monitoring through third party verification. (The EEA also places considerable emphasis on the benefits of involvement, learning and awareness when it suggests that environmental agreements appear to be of most use as complements to other policy measures regulations and fiscal instruments. In these situations, they can make a valuable contribution, especially in terms of their ability to raise awareness, create consensus and provide a forum for information-sharing among different parties).[62]

The OECD appears to be more cautious than others about the possibility of the success of voluntary agreements and more enthusiastic for the government to wield the big stick of regulation behind its back, when agreements are being negotiated as well as during the life of an agreement. Much of the literature quoted above calls for a multi-pronged approach. These additional options for governments are considered now.

Can regulation be designed to improve competitiveness?

Porter sums up the paradox facing business and government as: if innovation in response to environmental regulation can be profitable, if a company can actually offset the cost of compliance through improving resource productivity, why is regulation necessary at all? If such opportunities exist, wouldn't companies pursue them naturally and wouldn't regulation be unnecessary? That is like saying there will rarely be ten-dollar bills to be found on the ground because someone will already have picked them up. Certainly, some companies do pursue such innovations without, or in advance of, regulation. In Germany and Scandinavia, where both companies and consumers are very attuned to environmental concerns, innovation is not uncommon. As companies and their customers adopt the resource productivity mindset, and as knowledge about innovative technologies grows, there may well be less need for regulation over time. But the belief that companies will pick up on profitable opportunities without a regulatory push makes a false assumption about competitive reality, namely: that all profitable opportunities for innovation have already been discovered; that all managers have perfect information about them; and that organizational incentives are aligned with innovating. In fact, in the real world, managers often have highly incomplete information and limited time and attention.[63]

A growing body of work is showing that smart regulation can be effective in a way that improves businesses' competitiveness, whilst achieving real public benefits as well.[64] Some examples of this were discussed in Section 2, such as the German version of Best Available Technology legislation, which shows that specific forms of regulation will have to be developed that foster the dissemination of innovations and the development of new products and services. Market introduction, technology transfer, institutional design as well as science and education policies will all have to play their role.[65] Governments are able to adopt various policy measures and mechanisms to underpin and assist the development of the environment industry and the driving of innovation towards more sustainable outcomes. Instruments and mechanisms summarized in the tables earlier in this chapter, such as regulation, economic measures and attention to government actions and operations, are widely being used by governments to influence industry to innovate new technologies and processes.

History shows that voluntary partnerships, whilst a great start, are often not enough on their own to provide long-term solutions. Rather, they need to be supported by strategically phased-in regulation, regulatory frameworks or price signals and incentives to reward those businesses that are taking a lead. The wave of legislation regarding cleaner production (the Montreal Protocol in the late 1980s and 1990s) showed that with cost effective new strategies and clear phase-in times, business has easily met environmental regulation in the past. For example, in countries such as Germany and the Netherlands, as well as other parts of Europe, the environment industry has grown strongly as a result of environmental laws requiring companies to meet approved standards and actively reduce their negative load on the environment.

As Professor Michael Porter wrote:

> As other nations have pushed ahead, US trade has suffered. Germany has had perhaps the world's tightest regulations in stationary air-pollution control, and German companies appear to hold a wide lead in patenting and exporting air-pollution and other environmental technologies. As much as 70 per cent of the air pollution-control equipment sold in the US today is produced by foreign companies. Britain is another case in point. As its environmental standards have lagged, Britain's ratio of exports to imports in environmental technology has fallen from 8:1 to 1:1 over the past decade. In contrast, the US leads in those areas in which its regulations have been the strictest, such as pesticides and the remediation of environmental damage. Such leads should be treasured and extended. Environmental protection is a universal need, an area of growing expenditure in all the major national economies (US$50 billion a year in Europe alone) and a major export industry. The strongest proof that environmental protection does not hamper competitiveness is the economic performance of nations (over the last 30 years) with the strictest laws. Germany and Japan have tough regulations. In America, many of the sectors subject to the greatest environmental costs have actually improved their trade performance, among them chemicals, plastics and paints.[66]

Why do many governments and some global institutions still not see this? Michael Porter and Claas van der Linde took up the issue again in 1995 in *The Harvard Business Review* and the *Journal of Economic Perspectives*, arguing again that properly conceived regulation need not drive up costs.[67] They write:

> The need for regulation to protect the environment gets widespread but grudging acceptance: widespread because everyone wants a liveable planet, grudging because of the lingering belief that environmental regulations erode competitiveness. The prevailing view is that there is an inherent and fixed trade-off: ecology versus the economy. On one side of the trade-off are the social benefits that arise from strict environmental standards. On the other are industry's private costs for prevention and cleanup: costs that lead to higher prices and reduced competitiveness. This static view of environmental regulation, in which everything except regulation is held constant, is incorrect. If technology, products, processes, and customer needs were all fixed, the conclusion that regulation must raise costs would be inevitable. But companies operate in the real world of dynamic competition, not in the static

Table 11.11 *Strategies for effective regulation*

Focus on outcomes, not technologies; Best Available Technology regulation
Past regulations have often prescribed particular remediation technologies, such as catalysts or scrubbers for air pollution, rather than focusing on setting standards based on outcomes.

Develop the regulation with the relevant communities, stakeholders and businesses to ensure effectiveness[68]
Using interaction and building relationships and trust amongst stakeholders to improve communication and the effectiveness of regulatory approaches is recommended by modern regulatory theory, such as the post regulatory state. Even in an area as challenging as the tragedy of the commons, Ostrom and her colleagues are cautiously hopeful, pointing to examples where individuals and groups of CPR users have come together to forge their own solutions rather than waiting for governments or other institutions to impose rules and regulations. They stress that one of the most important lessons learned from empirical studies of sustainable resources is that more solutions exist than those Hardin proposed. Some of the most important recent case studies of community involvement with the development of regulation are the Florida Everglades,[69] The New York Water crisis,[70] and Canada's Coastal Action Program.[71]

Phase-in strict rather than lax regulation to inspire and reward real design solutions
Companies can handle lax regulation incrementally, often with end-of-pipe or secondary treatment solutions. Regulation, therefore, needs to be stringent enough to promote real innovation. Regulate as close to the end user as practical, while encouraging upstream solutions. This will normally allow more flexibility for innovation in the end product and in all the production and distribution stages. Avoiding pollution entirely or, second best, mitigating it early in the value chain is almost always less costly than late-stage remediation or clean-up.

Employ phase-in periods
Ample but well-defined phase-in periods tied to industry capital investment cycles will allow companies to develop innovative resource saving technologies, rather than force them to implement expensive solutions hastily, merely patching over problems.

Use carrots as well as sticks
Market incentives such as pollution charges and deposit-refund schemes draw attention to resource inefficiencies. In addition, tradable permits provide continuing incentives for innovation and encourage the creative use of technologies that exceed current standards.

Develop regulations in cooperation with other countries, or slightly ahead of them
It is important to minimize possible competitive disadvantages relative to foreign companies that are not yet subject to the same standard. Developing regulations slightly ahead of other countries will also maximize export potential by raising incentives for innovation. However, if standards are too far ahead or too different in character from those that are likely to apply to foreign competitors, industry may innovate in the wrong directions.

Ensure that the regulatory process is clear, bipartisan where possible, stable and predictable
The regulatory process is as important as the standards. If standards and phase-in periods are set and accepted early enough, and if regulators commit to keeping standards in place for, say, five years, industry can lock in and tackle root-cause solutions instead of hedging against the next twist or turn in government philosophy. Industry participation in setting standards should be encouraged from the outset.

Develop strong technical capabilities among regulators
Regulators must understand an industry's economics and what drives its competitiveness. Better information exchange will help avoid costly gaming in which ill-informed companies use an array of lawyers and consultants to try to stall the poorly designed regulations of ill-informed regulators. Minimize the time and resources consumed in the regulatory process itself.
Time delays in granting permits are usually costly for companies. Self-regulation with periodic inspections would be more efficient than requiring formal approvals. Potential and actual litigation creates uncertainty and consumes resources. Mandatory arbitration procedures or rigid arbitration steps before litigation would lower costs and encourage innovation.

Source: adapted and edited from Porter and van der Linde (1995a, pp121–134).

world of much economic theory. They are constantly finding innovative solutions to pressures of all sorts, from competitors, customers, and regulators. Properly designed environmental standards can trigger innovations that lower the total cost of a product or improve its value. Such innovations allow companies to use a range of inputs more productively, from raw materials to energy to labour, thus offsetting the costs of improving environmental impact and ending the stalemate. Ultimately, this enhanced resource productivity makes companies more competitive, not less.[72]

As a result, the companies acting early to address domestic regulations became conveniently positioned to internationally export the innovations and solutions developed as other countries began to tackle similar problems.

Increasingly, the environment is being regarded as an opportunity for innovation, and not as a threat to a company. This shift is related to a parallel change in environmental policies from cleaning-up activities towards integrated and precautionary measures. Whereas cleaning-up and pollution control measures necessarily add additional costs to companies, the new approach allows for cost reduction and innovation.

Raimund Bleishwitz, Wuppertal Institute

A summary of the strategies for government was presented in Table 11.1; some of these are explored in more detail in Table 11.11.

Effective economic measures to complement either voluntary or regulatory approaches

Carrots as well as sticks

If regulation simply ends up being the lowest common denominator then industry is simply required to operate above minimum standards and little progress will be achieved. However, the literature shows that, to date, voluntary measures, whilst achieving some gains, have not been as effective as was first hoped. This has led to renewed focus on the use of other market incentive mechanisms such as tax neutral shifts and permit systems. Experiences in many countries show that businesses leap at such opportunities and incentives that reward early adopters. Since tax burdens on business and society are already significant in most countries, there are plenty of taxes that could be cut with increased revenue from eco-taxes. Today nearly 95 per cent of the US$7.5 trillion in tax revenues raised annually worldwide comes from levies on payrolls, personal income, corporate profits, capital gains, retail sales, trade and built property; all essentially penalties for work and investment. At present, the governments of the world are mostly applying 20–50 per cent taxes on wages and profits and almost none on pollution and waste of resources.[73] Governments are overtaxing social goods and under-taxing social and environmental 'bads'. A tax-neutral shift would result in no citizen and few businesses being worse off whilst internalizing the presently externalized negative costs to the environment. Ernst Ulrich von Weizsäcker, whose uncle was President of Germany at the time, instantly mainstreamed the idea in Europe in his 1992 bestselling book, *Ecological Tax Reform*.

Tax neutral shift

Numerous overseas studies have shown that by putting taxes on environmental negatives, such as waste and pollution, and removing them from social benefits, such as work, both environmental protection and job creation can be achieved.[74] This outcome is often referred to as the environment and jobs 'double dividend'. As far back as 1975,

Table 11.12 *International environmental tax/levy reform*

Country	Tax/levy shift
Denmark	New or increased environment related taxes, including a carbon tax, have been used to reduce employer and income taxes.
Finland	New landfill and energy taxes used to lower income and labour taxes.
Netherlands	New energy tax used to reduce employer social security levy.
Norway	Proposal by Tax Commission to introduce new eco-taxes and to reduce environmentally harmful subsidies and payroll tax.
Sweden	New environment related taxes used to reduce income taxes, with reductions in employer taxes being considered.
UK	New landfill and energy taxes used to reduce employers' social security contributions.
Germany	New energy taxes to reduce employer and employee pension contributions.

Source: OECD (1997a); Hamilton et al (2000)

Agnar Sandino argued in the *Swedish Journal of Economics* that an 'optimal' revenue code would make substantial 'Pigouvian'[75] taxes in order to pass the costs of pollution back to polluters and reduce the need for other taxes such as income tax. Studies also show that the double dividend boosts employment growth whilst also helping the environment. Environmental Tax Reform (ETR) shifts taxation away from environmentally and socially sound practices and places it on polluting and environmentally damaging practices. The ETR provides enormous potential for improving environmental protection, whilst simultaneously boosting jobs and the economy. It also has the potential to be a key driver for economic and environmental modernization.

Most governments already understand that this (ETR) can be achieved with reductions in income tax so that on average, taxpayers are no worse off, as shown in the European examples in Table 11.12. Along this line of argument, almost all EU membership states have adopted some kind of eco-taxes since the late1990s. The predominant aim is a moderate but steady increase in energy or resource prices. Such an increase leads to further innovations and cumulative effects. If designed together with a good policy mix and other tax reductions, the overall effects on international competitiveness would be positive. There is both increasing theoretical and empirical evidence from economics that fiscal and regulatory competition resulting from unilateral action contributes to increasing economic efficiency and does not have dramatic negative or destabilizing effects.

Sceptics may still argue why such measures are needed. Examples abound around the world that if negative externalities are ignored a terrible legacy will be left for future generations. Take the country of Nauru for example in the South Pacific. It is the world's smallest independent republic, having gained independence from Australia in 1968. It is a phosphate rock island of 21 square km in the South Pacific Ocean. A century of intensive phosphate mining, mainly by a consortium of companies from the UK, Australia and New Zealand, reduced 90 per cent of the island to an uninhabitable wasteland. Although phosphate sales gave Nauruans one of the highest per capita incomes in the developing world, the mining has destroyed their home. Now, with the phosphate gone, Nauruans have neither their island nor anything else much to trade. There is nowhere to farm. In 1989, Nauru filed a suit in the international Court of Justice against Australia for the damage done to the island before independence. Australia was ordered to pay Nauru AU$107 million in damages. Whilst the case of Nauru is an extreme one, it does highlight the problem of finite natural resources.

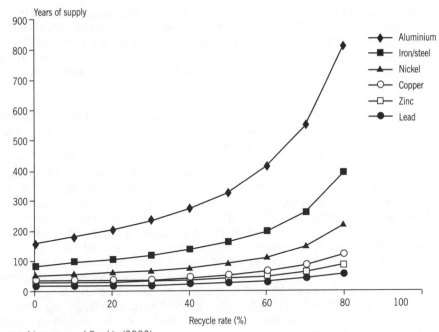

Source: Norgate and Rankin (2002)

Figure 11.3 *Years of supply vs. recycle rate for various metals*

Natural resources

Sustainability experts argue that our present economies are wasting scarce resources for future generations. In contrast, those economists who believe in the infallibility of the market argue that market price signals will feedback when a resource is scarce and when it is not, thus preventing society ever running out of resources or wasting them for future generations. There is truth in both of these positions. Prices do provide signals concerning the scarcity of resources, and in the absence of market failures these signals can lead to reasonable economic efficiency. However, we have shown that there are many cases where there are market failures, for example where there are externalities and situations like the 'tragedy of the commons'. In these cases the rate at which resources are exploited will not be efficient if we simply rely on market prices. What about a privately owned resource, though, like a mine? The owner of the mine has a clearly defined property right. Let us assume this owner is paying for the exact costs of the externalities of pollution from the mine so the rate of extraction from the mine is solely determined by whether the minerals are worth more in the future or the present? How much will copper ore be worth in 30 years time? If we assume resources will run out then one would assume that there would be a time, well into the future, when prices for raw copper ore will be significantly higher than today's prices. However, it is more than likely that the market can find substitutes for copper and the market may switch to using those substitutes around the time that the copper ore is exhausted. Hence, prices may not change significantly until many mineral resources have come close to the end of their supply.

Also, because mineral resources are present globally, if a nation exhausts its supply of a mineral that does not mean the price will change much in the global market for that commodity. This is why Nauru phosphate was mined to the point where all resources were exhausted without any significant market price signal from the global phosphate market. Whilst the local supply of phosphate had diminished to zero, the global supply of phosphate was sufficient to avoid the market signals reflecting local conditions. In Sections 1 and 2 it was demonstrated that developing nations with access to the most abundant and cheapest natural resources often have a lower gross domestic product (GDP) than countries like Singapore. In the academic literature this is known as the resource curse. In *The Natural Wealth of Nations*, David Roodham outlined in detail several additional factors contributing to this:

- Many studies show that, especially in developing countries, modern resource extraction does not do enough to impart skills to the managers and labourers it employs; skills that could then be applied in other industries.
- The wealth and profits in many developing countries, generated from timber, minerals and oil, tend not to have a positive impact on the country. While President of the Philippines in the 1960s and 1970s, Ferdinand Marcos granted timber concessions to political and military allies, the logging that followed generated US$42 billion in profits for 480 already well endowed and connected Philippine families. One doesn't need to be Einstein to realize what a difference could have been made if the government had instead charged market rates for the concessions and invested the billions in education, health and supporting community business programmes throughout the Philippines. The Harvard study by Jeffrey Sachs, quoted in Section 1, also found evidence that spending on family planning, infrastructure, education and health helped growth. Oxfam's 1997 Growth with Equity report on the Asian miracle concluded that those governments that spend the most on education, public health and infrastructure are the countries that exhibit the most growth. The report found, however, that if this same wealth were confined to political and social elites, it gave them disproportionate political power, which further prevented much needed social, economic and environmental reforms.
- As already stated, what is also most interesting is that the countries in the developing world which are dependent on key natural resources and lack diversity in their economy, are vulnerable to commodity price shocks.

Although, over the long term, extraction of natural resources may not be as effective for the overall well-being of national economies as, for example, the strategies employed by Singapore, resource companies are nevertheless creating real jobs and building real mining and timber towns. These jobs support families, putting food on the table for their children. However, the question is, are subsidies to these industries economically and environmentally justified? David Roodham and others have shown the following:

- These industries (fossil fuel, timber, mining) are capital intensive and, due to automation, often employ fewer people (per tonne produced) than even ten years ago.
- Studies have shown that some governments are subsidizing some industries to such an extent that it would actually be more cost effective to pay the workers the same wage not to work.
- And finally, extractive industries can be so destructive as to irreversibly destroy the environment and even the existing community structures. David Roodham illustrates this when he writes: 'Experiences in the Indonesian province of East Kalimantan illustrate how an extractive industry can harm a regional economy. Logging companies obtained title from the government to indigenous lands ... and employed 6 per cent of the workforce by the late 1980s. But they destroyed even more jobs by depriving cottage industries of forest access, according to the Indonesian Forum for the Environment in Jakarta'.[76]

In such instances, regardless of whatever short-term economic gain is made, the long-term well-being of the community has been so harmed as to beg the question, isn't there a better way? Yes, a resources boom is an opportunity for firms and the home or host nation to be investing in higher productivity outcomes, value adding to raw materials before export, and diversifying the economy to ensure that when this resources boom ends there are no significant job losses nor a blow-out in the nations 'balance of payments' deficit. It is a chance to be investing in R&D/Demonstration, and innovation.

There is much that the extractive industries can do too. They can innovate for sustainability. As the Argyle Diamond Mine in Western Australia showed, using a strategy of innovation for sustainability has not only extended the life of the mine by 20 years, numerous other cost saving innovations have been found and community goodwill is excellent. They can give back to the community to restore trust. They can support efforts to reduce corruption in governments. Numerous extractive industry companies have supported The Extractive Industry Transparency Initiative (EITI). The Initiative was officially launched by Tony Blair at the World Summit on Sustainable Development (WSSD) in September 2002. Its aim is to increase transparency over payments by companies and revenues to governments in the extractive industries.[77] They can agree to increase the amount of royalties returning to communities and the nation within which the mining, logging, etc. occur. For instance, BHP Billiton has created PNG Sustainable Ltd that will ensure all future profits from Ok Tedi will be used to support sustainable development projects in PNG. They can improve practices to get certified as best practice by legitimate third party certification. The World Wide Fund for Nature (WWF) is researching to develop a methodology to certify mining sites and mining companies. The Forest Stewardship Council and the Marine Stewardship Council already offer this opportunity to the forestry and fishing industries. There is much governments can do to help: to take the opportunity of a resource boom to assist economically wisely other successful parts of the economy and also to innovate to ensure that a lack of balance of payments deficits and other inflationary pressures are kept in check.

In Section 2, Fairbanks and Smith showed what firms can do, in any nation, to form with other businesses a cluster to improve outcomes for all those involved. In many sectors, firms that work with other relevant firms in clusters stand the best chance of achieving lasting competitive advantage in the 21st century. Despite the increased globalization of the world economy, there is mounting evidence that competitiveness depends on these local synergies, local clusters for which national and regional governments can play a vital role in ensuring that obstacles to these clusters' success are overcome. It is often argued that certain countries have economies that are too small to be part of a wave of innovation. However, consider Taiwan which, in the 1970s, had less skilled labour, capital and infrastructure than all OECD countries at that time – but Taiwan is now the world's leading producer of semi-conductors.

Professor Michael Porter's group's research suggests that competitive advantage is created and sustained through highly localized processes. Porter argues that 'The role of the home nation seems to be as strong as or stronger than ever.'

> Despite globalization, economic growth is being driven by 'global city regions', which have strong concentrations of emerging and traditional industries, supportive infrastructure and a highly educated population. In these global city regions, diverse knowledge clusters and networks are formed which allow maximum innovation to be combined with existing information in traditional industries to drive broad-based industry development. With globalization these local clusters are even more critical to national competitiveness than ever before.
>
> Peter Brain (1999) *Beyond Meltdown: The Global Battle for Sustained Growth*

As mentioned in Table 11.6, Italy provides one of the best examples of demonstrating the value of local synergies, clusters and business cooperatives helping to achieve higher than normal economic outcomes. The north of Italy is now significantly more prosperous than the south. Yet 1000 years ago the opposite was the case. Why has this changed? Several leading academics have studied this. In 1958 sociologist Edward Banfield's conclusion was that the culture of the south ran contrary to members of society banding together to act for the common good.[78] Instead, they were oriented towards 'Maximize the material, short-run advantage of the nuclear family: assume all others will do likewise'. They were more competitive than cooperative – and poorer for it.

Robert Putnam from Harvard, for example, notes that in both Northern and Southern Italy there were considerable investments in social relationships.[79] However, Northern Italy tended to be characterized by 'horizontal' ties that grew out of a long history of guilds and cooperative efforts. He argues that the 'horizontal civic bonds have undergirded levels of economic and institutional performance generally much higher than in the South, where social and political relations have been vertically structured'. Robert Putnam's 'Bowling Alone' article built on this to show that the roots of the difference go back to 1100 when the North never knew the centralized, autocratic, vertical-power-structure rule of Normans, and instead had small autonomous republics for many centuries. While the southerners lived in a hierarchical society, with every family dependent on the patronage of landowners and bureaucrats, the northerners depended on one another for work, for help, for money; and they formed hundreds of low-level, horizontal-bond organizations such as guilds and credit associations that built mutual trust instead of competition. In studying why particular regions of Italy were wealthier than others, he was surprised to find that the most powerful association was with the number of soccer clubs and choral societies. He wrote 'Good government in Italy is a by-product of singing groups and soccer clubs.' His analysis provided the basis for understanding how social capital – both the historical legacy and current social networks – have a significant effect on how an economy works. Markets are available to develop everywhere, but to bring together the required components of finance, government approval and community support requires the social infrastructure of networks and trust. The enduring 'tragedy of the commons' nightmare of southern Italy suggests that any part of the world high in social capital should place an extremely high priority on the preservation of that social capital. This human dimension is being increasingly acknowledged as being key to achieving both better economic and environmental outcomes.

Government–industry partnerships to improve innovation

Increasingly, businesses and government understand working with other businesses, government bodies, and other stakeholders as part of clusters to achieve greater outcomes. But also businesses' capacity to innovate also depends on factors outside the firm. Hence, firms are now working with a range of stakeholders to improve their innovation capacity. The ability of firms to innovate depends, in many nations, on a complex network of interactions with various external institutions. In many sectors, individual firms are part of a broader production system. How a firm's suppliers and distributors manage their own business, gain access to capital and deal with government regulations is as important to the firm as its own internal issues. Institutions in non-industry sectors also affect firms' ability to innovate. Government support for programmes can provide access to expertise, technology, laboratories, facilities and financing. Countries that facilitate the linking of firms with these government assets, are more likely to flourish than those that do not. Other sources of knowledge and technology exist, including university research units, Centres of Excellence, and technical standards organizations. Again, nations with effective linkages among these resources and firms are better off than those without. Institutions that finance the innovation process are critical players. Lenders and investors that understand

Table 11.15 *Green jobs around the world*

Country/region	Green jobs
Global	11 million pollution-control jobs worldwide at present. One of the fastest growing labour market sectors.
Australia	Green jobs growth of 38% between 1988 and 1993, one of highest growth sectors over that period. Growth strongest in waste management and clean production. Sustainable energy NSW: direct jobs growth of 9% per annum 1996–1998. Growth of 19% expected in 1999–2000. Other (unsustainable) energy industries had substantial job losses in the 1990s.
European Union	1 million direct jobs supplying environmental goods and services, 3.75 million direct and indirect jobs (in 1994). 190,000–320,000 new jobs in wind energy expected by 2010. Up to 294,000 direct jobs in photovoltaics by 2010.
France	418,000 jobs in environmentally related activities (in 1992).
Germany	956,000 jobs in environmentally related activities (in 1994). Growth of 520,000 jobs between 1984 and 1994.
US	480,000 direct jobs in remanufacturing (in 1998). Expected growth of 350,000 net jobs in sustainable energy by 2010.

Sources: ACF/ACTU (1994), Brown et al (2000), Ellis and Associates (1999)

recently, Japan, the Republic of Korea and other countries in East Asia have used a variety of mechanisms for market enhancement, in addition to securing the economic, social and institutional fundamentals. Sometimes these interventions were quite elaborate: the highly strategic use of subsidies, for example. At other times they were less intrusive, taking the form of export promotion and special infrastructure incentives. But the ability to choose wisely among these interventions and use them effectively is critical; ill-considered trade, credit, and industrial policies can and have cost countries dearly.' A brief explanation of the industry policy toolkit is provided in the following. Industry policy is a toolkit that governments use to manage these economic transitions to ensure that they are as painless as possible. Effective industry policy for policy-makers and governments would ensure that people are re-trained for the next areas of jobs growth. Numerous Asian countries, including Japan, South Korea and Singapore, have successfully used Industry Policy to rapidly catch up to the technological frontier over the last 40 years. This, plus the experience of the first industrial revolution, makes industry policy a very rich field of tested theories. Such knowledge is therefore very important if nations are to effectively assist their firms, cities and communities to make the transition to a truly sustainable economy. Countries also need to learn from what the best Asian economies have done over the past 40 years to escape the 'resource curse'. The toolkit to help nations make a transition away from significant dependence on natural resource export income, which was used by Japan, South Korea and the other Asian Tigers, is known as industry policy. It needs to work with and complement a nation's innovation policy and its national system of innovation policy.

Both macro- and micro-economics tend to focus on money flows, for example prices, the level of investment, taxes and subsidies. However, the impact of prices in the market can only be understood in the light of the elasticity or responsiveness of the market to those prices. For example, if products in the market are essential staples (i.e. the products are needed, the quantity needed is relatively fixed and no ready substitutes are available), the market will be highly inelastic: that is, highly unresponsive to either raised or lowered prices. At the other extreme, a luxury good, nowhere near its point of

Table 11.16 *Levels of economics*

Domain	Examples
Macro-economics	National accounts, monetary policy, interest rates, the level and structure of taxation, exchange rates, wages policy, unemployment, etc.
Meso-economics	Industry policy, regional economic development, and now also 'supply-chain transformation'.
Micro-economics	The use of targeted economic instruments to achieve issue specific changes in economic behaviour, the theory of the firm, firm level competitiveness, consumer behaviour, etc.

Source: Phillip Sutton, Green Innovations Inc

demand saturation, will be highly elastic. Demand will contract sharply if prices go up and increase sharply if prices fall.

Therefore, if there is a need to make significant changes to the structure and behaviour of an economy, attention needs to be paid to:

- nudging the economy in the desired directions using prices;
- facilitating change and increasing the responsiveness (elasticity) of the economy through any other channel for influencing the economy (other than via price or the quantity of monetary investment flows), for example by changing the technical, organizational and informational structure of the economy;
- increasing the key stakeholders in the market to be able to respond to a price signal;
- increasing people, especially people on lower incomes to be able to respond to a price signal through various measures.

For instance, simply increasing energy prices to 'encourage the conservation of energy and reduce greenhouse gases' will achieve little and potentially harm the poor if not combined with a much broader strategy to help business, families, schools, hospitals and universities improve energy efficiency in the first place. It is wise for governments as part of their industry policy to run a 2–5-year national energy efficiency strategy with government assistance and equity considerations built into it (the carrot). And then combine that with phasing in a market signal into the economy over 5 years, starting 2–3 years after the energy efficiency programme had started. If governments wait 2–3 years to use a market signal on energy prices this period should be long enough for the pay-back periods on energy efficiency initiatives to have largely paid for themselves and hence firms' energy costs should have been reduced substantially by this time. Governments should also address all the barriers for wiser energy and resource usage to improve the ability of the market to respond to a market signal. How to do this in the energy sector is well covered in papers like *Climate: Making Sense and Making Money* by Amory and Hunter Lovins (1997). In Section 4 these issues are discussed in detail.

Meso-economics is the field of economics that focuses on these critical non-price channels of influence. It is the branch of economics that deals the most directly with ways to change the elasticity or responsiveness of the economy and it is thus an essential complement to macro- and micro-economics. Traditionally, industry policy has been driven by the desire of governments and industry groups to foster economic development for the benefit of the community or firms. Now that we live in a massive interwoven global economy, the value chains or value webs that link each stage in the production of a product, whether service or physical good, are so complex that the starting point for analysis and action is usually geographically limited industry sectors.

First, imagine the sort of value chain or 'tree' that is created to show the transformation of raw materials through to a final product (as was shown in Figure 6.4). For just one product the related tree will be immensely complicated. Then imagine thousands of products, each with their own 'tree'. This starts to get very complicated and so, in a more simplified process, all the separate trees are tipped over, laid upon each other and compressed. From this we create a data set that can be more easily understood as a series of interlinked industry sectors, for example resource extraction, resource processing, elaborately transformed manufactures, infrastructure services, construction services, business services, information services, personal services, etc. This industry sector view is the foundation of industry economics or industry policy. Most industry policy proponents (e.g., government departments for industry development, industry associations, etc.) also have a geographical mandate, covering a nation or province or region, and so industry policy is often modified to introduce a regional economic development orientation. On the other hand, local governments and local economic development associations start from the regional development focus and then try to develop strategies for their region to tap into growth strategies that originate in the industry policy arena.

Traditional industry policy and regional economic development policy commence with the following assumptions:

- There are complex and widespread value chains to be tapped into (often global in extent).
- Industry sectors (that amalgamate these value chains) can be small or large, and declining, stable or growing.
- Local areas should try to harness or build local competences that make the area a desirable participant in the industry sectors (with preference often given to large and or growing sectors so as to maximize the local economic growth potential).
- Harnessing or building local competences requires not only general policies and investments that would help all types of business, but also more closely targeted actions that are built on detailed knowledge of the industry sectors and the local strengths and weaknesses.
- Both general and targeted assistance should focus on the creation of positive externalities, that is, positive side-effects where the benefits extend beyond the firm to whole networks of firms and, ideally, to the community at large.
- Assistance is most often important early in the development of a value chain, industry sector or local competence (the 'infant industry' argument). Therefore, firms should not capture programmes intended to assist them, in the early build-up phase, as a never-ending source of assistance. The same argument applies to structural adjustment assistance. For example, assistance for firms to transfer from one value chain to another, or to assist communities to wind down non-viable activities where there would otherwise be major social costs arising from the change.

Industry policy and regional economic development programmes, which affect both the supply and demand sides of the economy, can involve investment in or activity to foster:

- research and development;
- specialized infrastructure;
- specialized eduction and training;
- network and collaborative project facilitation, cluster development and partnership promotion;
- more sensitive and appropriate taxes and subsidies (including situation specific bundles such as 'feebates');[93]

- improved capital availability; and
- regulation via legal and economic instruments.

Because industry policy and regional economic development are founded on the specifics of products, firms, localities and communities, there is a wide range of policy tools available. As with anything, the devil is in the detail in terms of whether firms and nations will achieve the shift to sustainability. The field of meso-economics offers governments subtle tools and detailed strategies to more effectively and appropriately play its part in assisting an industry transition to a sustainable economy.

There still are some who believe that this should all be left to the market. They argue that the invisible hand of the market is the best way to ensure scarce resources are allocated efficiently. As we stated before, over the last 30 years in economics a far more sophisticated understanding of markets and market failure has evolved that can be used by governments to determine when it may be appropriate to act, and how. These developments in economics are somewhat theoretical, but they are foundational for all this discussion about the role of government. The economists who developed this new field of the economics of information were awarded the Nobel Prize for Economics in 2001 for this work. Hence, these exciting developments in economics are summarized in the next chapter.

CHAPTER 12

TOWARDS A DEEPER UNDERSTANDING

Those who believe that the market on its own is the most efficient way to allocate scarce resources would disagree with many of the previous suggested government measures. Giving free reign to the invisible hand of the market, they argue, is the best way to ensure the most desirable outcomes for society as a whole. In Section 1, and again in the introduction to Section 3, it was stated that over the last 30 years a far more sophisticated understanding of the market has developed that allows us clarity to see when markets may fail and when it may be beneficial for governments to act.

Markets and efficiency

As communities we have a range of goals, one of which is protecting the health of the natural ecosystems on which we depend. As neither our resources nor our lives are infinite, not all goals can be fully realized and somehow we have to make choices about what to do. In this context, efficiency matters precisely because we are interested in realizing as many of our goals as possible. Hence, the strong call for markets to be efficient. Governments and their detractors have often suggested that the state should not intervene in markets for this very reason. They claim that free markets allocate resources in the most efficient way possible and interference would only make matters worse. Is this really the case? Before we can answer this important question, we need to understand two main concepts: first what is a market?, and second how do economists define efficiency?

What is a market?

Markets are one of many methods societies have devised for allocating scarce resources. A market for a good or service uses what economists call the *price mechanism* to allocate the product. For example, the more demand exceeds supply in a well-functioning market, the higher the price will rise and vice versa. The relationships between different markets mean that price changes in one market will feed through into many other markets in the economy.

The market is therefore a decentralized method of resource allocation, as the information embodied in the prices of many different products throughout the economy enables people to adjust and coordinate their consumption, investment and production decisions without the help of some central institution for allocating resources.

How do economists define efficiency?

It might seem intuitive that efficiency is achieved when all the firms in an economy produce their products with the minimum possible amount of inputs such as labour, raw materials, and so on. However, this is not what economists mean when they say that the market allocates resources efficiently. This is because efficiency in production is only one aspect of the efficiency of the economy *as a whole*. For example, if firms were making their products with the minimum possible amount of inputs, but those products were not the ones that people actually wanted to buy, economists would not say that the economy was allocating resources efficiently. Even if firms were producing the goods that people wanted, if the goods were allocated to some people while others valued them more highly, economists would still not say that the allocation was efficient. The inefficiency exists because people could trade with each other for mutual benefit. For example, if a person has a bottle of beer but prefers wine, and another has a glass of wine but prefers beer, they could trade or swap goods and both be happier. Without creating any additional goods, the existing goods in the economy can be rearranged so that some people are made better off and no one is worse off.

It is this idea of making people better off 'for nothing' that informs the standard definition of economic efficiency. Formally, an allocation of resources is 'Pareto efficient'[1] if it is impossible to make anyone better off without making someone else worse off, as all the opportunities for mutually beneficial trades have been exhausted. This means that the very best way to distribute the resources, to make the population in general as 'better off' as possible, has been found and internal swapping, intervention and market manipulation will not provide a net benefit. In some ways Pareto efficiency is a 'narrow' or 'weak' criterion for evaluating the desirability of a particular allocation of resources. For example, not every Pareto efficient outcome will be regarded as desirable, as the criterion excludes distributional issues. Imagine a two-person economy where one person is allocated everything and the other has nothing at all. Such an allocation will, in general, be Pareto efficient as it theoretically fits the criterion that we cannot make either person better off without making the other worse off. Nevertheless, for most people this is not a desirable economic system, except perhaps for the person with everything.

Because Pareto efficiency fails to consider the fairness of the resulting distribution of resources, governments may wish to alter the allocation of resources even when the market is allocating them efficiently. Although important and fascinating, questions of equality are beyond the scope of this publication, where we focus on the efficiency of the market mechanism.

Limitations aside, this is how economists understand markets and efficiency. But when are markets efficient? Is it all of the time, or only sometimes? If markets cannot always achieve Pareto efficiency, can economists help us to understand exactly when markets will indeed be the most efficient method of resource allocation? We will answer these questions by looking at how economists' understanding of market efficiency has changed over time.

The classical understanding

Economists have long recognized that markets do not guarantee efficient allocations of resources. Adam Smith, generally recognized as the 'father' of modern economics, noted in 1776 that the market was not efficient in the presence of monopolies.[2] The monopolist can charge higher prices than those that would prevail if there were competition from other producers. Nor was the market efficient when supplying particular types of goods.[3] Private producers will not be efficient suppliers of 'public' goods such as roads and police protection, even if the market were competitive. Because individuals reap the benefits of roads or police whether they pay for them or not, private suppliers are unlikely to have enough paying customers to make production worthwhile. Therefore, more than two centuries ago, economists knew of some specific conditions under which markets were inefficient. They also knew of solutions to these inefficiencies. For instance, the government could 'break up' a monopoly and collect taxes to finance the provision of public goods. Whilst markets could not provide a watertight guarantee of efficiency, these discrete instances of market failure left market supremacy intact as the state's proper role was to fix these few failures and leave the market free to allocate resources in the most efficient possible way.

Perfect complete markets

The absence of monopolists and the need to deliver public goods are therefore necessary for Pareto efficiency. But is this enough? The answer is no, and it was first demonstrated mathematically in the 1950s by economists Kenneth Arrow and George Debreu.[4] They came up with a set of conditions that would guarantee Pareto efficient outcomes. Now known as the First Fundamental Theorem of Welfare Economics (FFTWE), the conditions state that if an economy has a complete set of perfect markets, the allocation of resources will be Pareto efficient. However, the assumptions made to develop the proof may not necessarily reflect the workings of real market economies, and, in order to understand how likely it is that these conditions will be met in real life, we need to understand what they mean.

A *perfect market* is one in which no participant exercises market power. Formally, a perfect market is one in which everyone is a 'price-taker', meaning no individual buyer or seller can influence the market price just by altering his or her own production or consumption. To understand market power, consider the following. If a single consumer decides never to eat tomatoes again, the price of tomatoes will be unaffected. In contrast, if a company, such as one of the handful of companies who together have a significant share of the world trade in cocoa beans, stopped buying beans tomorrow, the price of coffee beans could change. Hence the company exercises power in the market for coffee beans, while our single consumer exercises no power in the market for tomatoes.

If neither the buyers nor the sellers in a market can affect the price in this way, the market is perfect. Many real world markets are imperfect, even though they are not monopolies, because there are too few major buyers or producers. An economy has a *complete set of markets* if it has a market for everything. Here we must be careful about what 'everything' is. It is not sufficient to have a market for every good that could conceivably affect one's well-being, even those not traded in most conventional market economies, like biodiversity and clean air. A complete set of markets requires that the economy has a market for every possible good, in every possible physical location, at every possible time, in every possible 'state of the world'. For example, we require a market for umbrellas in Tokyo at 2 am next Tuesday, if it is raining and also a market for umbrellas in Tokyo at 2 am next Tuesday, if it is fine. One of the implications of the 'state of the world' requirement is that there exists a complete set of 'risk markets' where everyone must be able to purchase insurance for every conceivable adverse event.

So Arrow and Debreu showed that we achieve Pareto efficiency when (i) the economy has a market for everything, and (ii) each of these markets is perfectly competitive. Not even economists are so stubborn a breed as to maintain that real world economies actually meet these two conditions.[5] Despite the stringency of these conditions, however, most economists initially believed that Arrow and Debreu's conclusion was relatively robust. Although our world cannot be like the one in the Fundamental

Theorem, it is similar enough, so markets remain the most efficient way to allocate resources. However, over the past 30 years this belief has shifted somewhat as a result of a critical evaluation of Arrow and Debreu's assumptions about information.

The economics of information

The premises of any theorem make explicit the assumptions under which the conclusion is guaranteed to hold. However, some assumptions are made explicitly, whilst some are implicit assumptions about the nature of the world. In the case of the FFTWE, the completeness and competitiveness requirements are the explicit conditions under which the market will allocate resources efficiently. Implicit in Arrow and Debreu's work were the assumptions that information is fixed, costless and perfect. We know that information is not fixed, nor costless, nor perfect. The amount, nature and distribution of knowledge within a society change over time. Individuals and organizations must sacrifice time and money in order to acquire new information. Sometimes knowledge is retained by parties who have an incentive to conceal it, so that information is unevenly or 'asymmetrically distributed' between buyers and sellers. Economists such as George Akerlof, Joseph Stiglitz and Carl Shapiro argued that the kinds of assumptions economists made about information were important, because changing these assumptions would result in significantly different economic models. In the 1970s and 1980s, these and other pioneering economists set about including information in their models. The results were exciting. Rather than producing more complicated models making essentially the same predictions, the explicit inclusion of information resulted in models capable of predicting and explaining behaviour in many different markets, from those for labour to those for insurance and bank credit.

For example:

- People wishing to purchase health insurance possess more information about their susceptibility to illness than do their potential insurers. While the insurance company cannot distinguish between 'low risk' and 'high risk' insurees, those people who are more likely to need expensive medical treatment are more likely to purchase more insurance. If there are more 'high risk' insurees than the insurance company expects, the company will have to pay out on a higher than expected proportion of its premiums. Considering the asymmetric nature of information in this market helps to explain why insurance firms screen their potential clients so carefully, and why these markets are so fragile and prone to collapse.[6]
- Obtaining information about the productivity of white-collar workers can be difficult and time-consuming. It is easy to sit in front of a computer and look earnest while daydreaming or exploring the Internet. Rather than pay additional people to watch the employees, and employees to monitor the employees that monitor the employees, and so on, organizations may offer salary packages better than those their workers could find elsewhere. As employees aim to retain their higher-paying job, this mechanism induces higher productivity without the same degree of costly monitoring. As all organizations behave in this manner, white-collar wages will remain above the level at which supply for white-collar labour is equal to demand, even if the labour market is competitive.[7] This is in contrast to some earlier economic theories which argued that in a competitive labour market, wages would adjust to balance the supply and demand for labour.
- Importantly, in these and other new models, the market mechanism was shown to be inefficient in the face of imperfect information.[8] In 1986, Bruce Greenwald and Joseph Stiglitz[9] demonstrated that this conclusion is a general one, that is, that markets characterized by informational imperfections are not Pareto efficient,

since changes in the levels of access to information within the market can have a range of effects. Moreover, they are not necessarily the least inefficient way of allocating resources, as in simple situations involving a market with a single informational problem, there is always a government intervention which could make everybody in the market better off.[10] In more complicated settings involving multiple informational problems, welfare-improving government interventions will not necessarily exist, but the market mechanism remains inefficient. Hence the picture of efficient markets hampered by a cumbersome state bureaucracy is a crude caricature, but one which our culture unfortunately continues to accord the status of great art. The market mechanism is not efficient in the face of asymmetric information, and although each deviation from the world of Arrow and Debreu is a small one, cumulatively they form a rich, complex picture of the economy quite unlike the one in which information is always perfect and costless.

In addition to providing us with a better picture of the economy, the Greenwald–Stiglitz theorem also helps us to recast the old debate about whether or not there is a role for government in a market economy. The theorem shows us that there is indeed a role and that the relevant debate is not the existence of this role but its precise nature. Consideration will now be given to an important case study of why the economics of information is very useful for policy-makers by showing how, if it had been applied, it would have helped to mitigate the extent of the Asian economic crisis.

How did China escape the Asian economic crisis?

The 'economic miracle' of Asia has offered great hope to the world that the grinding poverty in, for instance, parts of Africa can be overcome. In its 1997 report, *Growth with Equity*, Oxfam, one of the world's leading development agencies, found that 'over the past three decades the region has experienced the most rapid and sustained growth recorded this century. Less widely appreciated is the fact that economic success has been accompanied by a silent revolution in poverty reduction. More people have moved out of poverty more quickly than at any time in history. The message that emerges for governments which are serious about growth is clear: 'get serious about poverty reduction and human development'. Ironically, just as people started to study Asia and learn from the 30 years of relative success before 1997, the Asian economic crisis hit, sending hundreds of millions back below the poverty line. The confidence that had grown in Asia over the previous 30 years was battered, as overnight many Asian countries' currencies plummeted. As is so often the case with an economic crisis, the banking systems in these countries were put under huge strain. In 1997–1998, the banking systems of a number of East Asian countries were in trouble, with a relatively high proportion of borrowers unable to maintain loan repayments. One such country was China. Yet while the financial systems of many of its neighbours collapsed, China emerged from the 'Asian crisis' relatively unscathed. Why was this the case? Does China's example offer us any strategies for preventing future crises, or at least mitigating their effects?

It turns out that theories of the economics of information discussed above can help us to answer these questions. Hence, what follows is a brief introduction to this important application of information economics. We begin by considering why it is that financial markets are important and why they can be fragile.

Financial markets: what they do and why they are fragile

Financial markets are one of the most important, complex and volatile sets of markets in a modern economy. They are important because they link the present with the future:

through saving some of their income today, individuals finance investment projects which contribute to production and employment in the future. It is this link with the future, however, that makes financial markets complex and fragile. In the market for an ordinary good such as apples, the apples and the money change hands at the same point in time. In financial markets, money is lent now for the promise of repayment at some specified future date. As the future is never certain, there is always a chance that these promises will not be honoured, and so financial markets are inescapably involved with risk.[11] We saw in the discussion of market efficiency that an economy allocates resources efficiently when there is a complete set of perfect markets, including a market for every conceivable risk. Even in sophisticated financial systems this is not the case, so a first set of market failures associated with financial markets stem from these 'missing' risk markets. A second set of market failures arises from the distribution of information between borrowers and lenders. Borrowers can fail to repay their loans for a number of reasons. Sometimes even honest, prudent borrowers who fully intend to repay their loans find that their investments are not as profitable as they expected. Not all borrowers, however, are honest and prudent; some may take out loans they have little or no intention of repaying, while others may take on excessively risky investment projects with slim chances of large profits but significant chances of failure. The problem for institutions that make loans is one of asymmetric information: borrowers possess more information about their character and the nature of their investment projects than do lenders. As all borrowers have an incentive to appear honest and prudent, it is often difficult for banks to tell genuinely creditworthy borrowers from unscrupulous and risk-loving ones.[12] If banks make too many loans to the wrong types of borrowers, they run the risk of becoming insolvent.

We know from the Greenwald–Stiglitz theorem that free markets are inefficient in the face of asymmetric information such as that between borrowers and lenders. This inefficiency, coupled with the importance of financial markets to the economy as a whole, means that there is a theoretical justification for governments to intervene in financial markets. In practice, governments do regulate financial markets in a variety of ways, providing deposit insurance, making laws against insider trading, monitoring the solvency of banks, insurance companies and other financial institutions, and so on. Such regulation and surveillance not only protect investors, they make financial markets work better: if people have confidence in the workings of financial markets they will be more willing to lend money, and those with genuinely creditworthy projects will have access to the funds they need. So the economics of information provides us with the theoretical foundations for the financial regulations we observe in 'developed' market economies such as the US and the UK. However, building a robust financial system takes time. 'Less-developed' and 'emerging' economies are more vulnerable to economic shocks such as financial crises, but generally have less capacity to carry out effective regulation and surveillance of their financial systems. It is essential that this combination of enhanced vulnerability and constrained regulatory capacity be considered when advising these countries on how to integrate themselves into the international financial system.

International financial markets and developing countries

The appropriate way for emerging and less-developed countries to integrate themselves into international financial markets has been a topic of heated debate, especially since the flawed integrations which contributed to the Asian financial crisis. At the centre of this debate are the questions of when, how and at what speed developing countries should remove restrictions on the way money flows in and out of their economies.

There are advantages to being able to receive funds from overseas investors. If that money can be used to fund appropriate investment projects (building new plants, buying new capital equipment, and so on) it can contribute to production and employment in future periods. Those who have lent the funds to the developing country also benefit from reducing the riskiness of their investment portfolios through diversification. However, if money can flow into a developing economy, it can also flow out. Foreign Direct Investment (FDI), the kind of investment that goes directly into financing new plant and equipment, is long-term investment in a country which is unlikely to be withdrawn hastily. But this is not true of all investment flows. Speculative 'investments' are very short-term (typically less than 24 hours), and are essentially bets on movement in prices such as exchange rates.[13] Not only does this kind of investment not build factories or employ people, it tends to be countercyclical: money flows out in downturns, and in during booms, destabilizing already vulnerable economies. As part of their integration into the international economy, developing countries have often been encouraged to dismantle restrictions set up to mitigate the effects of these large, short-term capital flows.[14] It was suggested that such liberalization was necessary in order to attract the foreign investment which would help developing countries' long-term growth. However, this advice ignores the fact that it is perfectly possible to attract direct investment whilst retaining restrictions that mitigate speculation, limit the involvement of foreign banks in the economy, and so on.[15] This is exactly what China has done. The Chinese economy is one of the biggest recipients of FDI in the entire world, but has received this investment without undertaking the recommended kinds of financial market liberalization. This in turn protected China from the Asian crisis: short-term investment could not flow out of China because it was not allowed to enter in the first place.[16]

None of the above should be interpreted as advocating regulation for regulation's sake, or suggesting that all and any financial market regulations are beneficial. What we are suggesting is that, given the fragility of domestic financial systems, especially in developing countries, and the devastating consequences for the whole economy when they collapse, careful attention should be paid to the speed with which financial market regulations are dismantled and the order in which they are removed. This point is now also policy for the institution responsible for the stability of the international financial system.[17] As we said, classical economic theory, which does not take asymmetric information into account in its models, predicts that opening up to foreign capital inflow leads to higher economic growth. It adds foreigners' savings to domestic savings, lowers the cost of capital by spreading risk, and supposedly helps develop a country's financial sector. This was one of the main reasons Thailand liberalized its financial markets, to hopefully turn its country into a financial centre like Hong Kong. However, when International Monetary Fund (IMF) Chief Economist, Kenneth Rogoff, checked to see what empirical evidence there was to support the theory, the discovery he made was sobering. In his recent report on these issues for the IMF he stated, 'An objective reading of the vast research effort to date suggests that there is no strong, robust and uniform support for the theoretical arguments that financial globalization per se delivers a higher economic growth.'[18] To be clear on what he means here is important. Rogoff is not saying that increased trade has not helped economic growth. He is saying that there are no concrete proven links between increased trade in financial capital, increased openness, and deregulation of the financial market leads and increased economic growth. For all the reasons listed above, Rogoff could not find any evidence of the benefits from liberalizing capital accounts in developing countries. In fact, he found the opposite: 'The evidence suggests that instead, countries that are in the early stages of financial integration have been exposed to significant risks in terms of higher volatility of both output and consumption.'

The IMF publicly states that it never encouraged countries to liberalize short-term flows through the banking sector, which is what turned out to be the Achilles Heel during the Asian crisis.[19] Finally, in examining the causes behind so many currency crises amongst developing nations, the report concedes that there is empirical evidence to support a range of serious criticisms of the global financial system. 'First, international investors have a tendency to engage in momentum trading and herding, which can be devastating for developing countries. Second, international investors may, together with domestic residents, engage in speculative attacks on developing countries' currencies, thereby causing instability that is not warranted based on the economic and policy fundamentals of these countries. Third, the risk of contagion presents a major threat to otherwise healthy counties, since international investors could withdraw capital from these countries for reasons unrelated to domestic factors.'[20] The lesson is that if the IMF and governments had listened to their economists and used the latest modern economics of information, the pain of the Asian Economic crisis would have been far less severe. The success of China, in weathering the storm of the Asian economic crisis through wise government approaches, shows the value of these new developments in economics to help all governments better evaluate policy and institutional frameworks. Rogoff's report concluded that: 'The analysis suggests that financial globalization should be approached cautiously and with good institutions and macro-economic frameworks viewed as a precondition... A growing body of evidence suggests that the quality of domestic institutions has a quantitatively important impact on a country's ability to attract foreign direct investment, and on its vulnerability in crises. There is accumulating evidence of the benefits of robust legal and (prudential) supervisory frameworks, low levels of corruption, high degrees of transparency and good corporate governance.' The IMF is now also strongly warning developing countries of the dangers of liberalizing their capital accounts and admits publicly that 'the experience (of the Asian economic crisis of 1997) revealed that the IMF had not kept up with the rapid developments in international capital markets, a deficiency it has tried to rectify through a number of steps taken over the last couple of years'.[21]

Anti-monopoly legislation: competition policy

To date we have used the term 'market failure', which may surprise some readers. However, the concept of market failure and the notion that when markets fail there may be a role for government is a very old one in economics. Adam Smith himself acknowledged that serious market failures occur when monopolies form. If a firm is able to become a monopoly, this allows price fixing and numerous other results that ensure that the market cannot work efficiently. Braithwaite and Drahos argue that the best chance nations have to raise standards is if their firms are as efficient as possible.[22] To ensure this, governments have a role to play in making sure there is good competition policy and regulation to encourage competition. It doesn't help standards in the long run if firms are protected from the winds of competition. In Section 2 the idea was discussed that competition in the real world can be far from perfect, and thus allow companies to ignore resource productivity savings. Hence, Drahos and Braithwaite argue it will help to ensure standards rise if competition is also enhanced globally.[23] Competition law allows businesses, who are the victim of a much larger corporation for example, to launch court cases against monopolistic practices. When business players unite to check the predatory practices of one or more of their own kind, they create positive externalities for citizens. Sometimes these externalities have a global reach. Competition law is a way of constituting these externalities.

The Greenwald–Stiglitz theorem helps us to recast the old debate about whether or not there is a role for government in a market economy. The theorem shows us that there is indeed a role, and that the relevant debate is not the existence of this role but its precise nature. We must, however, stress that although the Arrow–Debreu conditions for Pareto efficiency will never be achieved in a real economy, many real world markets approximate perfection to such a degree that government intervention would certainly be more costly than beneficial. As outlined above, the strength of the market mechanism

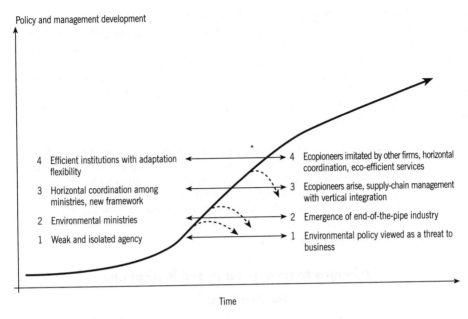

Policy and management development

4 Efficient institutions with adaptation flexibility

3 Horizontal coordination among ministries, new framework

2 Environmental ministries

1 Weak and isolated agency

4 Ecopioneers imitated by other firms, horizontal coordination, eco-efficient services

3 Ecopioneers arise, supply-chain management with vertical integration

2 Emergence of end-of-the-pipe industry

1 Environmental policy viewed as a threat to business

Time

Source: Bleishwitz (2002)

Figure 12.1 *Stages in environmental policy and management development*

derives from the information provided by prices when these are determined by the free interaction of buyers and sellers. The prices in 'quasi-perfect' markets do provide important information which helps the many different actors in an economy to co-ordinate their plans without the help of a central authority. It is folly, therefore, to suggest that even the most benevolent of centrally-planned states could acquire the amount of information necessary to replace such markets. Second, even well-intentioned governments are not perfect either. Politically powerful interest groups can exert undue influence over policy processes, regulatory agencies can be 'captured' by the groups that they were designed to monitor, a lack of 'hard' budget constraints can create incentive and inefficiency problems, and so on.

As both governments and markets can fail, considering the strengths and weaknesses of both, building-in mechanisms to stop corruption should help inform a mature, sophisticated dialogue about their appropriate roles in creating communities and a society which flourishes both now and in the future.

So far, consideration has been given to how market and informational failures can be significant contributors to environmental degradation and economic inefficiency. A range of mechanisms have been discussed, that now exist, with which government can address these failures to achieve a natural advantage. It is time now to consider what governments need to do to address the challenge of achieving a sustainable future and its impact on our traditional institutional approaches. Dr Raimund Bleischwitz, Head of the Factor Four Research Desk at the Wuppertal Institute, in his report *Governance of Eco-Efficiency in Japan*, states that Institutions shape the direction of technical progress, as well as the speed by which a society adapts to new framework conditions. He summarizes the stages of environmental policy and management development in Figure 12.1.

Dr Bleishwitz continues to report that, 'We should make the point that there is no "optimal" institutional framework which can be applied in each country at each stage of economic development. Rather, there is huge institutional diversity, resulting from different formal and informal mappings that are reflected in quite different modes of doing business and economic policy. Institutions need to evolve locally, relying on specific experience and careful experiments.'[24] However, this should not discourage us from learning from the success stories of other countries' institutions. Work, such as that being undertaken at the Centre for Resources and Environmental Studies at the Australian National University, shows that despite great institutional diversity, common themes and lessons are emerging, as summarized below.

> *If institutions are to protect people and a broad portfolio of assets, they must respond to and shape the major changes that will unfold over the next 50 years: urbanization, technological innovation, economic growth, shifting social values, changing scarcities for environmental and natural assets, and stronger linkages amongst nations. Institutions must be stable, but they must also be capable of changing and adapting, and new institutions must emerge.*

World Bank Development Report 2003[25]

Challenges to governments and institutions[*]

Stephen Dovers

EDITORS' NOTE: Institutions can be either significant allies or obstacles to achieving sustainability and understanding the issues and challenges for institutions in addressing sustainability is critical to assist nations achieve genuine progress. We invited Dr Dovers, a world renowned expert in institutions and sustainability, to provide an overview of how institutions are tackling sustainability issues.

Sustainable development presents a challenge to the way in which modern societies organize themselves and the activities in which they engage. Governments the world over have pledged themselves to at least rhetorical policy positions. This has required the restructuring not only of relationships between human and natural systems, but also of relationships between governments and the institutional system, particularly the elements of the system that determine the transactions and directions of societies, like communities, research communities, industries, traditional knowledge systems, etc. Having realized the limits of a narrow environmental policy based on simplistic regulatory, end-of-pipe measures, it is certainly being recognized that whatever governments seek to do at the local, regional or national level, the larger challenge is the development of systems of 'governance for sustainability', inclusive of more than just government and the usual major interests. The long-term goal of sustainability and the operational challenge of genuine sustainable progress refer to fundamental and structural inconsistencies between natural and human systems. As such, sustainable development may best be thought of as a higher order social goal, much like democracy, equity or the rule of law, and should have the same weight and priority as these social goals, which have taken centuries to develop even with strong commitment throughout society to achieve them.

However, we do not have centuries to achieve sustainable development. What follows is a discussion of the policy and institutional implications of genuine sustainable progress that will allow us to move quickly in response to such a challenge. The focus will be on

---

[*] This section was co-authored by Dr Stephen Dovers, Senior Fellow at the Centre for Resources and Environmental Studies, Australian National University. Some of this material is expanded on in Connor and Dovers (2004).

three main issues: the underlying attributes of policy problems, policy and institutional challenges, and the different but interrelated elements of human systems. In Section 1, sustainable development was described in terms of broad principles (e.g. inter-generational equity, precaution, integration of ecological, social and economic policy), or subsidiary issues (e.g. biodiversity, climate change and human development). These descriptions usefully flesh out the nature and implications of the sustainability agenda.

Attributes of policy problems in sustainability

Another approach is to identify the attributes of policy problems that are common across issues and which can better define the policy and institutional challenges. Significant problems in sustainability policy more often display the following attributes, especially in combination, than do problems in more familiar policy domains such as service delivery or economics:[26]

- broadened, deepened and highly variable spatial and temporal scales;
- the possibility of absolute ecological limits to human activity;
- irreversible impacts and related policy urgency;
- complexity within and connectivity between problems, both within and across the three arenas of environment, society and economy;
- pervasive risk and uncertainty;
- often cumulative rather than discrete impacts;
- important assets not traded in formal markets, and thus rarely assigned economic value, such as ecosystem services;
- new moral dimensions (e.g. other species, future generations, the world's poor);
- 'systemic' problem causes, embedded in patterns of production, consumption, settlement and governance;
- difficulty in separating public and private costs and benefits;
- lack of available, uncontested research methods, policy instruments and management approaches;
- lack of defined policy, management and property rights, roles and responsibilities;
- sheer novelty as a policy field;
- intense demands (and justification) for increased community participation in both policy formulation and actual management.

These attributes support a view that sustainability problems are, at least sometimes, different in kind, and possibly in degree, to more 'traditional' policy problems against which existing policy and institutional capacities have been developed and can comprehend, both in modes of analysis and operational policy systems. Those in the sustainability field are generally sympathetic to this claim, whereas those in traditional policy-oriented disciplines (e.g. law, public policy, neoclassical economics and public administration) may be less prepared to accept it. If the claim is true, then at least for some aspects of sustainability, there is a clear case that existing policy-oriented knowledge systems (including formal disciplines), and existing policy processes and institutions, will lack explanatory power and operational purchase on sustainability problems. Therefore, new understanding and capacities are needed. If societies are to respond to sustainability so as to create a coherent and powerful policy field, then interpreting sustainability in terms of generic rather than specific policy and institutional tasks is a useful approach. Table 12.1 does this by re-interpreting one version of what sustainability means: the goal, objectives and principles stated in Australia's 1992 National Strategy for Ecologically Sustainable Development (ESD).[27]

These 'ESD principles' are expressed or referred to in many hundreds of policies at all three levels of Australian government, and in more than 120 statutes.[28] While the principles are from one jurisdiction, they are consistent with international policy statements. In Table 12.1 the objectives and principles are stated as challenges for policy and institutional reform; that is, if these objectives and principles say what we think sustainable development means, then what do we need to know and do to fulfil the policy statement? Column (C) states sustainability principles more as operational challenges than their original form, to serve as the basis of a brief exploration of their implications for institutions and government.

Clarifying government, governance and institutions

So far, government and governance have been separated, and sustainability has been framed as a policy and institutional challenge. These terms need clarification if challenges such as those above, and the role of specific levels of government are to be clearly comprehended. 'Government' is a reasonably well understood human institution, and there is a valid base for the belief that government has an especially crucial role, given sustainability's long-term horizons, often non-local implications, and strong public good aspects. Integrated, whole of government approaches are needed to achieve complete responses to sustainability. However, the way in which local and other communities, disciplines, professions and private interests interact in a coordinated manner (the broader system of governance) is not well understood. Government responses and actions occur within complex and dynamic patterns of governance and institutions which are constantly evolving. Such evolution needs to be consistent with sustainability, that is, more inclusive and sensitive to long-term considerations.

Another way of expressing this is that governments and their agencies, at the various levels that exist in a given country, are one element within complex and dynamic institutional systems that have evolved, and continue to evolve, to manage joint transactions and goals in modern human societies.[30] Within institutional systems, policy processes are driven by organizations and interests (broader policy communities, tighter policy networks, local and epistemic communities), both within and outside of government, applying a range of policy instruments. Given that these multiple elements operate as nested hierarchies across scales, addressing difficult, interdependent problems, it is clearly inadequate to apply convenient notions of simple policy or institutional strategies, or favour one organizational scale over another.

Importantly, human institutions, and therefore to some extent the organizational forms and policy processes shaped by them, reflect past rather than present or future understandings and imperatives. Thus, in terms of the deeper institutional reform that is widely perceived as necessary for sustainability, and given that the roots of the sustainability challenge lie deep in patterns of production and consumption, settlement and governance, we are prisoners of history, caught within an institutional system that is outmoded.

One characteristic of persistent, influential institutions is 'goodness of fit' within the operating environment.[31] However, innovative institutional reforms for sustainability, need, at least to some extent, to 'not fit': this defines a core tension in sustainability reform that is 'radical' enough to drive sustainability, but 'mild' enough to be tolerated by the wider system.[32] Given the urgency of the challenge, it is important to take a reasoned view of the nature of institutional change. As deeper, structuring rules and patterns notwithstanding occasional revolutions or upheavals, institutions for the most part change slowly and in uneven and incremental fashion, with multiple cultural, organizational or legal changes marking more profound institutional shifts over time. Given the depth and complexity of institutional systems and the systemic nature of the causes of sustainability problems, rapid institutional change is unlikely.

Table 12.1 ESD (sustainability) *principles as policy and institutional challenges*

(A) ESD goals, objectives and principles	(B) Summary descriptor	(C) Core meaning as target for learning
Development that improves the total quality of life, both now and in the future, in a way that maintains the ecological processes on which life depends.	Goal.	Too general: see objectives and principles below.
Objectives		
1 To enhance individual and community well-being and welfare by following a path of economic development that safeguards the welfare of future generations.	Sustainable economic development.	Policy processes and institutional arrangements that embed long-term considerations in economic policy and planning, and the implications of economic policy for individual and community well-being.
2 To provide for equity within and between generations.	Inter- and intra-generational equity.	Policy processes and institutional arrangements focusing on multiple dimensions of equity over the long-term.
3 To protect biological diversity and maintain essential ecological processes and life support systems.	Biodiversity and ecological processes.	Policy processes and institutional arrangements that give high priority to biodiversity and ecological processes as social and policy goals, across all policy sectors.
Principles (to inform policy-making at all levels)		
1 Decision-making processes should effectively integrate both long- and short-term economic, environmental, social and equity dimensions.	Policy integration.	Policy processes and institutional arrangements that integrate ecological, social and economic considerations, or encourage or demand such policy integration, enable research on or develop methods for such integration.
2 Where there are threats of serious or irreversible damage, lack of full scientific certainty should not be used as a reason for postponing measures to prevent environmental degradation.	Precautionary principle.	Policy processes that explicitly inform decisions in the face of uncertainty, ensure proper consideration of risk and uncertainty, or seek to enhance the information base for decision-making in the long-term.
3 The global dimension of environmental impacts of actions and policies should be recognized and considered.	International commons policy.	Processes and arrangements that account for international threats to sustainability or opportunities for improving prospects for sustainability through international coordination of policy and action.
4 The need to develop a strong, growing and diversified economy which can enhance the capacity for environmental protection should be recognized.[29]	Sustainable economic growth.	Processes and arrangements that link economic policy with environmental policy, or to establish whether such links can or do exist.

Table 12.1 *continued*

(A) ESD goals, objectives and principles	(B) Summary descriptor	(C) Core meaning as target for learning
5 The need to maintain and enhance international competitiveness in an environmentally sound manner should be recognized.	International competitiveness.	Processes and arrangements that help explicate, review or ensure environmental (and social) benefits, or avoid the negative impacts of international law, trade, policy and interactions.
6 Cost-effective and flexible policy instruments such as improved valuation, pricing and incentive mechanisms should be adopted.	Policy instrument choice.	Identification and application of innovative policy instruments, and/or processes and arrangements to research, monitor, select and test new approaches to instrument choice and application (not only market mechanisms as implied in the principle).
7 Decisions and actions should provide for broad community involvement on issues which affect them.	Community involvement.	Processes and arrangements that encourage, allow and maintain community participation in policy debate, formulation and implementation, and on-ground management.

Note: ESD = ecologically sustainable development.
Source: Connor and Dovers (2004)

Indeed, fundamental redirection of policy and institutional systems is best thought of as occurring over generational or even longer time spans.[33] Such a sobering outlook is confirmed by experience with the 'natural partners' of sustainability, and other higher-order social goals such as democracy, equity and the rule of law. Hence, a critical question arising is: at which scales can different challenges be most appropriately addressed?

Available scales of sustainability governance

While it is generally accepted that management, policy and institutional reform and activities need to occur at multiple scales, and must involve ongoing coordination across scales, the full range of available spatial/administrative scales is not always fully acknowledged in discussion, either of the larger sustainability challenge or in the context of specific problems. Some discussions concentrate on the basic levels of government (e.g., national, regional and local), whereas others, including those less favourable to the idea of government as leaders in sustainability policy, concentrate on other scales or bases of human organization, including governance or ecological function.

Other discussions again are framed around quite different bases for policy and institutional development, cutting across spatial-administrative scales. The following seeks to capture this range, identifying the key 'scales', including non-spatial bases for policy and institutional reform, along with a brief explanation of each:

- Supra-national, being inter-governmental constellations including international, multi-lateral and bilateral, 'regional' organizations of government, trade zones and various groupings of nation states (e.g., Go8, OECD, G77), and groupings of commercial interests or non-governmental organizations (NGOs) across similar scales.

- The nation-state, which despite the perceived erosion of sovereignty and state power in recent years, remains the primary location of legal competency and the point of coordination with supra-national processes and law, and between those and sub-national policy and processes.
- Legally-competent sub-national, including state, provincial and territorial ('regional') governments, local governments and in some cases other formal layers of government. Noting that the powers and capacities of these layers vary significantly between, and even within, countries.
- Non-traditional sub-national scales, such as 'regional', bioregional or catchment, where policy and management are increasingly being framed, but where organizational arrangements typically lack a statutory base or independence of resourcing or activity.
- Household, land parcel, firm, etc., that are the fundamental social, legal and economic loci of much human responsibility and activity, and which underpin the logic of most policy interventions that seek to influence human behaviour. The individual scale exists below these.
- A range of (often interrelated) non-spatial 'scales', or loci of policy responsibility or human activity, including: resource sectors, firm type or industry category, environmental issues, demographic stratum, language or cultural group, communities of advocacy or interest, professions, etc. Most policy is made and implemented with primary focus on such loci or concerns, rather than on the spatial-administrative scale that is better regarded as a means, or one possible means, to the end.

The difference between legally competent and less or incompetent is crucial, given the key role played in institutional systems by the rule of law. Too often in the past, and certainly now, hopeful initiatives at non-traditional scales of policy and governance (e.g., regional, catchment) have not been supported by legal, administrative or other capacities, and therefore have been short-lived. Commonly, policy or institutional reforms and arrangements involve more than one, and usually more than two, of the above scales and a mixture of spatial-administrative and non-spatial scales.[34] That is, the logic of a policy intervention is most often to address a non-spatial process or phenomenon, not the jurisdictional basis for doing so, no matter how deeply ingrained or powerful the jurisdictional rationale is. Government is a means, not an end in itself.

Scaling responses

How, then, is the decision made as to the best scale/s over which to frame a policy or institutional response to sustainability? Using the challenges set out in Table 12.1 as an example, it is apparent that a range of policy and institutional reform options exist for any given challenge. The following sets out some viable options for addressing a selection of the principles translated as policy challenges in Table 12.1, and the scales of government or governance where they would logically be implemented:[35]

1 **Policy integration principle** (*Principle* 1, *Table* 12.1). The integration of ecological, social and economic imperatives and policy is central to implementing sustainability. Several prime options for integration exist, and we can note the scales at which they apply:

- Strategic environmental assessment (SEA), a procedure for assessing the environmental, social and economic implications of higher order policy proposals (as opposed to traditional EIA at project scale), applicable at national and state/provincial government level.
- Portfolio and Agency Redesign within public bureaucracies, aimed at either locating responsibility for sustainability in a central location (e.g. office or commissioner for sustainable development), or organization of larger portfolios and departments that incorporate a wider range of policy responsibilities than simply 'environment'. This strategy is clearly relevant to national and regional government.[36] There is little available information on the frequency of 'integration' through reorganizing government agencies.
- Triple-bottom-line accounting, largely developed and intended for the private sector, but increasingly proposed as relevant to the public sector as well. Relevant to any scale of government.
- National Councils for Sustainable Development (NCSD), of which +70 credible councils have been created in the past decade, aimed at inclusion of non-government interests into the policy process, but also to bring environmental, social and economic interests together. The Network of Regional Governments for Sustainable Development (nrg4SD) demonstrates that there is no reason why regional governments should not wish to enable an inclusive, integrative body such as an NCSD.
- Statutory Expression of Sustainability Principles (e.g. from the Rio Declaration) in a wide body of law, to require taking account of these across policy sectors: i.e. imposing this requirement on public agencies through statutory objects and defined decision-making procedures as well as on private sector decisions. While clearly a primary responsibility for national governments, such expression is just as relevant to regional government in areas of sufficient legal competence as well.

2 **The precautionary principle** (PP) (*Principle 2, Table* 12.1). The PP is a broad policy principle that requires differing approaches to implementation in different contexts. The PP does not recommend a pro-sustainability outcome, but requires a defensible process for dealing with uncertainty through approaches such as risk assessment or risk management procedures, population viability analysis, research and monitoring, safe minimum standards, etc. The expression of the PP as a statutory object is a national and regional government responsibility, but the application of it is relevant at any scale of decision-making.

3 **The international dimensions of sustainability** (*Principles 3 and 5, Table* 12.1) invite a primacy of responsibility for nation-states through treaties and their implementation and development aid. However, the nation-state does not have the only leverage, as the nrg4SD and Local Agenda 21 demonstrate that international coordination is relevant at other levels of government. NGO and industry networks are also significant.

4 **Policy innovation and instrument** (*Principle 6, Table* 12.1) is usually considered the domain of national, regional, and to a lesser degree, local government. However, with approaches such as market- or community-based policy or institutional change, instrument choice and implementation are also matters for non-traditional organizational scales (e.g. catchment), the private sector and local communities. The broad range of available policy options, the need to coordinate mixes of instruments, multiple implementation contexts, and various criteria against which instruments are selected, mean that innovative policy design requires negotiation across groups and scales. Nevertheless, legally-competent scales of government, especially national and regional, are core to effective policy instrument implementation through powers such as

taxation, land use planning, definition of property rights, education funding, curricula design and definition of inclusive procedures, etc.

5 **Community involvement** (*Principle* 7, *Table* 12.1) refers to involvement of non-government actors in higher-order social and policy debate, policy formulation, implementation, monitoring and evaluation, on-ground management, and enforcement of regulations and procedures. Thus, different forms of involvement are more relevant at different scales of governance through many different strategies and programmes. For example, representative advisory boards, public inquiries, management committees, co-management, participatory research and community-based monitoring. Many governments are more willing to pass on environmental management responsibilities and tasks than to hand over actual power.

The conclusion is of course that, more often than not, there is no single most appropriate scale at which such policy or institutional options should be implemented. Typically these options can, and should, be implemented across multiple, interdependent scales, and the choice will be dependent on the specific problem being addressed, and the particular legal, political, social and environmental context. Moreover, cross-scale coordination is not simply optimal but essential as, if one scale of purpose or implementation fails, then the entire interdependent policy or institutional strategy may also fail. However, such a strict hierarchical logic may inhibit innovation if the quality of policy advice is defined by the most reluctant or stubborn level of government, be that national, regional or local.

Whatever the scale of policy and institutional reform, the common attributes of sustainability problems invite the application of consistent principles to inform the policy and institutional design, often enabled by government, that can lead to the development of new systems of governance. The next two parts of the chapter will explore this further.

Principles and elements of policy and institutional reform

This section proposes key principles for positive institutional change for sustainability, drawn from the institutional literature, sustainability principles and the theoretical and applied literature discussing them, the adaptive management literature, and two major studies. The term 'positive institutional change' means programmes of reform that evidence a credible commitment by those involved, especially government, to significant institutional change that is consistent with the nature of the sustainability problem. The first set of principles are the five core attributes of 'adaptive policy, institutions and management' for sustainable development, proposed and utilized in the reviews of Australian policy experiences that were part of a three-decade review of policy and institutional development for resource and environmental management in Australia.[37] The 20-odd component reviews analysed areas including regional and catchment management, legal processes, state of environment reporting, environmental protection, intergovernmental and parliamentary processes, and so on. The study proposed five key attributes of adaptive policy, institutions and management, identified from previous analyses, institutional theory and the emerging field of adaptive management:

1   **Persistence**: allowing sufficient time for policy and institutional 'experiments' to be conducted and lessons accrued.
2   **Purposefulness**: through a widely recognized set of core policy principles (e.g. continually evolving principles of sustainability).
3   **Information-richness and sensitivity**: especially over time, referring not only to information gathering but to its wide ownership and application.

4　**Inclusiveness**: through clearly understood, sustained public participation in both higher level policy and on-ground management.

5　**Flexibility**: to encourage adaptation and improvement, so persistence and purposefulness do not develop into rigidity.

The second study explored leading international examples of institutional and deeper policy change for sustainability, utilizing a conceptual and analytical approach developed from the fields of institutional economics and policy learning.[38] The aim was to better understand the key component elements of institutional change, through identification and analysis of the main variables that shaped five significant examples:

1　**European Union**: the environmental policy of the EU over the past few decades is the world's leading example of inter-jurisdictional policy and institutional development in the environment and sustainability (and other) fields.

2　**New Zealand's Resource Management Act (1991)**: arguably the world's most significant example of national-scale legislative, organizational and policy reform driven by sustainability concerns, where environmental responsibilities were allocated across national, regional and local scales.

3　**Strategic environmental assessment (SEA)**: SEA's progress with the definition and implementation in various jurisdictions, is now a significant operational policy option for integrating environmental, social and economic considerations at higher levels of policy formulation.

4　**National Councils for Sustainable Development (NCSD)**: the NCSD has been established, along with equivalent bodies, in more than 70 countries since 1992, representing cross-sectoral and inclusive mechanisms for policy discourse and coordination at the national scale.

5　**Property rights instruments (PRI)**: drawing particularly on the experience of individual transferable quota in fisheries, as 'transformative' policy instruments exposing the nature of policy change within institutional and cultural systems.

These two studies, particularly the latter, allowed the identification of key elements of more successful institutional and deeper policy change for sustainability. The five principles of 'adaptive institutions' were found to have useful analytical and prescriptive value, but are rather general. A more detailed iteration is given in Table 12.2, as the key attributes of adaptive institutions and organizations. The importance of each attribute will vary from case to case, and the (tentative) list in Table 12.2 is neither exhaustive nor meant to be a strict 'recipe', but rather a set of key considerations for either analytical or prescriptive use.

From the second study were developed general, empirically derived principles that can assist in understanding the potential for institutional change and related policy learning consistent with the idea of sustainability. The seven principles below are organized under two broad classes of the 'objects of learning' used in the study. These are defined by drawing on the policy learning literature and the nature of sustainability challenges: problem (re)framing, and (re)organizing government. The nature of the sustainability problem makes it impossible to cleanly separate either these two categories or the principles developed under them, as they are strongly interrelated. The following is a sharp summary:

1　**Problem (re)framing** relevant to the formation of a widely-understood and coherent social construction of the sustainability problem:
　　• 　Institutional accommodation of the sustainability discourse: recognizing that sustainability is still very much a new, complex and contested idea, not fully understood, appreciated or endorsed in policy communities and the wider

Table 12.2 *Attributes of adaptive institutions and organizations*

Attribute	Explanation
Purposeful mandate	An accepted vision and set of goals with a matching mandate to pursue them (i.e. sustainability principles).
Longevity	Sufficient longevity to persist, experiment, learn and adapt (including maintenance of institutional memory).
Properly resourced	Sufficient human, financial and informational resources.
Legal basis	A clear basis in statute law (or, less commonly, customary or common law) ensuring transparency and accountability, and a higher probability of persistence.
Independence	A degree of independence from short-term political pressures, and thus not relying on easily changeable mandate or resources.
Informed and informing	High priority on information generation, use and wide ownership, and an emphasis on long-term monitoring and evaluation. This encompasses ecological and socio-economic information, policy and management monitoring, and multiple sources of information (scientific, community, traditional, etc.).
Multi-functional	Integration of research, planning, management and/or policy roles, so that these are not kept separate or poorly connected. Achievable internally or in coordination with other parts of an institutional system.
Applied	An applied/grounded focus (e.g. region, issue or sector), to ensure that policy and management prescriptions are operational and evaluated. Achievable internally or in coordination with other parts of an institutional system.
Integrative	Integrating environmental, social and economic aspects, and pursuing cross-sectoral, cross-problem and/or cross-cultural views. Achievable internally or in coordination with other parts of an institutional system.
Coordinated and coordinating	Maintenance of linkages with other parts of the institutional system (policy processes, organizations, knowledge communities, etc.), in recognition of the interconnected nature of sustainability problems.
Inter-jurisdictional (where necessary)	Cognizant of and capable of handling issues and human or natural processes cutting across spatial-administrative boundaries (local, regional, national).
Participatory	Participatory structures and processes that are transparent, genuine, predictable and maintained. Participation appropriate to the context, recognizing and choosing from a wide range of participatory options.
Comparative	Ability and mandate to engage in comparative analysis across sectors, issues and methods (whether concurrent or sequential).
Experimental	Mandate and ability to experiment with approaches and methods, and to move across disciplinary and professional boundaries.
Politically supported	Having political support at government, community and industry levels to enable establishment and favour persistence.

Source: Based on Dovers (2001); Dore et al (2003)

population. Such understanding is a long-term project, and thus an ongoing discourse around the idea is required and needs to be encouraged and maintained by (not only, but especially) governments through the creation and maintenance of conducive institutional arrangements and persistent discursive, policy-oriented networks.

- Normative change: advancing policy and institutional change for sustainability begs the acceptance of this strategy as necessary and valid by a sufficiently large group within the populace, which implies widespread normative change. Thus, change in the underlying institutional system is interdependent with normative change in the population.
- Legal change: recognizing that the law, constitutional documents, statutes and the common law are crucial to more profound institutional change, and that proposals for change need to incorporate an agenda of supportive (or at least not obstructive) legal change. Key to this is statutory expression of sustainability principles (especially precaution and policy integration) and accumulation of an understanding of their meaning and implementation strategies.
- International law, policy and drivers: recognizing that the international level has driven the (albeit vague) sustainability agenda. However, more recently, the interaction between the supra-national and national levels (and the regional, in the case of nrg4SD) has been crucial to (i) the maintenance of the agenda, (ii) communication of experiences in institutional change, and (iii) allowing the comparison between nations who are leading and those more reluctant that it is so valuable in enlivening debate in the latter. This principle can be extended to the domestic level, and national-to-sub-national interplay between laggards and leaders.

2   **(Re)organizing government** to inform the organizational logic of sustainability in the landscape of public policy and organizations:
- Integration of policy and practice: recognizing that integration (ecological, social and economic) is crucial to the sustainability idea, and requires purposeful and sustained development of policy processes and standards for it to occur (e.g., through structural reform of government, law reform, SEA, etc.).
- Subsidiary: recognizing that policy responsibility should reside, and decisions should be taken, at the most effective and appropriate level for political (democratic), administrative (e.g., economies of scale) and substantive (e.g., the nature of sustainability problems) reasons. However, in the case of sustainability, where most issues must be handled at multiple scales, this demands a sophisticated discussion and flexible implementation of the idea of subsidiary.
- Reiteration: recognizing that sustainability is a long.term social and policy project to undertake in the face of considerable uncertainty about both environmental and social conditions and the efficacy of policy strategies. Responses to sustainability will involve reiteration of the problems and the response, and unless such reiterative capacity is designed into institutional and policy systems, the result is more likely to be ad hoc. The persistence and flexibility of policy processes, and thus of the institutional systems in which they take place, are therefore critical considerations when developing proposals for reform.

While these are general principles, they are operational in the sense that their careful consideration and implementation will be more likely to render policy and institutional change effective in the long-term (if more complicated in the short-term). The overlaps between the seven principles above and the five drawn from the Australian experience can be viewed as confirmation rather than redundancy.

Is there 'credible commitment' to sustainability?

These two studies, particularly the latter, allowed the identification of key elements of more successful institutional and deeper policy change for sustainability. However, the 'credible commitment',[39] of whichever level of government, to sustainability principles is particularly important. This is the acid test: what government is prepared to force itself to do, as opposed to promise or encourage others to do. Consistent with the principles and arguments in this paper, the following are proposed as the core areas and reforms that would need to be seriously addressed, in a given jurisdiction, to justify a credible commitment to sustainability.

The presence of a comprehensive, integrated policy platform on sustainable development:

- Mandatory mechanisms to ensure consideration of longer-term ecological and social issues in policy-making: includes the guarantee of persistence of efforts, and provisions for reiteration and review.
- Reform of the organization of government to allow whole-of-government approaches to sustainability: must include sufficient influence over traditional sectoral and portfolio-specific agencies and imperatives to effect actual policy change.
- Implementation of policy integration mechanisms to enforce transparent incorporation of sustainability principles in all policy sectors and agencies, via procedures such as SEA.
- Processes to identify and implement necessary changes to the wider body of statute law: to embed sustainability into the objectives and processes of all public agencies and policy processes, through a wide-ranging legislative review and binding statutory expression of sustainability principles.
- Where necessary, and especially in federal systems, substantial renegotiation and reform of intergovernmental policy and statutory arrangements to allow more coordinated and effective responses to sustainability problems: includes the transfer of responsibilities and matching resources to the most suitable scale (subsidiarity principle), noting that this applies to both regional and national governments.
- Inclusion of the broader community in policy processes: encouragement and empowerment of community-based management approaches, including guarantees of ongoing capacity and support, and the transfer, where appropriate, of legal competence and decision-making power. An inclusive, higher-level body with defined roles (e.g. NCSD) would be part of this participatory strategy.
- (For developed countries), reform of development aid and trade policy to prioritize sustainability and renewed commitment to, and plan for the implementation of, the 0.7 per cent of GDP target for aid.

In all the above, the mere presence of such mechanisms is the smaller part of the challenge: the descriptors of 'firm implementation', 'mandatory', 'independent evaluation' and 'influence over other sectors' will determine the quality of the institutional response.

We now consider several of the most encouraging examples from governments around the world:

- Dr Steve Dovers discusses overleaf developments globally concerning NCSDs.
- To achieve sustainable development will require significant innovation. How do we adapt National Systems of Innovation to meet the challenge of sustainable development? In Chapter 13, Dr Paul Weaver writes of the lessons learned from the 5 year Netherlands Sustainable Technology Development Project.
- In Chapter 14, Professor Peter Newman writes on the Western Australian State Sustainability Strategy which is widely regarded as one of the best, if not the best, in the world at the regional government level.
- In Chapter 15, Emeritus Professor Val Brown discusses local government perspectives.

> *Many welfare enhancing opportunities can be realized only through coordinated activity, guided by institutions and policy.40 Because of differences in law, norms, and systems of government, the political and legal domain for coordinating activity is frequently the nation. Much private sector activity is national in scope, and currencies, trade policies, safety regulation and the like substantially circumscribe the markets. Furthermore, many externalities spill outside municipalities and regions, the nation is also the level at which interests can be balanced, either directly or by facilitating negotiation amongst localities. In fact, the national government plays a special role in providing the legal framework and in creating an enabling environment for partnerships in which private sector, civil society, and all levels of government can contribute.*

World Bank Development Report 2003

National Councils for Sustainable Development (NCSDs)[41]

Stephen Dovers

Agenda 21, the blueprint from the first world summit on sustainable development (known as the Earth Summit) in 1992, outlined how we can all play our part to help achieve sustainable development whether we are engineers or business people or teachers. Agenda 21, together with numerous other statements, also argues that furthering the sustainable development agenda will require ongoing collaboration between governments, the private sector and community organizations ('civil society'), in the development and implementation of national policy that integrates ecological, social and economic dimensions over the long-term.[42] NCSDs are promoted as a core element of such an approach, for particular purposes and at a particular scale. NCSDs are necessary but not sufficient, complementing other policy and institutional responses at other scales, in the community sector, or with respect to specific issues. Nonetheless, as the primary available model for creating inclusive policy dialogue at high levels in the institutional system, NCSDs deserve attention even at this formative stage in their development. The features of an 'ideal' NCSD, as perceived by their proponents and many of their members, have been proposed as including:[43]

- A focus across the field of sustainable development (i.e. long-term and integrative ecological, social and economic dimensions), rather than shorter-term or on specific issues, sectors or portfolio areas.
- Membership across different levels of government, non-government stakeholders and academic, scientific and professional communities, giving the body a prominence only possible through broad consensus amongst key groups.
- Enough status within the institutional system to influence policy and institutional change, conferred by the nature of the membership, the status of leadership within that membership, legal or policy mandate, or the perceived value of roles filled.
- Ability to engage in ongoing discussion and development of policy options, recognizing the long-term and difficult nature of policy and institutional development for sustainability, whether such longevity is provided by statute, evolving links within the institutional system, or by other means.
- Clear roles related to sustainability, that are perceived as useful through the policy community for their value in validating the effort of members and contributors, and to avoid being seen as merely a 'talking shop'.
- Linkages, through membership, roles and information transfers, to other parts of the institutional system relevant to sustainability.

Beneath the rhetoric and actual development of NCSDs around the world, few current arrangements compare favourably with the ideal, although some do better than others. It is, however, not easy to analyse NCSDs, as they are a recent phenomena, making it difficult to judge their achievements.

Features of NCSDs

The Earth Council provides a coordination service and other support for NCSDs, particularly in developing countries. At mid-2002, the Network listed over 130 countries as having a central coordinating agency or body for sustainable development, while the UN listed 150 countries as having a coordinating mechanism for sustainable development.[44] However, many of these are units within government. It seems that around 70 countries have an inclusive body that reflects to some extent the above ideal. Of these NCSDs or equivalents, there is great variation in form and function, and the detail cannot be covered here. Besides, there is very limited accessible material available on individual NCSDs, and even less on the whole set. However, we can note some main features and make general observations on effectiveness and constraints, before profiling a few councils.[45] Roles vary widely, but commonly include: policy discussion, education, advice to government, review of policy experiences, consideration of international dimensions, and research and development. Many use working groups and external advice to undertake specific tasks. Few councils enjoy a continuity of either human or financial resources, or a solid legal or administrative basis. The most detailed review was undertaken for the period 1999–2000, containing summary reports from 27 countries, commentary on specific roles and issues, and a review of positive and negative experiences across the range of councils.[46] The following issues emerged:

- Councils were beginning to demonstrate their value as 'outreaches' of the UN Commission on Sustainable Development at the national scale. A further potential role exists in enabling regional dialogue amongst countries on specific issues and on sustainability generally.
- Some councils have demonstrated an ability to advance policy integration (ecological, social and economic) and integration of the various components of environmental policy (e.g., water, energy, fisheries, forests, etc.), even where the structure of government does not suit cross-sectoral linking. This could serve to 'mainstream' sustainable development.
- However, sustainable development is still often viewed as an 'environmental' matter, to be handled by the environment agency or minister.
- A challenge for NCSDs (and others), remains the integration of information, dialogue and policy across spatial and administrative scales.

Specific NCSDs as examples

Belgian Federal Council for Sustainable Development

This council is interesting due to its membership arrangements, focus on the sustainable development field, and range of activities.[47] Known by the FRDO–CFDD, it was established under law in 1997 to replace the previous National Council for Sustainable Development that had operated since 1993. The enabling law deals with federal policy on sustainable development, and lists the tasks of the council being to:

- advise federal authorities on sustainable development, either at the request of the government and parliament or on its own initiative;
- operate as a forum for debate on sustainable development; and
- 'sensitize' organizations and individuals regarding sustainable development.

Activities of the Council are undertaken by working groups in areas such as scientific research, international relations, socio-economic dimensions, biodiversity, and energy and climate. The membership of the Council is prescribed, with representatives of federal and regional governments and their agencies having advisory roles, whilst private sector, non-government and expertise-based members hold voting rights. This majority of civil society members is rare and progressive. The voting membership of the Council is as follows:

- four presidents and vice-presidents;
- six representatives from environmental, six from development and two from consumer NGOs;
- six representatives from labour and six from employer organizations;
- two representative from the energy production sector;
- six scientists.

Together with non-voting participants and advisers seconded for specific purposes, the Council involves and draws on a substantive representative and expertise base, supported by a dedicated secretariat. A sense of the work of the Council, in the form of submissions to government, can be gained from the list below:

- in 2001, to the European Union (EU) green and white papers on a sustainable development strategy, and integrated product and chemicals policy;
- in 2000, to the Belgian Government on wind energy, the EU's sixth Environmental Action Plan, and the federal sustainable development plan;
- in 1999, to the Belgian Government on taxation and climate change, and implementation of the Convention on Biological Diversity.

In 2002, the Council prepared a document for the Belgian Government regarding the World Summit on Sustainable Development (WSSD). As a statement from a representative body for its national government to carry to the international level, the content and its construction of a systemic sustainability policy agenda was impressive. Among the priorities proposed for the federal government to champion and implement are: integration of ecological, social and economic policy; utilizing sustainable development as a whole of government framework; indicators and targets for sustainability policy; transport and energy as priority sectors where policy must drive change in unsustainable trends; democratization of global institutions; and human development. This is a more progressive policy approach to sustainability than that mounted by any national government.

Canada: National Round Table on the Environment and the Economy (NRTEE)

Canada's NRTEE is the longest standing NCSD-equivalent, and has adapted its focus and mode of operation over time. In 1986, the Canadian Council of Resource and Environment Ministers established a National Task Force on Environment and Economy.[48] The Task Force recommended the establishment of round tables on environment and economy as multi-stakeholder, consensus-driven advisory bodies at national and provincial levels. These were established between 1988 and 1991, becoming Canada's principal response to sustainable development. This was pre-UNCED in 1992. Here we only consider the National body, but note that the coordinated development of the Canadian round tables is interesting. The current NRTEE arrangement was set in legislation in 1994. As an independent advisory body, its members are high profile individuals nominated by the Prime Minister, to whom NRTEE reports. It is tasked with identifying issues with both environmental and economic implications and actions that will balance economic prosperity with environmental preservation. Members come from government, business, NGOs, academia and First Nations, and are supported by a sizable secretariat. The NRTEE oversees programmes undertaken by task forces that include members as well as others from government and elsewhere.

Over time, the NRTEE has built up a sizeable record of reports, meetings and dialogue processes. The emphasis has shifted over time as projects are completed and as the understanding of and approach to them have evolved. Recent and past programme areas illustrate the range, continuities and change in focus issues:

Past programmes:
- sustainable development issues in the future;
- health, environment and economy;
- Aboriginal communities and non-renewable resources development;
- brownfield and contaminated sites;
- climate change;
- sustainable cities; and
- greenhouse gas emission trading.

Current programmes:
- environment and sustainable development indicators;
- eco-efficiency;
- ecological fiscal reform;
- domestic emissions trading;
- conservation of natural heritage;
- urban sustainability; and
- national brownfield redevelopment strategy.

The Roundtable also prepares a budget submission each year and, of the increase of C$700 million in federal environment spending in 2000, up to half has been credited to NRTEE budget proposals.[49]

United Kingdom: from round table to commission

The UK's Sustainable Development Commission was established in 2000, consolidating the approach taken with the previous non-government Round Table on Sustainable Development established in 1994 and the British Government Panel on Sustainable Development. In keeping with the ongoing devolutionary trend in the UK, the Commission has been established collaboratively with the Scottish Executive, Welsh Assembly and Northern Ireland Executive.[50] It is sponsored through the Cabinet Office, and reports to the Prime Minister and first ministers/secretaries in Scotland, Wales and Northern Ireland. The basic roles of the Commission are to:

- review progress on sustainable development, and identify policies and processes operating to retard progress;
- identify unsustainable trends requiring policy action;
- develop an understanding of sustainable development and required responses; and
- encourage good practice.

The Commission is chaired by a prominent environmentalist and the membership totals 22 and includes prominent figures from regional and local government, environmental, health, consumer and development NGOs, business and farming representatives, and academics. It is supported by a secretariat of nine. The 2001–2002 work programme provides a summary of the focus of the Commission, organized into five project areas and four sectors:

Project areas:
1 'Productivity Plus': examining the reconciliation of economic growth, social progress and environmental protection.
2 'Climate Change': judged the single most important issue.
3 'Food and Farming': with an emphasis on the total production system.
4 'Regeneration': focusing on policy integration in community and economic regeneration programmes.
5 'Communicating Sustainable Development'.

Sectors:
1 Business: covering sectoral strategies and business leadership.
2 Central and local government.
3 English regions.
4 Devolved areas.

Although only recently established, the UK Commission has interesting attributes. The move from a Round Table with vague roles and separate government Panel to an integrated and more substantial Commission with clearly defined membership and functions suggests an evolving appreciation of the potential for an NCSD-style approach. The membership reflects a broad construction of sustainability, including development, health and consumer interests as well as environment. The focus on regions evidences co-evolution of sustainability concerns with broader political change and institutional shifts in a particular national setting.

NCSDs and international agreements

The three NCSDs above are all from developed countries. What about NCSDs in developing countries? A review of six developing country's councils' roles, in localizing the implementation of global environmental conventions (GECs), drew broad conclusions about the effectiveness of NCSDs in assisting the communication and operationalization of international agreements.[51] The six case studies were Burkina Faso, Costa Rica, Dominican Republic, Mexico, the Philippines and Uganda. In addition, the review focused on the uptake and use of multi-stakeholder integrated sustainability planning (MISP), a broad framework methodology.

Overall observations from the six case studies include:

• The importance of multi-stakeholder approaches, sufficient legal and policy settings, education and capacity building, and the monitoring of and learning from regional and local projects.
• There is too little attention paid and no resources assigned to achieving synergies that can occur between GECs when they are implemented. Similar demands arise from different GECs for policy development, information and capacity building, but these tend to be dealt with separately. Efficiency and effectiveness can be enhanced by recognizing such commonalities.
• The presence of an NCSD had a positive effect on understanding, communication, implementation and recognition of synergies across conventions, through their ability to create links and dialogue across jurisdictions, policy agencies, professions and groups.

General observations

NCSDs are mostly quite recent and experimental, however, the more impressive NCSDs demonstrate the potential to add value to the more standard administrative and policy arrangements in the near-term, and maybe even to drive long-term change. Reviews of NCSDs to date report some positive impacts. Of interest are those cases outlined above where initial arrangements have been replaced or reformed, creating 'second generation' and stronger NCSDs that are more embedded in the institutional system (Belgium, the UK, Canada). However, the limits of the NCSD model should be appreciated – they are not major institutional reforms in their own right. They are organizational interventions in the institutional system that might contribute to transformations over time, and they represent a recognition of the need to expand policy learning opportunities across different parts of the policy community and the broader public.

CHAPTER 13

NATIONAL SYSTEMS OF INNOVATION

Paul M. Weaver

EDITORS' NOTE: Harnessing national systems of innovation is key to achieving sustainable development. The Netherlands has emerged as an early leader in applying its national innovation capacity to focus on the challenge of a sustainable future. When the editors learned of the work of the Dutch Sustainable Technology Development programme through project mentor Philip Sutton, we were greatly encouraged as the work is truly ground-breaking. After making contact with one of the key authors of the publication based on the research, Paul Weaver, we invited Paul to consider writing a piece for this publication drawing on his experience to provide guidance for nations seeking to focus their national innovation towards achieving a sustainable future.

Practice makes perfect

The line of argument that we have taken leads us to conclude that there is a need for all nations to adapt their national systems of innovation to meet the challenges and opportunities of sustainable development. In sum, the key to national competitiveness lies in national innovative capacity, which in turn is strengthened and reinforced dynamically and recursively as it responds to and influences society's needs. A priority need as we enter the 21st century is for future development to be sustainable and for future products, processes and services to be produced with much higher eco-efficiency. The future prosperity and well-being of citizens worldwide depends on this, as does the wealth and prospects for individual nations.

Just as labour productivity improvement has been the guiding theme of past growth-oriented development, resource productivity improvement will be the dominant theme that drives and coordinates innovation in the 21st century, which increasingly will be

This chapter was written by Paul Weaver, Director of the Research Centre for Eco-Efficiency and Enterprise; the work reported is in part based on the research project Adaptive Integration of Research and Policy for Sustainable Development (AIRP-SD), which was financed within the EU Improving Human Potential programme by the Strategic Analysis of Specific Political Issues (STRATA) activity. The author gratefully acknowledges the support received from the EU. The views expressed in the chapter are those of the author and may not in any circumstances be regarded as stating an official position of the European Commission.

concerned with the qualitative aspects of how economic output and wealth are produced. The pressure of a growing world population and a growing world economy as citizens everywhere seek to secure a decent standard of living on a planet with limited resources and limited capacity to absorb and process wastes ensures that this will be the case. In turn, the high levels of eco-efficiency and resource productivity improvement that will be needed in the coming decades – improvements of an order of magnitude at least – will require 'systems level' changes in the way that needs are met, jobs are created, income is earned and export sales are generated. In their turn, these will depend upon changes in the institutions that support development and that provide the contextual framework for innovation and decision-making. Given the lead times involved in achieving resource productivity improvements of this magnitude, work on strategic long-term restructuring of our economies and societies needs to be underway already if the sustainability challenge is to be met. As indicated in earlier chapters, the state has a significant role to play here, as it is best positioned to co-ordinate long-term economic and industrial strategies and policies.

This is why sustainable development is so great a challenge. It defines a wholly new development paradigm. It calls for innovation across a broad set of fronts: structural, social and technological. Perhaps most importantly, it calls for innovation in the innovation system itself in order to re-orient innovation efforts towards new goals, to make these efforts more efficient and to accelerate the pace of progress on resource productivity improvement so that this overtakes and runs increasingly ahead of economic growth. Only then – and only if achieved eco-efficiency gains are used to reduce environmental pressure and secure poverty reduction – will the stress on the planetary system that underpins our economies, our societies and our welfare be reduced.

Sustainable development implies a new industrial revolution that will see new concepts of 'well-being' and new models of 'competitiveness' emerge. Living standards and life quality within countries will increasingly depend upon the resource efficiency with which vital needs are met. In the richer countries with ageing populations, a backlog of environmental problems and a need to restructure physical infrastructures to fit the new context, there will be many claims on increasingly scarce capital. Reducing the resource cost of comfortable living will be an imperative for the future well-being of societies with large numbers of non-working citizens, whilst in the productive economy, increasing resource productivity will be an imperative for securing the highest possible marginal productivity of labour and capital, as well as of natural resources. Competitiveness and what determines it will be redefined. Economic leadership in the 21st century will lie with those nations that seize the opportunity of responding to the sustainability challenge. They will make their own economies more robust and resilient in a world characterized by high resource prices, high waste disposal costs and increasing threats to conventional energy and material supply chains. They will also lead in the technologies and associated know-how of the new 'resource productivity' development paradigm. History shows that leadership processes are dominated by positive feedback and that an early lead in meeting an innovation challenge often brings long-lasting competitive advantage. First movers will have the best chance of becoming long-term front-runners.

The Dutch – with their national Sustainable Technology Development (STD) programme – have been the first movers; or, at very least, they are among the set of first movers. This chapter looks in greater depth at questions surrounding the decision by the Dutch to tackle the innovation challenge that sustainable development poses. Precisely what is the challenge? How have the Dutch responded and why should they be among the first to adapt their national system of innovation? What has been happening in the Netherlands and in other countries in the period since the national STD programme ended? Is it possible to evaluate the Dutch programme and other innovative programmes to assess the impacts on their respective national systems of innovation and to identify general and transferable lessons for other countries?

Innovation systems are part of today's development paradigm

Sustainable development poses special challenges for innovation systems.[1] The Dutch were very early in realizing this. Nonetheless, a precise diagnosis of the problem was not made until after the Dutch STD programme had completed and was first formulated in a background report to an evaluation study (the Adaptive Integration of Research and Policy for Sustainable Development Project funded by the STRATA Program of the EC) that sought to assess the influence of the Dutch programme and other sustainability-oriented research and technology development programmes.[2] The diagnosis suggests that today's national innovation systems and the prevailing development paradigm are closely linked because they have co-evolved. In effect, prevailing systems of innovation and the prevailing development pathway are mutually supportive and re-enforcing. The institutions involved in the generation, commercialization and diffusion of new products, processes and services, including the institutions of science, government, business and finance, as well as the systems for determining research and technology development priorities, financing research and development, establishing the incentives and regulations that provide the reference frame and context in which discovery, invention, innovation, diffusion and development decision-making take place, are all part-and-parcel of the same prevailing development paradigm. By contrast, sustainable development implies paradigmatic change – innovation for a new development paradigm.

Interestingly and in a similar vein, this same report also put forward the important hypothesis that principles for the design of an appropriate innovation system in support of sustainable development can be derived from the concept of sustainable development itself and from characteristics of the developmental system of interest. It also advanced and tested the hypothesis that innovation efforts in support of sustainable development and the outcomes from those efforts are not only influenced by the innovation context, but recursively impact upon their context. In short, appropriately designed innovation efforts that target systems-level change and practise the principles of sustainable development will strengthen the innovation system itself, so providing a mechanism for leveraging the effectiveness of future sustainability-oriented innovation. At issue is whether it is possible to initiate new innovation trajectories and begin such a virtuous cycle from within the context of prevailing institutional and organizational arrangements that have been developed over generations and are arranged specifically to support business-as-usual.

The challenge to innovation systems

A first concern is to develop a typology of the challenges that sustainable development poses as a basis for suggesting what forms of restructuring and reorientation of national innovation systems are required and what kinds of new scientific, social and governance capacities and capital need to be built or strengthened.

In principle, efforts to improve environmental performance can follow one of three tracks.[3] Research and innovation on a short-term track is concerned with fine-tuning already existing approaches to meeting needs. It has a time horizon of up to five years. Research and innovation on a medium-term track is concerned with more substantial product- or process-integrated technological improvements and reorganization. It has a time horizon of 5–20 years. On both of these tracks, however, improvements take place within the context of the prevailing development paradigm, are consistent with it and do nothing to change it. In turn, this strictly limits the scope of the improvements that are possible. The third track, by contrast, is concerned with the design of completely new system-level solutions, which are conceived in terms of fundamentally different sets of technologies, institutions and social arrangements and which are consistent with sustainability values. These are path-breaking solutions, since they are not consistent with a continuation of the prevailing development paradigm and trajectory, but imply changes in the direction of development and the creation of a new paradigm. The time scale is commensurately long, 20 years or more, but the scope for performance improvement is high because system-solutions can be designed from the outset to be intrinsically compatible with sustainability objectives. In principle, this 'third' track corresponds to innovation for sustainability.

The challenges for innovation on this third track are of a different order from those on either short- or medium-term time tracks. They are broad, conceptual and strategic challenges, they imply new tasks and they call for different approaches to innovation and different capacities. Sustainability-oriented innovation must be concerned with ambitious performance improvement targets. Entirely new systems-solutions cannot be developed in convenient isolation but must be contextualized within a holistic vision of a sustainable future defined by its own paradigmatic cluster of technologies, institutions and social arrangements. Whereas innovators working to improve existing solutions can take the paradigmatic framework conditions for granted, those working on sustainable solutions must base their work on the belief that these will change. Moreover, they must work towards changing them if new solutions are to be implemented.

This means that innovation for sustainability cannot be restricted to designing and evaluating solutions, but must also engage with the *process* of designing and implementing paradigmatic change. This is a strategic management challenge that requires special ways of working and a special toolkit to deal with the issues entailed, such as creating visions of sustainable futures, handling the dynamics of co-evolutionary change on several innovation fronts, handling uncertainty that is inherent when shifting into realms not previously experienced and communicating with stakeholders and decision-makers about options and their implications. The normative nature of sustainability implies that the challenge is prescriptive, rather than predictive. The challenge is not to forecast the future, but rather to envision a desirable socio-economic future that meets macro-sustainability constraints and conforms with society-agreed concepts of what constitutes a good quality of life, to set this as a target state and to work towards its realization. The challenge of managing change and transition is a multi-level one, since different spatial levels of the development system (local, national, regional, global) are interdependent. This means that sustainability research may be targeted on development problems or transition-management problems that are manifest on any scale, but that 'solutions' will always need to designed and evaluated to take into account the links with other scales.

Sustainable development implies the need to consider a broad set of economic, social, environmental and political criteria and to be concerned for spill-over effects that cross over spatial, temporal and scale boundaries. This implies that these same criteria are integrated into every step and stage in the process of finding, evaluating and implementing solutions. It implies the need for multi-objective, multi-criteria methods and tools for analysis. And it implies widening the boundary of analysis to encompass all significant cross-over impacts so that these are internalized into analysis and impact assessment. The need to take many disparate criteria into account complicates the search process, since it engages non-market values and implies the need for decisions to be made over the relative importance of different criteria and for compromise and trade-off among objectives. The selection of criteria and the relative weighting of each cannot be established by reference to markets or by scientific supposition, but can only be determined and legitimated by stakeholders and their representatives. Moreover, the criteria and weightings are likely to change as stakeholders' understandings change and, with it, their values and attitudes. In turn, this implies that scientists cannot search for solutions alone, but are engaged as one of the agents in a process of social problem-solving.

As there are no 'cure-all' solutions in sustainable development, there is a need to ensure that understanding of the sustainability threat and appreciation of the objectives and principles of sustainable development are widely diffused into all spheres of development decision-making within society, politics, business and science.

Complexity and uncertainty

In sustainable development the focus is no longer just the techno-economic system that delivers economic growth, but the whole socio-ecological system embracing the natural world, the cultural world and interactions between the two. Over recent years, there has been a stunning advance in our understanding of the planet, its history of transformations and its present dynamics. We now know that the natural world is a complex, hierarchically structured system characterized by non-linear dynamics. It belongs in the class of evolving, self-organizing, 'dissipative systems', which are far from thermodynamic equilibrium, which have multiple stable states, which are characterized by the potential for irreversible change and where discontinuous behaviour and structural change are the norm. By implication, the understanding needed for environmental change covers processes that operate over an enormous range of scales, interactions that operate with wide ranging time lags and impacts that depend on threshold effects. The inherent complexity of the natural world leads to inevitable uncertainty. It is intrinsically impossible to understand perfectly and completely so complex a system whose behaviours may be, in any event, intrinsically chaotic.

This is all the more important when interactions between mankind and nature are increasingly mediated through more powerful technologies. The combination of uncertainty, powerful technological interventions, the potential for irreversible ecological change and the limited capacity of humanity to adapt or respond when ecological change undermines the very basis of human survival or life quality constitutes a powerful case for a precautionary approach. This is certainly the case when planetary stability is at stake and may also apply when the livelihoods and quality of life of large numbers of vulnerable people are threatened by a technology or a development whose impacts cannot be known in advance. To exercise precaution demands considered judgement of potential benefits and risks of development choices, as well as concern for the distribution of these across society and generations in relation to the vulnerabilities of stakeholders in the event of problems.

There are comparable difficulties in dealing with the human and institutional systems, science included, that are integral to the process of development and the search for sustainable development. In sustainable development, we are dealing with a decentralized and distributed innovation system with many individual but interdependent actors and many stakeholders. As the stakes involved in a shift to sustainable development are high, there is a need to reckon with the interests and strategies of the various stakeholders and also with the uneven distribution of power in human and institutional systems. Human decisions and actions are frequently based upon what effectively amount to gaming strategies, where the purpose is to pre-empt the behaviour of another actor or provoke a particular response. Thus, the social systems that interact with the natural world are, in their own ways, just as complex, unpredictable and unfathomable as the natural system. Social systems are complex. Indeed, as Funtowicz and Ravetz point out, they are reflexively complex.[4]

Challenges to the organization and culture of science

One consequence of complexity is that no single scientific discipline or field of expert knowledge will be able to capture all that is relevant to the analysis of development problems. Furthermore, each field of expertise, while bringing to bear important insights to the problem, will necessarily introduce its own subjectivity relating to the artificial boundaries used to frame the problem and to the theories and methods used to analyse the problem. The assumptions introduced to enable a complex real world system to be analysed in parts, as if each existed in isolation, and to enable each part to be treated as if it were a simple or merely complicated system,[5] rather than something elementally or functionally embedded within a complex system, effectively ensure that each system subjected to disciplinary scrutiny is, in effect, artificial. The system analysed by each discipline and the image each discipline holds of the world and its phenomena reflect its own cognitive understanding. Each is, at best, partial, distorted and subjective. It follows that no single discipline or approach can capture all that is relevant, that it takes a plurality of approaches to obtain the best possible image of reality or to gain the best possible diagnosis of problems or solutions and that no one discipline or perspective is privileged with a more valid insight than others.

Thus, the tasks inherent in sustainable development are totally different from those for which Western science and modern innovation systems were conceived. Funtowitcz and Ravetz argue that, conceptually and organizationally, modern science has been constructed around a model of the relationship between mankind and nature as one of conquest and control rather than one of respecting ecological limits, managing problems, expecting surprises and adapting to these.[6] Furthermore, the power and influence of modern science are derived from its facility to tackle problems that can be neatly bounded. Modern science is based upon two complementary traditions: a tradition of breaking down complex real world systems of interest into parts and a complementary, although less well developed, integration science for combining the understanding obtained through disciplinary study of the separated parts. This structure and organization of science was developed and institutionalized long before the problems of complexity, uncertainty and chaotic behaviour were recognized. The result is that conventional science is well equipped to deal with the large number of problems and questions that are manageable within fairly narrowly defined system boundaries (problems that concern simple or complicated systems), but ill equipped to deal with complex systems and complex developmental problems.[7]

The strength of conventional science is that it provides for elegant theory and for a high level of certainty and reproducibility of scientific findings, especially when experimentation is conducted under controlled conditions where all variables other than those under investigation are held constant or are externalized. However, this strength is offset by several weaknesses. The initial splitting of real world phenomena into discrete sub-systems of interest and the initial matching of phenomena with study approaches are based upon cognitive understandings about what is and what is not important, about what should and what should not be studied and about how phenomena of assumed interest should be studied. An inevitable subjectivity surrounds the initial compartmentalization and choice of analytical method. In addition, the artificial simplification introduced by delineating system boundaries may also restrict the applicability of findings to real world problems or lead to unintended and unforeseen consequences when knowledge is applied, since only those impacts that fall within the system boundary will have been analysed. Furthermore, each discipline has its own terminology and conventions and makes its own set of simplifying assumptions. These are often mutually inconsistent, making the theory, methods, data and knowledge from different fields of study incompatible and reducing the possibilities for building the composite picture through integration science.

The major concern from the perspective of sustainable development, however, is that phenomena that arise through system interactions and which lie in the 'grey areas' between disciplines may fall out of consideration altogether. In the process of breaking down real world systems into parts, most of the links and relationships that are the central concerns of sustainable development – the links between the natural and social systems or between levels in hierarchical structures or between time periods – are severed and are not studied by the specialized disciplines. Relatively new academic fields such as resilience and complex systems theory seek to address these issues by integrating the social and natural sciences. Due to the complexity and non-linearity of complex natural and human systems, scientists, economists and engineers all have to make assumptions when constructing their mathematical models. In sustainable development our very concern is for relationships, phenomena and problems that lie at the interfaces between different scientific fields. Moreover, the very fact that these are today's major societal problems in part reflects their past neglect by the prevailing scientific paradigm which, consistent with the prevailing development paradigm to which science is recursively related, has externalized them from consideration and importance.

The danger that scientific efforts will be misplaced is heightened when the scientific agenda is set through processes that are introspective or are dominated by narrow interests and concerns vested in the prevailing development paradigm. Yet today this is the norm. This, in turn, reflects the status and influence science has attained through specialized study and also illustrates the emergence and institutionalization of a corresponding scientific 'culture'. Each specialized disciplinary field has its own body of theory and methods. Its practitioners come to share a common language and terminology. They publish their work in their own set of peer-reviewed journals. They set their own research agendas. Students are taught in the disciplinary strictures and are moulded to conform to the accepted norms of their discipline. Membership of a discipline or specialist scientific profession depends first upon success in examinations and then upon success in research and publication, which in turn depends upon conforming to the accepted disciplinary norms and achieving peer approval. The parallel between path-dependent science and path-dependent development (to which science contributes) is clear.

Another facet of scientific culture that arises from analysing bounded systems along the tradition of experimental science is the image of science as neutral and objective with a purpose to establish hard facts and truths. The 'science of parts' places importance on scientific certainty. Whilst there are notable exceptions, overall a narrow enough focus is usually chosen in order to develop data and tests that can be used to reject invalid hypotheses. A major hindrance to progressive research is the pressure to narrow uncertainty to the point where acceptance of an argument among scientific peers is essentially unanimous. Thus a culture is developed where scientists are reluctant to present findings or recommendations until there is a strong basis of scientific evidence that puts these beyond doubt. The approach is conservative and unambiguous at the price of being incomplete. But the danger of this approach is that in being so focused it will miss critical areas and is not appropriate for sustainability.

One response has been to use relatively simple systems to develop new experimental methods, mathematical approaches, statistical analyses and models that can better approximate complex reality. In this way we may be able to better appreciate uncertainty and distinguish the different types of uncertainty that characterize our systems of interest. Nonetheless, the insights of chaos theory, behavioural psychology and resilience theory mean that, whichever approach to modelling is taken, there will always be some irreducible uncertainty about the behaviour of our systems of interest and therefore also about the outcomes of management interventions in those systems. Given the intrinsic limit to our capacity to model the behaviour of our systems of interest, the issue switches to one of how best to manage such systems. The challenge is to develop a different *management approach* based upon regarding uncertainty less as an obstacle to action and more as a source of creativity and inspiration for the development of intrinsically safe interventions. The challenge to science in support of such a management approach is to shift towards a 'whole system'/'design for sustainability' approach. Such a shift can be seen in the traditionally reductionist field of chemistry. Originally, environmental chemistry was concerned simply to measure levels of pollutants in the environment. But, since the early 1990s, chemists are increasingly seeking to design chemicals for dissipative uses so that these are intrinsically benign. They are beginning to 'design-out' toxic chemicals. Such shifts will greatly assist policy-makers looking for solutions-oriented approaches to sustainable development.

Neither reductionism nor a search for certainty are compatible with the realities of sustainable development or with the needs of policy-makers facing urgent problems and decisions.[8] Nor is it consistent with the realities of the policy-making process. A focus on whole system design for sustainability can at least deliver relative certainty over what can be done to reduce our ecological footprint and, at the same time, can be used to integrate environmental, economic and social criteria into solution designs. Several initiatives within national innovation systems around the world are beginning to rise to the challenge. The Commonwealth Scientific and Industrial Research Organisation (CSIRO) in Australia, for example, has several programmes seeking to help do this, including the Social and Economic Integration (SEI) programme. It is part of an organization-wide strategy to ensure CSIRO delivers value to the Australian community through better diagnosis of complex problems and more rounded, creative and enduring solutions.

Challenges at the science–society and science–policy interface

Even though the specifics of sustainability problems are relatively new, an established body of theory and methods has been developed in relation to analogous complex problems. This body of theory and experience suggests that problems characterized by a large number of potentially conflicting objectives, high degrees of uncertainty and risk, potential irreversibilities, large numbers of stakeholders, high stakes, unavoidable subjectivity and context specificity, cannot be handled satisfactorily by centralized decision-making structures and processes. Instead, they are best analysed and resolved in a decentralized fashion through participatory processes that engage the relevant actors and stakeholders in a constructive social process of mutual learning and decision-making. Thus, innovation for sustainability calls not only for interdisciplinary working, but also for transdisciplinarity, inter-agency working and stakeholder engagement. Innovation for sustainability must integrate knowledge, values and actions from different domains, both formal and informal.

Since uncertainty is high, the analysis of uncertainty becomes a topic for analysis in itself. Moreover, through the connection between science and implementation an opportunity is created to learn about the systems under management, since every policy and management action will necessarily be taken on the basis of incomplete science and will represent a test of the underlying hypotheses upon which the policy or management action is predicated. This essentially describes an 'adaptive management' approach[9] that is sometimes used in the management of renewable resources, but which could form a useful general model for sustainability-oriented innovation. The essential point here is that in the case of sustainability there is a special need for continuous learning and adaptation, since the system of interest is not only incompletely understood, but it is also a moving target, evolving in part because of the impacts of management actions. Under these circumstances, management actions need to achieve not only the social goals desired, but also an ever changing understanding of the system under management. Policy and management actions can be designed specifically to test hypotheses, probe the system and, so, reduce uncertainty. This puts a premium on the quality of the science-policy interface and, also, on the levels of societal trust in policy-makers and scientists.

The foregoing comments also help to throw light on the links between risk, uncertainty, experimentation and learning, which is useful for operationalizing the precautionary principle. Clearly, risk cannot be avoided in situations of uncertainty. Moreover, a balance has to be struck between the risk inherent in inaction and the risks of acting on the basis of incomplete knowledge. When issues and the responses are local, or even regional, actions can be designed as management and scientific experiments whose purpose is to generate both understanding and solutions at the same time. But when problems are global, such as in the case of climatic change, a very different approach is needed.[10] Good experiments are meant to fail, but the experimenters should live to learn from their experiment. Holling proposes the general rule here that risk taking is appropriate only when errors are affordable. Put differently: 'We should not take risks with elements and qualities that underpin societies, economies or nature, especially when these are inherently planetary in scale, since these are the very foundations upon which sustainability with opportunity is based. Such elements and properties should be protected and preserved'.[11]

This raises the more general issue of communication at the science–policy interface. In principle, science is needed to supply the underpinnings of informed action while policy and management responses are needed to create an enabling framework for sustainable development. However, the two communities – scientists and policy-makers – all too often suffer from a communications gap. The issue is complicated, because the quality of communication at this interface is a function not only of how science is organized, but also of how policy-making and government is organized. Several studies confirm that the barriers of communication and comprehension at the science—policy interface are bound up with the compartmentalization that exists in both spheres: the disciplinary compartmentalization of science and the separation of governmental responsibilities across different departments and agencies. There needs to be interdisciplinary 'systems-level' science in order to develop integrated systems-level solutions. But, integrative systems-solutions and integrative policy proposals depend on integrative policy responses.[12]

Myers notes that many problems of unsustainable development arise precisely because governmental agencies do not act in systematic fashion and do not address those grey areas that fall between agency spheres of activity. Just as the disciplinary division of science externalizes important impacts from scientific consideration, so the division into governmental agencies, departments and ministries can lead to neglect of impacts that fall outside agency or departmental responsibilities. The divisions may mean that the institutions of government find difficulty in developing integrative responses to systems-level solutions even when these are proposed by science. One implication is that the capacity of government to develop integrated policy responses may be a contextual factor in the success of innovation. Another may be that building this capacity is a potentially important element in adapting our national innovation systems to fit them better to support sustainable development.

In sum, the requirements of sustainable development imply the need to reorient innovation efforts towards new thematic priorities and new process challenges. They specify new roles for scientists within the process of sustainable development as initiators, facilitators, coordinators and mediators in societal processes of complex problem-solving and decision-making. These roles are additional to the traditional roles of science and technology in providing information and technical means. They specify new tasks in relation to the handling of risk and uncertainty, and pose special requirements for communicating with a wide range of non-scientific actors and stakeholders as well as with policy-makers. They imply new ways of working, focused on inclusive and interactive approaches. They also specify a wider set of goals and outcomes for science and technology, which in turn holds implications for research management, research evaluation and research funding. New funding models are needed to enable innovation challenges to be re-conceptualized from first principles, to translate these into research proposals, to build transdisciplinary research networks and consortia and to cover the additional costs that are implied for stakeholder participation and for communication.

The Dutch National Sustainable Technology Development (STD) programme

At issue is the potential contradiction that sustainability research, which by definition is aimed at changing development trajectories and paradigms, is today dependent on prevailing national innovation systems for recognition, resources and steering. This situation is hardly likely to liberate innovation for sustainability – or to initiate the virtuous cycles referred to earlier – unless special provisions are made at the outset expressly for this purpose. The Dutch were early to recognize this and to establish a special programme of research and technology development with a mandate not only to explore radical new ways of meeting needs in the long-term future, but also to strengthen the national innovation system in its capacity to support sustainable development, especially by developing and testing research methods and innovation management processes appropriate for supporting sustainable development.

The Dutch STD programme was developed against the backdrop of a policy commitment by the Netherlands to sustainable development and a set of background studies made in the late 1980s and early 1990s. One such study estimated the scale of the resource productivity improvement that the Netherlands should target by the mid-21st century in order to meet its policy goal, placing this at an order of magnitude or more.[13] Around the same time, an inquiry by a special Dutch Commission for Environmental Policy concluded that incremental innovation would be incapable of meeting such a target. The mismatch led to a review of the status of Dutch research activities and the decision to re-direct some of the innovation effort towards long-term sustainability objectives and related capacity building. The background reports provided not only the justification for a research programme aimed at supporting sustainable development, but also provided pointers to the approach to innovation that such a programme should adopt. It was argued that innovation for system renewal implies a search for systems solutions consistent with a shift in the development paradigm and that successful innovation will therefore depend upon pre-empting future social and institutional contexts and integrating these into technology designs. The STD programme was therefore established as a programme for long-term technological innovation in support of sustainable development. It was designed to have critical mass and wide-ranging scope, to take a long-term time horizon and to target jumps in eco-efficiency. It was designed to be process-oriented. This means that the STD programme was focused on influencing the micro- and macro-innovation contexts and on developing new innovation methods and processes rather than on promoting specific technologies.

These defining aspects were reflected in the STD programme aims and objectives. The programme (1992–1997) was established with a mandate for 'learning by doing'. Its aims were: (i) to use a set of case studies to develop and illustrate a methodology for exploring long-term, systems-level solutions to meeting the needs of future generations; (ii) to initiate several new innovation trajectories (illustration processes) aimed at long-term renewal of production–consumption systems; (iii) to create new transdisciplinary networks of scientists, technologists, business managers, investors, policy-makers and societal stakeholders engaged in searching together for new solutions; (iv) to induce policy measures and social innovations to facilitate the process of innovation for sustainable technologies; (v) to embed programme outcomes in the national innovation infrastructures and institutions so that these would continue to be used and developed after the programme itself had ended; and (vi) to leverage the impact of the programme by disseminating a proven innovation methodology along with any transferable lessons learned.

Programme funding of €12 million came from a combination of sources – 85 per cent from government and the remainder from public and private sources. The government proportion was funded by five Ministries: Agriculture and Nature Conservation; Education, Culture and Science; Economic Affairs; Housing, Spatial Planning and the Environment; and, Transportation, Traffic and Water Management. Hence the programme is widely referred to as the 'Inter-Ministerial' STD programme.

The programme hypothesis was that the prospects for sustainable technology development could be improved by manipulating or modifying innovation processes. The STD programme was therefore aimed at developing new innovation methods and enabling actors and stakeholders in technology development to gain first experiences with these in the course of making some first strategic reviews of how needs might be met in the long-term future. A preliminary innovation methodology was developed centred around a series of tasks to be performed and outcomes to be attained, tools for accomplishing these, and a multi-step, iterative working schedule. The core of the STD programme's activity involved testing and refining the methodology using case studies in five key areas of future need and a set of 15 illustration projects deriving from these, each exploring possible new solution trajectories.

The essence of the STD method lies in the mutually supportive use of 'need-driven' approaches to problem redefinition, 'backcasting' and the development of new innovation networks to explore the challenges to innovation and technology development posed by sustainability. The starting point for the creation of a new innovation network lies in redefining an innovation challenge from first principles in relation to a key area of future need. The expectation is that sustainable systems solutions and technologies will transcend traditional sectors. Research and technology development (RTD) processes are, therefore, most likely to be successful if the challenge is re-conceptualized so that the search starts, not from the existing solution, but from the need that the solution is intended to fulfil; for example, for warmth, nutrition, mobility, etc. For each need, a new network is built around a new definition of the challenge that the need presents for innovation and sustainability. The network is then encouraged to develop a range of promising new solution concepts and to bring at least one to the stage of an outline 'design' capable of being communicated to others. For this, network members should develop a shared expectation or vision about how the need might be met in the long-term future, using sustainable technologies embedded in a compatible socio-economic context. By describing a pathway linking their vision of a target long-term sustainable future system state back to the present day, members of a network are able to define actions that should be taken in the near term to realize this vision.

Because the pathways must be described through a logical sequence of coherent interim states, the traced pathways help to identify the main technological, structural and social challenges that will be faced and by when these should be overcome. Since each pathway is drawn back to the present, the first actions will be ones that can be taken today. By implication, each pathway describes an evolutionary way forward towards trend-breaking technological and paradigmatic change. Backcasting is therefore the hallmark of the method. It is the main mechanism for incorporating a co-evolutionary, dynamic systems perspective into the innovation process and it is used to relax unnecessary constraints on solutions, such as to reduce the influence of existing technological solutions, while it reintroduces some necessary, but usually missing, constraints, such as those implied by the need to meet eco-efficiency targets and to avoid unacceptable spill-overs.

As conceived in the STD programme, the innovation process involves a set of tasks to be undertaken in sequence, each associated with one or more targeted outcomes. The programme formalized these into a step-by-step working schedule, which sets out the tasks and anticipated outcomes, and proposes tools that can be used to accomplish each task.[14] The various steps in the schedule fall into three main phases of activity. The first phase is designed to develop a long-term vision based upon a strategic review of how a need might be met in the future. This entails an orientation analysis to see how needs are presently met and to clarify current and likely future sources of unsustainability if trends are unbroken. The sustainability challenge is then redefined within robust trends (such as demographic trends) and from first principles to identify criteria that solutions should meet as well as opportunities for radical new solutions that might be opened by breakthroughs in basic science. Preliminary sketches of possible solutions are then set out and backcasting is used to reveal how each solution could be brought about. The second phase is designed to evaluate solutions and pathways and to clarify which actions should be taken in the near term. The third phase is concerned with implementing the action plan.

The results of this process have been remarkable. Research has shown that far from being impossible, major Factor 10 plus resource productivity improvements are possible over the next 30–50 years. The results are summarized in the Table 13.1.

The Netherlands context

Why is innovation for sustainability so important for the Dutch? The probable answer links back to Porter's thesis about the competitive advantage of nations. The Netherlands is a small country with around 15 million people and one of the highest population densities in the world. It is one of the world's most highly urbanized societies. Its low elevation, flat terrain, long seaboard and position in respect to some of Europe's major river systems present both challenges and opportunities. On the 'challenge' side, the water table is high and drainage is slow, which renders the Netherlands vulnerable to water and soil pollution, a problem that is made worse because the river systems carry pollution from several upstream European countries into the Netherlands and because the Dutch economy generates high levels of soil- and water-borne wastes from value-adding activities linked to the processing of imported feed-stocks. Pollution levels often seriously exceed local eco-capacities. Furthermore, the country is prone to inundation from the sea and from the rivers, which have high seasonal fluctuations in water levels. These conditions render the Netherlands especially vulnerable to climate-induced sea-level rise. With the exception of onshore (Slochteren Bell) and offshore natural gas deposits (an economic mainstay but already dwindling and expected to run out within 20–30 years), the Netherlands is poor in natural resource terms.

On the 'opportunity' side, the river estuaries and strategic location in relation to Germany, Switzerland and central Europe provide natural advantages for transport and trade. The Netherlands provides port and associated water, road, rail and air transport and logistics facilities for a huge European hinterland. Based around its port and transport facilities, the Netherlands has developed a strong trading economy, which adds value to imported raw materials and exports final products. Thus, the Netherlands has a strong refining and petrochemicals sector even though it has only limited domestic oil reserves. Equally, the value of its agricultural and food product trade – based in part

Table 13.1 *Results of the Dutch Sustainable Technology Development programme*

	The challenge set	Achievements
Overall		Factor 10–50 in 50 years from 1990 (i.e. by 2040) – depending on the issue (e.g. fossil carbon emissions Factor 25 (p42), oil Factor 40, copper Factor 30, acid deposition Factor 50) (p43). Table of specific Factor improvements needed without adjustment for population growth and poverty reduction ranging from 20% to 99% improvements (p41).
Nutrition		
Sustainable multifunctional land use		Factor 20 (95%) over several eco-capacity criteria (p100).
High technology closed-cycle horticulture		Wastage of CO_2 can be cut by Factor 8 (87%) and water by Factor 18 (94%) (p116).
Novel protein foods	Average Factor 20 improvement by 2035 (p145)	In general in many cases: Factor 20–Factor 30 (95–97%) 1/2 to 1/5 $ cost (p104). Specific examples: Lupin cheese Factor 9–Factor 21 (89–95%) improvement on dairy cheese production (p112), potato-derived pasta Factor 8 (87%) improvement over normal pasta (p112), by 2035 novel food protein could be produced more efficiently than pork today by a Factor 80 (99%) or Factor 60 (98) better than meat in 2035 (p143).
The water handling system (does not deal with water use efficiency measures)	Factor 20 improvement (p158) by 2040 (p159)	Some of the most important actions need to be taken on the demand side by system users in households, businesses and industry (p152). Abiotic depletion can be reduced by Factor 3 (67%) and aquatic eco-toxicity by Factor 4 (75%), fossil energy use by Factor 1.25 (15–20%), solid waste production by Factor 1.3 (25%).
Clean domestic textiles	Factor 10–20 (p 176) by 2040 (p186)	*Household by 2025:* Factor 2.5 (60%) for energy, Factor 4 (75%) for water; Factor 5 (80%) for detergent (p 194). *Neighbourhood by 2025:* Factor 2 (50%) for energy, Factor 10 (90%) for water, Factor 10 (90%) for detergent (p 195). *Centralized by 2025:* (no conclusions reported). More efficient technologies expected to be cheaper: less than half the cost possible even by 2005 (p197).
Chemical and industrial materials	By 2040 no fossil fuel use to source industrial organic chemicals/materials and Factor 20 improvement in efficiency of eco-capacity use (p215).	Many promising technology changes identified but no quantitative results reported.

Table 13.1 *continued*

	The challenge set	Achievements
Sourcing organic chemical feed stocks	To supply sufficient biomass to source organic chemicals and materials (plastics, liquid fuels, etc.), and to find effective chemical pathways from biomass to needed organics chemical materials.	The quantity of biomass that can be produced is adequate for chemicals and materials, but there is a shortfall for liquid fuel (p221). Feasible synthesis routes were available for practically all major commodity products. The quantity of phenolic compounds sourced from biomass may not be adequate (p245).
Biomass production on saline soils	To find halophytic plants that produce useful biomass as feedstock for the production of chemical products so that biomass production can be expanded by utilizing otherwise unavailable salinized land.	Several appropriate halophytic plants are available.
Motor vehicle propulsion		
Hydrogen fuel/ fuel-cell cars	To find alternative renewable energy 'carrier' fuel(s) (with high end-use conversion efficiency to offset any inefficiency of initial production (p249) that can provide the based for a significant Dutch industry to replace fossil fuel oil in the refinery sector (p248).	Hydrogen fuel (or hydrogen-rich liquid carriers, such as cyclohexane and methanol) were identified as possible alternatives (p248). A hydrogen-fuelled fuel-cell car could have an increased energy efficiency of Factor 1.75 (43%) compared to conventional internal combustion engine cars (p263). Renewable energy use with carbon removal from the fuel and carbon sequestration could enable CO_2 to be removed from the atmosphere (p265).

Note: Page numbers refer to Weaver et al (2000a).
Source: Weaver et al (2000a) summarized by Philip Sutton

upon importing soybean feedstock and exporting pork, but also upon glasshouse horticulture – is among the highest in the world despite the small land area. Another major industry is electronics.

The challenges of managing a difficult environment and of constructing a viable economy and society in the Netherlands have demanded long-term development strategies, the coordination of intrinsically interdependent but individual actors and the development of highly specialized environmental engineering knowledge. To meet these challenges, the Dutch economy, society and its institutions have developed in special ways. The Dutch society is characterized by a bottom-up, consensus model of decision-making. There is also a strong tradition of cooperative working, for example across ministries and across public and private sector agencies. The economy has developed on a 'knowledge-basis' to complement its trading, transport and value-adding roles. As well as specialized knowledge in the bulk and fine chemicals, fuels, electronics, horticulture and agri-food sectors, expertise has been developed in spatial planning, environmental management and environmental technology. Coastal engineering, water engineering, wind power and soil management are examples of specialisms with long-standing roots and traditions. Science – including the generation, dissemination, transmission, application, and embedding of knowledge and expertise (often in the form of technological hardware/software and of specialist knowledge institutions) – has played a major role in securing the strong economic situation that the Netherlands enjoys today. Expertise and technologies that embody specialized knowledge are exported and so generate income and add to the competitiveness of the Dutch economy. Today, Dutch per capita income is among the highest in the world.

Nonetheless, the Dutch economy is intrinsically vulnerable to environmental change and to natural resource scarcity. Approximately 70 per cent of Dutch GDP is derived from the use of imported eco-capacity.[15] The Dutch are acutely aware of the need to restructure their economy to make it more sustainable in a future context of natural resource scarcity and growing international competition for available resources. The Dutch are equally aware that, on a per capita basis, their consumption of natural resources is among the highest in the world and their per capita contribution to globally-relevant emissions of pollutants, especially greenhouse gases, is high. Since the Netherlands is vulnerable to rising sea levels and is unable to avert this through actions it can take directly itself, its capacity to influence other nations is important. The feeling within political circles is that the Netherlands will have to lead by example if it is to encourage other countries to reduce their greenhouse gas emissions. For analogous reasons, it will also have to demonstrate commitment to a more equitable sharing of global eco-capacity. While seemingly an onerous obligation, this is considered a no-regret approach since the understanding is that in a future world of insecure resource supply and higher material, energy and waste-disposal costs, resource productivity improvement will become increasingly important as an element in international competitiveness and economic security.

Thus, the Dutch are especially concerned about sustainability because of unsustainabilities and vulnerabilities that are inherent to their economy and society. But the Dutch are also used to environmental threats and have long-since learned to turn environmental adversity to economic advantage in fields such as water and soil engineering, becoming experts in winning land from the sea, soil drainage and remediation, and harnessing wind energy. Moreover, because collective welfare has depended historically on environmental management measures, which for success have relied on agreeing long-term strategic responses and co-ordinating decentralized actions, the stock of organizational, institutional and social capital relevant for sustainable development is stronger in the Netherlands than in most other nations. The foregoing goes some way to explaining the high importance attached to sustainable development in the Netherlands and to appreciating how Dutch understanding of the concept is translated into actions. Sustainable development was adopted as a macro-economic policy objective in the first Dutch National Environmental Policy Plan (NMP1) as early as 1989. In the Dutch context, especially, resource productivity improvement is the most viable strategy for sustainable development.

Recent developments

The full impacts of the STD programme will only emerge in the very long term (20+ years) and the programme's influence on these will inevitably be difficult to separate from other influences. Any commentary on the effectiveness of the STD programme at this time must, therefore, be based largely upon interim results and early indicators of the influence of the programme that can be directly inferred. This reservation notwithstanding, there is sufficient evidence to show that the STD programme was successful in making an identifiable, positive contribution to sustainable development. The STD programme successfully opened new approaches for operationalizing long-term, sustainability-oriented innovation activities. A methodology was developed through 'learning by doing' processes to meet future needs for nutrition, shelter, mobility, water and materials. In addition, nine of 15 innovation trajectories begun by the programme are still continuing today. In regard to improving the context for the diffusion of sustainable technologies, large numbers of actors and stakeholders were exposed to the programme and (with varying intensities of engagement) became aware of the potential role of innovation in sustainable development and the factors upon which a significant role for technology is likely to be contingent.

Possible new 'production–consumption systems' – were described in respect to all five thematic priorities. As well as technological solutions and supply-side approaches, the programme explored new organizational and business arrangements as well as some demand-side (sufficiency oriented) solutions to the extent that these had a technological component. Albeit that most projects were linked to Dutch economic and social priorities, the case studies have wider significance because they addressed basic needs relevant for people everywhere. The programme effectively demonstrated that, in some key areas of need, substantial eco-efficiency improvements can be realized. But results also warn of the difference between technology-specific eco-efficiency improvement and the capacity to deliver real improvement at the level of production–consumption systems, which depends also on rates at which new solutions replace existing ones. Importantly, the programme demonstrated synergy among new technologies and co-dependence among technological and non-technological components of the systems-level solutions it described, clarifying that technological innovation is contingent on social and institutional innovation and specifying what kinds of innovations would be needed on different fronts in order to deliver new production–consumption systems.

There is sufficient evidence to speak of a major influence of the STD programme on increasing the public understanding about sustainability and its implications as well as on the strategies, policies and practices in government, business and science. The success of the STD programme in transforming understanding can be seen in the shifting attitude in the Netherlands towards technology and its role in sustainable development. The programme contributed to a deeper and wider awareness within society of the challenge posed by sustainable development and to a more mature appreciation about the role of technology and innovation, including that technology alone cannot deliver sustainability. The programme provided business and government with approaches to make 'sustainability' operational. Moreover the programme has certainly influenced the policy context. The two currently active National Environmental Policy Plans – NMP3 and NMP4 – were both influenced by the programme and the fact that they are run in parallel reflects a new appreciation of innovation as a multi-track process. NMP3 stresses short- and medium-term policies while NMP4 addresses longer-term issues concerned with the sustainability transition and has a time horizon to 2030. The roots of the transition approach taken in NMP4 can be traced directly to the STD programme.

Both the methods pioneered in the STD programme and the innovation lines it initiated are being developed in ongoing research programmes in the Netherlands, such as the Economy, Ecology, Technology (EET) programme.[16] In addition, an important impulse has been created by the decision of the Dutch Government to hypothecate part of the natural gas revenues to fund work to strengthen the economic structure of the Netherlands, including the knowledge infrastructure. The purpose is to anticipate the ultimate depletion of the natural gas reserves and adapt the Dutch economy and society for that eventuality. Most of the funds are dedicated to physical infrastructure projects, but around 5 per cent of the total available sum has been earmarked to strengthen the Dutch knowledge infrastructure as part of the overall restructuring programme. An inter-ministerial working group (ICES-KIS) provides advice on the use of the funds. Every new cabinet decides on the size of the fund. In practice this means four-year rounds.

Two ICES-KIS funding rounds have already been completed (1994–1998 and 1998–2002). These have established research centres, programmes and projects some of which are devoted to sustainable development. A third funding round is just about to start. In the 1994 round (ICES-KIS I) there was an unstructured call for proposals. By contrast, the 1998 round (ICES-KIS II) was preceded by an investigation of strengths and weaknesses in the Dutch knowledge infrastructure. This resulted in the identification of six priority themes. Transition management, innovation and sustainable development were well represented, leading to programmes such as NIDO, HABIFORUM and CONNEKT.[17] These programmes, which continue work on the lines of the STD programme, are described and evaluated elsewhere.[18] A similar investigation preceded the latest funding round, which is distributing €800 million. Systems renewal and sustainability constitute two of the five themes being promoted through ICES-KIS III. Funds have been allocated, among others, for projects concerned with the development of the off-shore wind potential, the capture and storage of carbon-dioxide, the development of biomass as a feedstock, the long-term transition of agriculture and multifunctional land use.

The STD programme has also had an influence beyond the boundaries of the Netherlands. Within Europe, countries tend to look over each others' shoulders to see what is happening elsewhere. The cooperative research programmes of the European Commission also facilitate comparative analysis and the identification and transfer of good practice. It is certain that the Dutch STD programme influenced innovation efforts in other countries. The German parliament, for example, kept a watching brief on the STD programme, so learned from it and built lessons into the design of subsequent German programmes. This said, it is difficult, if not impossible to separate out or to quantify the STD-influence vis-à-vis other influences on other national programmes within Europe.

More useful is to look at each programme as representing some new ideas and some borrowed ideas. Our interest, after all, is continuously to find more effective ways to innovate for sustainability and to find ways that meet innovation needs in specific innovation contexts at specific times. Thus, each programme should therefore be considered and evaluated on its own merits, at the same time as looking both for similarities and differences among and between programmes. By default, each national programme represents a hypothesis (or set of hypotheses) on the part of its designers and managers about how sustainability-oriented innovation should be performed in that particular national context and its execution represents a test of those hypotheses. At issue, then, is to evaluate each research programme using a consistent evaluation method, so that its overall effectiveness and the effectiveness of any innovative approaches used in respect to its structure, procedures, content, goals or method can be assessed as a basis for identifying good practices and their transferability.

Lessons from the Dutch and other programmes

In order to learn from experience with innovative sustainability-oriented programmes, the AIRP-SD project (referred to earlier in this chapter) has made consistent evaluations of a set of recently-completed or on-going sustainability-oriented programmes. These include, among others, the Socio-Ecological Programme (Germany), the Programme on Technologies for Sustainable Development (Austria), the Ecocycle Programme (Sweden), the Zero Emission Research Initiative (Japan) and the STD programme (the Netherlands). The project objective was to find how best to design and administer innovation programmes in support of sustainable development. An answer to this question clearly depends upon using a consistent evaluation methodology based upon external reference standards for judging programme completeness and quality. But, whereas evaluators usually have an established reference standard to structure their evaluations, in regard to innovation efforts in support of sustainable development there is no established reference model for how science efforts should be designed and no firm basis of experience over which research designs have worked well in the past or have worked better than others. Indeed, to find answers to these questions was the purpose of the AIRP-SD research. Thus, an ancillary objective of the AIRP-SD project was to design an appropriate method for evaluating research programmes.

The lack of an established body of theory and practice at the start of the AIRP-SD project suggested the need to develop both through an iterative, heuristic procedure, beginning with tentative hypotheses about the nature of the research processes that might support sustainable development and then testing, refining and validating the hypotheses through the evaluation process itself. The first set of working hypotheses was based upon what can be deduced about innovation for sustainability from the concept of sustainable development itself or from the nature of the socio-ecological system of interest or from experience in handling analogous complex problems.

The AIRP-SD project identified three connected objects for evaluation: (i) the outcomes of research programmes; (ii) the quality of research design, process and management; (iii) and the innovation context. In addition, using the normative–deductive approach described above, the project specified a set of goal-oriented and process-oriented sustainability principles. These include: the maintenance of ecosystem function and diversity; intergenerational equity; intragenerational equity; broad participation; promoting actions to face vulnerability and build resilience; precautionary action; knowledge sharing and mutual learning; transparency and justification of decision-making; global and systemic approaches (which include spill-over impacts); and, the use of appropriate issue–scale boundaries (space–time boundaries) in problem analysis. Again, using a normative–deductive approach and reflecting upon the challenges that sustainable development poses for innovation, the project set out a broad set of generic outcomes that innovation for sustainability could target including: visions and indicators of desirable socio-economic futures; new solutions to development problems consistent with such visions (e.g. new production–consumption systems or elements thereof); models and information in support of transition processes; new supporting scientific capital and capacities; and new supporting social capital and capacities.

The approach of AIRP-SD was that research programmes could be evaluated on the basis of the strength of their contribution to these outcomes, that the quality of the research design and process could be evaluated on its degree of conformity with sustainability principles, and that the context for innovation could be evaluated on the basis of the status of the national innovation system in relation to how well this facilitates meeting the sustainability challenges faced. As working hypotheses, the project was developed from the propositions that: contextual conditions influence both innovation efforts (level, design quality, orientation, etc.) and innovation outcomes; research design and management quality influences the nature and quality of innovation outcomes; and contextual conditions, research design and process characteristics and programme outcomes are interconnected dynamically through a feedback loop. To test these hypotheses, evidence was collected for each of the nine programmes to enable judgements to be made about programme contexts, designs and outcomes. Judgements were made about the strength (strong, weak, neutral) and direction (positive, negative) in relation to how well contextual conditions facilitate innovation for sustainable development, in relation to how well programme management and design conform with sustainability principles, and to how well programme outcomes contribute to sustainability goals. Each of several features of programme contexts, research designs and outcomes were first evaluated separately and then the links between the evaluation objects were analysed. In this second step, it was possible to evaluate the influence of each feature of a programme design on programme outcomes, the influence of each feature of a programme design on all other design features (to explore synergies), the influence of context on programme design (to explore context dependency and transferability of innovative design features) and to evaluate any programme-induced changes in context.

Clearly, good practice may be context specific in some instances, but may also be in the form of generalizable lessons. There was certainly a good deal of conformity across programmes about the importance of adopting liberating financial and administrative models, reconceptualizing the innovation challenge, setting ambitious targets, adopting a systems approach, adopting a co-evolutionary approach, practising transdisciplinarity, using iterative and participatory procedures, using multipurpose and multifunctional tools/methods, etc. It also seems to help to have either an influential, respected and charismatic person to make the initial breakthrough by taking the fight to the funding agencies or a creative administrator in a funding agency who is willing to risk some percentage of a research budget on long-term efforts aimed at scientific renewal. Findings from the AIRP-SD project support the hypothesis that research programmes that are designed, administered and implemented in conformity with sustainability principles and goals and which practise the principles of sustainability deliver outcomes that support sustainable development. Furthermore, there are clear synergies among design features of successful programmes. By way of example, broad participation and transdisciplinary working is an important design feature for sustainability-oriented innovation. So is an iterative research procedure. But the presence of both in the research design is what provides an opportunity for mutual learning and enables assumptions and positions to be revisited in the course of a programme, paving the way for a dynamic adjustment in the research process, which is needed to build compromises and to handle risks and uncertainties. Just as sustainable development represents a coherent, integrated, systems approach to finding solutions to development problems, innovation in support of sustainable development needs to adopt a compatible systems approach. This requires that the approaches taken to research management and design integrate sustainability principles and objectives into each and every aspect of process.

Recommendations for sustainability-oriented research programme design and conduct are summarized in Table 13.2[19] and in the following paragraphs. These cover appropriate financial models, organizational models and research models for sustainability-oriented RTD programmes together with suggestions for managing cross-cutting aspects of programmes, including knowledge management, communication and dissemination, and the handling of risk and uncertainty. Detailed results and examples of good practice are reported elsewhere.[20]

Financial model Given the multiplicity of objectives that sustainable solutions are asked to meet and the trade-offs between these that are implied, a diversity of funding sources (co-funding arrangements) together with flexible funding mechanisms that are oriented to problem-solving (phased funding arrangements with in-built decision moments) are best suited to provide for the independence and integrity of researchers and research results. Such financial models also enable innovative 'checks and brakes' mechanisms to be incorporated. Because learning and sharing knowledge are key components of the sustainable development process, funding should cover the creation of knowledge partnerships, training activities and quality assurance procedures. Dedicated funding is specifically required for promoting internal cross-learning among programme projects or components and for promoting external knowledge sharing with stakeholders and the general public. Owing to the long-term nature and inherent uncertainty and complexity of sustainability-oriented research, a balance is required in financial management between traditional approaches and openness. Schemes and criteria for programme evaluation are needed that allow for uncertainty and risk.

Organizational model Considering the high degree of complexity and uncertainty surrounding the objects and modes of sustainability-oriented research, flexible management and decision-making patterns (adaptive management) embedding change as a structural factor and oriented towards participatory problem-solving are needed. Openness, transparency and accountability of management are important guiding principles for the good governance of programmes. Continuous quality assurance procedures by processes that engage an extended research community and mechanisms for extended consultation/participation with stakeholders across societal sectors are needed. Because socially robust (shared) decisions are highly desirable, there is a need to re-define success factors for management away from simply financial factors so that these include the guiding principles just listed: participation, openness and transparency. Managers' profiles and selection criteria might be modified accordingly and enhanced via on-going learning. Equally, because sustainability research transcends natural and social sciences, management and research teams should engage multi-disciplinary capacities to enable new forms of problem conceptualization and new pathways for solving problems to emerge.

Research model Quality checks are needed at the exploratory and initiation phases of research programme set-up to ensure all required aspects and stakeholders are duly considered and to ensure internal consistency. There is a need to ensure complementarity and coherence among components of research design and process. The programme design should preferably be inter- and trans-disciplinary, long-term oriented, implementation oriented, vision led and system based including global concerns. Broad participation mechanisms from exploration and initiation phases are needed with repeated moments of participation throughout the research programme in order to build a basis of shared knowledge and supporting 'language' to allow an interchange of knowledge and information as well as to promote discussion and bargaining of values. The selection of activities for funding should be open to scrutiny via transparent criteria. Accountable evaluation methods are required based on transparency and upon input from representatives of multiple interests. Multifunctional approaches and tools should be used in the research to develop and to evaluate developmental options and these should be justified in terms of legitimacy, fitness for purpose, reliability, etc. Quality assurance procedures are needed at each outcome level.

Knowledge management, communication and dissemination Science for sustainable development implies a paradigm shift in research, development and innovation. The main issues for knowledge management relate to sustainability awareness raising, knowledge sharing, mutual learning and quality assurance to assure legitimacy of both research and practice. Essentially, these call for a new model of science for policy based on a co-production of knowledge. In turn, this calls for a democratization of the research process, which requires extended participation across societal sectors and accountability of different perspectives. This requires mediation structures, spaces and processes to be created within RTD programmes to enable different types of knowledge to be exchanged and mediated into useful input for sustainability research, especially in relation to problem-framing, the creation of shared visions and the evaluation of research processes and products. Inter- and trans-disciplinary research implies a 'mixed' community of researchers and research users, so knowledge has to be prepared for many different audiences if sharing is to be successful. Time must be invested in developing and clarifying meanings and a common language. Equally, when dealing with external audiences, training and dissemination efforts should be tailored for specific target groups. The range of such groups necessarily extends in sustainability-oriented research well beyond the usual scientific peer groups of normal science. In essence, sustainability research can be considered as a platform for multiple languages, perspectives and scales; this needs to be operationalized through methods that create contexts of dialogue among diversity and plurality. Quality checks by peer reviewers and by users (extended peer reviews) are needed at all stages in the research in order to attain socially robust research processes and products.

Uncertainty and risk The management of uncertainty and risk must be considered explicitly in the research design, not only because sustainability problematiques are inherently prone to uncertainties, but also because programme outcomes may be further sources of uncertainty and risk when RTD programmes are highly innovative and are concerned with innovation in situations characterized by vulnerability. Management of risk and uncertainty in such cases depends upon establishing assessment activities and on creating resilience conditions for adaptation, such as strategies for coping with unintended effects. Risk and uncertainty management activities therefore need to be transversally integrated into programmes in a recursive and reflexive way. Equally, special efforts are needed to communicate uncertainty and risk. Essentially, uncertainty, lack of knowledge and potential risk are drivers for more inclusive and accountable governance agendas. Hence the communication of uncertainty and risk – as ever, tailored to the needs of specific target audiences – is an essential step in attaining shared decisions and policies.

Concluding remarks

Thus, in designing research programmes that are intended to support sustainable development, there is a special need to consider programme structure and process alongside programme content since these are important features of design that have been found to impinge strongly on the success of programmes, especially in the extent to which they enable a research programme to practise the principles of sustainable development and, through this, to build new capacities, competencies, processes and structures that are intrinsic to sustainable development.

Just as important for our national innovations systems is that results from the AIRP-SD project support the possibility of establishing a positive feedback loop through which successful sustainability-oriented research programmes might leverage the effectiveness and sustainability impact potential of future efforts in support of sustainable development, including future sustainability-oriented programmes, by inducing changes in innovation contexts, in innovation policy and in innovation capabilities and capacities. The way to strengthen our national innovation systems, so that these target and support sustainable development, is therefore to thoroughly integrate the principles of sustainable development throughout a set of pioneering RTD programmes. By practising sustainability principles in innovation processes, we change both the processes of innovation and, over time, the structures that characterize and define our national systems of innovation and their applications contexts, making these increasingly more open to and supportive of development that will be more sustainable. In sum, the applicable adage here is that, as in many other areas, 'practice makes perfect'.

Table 13.2 RTD *programmes for sustainable development: from start to finish*

Many reference manuals and guidelines on RTD programme design and management exist already, describing principles and methods which are often applicable also to sustainability-oriented RTD programmes. For this reason, we concentrate here on those special recommendations for RTD programme management and design that are specific to – or especially important for – sustainability-oriented RTD. Clearly, since contexts vary markedly between countries, flexibility is needed in setting up sustainability-oriented RTD programmes. In effect, there are few hard-and-fast rules that can be articulated for the design and management of sustainability-oriented programmes, but rather a framework of broad principles which needs to be interpreted flexibly according to the application context. This table focuses on issues that will need to be resolved in the course of programme set-up and gives some practical hints, especially about potential pitfalls in programme set-up and ways of avoiding these.

Phase or element	Practices	Pitfalls
Contextual conditions	Context influences: • The possibility to set up sustainability-oriented RTD activities. • The design characteristics of the RTD activities. There needs to be a sense of urgency in science, policy and society for the sustainability challenge to be taken up through RTD.	There is seldom consensus within science, politics and society on the urgency of the SD challenge. Framing the issue solely in terms of SD is unlikely to be helpful in gaining broad support for tackling SD problems. More useful is to transform the SD problem into a challenge that has a broad base of potential support; i.e. one that appeals to many parties to work on and that may even be perceived by 'SD-non-believers' as holding potential benefits.
Initiation	Given the urgency of many SD problems, there may be a wide range of potential research initiators from among the set of affected parties and stakeholders. To be effective, initiators should be in a position (or hold a role) that gives them access to the major actors implicated in the problem and its potential solution. Initiators will be inspired and/or supported by different actors, including NGOs, industry, academics, civil service, etc.	Timing is critical. A good proposal at the wrong moment may lose the opportunity for years to come. Therefore, the ground needs to be prepared by the initiator and supporting parties before launching the proposal to ensure a receptive context.
Exploration	The initiator(s) prepare a rough sketch of the programme, its basic principles and its goals in relation to the problem it seeks to address. This is the first opportunity to embed sustainability principles into the programme design and objectives. On the basis of this rough sketch, individuals and organizations potentially important for the problem solution need to be identified and invited to explore the	Not spending enough time or care during the exploration phase risks problems later, including loss of time in later phases of a programme. This is a real and big risk, which has beset many programmes. Exploration is not an open bottom-up exercise. The initiator should have a clear vision on the challenge and be able to explain and defend it, but the vision should not be so detailed that

Table 13.2 *continued*

Phase or element	Practices	Pitfalls
	outline programme to see whether the challenge is recognized, whether there is sufficient support for the programme, whether and how changes might be made to the programme that would broaden the appeal, to allocate roles in the programme, and to determine which networks are essential for the ultimate success of the programme, i.e. which parties may in the end be interested to implement the results, so that they might be involved from the beginning. During this process of exploration the circle of involved parties may be widened on the basis of suggestions and support from the parties already engaged. The exploration results in a programme draft.	it is closed to modification, to filling in or to re-interpretation from the position of the stakeholders party to its discussion. In a final plenary meeting with the various parties involved in the exploration phase, the parties will need to recognize themselves and their contributions in the draft programme and its vision.
Process monitoring	Usually sustainability-oriented RTD programmes are not stand-alone programmes but rather are part of a learning process towards a transformation of society. To make the experiences and 'lessons' of one programme or project available for new programmes and projects (and for educational purposes more generally) monitoring and reporting processes need to be established already from the very beginning. This covers, also, the need for comprehensive descriptive materials about programmes and projects, including relevant policy documents, descriptions of management structures and principles, decision-making processes, involved parties, financing and organizational aspects, etc.	For many national programmes, monitoring is a condition for approval; however, monitoring is often perceived as a burden, which should be reduced to the bare minimum. Adopting such an attitude risks losing many chances to learn even in the programme itself. It is strongly recommended therefore to set up a monitoring plan with elements to be monitored and with a clear responsibility for its implementation and maintenance right from the beginning.
(Provisionary) principles and mission	The programme draft should contain the objectives of the programme, its mission and its provisionary principles. These should be in line with SD principles and reflect aspects such as how risk, transparency, participation and communication will be handled.	Constituting a programme draft is not an administrative operation. It is an essential element in the processes through which both creativity and support are to be gained. The operation should be iterative. In iterative processes, creativity may be developed in small groups or by individuals, but the results have to be checked and amended in larger supporting groups of potential partners and stakeholders.

Preparation	From the initial exploration phase, the programme draft has to be research transformed into a full proposal that fulfils the requirements of investors and others who will play decisive roles in the execution of the programme. The programme draft must also win their trust. The efforts to be delivered and the process of research to be undertaken should be clearly described. The proposal should be ready for start-up including the availability of main staff and the commitment of relevant institutions and organizations.	There is a tension between the inherent flexibility needed in SD-oriented research and the unpredictability as regards programme outcomes on the one hand and the need for certainty of RTD investors about the work to be undertaken and the products to be delivered on the other. A compromise can be achieved by building GO/NO-GO decision moments into the funding arrangement with judgements about programme continuation based upon the monitoring of interim results, especially interim process-related outcomes.
Profiles of people	The nature of sustainability-oriented research and RTD programmes justifies additional requirements on the part of the engaged scientists and staff that go beyond the normal requirements on employees merely fulfilling their routine functions. In particular every researcher, research manager or member of a steering body should have a sense of the meaning of sustainable development and its implications for the conduct of the research (e.g. transdisciplinary attitudes and skills, participatory research processes, etc.). A 'champion' who leads by example is needed. Members of steering bodies should preferably act on the basis of their authority in the field rather than as representatives of interested parties (i.e. genuinely be willing to provide independent judgement and advice). In the spirit of working towards alternative futures, those who will live in those futures and have a vested interest in them, should be engaged in the work. Young scientists should be encouraged to be active in sustainability-oriented RTD programmes.	It would not be the first time that for understandable reasons (lobbies, time pressure, lack of availability), risks are taken in the appointment of the personnel who will perform crucial functions in the research. Time spent searching for appropriate personnel will be well spent.
Organizing support and commitment	Organizing support for and commitment to a programme among partners (actors and stakeholders) is essential for the conduct and success of a programme and is a central objective of its communication activities. Mutuality and interaction are in turn characteristics of the communication in support of commitment-building. Effective communication depends on integrating basic SD principles into	Creating false or inaccurate expectations about results is to be avoided since even if this helps win early support for and commitment to a programme from partners, disillusionment in later phases is counterproductive and can lead to a potentially damaging loss of trust and credibility in the programme. Co-funding by industry offers multiple potential benefits beyond the

Table 13.2 *continued*

Phase or element	Practices	Pitfalls
	the communications strategy (which will enhance almost all aspects of the programme) and on developing an awareness of the needs, sensitivities and interests of specific partners with whom communication and dialogue needs to take place. In the very first phases of establishing a programme, an inventory should be made of organizations and individuals likely to play a role in the success of the programme and the take-up of its results. This inventory seeks to establish the interests and positions of organizations and individuals (their currency) in their playing field (their arena). An inventory may serve to help make potential benefits of the programme explicit to potential partners or to add value to the work of the programme and its outcomes from the perspectives of partners and so help enlist their involvement and support. It may deliver a basis for negotiations on funding or on the active participation of potential partners. Continuous updating of this inventory is advantageous during the whole life of the programme.	research investment itself; it may strengthen industry commitment, increase the chances that results will be implemented in practice and provide opportunities to reach out to other partners through industry networks. The other side of the coin is the risk of focusing too strongly on the interests of the co-funder and thereby of under-representing the interests of other stakeholders. This puts adherence to SD principles at risk.
Communication model	Communication is a continuous activity from the beginning to the end of a programme with a fluent change over from internal communication to external communication and vice versa. Provisions have to be made to disseminate the knowledge gained in the programme adequately and to assure its effective use.	Communication is frequently considered as a side issue to which not too much time and money should be spent. In sustainability-oriented programmes, the contrary is the case; communication is an essential responsibility and one of the most important. The whole palette of communication means, from bilateral to public, internal and external, has to be used. Communication principles have to be established from the start, corresponding to SD principles on participation and transparency. Within this frame, however, different forms and attitudes are possible and are necessary in order for communication efforts to be tailored to the needs of specific stakeholders.

Organization model	Continuity, credibility and trust are requirements for any organization. In SD-oriented research, which requires flexibility, confronts uncertainty, and must work with stakeholders having a range of often-conflicting interests, credibility and trust are even more important. A constitutional document establishing the programme and describing the roles, tasks, rights and responsibilities of the various parties may be the basis of commitments to it by various organizations, institutions and individuals. The programme constitution is likely to include a programme steering group to which the programme management is responsible and a broadly-based expert consulting or sounding board whose members have authority in their own personal capacity. A specific organizational problemhas to be solved when the programme is carried by a bureaucratic organization, such as a ministry or large scientific institute. A positive characteristic of such organizations is that they create and maintain certainties (for public, politics, clients), which tends to make them trustworthy. However, sustainability-oriented research is intrinsically engaged in a search for systems-level and paradigmatic change that takes us beyond the realm of past experience. By definition, it implies uncertainty. To be involved in such research implies a risk of loss-of-trust for the organizations concerned.	Insufficient distance (figuratively and literally) of the programme to its commissioner may lead to continuous tensions within the programme and attempts to interfere in it by the commissioners (e.g. for economic or political reasons). This intrinsic tension requires some distance to be created between the programme and its commissioner.
Financing	Especially when public money is at stake, an optimum has to be found between the need for independence of the research and the need to give account for expenses. This means that the research efforts, the administration, the research process (principles, domain of research), a rough time schedule, a beginning and an end in time, all have to be established and assigned. In this balance, trust in the programme leader and in the programme management capacities plays a key role. The best way to ascertain real interest in the programme and the commitment to it of private parties is through their participation, be it in cash or in kind. Substantial financial contributions should not be expected: within prevailing socio-economic structures, private	To reduce the risk of non application of research results, the participation of stakeholders (more specifically those with the potential to play a decisive implementation role) is essential. However this holds the danger of biasing research towards the production of potential private benefits. Societal aspects like inter- and intra-generational equity tend to be under-developed. The use of a 'factor concept', such as an ambitious eco-efficiency target grounded in the wish to meet the (basic) needs of whole future generations may be one of the countervailing means.

Table 13.2 *continued*

Phase or element	Practices	Pitfalls
	investment in long-term research with high risks and great uncertainties (and with the objective to change production systems) is unlikely. Strategic considerations relating to the future survival and role of a company in new markets constitutes the most likely argument or driver for private parties to participate in sustainability-oriented programmes.	
Programme management	SD principles should be applied not only in the research execution but also in the research management. This is an extra requirement over and above the usual norms of sound programme management. In view of the characteristics of SD research (complexity, uncertainty, many stakeholders, high stakes, contested facts, etc.), programme management has to pay specific attention to striking pragmatic balances within an overall systems approach (e.g. balancing tensions over the means, capacities and timings of contributions by various parties, bridging tensions between the development of creativity and of broad support, shaping forms for participation and transparency, etc.). A repeated, iterative approach is needed throughout the research process from problem definition and goal setting to implementation, through which outcomes at each stage might be shaped in a creative setting and checked and amended in a supportive setting with relevant stakeholders (social process). Synergies between projects within the programme should be sought to strengthen opportunities for new perspectives on solutions to emerge and to help inter- and trans-disciplinary working.	Sticking to existing paradigms and/or focusing on disciplinary contributions may block creativity in finding breakthroughs. Nonetheless, there is a need early on to establish clear definitions, understandings and ground-rules for the research process among participants in order to avoid problems in later phases.

Source: Adapted from Jansen et al (2003)

CHAPTER 14

SUSTAINABILITY IN THE WILD WEST (STATE GOVERNMENT)

Peter Newman

EDITORS' NOTE: This chapter was written by Professor Peter Newman based on his experience having recently developed a comprehensive government sustainability strategy, covering 42 areas of the Government of Western Australia. Professor Newman is Professor of City Policy and Director of the Institute for Sustainability and Technology Policy (ISTP) at Murdoch University. The ISTP is now the largest such body in Australia, with 70 PhD students, 150 undergraduates, and 100 Masters students, all studying for degrees in sustainable development. Peter also has recently become Sustainability Commissioner for the state of New South Wales, Australia.

Sub-national government is critical to achieving sustainable development, not only as an important mechanism for managing local clusters to help drive eco-innovation this century. Whilst the achievements of Local Agenda 21 are well known, and the network of National Councils for Sustainable Development (NCSDs) has over 70 national members globally, the achievements globally of state governments have been much less well reported. Yet for countries like China, the US and India, with such large populations, or countries like Australia that cover such large areas of the planet, state/regional governments are a key level of government that will play a major role in whether or not we make the shift to a sustainable future. And given that the directions taken by China, the US and India will be critical to whether we make overall progress globally towards sustainable genuine progress, the critical role of regional/state governments in those countries, and hence around the world, cannot be overstated. In addition, state governments, responsible often for managing energy and water utilities, cities and surrounding regions, are therefore critical to operationalizing Sustainable Genuine Progress this century. The lack of recognition of the importance of regional/state government level to sustainable development, the lack of an international Agenda 21 regional government network, goes a long way to explaining the lack of progress since the Earth Summit in Rio de Janeiro in 1992.

The Fremantle Declaration: 'Passing the Torch to the Regions'

In order to progress this, a group of regional and state governments agreed to form an International Network of Regional Governments for Sustainable Development (nrg4SD) at the World Summit on Sustainable Development (WSSD) in Johannesburg in 2002. Those involved are making a serious attempt globally to build the network, holding conferences every six months, around the world, to build their membership and to build the momentum. With the failure of the nations attending the WSSD to agree on any real plan to operationalize Agenda 21, this relatively new state/regional government global network has taken on new importance. As Hunter Lovins stated at the Fremantle event: 'The torch has been passed to the regions.'[1] The Fremantle conference produced an academic declaration summarizing these emerging themes and issues for state/regional governments globally.

Fremantle Declaration
'Passing the Torch to the Regions'

Academic Network of Regional Governments for Sustainable Development
Western Australia, September 2003

Sustainability is the key imperative for the world.

Evidence such as ecological footprint analysis confirms that current practices cannot long endure. Conference delegates from states and regions around the world expressed great concern that current patterns of development, consumption and production are unsustainable and that there is an urgent need for action.

Conference presentations demonstrated that enormous opportunities exist to change the way in which human kind lives and relates to the earth. More sustainable practices were shown not only to be cost-effective but also to convey decisive competitive advantage and to enhance quality of life.

The transition to a sustainable future will require every community to shape its own vision for a preferred future, supported by blueprints and action agendas backed by a genuine commitment to implementation. The conference presented abundant inspirational examples of governments, industries and communities who are implementing more sustainable approaches. What is now needed is the political will to apply these lessons in every community and company.

It is clear that an integrated 'whole of government' approach must guide this process. But the conference consensus was that the regions are the most effective level of government at which the transition towards sustainability can be implemented. States manage land and cities, and are closer to the communities and industries that have the ability to implement real change. Growing networks at national, international and local levels can help, but regional government cannot escape taking responsibility for leading the transition to sustainability. Through the development of operational linkages between the regions around the world, active partnerships and technology transfer, the regions can promote best practices and ensure efficient action. Capacity building and community awareness are the next imperatives for action.

The torch has passed to the regions.

Sustainability encapsulates a different approach to government that is still being worked out around the world. Because it is a global discourse, it is possible to do something quite innovative on a world scale in, for example, WA. Because of the opportunity provided by a government with a commitment to sustainability, this opportunity has been taken up. A comprehensive assessment of 42 areas of government has been conducted and, after a two year process, the State Sustainability Strategy has been completed. Hence the WA story thus far forms a key part of this section, outlining its framework, key action items and process, how it has been accepted and what is being done to implement it. We ask the fundamental question: is there any real change occurring towards sustainability in WA? Using Patsy Healy's three levels of policy change – language, thinking and culture – we suggest that substantial moves along the first two levels have occurred but not the third.

The Western Australia State Sustainability Strategy: is change happening?

The Government of Western Australia manages an area of land the size of Western Europe, but with a population of only 1.8 million. The state has extensive mineral, gas and agricultural resources and is the only developed country area to have one of the top 25 'biodiversity hotspots'. This chapter outlines the strategy, its framework, key action items and process, to ask the question: 'Is change happening?' This is of particular interest as few state or sub-national governments have yet completed such a sustainability strategy, with nations and local governments being more than a decade ahead on such matters.[2]

In February 2001 the Gallop government was elected in WA with a mandate to stop the logging of old growth forests (WA is the only place in the world to do this with substantial ancient forests remaining), and a commitment to develop a comprehensive State Sustainability Strategy.

> *The Government has put sustainability at the very heart of what it does because we recognize that it is a way of making our State a better place to live – it provides a way of integrating environmental protection, social advancement and economic prosperity.*
> Hon Dr Geoff Gallop MLA, Premier of Western Australia[3]

The definition of sustainability adopted in the WA State Strategy is: '*Sustainability is meeting the needs of present and future generations through an integration of environmental protection, social advancement and economic prosperity.*'

The important words here are: 'future' – as governments generally don't tend to make decisions for our children and grandchildren – and 'integration' – as governments generally don't bring environmental and social factors into the mainstream of economic development, but instead treat each of the three areas as distinct 'silos' of thinking, institutions and decision-making. The overlapping circles in Figure 14.1 set out the new integrating disciplines of ecological economics, 'sense of place' or place management, and community health. The integration of all three areas is the new challenge required before real change can be anticipated towards sustainability.[4] This challenge was put before the WA public and government over a two year process from mid 2001.

The Strategy fills out what is meant by sustainability by developing a set of 11 principles of sustainability, 6 vision statements for WA, and 42 areas of government activity that require focused attention to see what sustainability means for them. The 11 principles are set out in Table 14.1.

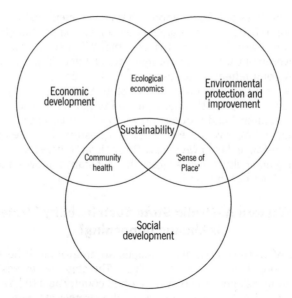

Source: Professor Peter Newman, Murdoch University, Perth

Figure 14.1 *Integrating disciplines of ecological economics*

The conceptual basis of the Strategy also suggests that as well as long-term perspectives and the simultaneous integration of different disciplines, sustainability requires two other dimensions: (i) the integration of different sectors of action;[5] and (ii) the integration of global and local thinking and action.[6] These are set out in Figures 14.2 and 14.3. Each circle has its own legitimacy and value, but when the partnerships between these are located, then real and permanent change can be achieved. The global dimension is especially important as it raises the sights of communities to consider their issues in a global context a matter of importance to communities that are geographically removed from major population centres in the world.[7]

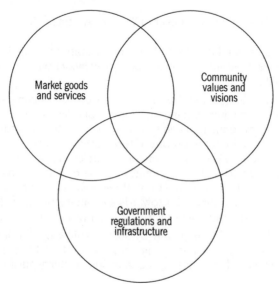

Figure 14.2 *Sectoral dimensions*

Table 14.1 *Principles for sustainability*

FOUNDATION PRINCIPLES

Long-term economic gain: Sustainability recognizes the long-term needs of future generations (as well as the short-term) for economic health, diversity, innovation and productivity of the earth.

Access, equity and human rights: Sustainability recognizes that everyone should have their interests recognized and share in the fruits of development, that an environment needs to be created where all people can express their full potential and lead productive lives, and that dangerous gaps in sufficiency, safety and opportunity endanger the earth.

Biodiversity and ecological integrity: Sustainability recognizes that all life has intrinsic value, is interconnected and that biodiversity and ecological integrity are part of the irreplaceable life support systems upon which the earth depends.

Settlement efficiency and quality of life: Sustainability recognizes that settlements need to reduce their ecological footprint (i.e. less material and energy demands and reductions in waste), whilst they simultaneously improve their quality of life (health, housing, employment, community...).

Community, regions, 'sense of place' and heritage: Sustainability recognizes the reality and diversity of community and regions for the management of the earth, and the critical importance of 'sense of place' and heritage (buildings, townscapes, landscapes and culture) in any plans for the future.

Net benefit from development: Sustainability means that all development – particularly development involving extraction of non-renewable resources – should strive to provide net environmental, social and economic benefit for future generations.

Common good: Sustainability recognizes that planning for the common good requires acceptance of limits to consumption of public resources (air, water, open space) so that a shared resource is available to all.

PROCESS PRINCIPLES

Integration: Sustainability requires that economic, social and environmental factors be integrated by applying all the principles of sustainability at once, and seeking mutually supportive benefits with minimal trade-offs.

Accountability, transparency and engagement: Sustainability recognizes that people should have access to information on sustainability issues, that institutions should have triple bottom line accountability on an annual basis, that regular sustainability audits of programmes and policies should be conducted, and that public engagement lies at the heart of all sustainability principles.

Precaution: Sustainability requires caution, avoiding poorly understood risks of serious or irreversible damage to environmental, social and economic capital, designing for surprise and managing for adaptation.

Hope, vision, symbolic and iterative change: Sustainability recognizes that applying these sustainability principles as part of a broad strategic vision for the Earth can generate hope in the future, and thus it will involve symbolic change that is part of many successive steps over generations.

Source: Government of Western Australia (2003)

The geographical scale is also important because, in many ways, sustainability has been addressed at the global, national and local levels for 10–20 years – but not at the regional or state level.[8] This level is where the land is managed, cities are managed, transport, energy, water and industrial systems are managed. It is necessary to apply sustainability at this scale and hence the WA Strategy has significance as it is one of the first to do this.

Figure 14.3 *Geographical dimensions*

Process for developing the strategy

The Sustainability Policy Unit was established in June 2001 and the first steps towards sustainability were to try and think about what it meant through public discourse. Work on the Strategy was begun by developing a series of 18 public seminars and developing a set of case studies and background papers using students and academics. This unique partnership between universities and the State Government was symbolic of the value that can be gained when a common cause can be identified. The resulting material has been placed on the Sustainability unit website and has created considerable interest as well as a strong base upon which to develop policy. The case studies are able to show what is already happening in WA on sustainability and the background papers summarize what has been achieved in other parts of the world. A consultation paper was released in December 2001 and public submissions and agency submissions were received until February 2002. These were then developed into the 240-page draft State Sustainability Strategy, which was accepted by Cabinet and released for four months of discussion in September, 2002. Public workshops and seminars as well as presentations to industry and community groups then began and 150 were held during the submission period. The final strategy was formulated along with an action plan and a set of partnership agreements, and released in September 2003. Thus the State had a period of over two years to think through the concept.

Public engagement

The Strategy process has been received with considerable interest. The evidence for this comes from the fact that many thousands of hits a day are received on the Sustainability website, with over one-third from overseas; there has also been consistently good attendance at all the meetings, and the demand for presentations was unprecedented. Perhaps of greater significance, however, has been the level of engagement by people in the Strategy discussions. As stated by Björn Stigson, who presented at one of our workshops:

> *I am impressed by the work that you and the Government of Western Australia have been doing to create a sustainable development strategy for your state. I have*

not come across any similar extensive process as that you are going through anywhere else in the world. It will be very interesting to follow how the next phases of your work will evolve.

Letter to Peter Newman from Björn Stigson, President of the World Business Council for Sustainable Development, 12 December 2002

At every meeting in the city, and in other regions, the notion of sustainability has intrigued people and demanded responses that went beyond their commonly held views. At all meetings, the notion led to people discussing what the legacy of current development plans were, and hence people engaged easily in issues of ethics and values. This appears to be one of the most significant characteristics of sustainability, that it encourages and enables values-based discussion on future issues rather than just expert opinion. At no stage did the discussion become party political except to recognize that it was an innovative government that had agreed to unleash this public discourse. The question is therefore posed: is the State Sustainability Strategy bringing about significant change towards sustainability in WA?

The policy change process

Professor Patsy Healy has suggested that policy change has three levels of increasing depth:[9]

1 changing language;
2 changing thinking;
3 changing culture.

In the processes that have begun so far on sustainability in WA, it is possible to suggest that there have been clear changes in language and some changes in thinking, but very little change in general culture – yet. There has so far been little media interest, and educational processes are only just beginning. Little can therefore be expected in terms of culture change. Nor would it be anticipated when there is such intense dialogue over the new concept. There are many steps to take before general society can be engaged. However 'vocabulary' and 'thinking' are obviously being addressed in this policy arena, and to some extent a change in the culture of government agencies has begun. Some of the detail supporting this assessment is set out below.

New language

Perhaps the best way to understand what occurred in the months after the release of the draft State Sustainability Strategy is to quote from a document written by a consultant David Galloway who used the Sustainability Strategy as the basis for a public design process in Margaret River for a new development. He began his report with the following box that summarizes two approaches to development.

The importance of the Sustainability Strategy is that it has given a chance for this new style of development to be better understood and articulated. It has enabled public vocabulary, and hence thinking, to be changed in a way that accepts that this is the best way for WA. This process has been occurring in parallel with many other areas of government that have been consistent with this approach and have indeed been essential to show that it has not been an isolated exercise by the Sustainability Policy Unit. Perhaps the best example of this is the front page story on *The West Australian* of Friday 3 January 2003, quoting a 'Sea Change' in approaches to coastal development. Many other examples in natural resource management, major projects and everyday government can also be cited and they are growing in number all the time. A further sign

---

Old style development is characterized by language such as:

Balance... Limited impact... Competition... Acceptable levels of... Meeting all statutory requirements... Consultation... Experts... Planning... No major effects... You can't have development without... Financial benefit... I'm only the... its not my responsibility... in the ideal world, but... Environmental Social Impact Assessment... It's not in the interests of...

Sustainability is characterized by language such as:

Net benefit... Change... Ongoing management... Efficiency... Inclusive... Innovation... Design... Best practice... Long term... Participation... Engagement... Altruism... Repair... Enhance... Sense of place... Sacred... Economic performance... Externalities... Broad based benefit... Partnerships... I'm responsible... Networks... Interdependence... Future...

---

that vocabulary is changing is the number of job descriptions that use 'Sustainability Officer'. There are seven of these job titles in WA local governments alone. Björn Stigson explained in his recent seminar in Perth that there are now 92 of his 150 global corporations making up the World Business Council on Sustainable Development that have Vice Presidents for Sustainability. However, there are now few Vice Presidents for Environment, as it is no longer a strategic issue, whereas sustainability clearly is.

New thinking

The notion of sustainability has not yet become common parlance and thus it has not yet touched general culture. However, the Sustainability Strategy has gone beyond the mere redefinition of words, to the level of changing how policy-oriented people think about development and the future. This is an important achievement. It will become an increasingly important element of how the government works, and has therefore created an important legacy for WA. The sustainability discourse has been developed throughout the government and, as suggested by Stigson above, it has begun to influence all levels of public policy discussion. The elements of this change in thinking are mainly about the principles (above) but also the detail of the actions suggested which begin to flesh out the meaning of the principles. These are briefly outlined here, although the document itself is the best source of information for the 336 action items.

Institutionalizing sustainability principles

The final State Sustainability Strategy has committed the government to creating a Sustainability Act which will enable the 11 sustainability principles to be embedded across the whole of government. Other legislation for each part of government can then refer to this as its context. Manitoba has such an Act, but few other state/regional governments have done this yet. The WA Act will establish the principles and require agencies to report on them. A Sustainability Roundtable will be established to enable sustainability to be facilitated through communities and business. The tasks of this broadly representative body will be:

- the implementation and further development of the state–local government partnership;
- a sustainability Partnership Agreement;
- community and industry Partnership Projects;
- regional Sustainability Strategies;

Figure 14.4 *How the Sustainability Strategy feeds into other strategies across government*

- global aid project facilitation;
- community education and awareness (including conferences and events);
- state of Sustainability Reporting; and
- revising the State Sustainability Strategy (every two years).

Embracing sustainability in agencies
All agencies have to develop Sustainability Action Plans based on a Sustainability Code of Conduct developed within the Department of Premier and Cabinet. This will encompass procurement, energy, fleet management, waste, water, triple bottom line reporting, and social responsibility (e.g. cross cultural training, access for people with disabilities). As well as these internal responsibilities, a range of agency strategies have begun to adopt sustainability principles and thinking in their areas of responsibility, as set out in Figure 14.4.

Contribution to global sustainability
The WA State Sustainability Strategy highlighted four key areas of global responsibility:

1 **Population, development aid and environmental technology** – suggesting that WA contributions to global aid, particularly at the village technology level, would be the most useful way to address the population issue.
2 **Biodiversity** – the globally significant biodiversity of WA is a global treasure and needs to be addressed in that context. The world's first endangered mammal species removed from the World Conservation Union list is the Western Australian woylie or brush-tailed bettong. Further strategies to pursue this kind of success are outlined.
3 **Oil vulnerability, the gas transition and the hydrogen economy** – A taskforce to examine this issue has been established, encompassing representatives from government, industry and the community to assist in the transition to pursue this kind of success.

Table 14.2 *Regional approaches to sustainability*

Economic	Environmental	Social
Regional Plans Regional Investment Tours	NRM Plans Regional Metabolism and Eco-efficiency Studies	Regional Stories (Indigenous and European) and 'Sense of Place' studies Community Aspirations and Place Management.

Source: Government of Western Australia (2003)

4   **Greenhouse** – a separate strategy has been developed in parallel with the State
   Sustainability Strategy to address this important issue.

Sustainability assessment

A new process that ensures simultaneous consideration of social, economic and
environmental aspects of projects and programmes, is being trialled and worked through
to ascertain the best internal process. The key will be an integration mechanism that can
ensure net benefit outcomes in environmental, social and economic areas pursued from
the start of an assessment.

Regional sustainability strategies

The next phase of the State Sustainability Strategy is to develop regional approaches to
sustainability. This is obvious in a state as large and diverse as WA, and many of the
elements of this are present in plans that are under way. However, there are some
suggested elements that are required to be integrated, including Regional Metabolism
and Eco-efficiency Studies in the environmental area, and in the social area 'Sense of
Place' studies that can tell the 'story' of a region (Indigenous and European) leading to
Place Management studies, and Community Aspiration studies that are based on
visioning processes. These are summarized in Table 14.2.

Natural resource management

In many ways, land has been managed at state level through a sustainability lens for
decades. One fishery has received WWF accreditation, forests' conservation has been
agreed and logging severely reduced with a shift to plantations, and agriculture still seeks
to clear land but is also concentrating on land care. Many of these issues were further
developed with a stronger social dimension, and with mining this focuses on how to
increase indigenous employment. The greater use of the planning system through
regions of local governments in NRM was also a feature of the State Sustainability
Strategy.

Planning and building

Sustainability will be brought more directly into the planning of cities through new
processes and guidelines. The Minister for Planning has called for a Sustainability
Scorecard approach to all urban development. Plans will need to demonstrate how they
address key sustainability criteria and those with a high score will be given bonuses and
assessment time benefits. A Toolkit and Guide to Sustainable Planning, Building and
Construction will be created to enable developers and councils to provide more
sustainable urban development. This will incorporate water sensitive urban design,
energy rating and greenhouse gas implications, solar orientation, public transport,
retention of trees, universal and accessible design. Broad planning issues about growth

management in Perth (capital city of WA) and other centres will be part of a visioning process on the new Plan for Perth. There will be a greater emphasis on the revitalization of older areas, especially in declining middle and outer areas (rather than continued urban sprawl) and ensuring there are dense, mixed use centres around rail lines.

Partnerships

A range of partnerships are being developed that can create ongoing implementation of the change in thinking due to the Sustainability Strategy.

- **Local government** This partnership arose from the submission provided by the WA Local Government Association suggesting that most of the State Sustainability Strategy recommended actions could be 'signed off' together. As local government is responsible for local town and regional planning, they have considerable power. However, there are many aspects that are stretching local government beyond traditional planning into new areas of sustainability. In the main, it is considered that this can best be handled by regions of local government formed around the appropriate bio-region (e.g., drainage and other NRM issues), or social/physical region (e.g., transport, waste, community services and affordable housing).
- **Researchers** The State Sustainability Strategy has suggested the formation of a Global Centre for Sustainability (GCS) as the basis of an integrated approach to sustainability research and the attraction of major international funds. The GCS has been agreed to by the four universities, TAFE and CSIRO, as well as the state government, and will draw industry and consultants into it as it begins to work in 2003. The notion of creating critical mass for the attraction of large-scale international projects is a long-term concept, but immediate projects are being investigated – particularly regional sustainability strategies, as they are increasingly seen as a requirement for aid delivery.
- **Industry** The involvement of some progressive industry in the development of the State Sustainability Strategy was critical to the change of thinking in WA. The reality of major multinationals who had over five years of experience in WA implementing sustainability within their own companies was a major source of encouragement to policy-makers and politicians in the development of the State Sustainability Strategy. The next stage will be the development of locally-applied codes of conduct for corporate social responsibility, for mining and petroleum, for eco-efficiency and industrial ecology. Also, the criteria for and facilitation of Sustainability Investment Tours are being established to try and attract ethical investments to WA.
- **Community sustainability** There are a number of key concepts guiding the application of sustainability to community, especially the role of community arts, community services, housing, health and education, in the development of 'sense of place' and social capital. The integration and focusing of these aspects to assist simultaneously environmental and economic development is the most difficult ongoing part of the State Sustainability Strategy. To assist the process of focusing an important new organization has been formed – the WA Collaboration – which combines peak civil society representation from conservation, unions, churches, ethnic affairs, welfare, indigenous, youth and active ageing groups. Funded by the Lotteries Commission, this group has been conducting extensive public consultation to develop a Community Sustainability Agenda. This has certainly contributed to a change of thinking in key social groups who have been the most recent part of the sustainability troika to be challenged into the process. The importance of the community in changing the culture towards sustainability cannot be underestimated, as only they can truly create the values and visions upon which sustainability depends.

The importance of these different partnership initiatives cannot be underestimated. Where political risk for sustainability is most difficult, there is the greatest need for new partnerships between all three sectors of society. The story of Perth is one of politicians overcoming bureaucratic advice over and over. The bus lobby belief that 'anything a train can do a bus can do better and cheaper' is not shared by the general public. Trains are therefore politically very popular and in WA they have been the basis of many election victories over the past 20 years. However, each step was a political risk, as advice said stick to buses. The patronage results have been stunning. More recently the Minister has had to pursue single-mindedly the redirection of our proposed southern rail so that it can be faster than traffic rather than slower. *This has meant overriding the bureaucracy with considerable community-based support. At each step that this partnership has been formed the result has been positive in all aspects of sustainability.* Political leadership was however essential. There are many other examples of innovative bureaucracies creating opportunities for Ministers to take political risks for sustainability and then winning over highly suspicious business and community. An example for us has been the Liveable Neighbourhoods Design Code which has created more dense, mixed use, transit-orientated centres and sub-centres with almost none of the expected political fallout from the market community.[10] It is interesting that this approach to development actually originated from some innovative urban developers, hence it has gone full circle in terms of a sustainability partnership.

New culture

The first steps towards changing culture can now be seen as the State Sustainability Strategy moves from new words into new thinking and new institutions. In particular, the key element of institutionalizing sustainability through a Sustainability Act and a Sustainability Roundtable will be critical to the cultural step. However, all of this has barely touched broader society. The State Sustainability Strategy is now beginning a process of education for sustainability in schools, and the first steps of defining an integrated household sustainability programme are outlined. These may become the basis for a more extensive application of sustainability in WA at the level of cultural change in future.

What have we learned?

The State Sustainability Strategy has been developed as a new way of approaching government. It builds on the global work of nations, states and local government in this area over the past 15 years. However, there are few sub-national areas that have developed anything quite as comprehensive: the State Sustainability Strategy covers 42 areas of government, whereas the Australian Government's National Strategy for Ecologically Sustainable Development (ESD) covered only 12 areas, having much less direct responsibility for many of the areas covered in the WA State Sustainability Strategy. The State Sustainability Strategy also has a much more coherent approach to the integration of social issues, as this has become a considerably bigger part of the sustainability agenda globally in the past few years. As the WA State Sustainability Strategy was undertaken as an election commitment, it had to begin with a lengthy process of definition and 'language change'. This quickly moved into a process of 'thinking change', as it challenged all areas of government in diversity and community to see what it meant to them. After a two year intensive engagement, the WA State Sustainability Strategy has, it appears, at least created change at the first two levels suggested by Healey. However, it has yet to reach the broader community. The question of whether it will depends on government, industry and community resources, but also whether the WA State Sustainability Strategy and the whole global process of sustainability is likely to continue to provide the key dialogue of our era. Evidence would suggest that this is likely. Consider the following three aspects:

Table 14.3 *A sample of the new initiatives for WA in this strategy*

Indigenous	Promote indigenous employment targets in major developments, joint management with indigenous people of National Parks, an Indigenous Protected Areas programme and Indigenous Regional Agreements to support indigenous sustainability.
Biodiversity	Develop a Biodiversity Conservation Strategy and Act, create 30 new National Parks under the policy to protect old-growth forests and five new marine reserves, assess the need for new reserves, and support the linking of major terrestrial reserves with areas of privately owned bush and regeneration, to help meet Australia's international obligations for biodiversity protection. • The Department of Fisheries is developing a process to assess all WA fisheries in terms of ecologically sustainable development and to report to Environment Australia and the WA community. • Develop a new vision for the Ningaloo Coast including fast tracking World Heritage nomination for Cape Range – Ningaloo Coast and gazette the extensions to the Ningaloo Marine Park and Cape Range National Park. • The Perth Zoo has adopted a comprehensive environmental management programme and aims to be the first sustainable zoo of the 21st century. • Bring Natural Resource Management into the local government planning system to ensure it has a statutory base.
Global warming	Implement a WA Greenhouse Strategy and continue to develop innovative contributions to the global greenhouse issue. • Respond to the findings of the Transport Energy Strategy Committee on short-, medium- and long-term transport goals for the transition from oil vulnerability, to gas, to the hydrogen economy. • Emphasize the revitalization of suburbs and, as part of Greater Perth, establish growth management to control urban sprawl. • Overcome car dependence through development that builds on the doubling of the rail system, revamp the Perth Bike Plan and introduce a SmartRider ticketing system for public transport with extra incentives, security and speed of operation.
Embedding sustainability within government	Develop a Sustainability Act which embeds the principles of sustainability, creates a Sustainability Roundtable and requires a State of Sustainability Report to indicate success in implementing the principles. The State Supply Commission will work with the Procurement Leaders Council to ensure that consideration is given to sustainability purchasing across the public sector. The State Supply Commission will administer the Sustainability Purchasing Policy. Purchasing guidelines and checklists to support sustainability purchasing for specific product and service categories, which will be further developed over time. Other states are doing the same: *National, Regional, State and local governments have a significant role to play in creating markets for eco-innovation.* 'Our AU$33 billion a year public sector can significantly influence the national whole (Australian) economy and provide leadership. For example, our vehicle fleet is around 5% of the national new vehicle market. That means our procurement decisions – plus those of the Commonwealth, the other states, territories and local government – can affect the economics of the cleaner vehicles market.' Bob Carr, Premier of NSW, Australia, June 2002.

Table 14.3 *continued*

Communities and sense of place	Support communities to participate fully in achieving a sustainable future • Involve the community in developing 'place management' approaches through an integrated community services framework to help prioritize and co-locate services. • Create an Education for Sustainability Competition based on student projects and school plans demonstrating sustainability. • Hold an annual sustainability ethics seminar 'Many Cultures – One Earth' and an annual Sustainable Living Festival. • Promote indigenous naming of regions, towns, suburbs and landscape features, to assist in the development of 'sense of place' in WA. • Use *Consulting Citizens: A Resource Guide* and *Consulting Citizens: Planning for Success* to promote effective public consultation and active citizenship. • Strengthen communities in their 'sense of place' through a neighbourhood renewal initiative, an Early Intervention Strategy, projects in sport, recreation, culture and the arts, and Regional Sustainability Strategies.
Water issues	Implement the State Water Strategy and continue to develop long-term solutions for water conservation and water supply including more community scale re-use applications.
Nuclear waste	Strengthen the Nuclear Waste Facility (Prohibition) Act 1999 so that it prohibits the transportation or storage of any nuclear waste in WA.

Source: Government of Western Australia (2003)

1   **Politics of hope** The WA State Sustainability Strategy document is inspirational, beginning to address many long-term issues of sustainability. Importantly, it represents the politics of hope when the context in the early 21st century around the world (and in Australia) is an emphasis on the politics of fear. This is probably one of the reasons for the very extensive engagement of people in the new idea and why it is likely to continue for some time: people need hope, and sustainability is offering the only politics of hope.

2   **Politics of partnership** The concept of sustainability demands an approach based on co-operation and partnerships, rather than competition. It therefore challenges at a fundamental level the kinds of agendas set by the World Trade Organization or national productivity commissions, that seek to ensure competition is observed as the key value in the economy. Sustainability challenges this, but not as a traditional left-wing approach which asserts greater state control over the market. Sustainability asserts that partnerships can create social and environmental improvement simultaneously with the competition-based economic agenda. This requires trials and demonstrations, new capacity building in government and industry, new institutions, and even new laws. It will fundamentally depend on the community asserting its values and visions for a better world, but there appears to be no other global agenda that is enabling that process to occur.

3   **Politics of globalization** Whilst there is a reaction to the mass consumption and 'Americanization' of the world, there is also a deeper sense that we are part of one Earth. True globalization is therefore lifting people to see beyond the traditional squabbles of nation-states to the development of new ways of thinking and living that ensure a global future. The United Nations have recently declared the decade 2005–2015 as the Decade of Education for Sustainability. This global agenda of sustainability is therefore not likely to disappear. The WA State Sustainability Strategy has taken the first two steps of a long walk towards change, and the final broader cultural change can be anticipated over the years to come.

CHAPTER 15

DELIVERING SUSTAINABILITY THROUGH LOCAL ACTION (LOCAL GOVERNMENT)

There is increasing global recognition on the significant role that local governments play in delivering environmental sustainability through cumulative local action. 'Think global, act local' has earned its place as one of the key concepts of the 21st century, clearly articulating that global agendas can only be achieved through local action. This chapter is based on the work of Valerie A. Brown and her colleagues through the Australian Local Sustainability Project and the ISA Forum Planning Group. In order to provide the general context to this work, we will briefly introduce a sample of the growing networks that have had a considerable influence over both the local and worldwide movement of local governments seeking to achieve tangible improvements in global environmental conditions.

A worldwide movement of local governments

Wayne Wescott, Martin Brennan and Yolande Strengers

EDITORS' NOTE: While state, national and global bodies assist in the establishment of broad-reaching sustainability agendas, it is at the local level that these actions are implemented. The International Council for Local Environmental Initiatives (ICLEI) is an organization that is driving the sustainability agenda by building the capacity of local governments. We asked Wayne Wescott, Chief Executive Officer at the ICLEI Australia/New Zealand, Martin Brennan, Partnerships and Political Support Manager, and his colleague Yolande Strengers to provide some insight into delivering sustainability from the local government level upwards.

Although local government has traditionally been seen as the most marginalized and least influential sphere of government in many countries around the world, it is now establishing itself as a leader and advocate to state and national governments. Local governments, and local government networks, are playing an important role in leading the global movement. The strength of the movement is most obvious through the presence and power of this part of the government sector at global events, such as the World Summit on Sustainable Development (WSSD) in Johannesburg in 2002. It is at such events that the cumulative effect of local government work around the world is recognized as a powerful and imperative part of implementing global sustainability agendas. There is some debate about the reasons behind local governments' growing focus on sustainability. One perspective is that the increase in focus can be partly attributed to the distinct and dynamic character of communities in which local governments operate. Local government constituencies often have direct access to challenge the power and priorities of local governing bodies, pressuring their councillors to take action on local environmental issues. Within Australia, the history of local government has paved the way for the management of holistic sustainability functions. Communities are now asking their governments to do more than their traditional roles of 'roads, rubbish and rates', by managing these domains in a sustainable way. Australian local government has now largely made the move from 'rubbish' to 'waste management', from 'roads' to 'sustainable transport' and from rates to 'triple bottom line' management.

Local governments wishing to achieve sustainable outcomes at the local level have formed a series of networks that build on the strength of this level of government and enable it to be heard at the state, national and global levels. ICLEI is one such organization that has provided local governments around the world with a solid platform to take action on local sustainability issues and ensure that those issues are being heard at all levels of government. The International Council for Local Environment Initiatives (ICLEI) was launched in 1990 at the World Congress of Local Governments for a Sustainable Future. The organization's mandate was to advocate for local government before national and international bodies, to increase understanding and support for local environmental protection and sustainable development activities. In Australia and New Zealand, ICLEI's campaigns and initiatives are delivered through a regional office, ICLEI-A/NZ. Campaigns that have operated through the regional office include:

- Water Campaign™: ICLEI's newest campaign is gaining local government participation from around Australia and has secured funding support from both state and federal governments, and several water retailers. Participation is growing at a rapid rate.
- Cities for Climate Protection™ (CCP™) Campaign: The Australian arm of the CCP Campaign has gained support from the Australian Government through the Australian Greenhouse Office, as well as support from several state governments. CCP Australia has the fastest uptake and largest local government participation base of any country in the world. There is already critical mass in Australian local government reducing greenhouse gas emissions through the CCP Campaign. The campaign now covers over 72 per cent of Australia's population including nearly all of the councils located in metropolitan regions. The sheer number of councils participating in this campaign, and ongoing interest from those that are not, indicates that CCP has cemented its place in Australian local government environmental management. Councils are using CCP as common terminology to refer to their response to global warming, as well as wider environmental issues facing local government. The Communities for Climate Protection (CCP) New Zealand Campaign has recently been launched, based largely on the success achieved by ICLEI in Australia.
- Local Agenda 21 Campaign: this includes a toolbox of local government projects and services, including the triple-bottom-line training system and a Green Purchasing Pilot Project.[1]

ICLEI-A/NZ uses a performance-based 'milestone framework' that takes councils through a series of steps to achieve environmental goals, building on work done internationally for the CCP Campaign in Toronto and Berkeley during the early 1990s. The approach breaks down complex issues into understandable tangible elements for the multiple stakeholders within local governments, and keeps all parties focused on actionable tasks. The framework requires councils to assess the extent of the perceived problem (Milestone One), set a goal (Milestone Two), develop an action plan (Milestone Three), implement the plan and demonstrate action (Milestone Four) and re-evaluate the problem over a period of time (Milestone Five). The performance-based approach also refers to a minimum standard of performance that ICLEI-A/NZ requires from its councils, in order to achieve each milestone. These expectations enhance the value of the campaigns by establishing concrete standards. This has also had the benefit of earning the respect of other government sectors.

Multi-level programme and political support

Without engagement at all levels, there is a risk that the campaigns may become personally or politically driven, or that they will not be continued beyond the timeframes of a councillor's elected term of office, or a chief executive's employment contract. The multi-level approach refers to the engagement of all levels of bureaucracy and elected member officials in a member or participant council. At a practical level, ICLEI-A/NZ works on the basis that local governments require support across all spheres of council operations and at the political council chamber. Using this approach, the organization aims to engage:

- officers who are implementing on the ground campaign work;
- middle-managers who are assisting in this process and managing the practical campaign components;
- directors and chief executives, who are budgeting and allocating resources to the campaigns;
- elected councillors, who are endorsing the campaign itself, cementing it into council policy, and advocating it to their constituency.

Analysis of campaign success

ICLEI-A/NZ bases its campaign analysis on the premise that the business case is a fundamental way to ensure that campaigns and initiatives deliver short-term tangible results and long-term culture change. The importance of quantification is applied across the organization's campaign framework, which requires councils to set targets and quantify their results. The annual CCP Australia Measures Evaluation Report is an example of the value of quantification. The report outlines the benefits of actions that councils have undertaken to reduce their local greenhouse gas emissions. In the period from July 1999 to June 2003 the 95 councils surveyed:

- reduced cumulative CO_2-e (carbon dioxide equivalent) emissions over the four year period by approximately 1.8 million tonnes;
- invested AU$3.3 million in greenhouse jobs;
- invested more than AU$67 million in greenhouse abatement.[2]

ICLEI-A/NZ uses these results as a feedback loop to its members and participants, to demonstrate achievements and the benefits of their commitment to these campaigns. The results are also used to build a case for further resource allocation or shared resources through government and stakeholder partnerships. By quantifying more than the environmental outputs of campaign participation, ICLEI-A/NZ is able to appeal to local governments and additional stakeholders by highlighting the multiple benefits that accrue from environmental action. In the case of CCP, the indicators used at this time are CO_2 emission reductions to demonstrate environment action, financial investment to demonstrate economic commitment, and job creation to demonstrate social and community benefit.

Sustainability Street: it's a village out there

Sustainability Street is a joint initiative of Vox Bandicoot and Environs Australia Projects (EAP), the project delivery arm of Environs Australia, the local government environment network. The central idea of the Sustainability Street approach is that we get together as local communities, learn something about ecological sustainability and then do what we can to encourage, assist or 'teach' other individuals or other communities to join the groundswell.[3] Sustainability Street is a community development and environmental programme gathering momentum across Australia, helping people transform their homes and neighbourhoods into sustainable green environments. An environmental education programme developed by environmental educators, Vox Bandicoot in collaboration with Environs Australia, it is based on the notion that everyone wants to create a safer and healthier living environment for themselves and their children. It also recognizes that humans are social creatures and the best outcomes for the community can be realized by bringing people together to pool knowledge and resources. The work is sponsored by companies and organizations from a range of societal sectors. The word 'street' is just a concept and refers to any geographically or socially connected group of people. A Sustainability Street community could be made up of people from down the street and across the road, or it could be made up of people from an existing group – as long the people involved want to get together to help create a better environment. Communities are informed about the programme at information sessions and are invited to participate. The idea is then to guide participating communities through a process where they learn about sustainability and learn how to ordain themselves as a group. It is fundamentally about getting organized as a local community around the important issue of ecological sustainability, showing that a group has skills that are greater than the sum of its parts and that a group is usually more effective at achieving things than lone individuals.

Facilitated sessions bring people together in the first instance and they are supported through the process with the following resources:

- **All Hands on For Sustainability** This is the central document that contains information on how to run a Sustainability Street programme.
- **The website** This is the central information portal for the greater Sustainability Street 'family'. Part of the website includes a 'Sustainoclopedia', which is being set up to demystify the language of sustainability for community groups. There are also online discussion forums for different Sustainability Street communities to interact with others in each group, or with the whole Sustainability Street 'family'.
- **Expert speakers and information** Through the networks that everyone can bring into the process, including official supporters of the programme, various and wide ranging expertise can be brought to communities as required.
- **TreeLess** A newsletter for communities.
- **Councils** Participating councils can bring various levels of support to the programme and can help direct communities to existing programmes and resources.

Essentially, the programme works on two levels:

1. **Sustainability in the home** As a starting point, communities come together to learn about sustainable living principles. The initiative is not another '101 ways to save the environment' programme; rather it's about 'learning how to learn' so that everyone can participate in the sustainability journey. A notional six month course covers,

amongst other things, three areas of daily focus: water, waste and energy, with the ultimate objective being biodiversity conservation.

2   **Sustainability in the community** The second part of the programme is about recognizing that communities are all unique, with different issues, ideas and resources. After all, who knows local issues better than the local community? Sustainability Street encourages people to identify local issues and to develop local projects using the various resources that already exist. It does not have predetermined outcomes for communities; rather it allows each community to determine what they would like to achieve and how they should go about it. At present, the programme has been focused on Victoria with 10 councils currently involved and the intention is to now broaden the programme nationally. The organizers of Sustainability Street believe that its success is due to its unique approach, its sense of community and 'localness', and most of all, the emphasis on having 'a bit of fun'.

Leadership in the local government sector: working from inside out[*]

Valerie A. Brown

The local government sector is often underestimated as a key contributor to progress towards sustainability. This part is based on a report on a collaborative study with 25 leading sustainability practitioners working in councils around Australia. The study explored their very different demographic profiles, mode of operations, and needs for the future. Surprises included the wide range of positions from which they were working, from junior project officer to CEO; the diverse entry points for introducing sustainability practice, such as organizational development, strategic planning and environmental services; and the variety of tools that they had used to make a difference. There was unanimous agreement that there was the nucleus of an active, vocal advocacy for sustainability right across the local government sector. However, individual sustainability practitioners felt very alone in their councils, even in cases where they had been recognized for their success. The sustainability practitioners came to the conclusion that, for sustainability to be advanced, the necessary strategic and personal support must be generated across the local government sector as a whole. Further, the local government sector should advise on local initiatives from the inside out, that is, from their own local knowledge to other agencies, not from other agencies and scales of government inward.

Internationally local government is constantly nominated as the delivery arm of sustainability practice. On the positive side, this places the local government sector in a key role as the interface between people and governance as a whole, as having locally appropriate management skills, as being in continual dialogue with their communities, and a place where the individuals in government and in the community know each other personally. On the negative side, it can mean that local government acts as the too-hard-basket into which unsolvable problems are thrown, the end-of-the-line for resources and influence that filter down from higher levels of government, and an opportunity for ambitious individuals to start their early career before leaving for better things. Both

---

[*] This section has been developed by Valerie A. Brown through the Australian Local Sustainability Project and the ISA Forum Planning Group.[4] Val is a well recognized and respected leader in local government sustainability and is currently a visiting fellow in the School of Resources, Environment and Society and the Centre for Resource and Environmental Studies (jointly) at the Australian National University. She is author of over 200 research papers and 12 books on links between human and environmental issues, and her work can best be summed up as 'thinking globally, acting locally'.

scenarios make their contribution to the reality that is local government. However, both come from the perspective that positions the government sector at the base of a top-down, bottom-up scenario. Whether the 'top' is government, business, specialist advisers, community or individuals, the local government equivalent is seen as the bottom rung of a high ladder, with less power, fewer resources and a lower level of expertise than anything above them (see Figure 15.1). This part proposes that this is not only a distorted perspective but one which, left to dominate, will neutralize any moves to sustainability.

Sustainability leadership in the local government sector

In both of the major global conferences intended to position governments in relation to sustainable development, namely, the United Nations Conference on Environment and Development (UNCED or the Earth Summit) in Rio de Janeiro in 1992, and the WSSD in Johannesburg in 2002,[5] local government played a key role. In 1992, the only action with specified outcomes and a due date that was signed off by the 92 national governments who attended the conference was the commitment to a Local Agenda 21 plan being in operation in the whole of their local government sector by 1996.[6] Since there was no delegation of resources, and since local government was not directly represented, it could not set conditions for success. This led to the goal being significantly underachieved in Australia, rather better in the UK and Canada where it was taken up by regions, and sporadically in Europe and the US.[7] In 2002 the local government sector, resourced to a great extent by the previously mentioned International Council for Local Environmental Initiatives (ICLEI), provided a strong presence, and offered some of the most active partnership projects.[8] At the same time, national governments could not agree on a joint action or even a joint communiqué. If local government is to take on a major global role as an effective unit of sustainability action, many questions must be considered. What is the underlying capacity of the local government sector to take on such a major task? What is the work going on in the local government sector that has allowed some councils to pursue sustainability as part of their core business, while others support increasing uncontrolled development? How does sustainability become incorporated into a local government authority, who does it, what does it take for the work to continue, and indeed for it to expand?

The answers cannot be found by evaluating the distinctive culture that is local government from the outside, from other scales and levels of government, as is often the case. The answers must be derived from inside local government, and from the sustainability practitioners themselves.

Profile of sustainability leadership

This part reviews the results of a project undertaken in Australia in 2003, the Integrated Sustainability Assessment Forum (ISA), which brought together 25 of the most respected Australian local government sustainability practitioners, as identified by awards, peer recognition, and frequent references as role models. The group of sustainability leaders worked together for over six months of discussion and review, in order to identify their personal and professional needs to advance sustainable development in the local government sector as a whole.

Based on needs established by research funded from an Australian Research Council grant to a University of Western Sydney (UWS) research team, the original aims of this Forum project were to:

* draw together in one place the suite of tools best incorporating sustainability into Australian Councils;

- explore how they fit together;
- discover whether they form a more-or-less complete sustainability package.

Members of the collaborative action research team (a social ecologist, an environmental scientist, a community development specialist and two of the sustainability leaders) designed a collaborative process whereby the 25 'sustainability leaders' agreed to take part in a preparatory email discussion group over three weeks, followed a month later by three days attendance at a participatory forum. Overall, 17 local government sustainability staff members, members of two national sustainability policy organizations, and the three university-based researchers above, participated as equal partners throughout the process. The Forum was designed as a consultation between peers, maximizing participation and discussion. It was assumed that, in an emergent and dynamic field such as sustainability, no one could be leader or follower – everyone's experience was equally valuable, and equally valid. The aim of the process was to achieve a synergy of the experience of the contributors through participation in open dialogue, rather than merely exchange of information. The design involved:

- a literature review and recollections by Forum participants of the work of all Australian Councils and organizations who had achieved recognition of leadership in managing for local sustainability;
- an invitation to 25 selected leaders to contribute to the consultative Forum;
- email discussion groups prior to the workshop responding to questions raised by the local sustainability review, and by the participants themselves;
- collation of review and email discussions as pre-forum briefing sent to participants;
- three-day participative workshop identifying issues and solutions for incorporating sustainability practices and tools in the local government sector;
- preparation of the Forum report as the basis for the development of sustainability practice in the local government sector.

Three questions were posed to, and by, participants each week for three weeks prior to the Forum. The responses provided the criteria for outcomes of the workshop, the set of integrating frameworks being used by participant councils, and the key strategies being used to introduce sustainability practices into councils. The first set of questions covered who the people were, their roles on their councils, their greatest needs and the tools they were currently using. Keep in mind that the organizers expected the outcome of the workshop to be the development of a comprehensive package of Sustainability tools appropriate for the local government sector. The first interesting finding in the responses was the wide range of positions from which the participants came, the second the diversity of their experiences in establishing sustainability, and the third the number of tools. Contrary to expectations, there seemed no common package, theme or set of skills. This led to concern that there would not be a concerted and agreed outcome of the Forum. As we shall see that concern was mistaken. The organizers were simply looking in the wrong place.

As an example of the diversity of positions from which sustainability had been introduced into their councils, the roles of the practitioners ranged from Council Chief Executive Officers through strategic planners to junior part-time project officers. There were three things their activities did have in common. One was the *strategic nature* of their intervention, another the *originality* of their thinking. The third common dimension was their *deep commitment* to the pursuit of sustainability. Some examples of their strategic use of their chosen tools follow:

- The Chief of Management Services designed, and implemented across the whole Council management team, a self-development programme that included a sense of identity with and respect for the environment, and a sensitivity to change, in themselves and in others. This allowed a fertile proving ground for new ideas to be considered on their merits, rather than simply threatening the status quo. It also infused decisions across the whole of Council with a respect for the uniqueness of their environment. This led in turn to leadership in other areas of sustainability practice, such as integrated regional sustainability reporting and cumulative impacts of council decisions. This was therefore a strategic intervention with a flow-on effect.
- A part-time Sustainable Development Project Officer was allotted the task of developing a conservation strategy for Council, its first. Develop it she did, consulting up and down the Council hierarchy of management and experts, running community consultations with sausage sizzles, and picnics on the beach. The first year everyone within the Council and their community was surprised and gratified to have such an excellent Conservation Strategy. The second year the strategy won an external prize for its range and its scope, and the extent to which it was being implemented. The consultations moved on to considering sustainability as the logical next step to conservation. The third year, the title and contents of the Strategy, with all parties' approval and consent, suddenly re-emerged as a Sustainability Strategy, an almost painless major shift in policy and practice, supported by all players. This could perhaps be called an acorn affect: a small seed, well-nourished, produced a major new initiative.
- The Head of an environmental services branch of one council established a Sustainability Office with a small State environmental education grant. Its staff was small, but its reach was wide. Three full-time staff were assigned as 'Sustainability Ambassadors', for industry, community and schools respectively. Their task was to bring sustainability into the core of each of their sectors, and to find ongoing support for the programmes within sector resources. This was achieved within two years, with a 'whole-of-council' pride in their work.
- Another environmental manager in another council proposed a whole-of-council accounting scheme, whereby all programmes were subject to an integrated triple bottom line tool, and assessed against the precautionary principle, for social, economic and environmental costs. As the scheme was trialled through the Council, it called attention to the existing fragmentation, and even conflict, between how decisions were currently being made. This led in turn to a review of the design of the whole Council's strategic plan. Different as each of these last two were in detail, both strategies acted as a snowball, gathering other parts of the Council and its advisers as it went, until the whole-of-council was involved.

The list of potential tools was collected and discussed during the email sessions. It was expected that there would be discussion on the relevant merits of the tools. On the contrary, as the email exchange continued, discussion moved from which were the more valuable tools and strategies, to another plane. All these sustainability experts began to agree that the tools themselves were not the deciding factor on the extent of change towards sustainability in a council. The tools were useful, but it was essential that there be a wide range, because it was the opportunities to use them effectively that were the deciding factors. And that depended on the strategic skills of the operator. The pen pictures of the workings of some of the strategic operations confirm these conclusions. Whether from a flow-on, an acorn or a snowball effect, it became clear that the crucial learning would come not from sharing recipes or skills, but from sharing experiences on how to operate strategically within the local government sector as a whole. Any thoughts of the three-day-forum being an opportunity to collect and publish a toolkit vanished. The outcome of the three-day Forum became an open question.

A summary of the Sustainability Practice tools in use among just these 25 people – this paints a vivid picture of the variety of choices they each had of where to begin:

- Sustainability Strategies replacing or influencing Local Environment Plans and Local Development Plans (which are legislated) and Environmental Management Systems (which are not).
- Integrated Sustainability Assessment Tool (using the Precautionary Principle).
- Town Planning procedures, Place management, Local Agenda 21, Healthy Cities, Main Street: existing strategies that could be converted to sustainability.
- State-of-the-Environment Reports, Community Score Cards, which were used as planning documents (although many were left on shelves).
- Linking community, expert and government in collaborative planning workshops and projects to address local priority needs, using guides such as the Community-based Planning Action Handbook.
- Cities for Climate Protection: a global set of rules and standards for reducing greenhouse emissions that many councils agreed to follow.
- Cool Communities: a programme of greenhouse gas reduction that left it entirely up to each council and their community to design their own initiative.
- Triple Bottom Line decision-making, accounting, toolkit: this involved much cross-fertilization between social, ecological and financial accounting methods.
- Sustainability Awareness projects abounded: green-web, common ground, no waste, water wise; the list covers every aspect of local community existence.
- Strategic Impact Analysis Matrix, an analytic strategic planning tool developed across the local government sector as a globally comparable tool.

The design of the three-day consultative forum was based on an open learning, collaborative design, more technically described in its pure form as 'Open Space.'[9] It was planned that the participants would set the agenda for the three days in an open market of topics when they first met. This meant that the considerable learning from the email discussion groups could act as a springboard for the Forum. Everyone could start together on a shared learning leap, rather than explore the issues all over again. It also allowed the Forum to begin knowing that the outcome was unknown, quite contrary to the usual workshop design with built-in goals.

The key issues generated in the open space were assigned to small group discussions, with the following issues emerging as first-level priorities.

'When everything is said and done – more is said than done'

Results such as these, from the first round of discussions, carried a clear message of powerful negativity. Here were the most successful local government sustainability practitioners in the country, but when they got together, they were telling each other it was all much too hard. Moving on: the early pessimism of the Forum evaporated in the second round. It seemed as if the people working at the heart of sustainability action, even the most successful, needed space to share the difficulties, when in the larger council workforce, they could show only their optimistic faces.

The next discussions generated a short list of recommended communication processes:

Table 15.1 *Key issues*

1 We're not sustainable	• Need a vision for public and government • Sustainability is dynamic – progress is better or worse e.g., recycling
2 A lot of misreporting	• Need some good data management and auditing • Inform/engage both the community *and* management
3 Lack of accountability, organizational ownership and budgeting	• Accounting within the budget–framework: e.g., corporate plan, annual report
4 Isolation within and between levels of government	• Local government disempowered, state government decisions often counter to sustainability, Commonwealth (EA) is retrograde and exclusive • It hurts!
5 Environment is forgotten as the bottom line	• Environment is a fundamental • Information and risk assessment • Should do National Competition Policy approach to triple bottom line
6 Black market decision-making	• Local government has an election accountability framework, sustainability needs to be part of the political election process • Decisions are a secret rite: need to make them transparent and accountable

1   Define genuine progress:
   • needs to be tangible;
   • recognize that needs evolve over time;
   • be made up of inclusive processes.
2   Tell the big picture story:
   • have a comprehensive toolkit;
   • meaningfully combine data sets in a strong summary;
   • make themes similar, but indicators different for each locality.
3   What are the synthesizing processes for getting to the big picture story?:
   • shared futures vision;
   • systems analysis;
   • use of maps/geographical information systems (GIS) to give feedback to local communities.

These items all need to be taken together with a guide to implementation issues as outlined in Table 15.2.

Sector-wide action

One of the principal concerns had not been on the agenda before the workshop, but emerged as one of the strongest during the discussion process. This was the position of the local government sector as a whole. On the third day, the Forum participants began to converge on a common theme, again one that emerged unexpectedly. Given the shared concerns, the group began to consider the need for whole-of-sector initiatives. They began to consider the value and assistance from outside each council, such as the Environmental Resource Officers in the State's Municipal Association, the strongly-

Table 15.2 *Implementation issues and actions*

Issues	Actions
1 Don't be scared of engaging the community or of divergent views	Consult, engage, and respect all stakeholders: community, experts, councils and staff and integrators
2 Emotive vision statement that leads to practical action	Combine action plans
3 Sustainability is context dependent	Know the context, i.e. trends, people, attitudes, values, etc.
4 Accept that sustainability evolves and changes everyday not once a year	Build flexible incremental strategic processes
5 Short-term political thinking conflicts with long-term thinking	Match community visions with Council strategic plans

established global programmes of ICLEI, and the range of national professional associations. Nevertheless, the strong movement that emerged at the end of the three days was for a concerted programme of sustainability advocacy, generated and supported not from outside, but from inside the individual councils. There was a flavour of '*It's up to us to put our own house in order*'.

The intra- and inter-governmental actions agreed upon can be summarized as follows:

- Local government will need to lead by example and take the lead in establishing partnerships with state government to implement sustainability, rather than wait for state or federal governments to take the lead.
- Talk to state governments about establishing a department or Minister/Commissioner to 'join the dots' (connect the departments and the councils) and to ensure that there really is responsibility and accountability.
- Convey the message throughout the local government sector that sustainability is not an expensive optional extra – it can provide better outcomes and a better way of doing things. Promote 'Sustainability as a better way of doing things' as a key message. This should be targeted to state and federal governments, and industry.
- Elevate internal sustainability networks to coordinate information and research, bring people together, engage the media, work with local educational institutions, lobby different interest groups.

Sustainability advocacy in the local government sector

A final plenary session on the context of sustainability in the local government sector drew some conclusions for the future. The following summary was prepared by a 'synthesis group' made up of a range of Council staff positions, the research group and the Forum facilitators:

- **The context** Strong frustrations were often expressed by the workshop participants, largely because the processes in which participants are involved is leading only to incremental improvement. The hidden 'black market' of decision-making (i.e. external power politics) is a major barrier, as is protection of professional territories. Others within councils who are not sustainability practitioners see the required changes as threats to their own positions and budgets, and work to conserve these.

- **The change processes** Visibility of the sustainability processes is important – being out there and getting involved as part of the democratic process. This requires training of individuals within councils and marketing the 'sustainability thing' (through the media and other avenues, each with the appropriate 'spin' for the audience). There is a need to get government involvement and as professional sustainability practitioners, we need to inform the electoral as well as the administrative process.
- **The key players** Individual councils have to work to bring the other levels of government into play. Other agencies such as ICLEI, environment action networks such as Environs Australia and the state municipal associations each have a role to play. It is also important to engage the public and to build their understanding of the risk issues involved. Because of the complexity of the issues and the strength of knowledge available, if we share our expertise, we can make a greater impact if we work in teams within the local government sector itself, not dispersed as representatives into other sectors.

The final recommendation made by the ISA Forum members addresses how to continue the momentum generated. Their answer was – '*through a sustainability advocacy forum operating within and alongside Local Government*'. The Forum members gave themselves a title 'The Baton Group' for taking over and running with the sustainability baton on behalf of the local government sector. A research brief was prepared, as follows:

> *Undertake research into model organisations and their ability to deliver frameworks for success, funding sources and support available, and costs associated with, establishing and sustaining an integrated sustainability practitioners forum respected for its input to the move towards tangible sustainability.*

The open learning process brought the 25 local government sector sustainability leaders together, allowing the group to spontaneously generate a new understanding of the needs of sustainability in the sector. A series of unexpected outcomes emerged from the steps of the process. First, practitioners responsible for a wide range of roles and activities were able to come to close agreement, not on a set of practical tools as expected, but on the strategic nature of their interventions. Neither the level of appointment, nor the professional background of each innovator seems to have been as important for their success as their personal style and level of commitment to sustainability. Second, the strategic directions were not in any one direction, but diverse and innovative and matched to each council's particular culture. Examples have been summarized above as flow-on, acorn and snowball effects, but there were many more. These outcomes suggested that it was the sustainability leaders' capacity to act as change agents within their own particular council, and their skill in strategic thinking that led to their success. This has important implications for sustainability in-service and professional training programmes everywhere. The third, and for the ISA Forum participants, the most important outcome was the re-direction of the collaborative research resources available to the Forum from the ARC Grant of the Local Sustainability project. Prior to the workshop this had been notionally allocated towards producing a manual containing the sustainability tools recommended by the sustainability leaders. The ISA Forum asked that the resources (funds and team time) be allocated for the purpose described in the last paragraph of the previous section: namely the exploration of the potential for the group to form a sector-wide set of sustainability advocates.

Figure 15.1 *Top-down, bottom-up*

In research terms, the most important finding was the discovery that the Forum group had spontaneously changed the local sustainability landscape. If we change the orientation 180 degrees, from the familiar top-down, bottom-up, from larger scales of governance down and back up (Figure 15.1); to inside-out, outside-in (Figure 15.2) with each local government authority at the core of its operations, we have another, equally valid, reality and one much more conducive to managing for sustainability, locally and globally. This shift of perspective refocuses not only the relationships between local governments and other governments but with their communities, specialist advisers, key individuals as change agents and, above all, the holistic overview of who they are and what their mission is.

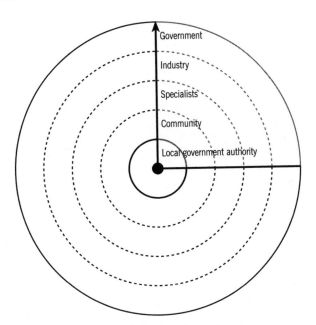

Figure 15.2 *From the inside-out*

The challenge of sustainability has been expressed as:

> *The achievement of sustainability objectives will require holistic actions by all sections of society (personal, business, political, legal and government), and will require considerable cultural change to societal customs and aspirations. This necessitates the development of transitional pathways from the present situation to the preferred future.*[10]

Engineers Australia Sustainable Energy Taskforce (2001, p12)

The local government sector is usually not seen as an autonomous player, but regarded as sandwiched between the States that set their parameters, and communities that tell them what they want. In this review of the sector's sustainability leadership in Australia, the strategic and holistic capacities of the sustainability advocates marked their work as different from other fields of action. They were able to re-think their cultural systems, and develop the transitional pathways, working as collaborators with their council peers. Their processes of social learning and organizational change, working from the inside-out, rather than the outside-in, can well stand as an option for other sustainability initiatives.

SECTION 4

SUSTAINABLE CITIES: THE CHALLENGE OF THE 21ST CENTURY

CHAPTER 16

TOMORROW'S MEGA-CITIES: HOW WILL THEY DEVELOP?

Cities are increasingly being seen as critical to the economic success or failure of regions, states and nations. Despite increasing globalization, many experts see economic growth being driven by these 'global city regions', which have strong concentrations of emerging and traditional industries, supportive infrastructure and a highly educated population.[1] In these global city regions, diverse knowledge clusters and networks are formed that allow innovation to be rapidly combined with existing information in traditional industries, driving broad-based industry development. Despite globalization these local clusters are even more critical to national competitiveness than ever before.[2] One of the most successful cities has been the Indian city of Bangalore, otherwise known as Silicon Valley II. But as a result of its economic success, the scale and speed of growth of Bangalore is unprecedented. It is creating challenges to urban planners and the urban infrastructure never seen before. This has been mirrored in numerous other rapidly growing cities throughout Asia. Such is the mainstream concern about these issues that *Newsweek* magazine dedicated a special issue on Asia's urban explosion.[3] The edition argued that 'the stresses [of urbanization] will either make the region or doom it'.

In this rapidly urbanizing world, cities are not just important for achieving sustainable economic growth but also for achieving sustainable development. The world's cities take up just 2 per cent of the Earth's surface, yet account for roughly 78 per cent of the carbon emissions from human activities, 76 per cent of industrial wood use and 60 per cent of the water tapped for use by people. Cities are home to more people than ever before and the existing and potential future negative environmental impacts are significant. In 1900, only 160 million people, one tenth of the world's population, were city dwellers. In contrast, soon after 2000 half the world (3.2 billion people) will live in urban areas.[4] As Figure 16.1 shows, many developing countries are undergoing urban transition with relatively high urban population growth rates.

Industrialization in developing countries has led to urban health problems on an unprecedented scale. Cities around the world affect not just the health of their people but the health of the planet. In response to this, there is now a growing level of commitment to creating sustainable cities.[5] Citizens and local leaders from Curitiba in Brazil, to Chattanooga, Tennessee, in the US and Vancouver in Canada, are already showing the way as they overcome financial and political obstacles to put ideas for

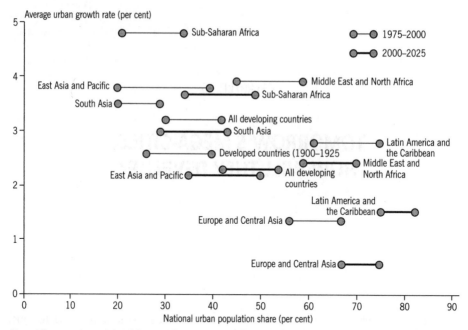

Note: All averages weighted by population. Lines indicate increase in share of urban population between end-point years (25-year increments).

Source: World Bank (2003)

Figure 16.1 *Average urban growth rate*

ecological sustainability into action. But overall internationally we still have a long way to go.

China, for instance, has reported 3 million deaths from urban air pollution over two years. China is growing economically at ~10 per cent per annum, and with a population of over a billion the development choices China makes on development and urbanization in the next 30 years will be critical to whether globally we can achieve sustainable development. As Mark Diesendorf writes: 'The desire of many of China's 'New Rich' to emulate the more extreme manifestations of the American/Australian way of life, with big cars, big houses, junk food and conspicuous wastage of everything, is undermining China's potential for sustainable development. For instance, in several cities, the number of cars is growing at 15 per cent per annum. New urban areas, that are under construction on the outskirts of existing cities, are being built at lower densities, thus encouraging car use and discouraging cycling. China stands on a knife-edge between sustainable and unsustainable development. Its future and the future of this whole planet depend on whether wise minds will guide China on how to leapfrog over the mistakes made in Western economies, to create a better China and a better world.'

Therefore we start Section 4 with a snapshot of China to reinforce the importance of this section's discussion on sustainable cities and whether leapfrog technologies will be adopted or not. It is vital that the West acknowledges its mistakes, and leads on sustainability and encourages by example China and developing countries to follow. If nothing else, it is vital for global security this century because today the USA imports more than 50 per cent of their oil, Europe 70 per cent and it is estimated that China will import as much as 40 per cent of its oil within ten years with much coming from the Middle East.

In Section 3 the role of government in achieving sustainable development was discussed in detail. In those discussions it was implicit that there were just three levels of government in any nation – national, regional or state, and local. But there is another level of government emerging that will be critical to whether or not sustainability is achieved in mega-cities around the world – municipalities. Mark Diesendorf discusses this and other issues pertaining to where China is at, and some actions that any country could take to assist China's transition to a sustainable economy for mutual benefit.

Having considered the current situation in China, Alan AtKisson then reports a stunning new vision for the future of sustainable cities proposed by the remarkable Indian team responsible for the award-winning Goa 2100 Sustainable Cities project. The Goa 2100 team proposed an integrated approach to sustainable cities that also ensured the whole region, not just the city within it, achieved ecological sustainable development. This award-winning submission demonstrated that not just a sustainable city but a sustainable region could achieve ecological sustainability within 30 years cost-effectively.

In the chapters that follow, we explore exciting, innovative, emerging technologies and new policy approaches in the energy, built environment, transport and water sectors that will help any city and region become sustainable. Through these chapters we seek to show not just that significant cost-effective progress is now possible but there are already demonstrable benefits to those cities, regions and nations leading the way. We trust that these chapters provide further evidence and support to the notion that it will be possible to make significant strides to ecological sustainable development more quickly than previously hoped. As we explained in Section 1, achieving ecological sustainable development is not an academic exercise. It is vital that we do achieve this as fast as possible, because the sooner we do, the more likely we are to succeed in sustaining the vital species and ecosystems upon which life depends.

Governance of municipalities: a snapshot of sustainable development in China

*Mark Diesendorf** *

EDITORS' NOTE: This part has been contributed by Professor Mark Diesendorf as a summary of his extensive work in this area. The piece is intended to provide a context to the importance of the role of municipal government in the mega-cities of the Asian region.

An understanding of the operational levels of government in the growing mega-cities is important for achieving sustainable development as many of the decisions influencing sustainable outcomes are made at this level. In China, which is divided administratively into 23 provinces, five autonomous regions and four municipalities (the cities of Beijing, Tianjin, Shanghai and Chongqing), each divisional government is appointed by, and responsible to, the central government. Each municipality, province and autonomous region is further subdivided. The subdivisions then have their own governments that are appointed by, and are responsible to, the respective higher level governments. To implement sustainable development, the goals, policies, directives and broad laws are all established by the central government. Then it is the responsibility of the provinces, autonomous regions and municipalities to implement them.

* Dr Mark Diesendorf is Senior Lecturer at UNSW's Institute of Environmental Studies, Director of Sustainability Centre Pty Ltd, Honorary Professor in Geosciences at the University of Sydney, Adjunct Professor of Sustainability Policy at Murdoch University, and vice-president of the Australia New Zealand Society for Ecological Economics.

China is planning for its environmental protection sector to grow at 15 per cent per annum over the first five years of the 21st century. To achieve this, China has strengthened environmental legislation and is investing the equivalent of US$12 billion between 1998 and 2007. The reduction in air pollution in Beijing since 2000 has been spectacular and there can be no doubt that preparations for the Beijing 2008 Olympics have driven this action in part. However, environmental improvement is also motivated by the desire to modernize industry and make it more efficient, and to create better living and working conditions by reducing pollution. Environmental improvements are being planned for much of China. The principal barrier is funding. China's future pathway could determine the success or failure of global sustainable development. If, in the future, China seeks a 'standard of living' (i.e. a level of wastage and environmental destruction) equivalent to that of the average Australian or American in 2004, then it is unlikely that human society has much of a future on Planet Earth. If, through excess demand for water, China becomes an importer of staple foods, then world food prices will increase and so will hunger in many poor countries.

At present, the US has the world's largest 'ecological footprint' and greenhouse gas emissions. In 2001 US President George W. Bush announced that he would not sign the Kyoto Protocol to begin the process of reducing emissions, because developing countries such as China were not part of the process. About the same time, it was revealed by a US government agency that China's emissions had been declining every year since 1997, despite very high rates of economic growth. As this material was being written, China announced that it would ratify the Kyoto Protocol. Meanwhile, US and Australian emissions continue to climb steeply. Not only is sustainable development official government policy in China, but it is also being implemented in some regions at a pace that far outstrips anything seen in Australia. In 2001 Shanghai announced that it would build the first commercial very fast train line based upon magnetic levitation, which is cutting edge German technology. The Maglev will connect the new Pudong international airport to the city's rapidly growing subway system, a distance of 30km. In 2003 the train commenced operation as a tourist experience and in 2004 it will run a frequent service. Furthermore, Shanghai, Beijing, Shenzen, Qingdao and Chengdu are building or planning new underground railway lines and in some cases light rail lines at ground level.

The transformation of Beijing, Qingdao and Nanjing is driven in part by China's goal of achieving a Green Olympics in 2008, thus emulating the Sydney 2000 Olympics. However, the determination to achieve sustainable development in Shanghai, which is not an Olympic city, cannot be explained in this way. In the city's urban planning exhibition, which attracts thousands of visitors each day, it is stated that Shanghai wants to become one of the world's leading commercial cities in the 21st century. To do this, one of the displays explains, Shanghai must clean up the air and the river. There is a strong recognition that sustainable development is good for business, tourism and citizens. The Chinese Government's investment of US$12 billion over the period 1998 to 2007, is not only being spent in Beijing. Cities in China are closing their most polluting factories and moving others away from residential and commercial areas. They are encouraging the modernization of industry, a programme that has, among other things, produced steady improvements in the efficiency of energy use over the past decade. Although coal is a major energy source in China, as it is in Australia, residential coal burning is gradually being replaced by the less-polluting natural gas for domestic heating and hot water in some cities. Recently a contract was signed to sell a huge quantity of natural gas from Australia's North-West Shelf to China. While further assisting the reduction of coal-burning in China, this will also reduce Australia's options for using natural gas as a transitional fuel to a sustainable energy future. In China, subsidies to the production and use of fossil fuels have been largely removed. In this regard, Australia, the US, Russia and Germany still have much to learn. In Australia, over AU$6 billion in subsidies are directed annually to fossil fuels, dwarfing the funding of sustainable energy.

In the northern part of China, where there is a huge demand for water for agriculture and industry, the once-mighty Yellow River often ceases to flow. To grapple with this serious problem, many northern cities are starting to charge substantial prices for water and for releasing polluted wastewater into the environment. The new pricing systems will encourage China's economy to become much more efficient in its use of water. Once again, a country such as Australia, which wastes the major proportion of river water diverted to irrigation, has something to learn. With limited funds, the Chinese Government is trying to redress the economic disparities between the east and west of the country. However, current economic restructuring is throwing millions of people out of work all over the country, thus increasing the gap between the rich and poor. Without a PAYE tax system, it may be impossible to create a national social security system, and so social sustainability faces difficulties over the foreseeable future.

China's commitment to ecologically sustainable development offers business opportunities to Australia and the rest of the world. 2002 included a visit to an innovative, environmentally sound, paint factory which has just commenced production in the small city of Yantai in north-east China. World Wide Paints is a joint venture between Chinese manufacturing skills and Australian research and development (R&D) expertise. Its manufacturing process produces essentially no liquid, solid or gaseous wastes, apart from a modest level of greenhouse gas emissions arising from energy use. Furthermore, the paints produced at Yantai contain extremely low levels of volatile organic compounds (VOCs), chemicals which are both toxic and carcinogenic. Most ordinary paints contain much higher levels. Managing Director, Richard Bell, says that his next step will be to eliminate VOCs entirely from all the company's indoor paints. Other environmentally sound joint ventures between Australia and China have been established in solar hot water and architecture. Australia's or any country's research and development expertise and China's large market offer mutual benefits. The areas of priority are wastewater management, efficient use of water, air pollution control, solid waste management, restoration of land damaged by erosion and desertification, efficient energy use and, in the more remote areas, renewable sources of energy.

If we consider Australia as a case study, potential inhibitors of further opportunities for 'green' trade and joint ventures between Australia and China are:

- A lack of understanding by Australians of the Chinese way of doing business. However, there are a number of cross-cultural advisers and facilitators who can assist.
- Inadequate marketing of Australian products in China.
- The high prices of Australian-made products that are exported to China. These can be reduced by manufacturing at least part of the product in China.
- Shortage of investment capital in China. An Australian company that brings its own finance to China has a much higher probability of success.
- Concerns about protection of intellectual property. Since China joined the World Trade Organisation, it has begun to strengthen its laws to protect Intellectual Property and its enforcement process. However, in the interim, some Australian companies prefer to use British or Australian law for contracts.
- Cost of building business links with China. This can be greatly reduced by seeking a cross-cultural facilitator who markets a product as part of a group of mutually compatible green products. From experience, Austrade, the Australian Government's export promotion, support and advisory department, appears to be doing an excellent job in China.
- The impact upon China of advertising and mass media promoting the 'consumption society', western style.

There is much then that any country can do to assist the many wise minds in China who have the potential to chart a new course and leapfrog the traditional Western development paths. There is much knowledge that can be shared. This section outlines some of the emerging technologies, often from the West, that can assist. But equally there is much the West can learn from the East. The challenge of genuinely achieving sustainable cities is so great that it is important that knowledge in this area is shared widely.

Cities can make significant progress if its citizens align their consumption with realistic needs, produce more of their own food and energy, design efficient transport systems and put much more of their waste to use.[6] The transition to sustainable cities requires a shift to a sustainable built environment and infrastructure with sound urban, social, economic and environmental planning and governance. We will cover these issues in depth in the rest of this section. But the transition to sustainable cities actually requires a re-thinking of the urban–rural relationship at a fundamental level. Cities depend of the rural sector for food, energy and water – in effect, most of its resources. This is leading to a new approach that comes from the East, from India, called RUrbanism.

> 'RUrbanism' is the sustainable integration of rural and urban communities. It is a sophisticated new set of design principles and practices governing land use, energy, transportation, governance, and all aspects of economic, ecological, and social development for a major city. Most importantly, it is a new framework for thinking about how to put an existing city onto a pathway toward genuine sustainability – particularly a city in the developing world, but the framework could apply in many other urban/rural contexts.

As described by Alan AtKisson, Board of Advisors, Goa 2100 Project

It was one of many exciting insights that arose out of the significant award-winning work of the Indian Goa 2100 Project team. Alan AtKisson reports on this remarkable work.

The Goa 2100 Project: a breakthrough project from India

Alan AtKisson

EDITORS' NOTE: This part has been contributed by Alan AtKisson,[7] adapted from project documents produced by the Goa 2100 Team including Aromar Revi, Rahul Mehrotra, Sanjay Prakash and GK Bhat. Speaking of the project Alan AtKisson said 'Goa 2100 is truly a breakthrough project, with many design features and analytical elements that must be studied closely to be understood and appreciated. I should note that I served on the project's Board of Advisors, reviewed some of their technical work, and assisted with the writing and editing of their final presentation to the Jury at the World Gas Convention. However, my role in the project was very small, and I performed these services voluntarily, as did nearly all of the members of the design team as well, who deserve to go far with this work. Goa 2100 marks that rare coming together of enormous professional competence and creativity with the passion to make a positive difference, the very definition of a labour of love.'

In the year 2000, the International Gas Union (IGU) boldly decided to 'explore the future of cities and urban communities in the next one hundred years.' The IGU commissioned a multi-million dollar international competition on Sustainable Urban Systems Design

(SUSD), with winners to be decided at the World Gas Congress 2003, in Tokyo. Competitors were instructed to:

- develop a clear vision of sustainable cities;
- provide process proposals for the transformation of existing cities into sustainable cities over a period of a century; and
- recommend how energy systems (and gas) could contribute to urban sustainability.

Ten Finalists were chosen from among 60 national teams, and the Finalist projects were awarded approximately US$75,000 each to further develop their design proposals and participate in international meetings during the course of two years. A blue-ribbon international jury of seven well-recognized experts and sustainability leaders was assembled to guide the process and review the proposals, culminating with a presentation in Tokyo and the awarding of prizes. Goa 2100's award, (one of three Special Jury Awards, with the overall winner being Vancouver, Canada), was earned on the basis of the extraordinary creativity and intellectual rigour of the model. The prize was earned despite the fact that the Indian team had far fewer resources than other teams. For example, the US entry had a budget of US$5 million, raised from a variety of sources, while the Indian team was limited to the original US$75,000 grant from the competition organizers, and the 'sweat equity' of the team members. The team behind Goa 2100 and the RUrbanism design framework was pulled together from some of India's most innovative design and consulting firms, with experience all over the country, and supported by a network of volunteer international advisers. The team chose the small state of Goa, a former Portuguese colony on India's west coast, because of its already good quality of life and relatively high levels of human development. The city of Panjim also reflects many of the common challenges faced by India's growing cities, whilst also having the resources, governance culture, and institutional base that make sustainability transition a clear possibility.

The era of 'RUrbanism'

The term 'RUrbanism' was introduced by the designers of Goa 2100, and the project is a model of RUrbanism in practice. It introduces a wide array of new design concepts and analytical tools to support sustainability planning and a transition to sustainability.

But the applications of RUrbansim, and the tools developed for Goa 2100, are not limited to the cities of India or to the developing world. Many cities around the world, at all levels of relative economic development, are facing the challenge of better integration between growing urban centres and the often distressed rural communities that support them with food and natural resources. And all cities are facing the extraordinary challenge of transition; of moving from today's unsustainable land use and infrastructure patterns to new patterns that will be both viable and elegantly liveable in the long run. Goa 2100's tools, and the RUrbanism design framework, offer cities a vision of how serious transformation can happen, in everything from urban form, to resource flows, to the mix of paid work and unpaid community engagement that comprise a vital community. It also offers powerful, quantitative methods for planning such a transition, from finding the optimal size and shape of built infrastructure to financing the process of rebuilding over several decades. This part describes the basic methodology of the Goa 2100 project, and provides examples of how the method was applied. Two caveats should be noted at the outset:

1   At time of writing (November 2003), the project design team was beginning discussions with the Government of Goa about how to take Goa 2100 from prize-winning visionary model to real application, and the project designers expect this will result in far-reaching changes to the model itself.

2   This part can only touch on general features of the Goa 2100 model, which includes extensive quantitative analysis. The interested reader is referred to the project designers to explore the model in more detail.

Foundation: comprehensive data-gathering and benchmarking

The team began by collecting a large amount of demographic, socio-economic, planning, natural resource, economic, energy, transportation and institutional data. They consulted with leading Goan citizens, made field visits to rural settlements in the surrounding Mandovi basin, and inspected nature reserves, forests, industrial and commercial locations, and various institutions to get a first hand feel of the local culture and challenges. Then they mapped Greater Panjim in detail, using satellite and remotely sensed data, along with 'ground-truthing' using global positioning satellite technology (GPS). People were sent out on motorcycles and mini-vans with hand-held GPS systems to develop geographic information systems (GIS) maps. The result was a complete topographical and land use model for the area, probably the first of its kind for the region. (None of the other international teams had to do this part of the process, because pre-existing digital map databases were available to them.) Based on this mapping data, the team forecast long-range trends for the Mandovi basin including:

- future land use challenges;
- the potential carrying capacity and 'ecological footprint' of existing urban systems;
- economic, development and poverty related challenges;
- energy, transportation and water resource constraints and opportunities;
- environment and climate change related challenges;
- heritage and conservation potential;
- cultural and institutional capacity.

The team considered these trends in relation to the South Asian cultural context and the global 'state of the art' regarding sustainability planning. They reviewed a wide variety of sources, including the IPCC's (Intergovernmental Panel on Climate Change) long-term climate change scenarios, the results of the Global Scenarios Group, various sustainability reporting and indicator systems, and more. They found most of the global studies to be lacking critical regional variables, or to have built-in assumptions that were contrary to key operational dynamics in South Asia generally and Goa particularly. This finding would strongly influence the development of their model, as would a finding that there were large gaps in international practice when it came to the design of sustainable infrastructure in the urban context. The Goa 2100 team realized they would simply have to invent a great deal of new methodology.

Intensive quantitative analysis

To fill one of the gaps in international best practice, the group undertook a detailed study of resource and security needs for a set of ten settlement types of varying densities in Goa and adjacent regions. This empirical study of built form and settlement structure enabled the group to create new quantitative models, including a 'Resource Security Index' for water and energy needs (see Figure 16.2). They performed detailed sensitivity analyses, and found that there were optimal values for the density and height of buildings in Panjim; values where water and energy were most efficiently and securely provided.

This was one of the most important insights of the project, as it enabled planning decisions to be framed around optimal densities of 150–300 persons per hectare: the most efficient and secure densities for providing water and energy to city residents. At those densities, major land use changes were possible, changes that would support the regeneration of the surrounding landscape and the lowering of urban ecological

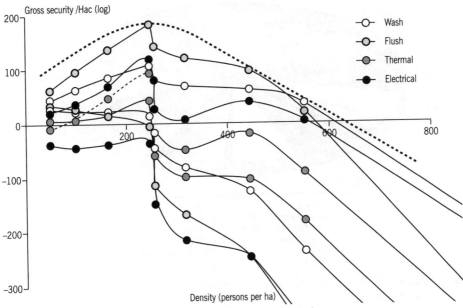

Figure 16.2 *Resource Security Index*

footprints. Goa could essentially be condensed, almost back to its scale during medieval times, without resorting to high-rise, resource-intensive development. When it came to the buildings themselves, the group extended the design principles of Christopher Alexander[8] using integrated life cycle analysis and other methods. A new set of principles for sustainable infrastructure design was developed for the static (long-lasting) and dynamic (fast-changing) elements of the city. The resulting design 'vocabulary' for the project involved a major reliance on organic materials and recyclable organic materials, using advanced biotechnology and nanotechnology (both existing technologies, and technologies expected to be developed in the decades ahead). This made possible a rebuilding plan that envisions the use of a large proportion of local materials to produce high-efficiency systems with high structural integrity; systems that were modular, adaptable, and ultimately recyclable.

One of most innovative features of the Goa 2100 project was its analysis of the entire 'temporal economy' of the city and region. Using comparative time-use studies from around the world, and adapting assumptions to the South Asian context, the team modelled the time-use of Greater Panjim and created a 'Time-use Budget' for both the present day's citizens, and for the citizens of a post-transition, sustainable Panjim, 100 years from now based on an estimated 2.7 billion person hours per year, as shown in Figure 16.3.

This analysis led to a key discovery: that time should be considered as an additional resource when considering the financing of a transition. It also calls attention to the fact that how people spend their time is a key element of both their quality of life, and the sustainability of a society. The Goa 2100 model – which allows for more than adequate personal, leisure, household and community time, in addition to the needs of work, childcare, education and many other factors – appears to be the first sustainability analysis of the time-use of an entire city. The intensive quantitative analysis of Panjim's transition to sustainability continued to stretch the boundaries of what was possible given existing data and basic spreadsheet technology, and along the way, the group stretched the capabilities of Microsoft Excel to its limits. They modelled demographic,

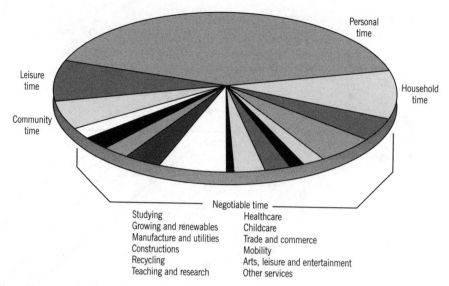

Studying
Growing and renewables
Manufacture and utilities
Constructions
Recycling
Teaching and research

Healthcare
Childcare
Trade and commerce
Mobility
Arts, leisure and entertainment
Other services

Note: the sectors for 'Negotiable time' are in order reading from 'Studying' on the right to 'Other services' on the left.

Figure 16.3 *Greater Panjim time-use budget* (2100)

economic and technological change processes. They analysed the succession process of urban land consolidation, forest regeneration, and the interpenetration of productive rural lands with urban structures. They incorporated hundreds of different factors, from technological advances and India's general plans for industrial development to finding the right energy mix (wind, natural gas and clean coal, with hydrogen and the electricity grid as energy carriers) that met the conditions of Goa and the need to stay within the sustainability boundaries for carbon dioxide emissions.

When it came to financing the project, they integrated traditional public and private capital investment schemes with the time-use modelling described earlier, and the breakthrough accounting concept of 'Lifetimes', that is, translating the available time in a human society to its imputed economic value, and thereby cross-linking economic, social and environmental accounting systems. They categorized different kinds of time-use by age, livelihood and uses of time that were non-negotiable (e.g., sleep), partially negotiable (e.g., level of educational training) and fully negotiable (e.g., leisure). They considered the community engagement and governance needs for managing a sustainability transition, much of which is not formally paid for in the market economy, but all of which adds 'economic value' to the process that is generally unaccounted for. By combining the time-and-money accounting of the costs of transition, they firmly established that a full transition to sustainability was both possible, and affordable. In their final estimates, they discovered that an investment of only US$60 million per year, coupled with the time investments of citizens from many different sectors (paid and unpaid) could accomplish the transition in just 30 years, much faster than the 100-year time period that the rules of the competition had stipulated, and at far lower levels of financial investment than most would expect.

The group calculated that this system of RUrban redevelopment, if adapted to develop a network of cities and linked urban areas along India's western coast, could support over 120 million people sustainably, providing realistic alternatives to mega-cities like Mumbai. The team had originally started with the city of Mumbai with a population of over 18 million, but abandoned the exercise after four months, when they

Table 16.1 *Design principles for Goa* 2100

Three goals for the sustainability transition	1 Sufficiency and equity: well-being of all people, communities and ecosystems 2 Efficiency: minimal throughput of matter–energy–information 3 Sustainability: least impact on nature, society and future generations
Seven organizing principles for sustainability	1 Satisfying the basic human needs of all people and providing them an equal opportunity to realize their human potential 2 Material needs should be met materially and non-material needs non-materially 3 Renewable resources should not be used faster than their regeneration rates 4 Non-renewable resources should not be used faster than their substitution rates by renewable resources 5 Pollution and waste should not be produced faster than the rate of absorption, recycling or transformation 6 The Precautionary Principle should be applied where the 'response' time is potentially less than the 'respite' time 7 'Free-energy' and resources should be available to enable redundancy, resilience and reproduction
Five strategies for land use management	1 Enable a long-term ecological succession from forest to cropland to city to forest 2 Design the landscape first; situate the city in the interstitial niches 3 Land use transitions governed by the demand for ecosystem services, resource potential, natural ecological succession and contiguity 4 Identify static and dynamic elements in the city, design the former, and provide a dynamic vocabulary for the latter to co-evolve with the landscape 5 Devolve governance and taxation to the lowest viable level
Six tactics to manage physical stocks and flows	1 Use less with Factor 4 technologies for supply and social limits of sufficiency and equity on demand 2 Grow your own, tapping harvestable yields as autonomously as possible 3 Build two-way networks for security: every consumer is also a producer 4 Store a lot because renewable resource yields are often diurnal and seasonal 5 Transport less over shorter distances using least life cycle cost technologies 6 Exchange using intelligent wireless networks to enable real-time trade and delivery of goods
A dynamic fractal morphology	1 Cellular structure: nuclei, cores, spines and skins 2 Hierarchical networks adapting to topography 3 Optimal densities, settlement structure and heights enabling security 4 Contiguous and hyperlinked with interpenetration of living net 5 Dynamic consolidation and nucleation around fractal boundaries and surfaces

realized that such large centres cannot make the transition to sustainability without radical surgery and deconstruction.

Envisioning RUrbanism

This extensive exercise in quantitative analysis and modelling was the foundation for the visionary re-imagining of Panjim, following the newly framed principles of RUrbanism. These were defined by the design team in terms of three 'overall goals'; seven 'organizing principles for sustainability'; five 'strategies for land use management'; six 'tactics to manage physical stocks and flows'; and a set of descriptions for the urban form that they grouped under the heading, 'A Dynamic Fractal Morphology'.

The goals, principles, strategies and tactics both grew out of, and helped to frame, the quantitative analyses that underlay the model, and these are critical to the sustainability and feasibility of the project. Concepts familiar to many in sustainability – from 'Factor 4' efficiencies to the 'Precautionary Principle' in implementing new technologies – are fully integrated. But perhaps the most novel and exciting element of the model is its 'dynamic fractal morphology'; in a few words, how the city looks. The design takes life itself, living biological systems, as its basic starting point. The city is re-imagined as an organism, with cells, skeletal structures, circulatory systems, and skin as the metaphors and models for the buildings, neighbourhoods, transportation systems, and the meeting points between city and rural or natural spaces. Just as, say, the gills of a fish allow for the maximum meeting of surface area between the fish's circulatory system and the oxygen-rich water, so does the spine-and-filament structure of post-transition Panjim make possible the complete interpenetration of urban settlement and rural land. Urban and rural meet each other in many small pockets, where dwellings jut out, and rural land juts in (see Figure 16.4).

One can imagine nearly everyone looking out of their windows onto rice paddies and vegetable gardens, and beyond to forested and natural resource lands. The boundaries between city and country remain clear, and yet country is much closer to city, and their interdependence is plainly visible to all, and indeed experienced by them daily. The spines allow for some interpenetration of green space with urban form as well, as the 'vertebra' of urban clusters are both linked together and separated by natural or agricultural patches. Some structures are underground, some above it, but nothing is higher than six stories, making the scale quite human, and meeting the conditions for optimal resource efficiency and security as previously highlighted. Water is collected for re-use everywhere, and off every surface where rain falls. The staple diet of fish, rice, and curry is largely produced within the sight of the city. Meanwhile, the buildings, infrastructure and transport systems are a mixture of high- and low-tech; bicycles, rickshaws, fuel-cell vehicles, light rail and fuel-cell ferries coexist peacefully, meeting different needs appropriately, with an average point-to-point transfer time of only 20 minutes across this condensed RUrban landscape. Energy comes from a mix of highly efficient, low-emission sources; the materials are nearly all drawn from regional sources and easy to recycle or re-use. Culture and dress are adjusted to climate, rather than the other way around, and the architecture preserves the best of Goa's mixed cultural heritage, while shaping the rebuilding of less efficient or attractive structures along futurist and aesthetically appealing lines.

In sum, RUrbanism involves transforming the city into a symbiotic partner with both nature and rural culture, and a net producer of resources and value, rather than a parasitic consumer. This fundamental feature of RUrbanism was particularly appreciated by many Judges on the international Jury. 'I like the proposal of India, especially the interrelation between urban areas ... with rural ones' noted Cassio Taniguchi, Mayor of Curitiba, Brazil (a city widely acknowledged as a world leader in sustainable design). And Professor Ernst Ulrich von Weizsäcker, noted German expert and co-author of the book

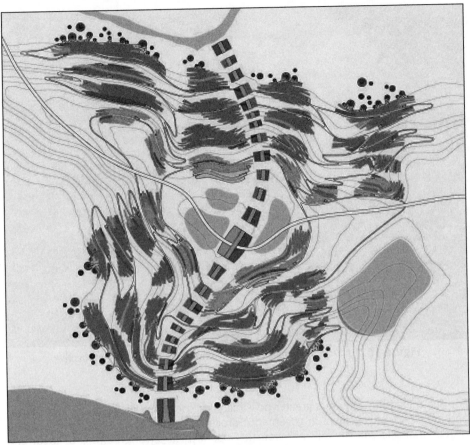

Figure 16.4 *Dynamic fractal morphology: nucleus land uses*

Factor Four, commented that 'there was one expression [from the Goa 2100 presentation] which impressed me a great deal: that the city should not colonize the rest of the world. This is something most memorable from the entire competition.'

The implementation of a dream

How would such a transition happen, in real-world terms? The financing questions have already been addressed; the major strategic challenges are therefore cultural and political. Part of addressing this challenge, design team members believe, involves placing this vision for Goa right in the heart of India's overall vision for its future, as a highly developed society where traditional farming and advanced technologies are both integral to future economic self-sufficiency and indeed global leadership. A sustainable Goa is a secure and economically dynamic Goa, with the city of Panjim – now a site of a proposed export centre for wind-turbines and advanced biotechnology and materials, along with a world class music conservatory and a world heritage site – modelling the mixture of prosperity and cultural integrity that the country imagines for itself. But perhaps the most important challenge that Goa 2100 identified was the transformation of current institutions and systems of governance. The sustainability transition clearly requires changes to values and ethics: sufficiency, equity, and the ethic of using a minimal throughput of matter, energy and information with the least impact on nature, society and future generations. These were identified as key goals for the project, and they require changes in how a society like Goa governs itself.

Figure 16.5 *A receding Gandhian dream: convergence of quality of life between rural and urban areas*

For one thing, they require a greater possibility for social and life style transformation, and more civic engagement in governance processes generally. The beginning of these transformations can already be seen in Goa, with its strong culture of local and community-based governance and a moderately open government. The Goa 2100 design team projected that 'a high quality of life, built around local communities and institutions of governance, can help reduce consumerism and physical flows, creating a vibrant urban culture within a dense yet dispersed city.' However, they also acknowledged that this is the least developed area of the Goa 2100 proposal, and an area that would require considerable thought and debate, as the project made steps from vision towards reality. But the effort to think through the real-world implementation challenges would clearly be well worth it. As noted by the design team: 'This [project] demonstrated that by 2050, up to 120 million Indians could live on the western coast meeting their basic needs without endangering the resource base or biodiversity of the region. This has special meaning in India (which would still have half its population living in rural areas in 2050) where a convergence of quality of life between rural and urban areas has been seen as a receding Gandhian dream' (see Figure 16.5).

A breakthrough project in urban planning
Goa 2100 is an important breakthrough in urban planning for at least two reasons:

1   The concept of RUrbanism introduced by the project design team has the potential to reshape the development of cities, especially in the case of small to mid-size cities that are expected to grow enormously over the next 50 years. It offers a new framework for thinking about the relationship between cities and their surrounding lands, and for building cities to make that relationship far more sustainable, as well as more beautiful.

2   Many of the analytic tools developed by the design team are both new and of immense potential utility. They include new ways of accounting for the time economy in the context of transition planning; analysing the optimal scale and form to ensure maximum resource efficiency and security, and many other relatively simple spreadsheet models that make possible a wide variety of scenario analyses, using different demographic and technological assumptions. These need to be further developed and tried in a variety of other urban planning contexts, but they are clearly a major step forward.

This author, at least, hopes that the team involved in Goa 2100 will have the opportunity to do just that, and to see elements of their remarkable vision for Goa and Greater Panjim to become a reality not just in Goa, but in many locations around the world.

CHAPTER 17

PROFITABLE GREENHOUSE SOLUTIONS

Michael H. Smith and Alan Pears

EDITORS' NOTE: The development of this chapter has been led by co-editor Mike Smith, TNEP Secretariat member, with support from mentor Adjunct Professor Alan Pears, a senior lecturer at the Faculty of the Constructed Environment in the RMIT School of Social Science Planning. Alan was named on Anzac Day as a recipient of the Centenary Medal, one of the nation's highest honours awarded for achievements or contributions at the time of the centenary of federation, for outstanding service to public policy on climate change and the environment.

Energy systems: drivers for change

Energy is big business. The electricity industry is one of the highest investment sectors in the world. A quarter of the world's development aid goes into building energy systems and every nation's energy system imposes significant costs on government and ratepayers directly and indirectly. Since 1970, world commercial energy consumption has grown at an average annual rate of 2.5 per cent. Interest in how we meet our energy needs is increasing for many reasons. All economies are becoming increasingly reliant on energy and we are reminded of this on days of extreme temperature when energy utilities around the world are stretched close to capacity. As we described in Section 1, if nations had made good energy efficient buildings, homes and heating and cooling equipment a greater priority, the taxpayer would be much better off. This is because the entire system is presently designed to meet these peaks and then carries a redundancy during the predominant non-peak periods. Peak energy demand is often subsidized due to limitations of metering and political sensitivities: for example a recent study undertaken in Sydney, Australia, estimated the real cost of supplying summer peak electricity demand at more than AU$3.80/kilowatt-hour, compared with a price of 12 cents. Greater energy efficiency would have avoided the need to build extra supply capacity and overall reduced costs to taxpayers.

Current interest in alternatives to oil is influenced by the fact that nations are increasingly dependent on oil from politically unstable regions of the globe. Protecting these oil interests is becoming increasingly expensive. Many believe we are coming to the end of the oil age. In The Economist,[1] Sheikh Zaki Yamani, a Saudi Arabian who served as his country's oil minister three decades ago stated: 'the Stone Age did not end for lack of stone, and the oil age will end long before the world runs out of oil.' *The Economist* goes on to write: 'he made this prediction because he believes that something has fundamentally changed since the first oil shock. Finally technological advances offer a way for economies, especially those in the developed world to diversify their supplies of energy and reduce their demand for petroleum, thus loosening the grip of oil and the countries that produce it. Hydrogen fuel cells, very high efficiency equipment and other ways of storing and distributing energy are no longer a distant dream but a foreseeable reality ... and with the right policies it can be made both possible and economically advantageous.'

Rocky Mountain Institute, who have undertaken a great deal of work in this area writes: 'The chairs of eight major oil and car companies have said the world is entering the oil endgame and the start of the Hydrogen Era. Royal Dutch/Shell's planning scenarios in 2001 envisaged a radical, China-led leapfrog to hydrogen (already underway): hydrogen would fuel a fourth of the vehicle fleet in the industrialized countries by 2025, when world oil use, stagnant meanwhile, would start to fall. President Bush's 2003 State of the Union message emphasized the commitment he'd announced a year earlier to develop hydrogen-fuel-cell cars.'[2]

Vulnerabilities in the energy system

Another area of interest and driver for change comes from the fact that modern OECD (Organisation for Economic Co-operation and Development) energy systems have vulnerable systems architecture. The modern grid is complex, sometimes beyond full understanding, requiring complex control and synchronism requirements that often only a few engineers truly understand in its entirety. If we had our time over again and were given the opportunity to re-design our energy systems from scratch, it is clear that we would not design them this way. Given the opportunity, we would design our energy systems to be much safer, more robust and resilient. Complicating factors include the fact that our current energy system and its dependence on oil and nuclear energy means that we have hazardous fuels, often in or near cities. If the electricity grid fails, then other systems such as gas grids, which depend on electricity, will also fail. The system is constantly weakened by the retirement of key staff who helped build these vast modern grids. But the most topical area where our highly centralized energy systems are vulnerable is sabotage.

A small group of people changed the world forever on 11 September 2001. The present highly centralized energy (power stations with usually only a few transmission lines, oil pipelines) and water supplies (large dams with usually only a couple of pipelines to major cities) present targets that are highly vulnerable to attack. These centralized energy and water systems are often located far from the end user, requiring long transmission lines or pipelines for water. The length of these transmission lines and pipelines make it prohibitively expensive to police them. Forty years ago the US Defense Electric Power Administration warned: 'main transmission lines are extremely difficult to protect against sabotage as they are widespread over each state and traverse remote, rugged and unsettled areas for thousands of miles.'[3] Concerned about these issues in the wake of the OPEC oil crisis of the early 1970s, the Pentagon commissioned a major study to assess the vulnerabilities and weaknesses of the US energy system. The final report – authored by Amory Lovins and Hunter Lovins, released on 13 November 1981 by the Federal Emergency Management Agency, and subsequently published as the book *Brittle Power*[4] – showed that 'the energy system of the US was vulnerable to terrorist threats, blackouts, technology breakdowns and disrepair, natural disasters and energy shortages'. It demonstrated that domestic energy infra-structure is often fatally vulnerable to disruption (by accident or malice) and it showed that 'A resilient energy system is feasible, costs less, works better, is slowly happening in the market, but is inhibited by current US energy policy'.

Alexandra de Blas, ABC award-winning journalist in Australia, interviewed Jeremy Leggett, Chief Executive of Solar Century London shortly after 11 September 2001 and asked 'is the war against terrorism and heightened awareness of national security, actually having a noticeable impact on thinking about renewable energy?' Leggett replied, 'Yes, since the horrific events of September 11th, we've been called up by a number of people interested in the new world we live in where evidently terrorists can conceive of flying civilian laden jet airliners into nuclear power plants, or quite easily blowing up oil and gas pipelines that come from the frontier areas where these fossil fuels are going to have to come from. One of the inquiries has come from the armed services in the UK, interested in how quickly we could move to a world that was powered by renewable micro power, and where there are no nuclear power plants and no need for imports of oil and gas.' Countries like Israel that have smaller scale distributed energy supplies, such as solar hot water on roofs of 100,000s of houses, have invested in a wise technology that has delivered a decentralized robust system. In the 21st century we now have the enabling technologies to allow us to decentralize our energy and water sectors: that is, to make a higher percentage of them more resilient and less vulnerable to sabotage, accidental stoppage and other impacts on the system.

Making electrical resources the right size

There is a historic shift occurring in the energy sector towards encouraging energy efficiency and smaller scale distributed renewable energy networks, with complementary changes to regulatory frameworks; because it is profitable.

Globally, wind power generation capacity is growing at a faster rate than nuclear power ever did. Wind power is now cost competitive with coal in areas of high average wind speed. Hence, there is an opportunity for communities, business, energy utilities and government to work together to find a new way forward where everyone wins and

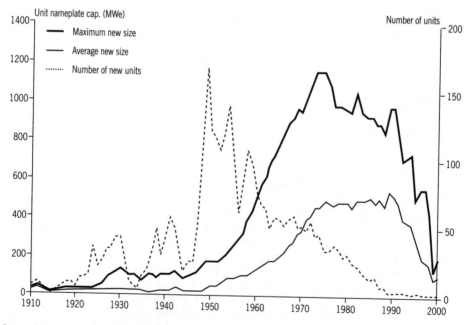

Source: RMI analysis from EIA (2000)

Figure 17.1 *Maximum and average sizes of new generation units (fossil-fuelled steam utilities, 5-year rolling average) by year of entry into service*

achieves greater profits. Such an opportunity, highlighted by Hunter Lovins on her recent tour to Australia, has been realized in Sacramento, California where the residents voted to shut down a 1000 MW nuclear power plant resulting in the power company losing roughly half of its capacity overnight. Traditionally, an energy utility would have simply invested in new supply and built a new coal fired power station. Instead the utility first invested in efficiency to help their customers use less energy but retain the same quality of life. They then invested in a wide range of alternative forms of small renewable distributed energy systems to learn how best to use the emerging technology. The result is that over ten years they have increased regional income by US$130 million. Had the plant kept running, energy prices (rates) were estimated to have increased by 80 per cent; instead, these investments have kept rates at the same level for a decade. A number of firms in Sacramento had stated that if rates increased that much they would have to leave the state. Hence, by keeping rates constant they were able to retain over 2000 jobs that would otherwise have left the state. In addition, since renewable energy and efficiency improvement are more labour intensive and less capital intensive, the strategy created 880 new jobs. Finally, the programme eliminated the utility's debt.

This is an example of a broader historic shift in the scale of electricity supply currently underway from 'big is always better' to the 'right size for the job'. This is the subject of the recently published, *Small is Profitable: The Hidden Economic Benefits of Making Electrical Resources the Right Size*[5] voted one of the three 'books of the year' for 2002 by *The Economist* magazine. In *Small is Profitable*, Amory Lovins et al describe this historic shift as follows, 'as one industry team stated in 1992, 'From the beginning of [the twentieth] century until the early 1970s demand grew, plants grew, and the vertically integrated utilities' costs declined. Looking back on the 1990s, it is now obvious that a reversal [in this trend] has actually occurred. In 1976 the concept of largely "distributed" or decentralized electricity production was heretical, in the 1990s, it became important, by 2000, it was the subject of cover stories in such leading publications as the *Wall Street Journal*, *The Economist*, and the *New York Times*, and by 2002, it was emerging as the winner in the marketplace.'

The change is exactly the sort of 'inflection point' described by Andrew Grove of Intel in his book, *Only the Paranoid Survive: How to Exploit the Crisis Points That Challenge Every Company and Career.*[6] Just as the critical mass of enabling technologies in IT has led to a remarkable shift in how we communicate over the last 30 years, examples such as the experience in Sacramento are showing that over the next 30 years we could see another similar wave of innovation in how societies meet their energy needs. *Small is Profitable* shows that there is now a critical mass of enabling innovations making integrated approaches to sustainable development in the energy sector economically viable. *Small is Profitable* shows that advances in energy efficiency improvement, demand management, renewable energy, co-generation, fuel cells, and new fuels like hydrogen are not simply a list of interesting options but 'a web of innovations that all reinforce each other.' It states, 'These developments form not simply a list of separate items, rather their effect is thus both individually important and collectively profound.' *Small is Profitable* describes 207 ways in which the size of 'electrical sources' (devices that make, save or store electricity) affects their economic value. It finds that properly considering the economic benefits of 'distributed' (decentralized) electricity sources typically raises their value by a large factor, often approximately tenfold, by improving system planning, utility construction and operation (especially of the grid), service quality, and by avoiding societal costs. Other drivers for distributed energy include changes to market incentives that require that energy utilities are systematically required to purchase renewable energy.

What Lovins et al are arguing is that we stand on the cusp of a wave of innovation in the energy sector. However, the book does more than that. In showing how utilities and firms in the energy sector can earn significant revenue through energy efficiency improvement, greater use of distributed energy systems and wise regulatory changes, it also shows how any nation over time can achieve deep cuts in greenhouse emissions. *Small is Profitable*, as the title suggests, is about how to improve the profits of energy companies and the well-being of nations overall. In doing so, however, it also shows how deep cuts to greenhouse gas emissions can be profitably achieved over the next 30–50 years. Hence, it is a key work in helping us to solve the human induced global warming problem and reduce the vulnerability of our energy systems in multiple ways.

Threat of climate change

Another major driver for change in the energy sector comes from the threat of climate change if we continue on our present path. As Sir John Maddox, ex-editor in chief of the premier science journal, *Nature*, states: 'There is no serious doubt that global warming will occur if the addition of greenhouse gases to the atmosphere continues unchecked. Moreover, the end point would be global catastrophe'.[7] Australia's Environment Minister, Dr Kemp, at the launch of *Climate Change: An Australian Guide to the Science and Potential Impacts*,[8] summed up the situation when he said that the question was no longer 'Will the Climate Change?', but rather 'How will it change?', followed by 'What can we collectively do to reduce the threat?' With the exception of a few climate sceptics and some industry groups, the majority of the world's scientific community, academies of science and governments now recognize that a continued increase in man-made greenhouse emissions will cause climate change. Of the last 100 years, eight of the warmest years on record have occurred in the last decade (see Figure 17.2).

Most of the energy we use contributes to greenhouse emissions and the costs of inaction will be significant for future generations.[9] Munich Re and UNEP forecast that climate change would cost the global economy US$300 billion per annum by 2050. However, studies and figures like this do not begin to communicate the potential tragic

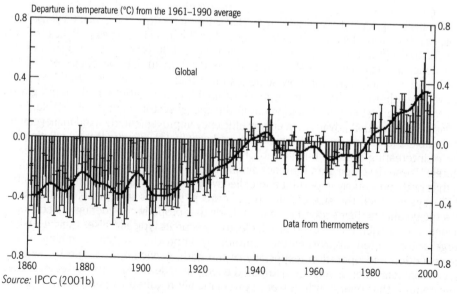

Departure in temperature (°C) from the 1961–1990 average

Source: IPCC (2001b)

Figure 17.2 *Trend in global temperature – IPCC 2001. Departures in temperature (°C) from the 1961 to 1990 average from 1880–2000*

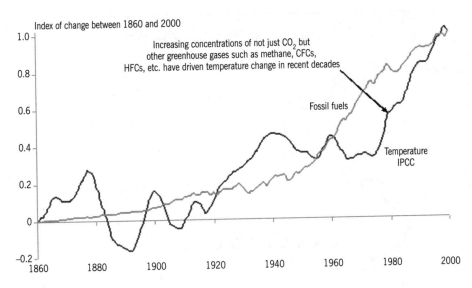

Index of change between 1860 and 2000

Source: Dr Alan Pears

Figure 17.3 *Comparison of trends in global fossil fuel use and global temperature (10 year rolling average), 1860–2000 – temperature change approx 0.76°C*

human dimension of the costs of global warming. The consequences of climate change are not simply environmental.

The human cost of climate instability

Norman Myers, of Oxford University, predicts that, based on the results from current climate models, climate change could increase the number of environmental refugees sixfold over the next 50 years to 150 million.[10] Myers states: 'In 1995, environmental refugees totalled at least 25 million people, compared with 27 million traditional refugees (people fleeing political oppression, religious persecution and ethnic troubles). The total number of environmental refugees could well double by the year 2010 and increase steadily for a good while thereafter as growing numbers of impoverished people press ever harder on overloaded environments. When global warming takes hold, there could be as many as 200 million people overtaken by sea-level rise and coastal flooding, by disruptions of monsoon systems and other rainfall regimes, and by droughts of unprecedented severity and duration.'[11]

A World Bank analysis shows that Bangladesh would be hardest hit, losing half of its rice production, the food staple of its 140 million people (see Figure 17.4). At current rice prices, this would cost Bangladesh US$3.2 billion.[12]

It is recognized that an island becomes 'lost' long before the water level covers the island: it is lost at the point where the rising water level enters the food chain rendering traditional crops, such as Babai or Taro, breadfruit and bananas inedible.[13] On the Pacific island of Tuvalu, increased salinity is forcing families to grow their root crops in metal buckets instead of in the ground.[14]

The consensus on the gravity of the situation stems from the fact that there is overwhelming scientific evidence that human-induced climate change is currently under way. This evidence has been extensively reviewed by over 4000 climate scientists worldwide who constitute the Intergovernmental Panel on Climate Change (IPCC). The basics of the climate science of the greenhouse effect are very simple. Greenhouse gases

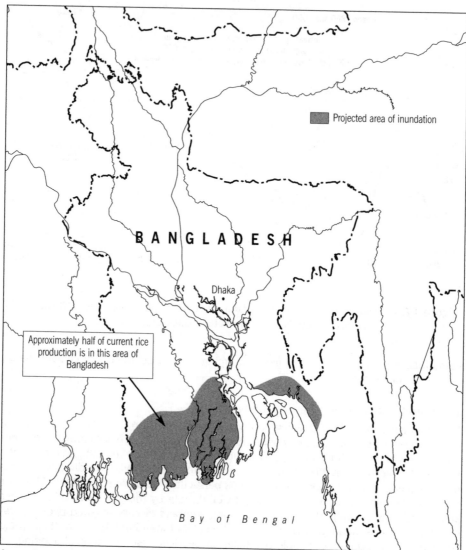

Projected area of inundation

B A N G L A D E S H

Dhaka

Approximately half of current rice production is in this area of Bangladesh

B a y   o f   B e n g a l

Source: Figure 2.4 from World Bank (2000, p100)

Figure 17.4 *A one metre rise in the sea level would cut Bangladesh's rice production approximately in half*

happen to absorb radiation at frequencies emitted by the Earth. They then re-emit radiation in all directions, so half of the absorbed radiation is returned to the Earth. So the Earth then receives more radiant energy – from the sun and from the greenhouse gases. Since it must move towards thermal equilibrium, its temperature must increase to increase its radiant heat transfer to space, to balance the extra heat it is receiving. Hence, these atmospheric gases act like a greenhouse. What is being debated is whether the increased concentration of these man-made greenhouse gases (largely the result of burning fossil fuels) is sufficient to cause temperature change. Climate change can also be brought about by natural phenomena.

As was demonstrated in Section 1 in Figure 2.3, there appear to be natural oscillations in the concentrations of these greenhouse gases in the atmosphere. Changes in volcanic action and the sun's level of activity have also been shown to influence climate change historically. Hence, the International Panel on Climate Change was established to investigate these complex issues and assess the scientific, technical and socio-economic information relevant for the understanding of whether there was a risk of human-induced climate change. They found that there is overwhelming evidence that man-made greenhouse gas emissions are causing global warming, a finding supported by recent studies showing that human-induced climate change is statistically significant.[15] Their findings have been corroborated by all of the academies of science globally, including the US National Academy of Sciences. In 2002, the Academies of Science in Australia wrote: 'Even with significant future global reductions of emissions it is expected that most of Australia will warm 0.4° to 2°C by 2030 and 1° to 6°C by 2070. These changes are likely to result in increased pressure on water resources, increased intensity of tropical storms, increased bushfire risk, damage to ecosystems and threats to human health.' Dr Colin Butler from ANU's National Centre for Epidemiology and Public Health writes: 'Climate change, at least in the next generation or two, is likely to adversely effect human health through at least three major pathways:

1   Increased extreme weather events (including intensified droughts, flooding and moderate sea level rise) that cause, and are predicted to increasingly cause, indirect damage to health and well-being via effects on food and economic security, or more directly via heat stress or (beneficially) less cold stress during warmer winters.
2   Changes in the distribution and possibly behaviour of disease-transmitting insects.
3   By interacting with other factors that affect ecosystems, such as invasive species, changed biodiversity, and new patterns of plant and animal disease.

In the more distant future, yet not so far away that it can be safely ignored, climate change may have even more drastic adverse effects on civilization. Three such risks are massive sea level rise from the collapse of the Greenland or Western Antarctic Ice Shelf;[16] runaway greenhouse gas accumulation from the failure of the terrestrial carbon sink (for example as forest ecosystems change from net sinks to net sources of carbon);[17] and a significant weakening of the oceanic 'conveyor belt' which warms Western Europe'[18] (Figure 17.5).

This 'global conveyer' is a massive current in the world's oceans and is largely responsible for the warming of both Northern Europe and the Eastern US, and for the UK's relatively temperate climate in comparison with Labrador, with which it shares latitude. The current is driven by a delicate balance of differential salinity levels and water temperatures in the world's oceans and receives no mechanical mixing. The current acts as a conveyor by drawing the warm water from the tropics north where, in the North Atlantic, it cools, increases in density, sinks and flows south. As a classic convection current, this sinking has the effect of drawing water from the south and in so doing perpetuates the cycle. A key factor in the behaviour of the current is the non-uniform salinity of the ocean. As the conveyor current flows north through sub-tropical high pressure zones, its salinity (and therefore density) increases due to a combination of reduced rainfall and increased evaporation. The resulting increase in density, combined with cooling resulting from proximity to the polar regions, leads to the massive 'sinking' of the current that occurs to the north of Iceland. Were this conveyor current to collapse, it would effectively turn off the heat, resulting in climate change across most of the Northern Hemisphere. The 'off switch' for the current is a warming of the earth's atmosphere. The theory assumes that as temperatures increase so does rainfall, runoff and the melting of the Arctic glaciers, all of which contribute increasing volumes of fresh water into the current. The resulting decreased salinity of the current in the North

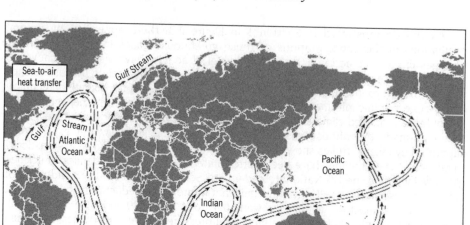

Source: IPCC (1995)

Figure 17.5 *The Gulf Stream is a part of the Atlantic conveyor that transports warm water past Northern Europe*

Atlantic will lower its density and therefore its tendency to sink. Consequently, the current loses it primary driving force and slows down.

The scenario outlined in the recently published Pentagon report discussing scenarios of Abrupt Climate Change is currently seen to have an extremely low probability of occurring in the next century, let alone this century. Some scientists argue that there is not the same amount of glacial ice as there was during past slow downs of the Atlantic current and so even if there were very signfiicant global warming a significant slowing down of the current is not possible. Canadian scientists Andrew Weaver of the University of Victoria and Claude Hillaire-Marcel of the Université de Quebec à Montreal tackled the subject in a *Perspectives* article entitled, 'Global Warming and the Next Ice Age'. The scientists' review of the literature concluded: 'It is certainly true that if the AMO [Atlantic Meriodonal Oscillation] were to become inactive, substantial short-term cooling would result in western Europe, especially during the winter. However, it is important to emphasize that not a single coupled model assessed by the 2001 IPCC Working Group I on Climate Change Science (4) predicted a collapse in the AMO during the 21st century. Even in those models where the AMO was found to weaken during the 21st century, there would still be warming over Europe due to the radiative forcing associated with increased levels of greenhouse gases. In light of the paleoclimate record and our understanding of the contemporary climate system, it is safe to say that global warming will not lead to the onset of a new ice age. These same records suggest that it is highly unlikely that global warming will lead to a widespread collapse of the AMO, despite the appealing possibility raised in two recent studies, although it is possible that deep convection in the Labrador Sea will cease. Such an event would have much more minor consequences on the climate downstream over Europe.' In the same issue, pioneering oceanographer Wallace Broecker dismisses the recent report rejected by the Pentagon that is predicated on a similar scenario. He comments in his letter, 'Exaggerated scenarios serve only to intensify the existing polarization over global warming.'

However, other scientists argue that more research is needed to better understand what did occur in the past and therefore better understand the risks for the future. A team at the Massachusetts Institute of Technology has discovered that for at least the last 1.5 million years, the Earth has undergone rapid and dramatic climate changes similar to those observed in ice cores from more recent times. 'Ten years ago, we had no idea that climate could change this quickly,' said Maureen E. Raymo, associate professor of Earth, Atmospheric and Planetary Sciences at MIT. Publishing their results in the 16 April issue of Nature, 1999,[19] Raymo and her colleagues at MIT and at Woods Hole Oceanographic Institute report that millennial-scale climate instabilities, swings of as much as 10° Celsius within a few decades, are not restricted to the large glacial periods of the last 700,000 years but existed much further back in time. 'Our results suggest that such millennial-scale climate instability may be a pervasive and long-term characteristic of Earth's climate, rather than just a feature of the strong glacial–interglacial cycles of the past 800,000 years,' the authors wrote. Raymo and her colleagues show that these climate changes are tied to changes in the conveyor-like circulation of ocean waters that deliver tropical heat to the northern Atlantic in surface currents while exporting salt-heavy deep waters cooled by Greenland's winds to the south.

Consequently, there is a need for greater research on these phenomena to better understand these processes and reduce the uncertainty about predictions. While the rapid climate change events of history have not been the result of man-made pollution, it was concluded in a US National Academy of Sciences report, released in 2000, that such abrupt events could be triggered by human activity.[20]

Hollywood's movie about the shutting down of the Atlantic conveyor *The Day After Tomorrow* in May 2004 at least starts with the scientist theorizing that it may take 100 or more years to see the current slow down and stop. From then on, by implying that the current could stop tomorrow and bring in a global ice age, the film becomes science fiction. That said, the movie has sparked significant media coverage of global warming issues and much debate. The UK Government's chief scientist, Sir David King, said *The Day After Tomorrow* will increase the public's awareness. But he added that it plays fast and loose with some of the science of climate change. 'I welcome the movie in the sense that it raises the profile of a critically important public debate about global warming and the need to persuade governments to take action now.' Sir David said. 'The science is bad, but perhaps it's an opportunity to crank up the dialogue on our role in climate change.' NASA research oceanographer William Patzert said of the premise that most people, including the film-makers, acknowledge that time had to be compressed to keep the audience's interest. When scientists who study climate refer to abrupt changes, they refer to decades, if not hundreds or thousands of years. 'Fox is not going to make a movie that goes on for 10,000 years,' Patzert said.

The real concern, as was outlined in Section 1, comes from the variety of ways human activities are altering nature and increasing stress on ecosystems. There are still real threats and risks of ecosystem collapse because climate change is coupled with other changes to the planet's ecosystems. If we continue to reduce the resilience of our ecosystems, either way they may not be able to cope with climate change this time. We are also no longer a nomadic species, rather our civilization is not easily moved, dismantled and rebuilt. Our infrastructure is not particularly flexible. Hence, the effect on civilization of rapid climate change would completely stretch societies' and nature's ability to cope and adapt. If we continue to destroy wilderness corridors, species will not be able to migrate to cope with climate change in the future as they did in the past. We honestly do not know whether such degraded ecosystems will be able to cope with rapid climate change, as never before has one species conducted such an experiment with the planet as we are doing today.

Therefore, the world's most authoritative body on climate change, the Intergovernmental Panel on Climate Change, has warned that the nations of the world will need to shift to a low-carbon future in order to avoid dangerous changes to the global climate. According to the IPCC, stabilizing concentrations at double pre-industrial levels will require deep cuts in annual global emissions, eventually by 60 per cent or more. In 2002, Dr Kemp, Australia's Environment Minister stated that, 'Some have talked about stabilizing global greenhouse gas concentrations in the atmosphere at broadly double pre-industrial levels by the end of the century as being consistent with temperature changes of 2°C or less, and those temperature changes in turn as being consistent with avoiding the most dangerous outcomes for humanity and nature... By the end of the 21st century, if we are effectively going to address the issue of global warming, we will need to see a global reduction in greenhouse gas emissions of between 50 and 60 per cent.'[21]

Greenhouse solutions that do not cost the earth

In the last five years, a large body of literature and reports has emerged to demonstrate that, even at today's prices and even assuming no new 'silver bullet' technologies, nations can viably achieve deep cuts of 60 per cent of greenhouse emissions over the next 50 years.[22] Obviously such significant decoupling of economic growth and carbon emissions will not happen overnight. However, if phased in over 50 years, the economic impacts do not impose significant costs on the economy; rather they can create more energy efficient businesses, less congested traffic in our cities and create new export opportunities for firms and nations that lead. Prime Minister Blair announced his government's intention to put the UK on track to reduce its emissions of CO_2 by 60 per cent by 2050. A detailed study by the UK's Department of Trade and Industry[23] concluded that the economic costs of these actions in the UK would be small, costing the UK about six months of GDP between now and 2050. And these calculations make no effort to tabulate the benefits of climate action, but these are believed to be substantial. In a more recent development, the UK announced its intention to have 10 per cent of the nation's electricity come from offshore wind by 2010. Noting that the UK is likely to face increasingly demanding carbon reduction targets, the study concludes that credible scenarios for 2050 can deliver a 60 per cent cut in CO_2 emissions (see Table 17.2).

Like the climate system itself, energy, transport and urban systems have great inertia. They take decades to change. This means that, in order to achieve deep cuts in emissions and avoid the worst effects of climate change, early planning and action is needed. European nations such as Sweden, France, Denmark and the Netherlands have made significant reduction commitments. Sweden has recently committed to a 50 per cent reduction by 2050 and has called for a European-wide target of 60 per cent by 2050. France has also taken a very aggressive position regarding its longer-term commitment, promising to reduce emissions by 75 per cent by 2050. Denmark, meanwhile, has renewed its commitment to a 21 per cent reductions target by 2010. Wind now generates 20 per cent of Denmark's electricity needs. In the Netherlands, policy-makers are developing a detailed 50-year plan for GHG (greenhouse gas) reductions. Bodies in the US have also done significant studies.[24]

The reason deep cuts to greenhouse emissions are possible is that in the past we have generally asked the wrong questions when we are developing energy policy. For example, policy debate often focuses on the cost per unit of energy generated at the power station or gas wellhead. The reality is that it is the total real cost of delivering energy services that matters. None of us want coal or oil. What we want is the services they provide. These energy services include a number of elements:

Table 17.1 *Relative costs of actions to meet emission reduction targets for a business that normally achieves 15 per cent pa rate of return on investment*

Option	Cost/tonne CO_2
Buy permits on market	AU$7 to AU$50 (or more)
Buy credits from plantations	AU$5 to AU$30
Geo-sequestration of CO_2 from coal-fired power stations	AU$52 to AU$156 (long term US target AU$27)
Buy Green Power at 3-6 c/kWh extra	AU$22 to AU$60
Cogeneration – hypothetical case at 1c/kWh more than grid power	AU$10 to AU$15
Cogeneration at 0.5 c/kWh less than grid power	–AU$3 to –AU$5
Renewable energy at 5c/kWh above grid price	
Renewable energy at 3/kWh above grid price	AU$22 to AU$30
Renewable energy at 2 c/kWh above grid price	AU$14 to AU$20
Renewable energy at 1c/kWh below grid price	–AU$7 to –AU$10
Energy efficiency – 1 year payback (c/f 15% pa return)[25]	–AU$32 (–AU$8 c/f 33% IRR)
Energy efficiency – 5 year payback (c/f 15% pa return)	–AU$4.50 (AU$8 c/f 33% IRR)

Source: Adapted from Pears (2000); cost of buying permits for, offsetting or avoiding emission of 1 tonne of CO_2 based on Hamilton et al (2001)

- The cost of energy consuming equipment is also a component of an energy service. Oversized equipment often incurs higher up-front costs as well as being less efficient when operating outside its optimum conditions.
- The total cost of energy equals the cost per unit multiplied by the number of units – so improving efficiency can offset higher prices. It is perfectly feasible to offset the possible higher unit costs of environmentally preferred energy (where they really do cost more) by using less of it. Indeed, many businesses and households are already doing this.
- The price of energy includes many subsidies, such as a failure to include a price for greenhouse gas emissions. There are numerous additional subsidies, worth billions of dollars, to fossil fuel use.[26] Peak energy demand is often subsidized due to limitations of metering and political sensitivities.
- The price of energy should include the cost of delivering it to the consumer. But the present energy market arrangements blur transmission and distribution costs, and fail to give full credit to local energy sources that reduce the need for investment in supply infrastructure.

So most debates about the relative generation cost of coal, gas or renewable energy miss most of the real point, and the real costs and benefits. There is now a new body of empiricism,[27] and government funded energy efficiency programmes and worldwide business practice, showing the multiple cost benefits and reduced risks for businesses pursuing energy efficiency strategies.[28] Even if climate change were not a concern, it is worth businesses pursuing energy efficiency for multiple benefits.[29] Energy efficiency is by far the most cost effective way to reduce greenhouse emissions (see Table 17.1).

Furthermore, when debating the potential of new energy solutions we compare emerging cottage industries and small-scale production solutions with mature technologies that have been built over the past century with massive community input, or what some might now call subsidies. When we look at the overall economics, there are even more arguments to rethink how we satisfy our energy requirements.

In June 1999, the Australian Prime Minister's Science, Engineering and Innovation Council, which draws together high powered business interests and eminent scientists, issued a report that urged the Australian Government to go from the defensive to an attacking position on climate change policy. It observed that 'Kyoto has created a new business environment in which new industries, markets and technologies can flourish', and urged the Australian Government to adopt policies, including emissions trading, that would see Australia capture at least 5 per cent of the enormous world market for greenhouse technologies. Already numerous pro Kyoto Protocol ratification business groups and networks have formed globally; at the same time the major anti-Kyoto Protocol business body, the Global Climate Coalition, has all but collapsed with most of its members to date resigning.

Whether the Kyoto Protocol is ratified or not, many companies, business bodies and governments at all levels believe that it is inevitable that we will live in a 'carbon constrained' economy this century. They see the business opportunities. Business leaders increasingly understand this. Hunter Lovins and Walter Link write: 'Leading companies are starting to capture the potential for energy savings. As the world's largest cement manufacturer, Lafarge produces twice as many GHG emissions as Switzerland. By changing its manufacturing processes, however, Lafarge has reduced its GHG emissions by nearly 11 per cent below its 1990 emissions levels. By 2010, the company wants to reduce emissions by a total of 20 per cent per ton of cement. Lafarge is keen to continue this work, since it is realizing significant cost savings and strengthening its future competitive edge in its industry. Other manufacturers are following Lafarge's lead. By doing so, the industry as a whole is positioning itself to make a significant dent in global emissions. IKEA, the international home furnishings retailer, has set several goals for itself also. It will reduce energy consumption by 10 per cent across all of its international operations by the end of 2003, and plans to switch 10 per cent of its heat and electricity to renewables by the end of 2005. The company also aims to reduce carbon emissions from transported goods by 15 per cent across its European operations and increase the share of goods coming to its stores by rail from 20 per cent to 40 per cent by the close of 2006. IKEA also plans to have 75 per cent of its stores accessible to mass transit by the end of 2005, and hopes to increase home shopping and home delivery services to reduce the need for its customers to drive to stores.[30]

Such announcements are indicative that many executives are realizing that protecting the climate is not costly but profitable, because saving fuel costs less than buying fuel. Using energy in a way that saves money is therefore an important way to strengthen the bottom line and the whole economy. The European Union has committed to improved energy efficiency and use of renewables, which it sees as key to their competitive advantage in the 21st century. The Energy Intelligent Europe Initiative, signed by Members of the European Parliament from all EU member countries by 15 February 2002, calls for the integration of energy efficiency and renewable energy as the basis for European competitiveness and high quality of life. The EU is seeking to source 22 per cent of its electricity and 10 per cent of its energy from such clean sources as wind within ten years.[31]

President Clinton launched the 'Clean Energy for the 21st Century' initiative, estimating that energy technology markets in developing countries will total US$4–5 trillion over the next 20 years and reach US$15–25 trillion over the next 50 years. The independent commission concluded that any meaningful deployment of clean energy technologies internationally would require a long-term, integrated effort that focuses on public–private partnerships. One of the long-term goals of President Clinton's Initiative was to develop integrated renewable energy technologies with the potential to power the full range of energy services for the 2 billion people in developing countries that do not have electricity now.[32] As Clinton stated, 'There are really people who basically believe, first, that you can't really get rich, stay rich, or get richer unless you put more greenhouse gases in the atmosphere. And, therefore, they have to believe that global warming is a fraud, otherwise, they'd face the Hobson's choice of being poor or being toast. A couple of years ago, we got the Energy Department and HUD and the Homebuilders – hardly a left-wing radical group, the National Homebuilders Association – to agree to build a housing development at the end of the rail line in the Indio Empire around San Bernardino for low income working people, and promised them that they would pay a little more for these houses, that all had little solar reflectors in their shingles, better insulation, the best lighting, that we would lower their electric bills, on average, by 40 per cent. And two years after these houses were built and occupied, the average reduction was 65 per cent. That was all using existing, known technologies in voluntary partnerships. There is a US$1 trillion market out there right now. And we're very close to having cars that get 89 miles, to having fuel cells that are commercially viable, to all kinds of other breakthroughs, never mind the existing stuff that's out there now.'[33]

There is mounting evidence to suggest he is right:

- Wind power now supplies more than 10 per cent of Danish electricity and wind turbines are Denmark's fourth largest export worth US$1 billion annually and employing 12,000 people.
- In the early 1990s, Germany had almost no renewable energy industry, with brown coal and nuclear the major energy providers. However, by the end of the 1990s Germany was a market leader. In 1990, in response to concern over events like Chernobyl, the German Parliament introduced the Electricity Feed Law (EFL). The law required utilities to purchase electricity generated from renewable energy, and to pay a minimum price for it, in the case of wind and solar, at least 90 per cent of retail price. In 2000, the Renewable Energy Law was introduced which, along with a raft of changes, set per kilowatt-hour payments for renewable technologies on the basis of actual generation costs. These regulatory changes significantly reduced market uncertainty and helped create a large enough market to drive further innovation. It greatly helped to build confidence amongst investors to commit significant funds to this emerging market. As a result of real commitment to build the market for renewable energy, economies of scale plus new innovation have been driving down the cost of renewable energy.[34] Wind power costs have come down 80 per cent in the last 20 years.
- At the recent International Conference for Renewable Energies-Renewables 2004, 154 governments declared that renewable energy should and will play a major role in the energy economy of the 21st century. This was the largest ever meeting of government and private sector leaders on renewable energy, with over 3000 participants according to the organizers. The conference produced an international action programme that contains 165 individual commitments by governments, international agencies and private groups to promote the use of renewable energy, including:
  - China pledged to increase its use of small hydro, wind, solar and biomass power generation to 10 per cent of its generating capacity by 2010. With this and other commitments China has the potential to become a world leader in innovation in this area.
  - German Chancellor Gerhard Schroeder announced plans to increase Germany's use of renewable energy to 20 per cent of its energy supply by 2020. Importantly Germany also recognized its global responsibility for being a relatively high per

capita greenhouse gas emitter by committing to provide €500 million worth of low-interest loans over the next five years for renewable energy projects in developing countries.

- The World Bank also significantly committed to increase its renewable energy lending by at least 20 per cent annually over the next five years.
- The Japanese Government invests US$200 million annually in its solar rebate programme, and they now lead the world in the manufacture and use of solar photovoltaics (PV). As a result, solar PV production costs have dropped by 75 per cent since the mid-1990s.[35] Now there are over 4 million solar water heaters in use in Japan.
- The Japanese New Energy development organization's 1 million roof programme aimed to have 1 million homes equipped with photovoltaics by 2010. The programme also focused on the issue of aesthetics and utilized thin film amorphous silicon cells that had been integrated into glass roof tiles.[36]
- In Israel, solar water heating has been a mandatory requirement in all new household buildings since 1980, which means that today most homes use it. Over 700,000 households in Israel have solar water heaters.
- US Department of Energy announced in June 1997, the Million Solar Roofs (MSRI) initiative to facilitate the installation of solar energy systems on 1 million US buildings by 2010.

With these growing markets around the world it is not surprising that up to 320,000 new jobs in wind energy and 250,000 new jobs in solar thermal are anticipated in the European Union by 2010.[37] These are significant strategic market opportunities not to be missed.

The hydrogen economy

There is, however, much more that is possible. The Australian Prime Minister's Science and Innovation Council wrote:[38] 'The Holy Grail of global energy is to move to a hydrogen economy and to eliminate air pollution (other than water vapour) from all energy sources. The critical issue is the selection of the pathway by which this goal is attained. Widespread application of fuel cell technology for transport and for distributed generation (together with adopting energy efficiency approaches) will act as the spur for the development of a hydrogen production and distribution infrastructure.' There is a great deal of research underway to be able to use fuel cells in a range of applications that will help build the market a hydrogen economy.[39] Rocky Mountain Institute[40] has played a leading role in promoting wise approaches to the adoption of hydrogen and have shown that there are many incorrect myths regarding such a shift to a hydrogen economy.[41] RMI writes: 'A hydrogen industry big enough to displace all gasoline, while sustaining the other industrial processes that now use hydrogen, would be only several-fold bigger than the mature hydrogen industry that exists today, although initially it will probably rely mainly on smaller units of production closer to customers to avoid high distribution costs.'

Hydrogen production already uses 5 per cent of US natural gas, mainly in refineries and petrochemical plants. As decentralized production expands, the market for hydrogen to run fuel cells in buildings, factories, and vehicles, more centralized production methods and pipeline delivery will become attractive. An especially profitable opportunity will involve reforming natural gas at the wellhead, where a large plant can strip out the hydrogen for shipment to wholesale markets via new or existing pipelines. Professor Robert Williams of Princeton University points out that the other product of the separation process, carbon dioxide, could then be reinjected into the gas field, adding pressure that would help recover enough additional natural gas to pay for the re-

Table 17.2 *Deep cut strategies*[42]

Some of the profitable deep cut options to reduce greenhouse emissions		Average greenhouse gas reductions
Whole system design	Big energy and resource savings often cost less than small savings. Sounds impossible? In fact, engineers are showing time and again that through good engineering, resource efficiency up to an order of magnitude is possible, often for less cost than incremental improvements, through whole system design.[43]	Up to 90%
Hybrid cars and trucks	In the US, Europe and Japan hybrid cars cost only marginally more than the standard models, use 50% less fuel and are selling well.	At least 50%
Electric motors	The Australian Greenhouse Office have created the Motor Solutions online resource. They write that 'selecting the right motor results in large and cost effective savings and how whole of system design and management can achieve even greater savings.' The use of variable speed drive (VSD) (up to 50%),[44] high efficiency motors (28–50%)[45] and improved system management (48–55% for pumping systems,[46] and 30–57% for ventilation systems) are expected to deliver an average increase in electric motor system efficiency of 85% by 2050.[47]	Up to 60%
Buildings	The energy efficiency of the structure of the commercial building (excluding equipment) can be improved by, on average, 45% through improvements in design and construction.[48] The Thurgoona campus of Charles Sturt University (Albury, Australia) consumes less than half the energy of the comparable building it replaced.[49]	45% on average.
Lighting systems	Using efficient compact fluorescent lights and installing movement sensors can improve the energy efficiency of lighting.[51] According to the Lighting Council of Australia, 'In 1999, Australia spent approximately AU$5 billion on lighting. Well-designed, energy-efficient lighting and lighting controls can slash AU$1.25 billion a year off this bill'.	70% using a range of measures.[50]
Residential sector	Shift to a 5-star rating system for new homes delivers, on average, a 55% improvement[52] (from the current average in Australia of 1.5 stars). In the case of Victoria, Australia, wall insulation is mandatory yielding projected savings of 45% for new homes (from the average of 2.2 stars in those states).[53] Installing energy efficient equipment in the house will further reduce energy usage.	55% based on uptake of moderate performance improvements.

Table 17.2 *continued*

Some of the profitable deep cut options to reduce greenhouse emissions		Average greenhouse gas reductions
Improving conversion efficiency		
Co-generation	The Australian Department of Industry Tourism and Resources states that, 'Cogeneration, the simultaneous production of electricity and usable heat energy, is a technology which can deliver high thermal efficiencies – an ideal economic and environmental outcome.' Co-generation (coal and gas), that produces power and heat, has been shown by the World Energy Council to achieve an energy efficiency of 70–85%.[54]	70–85%
Fuel cells	High Temperature Solid Oxide cells developed by CSIRO convert natural gas or methane to usable heat and energy with 80% conversion efficiency, double that of present power generating systems.	50%
Pulsed combustion	CSIRO's combustion team have developed the revolutionary pulsed combustion technologies that promise to double thermal energy conversion rates for numerous domestic, industrial and commercial processes.[55]	Up to 70%
De-carbonization of materials		
Mineral products	• Investigating ways to re-use, recycle slag and other waste streams in construction materials • Cement and Lime Production. In Australia, the mineral products industries directly account for over 5 Mt of CO_2, 1.2% of the national total. CSIRO is pursuing a number of strategies to reduce these emissions: • Indirect fired rotary kiln technology (able to achieve considerable energy savings), • Accelerated microwave curing of concrete and ceramic products (saving energy and also estimated to reduce CO_2 emissions by 40%, at lower costs), and • Development of new binders capable of reabsorbing up to 80% of the CO_2 released in calcination.	Up to 50%
Eco-cements	The making of cement is responsible for 6% of global greenhouse gas emissions. The World Business Council has a cement sustainability initiative. Magnesium Cement: The new recyclable, low cost eco-cement is the first building material providing high thermal mass with a very low embodied energy. It can incorporate high proportions of waste and sets by absorbing carbon dioxide in porous or semi porous materials such as bricks, blocks, pavers and mortars and with organically derived fibre reinforcing, thereby becoming a net carbon sink. Teseco in Tasmania are selling magnesium cement and bricks in Australia at the present time.	40–50%

| **Straw bale** | Straw is produced in such quantities that they and rice wastes are burnt in states like California causing greenhouse emissions. Instead straw bales could be used in construction. New Information on this has been published by CSIRO as part of CSIRO's Building Technology Files (BTFs). CSIRO has recently conducted the most important tests to date that 'legitimize' straw bale as a mainstream building material including fire tests. The testing has proved that used in wall construction, rendered straw bales are suitable for use in bushfire-prone areas. They are non-combustible to the stringent tests that were carried out by CSIRO. Rendered straw bale walls now stand together with mud brick and rammed earth as the lowest embodied-energy building materials available. | Up to 70% |

Recycling and treatment of waste

Organic recycling	The Haber Process that makes Artificial Ammonia fertilizer requires 400 atmospheres of pressure and 500 degrees. Making a tonne of artificial ammonia uses 30 gigajoules. New methods to recycle organic waste have been developed that require no energy to run and also remove a significant percentage of the landfill waste stream, further reducing greenhouse gas emissions.	>90%
Capturing methane gas from landfill	The city of Toronto has cut its greenhouse emissions significantly since 1990, through, for instance, harnessing the natural gas from landfill.[56] The global warming potential of methane gas is 21 times that of carbon dioxide.	95%
Metal, plastic, glass and paper recycling	Reducing, reuse and recycling offers some of the easiest and biggest greenhouse savings. For example, metal recycling yields significant greenhouse gas emissions reductions: copper[57] (84%), nickel[58] (90%), aluminium[59] (95%), steel[60] (60%), lead[61] (65%), zinc[62] (75%).	Up to 90%

Reducing carbon intensity for energy generation

| **Renewables** | Costs are consistently falling for renewable energy sources such as mini-hydro, biomass, geo-thermal, tidal and solar power. Significant innovations are also occurring in harnessing energy from ocean waves[63] and ocean currents.[64] Wind Power in areas of high average wind is already cost competitive with coal-fired power stations.[65] Pacific Hydro Ltd (PHY) is one of the leading renewable energy companies in Australia, the South East Asian and Pacific area. On 6 June 2003, PHY committed to joining a venture to develop a dual-purpose wave energy generator. | Up to 100% |

Table 17.2 *continued*

Some of the profitable deep cut options to reduce greenhouse emissions		Average greenhouse gas reductions
Super-cables instead of traditional power cables	Being almost immune to resistance, superconducting power cables lose only about 0.5% of power during transmission, compared to 5–8% lost by traditional power cables. These cables also deliver more power, about three to five times more power than traditional power cables.[66] As the rapid growth of urban areas increases demand for electricity while limiting the space for overhead and underground cable installations, the ability of these cables to transmit more power, with less energy losses, using the same amount of space as traditional cable will be increasingly important.	Up to 97%
Bridging technologies–carbon sequestration		
Below ground storage of carbon dioxide	A demonstration of carbon sequestration; a six year project at the Sleipner Field in the Norwegian North Sea. Approximately 1 million tonnes of carbon dioxide has been sequestered each year over the last 5 years. There are significant R&D projects now to investigate this in many countries. For instance, the USA's FutureGen Project is an effort to advance carbon capture and storage technology as a way to reduce greenhouse emissions. The project is a US$1 billion, public–private effort to construct the world's first fossil fuel, low-pollution power plant. According to Dr Peter Cook, Chief Executive Officer Australia's CRC Greenhouse Gas Technologies, 'I think it's reasonable to regard it as a bridging technology. In other words, the technology between where we are now and where we hope to be in X-years time, when we'll be totally dependent maybe on renewables.' In Australia, the Coal21 initiative and the CRC for Greenhouse Gas Technologies are researching this area.	Up to 100%
Reducing greenhouse emissions from agriculture		
Less gas, more meat	At least 12% of Australia's greenhouse emissions stem from cattle and sheep. CSIRO is exploring ways to help sheep and cattle to digest rough and low nutrient pastures more efficiently. By modifying the bacteria in the animal's rumen, scientists have found livestock yield more meat, wool and milk – and less methane. Trials have shown live weight gains of about 20% in sheep and cattle, and 9% fleece weight gains. In digesting more of their food, the animals release 18–80% less methane through belching.	18–80% less methane.
Halt land clearing		
Provide incentives to farmers to preserve their biodiversity	Land clearing is widely recognized as the biggest threat to wildlife in Australia.[67] It causes dryland salinity, soil erosion and water quality decline and contributes a substantial proportion of Australia's greenhouse gas emissions. The State Premier of Queensland has declared a moratorium to land clearing in that state.	5% of Australia's greenhouse emissions come from land clearing.

Note: For an extensive overview of international work on 'Deep Cuts to Greenhouse Emissions' see Denniss et al (2004, ch 13).

injection. The carbon would then be safely 'sequestered' in the gas field, which can typically hold about twice as much carbon in the form of CO_2 as it originally held in the form of natural gas. The abundant resources of natural gas (at least two centuries worth) could thus be cleanly and efficiently used in fuel-cell vehicles, and in fuel-cell powered buildings and factories, without harming the earth's climate. The hydrogen provider would be paid three times: for the shipped hydrogen, for the enhanced recovery of natural gas, and a third time, under future Kyoto Protocol trading, for sequestering the carbon.[68] Another profitable approach will come from combining the benefits of fuel cells in buildings with high efficiency use of hydrogen fuel cell cars, cost effective synergies will be possible from which a broader hydrogen economy can be built, as has been championed by RMI for many years.

The Four Times Square, Condé-Nast building in New York is a sign of things to come. The construction costs of this building are the same as a standard commercial building but that is where the similarities stop. This building is 50 per cent more efficient to run. One of the building's innovations is the glass window panels which are actually photovoltaic. A fuel cell in the basement stores the energy from the PV cells, thus ensuring that the building will never be affected by a blackout. Because constant energy is essential in the digital age, the guaranteed ultra reliable power helped recruit premium tenants at premium rents. During the 2004 New York blackouts people came from all over the city to congregate around the base of the building, the only light source available.

Hydrogen cars have potential that extends beyond their use for transport. In Los Angeles there are already five hydrogen cars driving around from Honda and Toyota. Their performance compares well now with standard cars.[69] As part of a company or government fleet, these cars could in principle be re-fuelled with hydrogen to generate electricity whilst idle during the day, with that electricity being fed back into the grid. If all the cars on the planet were used this way it would generate in the order of approximately 15 times the total electricity currently generated.

Iceland is committed to a transition to a hydrogen economy, and other major economies, such as Germany, have significant targets for hydrogen car and fuel cells. Japan is similarly focused on R&D for commercializing and popularizing fuel cells, fuel cell vehicles and hydrogen infrastructure. Its hydrogen R&D focus is primarily aimed at achieving the technological advances necessary to enable high performance and cost effective fuel cells to penetrate the market, in particular, the use of fuel cells in vehicle and stationary energy markets. The Japanese Government has set some ambitious targets for the penetration of hydrogen fuel cells in these markets by 2010 and 2020, shown in Table 17.3.

The Australian Government commissioned a major study for Australia to investigate the possibilities for a hydrogen economy. The study found that hydrogen should be part of Australia's future energy mix and outlined detailed policies to enable this to happen.[70] The US Department of Energy has a similar vision for the US, outlined in Figure 17.6.

Many leaders in China also understand this. Rocky Mountain Institute's Bill Browning met with the vice-premier who is next in line to be Premier of China, Wen Jiabao. Wen Jiabao has been chosen, Browning said, 'because he's viewed as one of the most

Table 17.3 *Japan's targets for fuel-cell sales*

Year	In transport (Number of vehicles)	In stationary energy applications (Capacity in MW)
2010	50,000	2100
2020	5 million	10,000

Source: Japan NEDO (2003)

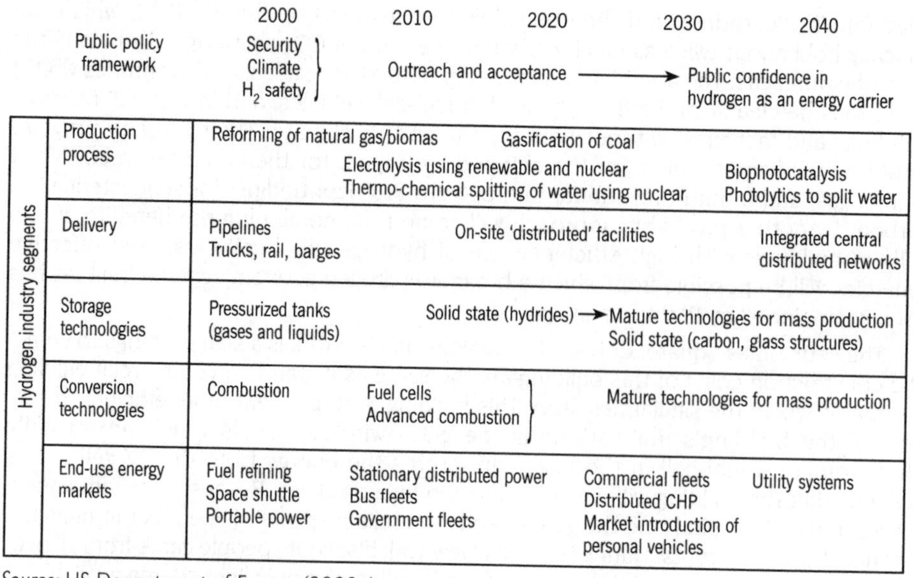

		2000	2010	2020	2030	2040
	Public policy framework	Security, Climate, H$_2$ safety	Outreach and acceptance ————→		Public confidence in hydrogen as an energy carrier	
Hydrogen industry segments	Production process	Reforming of natural gas/biomas Gasification of coal	Electrolysis using renewable and nuclear	Thermo-chemical splitting of water using nuclear	Biophotocatalysis	Photolytics to split water
	Delivery	Pipelines, Trucks, rail, barges	On-site 'distributed' facilities		Integrated central distributed networks	
	Storage technologies	Pressurized tanks (gases and liquids)	Solid state (hydrides) →	Mature technologies for mass production, Solid state (carbon, glass structures)		
	Conversion technologies	Combustion	Fuel cells, Advanced combustion	Mature technologies for mass production		
	End-use energy markets	Fuel refining, Space shuttle, Portable power	Stationary distributed power, Bus fleets, Government fleets	Commercial fleets, Distributed CHP, Market introduction of personal vehicles	Utility systems	

Source: US Department of Energy (2002a)

Figure 17.6 US Department of Energy: a national vision of the US's transition to the hydrogen economy

progressive and incorruptible of the country's top leaders. Countries like China are committing to applying real and sustainable solutions to their energy needs. 'His remarks were really astonishing'. In his discussion of China's energy strategy, he conceded that coal, nuclear, and natural gas will remain the most important sources for the near term, but China must focus on three things. The first is to clean up coal-fired power plants dramatically. The second is continuing the ongoing transition to natural gas. The third, and most important, Wen Jiabao said, is where the future of China lies. 'Our future is with solar and wind,' Browning said, quoting Wen. 'China has huge wind and solar resources it has barely begun to use. This is where we will focus our attention.' Even more importantly, Browning said, Wen Jiabao went on to say that all of the changes in energy presuppose that the nation will do the most important thing first: dramatically increase the efficiency of China's energy use.[71]

The *Shell International 2001, Choices and Possibilities Scenarios to* 2050 report argued that the leapfrogging by China to a hydrogen economy is its most likely course of action due to a number of factors. By 2010 China will be importing significant amounts of oil from politically unstable areas. It is less likely than other countries to, for instance, invest in other alternative fuels, such as bio-fuels, because China needs as much agricultural land as possible devoted to food production and to provide ecosystem services. Likewise, China lacks the rail infrastructure to meet its needs for electricity solely from coal. It has been estimated that if China attempted this, its entire rail network would be utilized by coal trains. Fortunately, there is a real alternative for China by virtue of its rich coal deposits that can provide a ready source of methane and hydrogen. It could make use of these, as well as indigenous technologies, to extract methane and hydrogen directly from its coal resources, allowing it to move energy by pipeline rather than by thousands of trains.

Major projects are underway around the world to both create climate neutral coal fired power stations, through sequestration, and also develop the best methods for coal to contribute to the hydrogen economy.[72] In addition, due to the size of its potential market and present lack of automobiles, China is probably the best positioned globally

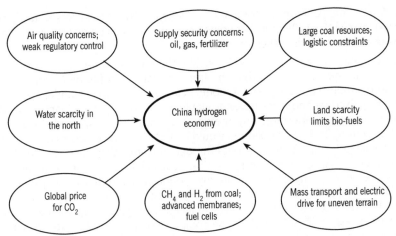

Note: China is able to exploit commercial fuel cells and advanced technologies to extract methane from indigenous coal resources in order to develop a fuel cell based energy system supported by a methane/hydrogen distribution grid.
Source: Shell International (2001)

Figure 17.7 A *Chinese leapfrog: drivers for China to shift to a hydrogen economy*

to leapfrog the west to mass produce hydrogen powered cars. Hypercar Inc now have a fully functioning Hydrogen-powered Hypercar demonstration model. All the technology needed is here, it just depends on which nation and which car companies decide to mass-produce them. All that is needed is to be able to produce 50,000 hypercars per annum to make it cost competitive with standard cars.[73]

A historic opportunity

The energy supply sector has, in the past, painted itself as the 'engine of economic development'. Given the technologies we have chosen to apply, and the types of industries we have chosen to base our economic development on, this has been true. However, recent economic studies show that if an optimized combination of energy efficiency, demand management and green energy is used the total life cycle costs of delivering energy related services are often reduced and other benefits such as increased employment add up.[74] The Allen Consulting study of Victoria's 5-star energy rating for housing shows that there are significant benefits for the economy of shifting investment from energy supply to improving the efficiency of the economy.[75] This is because the conventional energy supply sector employs few people (48,000 in 2000–2001, a fifth as many jobs per unit of value added as the average business),[76] absorbs enormous amounts of capital, and delivers low returns on investment.

Alternative ways of satisfying our energy service needs such as improved energy efficiency can create more employment and be less capital intensive. To illustrate this, the return on the net worth of the electricity, gas and water sector in 2000–2001 was less than half the average for all Australian business, excluding agriculture forestry and fishing.[77] In contrast, the Australian Government's Appliance Energy Efficiency Programme is delivering millions of tonnes of greenhouse abatement at a net negative cost of AU$30 per tonne.[78] Additionally, lower energy bills free up money for investment in other activities that deliver bigger economic returns than conventional energy supply, such as increased investment in energy efficiency improvement or renewable energy.

Why don't some economists, for instance those modelling the costs of ratifying the Kyoto Protocol, see this? Why is it that some economic models predict doom and gloom if nations ratify Kyoto, whilst others see net gain?

There are many reasons, but we will consider the three key ones. First, conventional micro-economic theory assumes that the firm maximizes profits by incorporating an optimal mix of labour, capital and other inputs in accordance with a standard production function, using fixed technologies freely available to all industry participants. It assumes that under perfect competition any inefficiencies will be eliminated. Under these assumptions, efforts to reduce pollution would be expected to add costs to an idealized firm that has already maximized its profits through implementing any cost effective cost cutting strategies. All economists know that real markets are far from theoretical perfection. However, many climate/economy models assume that perfect markets do exist and hence that all profitable energy savings must have already been achieved. On this basis, the modellers suppose, buying significantly bigger savings will be worthwhile only at higher energy prices. They then use complex computer models to calculate how high an energy tax is needed (based on historic elasticity), how much that will depress the economy, and hence what the 'cost' of protecting the climate must be.

On the other hand, bottom-up technological engineering approaches recognize barriers that may have inhibited firms from taking advantage of potentially profitable energy-saving opportunities. These bottom-up estimates typically predict that policy initiatives can induce reductions in energy consumption. As a result, they typically suggest less economic disruption from programmes to reduce global greenhouse gas reductions. Not only do other economic models derive the opposite answer from actually acknowledging that savings are possible through energy efficiency measures, but an enormous body of overlooked empiricism, including government-sponsored studies and worldwide business practice, shows that many of the technological breakthroughs that we need have already happened. What is more, these solutions are already being applied with remarkable results. In fact, through whole system design, achieving deep cuts to greenhouse emissions is often more cost effective than achieving incremental change.

Second, there are often significant information failures and gaps that can lead economists to make odd assumptions when modelling the impacts of climate change on economies. This was shown during the Australian Senate 'Heat is On' Enquiry.[79] A representative from the Australian Bureau of Agriculture and Resource Economics (ABARE), who are responsible for the main economic modelling used by the present Australian Government was asked by Senator Bolkus and Dr Clive Hamilton why ABARE had assumed there would be no negative costs on the Australian economy from climate change? Dr Hamilton asked 'Indeed, you have to ask yourself this. If you read some of their reports, ABARE will say right up front, "This does not take account of the benefits of emission reductions." They are quite up-front when they say that, and yet we know that in practice the results are used constantly to try to knock off policies to reduce emissions... Similarly, land clearing. ABARE's own study of land clearing in Queensland suggests – and it is not a systematic study – that the cost of reducing emissions by reducing land clearing would be about one or two dollars a tonne of carbon dioxide compared to the (previous ABARE) models' estimates of AU$30, AU$40 or AU$50 a tonne. So there is a very large chunk of emission reductions which can have almost zero cost, a very low cost. Why aren't they modelled?' The ABARE representative replied: 'That is a good question.' Clearly, economic modelling requires careful attention to the detail of what needs to be included in the models and what implicit assumptions are being made by the modelling approach. Seemingly small omissions such as ignoring the benefits to the Australian economy of emissions reductions can have a marked effect on the results and findings of such an economic modelling exercise. This is increasingly recognized by bodies such as ABARE.

In a major study called 'An Introduction to the Economics of Climate Change Policy', Professor John Weyant and his team at Stanford University have looked at a wide range of equilibrium models from around the world, including the ABARE GTEM model, showing the difference in the estimated cost of reducing carbon emissions according to the various models. They have tried to map the costs of emissions reductions in a consistent way and have compared the various models. It shows that ABARE GTEM is the highest of all of them. In fact, let us say you were trying to cut emissions by 20 per cent compared with the base case, then the ABARE GTEM (when this model is applied to the US) results for the US show a marginal cost of abatement approximately twice as high as the other models. So it is important for us to understand why it is that the GTEM model produces results like that. Issues such as whether ABARE has correctly assumed what is possible through energy efficiency or through reducing land clearing are therefore important in terms of the results predicted by their studies.

Professor John Weyant[80] identified five key areas where assumptions made by economists significantly affect the results of their modelling in this area. Two of the key assumptions in the models that Weyant refers to are the way in which economic models make assumptions about the substitute between different sorts of fuels and also the way in which the models deal with technological change, which is the critical issue that we are dealing with here. The conclusion that Weyant comes to, when he was talking about induced technological change, is that it probably does not make much difference in the short term but, over the longer term, say ten years or more, induced technological change could be a very substantial contributor to reducing the costs of reducing emissions. That makes sense, because we are actually talking about not only the development but also the adoption of new technologies which you would expect to take a decade or more to really have a big impact on the economy.

The way we look at energy use also shapes the possibilities we see for change. For example, the Australian National Greenhouse Gas Inventory (NGGI) allocates emissions according to the point of combustion, so 85 per cent of household greenhouse gas emissions and almost 90 per cent of commercial sector emissions are not allocated to these sectors. Instead, they are allocated to the electricity generation sector because they result from the use of electricity in these sectors. Hence, the NGGI does not reflect the significance of energy using activities in these sectors, which is a significant information failure in Australia.

At the same time, a significant proportion of emissions from mining and industry result from our (and other countries') voracious appetite for materials to build urban infrastructure, equipment and buildings. Approximately two-thirds of the manufacturing sector's greenhouse gas emissions are generated by the industries that process materials and chemicals for equipment and urban infrastructure, although much of this production is exported. Figure 17.8 shows the trends in material use in the US over the past century, which highlights the enormous quantities of materials now consumed. A large proportion of the materials consumed relate to urban infrastructure.

The use of energy varies widely within sectors. For example, 5 per cent of Australian households consume 15 per cent of household electricity.[81] Among office buildings, around 10 per cent use more than double the median level of energy.[82] By identifying these high consumers, programmes can be targeted to achieve large savings where they are likely to be most cost-effective. Figure 17.9 shows Victoria's waste stream for 2000. It shows the untapped potential for recovery of materials and conversion of wastes into energy.

Another significant information failure has been the lack of reliable data on wind resources for nations. If your company is in the mining industry, geoscience departments have all the information you need to know where to start, but until recently in Australia there was little data for wind energy companies to know where to invest. This led to wind

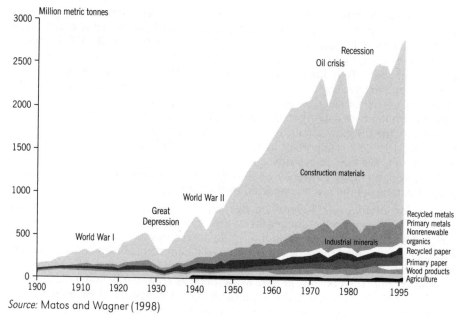

Source: Matos and Wagner (1998)

Figure 17.8 US *Consumption of materials*

energy companies investing in coastal areas creating conflicts because these areas had a high tourist value. Recently both NSW and Victoria have published with CSIRO wind atlases showing that there are many coastal and inland sites of note.[83] This will help government and, for instance, farmers to be able to decide whether their wind resources are competitive and worth investing. These are just a few of the traditionally significant informational failures preventing the most profitable greenhouse reduction options from being taken up by the market. Informational failures, however, are just one part of over 80 other regulatory, institutional and market failures that prevent these options from being adopted. One of the best overviews of how any nation can wisely address these barriers is Amory and Hunter Lovins' work, *Climate: Making Sense, Making Money*. This paper is highly recommended.[84] It clearly shows through inspiring case studies that businesses, governments and energy utilities around the world are addressing these key barriers for change with remarkably profitable results.

Third, concerning traditional economic modelling is the critical nature of the assumptions made by the economists of how the revenue from a carbon tax would be allocated. For instance, a net gain in employment and increased GDP could result if the revenues from an environmental levy on greenhouse emissions were used to reduce payroll tax, or business insurance (as they have done in the UK) and assist businesses in reducing their greenhouse emissions through targeting the most cost effective measures possible.

To date, much of the economic modelling on the effect of a carbon tax or emissions trading schemes on a nation's economy has assumed the resulting revenue stream will flow through the economy according to past priorities rather than in ways that would be most beneficial, such as being targeted to help industry achieve energy efficiencies. Nevertheless even the 1997 ABARE Megabare model, that made many such assumptions[85] showed that 85 per cent of the Australian economy would not be significantly affected, economically, for better or worse by a carbon tax. However, the results where not interpreted as showing that at the time. Later modelling, such as that shown in Table 17.4 gives similar results.

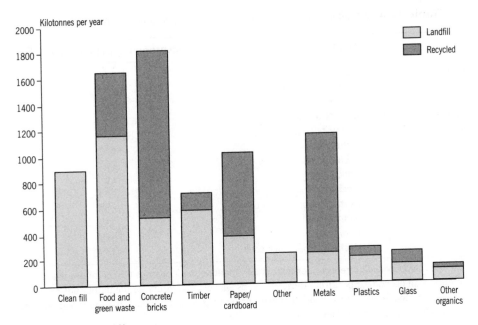

Source: EcoRecycle (2002)

Figure 17.9 *Victorian wastes* 2000–2001

ABARE for instance, now, after the recent Bonn Agreement, forecasts only a 0.18 per cent negative per annum impact on Australia's GNP if Australia ratifies the Protocol. Given that GNP is expected to increase by 40 per cent over the ten years, Australians would need to wait an extra three weeks before reaching the same level of GNP. Hence, when economic modelling does include an optimized combination of energy efficiency, demand management and green energy, the total life cycle costs of delivering energy related services are often reduced, and other benefits such as increased employment accrue.[86]

In Europe, carbon taxes are often introduced with corresponding reductions in taxes on labour, payroll or the insurance costs of business. In Denmark they use the revenue to target energy efficiency investment for business. This type of tax shifting, as recommended by *The Economist* magazine, can help to significantly reduce greenhouse emissions when combined with the profitable barrier busting strategies outlined in the *Climate: Making Sense, Making Money* paper recently mentioned.[87]

There are many cost effective energy efficiency savings out there because there have been significant barriers to businesses addressing them. There are still many cost saving opportunities to achieve energy efficiency in the economy because often there are significant barriers for firms, households, commercial buildings and industry to implement energy efficiency measures. For instance, PricewaterhouseCoopers consultants presented on this at a 2003 Sustainable Energy Authority Victoria (SEAV)/Business Council for Sustainable Energy (BCSE) energy efficiency conference in Melbourne. Apparently, if a business maintains old equipment, it can claim 100 per cent of the cost as a tax deduction in that year, but if it improves the equipment (for example by making it more efficient) that is considered to be a capital investment, and the tax deduction can only be claimed over the estimated life of the improved equipment. Even worse, equipment purchased before 1999 is eligible for accelerated depreciation (a higher tax deduction each year) if it is upgraded, but purchase of new equipment is ineligible for accelerated depreciation. So the least attractive option financially for a business is to invest in a new, more efficient plant. Even upgrading efficiency is less

Table 17.4 *Australian industry winners and losers for 'policy mix' greenhouse response*

	Sector	Percentage impact on activity, 2010
Winners	Electricity from gas	+6%
	Electricity from oil (!)	+2.4%
	Forestry	+1.0%
Neutral (+/− 1%)*	Most of the economy	
Losers	Electricity supply	−1.5%
	Natural gas	−1.5%
	Urban gas distribution	−1.5%
	Agriculture	−1.8%
	Black coal	−2.5%
	Electricity from brown coal	−7.5%
	Aluminium	−11%
	Brown coal	−12.5%
	Electricity from black coal	−13%

Note: The Allen Consulting report does not actually mention the industries that comprise the rest of the Australian economy, apart from those shown as winners and losers, so the author has presumed that they are unaffected. This is consistent with the findings of other greenhouse modelling projects such as ABARE's 1997 modelling reports.
Source: Allen Consulting (2000)

attractive than just maintaining equipment. Of course, this doesn't necessarily mean we should change the tax system, because it is designed to take into account many issues. But where are the incentives for energy efficiency to overcome these disincentives?

In Europe they have also given tax exemptions to a carbon tax gradually for industries that are energy intensive, in order to avoid conflict or capital flight and to allow ample time for energy efficiency measures to significantly reduce the carbon footprint of those industries. Hence, if market signals such as a carbon tax is applied with a wise policy mix that includes sensible tax shifting and programmes that use the revenue to target the most cost effective savings, this can even help the economy. The following is a summary of what any nation can do to ensure they do not miss this next wave of innovation in the energy sector.

Issue identification[88]

The key energy issues for ensuring nations seize these opportunities include:

- Development of a culture that makes energy waste an unacceptable activity (as is being done with water), and focuses attention on improving the productivity of energy use.
- Dramatic improvements in the efficiency with which energy and non-renewable materials are used, for both new and existing infrastructure and buildings.
- A shift from traditional, centralized, fossil fuel-based energy systems to diversified systems including renewable energy, cogeneration and energy efficiency improvement.
- Restructuring of energy markets so they make it more profitable for electricity retailers to save energy or sell renewables than to sell conventional fossil fuel-sourced energy, and to provide clearer signals to energy consumers of the costs and impacts of using fossil fuel-sourced energy wastefully, while ensuring equitable outcomes.

- Ensuring all new urban infrastructure, buildings and business expansion are compatible with a low greenhouse impact future, either through low emissions when built, or through flexible design so that low emissions solutions can be easily added as they become more cost-effective. This might include, for example, installation of hydrogen gas pipes to all houses in new developments.
- Utilization of local renewable energy resources (including wastes) and waste materials to replace non-renewables.
- Development of targeted energy strategies, such as management of peak energy loads, identification of high-energy users, etc.
- Assisting low-income households (many of whom rent or live in caravans or portable housing) to reduce energy costs while improving comfort.
- Development of tools needed to help identify energy waste in buildings and infrastructure, and to help set priorities for improvement. For example, rating schemes such as the Australian Building Greenhouse Rating facilitate benchmarking and targeting of high energy users, while the Australian Government's annual reporting of energy use by agencies[89] facilitates strategic energy management within the public sector, and could be applied more broadly.

Policy options

The nature of many decisions related to energy and sustainable cities is such that their implications are long term and their impacts are widespread. But there are numerous positive market based mechanisms that governments have to assist them. As discussed in the tragedy of the commons, arguably the most prominent reasons why markets for ecosystem services rarely exist are uncertainty about ecosystem processes and an inability to define and enforce ownership. But in the case of CO_2 and SO_x pollution, where it is relatively easy to identify and measure both the source and amount of pollution, markets can be easily created. Point source pollution issues like NO_x, SO_x, CFC and greenhouse gas emissions are the environmental problems that are most suitable for market creation. Take the experience to date with trading emissions in sulphur. Just before Congress approved in 1990 the cap-and-trade system for reducing sulphur dioxide emissions, industry predicted that the permit price would settle at US$1650 per ton. Environmentalists predicted that reductions would cost about US$330 a ton, or ultimately (said the optimists) perhaps US$250. The sulphur-allowance market opened in 1992 at about US$250 a ton; in 1995, it cleared at US$130 a ton. Therefore the cost of addressing sulphur dioxide emissions has ended up being over an order of magnitude cheaper than industry groups predicted.

The success of and experience in SO_x market trading schemes is spurring on many nations to set up their own national CO_2 emission trading schemes modelled on the successful SO_x emission trading schemes. The UK emissions trading scheme is off to a flying start.[90] Nearly 1000 companies transferred over 7 million tonnes of carbon dioxide during the first year. The EU will launch a European emissions trading scheme on 1 January 2005 that will allow regional governments with trading schemes to join the EU's trading scheme. In the US the Chicago Climate Exchange has been created for any businesses to join to either sell carbon credits (if they are below agreed targets) or buy carbon credits (if they are behind set goals). Experience with market solutions over the past decade has highlighted that, while they can allocate resources efficiently, the detailed structure of the markets and the extent to which they reflect long-term costs and limit the application of market power by entrenched interests strongly influences their effectiveness as policy tools.

It has also been found that regulation can be accepted in situations where allocation of costs is difficult. For example, the building industry has worked constructively with regulators to introduce energy efficiency requirements into the Building Code of Australia over the past few years, after resisting such action for decades. It has also been recognized that market mechanisms must operate within a regulatory framework anyway, so the dichotomy between market solutions and regulation has been found to be a matter of degree. For energy, the key issue is that most decisions that impact on energy use are made in a context where the energy implications are a minor component of the criteria. The reasons for this include the small cost of energy as a proportion of total costs, heavy discounting of future costs, split incentives where the decision-maker does not pay the energy bills and distortions of energy prices. Ignorance of the potential for energy savings is also a barrier, as is the early stage of development of the sustainable energy industry.

Given these barriers, there are no simple paths to sustainable energy in urban development. A comprehensive strategy is required that includes:

- education and promotion in relation to the benefits of sustainable energy;
- incentives for sustainable energy (which could include changes to energy markets, taxation, rebates, etc.);
- funding of pilot projects, for example application of energy efficiency and distributed generation to a new mixed use development;
- guidelines (evolving towards mandatory requirements) for incorporation of sustainable energy into new developments: for example, a greenhouse budget for all new buildings;
- development of evaluation and rating tools and their use to assess eligibility for incentives and/or application of mandated measures;
- provide information, and address any institutional information failures;
- enhance industry's, business's and the community's ability to respond to market mechanisms and price signals.

A fundamental problem we face in driving a transition is that all the regulatory and policy frameworks are still structured around traditional energy solutions. To drive a shift we need to:

- carry out modelling projects to help better understand how distributed systems might work and what infrastructure they could benefit from (e.g. local energy storage, advanced meters/voltage control/load management systems in homes and businesses, etc.);
- plan several new developments (preferably mixed used) from the ground up as energy efficient, distributed generation pilot projects, then build them and learn from experience;
- in parallel with the above, provide incentives and assistance to implement alternative models in targeted existing areas.

How can the uptake of renewable energy for residential and commercial properties be promoted?

This question is somewhat linked to other questions in this section. Ideally, packages are needed that combine energy efficiency improvement and renewable energy so that overall costs are reduced. However, capital cost may then be an issue, particularly where split incentives exist (i.e. the decision-maker does not benefit from future savings) so schemes that bring life cycle costs to the point of decision-making and/or allow the cost to be paid off via energy bills or mortgage payments are needed. It will be important to underwrite the risk so that individuals can feel confident to act.

Along with such schemes there is a need for a strong innovation/efficiency improvement programme for products and equipment used throughout the commercial and household sector, not just a mandatory standards programme. There are simply too many different kinds of products and equipment to be able to address each of them via standards within a reasonable timeframe. Training of designers and engineers to carry out quick assessments of energy efficiency potential of things from coffee makers to pizza ovens to cold rooms is urgently required, so they can get on with designing better solutions. It will also be important to ensure that investments in conventional energy infrastructure support the future adoption of sustainable energy options. For example, it is quite feasible to introduce tougher energy standards for hot water services to make them compatible with solar boosting. Solar pre-heaters can then be added to such systems at any time during their lives at minimum cost. At present, the solar systems must be installed up-front when there is often a shortage of capital or a split incentive situation. Of course, mandating solar hot water provides another path.

What are the barriers to utilizing renewable energy sources in residential, commercial and industrial areas and how might these be addressed?

The aim should be to encourage the adoption of a mix of sustainable energy options, including renewable energy, energy efficiency and demand management. For example, a household that uses less hot water through water-efficient showerheads, taps and appliances, needs a smaller solar hot water system than one that uses water wastefully. A recent study for the NSW Government shows how a mix of such approaches can deliver economically attractive outcomes.[91] Brief overviews of some of the issues are provided in key works from Watt and Outhred,[92] as well as Greene and Pears.[93] Key factors include:

- Energy is a relatively small cost for most people and businesses (in fact gas and electricity are, on average, less than 1.5 per cent of business input costs), and therefore does not attract much attention.
- Most decisions that impact on energy use are not understood to be energy-related by the decision-makers: businesses upgrade a photocopier because they want a higher speed model or new features, and rarely realize that this could impact on their energy use. Even where energy performance is a factor, it generally rates well-below other criteria such as price, aesthetics, status, reputation for reliability, etc.
- Split incentives such as the landlord–tenant problem mean that often those who have to pay for energy efficiency don't get the benefits.
- Markets are heavily stacked against energy efficiency as we now have many highly resourced marketing groups working for energy suppliers whose job it is to steal market share from their competitors, the overall effect of this marketing effort is an increase in energy use. Further, for energy suppliers, there is more profit at the margin from selling one extra unit of energy than from saving it, because a large proportion of their costs are sunk capital, which they have to pay for whether it is used or not.[94] Also, appliance and equipment markets are biased in favour of energy waste. For example, a salesperson selling boiling water units for an office kitchenette has a vested interest in selling a bigger model because it provides more profit for the same effort: but it is also less efficient. Similar pressures encourage the sale of bigger refrigerators and heating units and even houses.

Dealing with these barriers will require strong policy action, technology development, strong incentives to do things differently, as well as an education and cultural change programme that makes it clear that using energy wastefully is foolish. A new paradigm for the energy sector is showing that efficient use of energy is vital for nations that wish to catch the next wave of innovation.

CHAPTER 18

GREENING THE BUILT ENVIRONMENT

Cheryl Paten and Janis Birkeland with Alan Pears

EDITORS' NOTE: This chapter has been developed by lead author and The Natural Edge Project (TNEP) Secretariat member, Cheryl Paten. Mentoring and assistance was gratefully received from Alan Pears, co-director of environmental consultancy Sustainable Solutions and an Adjunct Professor in Environment and Planning at RMIT University in Melbourne, Dr Janis Birkeland editor of *Design for Sustainability* and the team from TNEP. Cameron Hoffmann is also acknowledged for his guidance on the chapter and a number of contributions included in the text. Working Group member Kate West is thanked for her review and comments during early chapter development. The editorial team would like to thank Bob Cameron for contributing some text and case study material. Thank you also to the organizations mentioned in the text, most of whom provided extra insight into the case studies.

> *We shape our dwellings, and then afterwards our dwellings shape our lives*
> Sir Winston Churchill, British Prime Minister, 1960

There are many well-documented examples of how our ancestors successfully used their surroundings to sculpt sustainable built environments. Attention to natural energy flows and to the properties of local materials was rewarded with comfortable shelters and small ecological footprints. However, over a time span of a few decades communities around the world have lost, or 'misplaced' much of their cultural knowledge. This has led to the adoption of many 'standard' practices that are not necessarily suited to the local context. While case studies demonstrate that architecture, planning, design and materials are all undergoing 'dramatic sustainability breakthroughs', why is our built environment generally becoming less comfortable and more resource hungry?

Green development may be viewed as developments which make significant progress in the pursuit of achieving a sustainable built environment: a return to a climatically, geographically, and culturally appropriate way of building, in combination with new technologies.[1] In reality, society is collectively such a long way from this goal that at present, any development that has benefited from a significant focus on sustainability issues is seen as a 'green' development. However, even when such examples consistently show significant improvements in economic, social and environmental well-being, there are people within the built environment industry who still think 'it's okay' to create inefficient buildings that guzzle materials, energy and water.

> *We are now in a transitional phase of industrial history in which companies are still inexperienced in handling environmental issues creatively... The early movers, the companies that can see the opportunity first and embrace innovation-based solutions, will reap major competitive advantages, just as the German and Japanese car makers did [with fuel-efficient cars in the early 1970s]. While Detroit spent its dollars fighting fuel efficiency standards, German and Japan[ese] manufacturers dominated the market.*
>
> Professor Michael Porter, Harvard Business Review[2]

In many countries there are still only a few examples that showcase the way forward in providing comprehensive sustainable solutions for the built environment. Will we now begin to see a national and international process of broad reform that is engaging the whole built environment industry? It is clear that we cannot rest only on the successes of our high achievers.

Building positive examples

Buildings around the world are demonstrating various principles of state-of-the-art green development that are good for the bottom line and better for employees and the environment. Examples provided in the following text include a property consultancy office and a state of the art headquarters of a non-profit organization in Australia, one of the world's best eco-tourism hotels in a developing country and an energy company's global headquarters in Japan.

When two members of The Natural Edge Project team visited a newly opened Queensland office refurbishment in October 2003, it was immediately clear that this was no ordinary office. The new sun shading features, thermosyphon wall and street front shops had dramatically transformed the western façade. Among the myriad of features were solar panels, a rainwater tank, waterless urinals, leased carpet, a solar hot water system and a staff worm farm.[3] It took almost an hour before someone noticed the smell, or lack thereof. There was none. The building had been open less than a week, but it was refreshingly free of 'new building odours'. The use of finishes such as Rockcote paints, Interface carpets, and low emission boards had virtually eliminated any trace of VOCs (Volatile Organic Compounds), while the biofilter planter in the foyer provided further filtering. The realization literally provided fresh appreciation of one of the many benefits of sustainable design.

When the PMM Group purchased this building (the shell of the former Ansett Transport Industries building) in Brisbane's Fortitude Valley, they decided it was important to 'walk the talk' with sustainable design. The aim of the building refurbishment was to provide an attractive, healthy and functional workplace for 120 staff, while at the same time showcasing sustainable design measures. PMM wanted to communicate a powerful message to the development industry by demonstrating that it is already viable and advantageous to adopt a wide range of sustainability measures in development projects, while maintaining commercial rigour. The design and commitment demonstrated in the building's construction will provide an ongoing educational and inspirational foundation for staff and client awareness and interest in sustainable design.

As a further example of innovative office design, Lend Lease's purpose-built Asia-Pacific headquarters '30 The Bond' at 30 Hickson Road, Millers Point in Sydney, represents a total commitment to the principles of sustainable development, and is an example of achievement within strict commercial parameters.

Source: PMM Photo Library

Figure 18.1 PMM *building, before and after renovations*

Employee workshops early in the process identified seven environmental aspirations: greenhouse gas reduction, indoor environmental quality, water management, materials selection, waste management, pollution and biodiversity. Employees ranked these aspirations, nominating reduction of greenhouse gases and the enhancement of indoor environmental quality, as the most important. The aspirations were then expressed in the design through the use of chilled beams, an operable façade, a full height atrium incorporating a heritage sandstone wall, a roof garden, and rapidly renewable and low-VOC (volatile organic compound) materials in the finishes. This building establishes new standards in indoor environment quality and biodiversity for a city office building. The design has also demonstrated significant greenhouse gas emission reductions through a commitment to the 'first base building design' 5-star rating in Australia, under the Australian Building Greenhouse Rating (ABGR) scheme.[4]

Source: Lend Lease Photo Library

Figure 18.2 Lend Lease's Asia-Pacific headquarters

The 60L (60 Leicester Street) 'Green Building' in Melbourne is an example of world class performance in terms of energy, greenhouse gas emissions and water efficiency in commercial buildings. The building focuses on reducing energy and water use, and minimizing waste and toxic exposure. As an employee working in the building explains, 'I love the whole building: it's clean and easy to breathe in. I feel more awake and not so tired after work'.

There are similarly striking developments internationally, and 'developing countries' have some of the world's best examples. Adjacent to the domestic airport at Mumbai, the recently built 245 room Orchid Hotel is the first five-star hotel to be built in Mumbai in 10 years, and the first in Asia to receive an Ecotel certification under ISO 14001. Although the rooms appear no different to any other hotel, on the bedside control panel is an 'ecobutton', part of a guest participation programme which invites the room occupants to save electricity by turning the room air-conditioning down by two degrees. There are a myriad of additional 'invisible' innovations throughout the building, with many of the innovative items in guest rooms made from recycled materials and sourced from local suppliers (including reusable cloth laundry bags, newspaper and shopping bags, coat-hangers made from compressed sawdust, tissue boxes and reed slippers). The hotel has achieved significant success as a result of these innovations, winning the corporate category of the 1999 annual Environmental Award of the International Hotel and Restaurant Association. The hotel is currently running at about 90 per cent occupancy year round.

Looking elsewhere to one of the most 'developed' countries in Asia, the Kyocera world headquarters in Japan is designed to place the highest priority on environmental issues.[5] The official corporate motto for this multi-billion-dollar corporation, 'Respect the Divine and Love People' is somewhat unusual in translation, but appears to have been very successful, with Kyocera being a leading producer and supplier of solar energy products worldwide. Opened in 1998, the 20-storey building was designed to be the world's most environmentally friendly corporate headquarters. According to the design team no sacrifice was made in space, comfort, or functionality to incorporate the facility's many environmental systems. The building even houses two world-class museums on its lower floors. Of particular note is a major innovation in solar panel technology. With 1392 solar panels on the south wall and 504 panels on the rooftop, at the time of opening this was the largest vertical solar energy system installed on any urban skyscraper. This creates a total output of 214 kilowatts, or 12.5 per cent of the building's electrical requirement, eliminating a significant amount of air pollution per year.

The solar-electric panels have also been installed in a unique array and have been adopted as a joint research theme between Kyocera and Japan's New Energy Development Organization (NEDO). This leading-edge project will be used to gather data on various solar energy systems operating long-term to help increase public understanding of solar electricity.

There is a growing list of green developments to learn from, with the previous examples providing a small snapshot. This chapter examines the key reasons for the building and development industry to change: to strive for truly sustainable development, genuine 'green development', in the built environment. This chapter will address what is limiting the building and development industry. We will look at how frameworks, operations and other innovations can address these issues and move the industry forward to achieve a large-scale change in performance. Readers are encouraged to read the key resources noted throughout this chapter to delve deeper into this material, and immediately begin putting into practice the actions discussed here.

Source: Kyocera Photo Library

Figure 18.3 Kyocera Building

The significance of greening the building and development industry

The built environment is regarded as Australia's largest asset. [In 2001, Australia's built environment represented a [AU]$100 billion-a-year infrastructure investment.] It's where we all live, where 95 per cent of the population work and where more than 90 per cent of the nation's GDP is generated. Thus, the technologies available for its design, planning, construction and operation will always be fundamental to the productivity and competitiveness of the economy, the quality of life of people and the ecological sustainability of the continent.

Brad Collis in Fields of Discovery: Australia's CSIRO[6]

In a recent article, How Green is thy City, the journal Business London asks whether, 'Under pressure to create environmentally-friendly buildings, could property developers be the new friends of the earth?'[7] The building and development industry currently wields one of the greatest influences on environmental and social conditions. Forty per cent of the world's materials and energy is used by buildings, with 55 per cent of wood cut for non-fuel uses consumed in construction. Thirty per cent of newly-built or renovated buildings suffer from 'sick building syndrome', exposing occupants to stale air or mould and chemical-laden air.[8]

Business-as-usual for this industry is clearly becoming a high-risk occupation.[9] In addition to issues of competition from more eco-efficient peers, there are an increasing number of regulatory requirements and associated fines and penalties for poor performance. Certain legislative frameworks now include the potential for personal liability as a result of corporate negligence. Consequently, companies which choose to ignore issues of sustainable development may experience higher insurance premiums or withdrawal of coverage, possible class action lawsuits, legal expenses, bad press and even consumer boycotts. This is in addition to the burden of unnecessarily high running costs and sub-optimal productivity.

On the flip side, common sense says that 'greening the built environment' is a way to make money and sell property. Companies that lead are gaining significant free publicity and are improving their chance of winning tenders. With the increase in requirements for sustainability initiatives in public infrastructure tenders, innovation in the area of sustainability is becoming a key point of differentiation. Within Australia, growth of the Listed Property Trust (LPT) sector[10] has led to increased scrutiny, by both community and institutional investors, of the development industry's sustainability behaviour. The Australian superannuation industry allocated, on average, approximately 10 per cent of its assets to LPTs at May 2003. For these investors, issues such as climate change, regulatory risks, water and waste management requirements and community and customer pressure highlight social and environmental aspects as key risks that need to be managed in the property sector.[11] Property developers who ignore these signals run the risk of being passed over by such investors.

One of the latest slogans in the industry, referring to the triple bottom line approach, is 'The bottom line of green is black'. There is a huge opportunity for the building and development industry to entice ethical investors to invest in green developments and green companies. Consumers are showing, through the growth of ethical investment funds in particular, that they want to direct savings to ensure a healthy retirement, and to ensure that these funds are used to create liveable environments for future generations. Developers globally have a significant ethical responsibility to society, local and regional economies, and the physical environments in which they operate. Not only does development alter the landscape and change patterns of human activity, it can dramatically change the well-being of individuals who live on or near the site, both now and well into the future. The following table summarizes key benefits to the financial bottom line, should social, environmental and institutional issues be addressed by the building and development industry. At the end of the day, companies in this industry will do well if they 'do good'; not all of these opportunities are found everywhere, but they appear frequently in daily business.

Table 18.1 *Reasons for change: key benefits to the building and development industry*

Economic	Social
Product differentiation	Indoor health
Market niche (health and productivity, green investment)	Higher work productivity for business occupants
Streamlined design costs	Reduced costs over the life of the building
Reduced capital costs	Satisfaction from doing the right thing
Reduced operating costs	
Increased market value (value premium) for the developer	**Environmental**
Faster leasing (absorption/ occupancy rate), increased rent for the building manager	Improved resource use
Customer mortgage and rebate incentives	Reduced building footprint (actual and ecological)
Public relations: word of mouth and referrals	
New business opportunities	**Institutional**
	Streamlined approvals
	Reduced liability risks
	Partnership and funded research opportunities,
	Keeping up with industry progress and regulations

Source: Material included from Wilson et al (1998)

Perceived barriers to change

With the benefits discussed above, why is the built environment industry so slow to move forward? Industry faces a number of barriers that may affect the success of implementing green developments, reflected in Figure 4.1 'Drivers restricting sustainable outcomes'. The following lists of specific barriers have been collated from a variety of sources, with key references noted. The lists are not exhaustive; the information, market and institutional failures described in the following section are inextricably interlinked. It is important to note that these issues reflect the current industry culture and perspective, rather than being a list of fundamental barriers to success.[12] They are *perceived* barriers and not necessarily actual barriers.

Information failures

Fundamentally, without a deeper understanding of the numerous impacts our buildings have on the global environment, communities, homes and workplaces, society is unable to see where the opportunities for improvement exist. Likewise, without a design process that is more inclusive and more rigorous in pursuing integrated design solutions, sustainable design cannot be realized and developed fully. As summarized in the *Hellmuth, Obata and Kassabaum (HOK) Guidebook to Sustainable Design,*[13] two things are needed: a greater base of information to inform decision-making, and a revised and expanded design process.

In Australia, the challenge is often not necessarily the lack of information, but the lack of access to this information; there is little opportunity for knowledge to flow to people who might make a difference. This is true to a large extent for educational facilities, government bodies and business including the built environment industry. Australia ranks near the bottom of major nations in its investment in building science, and research has long been hindered by widely varying building regulations within and between states. It is ironic that the results of the Commonwealth Scientific and Industrial Research Organisation (CSIRO) research have at times been incorporated into overseas building standards before they've been accepted in Australia.[14] (See Table 18.2.)

Market failures

Market failures of various kinds mean that the full benefits of many sustainability features in buildings cannot be captured either by the developer or the occupant. For example, water authorities are reluctant to reduce headworks' charges for buildings that limit their water demand or stormwater discharges, although this is improving. The difficulty of measuring other features such as indoor air quality means that the market finds it difficult to place a value on them. It is also true that a poorly constructed 'sustainable design' can give bad press when it doesn't perform, which can then unduly slow adoption of similar design opportunities. (See Table 18.3.)

Institutional failures

Within the development and building industry, there is a perceived overall lack of political will to drive innovation, such as market place reform, tax incentives, planning and development regulations. A report on innovation in the Australian building and construction industry in 2002[15] reflects that government can affect innovation in the building and construction industry in four ways:

Table 18.2 *Perceived information failures facing the building and development industry*

Knowledge and awareness	• Limited information about 'getting started'. • Lack of common terminology regarding aspects of the built environment. • Lack of reliable information regarding product source and manufacturing details, • Lack of information regarding the impact of architectural and design features. • Lack of training and education of all participants in the building industry, ranging from manufacturers of products and systems, architects, designers, private certifiers, installers and operators, to regulatory authorities and policy-makers. • Limited media coverage to promote discussion of built environment issues, contributing to a general lack of awareness amongst industry and the community.
Standards and guidelines	Standards and guidelines for planning and design often do not facilitate the incorporation of new techniques or practices.
Management syndrome	There is still an industry mindset of managing the environment (through mitigation or 'environmental management' measures) rather than managing development to enhance natural life support systems.[16]
Design dilution	Design features are diluted through the project, through lack of vision or information transfer, hindering the achievement of a holistic design approach.
Intellectual property	It is difficult to share information, forcing 'reinventing the wheel' scenarios within industry, due to the guarding of intellectual property, patenting processes and the fear of lawsuits.
Benchmarks	Despite the number of rating systems emerging in Australia, there is a lack of data available to a designer, purchaser or occupant, to assess how a building compares with some credibly formulated benchmark.
Design feedback	• Lack of stakeholder involvement during the design process, resulting in a built environment that may not address occupant's needs. • Limited resources allocated to research and development (data collection, analysis and definition) in the post-occupancy phase.
Future demands	There is still a lack of foresight into future sustainability issues. Although building uses are likely to change a number of times during a building's life, there is little consideration given to flexibility in the initial design.

Table 18.3 *Perceived market failures facing the building and development industry*

Financing	It is generally difficult to obtain financing for green buildings, with institutions still nervous about 'green' innovations, and the lack of other completed examples.
Tax disincentives and subsidies	The development industry still operates in an environment where tax incentives and subsidies promote existing products and their infrastructure, rather than more sustainable options.
Negating measures	Development features that are not sustainable are still often marketed to consumers, diverting capital from eco-efficiency opportunities in new buildings or refurbishments, to features that actually increase environmental impacts and ownership costs.
Rear-view mirror approach[17]	There are market analysis limitations with the current standard practice of looking at historic data to predict market trends, rather than evaluating emerging trends.
New vs. existing	Rating schemes and improvements are largely neglecting opportunities to refurbish existing buildings.
Modus vivendi[18]	There is a general reluctance in industry to trial new technologies, instead continuing to do what works, even though it may not be the best way.
Tendering process	• Few incentives exist to innovate in the design and construction phases of projects, due to non-descriptive project briefs and a lack of flexible pricing opportunities. • There is often a risk to tenderers of providing non-conforming tenders if they innovate.
Internalizing externalities	• Within financing institutions, there are a limited number of bank mortgage loans rewarding green buildings by taking a percentage off the mortgage loan. • Within the supply chain, externalities such as social and environmental impacts are often not included in product costs. • Within regulatory frameworks, building codes do not provide opportunities for reducing resource use.
Supply chain	There are few widely established supply chains for eco-efficient raw materials and products.
Split incentives	Developer/contractor/owner and owner/tenant divisions, or split incentives, often result in benefits of efficiency or improved performance measures not accruing to the party that initiated them, despite the clearly achievable overall savings.

1   as a major client: buying goods and services and creating demand for innovation;
2   as a regulator: developing and enforcing building codes and legislation;
3   as an educator: showcasing and promoting successful operators, success stories, and information sources;
4   as a custodian: creating a business environment through a tax system that encourages and rewards innovative businesses.

Government is in a unique position, as an industry stakeholder involved across the life cycle of buildings (i.e. as client, owner and tenant), to lead in the realization of this vision. However, government action still seems to be the exception rather than the rule. (See Table 18.4.)

Table 18.4 *Perceived institutional failures facing the building and development industry*

Political will	The short-term nature of political positions creates a short sightedness with regard to the future of the built environment.
Path dependency[19]	Systems, institutions, training, etc. favour dominant approaches and unintentionally discriminate against innovation (due to the sunk cost of prior investments) even where innovations are clearly the most cost effective.
Research and development	There has been a historical lack of government leadership in providing coordinated research and development into greening the built environment.
Education	There has been limited action by educational institutions to include 'sustainability critical-literacies' into material for professionals in the industry.
Professional accreditation	There is a general lack of sustainability-related professional accreditation requirements within the built environment industry.
Planning and development	Few local authorities have approval processes in place for the achievement of sustainability outcomes.
Regulation and incentives	• Although there are an increasing number of rating schemes and other performance measures, there is a lack of coordination. • There are limited government initiated incentives available to industry to encourage improvements in built environment performance.

From pioneers to systemic change: cultural reform

Given the information, market and institutional failings outlined above, it is clear that a critical shift is required to move forward: a behavioural change brought about by a critical mass of people willing to adopt and evolve sustainability principles and practices in the built environment. The impetus for greening the built environment is gaining momentum, with significant support and recognition for the need to change being demonstrated at all levels of society, from international bodies to national organizations, regional groups and local initiatives. Pioneers are also emerging in many areas of industry, including an increasing number of non-profit initiatives, partnerships, clusters and networks. Two leading examples are discussed below.

The Australian Council for Infrastructure Development (AusCID) represents those industry sectors involved in the area of private sector development of public infrastructure. Following a report card prepared with Engineers Australia in 2001, which highlighted the inadequacy of some of Australia's infrastructure, AusCID has produced a handbook on a 'Sustainability Framework for the Future of Australia's Infrastructure'.[20] It is intended that this framework will function as a driver to achieve the Council's strategic goals in the area of infrastructure development. As Dennis O'Neill, AusCID CEO, explains, 'Australia cannot afford to waste investment opportunities over the next 25–50 years. AusCID estimates the cost of making good the under-performing infrastructure, identified in the 2001 National Report Card, at around AU\$150 billion... the challenge of sustainable development is such, that a long-term vision and long-term plan of action must be produced... The opportunity offered by striving for sustainability also acts as a significant rallying call and incentive to build effective partnerships between governments and between public and private sectors, together with constructive discussion and concerted involvement of community stakeholders'.[21]

The Australian Green Development Forum (AGDF) was formed with support from a broad cross section of sectors including government, educational institutions, banking, product manufacturers, developers, industry representative bodies, community groups and a wide range of professionals in the development industry. As well as providing members with services such as information access, case studies of best practice, and listing and coordinating conferences and seminars, the AGDF provides opportunities for people with widely differing roles and interests in the development industry to share and learn from each other in a 'business community'. Partnerships created between AGDF members are intended to foster a greater appreciation of opportunities, methodologies and challenges in each other's respective fields: a natural business network. Such an approach also helps to broaden the collective understanding of what is necessary to achieve better functionality within the building and development industry. It is evident that regardless of a lack of formal systems, a critical mass is forming in the industry, with a number of internationally renowned Australian success stories.

In hosting the 2000 Sydney Olympic 'Green' Games, Australia clearly demonstrated its ability to be at the leading edge of a change to a 'greener' built environment.

> *In working with the Australians on the Sydney Olympic Village, I experienced firsthand how constructing all those green buildings, utilizing solar and wind power and using water technologies, galvanized the country. The Australians are now making great strides in green building technology, design and investment around the world.*

Bill Browning, Rocky Mountain Institute[22]

Given this momentum, regulatory and non-regulatory opportunities now need to be identified to facilitate the progression of sustainability initiatives in a whole-of-industry approach.[23] This is essentially Figure 4.3, the Platform for Change Diagram described earlier in Section 1, Chapter 4. Within this framework, an effective strategy for the built environment might include the following key elements, listed under the headings of information, market and institutional reform.

Information reform

Key opportunities for information reform are identified in Table 18.5.

Customer education, including feedback about the experiences of people living and working in both conventional and eco-efficient buildings, as well as promotion of credible and well-promoted rating schemes, can shift priorities. Already in Canberra, Australia, existing homes must be energy rated at the time of sale, and the rating displayed in all advertising: this can influence buyer perceptions and create an incentive for sellers to upgrade the performance of their houses. However, there is a long road to be travelled. For example, home and lifestyle magazines at present focus almost totally on aesthetics and image. They must be encouraged to rate the houses and buildings they present against environmental criteria, using house energy ratings, environmental ratings, etc., similar to the road tests in car magazines. When will there be a picture of a house with vast areas of unprotected west glazing described as scoring only two stars on its energy rating and rated by its occupants as uncomfortable in hot or cold weather? When will there be home improvement programmes tackling such a house and proposing smart strategies to shade the glass, provide movable insulation panels, or even reduce its glass area?

> *The process called sustainable development cannot be advanced quickly enough without a major contribution from engineering and technology.*

David Thom, Chairman of the Committee on Engineering and Environment of the World Federation of Engineering Organisations, 1991–1999

Table 18.5 *Information reform opportunities for the building and development industry*

Improved knowledge	Increased knowledge and awareness, through: • Including sustainability critical literacy requirements at the tertiary level for all disciplines associated with the building and development industry. • Providing sustainability critical literacy skills to senior management and politicians. • Training and certifying professionals and tradespeople to deliver eco-efficient buildings, including practical guidance towards suitable products. • Educating planning and development assessment officers to remain up to date with requirements and best practice options. • Providing education and information programmes for consumers, including homebuyers and prospective commercial building tenants.
Supporting information	• Development and refinement of rating and evaluation systems, as well as certification processes, supporting technical standards, model specifications and codes of practice within the building and development industry. • Provision of information relating to available products and making the most of technological aids such as the Internet.
Network and collaboration benefits	Increased awareness of sources of technical, product and processes information through associations, networks, advisory panels and media involvement.
Performance validation	• Obtaining information that validates performance, and using monitoring and measurement tools to assess the achievement of sustainability targets. • Research and analysis to quantify and document claimed benefits of eco-efficiency measures.
Simplification	Reducing the cost and complexity of implementing eco-efficient practices and products through improved design, increased economies of scale and technological development.
Information sharing	Facilitating information sharing within and between organizations and professions: a change in industry perspective to see the sharing of intellectual property as an opportunity rather than a risk.
Materials innovation	Innovation to create environmentally sound products, materials and systems that address the needs of the building and development industry.

There are a number of universities attempting to address innovation issues within the building and development industry,[24] and key funding injections are being made. The Cooperative Research Centre for Construction Innovation (CRC for CI) is an Australian example of a national research, development and implementation centre focused on the needs of the property, design, construction and facility management sectors, with a significant focus on sustainability. Underpinning the CRC is the most significant commitment ever made to construction research in Australia: a seven-year AU$14 million Commonwealth grant and AU$50 million in industry, research and other government funding and in-kind services.[25] This should, however, be put in context with the AU$20 billion or more spent each year in Australia on non-transport related energy.[26]

Within the education system, there is a clear need for tertiary institutions to be including sustainability 'critical literacy' programmes for all undergraduates, particularly for those seeking employment within the built environment industry. From engineers to accountants, to the trades, all areas of the industry must be exposed to the language and fundamental principles of sustainability so that the importance of sustainable developments can be understood and translated into daily business. This is discussed in Section 5, Chapter 22. Professional bodies are critical in implementing such material. Engineers Australia is an example of such a body leading the way in developing critical literacy material in Australia, through facilitation of the Engineering Sustainable Solutions Program.[27]

There is also a clear need for ongoing development of evaluation and rating methodologies, to clarify the criteria for good environmental performance. Manufacturers of materials, products and systems need assistance to identify the environmental strengths and weaknesses of their products so they can improve performance and promote their positive attributes. Specifiers, designers, builders, installers and customers generally need objective and accessible product-specific information to create a market 'pull'. A good example of a practical attempt at the provision of information is the materials flipchart, developed by RMIT's Centre for Design, for a major green housing development.[28] The Australian Council of Building Design Professions (BDP) has published an Environmental Design Guide that is continually updated with emerging issues, design notes and product and materials information.[29] *Ecospecifier*[30] is an excellent example of facilitating access to information about green products and resources that make economic sense. This web-based material database was used for the 60L project and many other developments, where it has contributed to improved environmental performance without jeopardising the 'bottom line'. According to RMIT (co-developer of *Ecospecifier*), with new products emerging almost every day, the database is facilitating improvements in a number of areas. For example, the building industry was dubious about using concrete with a 60 per cent recycled component, but its inclusion in Ecospecifier and subsequent implementation in 60L has helped to make this a standard in many projects. According to the project team, 'What exists is possible!'.

'Information hoarding' may not remain in the future culture of the building and development industry. Hellmuth, Obata and Kassabaum (HOK) provide an international example of the clear benefits of sharing intellectual property. HOK is a large international architecture, engineering, interiors, planning and consulting firm, designing almost US$5 billion in new construction and renovation each year. The firm has taken a huge step by sharing its accumulated knowledge on the industry through publishing a design guide on sustainability through the American Institute of Architects (AIA).[31]

> *The goal is, quite fundamentally, to redefine design quality in the built environment.*
>
> Sandra Mendler, HOK and Chair, AIA Committee on the Environment[32]

In 1995, an internal publication was compiled by HOK employees as a desktop reference to support project work. Through company leadership in recognizing the importance of the project, the writers were able to refine the publication and, in 1998, the company published the guide. In 2000, a revised edition was published by the AIA with additions and revisions from other organizations. From HOK's perspective, the impact of construction on the environment is great, but the ability to create meaningful improvements is even greater. Through this initiative, they have spread the word on their expertise, increased awareness of opportunities in design and have remained at the forefront of architectural consultancy. How many other companies have accumulated wisdom that could be developed, in a similar manner, to raise the profile of the company and accelerate progress towards an improved built environment? There are definite opportunities to be realized in this area for those who lead the way.

Market reform

When companies are spending an average of 70 times the amount of money (per 0.09m^2 per year) on employee salaries as on energy, for example, an increase of just 1 per cent in productivity can result in savings that exceed the company's entire energy bill.[33] When it is considered that productivity gains of 6–16 per cent, including decreased absenteeism and improved quality of work, have been reported in day lit buildings the case to consider sustainability design aspects is significant.[34] To a developer, these facts can mean higher lease rates and greater return on investment if the landlords and tenants understand the benefits, which include energy savings and productivity gains. While such facts have been available for a number of years now, there is clearly a need for the marketplace to make these opportunities visible: to promote new types of purchasing and leasing arrangements that provide such savings.

> *Providing ecologically sustainable real estate is becoming a key to deriving solid returns from real estate ownership and development... Property solutions in tune with the environment are being demanded by users and owners alike.*
>
> Nic Lyons, CEO, General Property Trust[35]

Key market reform opportunities are summarized in Table 18.6.

Table 18.6 *Market reform opportunities for the building and development industry*

Choice and decision-making	Help potential buyers appreciate the long-term economic, social and environmental consequences of life cycle choices at the point of decision-making.
Supply chain	Facilitate a more efficient supply chain so that good products are acknowledged, made known and made available to the development industry.
Building flexibility	Develop designs that can be built as smaller buildings but easily extended, or buildings that can be easily divided at a later date.
Market research	Use more innovative marketing research techniques.[36]
Performance disclosure	Require mandatory disclosure by developers of performance (including infringements) and benchmarking of performance, including indoor air quality, energy consumption, ecological footprint, etc. This provides communication of the cost, environmental and social benefits of urban sustainability to the community and other developers.
Financing opportunities	• Create markets through the formation of buying groups, collectives, green partnerships and clusters. • Increase awareness of 'feebate' incentives and of spreading costs and benefits through the business community.
True costing of externalities	Restructure pricing (i.e. by infrastructure agencies) to reflect cost savings resulting from eco-efficient building practices.
Business focus	• Encourage industry self regulation through Codes of Practice, frameworks and standards such as ISO 14000. • Provide incentives within industry groups, for businesses that initiate and foster sustainability related initiatives.
Green partnerships and green leasing	Encourage new-style leasing arrangements that reward reduced energy, water and materials consumption.
Tendering incentives	Provide incentives for sustainable design by allowing innovative or flexible payment arrangements and proposals in the tender phase of projects.

Urban design consultants, DesignInc, have been involved in two recent building projects that demonstrate cost savings associated with sustainable development that uses new technologies: Deakin University's Building T and the Geoscience Australia building in Canberra. The buildings were made possible through the leadership shown by Deakin University and Geoscience Australia, enabling pioneering research that is often difficult to undertake in the private sector. Both of these buildings incorporate passive heating and cooling systems, natural lighting and user controlled services to achieve substantial reductions in operational energy requirements. Both organizations took risks that would not normally be acceptable to private sector clients, but have still achieved downstream operational savings.

While individual companies can achieve marked improvements in building outcomes, it has also been shown in a number of instances that partnerships increase the potential for success even further. Demonstrated by the 60L building in Melbourne, where a team led by Councillor Peter Brotherton and assisted by Green Building Officer Alistair Mailer partnered with investor Mark Wootton to form the Green Building Partnership with two ethical investment companies, Surrowee Pty Ltd and Green Projects Pty Ltd. The 60L building is now owned and managed by the Green Building Partnership using a 'Green Lease',[37] which is generally believed to be the first lease of its kind in Australia. The lease is based on principles of shared responsibility, sustainability and waste reduction. In tandem with the lease, each tenant is required to comply with the building's Environmental Management Plan (EMP). Sustainable Solutions prepared fit-out guidelines for tenants, in conjunction with the Green Building Partnership, through a grant from the City of Melbourne. All tenants can access systems to separate and handle paper, beverage containers and residual materials and gain feedback on energy consumption and water use. Considerations, like bike parking facilities on the ground floor and water efficient showers on every level, support all tenants' work environments. The Victorian EPA and the Department of Sustainability and Environment provided assistance to communicate the message that 'Green Buildings Make $ense' to the commercial property development industry.[38]

Partnership approaches are delivering success stories worldwide. The Beddington Zero (fossil) Energy Development (BedZED),[39] in Sutton, is Britain's first urban carbon-neutral development. It is a powerful argument for the feasibility of a zero-carbon target for all new buildings. The BedZED design reconciles high-density three storey city blocks with high residential and workspace amenity. The BedZED partnership brings together four separate strands of activity, incorporating the experience and expertise of a number of organizations: it was developed over a five year period by Bill Dunster architects, in conjunction with engineers Arup, quantity surveyors Gardiner and Theobald and the BioRegional Development Group. The current design provides a balance between many competing needs while meeting the needs of the Peabody Trust to build a mixed tenure community on an existing brownfield site.

Institutional reform

Reform is required among institutional bodies to give effect to innovations, including integrated decision-making processes and sustainability performance standards. Opportunities for reform include the possibilities identified in Table 18.7:

While sustainability is a matter raised in most planning documents, a more significant paradigm shift within institutions is required for the built environment to be addressed successfully. The building and development industry relies significantly on planning frameworks. As such, there needs to be consistency in such frameworks, within and across government units, and with regard to the setting of clear performance objectives and compliance with sustainability standards. Across all levels of government,

Table 18.7 *Institutional reform opportunities for the building and development industry*

Vision in the planning system	Use sustainability principles as a foundation to underpin planning systems.
Clarity of approach	Provide a coordinated and clear approach to discussing and implementing sustainability initiatives, so that industry, the community, and all levels in all government departments are clear on how they may be involved.
Leadership	Lead, by setting ambitious sustainability guidelines on government building and infrastructure projects, and by setting standards, codes, benchmarks and incentive schemes that encourage improvement in the building and development industry.
Benchmarking, regulating and providing incentives	As confidence and expertise builds, incorporate eco-efficient building requirements in planning and building codes.

strategic policy directions, 'motherhood statements' and language such as 'should', 'encourage', 'consider', 'adequate' need to be translated into definitive planning, performance or design requirements.

To really move industry forward, government planning entities must have clear processes that send clear messages to industry. In general, governments are well placed to encourage the following planning measures for sustainable development:

- approval mechanisms that accommodate innovative sustainable design features;
- an improved approvals process that recognizes and rewards developments incorporating sustainable design features;
- performance based codes for energy, water and waste management;
- removing charges for services (e.g. headwork charges) that are not used;
- provision of feebates for developments that demonstrate measurable improvements in energy, water usage and waste management. These rebates could be funded from extra fees levied on less well designed developments;
- integration of department activities to minimize conflicting requirements;
- technical assistance and education in sustainable development principles and technologies for town planning officials, builders, designers and the public.

There are numerous local authorities in Australia and overseas considering integrating sustainability codes into their planning schemes, and assessment tools into their development assessment processes. Such tools essentially provide an initial sustainability checklist to determine whether developments comply with planning scheme requirements, followed by more detailed assessment protocols for more complex 'major' developments.

Rating schemes

There are many dimensions to sustainable buildings and major challenges in developing and applying objective criteria and analysis to the issues involved. Although Australia has a variety of energy and greenhouse rating systems, it is yet to develop a consistent national rating system for the environmental performance of a building as a whole.[40] Further, Australia's regulations are relatively limited in both scope and stringency compared with many developed countries. While regulations and policy responses to date have mainly focused on new buildings, the reality is that there is an urgent need to focus attention on existing buildings and, in particular, on major renovations and

Table 18.8 GRI *sustainability indicators recommended by* AusCID *for infrastructure projects*

Categories	Aspects	Indicators
ECONOMIC		
1 Direct economic impacts	Suppliers	1 EC3 – Cost of all goods, materials and services purchased.
ENVIRONMENTAL		
2 Environmental	Materials	2 EN1 – Total materials use other than water, by type. Report in tonnes, kilograms, or volume. Provide definitions used for types of materials.
	Energy	3 EN3 – Direct energy use segmented by primary source. Report on all energy sources used by the reporting organization for its own operations as well as for the production and delivery of energy products (e.g., electricity or heat) to others. Report in joules.
	Water	4 EN5 – Total water use.
	Biodiversity	5 EN7 – Description of major impacts on biodiversity – associated with the organization's activities and/or products and services in terrestrial, freshwater and marine environments.
	Emissions	6 EN8 – Greenhouse gas emissions. GHG emissions (CO_2, CH_4, N_2O, HFCs, PFCs, SF6). Report separate subtotals for each gas in tonnes and in tonnes of CO_2 equivalent for: • direct emissions from owned or controlled sources; • indirect emissions from imported electricity, heat, steam. 7 EN11 – Total amount of waste by type and destination. 'Destination' refers to the method by which waste is treated, including composting, reuse, recycling, recovery, incineration, or landfilling. Explain type of classification method and estimation method.
SOCIAL		
3 Labour practices and decent work	Health and safety	8 LA7 – Standard injury, lost day, absentee rates and number of work-related fatalities (including sub-contracted workers).
4 Human rights	Indigenous rights	9 HR12 – Description of policies, guidelines and procedures to address the needs of indigenous people. This includes indigenous people in the workforce and communities where the organization currently operates or intends to operate.
5 Society	Community	10 SO1– Description of policies to manage impacts on communities in areas affected by the reporting organization's activities, as well as description of procedures/programmes to address this issue, including monitoring systems and results of monitoring. Include explanation of procedures for identifying and engaging in dialogue with community stakeholders.
6 Product responsibility	Customer health and safety	11 PR1 – Description of policy for preserving customer health and safety during the use of organization's products and services, and extent to which this policy is visibly stated and applied, and description of procedures/programmes to address this issue, including monitoring systems and results of monitoring. Explain rationale for any multiple standards in product marketing and sales.

Note: The table contains a selection of indicators drawn from the Global Reporting Initiative (GRI).
Source: AusCID (2003, p25)

refurbishment projects. With over 7.5 million buildings in Australia, many of which are poor energy performers, there is a clear need for improvement.

Recent efforts have begun to draw together industry experience and integrate it into a coherent framework. This process is still in its infancy, and attempts to develop rating schemes to date have highlighted that a great deal of work is still needed to develop the knowledge base, products and services needed to deliver a 'greener' built environment. Nevertheless, some impressive projects have been completed and interest within the commercial building market has begun to grow.

Schemes such as the ABGR scheme for commercial buildings, and possibly new rating schemes for households, along with requirements to declare environmental performance at the time of sale or renting, are potentially important strategies. There have been a number of recent attempts nationally to develop more comprehensive evaluation and rating systems, such as NABERS,[41] BASIX,[42] LICHEE[43] and Green Star.[44] Internationally similar projects are underway with a number of design firms and organizations developing their own assessment and benchmarking tools to consult with globally.[45] An example of an exciting new development is the CRC for Construction Innovation's 'green calculator' that gives building industry professionals an immediate cost and environmental 'footprint' assessment of any commercial building. According to the leader of the CSIRO development team, Dr Peter Newton, the real-time calculator illustrates a growing competitive advantage in Australian research and development; the ability to combine the best research from contrasting fields coupled with industry-focused partners to drive real outcomes. 'It's a genuine world-first – and we're seeing real interest in it from the North American construction industry where there is currently nothing equivalent'.[46]

There is now a general perception within the industry that compulsory energy building ratings will be introduced – it is merely a matter of when. The Australian Building Codes Board introduced model regulations for housing in early 2003 (which are now under review), and will progressively introduce regulations covering non-residential building energy use over the next two years.[47] Large property organizations such as Mirvac, Macquarie Listed and Unlisted Property Trusts, General Property Trust, Investa Property Group and Colonial First State Property are using the ABGR scheme to build a reputation for their improved environmental performance. With the addition of tools to this scheme including 'Star Performer', a diagnostic tool that provides simple and effective energy efficiency advice, and the Tenant Energy Management Handbook, it is becoming easier to demonstrate improvements in performance.

There is the potential for a wide range of incentives, standards and schemes to be used, but the national context must be clear (for example through a national framework). Government could tip the balance towards innovation by demanding that each building and construction provider working on a government project should detail their innovation programme as part of the selection criteria. In the residential market, display homes could be required to display their environmental ratings in a prominent place and to display energy meters and information on the capital and running cost of the air-conditioning and heating equipment they have installed. Too often, display homes use large heating and cooling systems to overcome the serious energy-related weaknesses of their designs, but these are not visible to the potential homebuyers. Only after they move into their own dream home do they discover the reality in inflated power bills, by which time it is too late.

With the proliferation of rating schemes and similar tools, generally applied on a voluntary basis (driven by market incentives), there is the question of how or whether one or more should be made mandatory in development approval processes. At present, the tools are quite diverse with regard to whether they have mandated targets or mandated means of meeting those targets. When considering non-mandatory targets and performance measures, the provision of incentives may be necessary to give the broader assessment tools greater legitimacy. Given the potential breadth of sustainability assessment, it is clearly not possible to mandate performance against all possible assessment areas; however incentives can play a role in facilitating greater overall performance beyond core sustainability areas (e.g., energy and water). This debate clearly needs to be progressed to deliver clarity to the building and development industry.

Design practice reform

Design process elements

As Janis Birkeland summarizes in *Design for Sustainability*,[48] the built environment has derived from design 'of, for and by' the industrial order, rather than 'of, for and by' its inhabitants. Design practice reform is about ensuring that 'thinking green' is a focus of the entire design process, requiring collaboration and mutual incentives to drive the team to a new level of achievement. Rocky Mountain Institute (RMI) identifies four key design process elements of green development (see Table 18.9), the philosophy of which is also reflected in Birkeland's sourcebook and the HOK design guide.

Rockcote is a manufacturer of architectural coatings for buildings. Their proposed new building in Queensland's southeast hinterland town of Nerang is a champion project of the Urban Development Institute of Australia's Sustainable Urban Development Program, and is an example of what can result from consideration of such design process elements. The design team produced a building that echoes RMI's Design Process Elements and that emulates the company's sustainability vision.

According to Birkeland, to be considered an 'eco-development', the built environment should look at all of the following aspects, as a whole:[49]

Table 18.9 RMI *design process elements to encourage design practice reform*

Whole-systems thinking	Systems design means making system-wide improvements, not just remediation. We need to find fundamental material and energy efficiencies and synergies. Amory Lovins states: 'Any design element that has only one function is probably a mistake or a missed opportunity. We ought to strive for multiple and diverse functions of each element so we pay once and get many benefits.'[50]
Front-loaded design	Up-front building and design costs may represent only a fraction of the building's life cycle costs. When just 1% of a project's up-front costs are spent, up to 70% of its life cycle costs may already be committed; when 7% of project costs are spent, up to 85% of life cycle costs have been committed. As Bill McDonough states, 'People talk about heating a building... a cathedral. But it isn't the cathedral that is asking to be heated: it is the people. To heat the cathedral, one should heat people's feet, not the air 120 feet above them'.[51]
End-use/ least-cost	Design considerations must examine the future adaptability of the built environment and changing needs over time.
Teamwork	The old model of the financier talking to the developer, who talks to the architect, who talks to the construction professional, who talks to the real estate broker, who talks to the tenant, in a linear fashion, is counterproductive. Everyone needs to be communicating with one another simultaneously before a building or development project is actually considered.[52]

Source: Wilson et al (1998, pp37, 160–177)

- meeting social, economic, ecological and cultural needs in addition to being eco-efficient;
- improving basic environmental systems, not just reducing impacts (e.g., water and air quality, energy production, soil fertility, etc.);
- meeting human psychological needs (e.g., places for positive social interaction, communion with nature, sense of community);
- optimizing the use of urban space to increase biodiversity, natural habitats and ecosystem services (i.e. not relying on the surrounding region as a source or sink).
- improving community health and welfare (e.g., equity, sense of place, safety, healthy materials);
- increasing the conditions for biophysical-ecological welfare and increasing natural capital (i.e. not just respect carrying capacity);
- avoiding fibres, fuels, foods and processes that are linked to the fossil fuel supply chain.

In A *Pattern Language* and *The Timeless Way of Building*, Christopher Alexander and his colleagues explored ways in which society could relate traditional building methods which created functional homes, communities and towns with local skills and resources in an organic manner.[53] The methods would not be dictated by architects or planners, but largely by the people who lived there. In an attempt to capture the interconnected nature of functional spaces, the authors conceptualized a 'language' of 'patterns' that were ordered from largest to smallest, beginning with regions and towns, through neighbourhoods, clusters of buildings, buildings, rooms and alcoves, ending with details of construction.[54] The relevance of this system is the acknowledgement of the intrinsic connection between scales: each pattern is connected to the larger patterns which come above it, and to smaller patterns which come below it.

> *In short, no pattern is an isolated entity. Each pattern can exist in the world only to the extent that it is supported by other patterns: the larger patterns in which it is embedded, the patterns of the same size that surround it and the smaller patterns which are embedded in it... This is a fundamental view of the world. It says that when you build a thing you can not merely build that thing in isolation, but must also repair the world around it, and within it, so that the larger world at that one place becomes more coherent, and more whole; and the thing which you make takes its place in the web of nature as you make it.*
>
> Christopher Alexander et al[55]

This relatively simple means of describing the interconnectedness of the way in which spaces and systems work is one of the central ideas needed to implement sustainable additions to our built form. Indeed, the principles apply equally to the restructuring of our systems, the interrelatedness of programmes and policies and the machinations of society. It is holistic thinking condensed to a 'language' that can be grasped.

Two key examples of frameworks to guide the design process from a more whole and holistic perspective are Sim Van der Ryn and Stuart Cowan's Design Principles (summarized in Table 18.10), and William McDonough's 'Hannover Principles' as highlighted in Table 3.1.[56]

Residential buildings

As the focus in this chapter so far has been on commercial buildings, the following paragraphs examine some emerging opportunities for improvements in residential developments. In developed nations, many homes constructed in the post World War II

Table 18.10 *Design principles example: Sim Van der Ryn and Stuart Cowan*

1	**Solutions grow from place**	Ecological design begins with the intimate knowledge of a particular place. It is, therefore, small-scale and direct, responsive to both local conditions and local people. If we are sensitive to the nuances of place, we can inhabit without destroying.
2	**Ecological accounting informs design**	Trace the environmental impacts of existing or proposed designs. Use this information to determine the most ecologically sound design possibility.
3	**Design with nature**	By working with living processes we respect the needs of all species while meeting our own. By engaging in processes that regenerate rather than deplete, we become more alive.
4	**Everyone is a designer**	Listen to every voice in the design process. No one is a participant only: everyone is a participant-designer. Hone the special knowledge that each person brings. As people work together to heal their places, they also heal themselves.
5	**Make nature visible**	De-natured environments ignore our need and our potential for learning. Making natural cycles and processes visible brings the designed environment back to life. Effective design helps inform us of our place within nature.

Source: Van der Ryn and Cowan (1996)

'flight to the suburbs' are due for either demolition or renovation. While 'urban consolidation' policies are appropriate in some cases (i.e. increasing residential density combined with mixed use developments), this reconstruction process would take a long time, consume excessive resources and lead to incalculable waste to landfill. In the meantime, these old, leaky homes use fossilized energy for heating, cooling and ventilating. Higher standards of energy efficiency are being established for new homes, but these constitute only about 2 per cent of the total housing stock. Sustainability requires that something be done to plug the leaks in existing suburbs. Homes are one area where fossil fuel use could be eliminated without a loss of comfort. There is plenty of solar energy, and it can heat, cool and ventilate homes as effectively as gas or electric equipment – and with far less environmental and health impacts. 'Passive solar design' uses the building shape and materials to produce, store and distribute heat, coolness and fresh air throughout the building. This is much better than adding on 'energy efficient equipment', because mechanical equipment and fuels entail energy and pollution in production, transport, maintenance and eventual disposal.

It is essential to retrofit suburban housing stock to:

- reduce greenhouse emissions, waste, resource use and energy consumption;
- upgrade the housing stock without the extensive demolition and waste that accompany major re-developments;
- increase residential density without exceeding the capacity of the existing infrastructure or losing urban ecosystem services;
- convert them from dependency on toxic, petrochemical-based materials and energy to reliance on clean, safe and healthy passive solar energy systems.[57]

How can all of these imperatives be met in a cost effective way? Existing homes could be retrofitted at net zero cost to homeowners by using financial mechanisms that pay for the current construction work from the future energy savings of the building.[58] But while revolving funds for energy retrofitting have been established by some local councils for

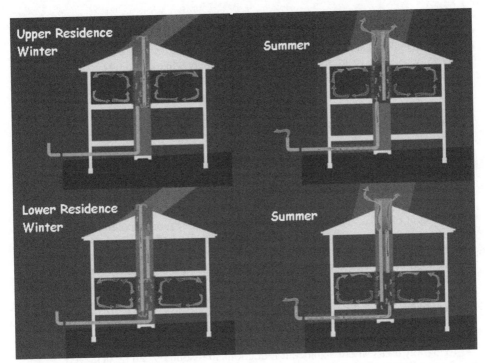

Source: Janis Birkeland[59]

Figure 18.4 *One example of a solar core design*

their own buildings, it does not appear to create an adequate incentive for the private home market. More is needed than simply a good return on investment; positive incentives are needed for homeowners or developers to retrofit existing homes with passive solar technology.

The 'Solar Core' is an example of a design concept that enables existing homes or apartments to be heated, cooled and ventilated with passive solar energy.[60] It works by collecting the solar heat in the attic of the second floor dwelling unit, storing it in the centre of the structure (in an existing fireplace or hall closet space), and distributing heating and cooling to both dwellings. The Solar Core is essentially a combination of a 'solar chimney' or solar stack (which draws hot air out of the house through a chimney type structure) with a vertical, centrally-located thermal storage container of earth blocks or small rocks, which stores and circulates heat and stabilizes the internal temperature. In winter, the hot air collected in the attic space and roof is delivered with a (solar boosted) fan from the attic space to the base of the Solar Core through pipes. This hot air heats the thermal mass of rocks as it rises. In summer, cool air would be drawn from below the house (or shady side in the case of slab-on-ground construction) which cool the rocks and drive unwanted heat out through the roof or chimney. North-facing windows or building shapes are not necessary, as the concept could be used on any roof not overshadowed by other buildings or tall trees.

The addition of second floor units with a Solar Core would not only provide an incentive for the conversion of existing homes to passive solar heating, cooling and ventilating, it would have many additional advantages. For example, it would reward good design, as only building additions that were ecologically responsible would be permitted. It would improve ecological and human health while generating economic development, new employment, and skilled jobs and training in 'constructive' forms of work (which cost less to create than jobs in most other sectors). It would also preserve consumer choice in life styles and housing, as the Solar Core would be compatible with any existing building style, by using the existing roof. In addition, it would preserve urban biodiversity, increase residential density and life quality, while avoiding congestion, urban heat sinks, storm water runoff and adverse impacts of other urban consolidation programmes.

The future in design approaches

> *Now more than ever ... we need people who think broadly and who understand systems, connections, patterns and root causes.*
> David Orr, one of the greatest environmental educators of our time[61]

The adoption of whole systems design approaches, that reorganize the design process around up-front consideration of issues and that include a wide variety of team members, is fundamental in achieving a reform of the design process. In addition, there are a number of other design approaches currently being discussed by the leaders in the field, such as:

* **Biomimicry**: capitalizing on what nature has been showing us all along: non-toxic, low energy, elegant solutions: Bio-inspired design.[62]
* **Material flows analysis**: mapping material flows through human and natural systems to identify areas where significant reductions in resources can be achieved.[63]
* **Energy flow analysis**: mapping energy flows through processes and comparing them with ideal energy requirements to identify potential areas for savings.[64]

An example of what such design techniques can achieve is the 30,100m², US$36 million mixed-use and naturally ventilated Eastgate building in Harare, Zimbabwe.[65] Old Mutual, a large property developer fed up with expensive imported air-conditioners, delivered an ultimatum to their design team that the building could not have any refrigerated air-conditioning. This was not an easy request for a building in the hot climate of Zimbabwe, so the team looked to biomimicry for a solution.

> *If we recognize that cities are ecosystems, like rainforests or coral reefs but built by humans, we can find meeting points between nature and technology.*
> Mike Pearce, lead architect on the Eastgate Building, Harare

Macrotermes bellicosus, a species of African termite, keeps its tall mound between 31 and 32°C, despite outside temperature oscillations between 2 and 46°C (this temperature range in the mound is optimal for the termites' main food, an edible fungus that termites 'farm'). A sophisticated ventilation design within the solid earthen structure makes this possible. Outside breezes are drawn in at the base of the mound, funnelled down to mud-cooled, subterranean chambers and then drawn up through the centre of the mound via a 'stack effect'.

The design team used this natural phenomenon to deliver to the client a passively cooled building. Giant fans were incorporated to imitate the termite's wing movements, and concrete slabs were used to store coolness. During Harare's cold, high-altitude nights, these fans draw in fresh air at the base of the structure. Seven times per hour, a complete change of air flows through the honeycomb chambers between all of the floors and out of the 48 chimneys on the roof. The stored coolness is released throughout the day as the air-exchange rate slows to 2 times per hour. As a result, the building uses less

Figure 18.5 *Eastgate Building, Harare*

than 10 per cent of the energy of an average Zimbabwean building its size, costs US$3.5 million less to build and offers rents 20 per cent lower than competitors (due to the lower energy bill). On all but the hottest days, this building provides a comfortable, quiet work atmosphere (3–4°C lower than outside air temperatures). Furthermore, in the six years since its construction, Pearce and his team of Arup engineers have improved upon the natural ventilation design and can now double its thermal performance.

An imminent new 10,000 m² office building, to be built by Melbourne City Council for its own occupation on Little Collins Street, has called on the same architect, Mike Pearce, as an environmental design director for the project, after his success on the Eastgate building in Harare. In addition, the design team includes a host of leaders in the sustainability field. According to Melbourne Lord Mayor John So, the building, known as Council House 2 or CH2, is being designed with sustainability considerations embedded into every part of it.[67] Forecast emission levels are 60 per cent less than that scored by a top-rating 5-star building under the AGBR scheme. Furthermore, in recognition of its aim for zero greenhouse gas emissions, the Council is exploring ways to offset all of CH2's greenhouse emissions by investing in renewable energy generation. This would enable the building to achieve a neutral or even positive net result for the project. The design process has included a two-week design group workshop session with the project team that established a conceptual framework for the project and produced the key strategies for the building design – its planning, envelope, structure and services.

> *This will be a win–win situation for everyone involved – we are taking a responsible, long-term approach to developing a building the council needs to have while setting an example of what must be achieved if we are to be a truly sustainable and thriving city.*
>
> Melbourne City Council Lord Mayor, John So[68]

Summary

In summary, developments highlighted in this chapter clearly show the benefits of greening the built environment, and there are many other national and international examples that demonstrate the social, economic and environmental benefits of a 'greener' built environment industry. The chapter also provides evidence of the wealth of ideas and successes internationally and in Australia that is not always acknowledged. We have discussed how perceived information, market and institutional failures are now beginning to be addressed, removing the barriers to industry change. It is time to seek out a large-scale change in performance. The language and actions required to achieve a sustainable built environment must become 'the norm', so that we can all benefit from more outcomes that will make our future generations proud.

CHAPTER 19

SUSTAINABLE URBAN TRANSPORT

Jeff Kenworthy, Robert Murray-Leach and Craig Townsend

Economic impacts of transport choices are significant[1]

Travel is so seamlessly intertwined with the range of activities comprising our daily lives that it is difficult to step back and clearly assess how it influences our quality of life, economy, and environment. In recent decades, we have grown accustomed to travelling further, faster and more frequently. Transport has many aspects, including movement in urban and rural areas, movement of people and freight, and movement by land, air and water. This chapter focuses on the global transport sector which directly affects a large and growing proportion of the world's population on a daily basis: urban passenger transport. Over the last half of the 20th century, privately-owned and operated motor vehicles have increasingly dominated urban passenger transport systems in many countries. As part of a balanced transport system, cars and motorbikes can bring flexibility and convenience that enrich our lives. However, with the rapid growth in private vehicle use our transport systems have become increasingly imbalanced, resulting in the problems from private motor vehicle exceeding their benefits.

The impacts of current motorized vehicles on air quality, human health and urban public spaces have been concerns for many decades now. In the 1990s 'sustainable urban transport' became a mainstream challenge to the notion that urban transport systems dominated by motor cars can be sustainable. In part this has been driven by the continued growth of car use in high-income cities, but also by the rapid growth in motor vehicle use in the large and growing cities of China, India, and South-east Asia. If these cities were to become as dependent on motor vehicles as many cities in Australia and North America, the global environmental consequences could potentially be extreme.

If China were to match the USA for levels of car ownership and oil consumption per person, it would mean producing approximately 850 million more cars and more than doubling the world output of oil. Those additional cars would produce more

This chapter was co-authored by Jeff Kenworthy, Associate Professor, Sustainable Settlements, Institute for Sustainability and Technology Policy, Murdoch University, Western Australia, Robert Murray-Leach, TNEP Working Group member, and Dr Craig Townsend, Planning and Transport Research Centre, Perth, Western Australia.

CO_2 per annum than the whole of the rest of the world's transportation systems.
UNEP, Sustainable Consumption: Global Status Report 2002

It has long been believed that building roads is good for the economy of cities while public transport is a financial drain. But a report to the World Bank (published as *Sustainability and Cities*[2]) prepared by researchers at Murdoch University is turning this way of thinking on its head. Professor Peter Newman says they've found that cities which emphasize walking, cycling and public transport are healthier financially and spend less of their wealth on transport costs. The six cities that came out the best were cities like Zurich, Copenhagen, Stockholm – very wealthy cities now which spend only 4 or 5 per cent of their wealth on transport, and yet they're the cities that are putting their money into public transport. And the cities still pouring money into freeways use up to 17 per cent of their wealth. Australian and US cities like Perth and Phoenix are wasting far more of their valuable wealth on just getting around. Our data would really question that freeway building has any economic rationale; unless you're building up the rail system (as in Perth) you are not going to help it economically. As soon as you put in big roads then you create a market for city sprawl and this is very expensive. If you build railways, particularly light rail, it concentrates a city as developers like building around it so it helps to stop the sprawl. Then you get a whole lot of flow ons. We now have major studies properly costing the real costs of different transport options including the hidden subsidies involved with each option. Around the world, changes to regulation is giving communities a real say in transport infrastructure investment by governments. The transport sector is a major contributor to greenhouse gas emissions, and globally it is one of the fastest growing areas, especially when aircraft transport is included in the figures. And our current oil dependent Western transport system is vulnerable to shocks. *The Economist* in their 'End of the Oil Age' article wrote, 'Oil still has a near-monopoly on transport. If the supply is cut off even for a few days, modern economies come to a halt, as Britain discovered when tax protestors blockaded some domestic oil deposits two years ago'.

This is important, especially within Asia, as cities are growing fast and the choices they make regarding urban planning and transport could make or break the resources of the region and arguably the globe. As was highlighted in Chapter 16, such is the mainstream concern about these issues that Newsweek dedicated an entire special issue on Asia's urban explosion. It wrote, 'Asia is becoming urban in half the time it took Europe and America. The stresses will either make the region or doom it.' Asia already is highlighting the importance of transport and urban planning in the economic outcomes of cities. When asked 'How do cities like Singapore, Tokyo, Hong Kong which have well developed public transport systems, fit into the model here?' by the ABC's Alexander De Blas, Peter Newman replied 'Well they came out even better. They're very dense and highly transit oriented and they only had 3 or 4 per cent of their wealth going into transport. This compares with the newly developing cities like Bangkok and Jakarta and Kuala Lumpur and so on which have put a lot of their money into roads and they're spending around 18 per cent of their wealth on transport. It's as though they are following an American model because that's what you do. It's patently not working when you go to these cities, they're impossible to get around in and the air pollution is a terrible problem and yet they haven't quite woken up to the fact that it's because they haven't followed a rail oriented model.'

Another impetus behind the sustainable urban transport critique is concern over the future availability of conventional oil supplies. World oil production is likely to peak in the first decade of this century, followed by declining yields.[3] This will have profound implications for the oil-dependent transportation sector, which will need to make sweeping long-term adjustments in both transport technology and urban planning.

Detailed analysis shows that if 'externalities' (costs borne by those not driving cars) are taken into account, then automobile use in cities is subsidized. This is contrary to claims by some automobile lobby groups in Australia that drivers more than pay their way,[4] contributing AU$12 billion in fuel excise and registration in exchange for only AU$7 billion in road works. While drivers also pay AU$8 billion in insurance premiums, however, the net cost of road crashes totals AU$15 billion every year.[5] If the additional estimated costs of AU$3 billion in noise and air pollution and AU$3 billion in tax deductions are included, the total annual subsidy for car use is at least AU$8 billion.

Drawing extensively from the global Millennium Cities Database for Sustainable Transport, a comprehensive and reliable source of data on transport related factors for a wide range of cities, this chapter examines the environmental, economic and social case for moving away from automobile-dominated transport. Current transport systems are responsible for significant greenhouse gas emissions which, along with energy use, is used as an indicator of the overall efficiency and pollution-intensiveness of transport systems. Focusing particularly on Oceania and Asia, this chapter looks at cities that are incorporating and providing a mix of transport modes, and how public transport and non-motorized modes can be incorporated through urban planning and design. Transport systems are influenced not only by physical planning factors, but also by individual and collective actions of governments, private companies and citizens. This chapter concludes by identifying some of the steps that various groups can take to realize the opportunities offered by sustainable transport.

Methodology of the Millennium Cities Database

The Millennium Cities Database for Sustainable Transport[6] was compiled over three years by Kenworthy and Laube (2001) for the International Union (Association) of Public Transport (UITP) in Brussels. The database provides data from 100 cities drawn from all continents. Data summarized here represent regional averages from 84 cities (which are listed in Table 19.1), together with their respective populations in 1995, the year for which all data was collected.

Characteristics of urban transport systems

While rising wealth is frequently associated with increased energy use and motorization, as will be seen later from the patterns of private and public transport, wealth alone does not provide a consistent or satisfactory explanation of transport patterns in cities. This is despite claims by a number of commentators that increasing wealth automatically tends towards higher auto dependence.[7] The relative income or wealth of metropolitan regions in this chapter is measured by the gross domestic (or regional) product (GDP) per capita (in US dollars), of contiguous urban areas rather than states, provinces or countries in which the metropolitan regions reside.[8] Based on GDP, the cities are split into two categories: higher income cities (average GDPs between US$20,000 and US$32,000) and lower income cities (average GDPs between US$2,400 and US$6,000). Global comparisons of urban transport systems indicate that those based around more private vehicles use a lot more passenger transport energy to generate an equal quantity of wealth. In the US cities in the database, 2.4 megajoules (MJ) of passenger transport fuel are used for each dollar of gross regional product generated. In the less car-orientated European and wealthy Asian cities the figure is 0.8–0.9 MJ per dollar. Zurich is a case in point, with an extremely high per capita income, but comparatively low car use and high public transport usage and service provision. It is important to first understand the wide variations that exist around the world in the patterns of transport in cities.

Globally, there are enormous variations in the magnitude of urban vehicle ownership and use. North American and Australian/New Zealand (ANZ) cities lead the world in car

Table 19.1 *Metropolitan areas in the Millennium Cities Database for Sustainable Transport*

USA	Canada	Aust/NZ	Western Europe		High-income Asia
Atlanta (2.90)	Calgary (0.77)	Brisbane (1.49)	Graz (0.24)	Athens (3.46)	Osaka (16.83)
Chicago (7.52)	Montreal (3.22)	Melbourne (3.14)	Vienna (1.59)	Milan (2.46)	Sapporo (1.76)
Denver (1.93)	Ottawa (0.97)	Perth (1.24)	Brussels (0.95)	Bologna (0.45)	Tokyo (32.34)
Houston (3.92)	Toronto (4.63)	Sydney (3.74)	Copenhagen	Rome (2.65)	Hong Kong (6.31)
Los Angeles	Vancouver	Wellington	(1.74)	Amsterdam	Singapore (2.99)
(9.08)	(1.90)	(0.37)	Helsinki (0.89)	(0.83)	Taipei (5.96)
New York			Lyon (1.15)	Oslo (0.92)	
(19.23)			Nantes (0.53)	Barcelona (2.78)	
Phoenix (2.53)			Paris (11.00)	Madrid (5.18)	
San Diego			Marseilles (0.80)	Stockholm (1.73)	
(2.63)			Berlin (3.47)	Bern (0.30)	
San Francisco			Frankfurt (0.65)	Geneva (0.40)	
(3.84)			Hamburg (1.70)	Zurich (0.79)	
Washington			Düsseldorf (0.57)	London (7.01)	
(3.74)			Munich (1.32)	Manchester (2.58)	
			Ruhr (7.36)	Newcastle (1.13)	
			Stuttgart (0.59)	Glasgow (2.18)	
Av. Pop. 5.74	*Av. Pop. 2.30*	*Av. Pop. 2.00*	*Av. Pop. 2.17*		*Av. Pop. 11.03*

Eastern Europe	Middle East	Africa	Latin America	Low Income Asia	China
Prague (1.21)	Tel Aviv (2.46)	Dakar (1.94)	Curitiba (2.43)	Manila (9.45)	Beijing (8.16)
Budapest (1.91)	Teheran (6.80)	Cape Town	Sao Paulo	Bangkok (6.68)	Shanghai (9.57)
Krakow (0.74)	Riyadh (3.12)	(2.90)	(15.56)	Mumbai (17.07)	Guangzhou (3.85)
	Cairo (13.14)	Jo'burg (2.25)	Bogota (5.57)	Chennai (6.08)	.
	Tunis (1.87)	Harare (1.43)		K. Lumpur (3.77)	
				Jakarta (9.16)	
				Seoul (20.58)	
				HCM City (4.81)	
Av. Pop. 1.29	*Av. Pop. 5.48*	*Av. Pop. 2.13*	*Av. Pop. 7.85*	*Av. Pop. 9.70*	*Av. Pop. 7.19*

ownership, with over 500 cars per 1000 people (US cities nearly 600). Western European cities have 414 cars per 1000, while Eastern European car ownership is more moderate at 332. All other groups of cities average between 100 and 200 cars per 1000 people, except for the Chinese cities which, in 1995, had a mere 26 cars per 1000 people, although this is growing at an enormous rate. Car ownership is always associated with wealth in the literature, hence a useful way of looking at the data is to express car ownership as a factor of wealth (i.e. cars owned per US$1000 of GDP). The ANZ and Canadian cities are the leaders in the higher income cities (25 to 30 cars per US$1000 of GDP), while US cities trail with only 19. Western European and prosperous Asian cities have only a fraction of the cars relative to their wealth (13 and 6 respectively). Lower income regions actually have relatively high levels of car ownership when their GDP is taken into account. Eastern European cities lead with 56 cars per US$1000 of GDP, but African and Latin American cities are not far behind with 48 and 41 respectively. Less prosperous Asian cities already have a rate of car ownership relative to wealth that is virtually equal to cities in Australia/New Zealand. Chinese cities, despite an average GDP of only US$2400, have almost the same rate of car ownership per dollar of GDP as

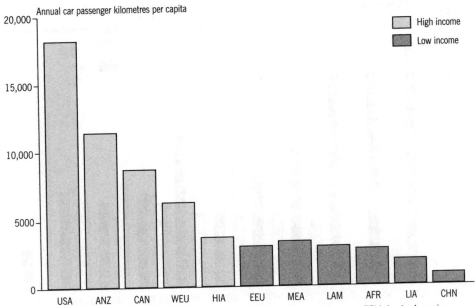

Key: REGIONS: Africa, AFR; Australia and New Zealand, ANZ, Eastern Europe, EEU; Latin America, LAM; Middle East, MEA; Western Europe, WEU; NATIONS: Canada, CAN; China, CHN; and the USA; INCOME: high-income Asia, HIA; low-income Asia; LIA

Figure 19.1 *Car use per capita in world cities,* 1995

Western European cities (11 compared to 13) which have an average GDP per capita of US$32,000.

It is not, however, car ownership per se that inflicts serious environmental, social and economic costs on cities. Car usage patterns are much more important in this respect and in this regard the difference between cities on a global scale are even more pronounced. Figure 19.1 shows the annual car use per capita expressed as car passenger kilometres for the eleven regions covered in this chapter.

These data clearly highlight that amongst high-income cities there are considerable differences in car use that are not explained by differences in wealth. For example, US, WEU and HIA cities have average GDPs per capita that are almost identical, yet their car use varies by around a factor of six. The numerous negative human health consequences of high levels of motor vehicle use in the cities of the developing and developed world are becoming global concerns. As the use of private motor vehicles grew in China between 1990 and 2000, annual traffic deaths have doubled from 50,000 to 100,000, and Asia as a whole now accounts for a significant proportion of the 1.2 million people across the globe who died in road accidents in 2000.[9] In many high-income cities the most severe effect of private motor vehicles is their replacement of walking. Lack of exercise is considered one of the worst threats to Australians' health after smoking, with 8000 people in Australia dying every year from inactivity[10] and obesity levels rising at an alarming rate, especially amongst children.[11]

If transport systems are designed around cars, people have to pay the costs of owning a car. In Australia, the average household spends over US$4500 a year on transport, 20 per cent more than they spend on housing.[12] In addition to these costs, a quarter of the population or more may not have driving licences in higher-income cities, making it harder to access work, healthcare and other social services. In lower-income countries the consequences of designing transport systems around cars are more

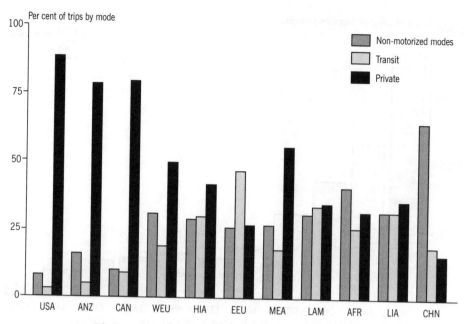

Figure 19.2 *Modal split for all trips in world cities,* 1995

severe, with less than eight cars per thousand people in India.[13] This has enormous social justice and equity implications. If urban transport priorities are directed primarily towards accommodating car travel through new freeways and parking facilities, this can threaten already viable urban transport systems including excellent networks of walkways and cycle paths that provide effective transport services to the majority of people.

Another variable that provides insight into private transport patterns is the percentage of all daily trips (all purposes) that are catered for by private transport. Not surprisingly, US (89 per cent), ANZ (79 per cent) and Canadian cities (81 per cent) head the list. By contrast, their wealthier counterparts in Europe and Asia have only 50 per cent and 42 per cent respectively of all trips by private transport. In the lower income cities, private transport caters for only between 16 per cent (Chinese cities) and 36 per cent (Asian cities) of all trips, with the exception of Middle Eastern cities where the proportion rises to 56 per cent. The extent of private transport use in many lower income cities often appears extremely high, due to the overwhelming visual and sensory impacts of traffic and its capacity to rapidly saturate the public space of a city. In fact, compared to public transport and non-motorized modes, private transport is a minority player in 7 out of the 11 regions in this study. Owing to their size, cars and other private transport vehicles have a huge impact, even at relatively low ownership levels, in urban environments not designed for them. At the moment many developing cities are either poised to excel in mixed-transport systems, or fall into auto-dependency. Some are building excellent public transport systems, but motor vehicle ownership and use is growing rapidly; motorbikes are becoming the dominant form of transport in many Asian cities, such as Ho Chi Minh City, where motorbikes carry 68 per cent of peak hour passengers.[14]

The most socially equitable and sustainable modes of urban transport are walking and cycling. These have few fossil fuel or greenhouse gas implications outside of the embodied energy in human food, bicycles, and pedestrian and bicycle infrastructure.

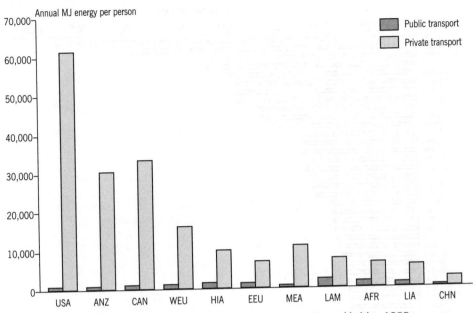

Figure 19.3 *Private and public transport energy use in world cities,* 1995

There is an extraordinary range in the extent to which these modes are still used in cities today, as shown in Figure 19.2.

As this figure indicates, only 8 per cent of all trips are made by foot and bicycle in US cities. Other automobile cities are a little higher, at 10 per cent and 16 per cent respectively in Canadian and ANZ cities. Eastern and Western European cities, high- and low-income Asian cities, Middle Eastern cities and Latin American cities, all have very similar levels of non-motorized mode use ranging from 26 per cent to 32 per cent of all trips. Walking and cycling account for 41 per cent of trips in African cities due to the majority low-income populations who rely heavily on walking, while the world leaders are still the Chinese cities with 65 per cent. The data reveal an extraordinary range in passenger transport energy consumption, with US cities leading the world at over 60,000 MJ per person of energy used for cars and motor cycles each year (see Figure 19.3). This is twice as high as the Canadian and Australian cities, and 4 to 6 times more than the Western European cities and wealthy Asian cities, such as in Japan. Even cities in the Middle East, where the most oil is produced, a figure of only 10,600 MJ per person is used.

By contrast, the level of per capita energy use for public transport in all cities is relatively small, ranging from a low of 419 MJ per person in Chinese cities to a high of 2158 MJ in Latin American cities. Considering the vastly different levels of usage of public transport in cities (see Figure 19.2), these data emphasize the relatively high energy efficiency of most public transport systems. The patterns of passenger transport energy use lead to the patterns of per capita CO_2 emissions shown in Figure 19.4 for each of the individual cities in the study. The difference between Atlanta, the highest, and Ho Chi Minh City, the lowest, is extraordinary.

Greenhouse gases are a useful indication of the wider pollution problems from auto-dependency. As cars and motorbikes make up more trips in developing cities and industry cleans up, transport is increasingly dominating air pollution. In Australia, private vehicles generate 70–80 per cent of oxides of nitrogen in urban air sheds,[15] and in Santiago, Chile, transport accounts for 86 per cent of ultra-fine particulates. In Beijing,

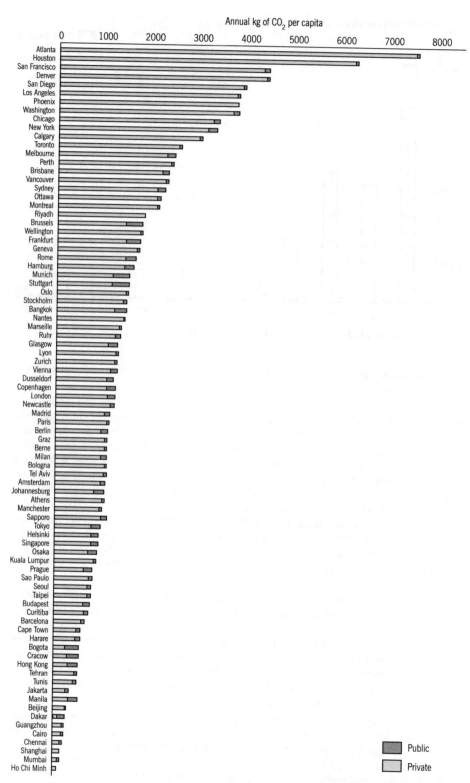

Figure 19.4 *Per capita passenger transport emissions of* CO_2 *in 84 cities worldwide*

the percentage of carbon monoxide emissions that came from transport increased from 39 per cent to 84 per cent between 1989 and 2000.[16] Pollutants, including carbon monoxide and nitrogen oxides, are linked to potentially fatal conditions including cardiovascular diseases, asthma, bronchitis and lung cancer. The World Health Organization estimates that, globally, one in 20 deaths are caused by air pollution, or 3 million deaths each year.[17]

As noted, many commentators suggest that urban transport energy use and greenhouse gas emissions inevitably grow as wealth increases. When lower- and higher-income cities are included together in cross-city comparisons, a moderate positive association between urban transport energy use, greenhouse gas emissions and GDP is observed. Amongst the higher-income cities, however, there is no statistically significant relationship between energy use, greenhouse gases and wealth despite a very wide range of GDP per capita. While in 1995 Hong Kong had a GDP per capita of US$22,969 and a per capita private passenger transport energy use of 4100 MJ, Sydney, with US$22,397, used 28,700 MJ per capita. Explanations for such differences in transport energy use (and by implication CO_2 emissions) are strongly linked to the modal share between private, public and non-motorized modes. The data in the Millennium Cities Database shows that energy consumption per passenger km is significantly higher for cars than public transport in every region. The significant factors underlying automobile dependence and energy use include the length of highways, number of parking spaces and the extent and quality of the public transport system, especially the kilometres of dedicated transit right-of-way and the amount of transit service provided, in particular by urban rail systems. Attempting to get rid of congestion through freeway building and other means, rather than building up the non-auto modes to help people avoid congestion, will not save energy or reduce CO_2 emissions, but will increase these factors in cities, and result in other negative environmental impacts. Strict limitations on freeway construction across a metropolitan area and limited parking in the central area of cities will assist in creating less auto-dependent cities with lower built-in energy demand and less greenhouse emissions from passenger transport. With regard to transit, Figure 19.5 shows the wide range of public transport use across regions, also emphasizing how high urban rail use is linked to much higher levels of overall public transport use (e.g. in Eastern Europe).

Lower income cities in the Millennium Cities Database provide comparatively high levels of transit service, but little of it is rail. Most of it is bus service, which is losing market share to cars and motor cycles due to unreliability and poor speed competitiveness mainly as a result of traffic congestion. Their level of transit use is low compared to many wealthier cities that anchor their transit systems heavily around speed-competitive rail systems. Rail can compete better with cars than buses due to smoother rides, higher speeds, greater reliability and greater presence and legibility in the urban system. The data in the Global Database shows that there are no regions in the world where the average speed of bus systems exceeds 26km/h, but metro systems average 34km/h and suburban rail 43km/h, in comparison to a general road traffic speed of 34km/h. In addition, rail modes (trams, light rail, underground, metro and suburban rail) are in virtually every instance more energy efficient than buses in the respective regions. They also have the advantage that in most cases, except selected suburban rail systems, they operate on electric power which may be generated from non-fossil fuel and renewable energy sources located outside of the cities. The Millennium Cities Database demonstrates the energy and greenhouse gas reduction potential and other benefits of managing and reducing the role of the automobile in urban transport systems and enhancing the role of public transport and non-motorized modes. In particular, the provision of rail infrastructure is critical for developing an attractive and well-patronized public transport system. However, in cases where this is not achievable due to existing restraints, a system of 'Bus Rapid Transit' may be a viable option.

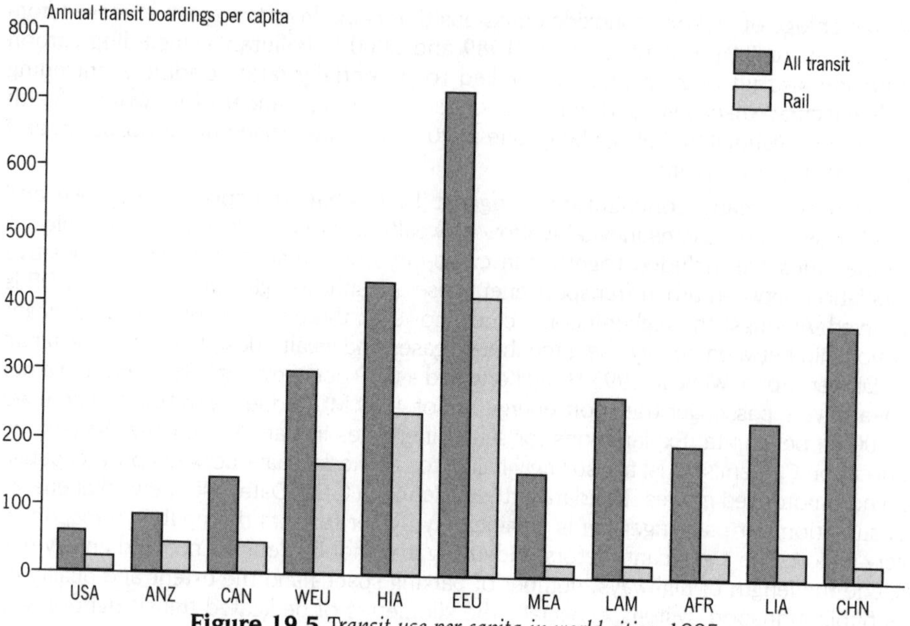

Figure 19.5 *Transit use per capita in world cities*, 1995

Sustainable transport systems

Private motor vehicles can provide a range of useful services, and are likely to continue to play an integral role in urban transport systems. The data for the different regions in Figure 19.3, however, show that cars can and do provide 50 per cent or less of the daily trips in many cities, including cities with a higher income level, where cars are more affordable relative to wages. A significant proportion of car trips in auto-dependent cities could realistically be transferred to public transport and non-motorized modes, with major benefits. It would appear very sensible from a social, environmental and economic perspective, and certainly from an energy and greenhouse perspective, to prioritize the protection and use of non-motorized modes by ensuring that facilities for pedestrians and bicycles are actively promoted and not eroded by motorization. This is especially urgent in rapidly developing cities. In China, where 65 per cent of trips are still made by foot or bicycle, their pedestrian and cycling advantage appears to be under increasing threat from policies against bicycles and the sheer scale of motorization.[18] Safe footpaths and cycling networks are minimum requirements for a society that walks and cycles. In the Netherlands, where a strong commitment has been made to cycling infrastructure, 28 per cent of trips are made by bicycle.[19] In cities like Adelaide, Australia, where until recently 'unpredictable' cyclists were seen as a source of danger to drivers, 1.2 per cent of trips are made by bicycle.[20]

There is a growing compendium of examples of innovative improvement of walking and cycling facilities. Pedestrian-only shopping-streets are growing in popularity with the realization that they increase retail sales.[21] In the city of Guangzhou in southern China, the pedestrianization of Beijing Road has seen a boost to business that has had shops in other parts of the city calling for the exclusion of car-traffic.[22] In Australia, the state of New South Wales has committed to expand the on- and off-road cycleway network by 200km each year.[23] Some of the most innovative uses of non-motorized transport are occurring in lower-income cities. Air pollution around the Taj Mahal, in India, sparked a renaissance in cycle rickshaws. Local agencies and the Institute for Transportation and Development Policy designed modernized, lightweight rickshaws that have raised the status of this mode and increased the earnings of their drivers, with over 30,000 units now sold across India.[24] In Mizrapur, cycle rickshaws are now used for part of the collection of street waste, lowering emissions, increasing hygiene and helping to beautify the city.[25] Improving public transport is also essential after decades of serious neglect in many parts of the world. It is often asserted that cars are simply more attractive than public transport. In reality, most people would naturally choose to use an excellent road network over a run-down public transport system. The task is to make an integrated and seamless transit, pedestrian, cycle and road network that will make sustainable modes of transport competitive with the car.

When people have come together in making bold commitments to sustainability, significant changes have occurred. In Perth, AU$400 million invested by the Government of Western Australia in extending and electrifying the rail network increased annual patronage of the rail network from 8 to 31 million between 1991 and 2001. The new Dehli metro system has also been a resounding success, carrying over 80,000 passengers per day and projected to turn a profit significantly higher than expectations.[26] While rail may be the ideal, a dedicated busway system can still avoid traffic and compete with the car. In Bogota, Colombia, the city has built the Trans Milenio, a Bus Rapid Transit (BRT) system where bus stations are connected by dedicated bus lanes, carrying 744,000 passengers a day. At only US$5.3 million per kilometre to construct,[27] this method is being promoted as an alternative to rail mass transit in cities of the developing world where funds to construct new rail systems are scarce. The famous case of Curitiba is detailed in the publication *Natural Capitalism*. BRT is currently being introduced in Jakarta, Dares Salam, Tehran and Dakar.[28] Many cities across the world are making real commitments to various aspects of a more sustainable transport system. For example, as part of Seoul Mayor Lee Mung-Bak's plan to reduce the proportion of trips made by car from 27 per cent to 12 per cent between 2002 and 2006, the Cheonggyecheon Expressway will be replaced with a BRT system.[29] Even the less drastic step of introducing bus-priority lanes has had great benefits in Kunming, China, where it increased bus ridership by 13 per cent and decreased the number of buses needed to provide the service by 50 per cent.[30] These examples indicate the range of options for improving the sustainability of transport systems, and the diversity of benefits that accrue from implementing them. With innovation and commitment, it is possible to increase the proportion of trips made by walking, cycling and public transport in many cities.

The importance of urban form

In addition to the transport factors discussed so far, there is the critical issue of the shape and structure of cities and how much they encourage or inhibit car use. It has been widely demonstrated how important urban form is in helping to explain the macro-patterns of urban transportation, especially the level of auto-dependence and transport energy use.[31] Urban density, a key characteristic or measure of urban form, is closely correlated with energy use. The Millennium Cities Database data suggest that car use, energy use and greenhouse gas production are positively correlated with each other while negatively correlated with population density.[32] Higher car and energy use cities, and the highest greenhouse gas producers, are low in population density, while the higher density cities have lower car and energy use per person and lower transport greenhouse gases. Average urban densities range from lows of 15 per ha in the US and ANZ cities up to 150 to 200 per ha in the Asian cities, including Chinese cities. On average, the lower income cities are more than double the density of the wealthier cities (109 vs. 52 persons per ha). Figure 19.6 shows the very strong relationship between urban density and per capita car use in the 58 wealthier cities in the database. In the high-income cities, 84 per cent of the variance in car passenger kms per capita and 78 per cent of the variance in per capita private passenger transport energy use is explained

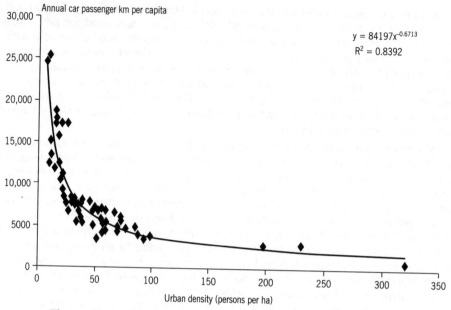

Figure 19.6 *Urban density vs. private car travel in 58 higher income cities*

by urban density. In the low-income cities, where other factors such as extreme variations in income affect the outcome, 47 per cent of their variation in per capita car use and 44 per cent of the variance in per capita private passenger transport energy use, can still be explained by urban density.

The results point clearly to the energy and greenhouse conservation potential of compact, mixed land use cities with extensive transit systems operating on a backbone of rail. Compact land uses can be combined with attractive environments for walking and cycling, which will save further energy and CO_2 emissions.

Sustainable urban development

In the last two decades attention has been intensifying on the development of compact cities in North America, Europe and Australasia. The growth in civil society support for compact cities through movements including 'Smart Growth' and 'New Urbanism' is partly driven by transport issues, but also by the view that compact cities can provide environments that better support the physical, social and psychological needs of people. There is considerable variation between these movements, but all share the tenet of designing cities around people, rather than cars. Compact housing designs are one element of compact cities which include a range of housing forms from terraces through to medium and high rise buildings. The important element is to ensure that ground level environments are attractive, distinct and human in scale, allowing people to develop a strong sense of place and attachment. Vancouver's West End is testament to the capacity of very high density housing to be incorporated into a highly desirable and beautiful residential location. A critical component in this process is the preservation of open space, and many communities, such as the Township of Edison, New Jersey, have introduced ordinances to ensure this is protected.[33] Mixing land use so that workplaces, houses and shops are all close to each other is a central pillar of developing compact, liveable neighbourhoods that are accessible by foot, bicycle and public transport. Mixing low- and high-cost housing also means that an area provides access to a range of people and their skills, reducing the need for commuting. Cities such as Toronto have policies to create an 'urban mosaic' of different socio-economic groups in any one area.

Urban growth boundaries and focusing investment into existing communities are critical steps in ensuring that cities remain compact. If inner cities are left to decay, those who can afford to will flee to new development at the urban fringe in a continual vicious circle. Revitalizing neighbourhoods, on the other hand, has the potential to give everyone a chance to live in an attractive suburb. The City of Portland is often cited as a successful example of urban growth boundaries (UGB), as its UGB has been in place sufficiently long enough for its effects to emerge. While there has been debate over the affordability of housing in Portland,[34] the city's policy matrix has seen greater urban redevelopment and infill accompanied by rapid economic growth and improved quality of life.[35] Developers have started to accept limitations on building at 'greenfield' sites at the edge of cities, as they have become more familiar with sustainability principles and the success of 'New Urbanism' styles of developments. Urban Ecology in Adelaide, Australia, for example, is one company constructing highly sought after properties in inner-city areas. In the US, many central city and inner-city areas are undergoing revivals, such as the 500 affordable houses built in a run-down area of Louisville.[36] Developers that continue to build on the edge of cities are currently subsidized by taxpayers, who bear the extra costs of providing services like health, police and public transport to these sprawling developments.[37] Diverting government incentives from unsustainable to sustainable practices must be a key principle in any future policies.

Integrating increased urban density with provision for pedestrians and cyclists and improved public transport brings multiplied benefits. Bus interchanges and rail are particularly important in this process, as it also encourages land developers to build around stations, further increasing the local density and accessibility. It appears that a fixed rail system has this impact by offering developers security for their investments, combined with the quieter, cleaner surroundings, due to electric propulsion. The Asia-Pacific region contains some significant examples of this type of integration. In Hong Kong, developers of high rise housing and commercial buildings were given concessions to develop around stations. This has resulted in high-density, mixed use development which is highly accessible by public transport, such as Tsuen Wan metro terminal, which is pedestrian friendly and contains a bus interchange, shopping centre and offices.[38] Similarly, Singapore's high rise public housing estates are built along an elevated and underground heavy rail system (the MRT) with highly integrated urban development at most stations.[39] Rail and light rail increase the real estate value of land around the line, a factor that has allowed the Toronto Transit Commission to generate additional revenue from its rail system.[40] Compact cities which are highly accessible by foot, bicycle and public transport are not only more attractive, sustainable and socially responsible, they make good business sense. Walkable neighbourhoods are more attractive for young staff, in particular attracting the entrepreneurial and IT companies to relocate.[41] Delivering economic, social and environmental benefits is one more step towards creating more sustainable urban futures.

Designing around the mind: understanding behaviour

Developing more sustainable urban travel patterns is not just about planning and providing transport, it is about helping people to *choose* more sustainable transport. Changing people's behaviour is not about manipulating minds, it is about understanding people's needs and how they work. Improving people's knowledge is the first step, because if people do not know, for example, which bus to catch, they are more likely to use their car. In South Perth, Australia, the TravelSmart® project provided households with personalized bus timetables, increasing the use of public transport in the project area by 26 per cent.[42] In Viernheim, Germany, the provision of individual travel advice (IndiMark®) resulted in the share of household's trips made by foot, bicycle and public transport increasing by 7 per cent, 10 per cent and 29 per cent respectively.[43]

TravelSmart has also focused on breaking habits. This involves helping people see that there are options apart from driving, and then encouraging them to try other modes of transport. Other examples of habit breaking include the 'World Car Free Days', where sections of cities are cordoned off from traffic and used to host social gatherings. Whether people will use alternatives to cars once they have tried them, however, is contingent on providing a good quality network of footpaths, bicycle lanes and public transport systems.

People choose which mode to take by *comparing* between walking, cycling, public transport and cars. If a new cycle lane is constructed, people will not necessarily start to cycle if driving is still far more attractive. There are a range of hidden biases in our societies which encourage car use. As discussed, car use is generally subsidized, as drivers do not pay the full cost of accidents, pollution and congestion. Since World War II, developed countries have been building cities around cars, and so driving is more convenient. The data in the Global Cities Database shows that the more freeways and parking that are provided in a city, the more that cars and motorbikes are used. On top of this, there are a range of tax breaks that favour driving. In Australia the annual tax break on company vehicles increases with the distance that they are driven. To ensure that people make sustainable travel choices, we need to make strong commitments to remove these biases, knowing that this means that in addition to cycling becoming more convenient, cars might become less convenient.

In many cities, enabling people to walk and cycle safely will entail 'traffic calming', which involves reducing the speed and volume of car traffic by narrowing or removing traffic lanes and changing the streetscape and the geometry of the road. In Singapore the incumbent government has been discouraging widespread car ownership and use through a number of highly coordinated measures. Singaporean citizens seeking to purchase cars must first bid for a limited number of 'Certificates of Entitlement' that allow them to buy a car, which is then heavily taxed. In the early 1970s an 'Area Licensing Scheme' was initiated where motor vehicles are charged for entering the central business district in peak periods, and its success at eliminating traffic congestion saw its expansion during the 1990s. The success of Singapore has boosted the confidence of other political leaders. In the face of strong opposition, London's Mayor Ken Livingstone recently committed to charging all cars that entered the city centre, with the result that traffic and pollution have been cut, businesses have flourished and bus service waiting times are down.[44]

Transport choices are also affected by cultural factors, and in many societies cars have ideological connotations with wealth or masculinity. In the UK children as young as four can identify the brand and model of a car and describe their status.[45] Individual adults refusing to see driving as a status symbol is part of the solution, but it is also important to remove tax-breaks and other implicit encouragements for car use. Government car fleets in particular should play a significant role in setting an example to the rest of the community, at the very least purchasing highly fuel-efficient and low emission vehicles. Policy-makers therefore have diverse and significant impacts on transport patterns.

Civil society and business

Until this point, the chapter has referred mainly to the actions of the public sector, or governments, in moving towards more sustainable urban transport systems. While urban transport planning was once viewed as a solely technical activity to be executed by 'value-free' experts, it is now acknowledged that it is an inherently political activity because it influences the distribution of costs and benefits within societies. There are a number of questionable assumptions held by many policy-makers that challenge the introduction of sustainable transport. For example, it is widely asserted that promoting alternatives to car use will damage local car industries. This view is countered by the examples of Japan and Korea, which became major car manufacturing nations while exercising strong restraints on domestic car use.[46] People who cycle to work are still likely to own cars for longer journeys, a fact that was recognized by Volkswagen when it included free bicycles with new cars in 1996. While planners working for the state may have certain designs or ideas for urban transport systems, civil society groups or private companies may circumvent or overturn the government planners. If state actions are not coordinated or congruent with the actions of communities (civil society) or businesses (the private sector) they will have little chance of success.

Even in situations where politicians actively attempt to please their constituents, they can only base decisions on what they see as the population's view. Studies from a range of countries, including Australia[47] and Norway,[48] found that policy-makers frequently underestimate the public's support for prioritizing funding transit over roads. As a result, the turnaround in US transport started when public consultation became mandatory for transport projects under ISTEA and TEA-21 legislation.[49] These highlight the importance of community consultation and public lobbying. Examples include the revival of light rail in the US city of Portland that was started by public opposition to an unnecessary highway development, or the upgrade of bus stations in Penang, Malaysia under pressure from the NGO Sustainable Transport Environment in Penang (STEP).[50] It is possible to develop sustainable transport systems with political commitment, and that commitment is starting to emerge, but it requires strong civil society action to represent the interests of those not generally represented well in the politics of planning, land development and transport policy.

Responsibility for sustainable transport lies not only with government, but is something that everyone can contribute to as individuals and through businesses, schools and community groups. People and businesses need to back up their stated desires and visions with concrete individual action. Workplaces, universities and shopping centres generate travel by staff, visitors and deliveries. Organizations can benefit from committing to sustainable transport not only by strengthening their environmental performance and image, but also by cutting financial costs and having staff that are healthier and more productive. Cyclists, for example, take up to five less sick days per year.[51] Green Travel Plans are a simple tool that organizations can use to develop more sustainable travel patterns. The key to Green Transport Plans is to research them, tailor them to the corporation's requirements and make strong commitments to implementation. Examples of successful Green Transport Plans are diverse because they are tailored to diverse organizations. Oxfordshire County Council in the UK limited their mileage reimbursement rate to a level suitable for efficient cars, saving US$180,000. Rijnstate Hospital in the Netherlands introduced a range of measures including charging for parking and public transport discounts, with the result that transit use increased 22.5 per cent.[52]

The first step in designing a Green Travel Plan is to talk with an organization's staff, customers and visitors, and find out how they travel, why they travel the way they do and what can be done to help them travel more sustainably. The second step is getting a group of staff together to look over the results of these investigations and then working out a plan that is appropriate for the organization's budget, activities and aspirations. The final step is to allocate roles and responsibilities, set targets, budget and execute the plan. The principle underlying these plans is simple: barriers to more sustainable travel need to be identified, and then overcome. For example, if staff do not cycle to work because they are concerned about the security of their bicycles, building a bike cage might encourage more cycling. If staff have to drive because they need to drop off children on the journey to work, starting a crèche in the office can enable them to take public transport to work, potentially reducing their travel time and making staff more productive.[53]

Schools encounter a particularly self-reinforcing transport problem. Parents who are concerned about their children being hit by traffic drive them to school, creating more traffic. The decrease in children walking to school is thought to be related to the increase in childhood obesity, and schools in many cities, like Christchurch in New Zealand, have started schemes known as 'walking school buses'. Vetted parents walk small groups of children to school, increasing the children's exercise and social skills. There are a range of options that can be undertaken, but innovation and commitment are the essential keys. Everyone can personally contribute to making transport more sustainable. The more people who walk, cycle and take public transport, the greater the pressure for governments to invest in footpaths, safe crossings, cycle lanes and public transport. In turn, this makes walking, cycling and public transport attractive to more people, creating a cycle of continual improvement. It also begins to set new norms for a community about what is 'typical' behaviour, helping to reinforce changes that are already underway. Using more sustainable transport does not have to mean sacrificing the use of a car for journeys to the beach, or the country or parts of town which are poorly serviced by public transport. It can simply mean using other forms of transport when they are suitable. Walking to local shops can be just as fast as driving when the time to park is taken into account, it saves money, and walking or cycling three times a day for ten minutes can provide significant health benefits.[54]

Moving to an accessible area can benefit people in multiple ways, as savings on transport costs can be significantly higher than the extra rent. In fact, a study from Melbourne, Australia, found that if the average household owned one less car over a working life they could retire with an extra US$580,000 in the bank.[55] Even if moving is not possible, it is still possible to save money and travel more sustainably. For example, if people share the drive to work with a colleague they can halve their petrol bill. When purchasing a car, efficient models are normally cheaper to buy and run and, unless people are planning to go off-road at least once a fortnight, it is normally cheaper to buy a car that is suited to the city and hire a four-wheel drive for occasional holidays.

Individuals, organizations and policy-makers can make changes that will increase the sustainability of urban transport today, and the environmental, social, medical and economic arguments for making these changes are clear. Changing the way that we travel is not a compromise; it produces benefits across all aspects of our lives. The tools for making this change are well known. We only have to choose to change.

CHAPTER 20

WATER: NATURE'S GOLD

Michael H. Smith with David Dumaresq[*]

Of all our natural resources, water has become the most precious. In an age when man has forgotten his origins and is blind even to his most essential needs for survival, water along with other resources has become the victim of his indifference.

Rachel Carson, Silent Spring (1962)

The World Water Forum has stated that some 2.4 billion people lack access to adequate sanitation, and 1.1 billion people are without access to safe drinking water. Current water management practices and lack of environmental sanitation contribute substantially to water-related diseases. Even in countries where a large part of the population has access to improved water, sanitation and the quality of water resources need improvement. At the World Summit on Sustainable Development (WSSD) in Johannesburg in September 2002, UN Secretary-General Kofi Annan identified water and sanitation as one of the five key areas in which concrete results were expected.

In 2000, Kofi Annan had already set forth the Millennium Development Goals. These included, in particular, the objective of halving the proportion of people without sustainable access to safe drinking water by 2015. The International Year of Freshwater was held in 2003, which further helped to publicize the seriousness of these issues. The goal of the Year of Freshwater was to raise awareness about the need to protect and manage fresh water, with the goal of accelerating the implementation of the principles of integrated water resource management. Such action is becoming increasingly urgent. According to reports, such as that issued by the UN and the Stockholm Environment Institute, by the year 2025 two-thirds of the world's population will be affected by water shortages.[1] The UN, in a separate report, showed that demand for water has doubled in the last 50 years.[2]

[*] The authors acknowledge the contribution of Mike Young and Jim McColl of the Policy and Economic Research Unit, CSIRO Land and Water, Adelaide. We thank them for giving permission to quote and paraphrase their work, upon which much of this chapter is based.

Key drivers for change

Water is taken for granted. Around the world it costs almost nothing. Consequently direct consumer cost is not driving the more efficient use of water in most markets. However, behind cheap water use there are many significant hidden infrastructure costs, most of which are paid for by the taxpayer or farmer. The ecological footprint and social impacts of our water usage are also very significant. Many rivers are in crisis, whether due to salinity, pollution or simply to the lack of natural environmental flows as a consequence of dams. Kader Asmal, Chairperson of the 2000 World Commission on Dams (WCD) wrote, 'On this blue planet, less than 2.5 per cent of our water is fresh, less than 33 per cent of fresh water is fluid, less than 1.7 percent of fluid water runs in streams. And we have been stopping even these. We dammed half our world's rivers at unprecedented rates of one per hour.'[3] Dams, inter basin transfers and water withdrawals for irrigation have fragmented 60 per cent of the world's rivers. By the end of the 20th century, there were over 45,000 dams in over 150 countries.

Some of the key findings of the landmark report from the WCD,[4] were:

- dams, especially shallow dams in the tropics, are significant greenhouse emitters due to rotting vegetation;
- cost performance data in the WCD knowledge base confirms that large dam projects often incur substantial capital cost overruns – for 250 projects examined, the average overrun was half as much again as the projected cost;
- poor accounting in economic terms for the social and environmental costs and benefits of large dams implies that the true economic efficiency and profitability of these schemes remains largely unknown;
- dams have been the biggest drain on aid budgets for the past 50 years, costing US$4 billion a year in the 1980s;
- so far, dam building has driven up to 80 million people from their homes;
- one of the most disturbing findings is that few dams have ever been looked at to see if the benefits outweigh the costs;
- a quarter of dams built to supply water deliver less than half the intended amount – in a tenth of old reservoirs, the build-up of silt has more than halved the storage capacity;
- by stopping the flow of silt downstream, dams reduce the fertility of flood plains and invariably cause erosion of coastal deltas;
- dam construction is one of the major reasons for the extinction of freshwater fish and the vanishing of bird species from flood plains.

In addition, there are significant indirect infrastructure costs. In the last two decades, whole system cost analysis has shown that water efficiency delivers far more benefits than previously imagined. Most nations' water infrastructure assets total tens to hundreds of billions of dollars, half of which is for metropolitan water supply and sewerage. By reducing the need for the construction of new dams, new treatment plants and reducing the maintenance of the pipes and associated infrastructure used to deliver and remove water, significant savings can be made. This is now widely understood and acknowledged. Sydney Water, Australia, for instance, expects to retrofit up to 80 per cent of Sydney homes for more efficient water usage under a AU$50 million programme entitled 'Every Drop Counts'. The target, ambitious even by world standards, is to reduce water usage by 35 per cent over a decade, and initial indicators have been promising. Subsidized appliances on offer to householders include not only the expected efficient showerheads but also rainwater tanks and mulchers.[5]

The latest studies are showing that we can use water much more efficiently through water recycling, reuse and the redesign of urban water systems over the next 50 years[6] (see Table 20.1). In Australia, CSIRO (Commonwealth Scientific and Industrial Research Organisation) has run a 5-year Urban Water R&D and delivery programme working with the major European Urban Water Network on urban water issues.[7] CSIRO's Australian Urban Water Program concluded that, 'Together with water conservation, water reuse and recycling provides a means of extending limited water resources. In some circumstances, there is potential to support three times as much activity as is possible under traditional water use practices where water is used once and then thrown away.'[8]

Urban water systems were designed largely to meet the health concerns of over 100 years ago, and ensuring clean water sanitation has had a profoundly positive effect on the overall health of OECD (Organisation for Economic Co-operation and Development) nations. But now, in the 21st century, innovations in water recycling and water treatment are making it possible to re-design urban water systems anew. For instance, as CSIRO's Professor Mike Young stated: 'One of the really interesting ones is how we use sewage water. Recent work by CSIRO's urban water programme is showing that the most profitable sewage treatment plants now are really ones that treat effluent, between 5000 and about 8000 or 10,000 houses, so rather than having sewage treatment plants right at the end of the city and taking all the sewage the whole way down, you would take the sewage from say, 5000 houses, treat it, and then actually pass it down in a dual system through the rest of the city.'[9]

There are numerous new efficiencies possible now and into the future, to reduce our dependence on large dams and prevent the need for expensive new dams to be built[10] (see Table 20.1).

However all this will amount to little unless water usage in rural agricultural regions is addressed because this is where approximately 70 per cent of freshwater usage occurs.[11] Most water used in rural areas comes from rivers, groundwater, bores and water stored in dams. There is much that can be done to improve significantly water resource productivity. The use of fresh water on farms has halved in Israel since 1984, while the value of production has continued to climb. Farmers in India, Israel, Jordan, Spain and the US have shown that drip irrigation systems that deliver water directly to crop roots can reduce water use by 30–70 per cent and raise crop yields by 20–90 per cent.[12] In the Texas High Plains, farmers using highly efficient sprinklers raised their water efficiency to more than 90 per cent while also increasing corn yields by 10 per cent and cotton yields by 15 per cent. Rice farmers in Malaysia saw a 45 per cent increase in their water productivity through a combination of better scheduling their irrigations, shoring up canals, and sowing seeds directly in the field rather than transplanting seedlings. Recycled water has been used for a number of years to irrigate vineyards at California wineries (US), and this use is growing. Recently, Gallo Wineries and the City of Santa Rosa completed facilities for the irrigation of 350 acres of vineyards with recycled water from the Santa Rosa Subregional Water Reclamation System. At Ararat, Australia, treated and recycled grey-water and sewerage (which previously went into a river) is used for irrigation and fertilizer adding AU$40 million per annum to the local wine industry in partnership with Southcorp Ltd. An AU$4 million investment to re-use grey-water now reaps an additional AU$40 million per annum from wine sales.

Much greater water efficiency can often be achieved through sealing irrigation channels and/or investing in sealed irrigation pipes and drip irrigation technologies. At the present time in Australia, most farming irrigation still occurs without the channels being sealed leading to significant water loss from evaporation or seepage into the soils. Hence, in principle, it is now possible for farmers to use water much more productively and thereby allow environmental flows of half the world's rivers currently damned to be at least partially restored.

Table 20.1 *A sample of some of the cost effective options to improve water efficiencies*

Using less water whilst still providing the same or better service

Retrofit homes	Water efficient showerheads can save over half the water used by the traditional showerhead. One of the largest users of energy of the home is water heating, therefore such an investment in showerheads will typically pay itself back within months.
Buy front loading washing machines	In Australia, the Victorian Government has made it compulsory for all new clothes washing machines to be front loading rather than top loading (which are 40–75% less efficient). Front loading machines also work better because the chemicals are more concentrated and clothes last longer because they are not agitated.
Indoor taps/sinks	Cheap gadgets that reduce the flow by at least 30% can be attached to indoor taps to reduce the amount of water flowing into sinks.
AquaLoc	A new invention called AquaLoc replaces the traditional tap seat and washer and lasts for at least 15 years. Reductions in flow rates of up to 70% are possible, and in most situations water consumption costs are reduced by up to 45% when the recommended models are installed. Organizations that also bear the cost of wastewater can often add another 20–25% on this figure from savings on sewerage usage. By reducing water consumption, AquaLoc reduces the energy required for heating hot water, and power cost reductions can be up to 60% with significant savings in CO_2 emissions as a result. The main benefit of this, however, is reduced maintenance.
Science laboratories	Some laboratories, believe it or not, still use respirators with tap water running for as long as is needed to create vacuums. Small desktop electric diaphragm pumps create better vacuums, thereby increasing lab workers productivity as much as fourfold whilst eliminating significant noise. These also pay themselves back through the water saved within two years.

Recycling/re-using water

Recycling water used for industrial cooling	In the Dutch industry the majority of this water use concerns the use of surface water in once-through coolers. A so-called open recirculating cooling system forms an ideal compromise, in which the benefits of water-cooling are preserved and the environmental disadvantages are reduced. Inside these systems, cooling water is recirculated in a cooling tower. The evaporation of a small part of the circulating water carries the largest amount of the heat away. The water intake that is needed to refill this part is a factor of 50–70 lower than the water intake of a once-through system with the same cooling capacity. Worldwide, the advance of these systems led to a strong reduction of surface water for cooling purposes.
Water recycling decreases discharge to sensitive water bodies	Take, for example, the release of water from the San Jose/Santa Clara Water Pollution Control Plant into the south San Francisco Bay that threatened the area's natural salt water marsh. In response, a US$140 million recycling project was completed in 1997. The South Bay Water Recycling Program now has the capacity to provide 21 million gallons per day of recycled water for use in irrigation and industry. By avoiding the release of this water, the conversion of salt water marsh to brackish marsh was prevented and the habitat for two endangered species was protected.
Embedding water recycling into major housing development	Mawson Lakes, in Adelaide Australia is a 31/2-thousand home for approximately 10,000 people. Attached to it is Australia's largest fully self-contained recycled water scheme. All the water for re-use is collected on site, and up to 70% of the water used by residents is recycled. Every house will be fitted with two sets of pipes and the recycled water will be used for toilets and gardening. A key challenge for recycling is storage, because the bulk of water falls in winter while the demand is in the summer. Mawson Lakes will store the water underground with the help of CSIRO's urban water project team (see below).

Rationale for dams in the past

Dams are a nation's protection against the ravages of drought. In addition, dams are also used to produce energy from which governments and business profit substantially. Hydropower currently provides 19 per cent of the world's total electricity supply, and is used in over 150 countries with 24 of these countries depending on it for 90 per cent of their supply.[13] Therefore, restoring environmental flows may also mean reducing a nation's potential power capacity. This is a major financial barrier to restoring environmental flows. Australia's Snowy Mountains Hydro-Electric Scheme of dams is a classic example of this, and will be considered next.

The real threat of droughts and floods has been the main rationale for building large dams. Australia is no exception. Australia is one of the world's driest continents. Although it has about 5 per cent of the world's land area, it only has 1 per cent of the world's river flow. Unlike water in other parts of the world, Australian surface water supplies tend to be highly variable. Consequently, in endeavouring to manage this extremely variable flow, Australia has made substantial investments in the development of dams and distribution systems. It stores more water per head of population than any country in the world, very few of Australia's surface and groundwater systems resemble their natural state. Australia has experienced severe droughts, such as the 1900–1913 drought, the worst recorded drought in Australia. But Australia also experienced deep droughts that were almost as bad in the mid 1930s, in the middle of the Great Depression and in 1946 whilst Australia was attempting to rebuild after World War Two. These two severe droughts within almost a decade of each other led to unanimous bipartisan government support for the creation of one of the largest engineering projects in the world, the Snowy Mountains Hydro-Electric Scheme.

Case study: the Australian Snowy Mountains Hydro-Electric Scheme

Much of the Australian continent receives little rain per annum, therefore the ecosystems' and rivers' surface groundwater largely comes from the rainfalls and rivers flowing from the Great Dividing Range on Australia's east coast, of which the Snowy Mountains form a significant part. The Snowy Mountains Hydro-Electric Scheme has significant storage capacity (4320 billion litres), and supplies water to the Murray, Tumut, Murrumbidgee and Snowy Rivers.[14] The Snowy Mountain Corp is required to release a minimum of 1026 billion litres per annum. This amount was determined using local rainfall data from the period 1880–1945. The design engineers built a scheme to provide both electricity and a certain amount of water westward along the Murray River sufficient to almost cover the longest known drought in that period; at that time this was the 13 year drought of 1900–1913. The whole scheme is designed to fail just once in 100 years. In other words, if the Snowy Mountains Hydro-Electric Scheme of dams had existed in 1900 at the start of Australia's worst recorded drought, at the end of 1912, it would have run out of water for 1913. The dams are designed to capture almost all of the water that falls in the Snowy Mountains catchment; it captures and diverts 99 per cent of the stream flows in the Snowy Mountains[15] and it is interlinked to allow water to be shunted between the dams. Engineers built the scheme to trap virtually all the water from the Snowy Mountains, including the snowmelt, through a remarkable myriad of mini-dams – tiny dams that collect the water of trickling montane streams.[16] This diversion of water from the high alpine country is for power generation. It does not provide the scheme with more water for irrigators, as all of this alpine mountain water would end up in the rivers anyway through either environmental flows or collection in the lower dams. Hence, in diverting water for energy, the mini-dams are responsible for much of the negative environmental impacts of the Snowy Mountains Hydro-Electric Scheme.

Table 20.1 *continued*

Storing water for later use	
Storing storm water in aquifers	Preliminary work by CSIRO's Urban Water Program shows that the Adelaide Hills could provide water for the city's needs all year round, with some to spare. 'The potential recovery from storm water alone would supply almost a third of Adelaide's current water needs', says Mr Andrew Speers, leader of CSIRO's Urban Water Program. In a normal year, Adelaide derives 40% of its water or 70 billion litres per year from the Murray River and 60% comes from the Adelaide Hills. Recycling just some of the city's wastewater and runoff could reduce Adelaide's dependence on the Murray to zero and reduce the use of water from the Adelaide Hills to less than half the current demand. This team won the inaugural Great Man-Made River International Water Prize award. Granted by UNESCO, the prize is for innovation in water resources management in arid and semi-arid areas. It rewards eight years of research, exploring the use of aquifers to store urban storm water and reclaimed water to be reused in irrigation.
Commercial buildings	Australian Conservation Foundation's 60L Commercial Green Building in Melbourne, Australia uses 90% less water than standard commercial buildings through a variety of measures including: minimizing the demand for water by providing water efficient fixtures and fittings, including waterless urinals and low flush volume toilet pans; using collected rainwater to replace 100% of normal mains water consumption whenever possible; 100% on-site treatment and reuse of grey-water (basins and sinks) and black-water (sewage) streams to produce reclaimed water for flushing toilet pans and irrigating the roof garden and landscape features.
Harnessing new sources of water more cost effectively	
De-salination breakthrough	Those living in the world's arid regions could enjoy fresh water courtesy of a British architect and his revolutionary seawater greenhouse. The pioneer building, which has won a series of awards, uses sunlight to turn salt water into fresh water for growing vegetables and for drinking water. The ingenious building, designed by Charlie Paton, operates at a fraction of the cost of traditional desalination plants, costing 21p to make 1000 litres of distilled water. At the heart of the design is a steel-framed greenhouse with 'evaporators' at each end made from corrugated cardboard. This creates a huge surface area, allowing fresh water to evaporate, leaving salts behind. These strengthen the cardboard, so that it will last indefinitely. The roof lets in light in the red and blue spectrums, which is needed for photosynthesis and infra-red and ultraviolet are used to heat air in a roof cavity to help to drive the evaporation processes. This first seawater greenhouse was built on Tenerife, partly with European Commission funds. A second is under development in Oman and there are plans for others.[17]
Savings to taxpayers	Cheaper ways to purify water. A recent study showed that the provision of adequate clean water to New York City by forests in the Catskill Mountains was equivalent to a capital investment of US$6–8 billion and an annual operating cost of US$1–2 billion for a plant to carry out the same service. The City took the option of maintaining water quality via ecosystem services by purchasing some small parcels of land, applying some covenants on the use of fertilizers in the catchment, and making a one-off investment of approximately US$1 billion to upgrade a few local sewerage plants. Hence, by taking ecosystems into account, NYC saved US$10 billion.

Source: Selected material included from Hawken et al (1999, ch 11) and Postel (1999)

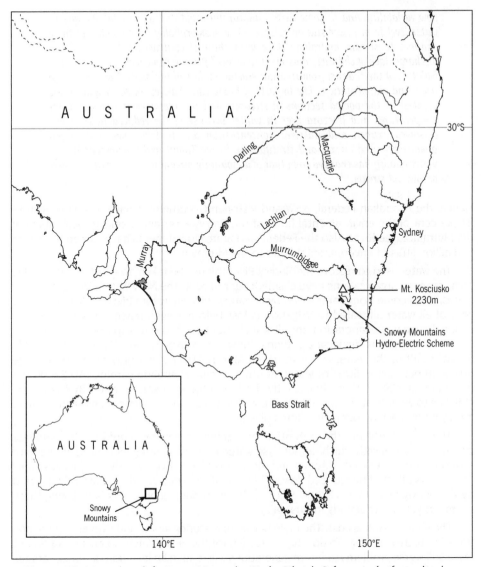

Figure 20.1 *Location of the Snowy Mountains Hydro-Electric Scheme, and other major rivers*

Environmental damage from the dams and the mini-dams in the high country is significant. The ecological resilience of the region has been diminished because water is being removed from the landscape, which makes it more fire prone in summer. The Snowy Mountains Hydro-Electric Scheme captures and diverts the headwaters of 12 rivers and 71 creeks,[18] as well as mountain streams. The 1998 Expert Panel Environmental Flow Assessment concluded that:

> the Snowy Mountain Hydro Scheme has impacted the hydrological, geomorphological and ecological condition of many streams in the Snowy Mountains. These impacts are particularly severe in the Tumut, Eucumbene, Snowy and Gungarlin Rivers, and some reaches of the Tooma and Geehi Rivers. The impacts of the Scheme on stream flow in most of these rivers are reduced flood frequency and magnitude, reduced volumes of flow at all times, reduced seasonal

flow variability, and in some cases unnaturally rapid and a-seasonal changes in water level from power station releases. The geomorphological outcomes of these changes to stream hydrology have been channel contraction due to reduced discharge, lack of channel adjustment to reduced flows in some reaches, resulting in isolation of the channel from riparian vegetation, loss of rapids, lateral isolation of pools and sedimentation. The impacts of hydrologic changes on water quality are greatest in the pooled sections of streams, and include warmer summer water temperatures and freezing over in winter because of the reduced flows, lower dissolved oxygen and nutrient concentration due to low flows, high algal productivity, and anoxia and stratification in the Tumut and Eucumbene Rivers. Water quality has changed from that of a mountain stream to that typical of a lake or lowland stream.[19]

Hence, the Australian Federal, NSW and Victorian Governments have agreed to restore 21 per cent of the environmental flows of the Snowy River and a smaller percentage of the Murrumbidgee River. Also the Federal and State Governments have agreed to restore 500 billion litres of environmental flows to the Murray river.

The water used to restore the Snowy River will not be taken away from irrigators (as some farmers' organizations have claimed) but rather, as the NSW Water Licence[20] clearly states, it will come from water saved by irrigators through water efficiencies. Over 17 per cent of all water allocated to irrigation is lost before it even reaches the farm due to channel seepage, evaporation and illegal abstraction.[21] The newspaper *The Australian*, showed that there is significant potential for water savings, writing: 'NSW is responsible for over half of the water taken from the Murray Darling, yet only earns on average [AU]$300 per million litres of water. South Australia is already earning [AU]$2000 per million litres. NSW is then significantly the least efficient users of water in Australia'[22] One has to wonder at the wisdom of rice growing in as dry a continent as Australia when it only returns AU$60 per million litres of water used.

There is, therefore, the potential for significant improvements in the resource productivity gains with which farmers use water, thereby allowing increasing amounts of environmental flows to the Murray and the Snowy Rivers. However, that still leaves many other rivers affected by reduced flows. There are another eleven rivers currently diverted by the Snowy Mountains Hydro-Electric Scheme of dams alone. Why is restoring these rivers not yet on the agenda in Australia?

The short answer is cost. The main barrier to restoring alpine and river environmental flows in Australia is cost. To do what is needed for the environment to ensure we do not leave still worse problems to future generations will require an injection of funds. Farmers need assistance to adopt the most water efficient technologies. But, if the environmental flows are restored to other rivers associated with the Snowy Mountains Hydro-Electric Scheme, this will take away revenue earned through power generation. The water in the Snowy Mountains Hydro-Electric Scheme is currently being used to produce power that provides a significant financial return for the Victorian, NSW State and Australian Federal Governments. The Snowy Mountains Hydro-Electric Scheme's own annual reports talk about power being lost through restoring mountain environmental flows. To genuinely restore the environmental flows from the Snowy Mountains Hydro-Electric Scheme will reduce revenue to government. For instance, the commitment of the Australian and State Governments of Victoria and NSW to restoring 28 per cent of the environmental flows or 290Gl of the Snowy River will cost approximately AU$400 million per annum.

But Australia is far less dependent on the Snowy Mountains Hydro-Electric Scheme for energy than when it was originally built. The peak energy period from the scheme is during the winter, but Australia's energy peak loads are in the summer due to the use of air-conditioners. It is also important to note that power generation is not the only source of revenue available to governments from the Snowy Mountains Hydro-Electric Scheme. For instance, the State Governments of Victoria and NSW and the Federal Government pay the Snowy Mountains Hydro-Electric Scheme as insurance to essentially provide a back up generator for the Australian Eastern Seaboard grid using Tumut 3 (the largest single power station and the last station on the Tumut side of the scheme).[23]

Much of the environmental damage of the Snowy Mountains Hydro-Electric Scheme would be remediated if the power generating aspect of the scheme, the chain of extremely small mini-dams, was gradually decommissioned. If these mini-dam systems were decommissioned it would not result in any less water for farmers, because all of this water, if allowed to follow environmental flows, ends up in the rivers, lower dams or groundwater (where it ends up anyway) after ensuring that the ecosystems in the higher alpine region have the water they need. But there are also competing needs in Australia at this time. The National Farmers Federation and Australian Conservation Foundation (ACF) estimate that it will cost Australia AU$65 billion to truly address the emerging salinity problem and address related issues in the Murray Darling Basin over the next 10 years. ACF have proposed a number of important methods whereby the private sector can be encouraged through changes to tax laws to assist in tackling this challenge.

Whilst there are many win–win opportunities to achieve Sustainable Genuine Progress, we have inherited infrastructure designed and built before environmental concerns were a mainstream issue. Therefore, in some areas becoming truly sustainable will cost. Restoring the environmental flows of rivers will be one of these costs. But the costs of acting now will be far less than the costs of addressing the problems in the future. By acting now, there is much land and many rivers that can be saved. But if we leave these problems to future generations it may be too late. Australian scientists now have enough information to both understand that the environmental problems are far worse than originally thought,[24] but also to devise improved ways forward. These and other factors, such as the recent drought in Australia, have meant that the issue of water management has finally risen to the top of the political 'to do list'. For instance, by 2020 if Australia continues with business as usual, it is possible that the Murray River's salinity will fail to meet World Health Organization standards over 50 per cent of the time. Most people incorrectly perceive rivers as narrow conduits. Many of Australia's most serious water problems stem from this assumption and the failure historically to understand ground–surface water connectivity and the long lag time groundwater systems take to respond to changes in land and water use. As much as 50 per cent of the Murray River is thought to have spent part of its life as groundwater.

As Professor Mike Young from CSIRO stated, 'The environment is the cruellest of all the things we have, crueller than the marketplace. It responds very slowly. The water system, particularly the groundwater and the way it flows through into the rivers, has lags of 20 or 30 years and we were ignorant about that and if you don't put the environment first, and the biophysical reality of the way rivers work, ultimately it delivers the disasters we're now seeing and they just get worse and worse. So, if you postpone [addressing issues related to] the environment, it bites you harder so I would put integrity [of the environment] first and designing systems that aren't ignorant, and deal with problems as they emerge. That's tough, but if we don't do that, we end up with the problems we now have and if we don't deal with them now, they get worse and worse and worse until finally we have a drain and we have massive severe problems.'[25]

Rural communities fear that, in addressing these issues, their personal welfare will be harmed. Their concern is understandable as the scale of the problem is significant. Many of Australia's rivers are dying. For instance, in the case of the Murray River (one of Australia's largest rivers), Professor Mike Young estimates that 20–40 per cent of irrigation water needs to be returned to its upper reaches so that it can be restored to a healthy working river.[26] This could require as much as 1500 billion litres of extra flow per annum, 1000 billion litres more than the present Australian Government has committed to restoring. To put this in perspective, South Australian farmers only withdraw 500 billion litres per annum presently. As Professor Mike Young said in an ABC interview, 'South Australia's irrigators use a bit over 500 billion litres so the magnitude of the problem that we're talking about now is one where somebody has to start at the bottom of the river down here and go up and talk to every irrigator all the way up to the top of South Australia and tell them they can't use any of their water. When you get to the border of South Australia and Victoria and NSW, you've only just spoken to a third of the irrigation that has to stop. You have to do it twice more... we were ignorant, we didn't know back in 1970 or 1980 and that hurts me.'[27]

Nevertheless, the business case for addressing and solving the problems of the Murray River is convincing. Restoring its flow and decreasing salinity impacts is a worthwhile investment.[28] The Wentworth Group have recommended that 100 billion litres of water should go back to the Murray each year for the next 10 years. The Wentworth group argue that we need to put the water into environment trusts. Mike Young explains that 'we can manage it in a clever way and work in harmony with the irrigation sector. And this would mean that in dry years we might be able to even put some of that water into irrigation when the environment doesn't need it all, and alternatively buy it back for floods when floods are needed. So if we can manage it really cleverly, we can come up with some innovative solutions.'[29] Whilst restoring the environmental flows of Australia's rivers is a critical issue to avoid far worse problems in the future, so is creating fair processes for such structural adjustments. Governments have in the past encouraged farmers to invest significant money in regions that now are increasingly faced with soil salinity, water and drought problems. Hence any structural reform has to incorporate assistance for farmers.

This will depend on the detail of implementation.[30] If governments like the Australian Government are going to spend taxpayers' dollars to partially restore the environmental flows and compensate irrigators for reduced access to water, then a significantly improved robust regulatory framework is needed. Efficient allocation and management of water requires a robust and consistent water allocation system taking into account both consumptive and non-consumptive uses and a method of implementation and management. The current system in Australia is leading to most unfortunate outcomes. Water trading to date has not brought environmental flows back into the river. This is because of the way states defined the entitlements of water usage. Trade has moved water to what is called higher and better uses, but has not actually kept the savings back, thus when somebody improved an irrigation system or moved the water to somewhere else, more water, not less has been used. Another major driver for change is the fact that the CSIRO reports that 80 per cent of farm profit in Australia comes from just 2 per cent of the national natural resources.[31] Hence changes are needed to make the rural sector more profitable. At this moment in time, Australia has a historic opportunity to genuinely create one of the best rural and urban water management systems in the world.

Creating a robust foundation and framework for water management

Economic and institutional reform: water property rights

The issues regarding effective water management are, in fact, fundamental issues concerning how we manage a 'public good', an area that has historically been poorly managed by institutions according to the World Bank.[32] Ideally, decisions to determine the public use of water are made on behalf of the community as a whole through various processes, be they legislative, regulatory or management oriented. As Professor Mike

Young states, 'no markets are excellent servants. If you set up the rules wrongly or incorrectly, they will tell you how badly you have got it wrong with glorified eloquence and you have salt in the river, you'll have no water left in the river and the market will happily destroy what you have, but if you put the framework together which is focused on solutions and a framework that has integrity, the market with equal eloquence and style will deliver the vision. Markets drive change. You set up the rules and the architecture in a way that has integrity, you'll have the best outcome you can ever have and that's what Australia (or any nation) needs.'[33]

At the very least, the title scheme that is adopted must maximize the value of the water in its beneficial use while ensuring the protection of its public good role, within the constraints imposed by the legal system and community expectations of fairness. Australia has traditionally been one of the leaders in the area of property rights; in many countries Torrens Title (the separation of a number of property rights) is known as 'Australian Title'. However, the water licensing systems in Australia 'are like the railways of 100 years ago; they do not connect effectively at state borders and stand in the way of national environmental and economic progress.'[34] Traditionally, water title has been linked with property title, both in relation to water extraction from streams and use of water that falls on private property. This nexus has now largely been broken in many parts of Australia allowing trading of water rights on a seasonal or permanent basis. This increased flexibility has undoubtedly had benefits, but it is essential to bear in mind that these links still exist. In particular, a water property title scheme must take into account special considerations for water, such as the variability in flows from year to year.

Effective water property title systems are ones which define interests in water and land in a manner that maximizes opportunity. Trading or portability of interests in water is seen as a necessary part of such arrangements, as is the need to manage the application and use of water. In defining different types of titles, water can be separated into a number of different categories:

*   water requirements for properties to remain viable (property water rights);
*   water requirements for the environment (environmental flows, future generations); and
*   water surplus from a property, area or region that can be transferred elsewhere (tradable flows).

There would be little debate as to the need for the allocation of a water entitlement to a property to ensure that the normal land use remains viable. Similarly, there is now general acceptance of the need for environmental flows. The issue, therefore, is not whether these needs exist, but how to quantify and specify them. The same could be said of transferable or tradeable flows, as there are already systems in place that provide for the transfer of water from one area to another and allow the trading of right of access to such water.

The initial reason for the transfer of water was related to the problem of some areas having a water surplus and others a water deficit. Other factors that determined the patterns of water transfer were transport, delivery and the options available for use. Transport was mainly along river systems, hence options for transfer were mainly constrained by catchments. Delivery was by way of open earth canals with flood irrigation; hence irrigation areas were developed in largely flat terrain with reasonably impermeable soils. Given the large volumes of water, its use was mainly in agriculture for crops with established markets. The climates in irrigation areas were more suitable for marketable crops than where the water surpluses occurred.

The prime purpose of a water trading system is to facilitate change in the patterns of water use. It is assumed that implementation of an effective water trading system can facilitate social change. The reason that such change does not occur naturally is that, having established water access rights, most do not see the benefit to them in such change. Addressing the rights and perceptions of those that currently hold water entitlements, and provide benefit to the community through their use, is at least as important as addressing the perceived needs identified by those suggesting change.

The Council of Australian Governments Agreements on Water Policy

In 1994, the Council of Australian Governments (COAG) established a number of guidelines for the reform of water policy. These included general principles for pricing and trading water and the separation of water allocations from land titles.[35] COAG understood that there are immense benefits in separating water access entitlements from land titles so there can be trade in both allocations and entitlements.

However, there was a great deal of uncertainty over the implementation of these guidelines. In some states there were a range of surface water entitlements, with some in perpetuity and some for set periods. These uncertainties acted as disincentives to investment in infrastructure for water efficiency improvements, and in the rural sector in general.

Hydrology

Nevertheless, in the last decade recognition of the need to manage our resources more wisely led to attempts at:

- *capping*: the setting of a limit on new licence allocations; and
- *trading*: the introduction of mechanisms to encourage economically inefficient water users to sell water entitlements and allocations to economically efficient water users.

Sadly, to date, capping has been applied on an ad hoc basis. In most States, groundwater resources remain uncapped. Farm dam development, forestry and other forms of land use are taking up water supplies for water catchments and river systems. Furthermore, the assumptions underlying the present trading arrangements are leading to more water being taken out of the rivers and groundwater, not less, thus diminishing the environmental flows of the rivers. Along the Murray River, water allocations are typically exceeding 20 per cent of the cap. Few trading arrangements presently recognize that when water use is technically inefficient, most of the water eventually returns to the river for use by others and the environment and helps to restore rivers' environmental flows. Presently, most irrigators are allowed to use the 'savings' they make from increases in water efficiencies within their existing allocation and expand their irrigation. This simply means less water is returning into the groundwater and rivers and as such the present arrangements are eroding the cap.

Consider the situation where a farmer switches from flood irrigation to drip irrigation; their water use efficiency would increase from 40–50 per cent to up to 85 per cent. This farmer is now using his allocated water as much as two times more efficiently as before. Sounds good so far! Now, let's say this farmer is allocated 1000ML/annum. Previously the farmer used most of it but now he finds he only needs to use half of it. Let's say this farmer then chooses to expand his irrigation to use the full allocation with drip irrigation. This means that >35 per cent of the water allocation is no longer being returned through the groundwater to rivers and downstream users. Likewise, if a farmer, using water inefficiently, trades part of his allocation to a farmer using water efficiently this will also take a significant amount of water out of the groundwater and therefore the river system.

Another serious flaw is the failure to account for the impact of increased forestry and other land use changes that reduce water yield. For instance, current plans to treble Australia's plantation forests by 2020 are expected to reduce flows in the Murray–Darling Basin by around 1300 billion litres. Young and McColl's work shows that even if governments proceed to reduce irrigation entitlements along the Murray river by 1500 billion litres to restore environmental flows and take no other action to fix the regulatory frameworks, factor in water uptake from forestry, in 20 years or so, the result will be less, not more environmental flows. Hence, as Mike Young states: 'it is clearly important to limit trading opportunities to the amount of water consumed.' He continues: 'trading rights without regard to the amount of water available to others and the environment is eroding existing systems. If we keep trading in gross rather than net terms, the extent of over-allocation will increase. So we've got to decide if we're going to trade on net use only, or monitor the gross total use and make regular entitlement and allocation adjustments.'

Other largely unaddressed issues to date include the National Competition Policy's recommendation that water prices should include the cost of externalities. A number of new proposals have begun addressing all these issues. One of these comes from the Wentworth Group of concerned scientists, formed in Sydney's Wentworth Hotel.[36] The Wentworth Group identified the features of water entitlement and allocation systems that have economic, hydrological, social, financial and environmental integrity. One member of the Group, Peter Cullen, summarized these in his keynote paper for Australia 21's *In Search of Sustainability* online conference. He also assisted a number of Australian businesspeople to contribute to the water property debate with his book, *Truth in Water Entitlements*, which outlined a Gold Standard of Water Entitlement. CSIRO's Mike Young and Dr Jim McColl's robust separation framework and other significant work was also integrated by this new group. Around the same time the Wentworth group was working on proposals for government, the National Farmers Federation and Australian Conservation Foundation also prepared a joint statement for action on water that was well received politically and shared many similarities with the recommendations from the Wentworth group.

In 2003, the COAG meeting provided significant impetus for a resolution to the water debate by committing to many of the recommendations of these documents. No country yet has got their water management entirely right, hence Australia now has an opportunity to genuinely create one of the best water management systems in the world.

The COAG communiqué below demonstrates the significant shift in Australia.

The COAG communiqué to develop a National Water Initiative

The Council of Australian Governments agreed that there is a pressing need to refresh its 1994 water reform agenda to increase the productivity and efficiency of water use, sustain rural and urban communities and ensure the health of river and groundwater systems. Investment in new, more efficient production systems is being hampered by uncertainty over the long-term access to water in some areas. Fully functioning water markets can help to ensure that investment is properly targeted and water is put to higher value and more efficient uses. However, current arrangements are preventing those markets from delivering their full potential. Furthermore, there are significant concerns over the pace of securing adequate environmental flows and adaptive management arrangements to ensure ecosystem health in our river systems.

A key focus of the National Water Initiative, as it is being developed by COAG, will be to implement a robust framework for water access entitlements that encourages investment and maximizes the economic value created from water use, while ensuring that there is sufficient water available to maintain healthy rivers and aquifers. The framework will be compatible between jurisdictions and reflect regional variability in the reliability of water supply and the state of knowledge underpinning regional allocation decisions. The key aims of this initiative are to:

- Improve the security of water access entitlements by clear assignment of the risks of reductions in future water availability and by returning overallocated systems to sustainable allocation levels.
- Ensure ecosystem health by implementing regimes to protect environmental assets at a whole-of-basin, aquifer or catchment scale.
- Ensure water is put to best use by encouraging the expansion of water markets and trading across and between districts and States (where water systems are physically shared), involving clear rules for trading, robust water accounting arrangements and pricing based on full cost recovery principles.
- Water-sharing plans based on best-practice system modelling developed through transparent processes involving all stakeholders, subject to review when necessary, and with regular reporting on progress.
- Best practice specification of the responsibilities of water users.
- Achieve an efficient water market structure and expand markets to their widest practical geographical scope, enabling increased returns from water use. Where applicable, and particularly in the Murray–Darling Basin, this will involve a review of the various water entitlement products, pricing policies, exchange rates and trading rules with a view to ensuring compatibility across jurisdictions.
- Best practice water pricing using the principles of user pays and full cost recovery, and include where appropriate, the cost of delivery, planning, and environmental impact.
- Establish new arrangements dedicated to the management of water at a basin, aquifer or catchment scale to deliver agreed environmental outcomes. For example, in the Murray–Darling Basin, a basin-wide system of mechanisms will be established to enable environmental water management, including through the market. A flexible trading model has the advantage of being able to purchase water for the environment in a cost effective manner when needed, and selling or leasing water back to other water users at other times.
- Provide water for the environment through targeted public and private investment in engineering works to improve 'leaky' infrastructure, based on rigorous investment criteria.
- Ensure accurate measurement, monitoring and reporting: this is raised to a new level of importance when there is increasing competition for water and where the proposed water management system depends on secure entitlements, market approaches, water recovery and environmental flow management.
- Assist jurisdictions to establish a robust and transparent regulatory water accounting framework that protects the integrity of entitlements.
- Ensure governments continue to invest in improving the scientific understanding of our water resources, and the industries and ecosystems that depend on them.
- Encourage water conservation in our cities, including better use of stormwater and recycled water.

The National Water Initiative will build on the achievements of the 1994 COAG Strategic Framework for the Reform of the Australian Water Industry, the Natural Heritage Trust and the National Action Plan for Salinity and Water Quality. Further details of the National Water Initiative were developed at the COAG meeting of 25 June 2004, in line with the original commitments of the 2003 COAG communiqué. Implementation of the National

Water Initiative will be overseen by the Natural Resource Management Ministerial Council in line with detailed implementation plans to be developed by each state and territory over the rest of 2004–2005.

A robust separation framework

Robustness

The COAG communiqué discussed how both the framework and accounting system for this new national water initiative needed to be robust. Robust systems have an architecture that can be expected to produce efficient and fair outcomes in an ever-changing world and will stand the test of time. This general point deserves to be emphasized, as all the work in this area provides much food for thought for policy-makers interested in how to make government policy robust. The central point of the rest of this section and the communiqué is the importance of creating a robust framework to provide a sure foundation within which reform can proceed fairly and equitably for both the environment and farmers. One of the greatest contributions to understanding how to create robust systems comes from economist and Nobel Prize Laureate Jan Tinbergen in the form of the Tinbergen Principle. This principle states that to attain a given number of independent policy targets through time there must be at least an equal number of policy instruments. Thus, to ensure arrangements for managing water allocation and use are robust, the components of existing systems must be separable from one another. Whenever any problem emerges in unseparated systems the entire system comes under review, negotiations are not straightforward and an opportunity is created to reopen old agendas. Therefore, one of the keys to creating a robust system for many of Australia's water problems lies more with separation than integration.

Water access entitlements: allocations and use conditions

Building upon this concept of fully specifying risk and the Tinbergen Principle, the features of a robust set of water-licensing arrangements separated from land title have been identified.[37] Fundamental clues leading to the development of Young and McColl's framework have come primarily from the limited liability company and share trading system, the Torrens Title system and from the banking system.

Key features of the proposed system include the aspects discussed in the following subsections.

Water shares

Using the limited liability share company concept, Young and McColl propose that water rights or 'entitlements' be formally described as a share, and managed in a system that is identical to the share registry. The entitlement holder would have a long-term share, defined as an unequivocally guaranteed mortgageable claim to a proportional share of any periodic water allocations. Governments grant entitlements that define the degree of access to the resource that can be expected over time.

Mike Young states: 'they must also specify precisely what can and what cannot be compensated through the courts. Share systems make it clear that risk is involved and that circumstances may change.'[38] For example, a change in mean annual rainfall, which forces an adjustment in the amount of water an entitlement holder receives (allocation), is a risk the entitlement holder has to carry. However, there are avenues for assistance that can be pursued. For instance if an administrative error is made, entitlements would also be registered under a Torrens Title system. Young states: 'the Torrens Title system requires that property should be defined on a register, not by distributed pieces of paper. This has been shown to significantly reduce the opportunity for fraud and misrepresentation of the true nature of an interest. In any dispute, the register is deemed to be correct.'

Water allocations

The second part of the robust system defines water allocations as a 'unit of opportunity' (usually a volume) distributed periodically. Jim McColl stated, 'An allocation is like a dividend … the periodic allocation is what you can extract annually on the basis of your share. Much like the management of money in the banking system, allocations would be credited to a formal account.' Trades and extractions from the common pool for irrigation, for example, would then be debited from these accounts and people could write water cheques and/or trades on the Internet at low cost.

Water-use licences

The final component of the robust system is the 'use licence': the right to apply water to land. This component allows the impacts of environment, neighbours and downstream water users to be specified and managed. The licence would specify the degree of use permitted. For example, a use licence may grant permission to flood irrigate a maximum of 500 hectares on a specified area of land. It would also define such things as pumping limits, drainage disposal requirements and obligations under the district or regional salinity management strategy.

Young and McColl argue that the use licences should begin by reserving pollution rights to the crown. It is vital that this is done, as it would then be possible to manage salinity and other water quality issues separately from quantity issues. These complex natural resource management (NRM) issues are all interrelated. Young and McColl point out that many salinity interception schemes, while reducing river salinity, also reduce environmental flows.

To conclude, a robust system is required that will enable river managers to manage both quality and flow issues simultaneously through time and over large regions.

Electronic trading

By separating water entitlements, allocations and usage, the trading of water could operate entirely separately from the management of water use. Entitlement trading would be possible using licensed brokers and clear trading rules, while allocation trading would be possible using electronic transfers and accounts, just like those used to manage a bank account. 'People could trade entitlements or allocations and not have a use licence,' McColl says, 'or, they could buy a use licence and then buy an entitlement from the market which would entitle them to a share of the common pool. Or, rather than holding an entitlement, they could buy periodic allocations on the market.' This situation would give farmers real choice in how best to use their allocation. For example, in a drought year, a farmer irrigating low-value crops might achieve a better return by selling part of his allocation. This would allow another user who might have high value crops, such as grapes, to buy the extra water for a better harvest. This scenario is happening to a limited extent now, but it could be made more efficient given proper specifications of the entitlement, allocation and use licence.'

Transitional arrangements

Sequencing

Australian water politicians are currently focused on the removal of impediments to permanent water access entitlement trading and securing an additional 1500 billion litres for environmental flows in the Murray. Similar targets can be expected to emerge soon for the other large river systems such as the Darling and several stressed coastal rivers.

The presence of market impediments and the fact that the real environmental costs are presently not being accounted, however, means that the value of water access entitlements, allocations and the use licences are less than they would otherwise be. In overallocated systems, like the Murray River, the result is a sequencing opportunity and a sequencing trap; if governments remove market impediments before a robust entitlement and allocation system is embedded, the cost of reform increases. However, if water is secured for the environment at the same time as market impediments and entitlement flows are reformed, then the market gains from this process can be utilized to reduce the need for transitional assistance payments.

Failure to pursue these reform sequencing opportunities and, in particular, to implement the politically easy options without addressing the underlying flaws is likely to result in the emergence of problems that will hinder opportunities to make further progress. As a general rule, it will be cheaper for governments to acquire additional water to assist the environment before impediments to permanent water trading are removed and before a new flawless water access entitlement system is put in place.

Conceptually the simplest option for governments would be the compulsory acquisition of all water licences at current value, the embedding of the necessary reforms and the sale of a new range of water access entitlements to the highest bidders.

Restoring environmental flows

There is a range of options for governments to help restore environmental flows. In the immediate term, for river systems that are not over allocated, existing systems can be retrained and run conservatively. In over-allocated and overused systems, water access entitlements of reliability will need to be reduced over time.

Relatively cost effective options of securing water access entitlements include:

- a pro rata reduction implemented administratively by reducing expected reliability and/or, by reducing the volume of water periodically offered for sale (as in Victoria);
- a pro rata reduction in the volume stated on each licence;
- acquisition of water licences by using market like processes, including open market like processes, voluntary lender and compulsory tender mechanisms;
- compulsory acquisition of either a proportion of each licence or closure of specific categories of water use and/or areas of irrigation;
- contracts involving investment by government in infrastructure upgrades (supply system and/or on farm) in return for the surrender of all or part of one or more licences.

Each option has its benefits, costs, equity and political implications. Pro rata reduction approaches can be expected to increase market activity and incur deadweight transaction costs, as those who cannot afford to give up water buy it back. In systems where two or more types of licence exist, it is possible to reduce the reliability of just one type of licence. Whatever approach is taken under pro rata reduction mechanisms, the most economically efficient water users can be expected to purchase water access entitlements or allocations from less efficient water users and from those simply investing and trading in entitlements and allocations.

The cheapest market acquisition approach known is the compulsory tender approach used for sulphur trading in the US. Under this mechanism, all licence holders are required to offer a proportion of their access entitlement for sale but can nominate any reserve price they choose. The result is the rapid emergence of a deep and mature market characterized by lower transaction costs than any other voluntary market process can deliver.

Young and McColl's preference is for all water secured for the environment to be placed in an independent Murray–Darling Basin-wide trust, empowered to maximize environmental outcomes by trading water. The trust, for example, might sell some allocations in a drought and use the resultant proceeds to buy back a larger volume of water in subsequent years when water is cheaper. How these options are mixed together is a matter that will occupy many government minds. After consideration of the options, the Wentworth Group has suggested a mixed approach with irrigators having the access entitlements reduced by 1 per cent per year for 10 years, following conversion to a robust form, with the remainder of environmental flow water purchased using a compulsory tender, or other similar mechanism.[39] A national public consultation on water allocation, river flows, water trading, environmental degradation and assistance is under way, and a paper on water property rights, prepared by the Natural Resource Management Ministerial Council's Chief Executive Officers' Group on Water[40] forms the basis of this public consultation and covers many of the principles raised by Young and McColl.

Conclusion

The United Nations is currently holding major conferences annually to address these and many more issues relating to water. Water is one of the basic rights of all people. Hundreds of nations have agreed with the UN's goal to ensure that the number of people across the planet without access to clean water is reduced by half by 2015. In *Factor Four* and *Natural Capitalism*, the authors showed the remarkable array of new ways that humankind can use water more efficiently. *Natural Capitalism* also showed that many of the regulatory failures in the energy sector also apply to the water sector. For instance, as with energy, water utilities are often rewarded for selling more water not less. Water utilities rarely operate in a regulatory environment that rewards them and encourages them to encourage water efficiency. Therefore, just as with the energy sector, there are insurmountable opportunities in the water sector to achieve dramatic resource productivity improvement.

The drought in Australia over recent years, and Australia's complex biophysical landscape has focused some of Australia's best minds on these issues. The new techniques for managing and treating water more efficiently and the new regulatory frameworks that these scientists, engineers and economists have developed are world class and of relevance to any country. The WCD has shown it is time to recognize that humankind has fragmented 60 per cent of the world's rivers leading to significant negative environmental and social impacts. If more efficient use of water is combined with these robust regulatory frameworks, it will give nature a chance to restore its resilience leaving a positive legacy for future generations.

SECTION 5

A NATIONAL COLLABORATIVE APPROACH: THE BIGGER PICTURE – BUILDING RESILIENCE

CHAPTER 21

INTEGRATED APPROACHES TO SUSTAINABLE CONSUMPTION AND CLEANER PRODUCTION

Christopher Ryan

Consumption and low impact affluence[1]

The growing attention to the issues of sustainable consumption is a natural outcome of decades of work on cleaner production and eco-efficient industrial systems. It represents the final step in a progressive widening of the horizons of pollution prevention; a widening which has gone from a focus on production processes (cleaner production), to products, (eco-design), then to product-systems (incorporating transport logistics, end-of-life collection and component re-use or materials recycling) and to eco-innovation and eco-effectiveness (new products and product-systems and enterprises designed for win–win solutions for business and the environment).

> *Action focused on consumption has highlighted the need to address the creation of new systems of production and consumption, systems that might be truly sustainable, environmentally, economically – systems that will enhance the quality and equality of cultural, social and physical existence for all people.*

UNEP, *Sustainable Consumption: Global Status Report* 2002

Development, prosperity, wealth – the economic, social, cultural and environmental factors that underpin our sense of quality of life – are dependent, ultimately, on the structure of our systems of production and consumption. However, in the lead-up to the first global conference on the human environment (Stockholm 1972), community, scientific and political debates targeted those systems of production and consumption as a potential threat to human survival. The next 20-year period leading up to the Earth Summit in Rio de Janeiro saw huge changes to global understanding of the relationship between economic activity and ecological systems. By 1992, there was a sense of

---

This chapter has been adapted for this publication by Professor Christopher Ryan of RMIT University, Melbourne, Australia from his report *Sustainable Consumption: Global Status Report 2002* (UNEP, 2002b). That report was produced for the UNEP Division of Technology, Industry and Environment (DTIE) for the World Summit on Sustainable Development (WSSD) held in Johannesburg in 2002.

optimism that preventative strategies heralded the potential of a *change of course*, in which industrial and economic development would become compatible with sustaining the global environment.

A critical review of achievements in pollution prevention, cleaner production and eco-efficiency can point to some real progress since Rio. However, whilst some gains are observable in production, consumption appears to be moving in ways that threaten sustainable development, bringing issues of 'sustainable consumption' and 'over-consumption' to the front of the policy debate. Discussions of consumption, over-consumption and sustainability are prone to a confusion in terminology which arises from the economic focus on consumption of goods and services (demand and volume) and the ecological focus on consumption of resources and generation of waste (ecological impact). The term 'patterns of consumption' has grown in usage as a way of expressing the linkage between these two aspects of consumption. Whilst the ultimate concern is the impact of resource consumption (and waste) on the biosphere, it is vital to recognize that this impact arises from the consumption of goods and services and the ways such goods and services are produced. How goods and services are produced, distributed and consumed affects the net resource consumption and waste which will result from their consumption. 'Patterns of consumption' is a loose term that aims to describe particular ways in which goods, services and resources are produced and consumed by some community or population.[2] Globally, unsustainable patterns of consumption demand attention and action. In particular, we see:

- growing disparities in levels of consumption between rich and poor countries;
- growing disparities in levels of consumption within developing countries;
- total growth in consumption of resources (particularly water, food and energy) in developed economies which is now so great that technical (eco)-efficiency improvements are being overwhelmed.

The inequalities in consumption between countries (and within countries) are so significant that they represent a fundamental distortion in progress towards sustainable development. There are critical resource areas where consumption levels within countries are threatening future development because demand is exceeding supply. The overall consumption of the richest fifth of the world's population is nine times that of the poorest fifth.[3]

> In the last 25 years the world economic output has more than quadrupled with significant rises of GDP in East Asia and the Pacific, Sub-Saharan Africa and Latin America and the Caribbean. Yet nearly 2.8 billion people live on less than two US dollars a day (India 82 percent of population, Indonesia 65 percent, China 55 percent, South Africa 37 percent, Brazil 17 percent).
>
> World Bank (2000) World Development Index

Increasing eco-efficiency remains the most optimistic strategy for sustainable production, at least in the short term, and has the strongest support of industry. In general terms, eco-efficiency reflects an increasing economic and technical focus on resource efficiency, after almost 200 years of emphasis on improving labour efficiency.[4] However, there is evidence that GDP (gross domestic product) is growing at a faster rate than improvements in resource or energy efficiency – consumption is outpacing the gains from improvements in production and products, which in most OECD countries has been significant.[5] There is increasing evidence of rebound effects, in which improvements in efficiency actually become a stimulus for increased consumption.

It used to be taken for granted that economic growth entailed parallel growth in resource consumption, and to a certain extent, environmental degradation. However, the experience of the last decades indicates that economic growth and resource consumption and environmental degradation can be decoupled to a considerable extent. The path towards sustainable development entails accelerating this decoupling process ... i.e. transforming what we produce and how we produce it.

Yukiko Fukasaku, Directorate for Science, Technology and Industry, OECD[6]

Throughout Agenda 21 there is a clear sense that a re-orientation of production and consumption is technically possible – and achievable – with the right approaches, the correct policy context and appropriate political action. Yet, as the evidence of technical improvements in production has grown, the contradictions have deepened, generating a new focus for concern and action – consumption.

Extravagant and wasteful consumption of affluent communities constitutes an environmental constraint ... on rich and poor alike, and demands the application of science, technology and policies to address the problem. Furthermore, the skewed consumption patterns between rich and poor might well mean that the point is being approached when – contrary to much past experience – the poor are poor in part because the rich are rich. Worse – the gap between the rich and poor is growing.

Norman Myers (2000)

Given the scale of global inequalities, progress towards sustainable consumption has to emerge from action taken within industrialized countries where the dominant models and aspirations for global development are generated. This point was made strongly in Agenda 21 and has been strengthened by the many meetings and reports since that time. Only developed countries have the resources to assist in the eradication of poverty and the economic and technical capacity to transform current systems of production and consumption, to achieve the levels of environmental efficiency necessary for a sustainable existence. Unless new aspirations for sustainable prosperity are widely and visibly embraced within developed countries, they will not become a global pattern. However, any action in developed countries has to be relevant to the conditions and the needs of developing countries and open to solutions and approaches derived from the experience and practice of developing economies. Change will occur only though North–South and East–West dialogue and collaborative projects.

Encourage and promote the development ... of programmes ... to accelerate the shift towards sustainable consumption and production, to promote social and economic development within the carrying capacity of ecosystems by addressing and, where appropriate, de-linking economic growth and environmental degradation through improving efficiency and sustainability in the use of resources and production processes, and reducing resource degradation, pollution and waste. All countries should take action, with developed countries taking the lead. This would require actions at all levels to: (a) Identify specific activities, tools, policies, measures and monitoring and assessment mechanisms, including, where appropriate, life cycle analysis and national indicators for measuring progress (b) Adopt and implement policies and measures aimed at promoting sustainable patterns of production and consumption, applying, inter alia, the polluter-pays principle (c) Develop production and consumption policies to improve products and services, while reducing environmental and health impacts (d) Develop awareness-raising programmes on the importance of sustainable production and consumption patterns, particularly among youth. Especially in developed countries, through, inter alia, education, public and consumer information, advertising and other media (e) Develop and adopt, where appropriate, on a voluntary basis, effective, transparent, verifiable, non-misleading and non-discriminatory consumer information tools to provide information relating to sustainable consumption and production.. (f) Increase eco-efficiency, with financial support from all sources for capacity-building, technology transfer and exchange of technology with developing countries and countries with economies in transition, in cooperation with relevant international organizations.

WSSD (2002) *Plan of Implementation*, Section 14, 4 September 2002

Thinking about consumption has provided a valuable approach to the analysis of current conditions and an important way to structure strategies for future development.[7] A critical issue is to identify strategies for action that do not depend on a simplistic division into separate spheres of action: production-focused (*producers, processes, technology facilities*) and consumer-focused (*needs, awareness, behaviour*). 'Production' and 'Consumption' ('producers' and 'consumers') is a limited way of thinking about systems of production and consumption which involve a complex set of interacting factors. Strategies for change will require these complexities to be focused into areas of action which can be communicated, understood and embraced by all stakeholders.

Patterns of consumption are a global issue

Which patterns of production and consumption provide the basis for a future in which there is global equity in quality of life and access to resources and a sustainable existence? And how are the concepts of quality of life in developing countries affected by the aspirations and goals of consumers and business in developed countries?

Nepal is ranked second only to Ethiopia as one of the poorest nations. The level of imports of cosmetics, soft drinks and cameras into Nepal belies the severity of the poverty of its people. The imports of cosmetic goods increased from US$227,000 in 1992/93 to US$1.5 million in 1997/98; cameras increased from US$220,000 to US$1.3 million; soft drink concentrates accounted for US$202,000 in 1992/93 and rose to US$823,000 in 1997/98. These statistics are alarming in a country where more than 53 per cent of the population lives on less than US$1 a day.

UNEP (2001) *Workshop on Sustainable Consumption, Asia Pacific*

'Scaling-up' current Western patterns of consumption as the basis of development for, say, China or India – adding another 2 billion 'Western style' consumers – is simply not a realistic option unless the risk of catastrophic collapse of the global ecosystem is considered acceptable.

If China were to match the US for levels of car ownership and oil consumption per person it would mean producing approximately 850 million more cars and more than doubling the world output of oil. Those additional cars would produce more CO_2 per annum than the whole of the rest of the world's transportation systems. If China were to match US consumption per head of paper, it would need more paper than the world currently produces. If China were to consume seafood at the per capita rate of Japan, it would need 100 million tonnes, more than today's total catch. If China's beef consumption was to match the USA's per capita consumption and if that beef was produced mainly in feedlot, this would take grain equivalent to the entire US harvest.

UNEP, *Sustainable Consumption: Global Status Report 2002*

Whilst the last ten years have seen real improvements in production processes and products, these have not been of the scale necessary to provide a realistic path for equitable global development based on 'US style' consumption patterns. Western economies have been supported by an entrenched social and cultural commitment to the link between prosperity and per-capita consumption of goods and services. Through global business, trade, advertising and communications, concepts of quality of life in developing countries are strongly affected by the aspirations and goals of consumers and business in developed countries. The impacts of this 'global aspiration system' are acutely evident in the concerns expressed in regional consultations on consumption and from the UNEP work on the emergence of a Global Consumer Class (GCC).[8]

The GCC is a term for middle to upper income earners from all regions of the world – approximately one-third of the global population. UNEP selected this segment of global consumers for a study, surveying over 700 consumers from six global cities – Sao Paolo, Sydney, Lagos, New York, Bombay and Paris, in 2000. The survey aimed to:

- discover similarities between consumers across the globe;
- interact directly with global consumers to find out about their consumption patterns and attitudes and concerns; and
- explore the feasibility of global/UNEP policy options.

The results of this survey confirm that there is a large global set of consumers with similar tastes and preferences, recognizing international brands and life styles. The importance of those results for policy-making is that 'counter-aspirations' observed in developing economies – such as recognizing the environmental implications of product choice – are also diffused amongst this set of consumers.[9] Any shift towards more sustainable consumption in developed countries is therefore likely to have a global influence. The important issue is to find ways of amplifying this potential, to ensure that developing countries grasp the business opportunities from increasing awareness. This suggests a focus of policies and action for the future.[10]

Recent history suggests that those living in wealthier countries do not intend to consume and waste less. Given that the other 80 per cent of the planet's people seek to emulate those consumption habits, the only hope for sustainability is to change forms of consumption. To do so, we must innovate.[11] This approach, altering patterns of consumption by changing the form of what is consumed and shifting the value of consumption towards less material and resource intensive products and services – requiring innovation in technology, business and social behaviour – underlies current policy approaches of governments and international agencies and has become fundamental to the idea of sustainable consumption.

Policy approaches and action

The UN has added a total of 14 points to its consumer protection guidelines to address issues related to sustainable consumption. These amount to a set of policy approaches and actions directed to governments, which '*should take the lead in introducing sustainable practices in their own operations*'. They note that responsibility for sustainable consumption is shared by all members and organizations of society and that those governments should act in partnership with 'informed consumers, business, labour organizations, and consumer and environmental organizations'.

The guidelines cover:

- Developing and implementing strategies that promote sustainable consumption through a mix of policies that could include regulations; economic and social

instruments in such areas as land use, information, transport, energy and housing.
- Removing subsidies that promote unsustainable patterns of consumption and production.
- Implementing programmes to raise awareness of the impact of consumption patterns and the health related benefits of sustainable consumption and production patterns.
- Encouraging the design, development and use of products and services that are safe and energy and resource efficient, considering their full life cycle impacts.
- Promoting the development and use of national and international environmental health and safety standards for products and services; such standards should not result in disguised barriers to trade.
- Setting up mechanisms for the impartial environmental testing of products and the provision of accessible information to consumers.
- Creating or strengthening effective regulatory mechanisms for the protection of consumers.
- The development of indicators, methodologies and databases, for measuring progress towards sustainable consumption.
- Promoting research on consumer behaviour related to environmental damage.

The sixth EU Environmental Action Plan, which came into force in 2002, includes a number of consumption-related policy approaches being developed under the broad goal to: ensure that the consumption of renewable and non-renewable resources and the associated impacts do not exceed the carrying capacity of the environment and achieve a decoupling of resource use from economic growth through significantly improved resource efficiency, dematerialization of the economy, and waste prevention.

Measures being considered include:

- Increasing support for research and technological development of less resource-intensive products and production processes.
- Introducing best-practice programmes for business.
- Shifting of the tax burden on to the use of natural resources, a virgin raw materials tax and the use of other economic instruments such as tradable permits to encourage the uptake of resource-efficient technologies, products and services.
- Removal of subsidies that encourage the over use of resources.
- Integration of resource efficiency considerations into Integrated Product Policy (IPP), eco-labelling schemes, green procurement policies and environmental reporting.

The above approaches are repeated in terms of waste management policies that also seek to decouple the generation of waste from economic growth.[12] The Integrated Product Policy (IPP) process in Europe includes experimentation with community product panels, multi-stakeholder panels which are focused on different categories/sectors of products and services to discuss needs, product improvement areas, consumption issues, etc.[13]

Summary of policy approaches for sustainable consumption

A summary of policy approaches for sustainable consumption is provided in Tables 21.1–21.4.

Table 21.1 *Production and product improvement focus (target: business)*

Goal	Approaches	Actions	Key actors
Un-link resource consumption and economic growth. Significant increase in eco-efficiency of production and consumption. (Global).	Dematerialization, decarbonization and detoxification of consumption. Reduce material/resource flows; increase use of renewable energy, eliminate toxics (or keep in closed cycles). Increase competition and innovation for new eco-products and services. Products and services that are resource efficient and safe from a life cycle perspective.	Green purchasing. Continuous improvement in performance standards. Independent evaluation of performance. Labelling of products and communication of product life information. Education, training and information on eco-design, LCA, for professionals and SMEs. Resource taxes; removal of perverse subsidies Integrated Product Policies. Polluter pays policies to follow global production chains.	Government Business (WBCSD) Design Education Research International agencies (WTO; UNEP)
Ensure green market information and product eco-design strategies 'shape' new production, products and services, in developing economies.	Develop and extend global information – ensure access in developing countries. High profile communication of case studies of eco-products and new environmental business development in developed economies. Use trade systems to support flow of eco-products and services from developing countries to developed markets.	Information provision to developing markets from best practice in developed countries (production and policies). Education and training support. International labelling schemes. Capacity building networks.	UNEP WTO Bi-lateral governments agreements (research and education)
Ensure new eco-products and services are 'designed to be desirable' – to project to the market as sophisticated, of high(er) quality, advanced. Ensure transfer of best environmental technology and production to developing countries.	Eco-design work to extend beyond technical, engineering changes (to reduce impacts) to include aesthetics, cultural expression, market values, creativity. TNCs and other industries of developed countries, to use only best available production facilities and technologies for investments in developing countries.	Link eco-design methods and strategies, closely to marketing. Consumer research on the positive values of sustainable products. Investment controls (target countries). Case study exposure and reporting. Consumer organization monitoring.	UNEP Education Research Eco-design Eco-design organizations Countries Business Consumers International

Source: UNEP (2002b)

Table 21.2 Information and awareness focus (target: consumers)

Goal	Approaches	Actions	Key actors
Ensure consumers can see the 'life behind the product' and make informed choice.	Labelling and product information reporting. Ensure product standards and claims to highest international levels.	Global labelling systems. Performance standards. Independent evaluation of performance. Best practice information.	Government Business Research International agencies (UNDP, UNEP, Consumers International)
Promote (global) ideas and examples of 'sustainable prosperity' or "low-impact affluence'.	Quality of life indictors adopted internationally. Market such ideas using the same techniques and positive images as selling products and 'product-accumulation affluence'. Case studies of high quality of life, low-impact living.	Develop WWF and UN DESA consumption data and indicators. Develop consistent de-materialization indicators. Data on health and consumption. Transfer skills and approaches from advertising and marketing to governments – producers of eco-products.	WWF UNEP UN DESA WHO Consumers International Government Advertising, marketing and communications professionals
Build on positive aspects of global consumer trends and youth awareness – concern about links between consumption and environmental damage – to increase demand on producers for improved products.	Continue work on engaging with consumers to understand their attitudes and concerns. Bring advertising and communications industry into network.	Regular consumer and other stakeholder dialogues. Continue UNEP/UNESCO Youth programmes. Link UNEP advertising and communications forum strongly to youth programmes. Youth TV and Music – content on consumption issues. Global communications Award scheme.	UNEP UNESCO Communications industry Advertising industry Consumers International

Source: UNEP (2002b)

Table 21.3 *Equality focus (target: international agencies and government)*

Goal	Approaches	Actions	Key actors
Ensure minimum consumption standards globally for key goods and services.	Development of essential infrastructure in water, healthcare, sanitation, electricity, education in all countries. Stimulate participation in decisions about consumption patterns.	Global action for human development. Reporting on consumption indices – guide to aid and investment. Multi-stakeholder dialogues.	Government Business International agencies World Bank
Increase access to information systems and information technology and local control of information hubs.	Appropriate local infrastructures. Community access to IT. Training in IT and communications.	Development of local IT networks. Work from communal access as starting point. Local information collection.	Government Education and research NGOs
Increase choice of eco-products and services in all countries/markets.	Development of local infrastructure and integrated product policies.	Capacity building and support programmes to help producers in developing countries. Government procurement programme to emphasize environmental criteria for product choice.	UNEP WBCSD Government
Strengthen consumer protection.	UN Consumer Protection Guidelines. Polluter pays policies.	Ensure awareness and implementation. Extend polluter pays policies in North to cover all of the global product chain.	Consumers Consumers International Government UN
Remove economic barriers.	(See OECD policy options in Table 21.4.)	Modernize tax systems to include resource taxes. Discourage perverse subsidies.	Government

Source: UNEP (2002b)

Table 21.4 OECD *policy instruments for sustainable consumption*

Actor	Action	Policy instruments	Example
Consumers	Use fewer resources	Financial Legal Social Other policy influences	Energy tax Speed limits in air polluted areas Water saving campaigns Public health campaigns
Consumers	Use better resources	Financial Legal Social Other policy influences	Solar power supply Temporary bans on using drinking water for gardens Green electricity schemes Physical planning regulations for local windmills
Consumers	Use fewer goods	Financial Legal Social Other policy influences	Motor vehicle tax Free motorway zones for car sharing Promotion of library Tax incentives influencing household size
Consumers	Use better goods	Financial Legal Social Other policy influences	Leaded petrol taxes Environmental standards in car maintenance schemes Promotion campaigns for fair trade coffee Agricultural policies promoting industrial food products
Consumers	Produce less waste	Financial Legal Social Other policy influences	Recycle premiums Local waste separation regulations Awareness campaigns on avoiding packaging Safety and hygiene regulations
Producers	Supply better goods and information	Financial Legal Social Other policy influences	Research gains Construction standards for efficient houses Voluntary reporting initiatives Information technology leading to greater transparency
Producers	Supply new goods or services	Financial Legal Social Other policy influences	Taxes/subsidies Product standards Network building of pioneers Labour cost policies
Retailers	Practise good housekeeping	Financial Legal Social Other policy influences	Taxes/subsidies Waste regulations Voluntary initiatives Physical planning
Retailers	Supply better goods and information.	Financial Legal Social Other policy influences	Added value tax exceptions Information standards Voluntary initiatives for subscription schemes for organic food Media policies
Retailers	Provide facilities for recycle and repair services	Financial Legal Social Other policy influences	Local subsidies N/A Promotional activities, e.g. local recycling week National labour cost policies

Table 21.4 *continued*

Actor	Action	Policy instruments	Example
Public authorities	Green procurement	Financial	Temporary financial incentives for buying green
		Legal	Procurement standards
		Social	Awareness campaigns
		Other policy influences	International harmonization and competition policies
Public authorities	Supply better infrastructure and information	Financial	Budget grants for innovative projects
		Legal	Environmental standards for use of materials
		Social	Consumer lobbying
		Other policy influences	General budget policies
NGOs, researchers	Information and advice, lobbying, research	Financial	Subsistence subsidies
		Legal	N/A
		Social	Research pioneers networks
		Other policy influences	Curricula development

Source: UNEP (2002b)

Industry attention and action

Changes and improvements over the last decade or so can be seen in companies' environmental performances, which have impacts both on production and consumption. The response to policy developments has principally brought about change in production processes and in product design. However, extended producer responsibility (EPR) and eco-labelling, is shifting attention to consumption issues, at least to end-of-life management and waste reduction. Thus, generally, along with improved environmental performance and eco-innovation there is growing business discussion of the idea of 'asset retention' or 'remanufacturing' – recapturing the value embedded in products through recovery systems, refurbishment, and upgrading combined with leasing.[14]

The World Business Council for Sustainable Development (WBCSD) launched a project focused on developing a better understanding of the concept of sustainable consumption in 1997. This addressed the issue that extrapolation of the consumption rates in developed countries to the rest of the world was not possible. The WBCSD was concerned to seek responses to that situation that did not include reducing consumption of goods and services, which would destroy the very premise for business to continue. In two reports, the WBCSD has sketched out a broad programme for business[15] dealing with both sustainable production and consumption:

- develop technological and social innovations to improve quality of life and tackle depletion of resources;
- practice eco-efficiency (more value with less impact, growing qualitatively not quantitatively);
- build alliances and move towards partnerships for progress; and
- provide and inform consumer choice (improving quality of life and increasing market-share of sustainability minded companies).

Strategies for the future

Moving forward, towards a fundamental change in the 'way that industrial societies produce and consume', will involve further attention to, analysis of and action on the following:

- Clarifying the focus for action on consumption.
- Developing better measures of 'consumption pressure' and 'quality of life', and putting them to effective use.
- Developing a useful schema for addressing the key elements and interactions that define systems of production and consumption that is simple enough to assist analysis and intervention.
- Supporting and enhancing localized campaigns of action to transform consumption of targeted resources or goods and services.
- Focusing production and consumption-oriented action on the transformation of products and services.
- Developing and promoting the idea of 'leapfrog change' (see later in this chapter).

Clarifying the focus for action on consumption

There is a tradition of using consumption as a measure of activity both within economics and the environment, although, as already emphasized, what is measured in each case is different. In economic terms 'consumption' refers to the volume and demand for goods and services; in environmental terms, the issue is the (ecological impact of) resource use and waste. However, another meaning of consumption derives from the substantial literature on consumerism and consumer culture, which tends to portray consumption as the most significant driving force of the economy and production. In the context of this voluminous literature,[16] the label 'consumption' can easily be interpreted as singling out the consumer and their behaviour/needs/wants as the focus and the target for action and change.

Thus, there is also confusion over whether 'consumption' is a system measure, or a shorthand for 'consumer behaviour'. These two broad meanings for consumption (as measure, and as shorthand for consumer behaviour) need to be clearly distinguished in discussions about sustainable consumption, particularly in developing action and policies.[17]

Developing better indicators

There is a need for indicators and meaningful feedback in order to work out where we are going and how we are doing and many groups are attempting to measure – and aggregate – consumption and its impacts for this purpose. The World Wildlife Fund (WWF) 'consumption pressure' analysis was, in their own terms, limited to sets of data that were consistent, recent and updated. Their index was based on resource consumption and pollution data from 152 countries, in 1995, and the results are shown in Figure 21.1. It represents an attempt to quantify the burden placed on the global environment by the inhabitants of these countries.

WWF used six components to calculate Consumption Pressure: grain; marine fish; wood consumption; freshwater withdrawals; carbon dioxide emissions, as a proxy for fossil fuel consumption; and cement consumption, as a proxy for land consumption.

Each of the six components was given equal weighting. This approach was adopted for simplicity, in spite of its limitations. Since the publication of that 1995 data, in their Living Planet Index of 1998, no updates to the consumption pressure index have been published and the research that would be necessary to improve the data sets has not

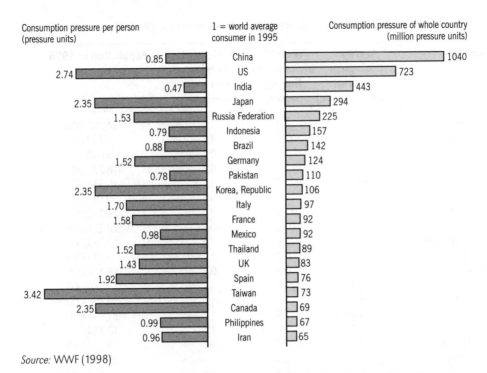

Consumption pressure per person (pressure units)	1 = world average consumer in 1995	Consumption pressure of whole country (million pressure units)
0.85	China	1040
2.74	US	723
0.47	India	443
2.35	Japan	294
1.53	Russia Federation	225
0.79	Indonesia	157
0.88	Brazil	142
1.52	Germany	124
0.78	Pakistan	110
2.35	Korea, Republic	106
1.70	Italy	97
1.58	France	92
0.98	Mexico	92
1.52	Thailand	89
1.43	UK	83
1.92	Spain	76
3.42	Taiwan	73
2.35	Canada	69
0.99	Philippines	67
0.96	Iran	65

Source: WWF (1998)

Figure 21.1 *Consumption pressure, a measure of the burden placed on the environment by people, 1995*

been carried out. The 1998 index was not well received by some countries and its underlying data and calculation methods were criticized. In the latest Living Planet Index (2002) the only comparative measure of overall production and consumption impacts is in the form of eco-footprint calculations for 72 countries. Calculations for a selection of countries are listed in Table 21.5.

Yet, as a limited and one-off 'first attempt', the 'consumption pressure index' has been very widely reproduced and referred to, both as an awareness-raising tool and as a 'measure' of consumption relativities and problems. Possibly it was a more accessible (or direct) concept than eco-footprint, as the latter uses 'equivalent land area' (required to produce the resources consumed and to ameliorate pollution) as its comparative unit. Whichever system is used (and the eco-footprint approach seems to be gaining in sophistication and credence), the need to develop a better set of measures, and to collect data, track and report (in an accessible way) on aggregate change, is clearly evident from the sustainable consumption literature. There are numerous proposals and publications of alternative measures to GDP which attempt to capture a more complex sense of prosperity and quality of life.[18] Measuring and reporting on quality of life is directly or implicitly called for in many of the strategic actions for sustainable consumption. Explicit and comprehensible feedback on quality-of-life conditions would seem (along with consumption–environment–impact data) to be an essential platform for sustainable development. None of the alternative 'green accounting' measures have managed to achieve the status and institutional commitment of GDP.

As mentioned above, industry sectors recognize the need for effective measurement, reporting and data exchange. From the industry sector reports to the World Summit on Sustainable Development (WSSD), it is clear that some measures of consumption (energy,

Table 21.5 Eco-footprint calculations for various countries

Country	Average ecological footprint (ha per person)	Available bio-capacity (ha per person)	Ecological surplus (ha per person)	Population in 1995
Argentina	3.0	4.4	1.4	34,768,000
Australia	9.4	12.9	3.5	17,862,000
Austria	4.6	4.1	-0.5	8,045,000
Bangladesh	0.6	0.2	-0.3	118,229,000
Belgium	5.1	1.7	-3.4	10,535,000
Brazil	3.6	9.1	5.6	159,015,000
Canada	7.2	12.3	5.1	29,402,000
China	1.4	0.6	-0.8	1,220,224,000
Czech Republic	3.9	2.6	-1.4	10,263,000
Denmark	5.9	4.2	-1.7	5,223,000
Ethiopia	0.7	0.5	-0.2	56,404,000
Finland	5.8	9.9	4.1	5,107,000
France	5.3	3.7	-1.6	58,104,000
Germany	4.6	1.9	-2.8	81,594,000
Greece	4.2	1.6	-2.6	10,454,000
Hong Kong	6.1	0.0	-6.1	6,123,000
Hungary	3.1	2.6	-0.5	10,454,000
Iceland	5.0	6.8	1.9	269,000
India	1.0	0.5	-0.5	929,005,000
Indonesia	1.3	2.6	1.4	197,460,000
Ireland	5.6	6.0	0.4	3,546,000
Israel	3.5	0.3	-3.1	5,525,000
Italy	4.2	1.5	-2.8	57,204,000
Japan	4.2	0.7	-3.5	125,068,000
Korea, Rep.	3.7	0.4	-3.2	44,909,000
Malaysia	3.2	4.3	1.1	20,140,000
Netherlands	5.6	1.5	-4.1	15,482,000
New Zealand	6.5	15.9	9.4	3,561,000
Norway	5.5	5.4	-0.1	4,332,000
Peru	1.4	7.5	6.1	23,532,000
Philippines	1.4	0.8	-0.7	67,839,000
Poland, Rep.	3.9	2.0	-1.9	38,557,000
Russian Fedn	4.6	4.3	-0.4	148,460,000
Singapore	6.6	0.0	-6.5	3,327,000
South Africa	3.0	1.0	-1.9	41,465,000
Spain	3.8	1.4	-2.5	39,627,000
Sweden	6.1	7.9	1.8	8,788,000
Switzerland	4.6	1.8	-2.9	7,166,000
Thailand	1.9	1.3	-0.7	58,242,000
UK	4.6	1.5	-3.0	58,301,000
USA	9.6	5.5	--4.1	267,115,000
World	2.2	1.9	-0.3	5,687,114,000

Source: Selection of countries taken from data from Wackernagel (2000)

water, etc.) are seen as necessary for effective management and strategic planning for sustainable development. Feedback can also play a role at the individual or small group (e.g., household) level, where the availability of information (or lack of it) can become a critical factor in changing motivations. There is, for example, simple software that gives individual computer users feedback on the implications of their printing decisions, as a measure of cumulative paper used, which appears as desk-top icons of (percentage of) trees consumed. Power and water suppliers in many countries have adopted a simple demand management feedback system by including relative monthly use figures (over past years) in their billing for consumers. This fills an information feedback gap that can change consumers' awareness of the results of their daily-use decisions. Recent work in many countries has shown that comparative consumption data (i.e. individual consumer use patterns compared with average use or a range of low, middle and high users) provides an incentive for users to modify their consumption patterns, Information technology offers enormous potential to expand consumption feedback at all levels (individual, community and aggregate) for many key resources.[19]

An alternative conceptual approach for describing systems of production and consumption

The UN Commission on Sustainable Development (UN CSD) definition of sustainable consumption as an 'umbrella term' talks of addressing needs, quality of life, equity, resource efficiency, waste and (environmentally-improved) goods and services. It emphasizes changes in patterns of consumption, referring to both the levels of utilization of goods and services and the way those goods and services are produced and delivered. The consumption of goods and services is not an end in itself; patterns of consumption reflect the existence of markets for goods and services – 'systems of production meeting the expressed needs of consumers'. The 'expression of needs' is a complex issue. Even needs which could be considered as universal (nourishment, health, shelter, mobility, etc.) are obviously expressed (and met) in different ways in different contexts. Even in a given context, the way those needs are expressed (and met) changes over time.

How needs are created and expressed and how they both shape, and are shaped in turn, by the market of goods and services, has been the focus of much theoretical analysis from a number of different perspectives. What is generally interpreted as expressed needs (derived from patterns of consumption) is an aggregation of the behaviour of individuals and groups of consumers, who are certainly not homogeneous in their priorities, concerns and choices. From a social and economic viewpoint, theories have attempted to focus on individual behaviour (which has often been depicted as 'irrational' or contrary to the theoretical 'best interests' of the individual) and the influence of group allegiances at different levels (family, age-group, socio-economic, etc.). From an environmental viewpoint it is often only aggregate 'patterns' that are of interest (in terms of total resource consumption, etc.). However, strategies for changing unsustainable consumption patterns need to be well attuned to differences in individual and group behaviour, because such strategies generally rely on building on (or modifying) behaviour that is (at least in some respects) different from the aggregate pattern.[20]

The OECD, like UNDP, examined a range of analytical frameworks, which have been used to explain the behavioural and infrastructural basis of consumption. These reflect various attempts by researchers to deal with the large number of factors which are assumed to influence systems of production and consumption:

- human needs and desires – social, cultural and biophysical;
- social and cultural structures;
- education;

- marketing and the media;
- availability and cost of products and services;
- availability and cost of resources;
- the quality and appeal of product form and function;
- technological development;
- economic development and levels of affluence;
- population size and demographics;
- infrastructure – physical structures, resource distribution and information systems.

A problem for developing policies and programmes is that these factors are not independent and their interaction can be complex.[21] It is difficult to decide where it is effective and practical to intervene. Policies and actions have involved a variety of stakeholders – not just 'producers' and 'consumers' – and have focused on resources, production, technology, products and services, information, economic factors, standards, education and training, knowledge systems and cultural values (etc.). These do not divide easily into 'actions for changing production' and 'actions for changing consumption'.

An alternative approach is needed which provides a practical way of describing the system (to guide intervention) but allows for more complex modelling of the real world. In the research and writing for the UNEP Global Status Report on Sustainable Consumption, a new model of the system of production and consumption was developed from an analysis of a large range of case studies of action to change patterns of consumption. This model has since been applied in a variety of 'local' campaigns to address particular areas of consumption pressure (e.g. water, tourism). In this model, the system is described from three perspectives: *provision* (the way that goods and services are produced and their systems of delivery and function); *motivation* (the incentives and disincentives which shape the market for goods and services) and *access* (factors which include or exclude consumers from participating in the market). These three viewpoints reflect an aggregation of forces, which affect patterns of consumption into three logical areas for analysis and action.

For example, a number of industrialized countries have introduced programmes to enable consumers to purchase 'green' electricity from the grid (usually at some premium value). Green electricity is produced from renewable sources such as wind, solar, tide, etc. Increasing the contribution of renewable energy to the total energy mix is one of the fundamental ways to reduce consumption impacts (reducing CO_2 per unit of energy utilized in production and consumption). For such schemes to be successful, each of the three areas – provision, motivation and access – have to be addressed through appropriate policies and programmes. Green power requires new structures of provision (it has to be generated and distributed via a grid); it has to be accessible to consumers (in terms of cost, information, mechanisms of purchase and accounting – production has to be audited to ensure it is matched to demand, consumers have to be able to select green providers); consumers have to be motivated to purchase and pay higher charges (to understand the environmental value of renewable power and their ability to contribute in this way to more sustainable consumption); and producers have to be motivated to invest in power production (through economic and market incentives). One state in Australia – New South Wales – recently reported that consumer take-up of their audited programme of renewable power saved 114,000 tonnes of greenhouse emissions in the year 2001, equivalent to taking 25,000 cars off the road.[22]

Systems of provision

Systems of provision are all those processes and infrastructures through which goods and services are made available for consumption. Provision[23] is more than production.

It is used to describe the combination of established industry processes and business practices, the accumulated physical production and delivery infrastructure and the corresponding social and cultural practices, which together define the ways in which life styles and particular sets of products and services become mutually supporting structures. This includes not just all the processes involved in the design, production, distribution and disposal of products and services (along with the necessary technical and organizational infrastructure), but also the shared set of expectations and established practices of consumption that affirm particular categories of products and services as 'necessary' for daily life styles to function. Considering systems of provision means examining the various ways in which the consumption of products and services and the use of resources (and production of waste) associated with that consumption, are determined by structures of creation, delivery, utility, disposal and information. Systems of provision also includes the collective and non-material goods and infrastructure which are not traditionally part of the market but are essential to quality of life – such as clean air and fresh water, natural capital,[24] etc. There is a progressive trend, in most developed economies, for many of these previously public, community-held, non-material goods and systems of infrastructure to be transferred to private ownership and control (into the market place). This shift is widely identified as a critical change in systems of provision that affect both consumer motivation and systems of access (increasing individual consumption of – private – goods and services).

Systems of motivation

The actions and behaviours of people, as citizens, as consumers, as workers and managers, can be attributed to motivations that arise from needs and desires (individual, social and cultural).

Traditionally, needs and desires are described in general terms as:[25]

- survival (biophysical needs and safety, safety and risk);
- acceptance (belonging, love esteem, status and power);
- cognition (understanding, exploration);
- aesthetic appreciation, (appreciation of form and beauty, comfort);
- self-fulfilment (personal improvement, stimulation, excitement);
- transcendent ideals (concern for others; political spiritual and moral beliefs).

From the sustainable consumption literature, there is broad agreement on the following aspects of consumer motivation:

- Ultimately all motivations are dependent on information and understanding (of options and implications of action). Information is a key aspect of systems of provision, which affects motivation. (It is also a fundamental determinant of access.) However, as sociological studies show and marketing people know, there is no simple, direct, relationship between information and awareness, and behaviour, which is influenced and modified by other factors.
- Motivations are both individual and socially contingent; they reflect personal concerns and social and cultural influences which are often weighed up in a conscious process (for example, in deciding whether to use a car or public transport when personal comfort and convenience is weighed against pollution, etc.). Social and cultural influences on motivations emphasize that consumers 'belong' to more than one group (based on kinship, class, age, religion, etc.) with sets of expressed needs that can be very different. (The UNEP Global Consumer Class survey highlights aspects of the multiple nature of group 'belonging'.)

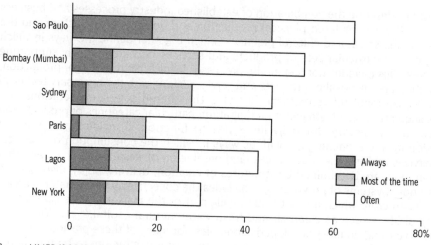

Source: UNEP (2002b) GCC Research MDB

Figure 21.2 *Global Concerned Citizens – UNEP Global Consumer Survey: Respondents who consider the 'life' behind the products they consume*

- Motivations also reflect habits and repeated sets of practices that relate to past experience and established routines. These are often reinforced by the development of infrastructures. This is one way that motivations are connected to systems of provision;[26] motivations reflect patterns of behaviours related to patterns of provision (for example, travelling by car in cities designed without effective public transport).
- Consumer motivations and behaviour are not consistent and stable over time; change can be sudden and rapid (use of the Internet is one example).

Various organizations and reports on sustainable consumption have focused on analysing the drivers which lead to 'over-consumption', or the desire to actively acquire and accumulate goods. However, it is very important to recognize that (some) consumers do see the connection between consumption and pollution/waste and are concerned about the 'life behind the product'. In particular circumstances, consumers can be motivated by longer-term interests rather than short-term, by collective and social goals rather than individual, and do act to consume responsibly. As the UNEP surveys on Global Consumers and Youth have shown, such behaviour is not limited by region or country (see Figure 21.2).

Discussion of sustainable consumption has a tendency to focus on consumer motivations and behaviour. As systems of provision highlight, consumption patterns reflect a market shaped by consumers and producers (and products and infrastructure). Policies and action aimed at changing systems of motivation need to also consider influencing the motivations of producers and businesses, product designers and 'infrastructure creators'. Analysing the motivations for business to improve environmental outcomes has identified factors such as:[27]

- market competition and 'recognition' of a 'green market';
- long-range planning (recognition of trends and potential future risks);
- regulation or potential of future regulation;
- improved relationship with customers;
- individual company personnel desires (to contribute, through work, to socially positive outcomes);
- protecting 'brand' image.

Systems of access

Patterns of consumption reflect systems and structures that control access to the existing market and to processes of influence in shaping the market. Critical factors affecting access include:

- **Income** Levels of income either widen or restrict access to the market. This is obviously most critical in conditions of scarcity where poverty is the major barrier. The increasing dependence of consumption on private income (with the reduction in public infrastructure), in all markets, has important implications for access.
- **Time** Along with income, conditions of life can make time a critical commodity and an important factor in access – to the market, to information, to political and social process which affect the market – consumer action.
- **Availability and ownership of infrastructure of essential goods and services** Provision affects access.
- **Availability and choice of products and services** ('no eco-lifestyles without eco-products and services' – WBCSD).
- **Information** An absolute determinant of access in all market conditions. Knowledge of goods and services, knowledge of 'life behind the product'. Awareness of quality of life issues with choices. Awareness of best practice possibilities.
- **Education and training** Along with information, this affects abilities to participate in shaping markets, in the utilization of opportunities.

Enhancing the potential of limited, localized actions

The complexity of production and consumption systems – provision, motivation and access – can be a significant barrier to taking action, with only large global or regional organizations and governments appearing to have the power and resources to tackle the problem. However, there are campaigns of action directed to reducing consumption of particular sensitive resources, or changing the patterns of consumption of specific goods or services, which offer another approach. These campaigns are not well recorded or analysed within the sustainable consumption literature, yet they represent a level of action that may have great advantages in terms of involvement and achievable outcomes. Unlike actions and policies intended to shift consumption patterns in whole economies, or which aim to change global conditions, these campaigns of action are often conducted in localized areas – regions, cities, towns, communities.

They include such things as: shifting modes of transport from cars to public transport, creating car free areas, reducing water consumption, reducing energy consumption, shifting energy consumption towards renewable energy and reducing household waste. Such campaigns arise when a relatively focused pattern of consumption is recognized as having detrimental localized effects. Ecotourism is another example; recent campaigns have been proposed (and are underway) to deal with the impact of mass-tourism in specific resort locations (such as islands). Although tourism is receiving some media attention (because of bed-taxes or proposals for visitor fees) only the creation of 'car-free spaces' and domestic waste management, seems to be well documented with a network of information and case studies. These have in part been assisted by high-profile journals and web-sites from organizations such as Adbusters, which have been able to bring the skills of advertising and marketing professionals to campaigns such as 'car-free-days'.[28]

Creating a global network and a database of case studies of such actions, would provide a valuable resource and inspiration for communities interested in dealing with local consumption issues, particularly in the critical resource areas such as water and fossil-fuel energy. Case studies could provide guidance for developing appropriate supply and demand approaches, highlight the role of new products and services and showcase the linkages between consumption, production, poverty-reduction, quality of life and policy development. Of course, such campaigns are usually limited to dealing with one particular resource, or impact area, and there is always the possibility that proposed solutions will exacerbate consumption problems in another area. They do, however, reflect an awareness of the need to address consumption-related impacts and they have the advantage of local(-ized) action which makes the engagement of multiple stakeholders more realistic. With the development of indices such as eco-footprints and improved monitoring of consumption patterns and impacts, there is the potential for such action to widen to a more holistic approach.[29]

Case studies of localized campaigns could be the basis of research to examine total life cycle changes resulting from campaigns for specific reductions in consumption, as well as providing an opportunity to test the appropriateness of indices for use at the community and regional level.

Improving products and services: the logical focus for production and consumption

Products and services form the link between production and consumption. Production systems deliver products and services to the market; it is these products and services that are consumed; it is the volume of their consumption, and the efficiency (in environmental terms) with which they are produced and used that is the critical issue. Products and services define systems of provision; they play a major role in systems of motivation; the range of products available affects systems of access. As the WBCSD suggests, there can be no eco-efficient living without eco-efficient products and services. In the last decade, products (and services) have become an increasingly important area for government policy as analysis and practical experience in industry has demonstrated that:[30]

- Environmental impacts from products has continued to rise (in gross terms) relative to impacts from production processes.
- A life cycle perspective on the environmental impacts of a product 'captures' the whole production-consumption chain.
- 60–80 per cent of the (life cycle) environmental impacts from products are determined at the design stage.
- When product-related environmental impacts are made explicit in the design process, there are well tried design strategies for reducing them ('eco-design').
- A focus on products is a good way to engage company interest and action because it focuses on their core business.
- The existence of new eco-designed products changes the market, projecting a new 'demand space' for product competition.

A focus on the creation of sustainable products and services, if considered from a life cycle perspective, results in changes to both systems of production and patterns of consumption. 'Well tried' eco-design strategies, developed for managers and designers in companies, tend to stress the technical and engineering aspects of such work (the use of quantitative life cycle analysis, the optimization of material use, the development of simple and reversible fasteners, the selection of recycled materials, the selection of technically efficient components, etc.). However, in practice, these technical, production issues only partly shape the outcome.[31]

Other factors enter the process, factors which play an increasingly important role in the creation of value and which reflect the complex forces that shape patterns of consumption. Products are not just enablers of change, as the WBCSD argument would suggest. The history of product design in industry since World War II demonstrates that designed products have played an increasingly central role in the shaping of consumption. Through the design process and with the increasing technical sophistication of the manipulation of materials, consumer products have become symbols of possibilities and potentialities as much as objects of function and utility. They are designed to motivate consumers, to create desire for ownership and possession, to communicate value, identity, status, enjoyment and fulfilment.

> *The process by which design incorporates ideas is by no means direct ... Manufacturers filter and distil ideas and add some of their own, all with the intention of making their products seem more desirable ... successful design is like alchemy: it fuses together disparate ideas from different origins, so that the form of the completed product seems to embody ... a single idea*
>
> Adrian Forty, *Objects of Desire – design and society since 1750*

The availability of new eco-products and services in the market affects the structures of provision and access and, as a result of the increasing sophistication of design, they also become an important motivational force for change. Any recyclable, water-saving, solar energy, package-free products that exist in a competitive market must have been designed to attract consumers, to create desire (to consume these objects rather than competing ones). Such products have the potential to re-shape consumer desires, behaviours and ideas of satisfaction and quality.[32]

Production-focused strategies (cleaner production, process redesign) have a solid history of achievement and established infrastructure. Consumption issues have drawn attention to the limits of such strategies and there are clear calls for the integration of action on cleaner production and sustainable consumption. The improvement of products and services through eco-design and the creation of a policy framework conducive to such development (e.g. the EU's Integrated Product Policy) is a logical and easily communicated focus for integrating cleaner production and sustainable consumption. The development of improved support tools and information about eco-products and eco-services and eco-design (particularly for small and medium-sized companies) in both developed and developing countries will be an important contribution to meeting demands from regulations, policy changes, standards and green procurement programmes.[33]

The overall strategic goal: leapfrog to new systems of products and services

The creation of sustainable systems of production and consumption is increasingly viewed as a process that will depend more on a radical restructuring of existing systems (including products, services, life styles, businesses and measures of economic value) than on incremental improvement. There is a growing differentiation between the terms eco-efficiency and eco-innovation, which is intended to emphasize this point. Eco-efficiency is the progressive improvement in the resource efficiency and environmental impact of current systems and businesses. Eco-innovation is the creation of new systems and businesses that alter fundamentally the current relationships between resource–consumption–waste and the creation of economic value. This has been labelled the 'next industrial revolution'.[34] In the desire to communicate the idea of change as a real discontinuity, another term has come into use:[35] 'leapfrog change'.

As UNEP DTIE's Director, Jacqueline Aloisi de Larderel stated: 'Developing countries complained "We are not yet consuming. We would like to have the same quality of life that you people in the North are enjoying". But for developing countries, sustainable consumption does not mean "not consuming"; it means, quite the contrary, namely leap-frogging. It means achieving a better quality of life for all, it means sharing between the richer and the poorer. Industries fear losing markets. In reality, sustainable consumption will bring new business opportunities.'[36] Leapfrog changes in systems of production and consumption, and in products and services, offer the possibility of a 'development path' which will link economic development with sustainable consumption. Leapfrog transformations of production and consumption systems will require changes in all aspects of systems of provision, motivation and access. This is therefore not only a technological transformation – it will have to encompass changes to patterns of living and to the balance between private and collective-community ownership of resources and infrastructure and changes in values and behaviours. The recognition of leapfrog restructuring and its effect on existing industry sectors, products and services is currently limited to a few leading companies, researchers and business schools; it is not as widely evident in the thinking of industry generally as the challenge of sustainable development demands. Talk of product stewardship as involving recycling of materials recovered from end-of-life products, is talking, at best, about limited transitionary activity. Recycling of materials quickly faces an energetic limit as consumption grows (each recycling path requires energy input for transport and for processing). Even the idea of dematerialization, when it is limited to light-weighting and miniaturization, is a transitionary approach which could quickly be overcome by growth in production and consumption of products unless there are sophisticated systems of remanufacturing and component refurbishment, upgrading and re-use.

However, in facing the reality of the limits of continued growth in product consumption, the implications and strategic directions of leapfrog change are beginning to appear. Growth in sustainable services and 'product-service systems', the creation of new businesses based on sales of services with very low infrastructure and resource demands, is being discussed in business and government sectors. These discussions are beginning to encompass the idea of new industries, new alliances and partnerships within current industry and new consumer interests, behaviours and patterns of living (sustainable prosperity). In talking of the future, the Automobile industry Sector Report to the WSSD, for example, speaks of the need for new kinds of partnership: The challenge of sustainable development requires new forms of partnership and co-operation. The auto industry is only one of a number of players affecting transport. For major goals to be achieved a joint commitment from all players ... is required. The role of the industry is to promote technological development and provide integrated solutions for transport and mobility... Designing and managing a complex transportation infrastructure and developing linked modes of transport will be a key issue for countries and their governments in the developing world. Through intelligent transport systems solutions, the efficiency of different means of transport can be further enhanced.

That report confirms that PSA Peugeot-Citroen has established a think tank to bring together urban planners, researchers and scientists, to study new mobility solutions to meet current needs and future challenges. This will study expectations and demands of city dwellers in Europe as well as in developing countries. The Tourism Sector Report (to the WSSD) refers to another development in business thinking about the 'experience based economy'[37] which describes what happens when 'a company uses services as the stage, and products as the props, to engage individual consumers in a way that creates memorable events and experiences'. It notes that the Tourism industry simultaneously thrives on this trend and is threatened by it, but that: 'Tourism products and services that demonstrate greater sensitivity to the environment, traditional culture and local people at destinations, can create such an experience, whereas tourism in the context of uncontrolled growth which puts increased pressure on the natural, cultural and socio-economic environment, risks diminishing the visitor experience.' Such thinking reflects the emergence of new ways of looking at products and services and new businesses. Product eco-design has been progressively moving from improvement (or re-design) of existing products towards the re-design of product-systems, incorporating, as a target, changes in consumer use-patterns, product-longevity, disposal-collection and systems of re-use and remanufacturing of components. New models of system change are receiving attention derived from different patterns of ownership of products and services (such as leasing and sharing) and the replacement of products with services.[38]

Addressing unsustainable consumption has exposed the necessity of leapfrog change in systems of production and consumption; it has also exposed the essential elements in such change. There are structural changes in provision and access – the creation of new products and services and the new infrastructures of production, use and disposal/re-use for those products and services. Governments and consumer organizations can help to create the right conditions (demand) for this to take place, but the focus of action will be business. Creating the right conditions will mean smart regulations (stimulating innovation and motivation for change) and the development of support systems – analytical and practical tools and training. These are changes aimed at a shifting the market for goods and services. But the analysis of consumption has also shown the need for concurrent action on changing motivation, attitudes, desires and expectations, of producers and consumers alike. Communication and promotion of leapfrog developments, the articulation and 'opening-up' of ideas and concepts of alternative patterns of living and sustainable (low-impact/high satisfaction) prosperity, will be as critical to creating sustainable consumption as the provision of the leapfrog products and services which will make such patterns of living possible.

CHAPTER 22

CHANGING HEARTS AND MINDS:
THE ROLE OF EDUCATION

The need for critical literacies in sustainability

To date, in this book, we have talked largely about how business, government, civil society, research organizations, etc. can step up to make the most of the opportunities provided to those who lead. We have shown inspiring examples of the benefits for those who already have. Change in these organizations occurred because an individual or a group of people effectively catalysed and then facilitated change. In earlier sections, we discussed significant signs that attitudes and values about sustainability are changing. What is lacking in many countries to achieve sustainable development is reliable information, and dissemination of that information to empower people, whatever their station in society, to act. But also importantly in this information age, we all need critical literacies to be able to most effectively and wisely use such information. David Orr, one of the world's leading environmental educators, has argued that the environmental crisis is actually a crisis of education: 'The crisis we face is first and foremost one of the mind, perceptions, and values; hence, it is a challenge to those institutions presuming to shape minds, perceptions, and values'.[1] This is now widely recognized. The recent major report from the New Zealand Parliamentary Commissioner for Environment, *Sea Change: Learning and Education for Sustainability*,[2] showed that 'The need for education to play a key role in addressing the challenge of sustainable development was articulated at the Earth Summit in 1992. All 40 chapters of its action plan Agenda 21, called for education. Governments from around the world agreed that education for Sustainability is 'critical for achieving environmental and ethical awareness, values and attitudes, skills and behaviour consistent with sustainable development and for effective public participation in decision making'. Agenda 21 also called on all countries to develop a strategy to implement education for sustainability.' The United Nations has now declared that 2005–2015 will be the Decade of Education in Sustainable Development.

In Australia, the federal government has set up the National Environmental Education Council and Sustainable Schools[3] committees to add value to existing initiatives and networks. There are now significant environmental education networks around the world, Australia is no exception. For instance take the SCRAP network. The Australian SCRAP network, *School Communities Recycling All Paper*, lead by Peter Carroll, began with just three teachers in Australia in 1992. It now services over 3000 organizations including over 2000 schools, and is the largest purchaser of products with recycled content in Australia. The *Australian Campuses Towards Sustainability* (ACTS) network is a similar network to SCRAP, but for the university sector. A simple email asking who was working on environmental management at university campuses in Australia led to its formation. This network has subsequently organized a sustainable campuses national conference every year led by 'quiet achievers' among Australian Universities.

Schools and higher education facilities around the world are major societal hubs. In addition to educating 'enrolled' students, they provide opportunities for families and community groups to become involved in projects. Professional bodies are also valuable hubs for interaction. They provide a conduit for information transfer, and an essential link between individuals, local groups and national and international networks. At a time when access to information can vary from 'nothing' to 'overwhelming', it is exciting to see the vast array of creative ways that such entities are facilitating learning and providing training and opportunity for students and the community. However, it is imperative that all education facilitators continue to explore new ways to work in collaboration; for example schools with universities, and universities with professional bodies. Of all sectors of society, our education sector has the greatest opportunity to truly empower us and our future generations to make a difference. It is therefore essential that all parts of the education sector work together, to ensure that society is learning, as quickly as possible how to achieve sustainable development.

Three more examples of capacity building in the education sector are provided below, through two school based programmes and a youth–professional body initiative.

The Australian Murray–Darling Basin 'Special Forever' programme is an example of the way school networks can help to provide communities with the information they need to make a difference. Commenced in 1993, the programme was created to raise awareness about salinity and land degradation issues in Australia's 1 million km^2 Murray–Darling Basin. A partnership between the Murray–Darling Basin Commission (MDBC) and the Primary English Teaching Association (PETA), the programme broadly addresses the need for information and education, to empower communities to address the salinity crisis affecting land in the region. From the equivalent of one funded position (originally with input from five people) and a small budget for administration and publication costs (a total of around eight cents per student per week), Special Forever ,at its peak, supported and directly involved hundreds of thousands of people and half of all primary schools throughout the basin. David Eastburn was the facilitator for the first four years of the programme. He believes that the secret of his success was that he did not prescribe to schools and communities what they 'had to do'. Rather he listened and offered choices and support for whichever direction they chose. The programme tapped into the innate desire of each community to take charge of their future, if simply supported with reliable information and contacts with others working on the same problems.

Two other inspiring examples are the Aranda Primary School in Canberra and the ACT Year 9 High School Exhibitions project that seek to address meaningfully the recommendations of the United Nations Educational, Scientific and Cultural Organization's (UNESCO's) International Commission on Education for the 21st Century.

Sustainable development in schools

Anna McKenzie

EDITORS' NOTE: Anna McKenzie, who taught at Aranda Primary school, facilitated the School Community Environment Program from 1992–1999 and then, with the ACT Education Department, developed in consultation with academics and teachers the ACT Year 9 Exhibitions project. She has summarized both projects here. Anna is currently a full-time teacher at Campbell Primary school, and writing her Master's thesis 'Productive Pedagogies through Year 9 Exhibitions'.

Constructive environmental education

In the late 1980s the media began reporting regularly about ozone depletion, global warming and disastrous events like Chernobyl. The media presented these issues in a very doom and gloom way. This meant that school children were becoming increasingly alarmed and wanted answers from their teachers to questions like, 'What is the hole in the ozone layer?'. As a teacher and parent, I was concerned that we give children not only knowledge but also hope for the future by providing safe, constructive ways that they could personally help the environment. I was concerned that if left to the media, students would see environmental crises as a 'fait accompli' rather than as an opportunity to make a positive difference. So through the efforts of like-minded parents and teachers and with the blessing of its Principal, Aranda Primary School began a process of change, teaching and learning in line with the principles of ecological sustainability. The school has successfully maintained a particular focus on environmental education since 1991, our environmental education programme having evolved as part of the whole school community's response to the pressing need for all of us to care for the earth. Its aim has been to promote ecological approaches to health and the acceptance of shared environmental and social responsibility. The project has been successful in effecting positive change in the immediate physical environment of the school, such as through land care and community arts projects, habitat creation and courtyard renewal. In so doing it has provided opportunities for students to initiate projects, engage in planning and implementation, involve their parents and make productive partnerships with the wider community, modelling good practice for effective community participation both now and in the future.

In the early 1990s Dr David Suzuki visited Canberra, including in his busy schedule a talkback radio programme called 'The Green Classroom', where a panel of school children interviewed him and others phoned in to ask him questions. On the panel were two children from Aranda Primary School who told Dr Suzuki that they were recycling paper, propagating plants, keeping worm farms and planting trees at their school. They asked him what more they could do to help the environment. He replied 'Don't just plant trees, create habitat.' David's comment profoundly affected us all and from that day on the environment programme at Aranda Primary School was never the same. Not only did children, staff and parents 'create habitat' by planting a forest of 4000 trees and shrubs, and a 'butterfly garden' of herbs, but also, spurred on by David Suzuki's comments, worked to expand the overall programme so that it became more holistic and integrated. All who participated were encouraged to think more deeply and holistically about their actions and their effect upon the environment.

Youth agency has been an important element of the programme, promoting initiative, participation and self confidence in our young people. For instance, over the intervening years many visitors to Canberra have wanted to see 'the forest in our school grounds'. Rather than a teacher hosting tours of the school grounds, it has been the Year 5 and Year

6 children, 10 and 11 year olds, who happily take on the responsibility of explaining the environmental initiatives to visitors. Students are also making valuable conceptual links between the formal curriculum and their day-to-day lives. For example, in a recent student-led project with the 'The Art of Choice' project team, the children decorated calico shopping bags, a gift to their parents to use in place of 'disposable' plastic bags. School–community action fosters a sense of ownership and belonging in students, making their school a special place: one which is familiar, responsive to their needs and where they have some control in decision-making and can make a positive contribution.

Adding value not load

UNESCO's International Commission on Education for the 21st Century has recommended that all schools provide creative opportunities for students to learn in a meaningful way. The commission's aim is to provide additional critical literacies beyond those commonly taught, such as functional numeracy and literacy. The ACT Student Exhibitions project is a showcase example of a school-based response to this call, a programme that has helped to reinvigorate teaching and learning in High Schools in the Australian Capital Territory. It is described in detail in the following paragraphs, to show how innovations in teaching can change the way we learn, without just squeezing more information and subjects into an already crowded curriculum. It is a real attempt to drive high school reform, with the purpose of teacher renewal and improving the learning process for all student types at schools. Although the example is school based, the concept is equally applicable to universities and other further education facilities. The ACT's Department of Education, Youth and Family Services has implemented a world class 'Student Exhibitions Program' for Year 9 students (14–15 year olds), which is based on providing students with an opportunity to develop additional 'critical literacies', to build their intercultural competence. Since 2001, it has involved 19 ACT government secondary schools.

In the Student Exhibitions Program, the word 'exhibition' takes on a whole new meaning. It is the title given to newly designed student-focused units of work which deal with issues of immediate concern to young people. These broad learning tasks are trans-disciplinary, problem-based and community focused, providing the real-world value and connection so critical for engaging young people. The exhibitions are unique in that they combine a rigorous curriculum focus that is underpinned by effective teaching strategies, and 'authentic assessment'; it assesses what students can do and what they have genuinely achieved. A special feature of the programme is the requirement for each student to present a selection of their work to a 'Roundtable'; a panel consisting of teachers, other students and community members. This gives students the opportunity to explain the main ideas that they have explored through their 'exhibition' and to present what they have learnt and how they have learnt it. In so doing students are 'taking the reigns': reflecting on and taking responsibility for both the processes and outcomes of their own learning. Such a public display of achievement adds significance and value to what students have done and provides real-life experience in preparation for interviews in their future lives. The programme focuses on four broad learning outcomes:

1   **Obtaining critical literacy skills** Critical literacies are different kinds of knowledge and skills, including literacy and numeracy, which students need in order to make sense of a wide range of oral, print, visual and multimedia communications. Broadened forms of literacy, such as social and environmental literacy, allow them to understand contemporary issues. Students are required to make judgements about what kind of knowledge is relevant and how to relate it to other areas of knowledge, and to present their findings in many different ways. They need to acquire 'real-world

literacy' to be able to critically analyse information in all aspects of their lives, from leisure to commerce, from a local to a global perspective.

2 **Building communities** This means engaging students in school governance, classroom negotiation, conflict management, making connections with the wider community and in school policy development. Students have the opportunity to engage cooperatively in community participation and democratic decision-making processes in a supportive environment that they can influence.

3 **Undertaking real life research and futures study** This involves students in working with government, business, community and other non-governmental organizations on socially-relevant and important research projects. It gives credence to the notion of students as producers of knowledge. Students not only grasp current limitations but also rise above negative assumptions to imagine preferred futures. They can position themselves in the world to seek new solutions and take new directions.

4 **Understanding cultural ethical and environmental heritage** This recognizes that existing knowledge and systems of understanding the world are important resources for all students. In a climate of increasing globalization and interdependence, the economic and population shifts taking place require a reinvention of processes for building social cohesion and citizenship that recognize diversities while still enabling shared activities and interpretations. By identifying and examining a range of experiences, identities and value positions, students can appreciate and understand difference for a more inclusive and sustainable world.

In essence, the programme approach takes important issues of real-world value and places learning in a social context rather than treating it as a separate activity. Exhibitions cut across the artificial boundaries that often separate the subject areas in many high schools. This trans-disciplinary approach, where students work in fields of knowledge, helps students to make connections in their learning by design not accident. The emphasis shifts from the learning of pieces of content to the application of knowledge. The scope of each exhibition task, the direction taken and the process for learning is negotiated between teachers and students so that the exhibition is tailored to meet student interests and needs. The tasks also have a strong information communication technology and information literacy component. Through taking a more active role in learning, students come to understand that they can be producers of knowledge, not only receivers. The exhibitions involve students in cooperative group work, building collaboration in order to solve problems. Students are also encouraged to conduct their own research using investigative tools, such as surveys.

As students engage in planning their own learning and assessment, teachers have the space to develop highly relevant, engaging and futures-focused curriculum. The programme has provided an opportunity for high schools and their communities to develop Exhibition tasks to fit their school setting. They also pave the way for students to take a more significant role in school governance. A summary of some of the tasks is presented in Table 22.1.

The ACT Government believes that the Student Exhibition Program is a major investment in preparing young people for the changes and challenges of the 21st century. The programme provides a vital forum for students to examine and act on environmental issues, with a focus on achieving a sustainable future. Environmentally-conscious decision-making also takes on a 'mainstream role' in school-based management and curriculum development. Exhibition initiatives build a practical sense of hope from working together collaboratively, engender a sense of social competency for dealing with problems as young people, and lessen youth alienation.

Table 22.1 *Examples of 'student exhibition programme' tasks*

Alfred Deakin High School	Students investigated the social and economic realities of living in a group house, including a visit to Canberra University to learn first-hand about campus living. Another task focused on waste minimization and recycling in their school, and moving towards achieving sustainable resource use.
Belconnen High School	Student volunteers worked with people with acquired brain injury (ABI) and developed a campaign to provide much-needed funding and to build community awareness.
Canberra High and Lanyon High	Students put the health of their student communities under the spotlight. Student-generated survey data lead to Canberra High students creating a breakfast club and inventing nutritious, portable breakfast foods for students to help them make a good start to their school day. Promoting personal responsibility for physical, emotional and mental health also formed the bases of Lanyon High's targeted campaign to reduce health risks within their student population and helped to strengthen school community participation.
Calwell	Students studied salinity issues, which included research into Aboriginal connections to country and the history of land use in Australia. Students worked with local agencies to measure and map salinity problems on nearby farms and to come up with recommendations for possible solutions.
Caroline Chisholm	Students designed and organized a youth forum celebrating the environment. Songs, plays, visual displays and interactive games that celebrate the environment across cultures keep their younger counterparts from neighbouring primary schools informed and entertained. Guest speakers from local water, land and wildlife protection organizations such as Cool Communities (greenhouse gas reduction) and Greening Australia (plant propagation and revegetation) stimulated discussion among young people to turn their talk into plans for future action.
Campbell High School	With the assistance of ACT Energy and Water Corporation (ACTEW) AGL, students installed a solar array on the roof of their school hall, providing the opportunity for students to monitor and examine alternative energy sources and to organize the launch of the initiative.

In summary, the Student Exhibitions Program provides schools with the opportunity to rethink the range and responsiveness of processes they provide and to improve learning outcomes for all the different kinds of students. It provides a coherent framework for teachers to make sense of many competing curriculum and 'extra-curricula' demands. It also broadens the scope of learning opportunities for students, building their capacity and belief in themselves as active, informed and socially critical global citizens, both now and in the future.

Key role of higher education and the professions

In 1997 UNESCO argued that the power of universities to educate provides humanity's best hope and most effective means to achieve sustainable development.[4] Universities, especially those in Europe and North America, increasingly recognize this and are now responding to the challenge of achieving sustainable development. There is the start of a shift in universities in Japan, Australia, New Zealand, Taiwan, Beijing, China and occasionally one or two universities in other countries of the Asia-Pacific.[5] Most encouraging has been the leadership shown by Japan in initiating the United Nations Decade of Education in Sustainable Development starting in 2005. Also encouraging has been the leadership from UNESCO in the formation of the Global Higher Education for Sustainability Partnership (GHESP) which already involves over 1000 universities globally including such institutions as Harvard and Cambridge.

Universities prepare most of the world's managers, decision-makers and teachers, and also play significant roles in national and global economies themselves. They train the next generation of teachers, who will in turn teach millions, and they train society's designers, whether they be engineers, industrial designers or architects. It is critical that universities understand the benefits of whole system design for sustainability in order to help achieve sustainable development. As the authors of *Natural Capitalism* wrote, 'By the time the design for most human artefacts is completed but before they have actually been built, about 80–90 per cent of their life cycle economic and ecological costs have already been made inevitable. We can make no better higher-leverage investment for the future than improving the quality of designers' mind-ware'.[6]

Take the built environment for example. As previously shown in Chapter 18, it is responsible for over 50 per cent of greenhouse emissions but surveys of the Australian construction industry show little knowledge of what sustainable development is, let alone any knowledge of how to apply it. So, the forthcoming United Nations Decade of Education in Sustainable Development cannot come soon enough. There is no longer any serious scientific doubt that every major ecosystem in the world is in decline. Universities are especially powerful by virtue of their research and curricula and are able to make a significant difference. The most important point that universities understand is that this will add value, not additional load. It will ensure that universities will equip graduates with the skills required to meet the needs of employers. With respect to the engineering profession, Jenni Goricanec and Roger Hadgraft at RMIT University write: 'In many books about engineering practice, engineering is described as problem-solving, particularly within the arena of technology and the technical. Engineers see themselves as producing devilishly clever technical solutions to social problems (bridges, cars, telephones, space shuttles, etc.). Rarely are they concerned about the impact of these devices on the natural, social or economic worlds. As we move forward into a world of massive change, the role of engineers will change to become decision-makers, not only of technical issues and technology, but also in a wider economic, social and environmental context.'

There are many hidden benefits if universities realize that the challenge of sustainability is in fact an opportunity, as Dr Daniella Tilbury explains in detail in her paper 'Environmental Education for Sustainability: A Force for Change in Higher Education'. 'When education for sustainable development is interpreted as a process of learning which enhances generic skills (in engineers' case including the social and environmental in design processes), rather than simply a competing content to be taught, it is relevant to all fields of learning.'[7]

RMIT contribute the following rationale in the context of engineering:[8] through [such] processes, students will be developing the graduate capabilities that will be essential to them in their future engineering practice: problem exploration and decision making, communication, teamwork, technical skills, sustainability and personal development. In the future the triple bottom line (TBL) framework will be used increasingly. Engineers will be required to base decisions on social, environmental as well as technical and financial concerns. If we are to achieve this kind of holistic triple bottom line thinking in our young engineers, how do we make this happen in engineering schools? The current approach is *bottom-up*. We give students a large number of fragments of mostly technical knowledge – fluid mechanics, solid mechanics, transport engineering, project costing, project management, etc. In some programmes, students will briefly meet environmental impact and social impact. Students may or may not bring all these things together in their minds in the design project in final year. How can we do this differently? We need to start at the top and work down. Students should see whole engineering problems in year one. They should be encouraged to pull them apart – to identify what knowledge and skills they need to resolve the problem. This process would typically deal with questions like:

- What is the *social need*? Who is affected? Who and what will be affected? This is a process of drawing a *boundary* around the system containing the problem.
- What are the *possibilities* for solution? These will include technical solutions, e.g. build a new dam, but must also include solutions from other domains, e.g. reprice the water (economic), use drought tolerant plants (environmental) and encourage water savings through an education campaign (social).
- What *criteria* will we use for choosing between these possibilities? What are our measures of performance (social, environmental, economic and technical)?
- To what level of detail do we need to *evaluate* each possible solution before we can choose among them? This may require data collection, calculations, community consultation, etc. At this point, students may need to learn new methods of analysis, negotiation, consultation, etc.
- Which alternative is *best*? How do we balance numerical and non-numerical criteria?
- How will it be *implemented*? What technical, economic, social and environmental measures are required?

Alongside this process of enquiry, more traditional modules of content may be arranged to help students to acquire the necessary knowledge and skills to explore and evaluate each solution possibility. Much self-directed learning will also take place in project groups. Through these processes, students will be developing the graduate capabilities that will be essential to them in their future engineering practice; problem exploration and decision-making, communication, teamwork, technical skills, sustainability and personal development. RMIT is one university that has embarked on a curriculum redesign of this kind. A spine of Engineering Practice courses runs through each semester. These project-based courses embed students in engineering decision-making. Supporting courses build the technical and non-technical skills for the projects. Students will grapple with sustainability issues throughout their programme and emerge ready for the competing demands of engineering in the 21st century. Other universities similarly are adapting their curricula.

Table 22.2 provides a list of examples of leading efforts globally to innovate curricula.

Harnessing universities' research capacity

Universities are increasingly establishing multi-disciplinary 'institutes of the environment' to build new partnerships and to create new opportunities for the host university. Australian National University (ANU) and RMIT University are provided as two examples of such research and innovation institute initiatives. Global Sustainability at RMIT (GS@RMIT)[9] is focused on development of the emerging multi-disciplinary field of 'knowledge around sustainability', both within and outside the university. The institute's vision is to be a leader in the intellectual and practical exploration, development and application of Global Sustainability in Australia and the Asia-Pacific region. Team staff are working across portfolios and schools within RMIT University to ensure that these

Table 22.2 *Other leading efforts globally to innovate curricula*

Business schools	World Resource Institute Project: BELL (Business-Environment Learning and Leadership).[10] The BELL syllabus is designed to prepare future business leaders to run more sustainable enterprises. It is currently being run in North and Latin America, and Asia.
Redesigning university degree programmes	Natural Capitalism Group (NCG) creates and delivers courses in sustainable business,[11] and works with universities and professional schools to (re)-design degree programmes to address sustainable development specifically for that course. For instance, NCG is the lead consultant for Presidio World College in the design of their new MBA in sustainable management. Clients of the NCG include: • UC Berkeley, Haas School of Business and Boalt School of Law (Berkeley, CA) • Stanford University (Palo Alto, CA) • Williams College (Williamstown, MA) • University of Iowa, College of Engineering (Iowa City, IA) • Presidio World College (San Francisco, CA) • UC Santa Barbara (Santa Barbara, CA) • North Fork Community Development Corporation (North Fork, CA)
Fully accredited MBA in sustainable management:	The Presidio World College MBA, with a concentration in sustainable management, is unique in the field of higher education in the USA. While individual units within MBA courses on business ethics and environmental management now exist, few programmes engage faculty and students in the process of integrating, at all levels, social and environmental values with the application of practical business skills. This programme is designed to prepare professionals to position their organizations, private, public or non-profit, to be leaders in the practice of Sustainable Management.'[12]
Engineering and SD curricula reform	Cambridge University has created the Engineering Centre for Sustainable Development. It is a centre for research and teaching in engineering for sustainable development that is seeking to address the pressing issues that face engineers in responding to the increasing demands being made in this area. Delft University of Technology, in cooperation with the Environmental Engineering and Education (EEE) network, hosted a conference on Engineering Education in Sustainable Development and the 2004 conference was in Spain.[13]
Sustainable development curricula for the developing world	Sudan Virtual Engineering Library – Sustainability Knowledge Network (SudVEL-SKN) is a pilot project supported by UNESCO in partnership with many international institutes and organizations such as WFEO. Databases such as this are needed in every country to draw out local material and ensure technology transfer from international sources into the curriculum of engineering students, material for researchers and professional development.[14]
Green Chemistry Institute and affiliates educational outreach programmes	Green Chemistry Institute, USA, is collaborating with the US Environmental Protection Agency's (EPA's) Green Chemistry Program and the American Chemical Society's Education and International Activities Division to develop green chemistry education materials and programmes. These are targeted at practising chemists, graduate and undergraduate university students, community-college students, and students in kindergarten to grade 12 (Program on Pollution Prevention and Green Chemistry Concepts).[15]

Table 22.2 *continued*

Teaching and learning for SD	UNESCO, in partnership with Griffith University (Queensland, Australia) has developed a multimedia teachers education programme called Teaching and Learning for A Sustainable Future.[16]
Murdoch University Institute for Sustainability and Technology Policy	The Institute for Sustainability and Technology Policy (ISTP) is one of the leading research institutes in the world integrating policy for simultaneously creating a better economy, an improved environment and a more just, participative society. The Institute was established in 1988 at Murdoch University to help create a better understanding of the roles and effects of science and technology for the benefit of all sectors of society.[17]
Make use of existing online resources and magazines	CSIRO's main magazine ECOS – Science for a Sustainable Future is now freely available online.[18] This is largely due to CSIRO wanting educational institutions, around the world, such as universities, to make use of it. An increasing number of databases and educational resources are becoming available online internationally.
E-list networks	There are many emerging web-based news groups and e-lists. Of note in Australia is the long running peer CSIRO Sustainability e-list network, based on submissions by academics on the latest research and events.[19]

sustainability principles and practices are incorporated into the university's vocational and technical education programmes. Their aim is to ensure that future graduates understand sustainability as it relates to their particular discipline and future career. They are also working with staff across the university to integrate sustainability into its operations, facilities and in its public reporting. RMIT University has many departments and centres tackling sustainability issues. The Centre for Design promotes environmental sustainability through a directed programme of research, consulting, professional development and knowledge sharing. The Centre is recognized internationally as a leader in the development of design methods and tools that support sustainable product design. The programmes focus on sustainability and eco-efficiency as a source of innovation and responsible business development. The Centre, for example, is working on a wide range of projects to address sustainability.

Many other universities have also set up such institutes with each being unique to that university. The ANU's multi-disciplinary National Institute for Environment is made up of over 500 academics, post-graduate and undergraduate students.[20] As such it has one of the greatest concentrations of expertise in the area of sustainable development of any university in the world. The scale, quality and dynamism of this institute is making it a model from which other universities can learn. Combined with its environmental management programme, this institute is helping ANU to walk the talk on sustainability. Along with other universities in Australia and internationally, this type of arrangement has helped pioneer and support multi-disciplinary research.

There are numerous creative, simple ways that governments and universities can work together to ensure the next generation is equipped for the challenges of the 21st century. For example, for the last four years undergraduate students at ANU have been given a modest budget and editorial control of a 100-page Green Guide from which up to 2000 copies have been printed per year for other undergraduate students. Since this green guide contains practical information relevant to anyone living in Canberra, the effort is undertaken in partnership with many other environmental groups and associations, including the Australian Association for Environmental Education. ANU has now course-accredited the guide so that undergraduate students in geography or information technology courses can work on updating it as part of their second or third year projects.[21]

In the end, change does not happen nor is sustained without leadership from staff and students taking the initiative. ANU have found that the creative arts also have a critical role to play in communicating ideas like Factor 10. The university's National Institute for Environment, ANU Green, and the ANU National Institute of the Creative Arts ran a month-long Factor 10 symposium in 2002. Over 5000 people visited the corresponding art exhibition and academics provided symposiums on why and how we need to achieve Factor 10 to achieve sustainable development.[22] With respect to the arts, it is interesting to note that the discussion paper on the Arts and sustainability was by far the most downloaded discussion paper from the Western Australian State Sustainability Strategy.

This is just a taste of the changes occurring in the university sector. The recent Australian Conservation Foundation Tela[23] paper 'Universities and Sustainability' provides a useful summary on best practice in the university sector globally.

Partnering with professional bodies to build capacity

While schools are generally able to involve communities through family involvement, universities, further education courses generally only reach students directly enrolled at their institution. Peak Professional bodies therefore play a leading role in this area of the education sector, in capacity building for sustainable development. Even within school environments, it is becoming evident that interaction with professional bodies is important in providing youth with role models and in bringing communities together. With the focus on the UN Decade of Education in Sustainable Development, there is an opportunity for professional bodies to establish partnerships with other groups in the Education Sector.

> *Engineers around the world understand that they have a tremendous responsibility in the implementation of sustainable development. Many forecasts indicate there will be an additional five billion people in the world by the middle of the 21st century. This future 'built environment' must be developed while sustaining the natural resources of the world and enhancing the quality of life for all people.*
>
> The Engineer's Response to Sustainable Development by the World Federation of Engineering Organisations, 1997

In January 2004 the University of Khartoum in the Sudan hosted a 5 day project to assist in the development of the Sudan Virtual Engineering Library – Sustainability Knowledge Network (SudVEL-SKN). The project was supported by UNESCO in partnership with Engineers Australia, the Australian Virtual Engineering Library (AVEL-SKN), World Federation of Engineering Organisations (WFEO), Sustainable Alternatives Network (SANet) and the Foundation Ecole d'Ingenieurs (EPF) through the International Institute of Women in Engineering (IIWE).

The project sought to illustrate how communication and collaboration between engineering institutions and organizations internationally can improve the transfer of technology and information needed to achieve sustainable development globally. A major challenge for institutions in developing countries is access to a growing amount of relevant international material to underpin the capacity building and training of engineers. The SudVEL-SKN database is intended to contribute to research, education and practice in sustainable development in the Sudan. The library will be a part of the learning environment for the University of Khartoum's Faculty of Engineering and

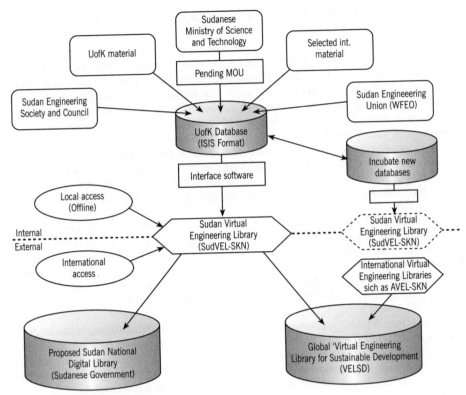

UofK = University of Khartoum.
Source: SudVEL-SKN Executive Report: Pilot Project 2003/04, written by Charlie Hargroves of The Natural Edge Project and Dr Iman Maaly of the University of Khartoum

Figure 22.1 *Sudan Virtual Engineering Library process diagram*

Architecture and Institute of Environmental Studies containing both local sources and a selection of international materials. The library will provide easy and efficient offline local access together with international access to students, researchers and academic staff. SudVEL-SKN will also provide Sudanese contributions to the UNESCO/WFEO Virtual Engineering Library for Sustainable Development and contribute to the Proposed Sudan National Digital Library. Databases such as this are needed in every country to draw out local material and ensure technology transfer from international sources into the curriculum of engineering students and researchers. The virtual library will serve as an information services unit in the field of engineering and sustainable development. The contents of the library will be as follows:

- Referral database of engineering institutes and organizations in Sudan.
- Referral database of Sudanese experts and faculty members in Engineering.
- Sudanese literature in engineering: research papers, thesis, dissertation, books, reports, etc.
- Selected international contents in engineering for sustainable development.

It is expected that the SudVEL-SKN will increase information transparency, promote research and higher education in engineering and assist projects in sustainable development throughout Sudan and the greater region. It is intended that the database will provide a resource to support research and education in the Faculties of Engineering at Sudanese universities and as a broader resource throughout the region and internationally.

As discussed in previous sections of this book, professional bodies are addressing sustainable development in multiple ways for multiple reasons. In 2003, members of The Natural Edge Project (TNEP) undertook discussions with past Engineers Australia President and TNEP mentor Barry Grear (then Vice President of Professions Australia), to develop a proposal for a roundtable to be focused on the theme of 'Achieving a Sustainable Future'. The aim of the Young Professions Australia Roundtable was to allow a selection of young professionals to actively focus on a particular theme, and develop material for their respective nominating bodies. The proposal was accepted and strongly supported by Council members. Roundtable members participated in a three month programme involving various small group activities, electronic discussions and teleconferences. At the subsequent forum, key findings of the participants included:

- all professional bodies should ensure base literacy in sustainable development;
- involvement by members within professional bodies, in public policy debate;
- increasing representation in professional body activities by younger members; and
- development of a greater level of linkage between professions and associated professional bodies, through the Professions Australia website, and by Professions Australia becoming a holistic centre of information and contact.

One of the main drivers for change in attitudes to sustainable development has been the insurance crisis and the significant rise in professional indemnity insurance. In addition, a requirement to pursue best practice in sustainable development is increasingly entering professionals' codes of ethics. They are also seeking to provide better services to existing members, and attract and keep new young professional members.

This desire to move towards sustainability is beginning to be discussed with other parts of the education sector. Professional bodies are now starting to require universities to ensure that graduates in engineering, for example, have a critical literacy in sustainable development. It is important that, rather than such initiatives being 'directives' from above, the potential for partnerships and other opportunities are identified to ensure that the message is translated to the students. The Young Professions Australia Roundtable is an example of such a step by a professional body. As mentioned in Section 4, Chapter 18, Engineers Australia is also taking a lead by facilitating the development of the Introductory material for the Engineering Sustainable Solutions education modules to be expanded into a series of level-one units in 2005 with support from UNESCO as part of the Decade for Education in Sustainable Development. The integration of such sustainability educational material into course curricula, for all undergraduate engineers nationally, will provide critical literacy skills that will equip this professional group to really make a difference in their careers.

With the Internet and email it is possible now to learn from best practice around the world much more rapidly. Young professionals, in particular, across the globe are getting organized to address sustainable development issues and acting as effective catalysts for change. Take Oz GREEN, an Australian non-governmental organization (NGO), which works with schools, youth, and business and has worked with communities on numerous Australian River catchments since 1993. Over the past 10 years Oz GREEN has achieved their aims in Australia by:

- Involving over 200 schools and tens of thousands of young people in conducting over 6000 water quality tests and environmental action planning.
- Training over 80 volunteer eco-team leaders to conduct sustainable living programmes in their own communities. Independently evaluated to achieve significant and measurable reductions in their environmental impact.

- Working on a one-to-one basis with over 500 small–medium industrial businesses to prepare pollution prevention plans. Independent evaluation shows that 71 per cent of businesses had completed or substantially completed the implementation of these plans within six months.
- Surveying and strategically questioning over 5000 industrial businesses.
- Training, mentoring and supporting 100 Youth LEAD'ers to implement eco-social projects within their own communities and beyond.

This is the tip of the iceberg in terms of what young professionals are doing globally to utilize and transfer their skills to assist sustainable development in developing countries and vice versa.

The power of individuals

Despite all the examples and points made thus far in this book, there are still many for whom worldly cynicism prevents them from seeing what they could possibly achieve. Despite the example of people like Nelson Mandela, some still doubt that an individual can make a difference. But as Professor Dexter Dunphy, one of Australia's leading experts on corporate sustainability and corporate social responsibility, writes 'what we do as individuals matters, even though we often can't see the results in our lifetime. If we act with vision and principle, our actions may be amplified beyond our dreams. If we act in accord with our deepest intuitions, we do not act in vain.' He relates a remarkable story of how one person, Peter Board, in the New South Wales Department of Education, as an individual, made a difference:

> At the beginning of last century, a young Australian returned from the US to become Director General of Public Education in New South Wales. His name was Peter Board and he brought a number of reforms into the school curriculum. One of these reforms was the introduction of a new subject: Natural Science. At the time, my father, Myles Dunphy, was a small boy attending the local Kiama public school. He was captivated by the new subject which encouraged him and his friends to seek out fossils, identify plants and insects. Out of that experience, Myles developed a love of nature which led him into bushwalking. He founded the first two bushwalking clubs in this country, explored and mapped much of the Blue Mountains and other remote areas. He began to realize that much of the native wilderness was under threat and he worked hard, with his mates, to mount public campaigns to preserve wilderness areas for future generations. He is known today as the Father of Australian Wilderness, because much of our superb heritage of national parks was envisaged by him. My brother Milo continued his work, lobbying politicians, running public campaigns, building the conservation movement. As a result my father's vision has been largely implemented. Few people today remember Peter Board, yet without his educational initiative it's unlikely that so much of our natural heritage would have been preserved 100 years later.

Professor Dexter Dunphy, son of Myles Dunphy, UTS Corporate Sustainability Unit, text edited from Ockam's Razor, ABC Radio

Almost 100 years later, the NSW Department of Education has made it compulsory for high schools in NSW to take students on excursions to national parks to appreciate the complex ecosystems that Myles Dunphy and his friends played a critical role in having protected. Through their efforts, more hearts and minds of the next generation will be touched through the beauty of NSW's national parks. The truth of course is that Peter Board did not simply bring about this change on his own. He, like most of us, was part of an organization, in his case the NSW Department of Education. Any reform has to be approved of by many people. Hence our effectiveness to make a difference in the real world depends significantly on our ability to work and communicate effectively with many people.

CHAPTER 23

ACHIEVING MULTI-STAKEHOLDER ENGAGEMENT

Many issues today cannot be addressed or resolved by a single set of governmental or other decision-makers but require cooperation between many different actors and stakeholders. Such issues will be incapable of successful resolution unless all parties are fully involved in working out the solutions, their implementation and the monitoring of results.

Hesphina Rukato and Derek Osborn, Co-Chairs of the United Nations Economic Development Forum on Multi-Stakeholder Processes, 2001[1]

As discussed in Section 1, the fundamental principle behind The Natural Edge Project (TNEP), and this book, is a collaborative, 'whole of society approach'. But how does one get started on any sustainability project? Every part of business, government and civil society must consider the improvement of economic, social and environmental performance. This chapter provides a perspective on multi-stakeholder engagement and processes to achieve engagement ('multi-stakeholder processes') illustrated by a tool used by a leading international consultant in the field, AtKisson Inc lead by TNEP mentor, Alan AtKisson.

What is multi-stakeholder engagement?[2]

Stakeholders are those who have an interest in a particular decision, either as individuals or representatives of a group. This includes people who influence a decision, or can influence it, as well as those affected by it. Terms such as 'multi-stakeholder dialogue', 'stakeholder forum', 'stakeholder consultation', 'discussion' and 'process' are commonly used by various professionals in the field. The meanings of these terms overlap and refer to a variety of settings and modes of stakeholder communication. The term 'multi-stakeholder processes' (MSPs) describes processes which aim to bring together major stakeholders in a new form of communication, decision-finding (and possibly decision-making) on a particular issue. They are also based on a recognition of the importance of achieving equity and accountability in communication between stakeholders. Based on democratic principles of transparency and participation, MSPs aim to develop partnerships and strengthen networks. They cover a wide spectrum of structures and levels of engagement, and can comprise dialogues on policy or grow to include consensus-building, decision-making and implementation of practical solutions. MSPs come in many shapes: each situation, issue or problem prompts the need for participants to design a process specifically suited to their abilities, circumstances and needs. They are suitable for those situations where dialogue is possible and where listening, reconciling interests and integrating views into joint solution strategies seems appropriate and within reach.

Where does multi-stakeholder engagement fit in?

It has been seven years since David Wheeler and Maria Silanpää published *The Stakeholder Corporation*,[3] about the same time as Shell faced Greenpeace off the British Isles over the Brent Spa oil platform, and the anti-Nike campaign was at its height. Stakeholder engagement has become the emerging norm since then.[4] Agenda 21 was the first United Nations (UN) document to address extensively the role of different stakeholders in implementing a global agreement. In each of its chapters, Agenda 21 refers to roles that stakeholder groups have to take to put the blueprint into practice, with stakeholder involvement described as absolutely crucial for sustainable development. The World Summit on Sustainable Development (WSSD) provided an important leap in 2002, when partnerships among multiple stakeholders became linked with inter-governmental decision-making. Member states agreed to consider a large number of sustainable development partnerships as part of the official outcome of the Summit event.[5]

Current issues with multi-stakeholder processes

MSPs have emerged because there is a perceived need for a more inclusive, effective method for addressing the urgent sustainability issues of our time. However, according to Hemmati,[6] it appears that stakeholder dialogues, ways of feeding them into decision-making and concrete follow-up, are mostly being organized and prepared on a rather ad hoc basis. There is a vast experience with participation at community levels and increasing experience at national and global levels. Yet studying and comparing the different approaches and distilling some common but flexible guidelines from a stakeholder perspective is lagging behind. Governments and inter-governmental bodies, industry, non-governmental organizations (NGOs), local governments and other stakeholders are trying out various approaches, resulting in many different set-ups being called the same thing. In addition, the relationship between stakeholder participation and decision-making remains unclear in many cases.

Looking forward: multi-stakeholder process design

Governments, businesses, international organizations, local groups and numerous other publicly engaged bodies are turning to MSPs for decision-making, as conventional politics is increasingly unable to integrate broad-based, consensual policies. MSPs can bring together those whose interests are at stake in crucial social, economic, developmental and environmental debates, and for whom finding practical solutions as well as ways in which these might be implemented is essential. Hemmati puts forward a framework for designing MSPs, which aims to contribute to the advancement of such mechanisms as well as producing practical solutions:

> *We need common yet flexible guidelines and to learn from experience. Sustainable development is a mixed concept, comprising values (such as environmental protection and equity) and strategies (such as healthy economic growth, stakeholder involvement and global perspective). Based on scientific and empirical analysis, we can look at what has been proven to work to address certain problems and/or how we can combine various tools in an effective manner. Such a discourse will lead to suggesting strategies for bringing a multitude of perspectives into*

decision-making; listening to each other; and facilitating meetings. Arguing for a multi-stakeholder approach in this manner will lead to suggesting strategies which increase creative thinking, commitment to implementation and multiplying effects, in order to address problems such as resource depletion and human and environmental security.[7]

Some people want to relate to shared values and a common normative vision, others need statistics that prove one approach will yield success with greater likelihood than another. But moreover, the main reason is that behaviour, and behavioural changes, are grounded in many factors such as: our beliefs, attitudes and emotions; the information we have; positive rewards (monetary or social); behavioural options; and social pressures. Proposing tools for sustainable development, such as MSPs, should be based on considering basic values and ideologies (as a set of criteria) as much as practical experiences and empirical knowledge of how such processes can work in various contexts.

Engaging the spirit

Many suggestions for designing MSPs are not new, and neither is the MSP approach. What authors like Hemmati and consultants like AtKisson Inc are trying to do is to ground them in values, experience and science, and to generate a more conscious and comprehensive dialogue about them. Even if the notion of MSP appears as just common sense, it seems that we have a problem practising common sense. As Hemmati concludes, 'problems do not go away just because we look away. Necessities don't disappear just because we become cynical. Haven't love (for each other and for our environment) and justice been preached for ages? Don't we know how painful war, poverty, disease, injustice and oppression are and how they destroy us and our societies? Don't we know that we need to listen to each other rather than fight in order to come to lasting, sustainable solutions? Haven't we learned that without pooling our resources of expertise and power we will not be able to tackle the complex and urgent problems we are facing? Well – yes. But life is a journey of learning and unlearning. What we understand in our minds, we won't necessarily put into practice. Have we really proven that we cannot do better? Whether humankind can indeed learn and change as a collective remains an open question. It will help if we try to do so together and consciously.'

Introducing the Pyramid: a versatile process and planning tool for accelerating sustainable development through multi-stakeholder engagement

Alan AtKisson

EDITORS' NOTE: As many of the challenges we face in achieving a sustainable future will ultimately call for wide involvement throughout society we must find productive ways to work together. One of the world's leading experts on achieving multi-stakeholder engagement for sustainability is Alan AtKisson and his colleagues at AtKisson Inc. We first met Alan at the Network of Regional Governments for Sustainable Development Meeting in Perth in late 2003, and being familiar with his work we invited him to mentor the development of our project and in particular provide a succinct summary of his proven tools for achieving multi-stakeholder engagement. Alan, author of *Believing Cassandra*, a book on how to think and do sustainability, together with his colleagues R. Lee Hatcher and Sydney Green have written the following piece to describe the theory behind their tools, the different ways they can be used and provide case studies to illustrate how such a process can work in practice.

The challenge of sustainable development creates unprecedented demands for learning, thinking, planning and decision-making. Economic, social, and environmental performance must all be improved, usually all at the same time, and often against a backdrop of one or more critically negative trends. All too often, these trends act together to reinforce each other. As if that were not complicated enough, the challenge is often compounded by the need to work in diverse, multi-stakeholder groups, and to achieve consensus on a set of actions that everyone believes will actually produce results. Finally, initiatives seeking to promote sustainability are often doing so under a sense of time urgency, with limited resources. They do not have time or money to waste on suboptimal solutions or difficult-to-achieve agreements. Building on a dozen years of work with sustainability and community development initiatives around the world, we developed the *Pyramid* process to address these needs. While the Pyramid as an integrated process was first introduced in 2001, it is built on basic sustainability tools and methods that we have been using since the early 1990s.

What is the Pyramid?

At its core, the Pyramid is a framework and a process for strategic planning. However, the framework can also be used as a training programme for sustainable development; as a team-building process to build mutual understanding; and as a workshop structure for building consensus on new goals and directions. The Pyramid incorporates two other frameworks previously developed by Alan AtKisson:

1   **The Compass of Sustainability**, a way of representing the different dimensions of sustainability, and of supporting true multi-stakeholder engagement acts as the base of the Pyramid.
2   **The ISIS Method**, a logical thinking process that helps groups develop a more systematic and strategic understanding of sustainable development.

The Pyramid combines these into a structured group process to provide training, planning or general decision-support for more sustainable outcomes. To set the stage for understanding the Pyramid process, we must first discuss these elements in brief.

The Compass of Sustainability

North	Nature	
South	Society	
East	Economy	
West	Well-being	

This simple wordplay is actually an adaptation of sustainability theory as first put forward by economist Herman Daly (and later reinterpreted by Donella H. Meadows). Daly proposed that these four elements, Nature, Economy, Society and individual human Well-being, were dependent on each other for their existence, and that each element was dependent on the one preceding it in a logical hierarchy. During a series of international meetings in 1999 on the topic of best practice in sustainability indicators, this hierarchy of dependence was challenged on a number of grounds. For example, in some cultures the overall Society is considered to be paramount, with individual Well-being looked upon as secondary to social needs. Also, there are now ways in which the health of Nature is arguably dependent on stable economies and social structures.[8] Out of those meetings the *Compass of Sustainability* was developed to stress, instead, the inter-

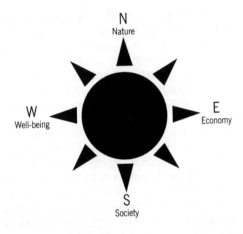

Figure 23.1 *The Compass of Sustainability*

connected nature of these four elements: all must be healthy for sustainability to be realized. The Compass metaphor also captures the sense of new directions that sustainability implies, as well as standing for the inclusion of all stakeholders: people come from all directions to participate in the process of sustainable development.

To briefly define the points of the compass:

- **Nature** refers to the ecological systems and natural resources.
- **Economy** is the process by which resources are put to work to produce the things and services that humans want and need.
- **Society** is the collective and institutional dimension of human civilization, incorporating everything from governments to school systems to social norms regarding equity and opportunity.
- **Well-being** refers to the satisfaction and happiness of individual people – their health, their primary relationships, and the opportunities they have to develop their full potential.

These categories have been used to structure formal sustainability assessments and indicator systems.[9] The Compass defines what sustainability is; and Pyramid supports users through the process of implementing sustainable development.[10]

The ISIS Method

ISIS is an acronym standing for the four steps in a sequential strategic thinking process – a process that is particularly well suited to the demands of sustainable development.

1   'I' is for 'indicators'. *Indicators* are signals that tell us something about the state of a system. They reflect the status of critical elements in the system, and help us determine how healthy that system is, and whether the trend is in a healthy direction. In assessing the health of your body, for example, a doctor first looks at common indicators such as your temperature, your blood count and whether you have any pain. If these reflect trouble, she might then look more closely. The combination of indicators is what usually tells the doctor what the trouble is likely to be. Indicators can be formal measurements, represented as charts, graphs and statistics; or they can be more informal, based on subjective perceptions. The Pyramid process can make use of both.

2   'S' is for 'systems'. *Systems* are groups of discrete elements that work together to make a whole. Systems are bound together by the laws of cause and effect, and governed by flows of information. A human body, a community, a rainforest or a company can all be thought of as systems. Understanding how the various elements work together is critical to managing a system successfully. With the ISIS method, using Indicators as a starting point, the user builds a systems understanding of how and where change is possible. This creates a more sound foundation for thinking about change itself.

3   The second 'I' is for 'innovation'. *Innovation* is the process of developing and introducing a change to a system. Any kind of change or intervention qualifies, from the application of a technology, to a change in the rules, to an alteration in the information flows. Innovations do not have to be 'new' in any absolute sense; old ideas can be 'innovative' if they are new to the system in question. At this stage, groups can use catalogues of best practices, brainstorming and prioritizing to identify promising options for making change, and selecting among them. The best innovations are those that hit the most effective leverage points, causing positive change in each of the four Compass Points.

4   'S' is for 'strategy'. *Strategy* is planning for the successful implementation of an envisioned change. Developing strategy involves consideration of all the factors likely to help or hinder the acceptance of a change, and the actions (including contingency plans) to be followed in seeing the change through to its conclusion. The more fundamental the change, the more critical it is to develop a sound and workable strategy. Once a group has identified its priority change initiative, it can use a variety of techniques, applied Innovation Diffusion Theory, 'SWOT' analyses, etc., to develop good plans for implementation of that change.

The ISIS method ensures that change initiatives:

- are developed in consideration of all the relevant trends and issues;
- are targeted at those spots in a complex system where change is most likely to create the desired outcome, as well as other positive benefits;
- draw on the full range of possible alternatives, and the creative thinking of a diverse group;
- are grounded in real-world thinking about implementation.

By following the ISIS method, the user stands a better chance of managing limited resources wisely, and successfully creating a change in the target entity, a change in the direction of sustainability.

What's new about ISIS?

ISIS may appear similar to other strategic planning frameworks on the surface; but in practice, it is quite different, in ways both obvious and subtle:

- First, the focus on Indicators ensures that the whole group is exposed to the widest possible range of available information about critical trends affecting the system in question. Traditional planning usually attempts only to identify 'critical issues or problems', many of which may be just the surface of a more complex set of issues. ISIS-based planning looks for longer-term trends as well, which may or may not be identified problems. Moreover, using the Compass of Sustainability ensures that the net is cast as widely as possible to ensure that nothing important is overlooked.
- Second, the Systems step encourages a group to contend with the complexity of multiple cause-and-effect relationships, and chains of such relationships. While

often confusing and difficult, especially in groups of widely varying experience, this is a critical step. Too often, planning efforts address symptoms, not causes; or proximate causes, and not root causes. The Systems analysis process creates a greater likelihood that a group will discover more effective 'leverage points' for creating beneficial change and help to build a complex shared 'mental model' of the target entity. In practice, multi-stakeholder groups tend to use the Indicators phase to teach each other about critical issues. They can interpret trends to each other, based on their differing experience and expertise. At the Systems level, they may be teaching each other about critical connections between trends; but they generally also discover new analyses that would not have been possible (or at least easy to come up with) had they been working on their own, in single-issue groups, or in a planning framework more focused on one area of expertise. At the Innovation level, groups do more than just brainstorm possible good ideas, as they generate ideas that are likely to have broad, beneficial, systemic impact, and then prioritize among those ideas.

- Finally, at the Strategy level, groups put these ideas to the 'real world' test, and build plans for implementation that are developed with the aid of applied Innovation Diffusion Theory or some other guide for enhancing their chances of success.

The ISIS method can produce, as a purposeful by-product, improved levels of inter-disciplinary understanding and innovative thinking. When coupled with the Pyramid framework for running group processes, it can support group learning, planning, and decision processes that are (to borrow language from NASA) 'faster, better, and cheaper'.

How the Pyramid process works

The Pyramid process can be a very effective way to support and accelerate a group's progress on the sustainable development journey, from the initial engagement with a vision of sustainability, through analysis and brainstorming, to a consensus on a credible and meaningful plan of action. Along the way, the process seeks to build a shared competency in trend analysis, systems thinking, strategic planning and consensus development.

The Pyramid process generally starts with a presentation to set the framework, beginning with an introduction to the Sustainability Compass (or some whole-systems sustainability framework). When the Pyramid is being used in a planning process, the use of the Compass from the outset will ensure that all Compass Points are represented at the table, helping to assure that the process is truly multi-stakeholder. The Compass also provides clarity of definition for what sustainability means in practice, and it can be supplemented with specific visions and principles to guide thinking. The greater this clarity, the stronger the foundation on which the Pyramid process rests. When Pyramid is the basis for a training programme, groups are introduced to sustainability via the Compass, and participants are then invited to sit in 'Compass Point Groups'. They are encouraged to choose a Compass Point that is not their usual point of reference, so they can get an experience of stretching to think from other people's perspectives. In both the training and planning context, the Pyramid process involves working through four levels corresponding to the four steps in the ISIS method. The Pyramid narrows as it grows, and this is reflected in the process as well: a large number of indicators are analysed to produce a somewhat smaller number of key systems insights. Then a large list of brainstormed initiatives must also be narrowed down to a smaller number of genuine options that all can agree on. Finally, there are usually just a few options for different strategic plans that can lead to successful implementation. In this way, the Pyramid process leads a group, step-by-step towards an all-important conclusion: an agreement to actually do something.

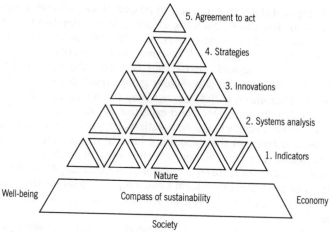

Source: AtKisson Inc

Figure 23.2 *Pyramid of sustainable development*

At the top of the Pyramid is the Capstone. In physical pyramid construction, the capstone is the last, crowning piece. In colloquial English, the word has come to mean a culminating event. The capstone of the Pyramid is Agreement. After working through a process of developing Indicators, analysing Systems, selecting Innovations, and creating Strategies, the group must then agree to take action. In sustainable development initiatives, which are so often characterized by multi-stakeholder partnerships, involving actors who represent different sectors, disciplines, or even cultural or political groups, the operative word is 'consensus'. Without full, shared agreement, implementation of even the most exciting ideas and strategies is not likely to occur. Pyramid brings together many of the ideas and practices that have become central to the concept of sustainable development. Indicator development, systems thinking, and the applications of innovation theory to strategic action have all become common to sustainability practice; Pyramid, with Compass and ISIS, brings these together into an integrated process.

Moreover, the structure of Pyramid guides a group through the process of first building a firm base of understanding, casting a wide net for relevant information and ideas, and then focusing and narrowing down to what is important, effective, doable and something that everybody can agree on. Throughout the process, Pyramid takes an inter-disciplinary, cross-sectoral systems approach. Strategic use of small group/large group discussion tasks mixes people together in different ways and supports the identification of important linkages and leverage points. Groups get practice in sharing ideas, expertise and experience, and in building consensus based on clear criteria. For these reasons, we believe Pyramid represents a genuinely new approach to group learning and strategic planning that is specifically designed for integrating sustainability into planning, decision-making and design. This model uses sustainability as a value-added methodology to focus on the problem, issue, policy or project at hand. In our practice, clients have often found it to be an improvement over their existing strategic planning methods in a more general sense.

Invented by AtKisson Inc in 2001, Pyramid has been used in a wide variety of settings, and in several different ways:

- As a training programme on applied sustainable development, Pyramid has been used by UN-sponsored training programmes in Asia, sustainability education centres, and the US Army, among others.

- As a strategic planning framework, Pyramid has been used by our firm with a wide variety of clients, both explicitly and in the background of our own planning. Its explicit use has been with clients such as foundation grant programmes and regional sustainability initiatives.
- As a workshop model for bringing multi-stakeholder groups together, building a common understanding, and generating initiative ideas, Pyramid has been used by sustainability initiatives at the city, regional and international level.

We present here three case studies that illustrate the use of Pyramid in practice, in each of the three contexts described above.

Magic Eyes/UNEP: Pyramid training for Asian change agents

In early 2002, AtKisson Inc undertook a Pyramid training session, supported by UNEP, with a leading Thai NGO called 'Magic Eyes', the popular nickname for the Thai Environmental and Community Development Association (TECDA).[11] The UNEP/Magic Eyes programme brings professionals in the media or government together for five days of instruction and discussion. The Pyramid process and related tools comprise about 40 per cent of the experience, and these elements of the training have consistently received very high evaluation scores from participants. In this and other training contexts, participants work in a simulation environment, with a pre-developed scenario, in this case, a South-East Asian village. The Pyramid process walks them step-by-step through the sustainable development process, starting with a Compass-based definition of sustainability, and a review of the key issues affecting the community.

Participants then break up into teams, one for each of the Compass points. For the duration of the exercise, they operate from the imagined perspective of a stakeholder who is naturally associated with that Compass point. The groups then go through a set of structured presentations and exercises over the course of two days. They develop indicators of the key trends for their community. They analyse how these trends link to each other. They create 'System Maps' showing how specific clusters of trends work

Source: AtKisson Inc

Figure 23.3 *Workshop participants placing capstone on Pyramid*

together, usually linking all four points of the Compass. They look for opportunities to make system-wide change through innovative initiatives, and practise coming to consensus on which initiatives they will pursue, and how. At each step, the groups share their learning, negotiate with each other, and physically build a model of a Pyramid, which reflects (with both words, connecting lines, and sometimes artistic embellishments) the things they have learned and accomplished.

By the end of the workshop, they have a thorough and systematic understanding of the sustainability challenges facing a typical Asian community, and a clearer sense of possible strategic avenues for positive change. They have also gained experience thinking and working their way to consensus about sustainability initiatives, an experience that they can directly apply in their professional lives.

Baltic 21: Pyramid-based strategic planning

Baltic 21, more formally known as 'Agenda 21 for the Baltic Sea Region', is a multi-stakeholder, international initiative, with a formal mandate from the 11 Prime Ministers of the countries surrounding the Baltic Sea (plus Norway and Iceland). Government agencies, business, research institutes and civil society are all actively engaged. When it became time to renew the Prime Ministers' mandate for Baltic 21, the group's steering council (called the 'Senior Officials Group') created a strategic planning process and Working Group. After performing its own extensive historical review, the Working Group engaged AtKisson Europe AB to support them in developing the new strategy. The Group adopted the Pyramid process and ISIS methodology. Baltic 21 had already been working with indicators for several years, and so participants quickly understood the value of bringing a systematic and logical framework to bear on the complex issues they were facing in the region. The Pyramid process was used both in the planning meetings themselves, and as the workshop model for a stakeholder workshop in Riga, Latvia, in January 2004. During the course of two days in Riga, 30 representatives from government ministries, private sector groups, inter-sectoral initiatives and NGOs worked together to produce a proposal for a new strategy for Baltic 21.

At each step of the Pyramid process, participants made important contributions to a broader understanding of sustainable development strategy in the Baltic Sea Region:

At the *indicator level*, participants reviewed the existing Baltic 21 sustainability indicators for the region, but then augmented these with a list of some 20 other trends that were critical to understanding regional issues.

At the *systems level*, they worked in small groups to analyse a handful of key trends in terms of their connections to other trends, through chains of cause and effect. This allowed them also to map the key decision points or influence points ('leverage points') where focused effort could bring about system-wide positive effects. The Systems level, in particular, contributed to a set of 'Key Insights' that ultimately framed the group's new strategy proposal.

At the *innovations level*, the group brainstormed a long list of new and existing ideas for targeted initiatives to effect change at those points of influence, and then prioritized them according to a set of criteria that fitted Baltic 21's identity as a regional, multi-stakeholder forum for collaboration. A preference voting exercise was used to bring the most promising ideas to the top of the list.

Finally, at the *strategy level*, small groups took the top-ranked initiative ideas, fleshed them out, performed 'SWOT' analyses on them, and developed proposals for implementing those ideas in the context of a coherent overall strategic vision, which had emerged from discussions after the Innovations level.

In summary, the proposal was to:

Source: AtKisson Inc

Figure 23.4 *Agenda 21 for the Baltic Sea Region participants in Pyramid process*

- Redevelop the Baltic 21 steering council, the 'Senior Officials Group', into a 'think-tank' for sustainable development issues in the region. This group would work through existing international channels to more directly inform and influence policy decisions.
- Create a set of 'Lighthouse Projects', larger-scale initiatives that were regional in scope and demonstrated the value of sustainable development in visible, tangible terms.
- Develop a 'Baltic 21 Fund' and other innovative funding mechanisms to support these projects with money, working through existing EU, regional and national funding sources.

By the end of this workshop, there was already a Capstone Agreement in place: a strong consensus, among essentially all workshop participants, that this proposal was the most effective role for Baltic 21 to play, given its identity and the strategic challenges of the Baltic Sea Region. The proposal left intact those elements of Baltic 21 that were working well, dropped some less-useful elements, and refocused the initiative's limited resources in a more powerful direction. The group recommended that the proposal be developed further by a Working Group and presented to the Senior Officials Group and other regional decision-makers in time for consideration by the Prime Ministers at their June, 2004 summit meeting.

While the proposal was amended somewhat in the lead-up to the Prime Ministers' summit, the strong consensus developed at the Riga workshop was still present in the proposal's final version.[12]

Woodford Correctional Centre: Pyramid workshop for new initiative development
One of the most innovative applications of the Pyramid process occurred in an Australian correctional centre. In a day-long planning workshop, a group of 20 staff came together from every division of the prison. The purpose of the workshop was to explore

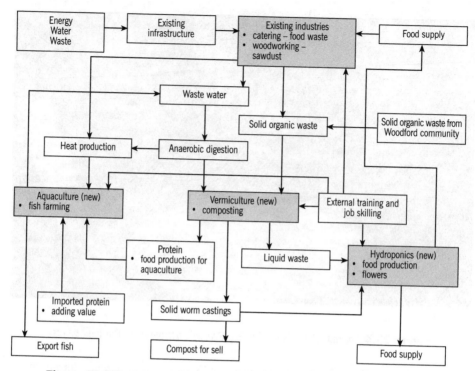

Figure 23.5 System map from Pyramid workshop, July 2003

ways to run the prison according to 'triple bottom line' sustainability principles. The result of the Pyramid process was a proposal for a new set of industries for the prison, work that inmates could perform that would support their rehabilitation, contribute to society and reduce the prison's consumption of resources and impact on the environment (see Figure 23.5).

Using a set of indicators developed for the occasion from prison records, the group mapped the energy, waste and water flows; the prison economy (its economic products include catering services as well as rehabilitated citizens); and the social systems that support training and development of inmates while maintaining a safe and quality work environment for prison employees. The systems analysis led to the insight that prison industries were the key leverage point in the system, that is, the most powerful place to introduce innovation. A change in the kinds of jobs prisoners performed could close waste and resource loops, reduce environmental impact, provide more beneficial economic products, improve training and rehabilitation opportunities for prisoners, and enhance the quality of life of prison employees.

At the end of the process, the workshop group had come to consensus on a proposed set of three new industries that could work within the special requirements of a correctional facility. These were:

1   vermiculture composting;
2   aquaculture fish farming;
3   hydroponic vegetable gardens.

These systems could absorb wastes from the existing catering services, while adding high quality products to those services, reducing the cost of importing food and other inputs.

They would expand the skills base of prisoners and prepare them for jobs in markets that are expected to expand. And they would help to create more pleasant work environments for the whole prison community (see Figure 23.5).

At the time of writing, these proposed new industries had passed a feasibility study by state officials, and prison management had begun seeking expressions of interest from potential developers. If successfully implemented, this industrial retrofit could amount to a revolution in thinking about how prisons can be run sustainably.

Concluding words from Alan AtKisson

While Pyramid is still a new process, it has already been used successfully in many different contexts and cultures. It has proven itself adaptable to a number of different sustainability frameworks, from 'Triple Bottom Line' to 'Natural Step' to our own 'Compass of Sustainability'. From the reports of users, we can say that it has produced satisfying, and in some cases quite exemplary, results. There is no easy way of testing the model to determine whether it accomplishes its stated purpose of 'accelerating sustainable development'. Such a test would require the close of observation of two very similar organizations or communities, one using the Pyramid process and the other not, over a defined period of time; and then comparing the results they achieve in measurable terms. Such a test does not seem practical or possible.

However, the testimonials of clients lead us to believe that the process works well on a variety of levels. Workshop leaders and participants report that the process:

* teaches them to think in a clear and systematic way about what sustainable development means, in tangible terms;
* helps them understand the complexity of the systems they work in, and gives them critical insights about how, and where, to make change happen;
* stimulates them with new ideas and creative thinking about what kinds of change are possible;
* supports their understanding of how different stakeholders view the issues, and broadens their perspective;
* makes it easier to achieve consensus on what actions are the most appropriate and effective next steps; and
* gives them a sense of energy and enthusiasm to pursue the difficult work of sustainable development.

Pyramid can also function as a longer-term strategic framework. At each level of the Pyramid, users can bring in a variety of other complementary tools and methods. For example, GRI reporting can be used at the Indicator level. More sophisticated system dynamics modelling can be applied at the System level. A wealth of organizational and management consulting techniques can be used at the Innovation and Strategy levels. By sitting on a base of clear principles and visions, and leading diverse groups through a disciplined 'building-up' process of information gathering, systems analysis, innovative thinking, strategic planning and consensus development, Pyramid can help any organization seeking to make sustainability a meaningful reality.

Building a network around a project: The Natural Edge Project

Karlson 'Charlie' Hargroves, Michael H. Smith, Cheryl Paten and Nick Palousis

There are many important issues and challenges that have not been covered in this book. Will AIDS undermine what progress has been made in Asia, Africa and other countries like India? Will farming subsidies in the North and other barriers to trade continue, and how do institutions involved with global trade address environmental issues? Can we make significant progress to achieve the millennium goals and halve world poverty by 2015? The ageing population is already a significant issue in OECD countries, but there is also a lack of opportunity in many developing countries for their youth. Growing up, anyone who reads or watches the media will be left to think that such problems in this world are inevitable. This book, and those upon which it has consciously been built, has shown that this is not the case. Rather the choices we make influence the future we build; another world is possible.

There are there numerous win–win opportunities when problems are addressed in a holistic integrated way. In fact, if our solutions do not deliver multiple benefits we need to go back to the drawing board. This book and online companion seeks to show what can be achieved by people both 'thinking outside the box' and looking for the synergies that may in turn provide additional solutions. For instance, one company's waste could be another company's resource. These synergies are often there if we look. But if they are not, we need to ensure that in future designs there is this capacity for synergies to evolve. More and more the challenge and problems we are faced with are long-term problems that need an integrated approach. However, politics is increasingly becoming about winning the daily media battle, the latest poll and the next election in a year's time.

The take-home message is that we can solve many of the current problems if we take holistic approaches and set up inclusive processes to involve the key stakeholders. We can solve these 'problems' if we can see that they are all integrated and seek to develop long-term whole of society approaches. So often governments, businesses and educators say we cannot do everything; we have to choose one problem, one project and address that. But we argue that misses the point completely. As this book has shown, there is now a wealth of case studies, living models like Curitiba in Brazil, showing what can be achieved through taking holistic approaches and looking for synergies. But taking integrated approaches will not always be easy. Involving the stakeholders in MSPs can be complicated, time consuming and hard to control. We live in a world where many economists do not know ecology, and many ecologists do not know economics, many business leaders do not know science and engineering and vice versa. We live in a world where, despite air travel, we still know so little about other cultures, other religions and ways of living. Therefore, one of the barriers to taking integrated approaches is there are few people who can communicate effectively across the disciplines, across what, in Australia, we call the 'silos'.

These are some of the main reasons for creating The Natural Edge Project (TNEP). In 2002 TNEP was formed by Karlson 'Charlie' Hargroves, Mike Smith and James Moody, a group of young engineers and scientists seeking to make a difference and influence the future. This attitude has led us to work with a wide range of groups within society on a number of progressive projects. Later in the project, James Moody resigned and two young engineers, Cheryl Paten (formerly Desha) and Nick Palousis joined the core group of TNEP, known as the secretariat.

This book and companion website, our flagship initiative of the project, seek to provide a multi-disciplinary resource to compliment current largely discipline-based university courses. There is a need for people to have the opportunity to be skilled in one profession, one discipline, but we also need more books and websites that help people to learn quickly at least the essence and language of other fields and a snapshot of what other fields of knowledge are seeking to understand. Amory Lovins has said that we need to learn a new discipline every six months. With this book and companion website, we have sought to make this as easy as possible for readers to do so. But above all, the message of The Natural Edge Project is one of hope. We have tried from day one, and each step of the way, to do what we knew was ethical and to act with integrity. We have asked ourselves what would be the most appropriate way forward at each point and at

Table 23.1 *Whole of society approach: sectors identified to approach*

Sector	Examples of supporting bodies in Australia
Business	Environment Business Australia, The Barton Group, Chambers of Commerce, Triple Bottom Line Australia, Business Council for Sustainable Energy, Hatch Associates, Arup Sustainability, Design Inc.
Professional bodies	Institution of Engineers Australia, Environmental Engineering Society, Environment Institute of Australia, Royal Australian Institute of Architects, Young Engineers Australia, [Institute of Professional Engineers of New Zealand, Environment Institute Australia and New Zealand (EIANZ)]
Educational bodies	RMIT Global Sustainability Institute, ANU's National Institute for Environment, National Environmental Education Council, Australian Association of Environmental Educators, Australian Virtual Engineering Library, Monash University Centre for Green Chemistry, Institute for Sustainability and Technology Policy – Murdoch University. [University Leaders for a Sustainable Future]
Events, festivals, media	Australian Innovation Festival, National Engineering Week, National Science Week, Australian Broadcasting Company Science Unit (ABC), Science and Engineering Challenge
Governments and agencies	Environment Australia, Australian Greenhouse Office, Department of Industry Tourism & Resources, State Offices for Sustainability and EPAs, Environs Australia, [International Council for Local Environmental Initiatives (ICLEI)]
NGOs, charities, foundations	Australian Green Development Forum, Australian Conservation Foundation (Blueprint for a Sustainable Australia), Nature and Society Forum, The Centre for the Encouragement of Philanthropy (CEPA) Trust
Research institutions	The Commonwealth Science Industry Research Organisation, Cooperative Research Centres, The National Academies. [UNEP International Environment Technology Centre, Rocky Mountain Institute, Forum for the Future (UK)]
Community advocates	Australian Collaboration (for a Just and Sustainable Australia), The Western Australian Collaboration, Our Community

each step of the way our partners and collaborators have appreciated this approach. For instance, the project is set up as a not-for-profit organization with all royalties, grants and revenue used to support further initiatives. It is the right way to honour the generosity of our co-authors, endorsees and partners, many of whom have dedicated their lives to making the world a better place, bestowing upon our team their lifelong work in order to reach new audiences.

This book project and website provided a catalyst for researchers and professionals, government public servants, activists and business people to engage and contribute their thoughts, and papers. We knew that if we were serious about building a platform for wise and constructive change we needed to involve as many leading stakeholders as possible in this project through a whole of society approach to sustainability. We decided that the most appropriate way to seek sponsorship to develop the project was to identify the main groups and bodies in society (arbitrarily grouped into eight fields as shown in Table 23.1) that would need to be involved to truly give the project the best opportunity to succeed, and we approached them in turn for support. Our goal was to seek both financial and in-kind support, with no group asked to contribute more than an eighth of the total budget to ensure that no one sector would be unevenly represented. Many groups who were unable to provide direct support volunteered hours of peer review and mentoring time to the project.

As our team was made up of young engineers and scientists with Charlie, Cheryl, Nick and James having previously been volunteer Presidents of state chapters of Young Engineers Australia, a group of Engineers Australia, and Mike being active in the science community, the logical place to start was the engineering professional body, the Institution of Engineers Australia, and the leading science research body, the Commonwealth Scientific and Industrial Research Organisation (CSIRO). The team approached both the Engineers Australia Director for Engineering Practice, Martin Dwyer and the Director for Marketing and Communication, Steve Williamson, with the proposal for the publication and the response was amazing! Within a very short period of time it was agreed that the Institution would become the administrative host for the project as a form of in-kind support, providing strong accountability as to the use of funds and also making the first financial contribution to the project becoming the first Foundation Partner. Since this time, the members of the project have received a great deal of mentoring and support from many of the Institution's leaders, such as Dr Peter Greenwood and Doug Jones (Presidents), John Boshier (CEO) and a number of staff members. During the formation of the project, our team received a great deal of mentoring from both Geoff McAlpine and Elizabeth Heij of the CSIRO and when we were ready to present the publication proposal, Geoff McAlpine arranged a meeting with Geoff Clarke, on behalf of Geoff Garrett, CEO of CSIRO and it was decided that CSIRO would also become a Foundation Partner along with Engineers Australia and make a strong financial contribution to the project.

A relationship with such bodies provided unique leverage points for change, such as that in education, given that the Engineering professional body in Australia accredits university courses and is looked to by practising engineers to provide leadership in the emerging fields of engineering. In addition to these groups, our team approached Ron Clarke, a world-record holding Olympic athlete, at the Centre for the Encouragement of Philanthropy in Australia (CEPA), as they had shown strong support for environmental education activities in the past. In this group we found a very receptive partner and together with a personal contribution from the projects co-founder, James Moody, we achieved the seed funding needed to allow the team to literally 'quit our day jobs' and focus on the development of the project. Without the initial support from Engineers Australia, CSIRO and CEPA Trust our team would not have been able to build a strong platform to develop our project, not only through the financial support but, equally as important, through the access to leading research and peer review. Building on from this, the team gained significant support from partners such as the RMIT Global Sustainability Unit, Queensland EPA Sustainable Industries Division, Environment Business Australia, Barton Group and, through the donation of our website, by Australian web developer Izilla.

With this support, the team was able to undertake an extensive programme to meet with a range of leaders in the field, both in Australia and internationally, to discuss the various issues and through discussion, many times one on one, learn from a wealth of experience and knowledge to create the thesis for this publication.[13] Following this, our team developed a précis of the argument we intended to develop in the publication and invited peer review and comments from our newly formed network. Realizing that we needed to ensure that the work built on from the best in the field, we approached the likes of Amory Lovins, Hunter Lovins, Bill McDonough, Alan AtKisson, Michael Fairbanks and David Suzuki and were given strong support in each case, which heavily influenced the development of the publication.

The project is supported by a number of structures to enhance communication channels and engagement from partners and supporters. The team approached a number of leaders in the field to join the projects Advisory Board to provide high level advice and mentoring. Additionally each of the organizations involved were invited to nominate an operational representative to the projects Steering Committee to provide a clear point of contact and input on operational issues such as peer review, the contribution of case studies and media related material. Finally, a Working Group was formed to engage other young professionals and researchers in sustainable development related activities.[14] The project is driven by the Secretariat who are accountable and responsible for all the day to day activities of TNEP. The TNEP Secretariat is currently made up of project founders Charlie Hargroves and Mike Smith along with Cheryl Paten and Nick Palousis.

Communication to the supporting network is achieved mainly through a quarterly update from the secretariat that can be subscribed to and downloaded from the project's website. TNEP does this to ensure that at each point project goals are clearly communicated, so that potential synergies are not missed and collaborations can be enhanced to reduce the resources and funding needed to deliver initiatives. To supplement the project updates, the secretariat issues periodic announcements of special events, partner information and achievements and developments of the project. TNEP is in a position to report on a range of exciting project opportunities over the coming years, including education material, additional publications, design guides, training materials and active partnerships within industry ranging from data collection and interpretation to development and post conflict reconstruction activities internationally. Your purchase of this book will help the project to develop a range of initiatives into the future.

Our team is grateful for the amazing level of support received in developing this project. In hindsight we set ourselves a difficult task of building a network around the development of the project and doing our best to ensure that the key groups, peak bodies and individuals were involved. This called for many hours of conversation, emails, proposal writing and research, adding significantly to our cost and time to deliver the publication. However, the genuine level of engagement achieved throughout the project by undertaking such a task truly highlights the saying that 'the process is as important as the product'.

With the generosity of TNEP's partners and the spirit of genuine partnerships we are confident that TNEP has now built up the start of a significant network that can help to achieve an ecologically sustainable future. We hope that this story of how TNEP formed and why it is built on a partnership model will inspire other young engineers and scientists to do the same in their respective countries. We hope that peak bodies globally support the genuine initiative of its young scientists and engineers, as CSIRO and Engineers Australia have done here in Australia through supporting our project. If you would like to know more about TNEP or follow its progress, please visit our website (www.naturaledgeproject.net). Charlie Hargroves, TNEP Coordinator, is the point of contact for further information on partnering with TNEP, collaborations, training, speaking and education material based on the material presented, and can be contacted at charlie@naturaledgeproject.net. For further enquiries about the content and research of this book and other TNEP projects please contact Mike Smith, TNEP Content Coordinator at mike@naturaledgeproject.net.

NOTES

Foreword by L. Hunter Lovins

1 The thesis behind this Foreword is being developed further into a publication now being prepared by Hunter Lovins and her colleagues with TNEP. Refer to Chapter 10 for a summary of the publication designed to enable leaders to put the ideas of this book into practice.
2 Atkins (2004).
3 Peters (2004); www.tompeters.com/reimagine/.
4 Drucker (2001).
5 Grove-White (1997).
6 www.solcomhouse.com/shell.htm.
7 *Business Wire* (2000).
8 *The New York Times*, 12 March 2004.
9 *New York Times* (2004).
10 Holliday et al (2002, p21).
11 Pers comm., Professor Peter Newman, Murdoch University, sustainability adviser to the Premier of Western Australia, September 2003.
12 Holliday et al (2002).
13 Willard (2002).
14 Hawken et al (1999, p245). Both *Natural Capitalism* (Hawken et al, 1999) and *Factor Four* (von Weizsäcker et al, 1997) document hundreds of such savings opportunities.

Foreword by Michael Fairbanks

1 The four constituents are from the forthcoming book, *The Prosperity Event: How Business Strategy Transforms Nations*, edited by Michael Fairbanks.
2 Ray (1998, p9).
3 Ibid, p12.
4 Amartya Sen discusses the difference between a stock and flow in *The Concept of Wealth* (1996).
5 Michael Fairbanks developed the heuristic of the seven forms of capital through a meta-analysis of recent literature on economics and social capital. Examples of the latter include: Coleman (1988); North (1990); Olson (1982); and Serageldin and Dasgupta (1997).
6 For the best practical example of this view of prosperity, look at James Wolfensohn's internal, but now widely accessible memorandum on the *Comprehensive Development Framework* (CDF), spring of 1999. The president of the World Bank has begun to implement a 'holistic' approach to development, around the concept of a 'social balance sheet'.
7 Sen (1996, p7).
8 Sowell (1998, p329).

9   Much of this rich literature is synthesized in Inglehart (1997).
10   Inglehart (1997, Ch 1) demonstrates these connections with the *World Values Survey* in the early part of this decade and concludes that 'far from being randomly related, *cultural, economic and political variables are closely related*'. This survey provided a broader range in the variation of data than had ever been available before. It is drawn from over 56,000 respondents in 43 countries representing 70% of the world's population. They varied from populations with a US$300 per capita income to US$30,000; and from long established democracies with market economies to just-former socialist countries, and authoritarian regimes. And these conclusions often appear to hold across levels of education, occupation and income. He also reports that for richer countries there is a point of diminishing returns where the subjective values become more important than the objective values.
11   Sachs and Warner (1995).
12   Krugman (1994, pp113–121).
13   Fairbanks and Lindsey (1997, Chs 1–7).
14   *Classic socialism*: Cuba and North Korea; *monetarism*: Chicago school, Chile between 1973 and 1983, Thatcher's United Kingdom. Keith Griffin (1989) at Berkeley categorizes four other archetypes of government strategy: *redistribution*; *agriculture-led*; *import substitution*; and *open trade*.

Introduction

1   Solow (1986, 1992); Stiglitz (2003).
2   Glenn and Gordon (1998).

Chapter 1

1   McDonough and Braungart (2002).
2   Anderson and Cavanagh (1996).
3   Braithwaite (1980); Castleman (1979, 1981); References cited in Braithwaite and Drahos (2000, p267).
4   Leonard (1988); Wheeler and Mody (1992); Jaffe et al (1995); References cited in Vogel (1995).
5   Porter and van der Linde (1995a, 1995b); Schmidheiny (1992); Panayotu and Vincent (1997); Holliday et al (2002).
6   Porter (1990, p648).
7   Benedick (1991, p55).
8   Braithwaite and Drahos (2000).
9   Porter (1990, p645).
10   Blazejczak and Lubbe (1993); Feketekuty (1993); Rowlands (1995, pp30–31).
11   Brown et al (2000); in addition, refer to the Green Jobs section of ACF (2000).
12   Weale (1992).
13   Brown, R. et al (1993).
14   Hawken et al (1999, Ch 6).
15   Lovins and Lovins (1997).
16   The Environmental Sustainability Index is an Initiative of the Global Leaders of Tomorrow Environment Task Force, World Economic Forum Annual Meeting 2002. In collaboration with: Yale Center for Environmental Law and Policy Yale University Center for International Earth Science Information Network Columbia University.
17   Rocky Mountain Institute, McDonough and Braungart Design Chemistry, Natural Capitalism, Inc, The Wuppertal Institute, Australian Conservation Foundation (Natural Advantage: Blueprint for A Sustainable Australia).
18   Porter and van der Linde (1995a).
19   Button and Weyman-Jones (1992).
20   Hawken et al (1999).

21   McDonough and Braungart (1998).
22   Hawken et al (1999, p116).
23   Birkeland (2002).
24   See Section 2 for further explanation.
25   The WBCSD was created in 1992 and in 2003 comprised over 160 major international corporations from more than 30 countries. It also benefits from a global network of 35 national and regional business councils and partner organizations involving over 1000 business leaders globally.
26   Womack and Jones (1996).
27   Swiss watches command top dollar around the world. The aluminium in each watch costs approximately 30 cents. Clearly, Swiss watch companies have identified and targeted being world competitive in the most profitable part of the supply chain.
28   It is widely recognized that it is in a nation's economic interests to add value (Value Adding) to its raw and natural resources before they are exported to command premium price for the export of these resources. Refer to the report of the MMSD Australia project, 'Facing the Future' (Sheehy and Dickie, 2002).
29   Collins and Porras (1994).
30   Foster and Kaplan (2001).
31   Ibid.
32   Ibid.
33   Porter and van der Linde (1995a, 1995b).
34   Anderson (1998).
35   Refer to the proceedings of the 8th International Greening of Industry Network Conference, 1999.
36   Foss et al (1999).
37   Commonwealth of Australia (1997, p28).
38   Gordon Moore first expressed Moore's Law over 30 years ago. Moore, the founder of Intel, noticed that his engineers had an amazing capability to double the processing power of the chips they were designing at a regular rate. He used this insight to come up with his bold prediction. This prediction has held true for the last 30 years.
39   Transaction costs are the costs of undertaking transactions between purchaser and seller, supplier and distributor.
40   Downes and Mui (1998).
41   The first economist to study transaction costs in business was Ronald Coase. In his 1937 article 'The Nature of the Firm' Coase suggested that it was the costs of transactions which dictated the size and core business of a firm. For example, a sheet of paper may only cost a fraction of a cent, but if you were to purchase it one sheet at a time the cost of your time would far outweigh the cost of the piece of paper. By purchasing the paper in bulk, you reduce the transaction cost of obtaining the piece of paper to an acceptable level. Coase took this idea one step further. He made the case that firms actually formed in order to reduce transaction costs. For example, in order to purchase reams of paper individually the transaction costs would still be high; firms would pool everything from marketing to the stationery cabinet (where reams of paper would reside). These transaction costs would even determine when firms would decrease in size; eventually the stationery cabinet (or department) would become too costly to maintain, and would become a prime candidate for 'outsourcing'; reducing these transaction costs still further. Coase eventually won the Nobel Prize for Economics for this research.
42   Lovins et al (2002).
43   Womack and Jones (1996, Ch 2).
44   This has been given names such as 'reducing our negative impact on the environment' by a Factor of 4 (a 75 per cent reduction in resource intensity) or a Factor of 10 (a 90 per cent reduction in resource intensity). In short we need to 'do more, with less for longer'.
45   Weaver et al (2000).
46   Benyus (1997).
47   When intelligent engineering and design is brought into play, big resource savings often

cost even less up front than small or incremental resource savings. Whole systems engineering allows companies to tunnel through the cost barrier and achieve multiple benefits. Chapter 6 of the book *Natural Capitalism: The Next Industrial Revolution* has numerous case studies of this.

48 von Weizsäcker et al (1997).
49 Pigou (1932).
50 Jones (1974, pp116, 127); Hammond (1946); For an introductory book on the subject that provides an overview of many of the issues relating to energy discussed in this book see Rifkin (2002).
51 This material was drawn from the United Nations Environment Programme Press Release, 'Impact of climate change to cost the world US$300 billion a year'.
52 Refer to the CSIRO Ecosystem Services Project. (Publications from the Australian Productivity Commission include: *Creating Markets for Ecosystem Services*, 19 June 2002, *Harnessing Private Sector Conservation of Biodiversity, Creating Markets for Biodiversity: A Case Study of Earth Sanctuaries Ltd Constraints on Private Conservation of Biodiversity, Cost Sharing for Biodiversity Conservation: A Conceptual Framework*.)
53 Costanza et al (1997).
54 WBCSD (1992).
55 Daily and Ellison (2003).
56 Ehrenberg (2003).
57 Every product we buy, every service we use, has an impact on the planet, otherwise known as an environmental load. This can be measured by measuring a product's ecological footprint. How large that ecological footprint is depends on the amount of energy and materials needed to make, transport, package, market and approve it. All products have this 'secret life' that most of us never consider.
58 Lovins (2004).
59 Ibid, pp20–21.
60 World Commission on Dams (2000).
61 The International Rivers Network (IRN) has developed a booklet providing background on the formation of the WCD, a detailed summary of the WCD's findings and recommendations, and responses from NGOs, institutions and governments to the report.
62 Sutton (2000).
63 Wilson et al (1998).
64 *Newsweek* Special Issue, 37, 'Boom Towns: Is Asia's Urban Explosion a Blessing or a Curse?'.
65 The World Federation of Engineering Organisations (WFEO) has identified megacities as a major area of concern for the future.
66 World Bank (2003, Ch 6).
67 Newman and Kenworthy (1999).
68 Kenworthy (2003).
69 Refer to Chapter 19 of this publication on Sustainable Urban Transport, based on the findings of a study of the Newman and Kenworthy (1999) study.
70 Kenworthy and Laube (2001).
71 Newman and Kenworthy (1999).
72 Lovins et al (2004), available online at www.oilendgame.org.
73 Fairbanks and Lindsey (1997).
74 Cited in Roodman (1999, p55).
75 Roodman (1999, p54).
76 Sheehy and Dickie (2002).
77 Romer (1994).
78 Romer (1993).
79 McMichael (2002); McMichael (2001); IPCC (2001a, Ch 5).
80 Lovins and Lovins (1982).
81 Klare (2001).

82   Robinson (2002).
83   Government of Western Australia (2002, p198).

Chapter 2

1   Raskin et al (2002).
2   WRI (2000).
3   In the United Kingdom, the Blair Government published a report on how a 60 percent reduction in emissions might be achieved. Stating that the UK 'is likely to face increasingly demanding carbon reduction targets', it concluded: 'Credible scenarios for 2050 can deliver a 60 per cent cut in CO_2 emissions, but large changes would be needed both in the energy system and in society'.
4   Turton et al (2002).
5   Allen Consulting (2003). Economic studies previously had notoriously struggled to factor accurately in energy efficiency and demand management strategies. Hence these more recent studies are significant.
6   ABC News in Science (2001) *Species on the Move Due to Global Warming*, 6 September.
7   Bright (2000, Ch 2, pp22–38.
8   Myers (1995); Myers (1996a).
9   Abramovitz and Dunn (1998).
10 USGCRP (1998).
11 Gliessman (1998).
12 USGCRP (1998).
13 Tainter (1988, p133).
14 McNeill (1975, p131).
15 CSIRO (2001).
16 ACF (2000, Ch 13).

Chapter 3

1   Toshiba's new de-colourable ink aims to boost paper recycling and contribute to reduced environmental loads. Toshiba has already developed a prototype de-colourable printing ink that can be easily rendered invisible by even low heat treatment or solvents and the new ink promises efficient cost effective paper recycling and allows the re-use of huge volumes of paper.
2   'The welfare of a nation can scarcely be inferred from a measurement of national income as defined by the GDP... goals for "more" growth should specify of what and for what', Simon Kuznets (1962), creator of GDP.
3   Smith, B (2003).
4   Hamilton and Diesendorf (1997, pp122–123).
5   Dodds (1997, p–122).
6   See for example work by Philip Sutton, Director of Strategy at Green Innovations: www.green-innovations.asn.au/Sustainability-meaning.htm.
7   An address to The International Society of Ecological Economists by the Federal Minister for the Environment and Heritage Senator the Hon Robert Hill, Australian National University, Canberra, 6 July 2000.
8   CSIRO (2000).
9   Table 3.1 represents a summary of the items contained in the various documents; for an expanded version refer to www.naturaledgeproject.net.
10 Dasgupta and Maler (2001); Hamilton and Clemens (1999).
11 Arrow et al (2003).
12 Pearson et al (2003).
13 Hamilton and Clemens (1999).
14 Hamilton (1998).
15 Pearson et al (2003).

16   By this criterion, sustainable development involves the maintenance of an overall stock of productive capital (including natural capital), where distinct capital items are weighted by appropriate dollar values, and these dollar values (shadow prices) indicate their degree of economic substitutability with each other.

17   Pearson et al (2003).

18   Hawken et al (1999).

19   von Weizsäcker et al (1997).

20   McDonough and Braungart (2002).

21   Birkeland (2002).

22   AtKisson (1999).

23   McDonough and Braungart (2002).

24   Birkeland (2002).

25   von Weizsäcker et al (1997).

26   As described in an interview with Professor Alan Pears of RMIT University, Melbourne.

27   *EcoGeneration: Magazine of the Australian EcoGeneration Association*, Issue 8, October/November 2001 pp14–15.

28   The Australian Federal Government's Cool Communities Program runs workshops on how most homes can be retrofitted cost effectively with adequate insulation and outside blinds on windows to dramatically decrease the need for air-conditioning.

29   Ken Henry, Head of Treasury Australia, Speech to the 30th Anniversary of the ANU Masters Program.

30   Such as the network of governments involved in the National Councils of Sustainable Development Network, Regional Government for Sustainable Development Network and with the International Council for Local Environment Initiatives.

Chapter 4

1   Keynesian economics is an economic theory proposed by British economist John Maynard Keynes. His major work came in 1936 in *The General Theory of Employment and Economics*. Keynes' ideas created a revolution in the world of economics called the Keynesian Revolution and he proposed the idea that governments use deficit spending in order to bring about economic recovery.

2   The Organization of Petroleum Exporting Countries (OPEC) was formed in 1960, but its strength and impact were not felt until 1973, when the cartel decided to raise oil prices dramatically by cutting back on world supply.

3   Greenwald and Stiglitz (1986).

4   For instance, recently the corporate scandals in the US and, to a lesser extent other countries, have led even conservative governments to acknowledge the role and importance of governments, regulation and accountancy standards.

5   Hanley et al (1997); Dovers (2001).

6   Hosted by the Government of Western Australia, the conference brought together both government delegations and the academic community from around the world to focus on the issue of the role of regional and state governments in achieving sustainability. Refer to Section 3 for the resulting Fremantle Declaration – Passing the torch to the regions.

7   Australian Treasury Department (2001).

8   Energy Efficiency Measures in the Building Code of Australia, Energy efficiency measures for houses were introduced in the BCA on 1 January 2003 (Amendment No 12). Regulation Document (RD2003-1) for multiresidential buildings (Class 2, 3 and 4 buildings).

9   Brennan (2003).

10   The WBCDS was created in 1992. It is made up of over 160 major international corporations covering 20 significant sectors, from more than 30 countries. It also benefits from a global network of 35 national and regional business councils and partner organizations involving over 1000 business leaders globally.

11   WBCSD (1997).

12 European Commission (2001).
13 World Bank (1997).
14 Again contrary to public perception economists have been working on the real costs of externalities like congestion costs to the economy for decades. The Nobel Laureate James Tobin was one of the first economists to study and attempt to quantify 'congestion costs' to the economy.
15 Newman (2003).

Chapter 5

1   Holm and Sorensen (1995) define globalization as the 'intensification of economic, political, social and cultural relations across borders'.
2   Braithwaite and Drahos (2000). The award-winning work of Braithwaite and Drahos provides clear frameworks and strategies forward for all actors. Their work, the result of over 500 interviews over 10 years, shows the range of people wishing to work for a race to the top.
3   Ibid, p519.
4   At present, basic trade rules dictate that imports of goods may not be restricted because of their environmental impacts on their production processes. The lack of environmental policies in the exporting country cannot be given as a valid reason to restrict trade unless the products themselves are the source of the pollution for the importing country. Hence, the WTO considers recycled and non-recycled paper 'like' products and cannot be discriminated against.
5   Heij (2002).
6   FOE, *Trade Case Study: US Ban on the Use of More Polluting Petrol in City Areas* (aka the 'Venezuela-Petrol Dispute'), Friends of the Earth International.
7   Heij (2002).

Chapter 6

1   Anderson (1998).
2   Fairbanks and Lindsay (1997).
3   Porter (1995).
4   Ibid.
5   Foster and Kaplan (2001).
6   Porter (1990)
7   The 'CSIRO Solutions for Greenhouse' website provides an extensive overview of how to cost effectively reduce greenhouse emissions.
8   CSIRO, Australia's leading science and engineering research body, provides up to date news on their latest innovations, and exciting business opportunities online including a free sustainability monthly electronic newsletter, edited by Elizabeth Heij.
9   UNEP's Industry Best Practice Database highlights industry as a partner for sustainable development in a series of reports developed by UNEP in conjunction with various industry organizations. The reports gauge the progress across 22 private sectors towards sustainable development.
10 Speech by George Yeo, Minister for Trade and Industry, at the Singapore-Stanford Partnership (SSP) MOU Signing on 25 February 2003.
11 Building the Future, *Australian Financial Review*, 10 December 2001.
12 Rocky Mountain Institute: Green Development Services CD-ROM of European green buildings, World Green Building Council.
13 Wilson et al (1998, p18).
14 *EcoGeneration*: Magazine of the Australian EcoGeneration Association, Issue 12, June/July 2002, p12.
15 Gipe (2002).
16 Sinclair Knight Merz (2001, p17).

17   McDonough and Braungart (2002) point out that the word 'eco-efficiency' was first used by the WBCSD in their 1992 publication 'Changing Course'. It seeks to encapsulate the idea of using fewer resources and creating less waste and pollution whilst providing the same or better services. According to the WBCSD, eco-efficiency entails the following: a reduction in the material intensity of goods or services; a reduction in the energy intensity of goods or services; reduced dispersion of toxic materials; improved recyclability; maximum use of renewable resources; increased durability of products; and greater service intensity of goods and services.

18   Amory Lovins interview, 'Natural Capitalism' as broadcast on Radio National's Background Briefing.

19   Cascio (1993); AMA (1996); Dorfman (1991); Littler et al (1997).

20   Collins and Porras (1994).

21   Gundling (2000).

22   Sonnenfeld (2004).

23   Braithwaite and Drahos (2000).

24   Ibid.

25   Fairbanks and Lindsay (1997).

26   For an overview of further case studies and reports on these issues we recommend the following sources: Smith, D (2000); UNDP (2001, 2003).

27   Smith, D (2000).

28   Deni Greene Consulting Services (2001).

29   Annan (1998).

30   Rainforest Action Network (2000) *Democrats to Citigroup: Show Us the Money! – Citigroup Receives Award from DNC: America's #1 Bank is #1 in Democracy Buy-Out*, Press Release, 17 August.

31   Corporate Governance is the system by which companies are directed and controlled. The goal is to improve the structures and processes of companies to improve their performance and make them more accountable to shareholders and other stakeholders. It covers issues such as the nature and structure of the boards, financial reporting, issues of transparency, conflicts of interest and separation of powers.

32   Chapter by leading sustainability consultant Molly Harris Olsen in Dunphy et al (2000).

33   Taken from a transcript from Hunter Lovins' presentation to the Sopris Foundation, 13 July 2002 Aspen, Colorado.

34   For further reading on organizational change Dunphy et al (2002); Dunphy et al (2000).

35   Arora and Cason (1995, 1996).

36   DeCanio and Watkins (1998).

37   Recent estimates indicate that in 1996 the Australian chemical industry had a turnover of AU$35 billion, and employed approximately 80,000 people, Environment Australia, *National Profile of Chemicals Management Infrastructure in Australia*, 1998.

38   Anastas and Williamson (1994).

39   Anastas et al (2000).

40   Anastas and Williamson (1998).

41   Quoted from the Foreword to Anastas and Williamson (1998).

42   Hawken et al (1999, Ch 6).

43   von Weizsäcker et al (1997).

44   Hawken et al (1999, p117).

45   Australian Greenhouse Office Motor Solutions Online: comprehensive information and guidance, as well as practical information and tools, to help you make the right choices about electric motors. Achieving best practice will improve motor system reliability, minimize energy costs, maximize profits and, ultimately, reduce greenhouse gas emissions.

46   Porter and van der Linde (1995a).

47   Foss et al (1999).

48   McDonough and Braungart (1998).

49   Ibid.

50 Benyus (1997).
51 The WFEO is a non-governmental organization (NGO) and was established with the support of UNESCO in 1968. The WFEO currently represents an estimated 15 million engineers. ComTech is the WFEO Standing Committee on Technology. Its purpose is the sharing, transferring and assessment of technology.
52 von Weizsäcker et al (1997).
53 DeCanio (1998).
54 Feldman et al (1997).
55 Drozdiak (2000).
56 Lovins and Link (2002).
57 Ibid.
58 NZBCSD (2002).
59 Dumaresq and Greene (2001).
60 Womack and Jones (1996).
61 Jones (2003).
62 Ibid.

Chapter 7

1   Australian companies can join the Buy Recycled Business Alliance network that already represents over AU$30 billion worth of purchasing power.
2   Porter (1990).
3   Forde (2003).
4   OTF Group is a strategy consulting firm based in Watertown, MA with project offices worldwide. The firm has led cluster competitiveness for the last 12 years in more than 25 countries and dozens of industries.
5   Clusters consist of all stakeholders in a given industry, including but not limited to private sector enterprises, suppliers, customers, labour, government, research institutes, training institutions, professional associations and other groups. Clusters promote firm-level competitiveness by increasing both the cooperation and competition among firms. The relationships developed within clusters accelerate product development and improve access to specialized inputs, market information and a skilled workforce. Developing strong clusters helps regions position themselves to respond to the challenges of the knowledge-based global economy.
6   Rogers (1995, p262).
7   See description of the Seven Forms of Capital (Cultural, Human, Knowledge, Institutional, Financial, Infrastructure, Raw Materials) in Fairbanks (2000).
8   Rwandan economic objectives and coffee sector data is from the forthcoming article by Rudasingwa and Donahue (2004).
9   Other stakeholders may include 'future generations'.
10 Figures from On The Frontier (OTF) Group Presentation (2002) *Rwanda Coffee Strategy and Action Priorities*, developed as part of the Rwanda Competitiveness and Innovation Program, 15 July.
11 Concept relates to the third principle of *Natural Capitalism* outlined in Hawken et al (1999).
12 The Jamaican energy sector example is based on preliminary meetings between the Natural Capitalism Group lead by Hunter Lovins, the OTF Group and Jamaican energy sector players in April 2003.
13 The cost figures estimated for efficiency technology are based on research conducted for the book, *Small is Profitable*, Lovins et al (2002).
14 There are over 2.5 million smallholding cocoa farmers (under 5 hectares) supplying 90% of the worldwide cocoa production according to the International Cocoa Organization.

Chapter 8

1   Mays (2003).
2   This articulation has been contributed by Dr Ian Woods, Senior Research Analyst, Sustainable Funds, AMP Global Investors, Australian Equities.
3   Lajeunesse et al (2001).
4   Figure 8.1 demonstrates the approach to assessing corporate sustainability by one investment institution.
5   Suzuki and Dressel (2002).
6   Responsible Shopper provides access to information regarding various products from clothing to shoes to toothpaste, investigating hundreds of companies on a range of issues, including sweatshops, pollution, ethics and discrimination.
7   IFC (2002).
8   Misra and Misra (2002).
9   Pfeffer (1998).
10 Jones (2001, p47) quoting Sir John Brown CEO of BP Petroleum.
11 Wilkinson et al (2001).
12 Sheehy and Dickie (2002).
13 The Federal Government of Australia has published online and in hardcopy 17 booklets of best practice in environmental management and mining. (Refer to Australian Government Sustainable Industry: Sustainable Minerals).
14 Robinson (2001).
15 Braithwaite and Drahos (2000).
16 Ibid, p269.
17 Ibid, p280.
18 Kumarasivam (1996).
19 Thailand Environment Institute (1999).
20 USAID (2002).
21 This material was drawn from the UNEP Press Release, 'Impact of climate change to cost the world US$300 billion a year'.
22 The Carbon Disclosure Project began on 1 November 2003 with a group of 87 institutional investors with assets of over US$9 trillion under management who wrote to the 500 largest quoted companies in the world, asking for the disclosure of investment-relevant information concerning their greenhouse gas emissions.
23 We will not attempt to debate here the relative merits or otherwise of the name given to this form of investment but concentrate instead on its salient attributes, and therefore we will assume for the purpose of this discussion that the terms are synonymous.
24 Mays (2003).
25 Garz et al (2002).
26 Dunstan (2003).
27 Deni Greene Consulting Services (2001).
28 Lewis (2002, p20).
29 Deni Greene Consulting Services (2001).
30 Margolis and Walsh (2001).
31 Schafer and Stederoth (2002).
32 Hildyard and Mansley (2001).
33 Geczy et al (2003).
34 Angel and Rivoli (1997).
35 Alfred Rappaport is one of the founders of the shareholder value mindset, which gained importance in the 1980s and is still growing and increasingly accepted worldwide. Rappaport has written a ground-breaking classic book on Corporate Strategy in relation to Shareholder Value creation, *Creating Shareholder Value – The New Standard for Business Performance*, 1986.
36 Garz et al (2002).

Chapter 9

1   In Australia for instance, ACF's Corporate Reputation Index for 2002, shows little change in corporate performance in Australia's top 100 companies from previous years. A 1999 review of 30 Australian organizations found that their standards of environmental reporting were very poor compared to global companies.

2   Suzuki and Dressel (2002, p46).

3   Lovins and Lovins (1997) Also highly recommended is Lovins and Lovins (1982, Ch 17).

4   Schaltegger et al (2000).

5   Lovins and Link (2002).

6   Refer to the 2002 Towers Perrin Report, *Worldwide Total Remuneration*, 2001–02.

7   Stiglitz (2003, p143).

8   Healy (2003).

9   Duty of superannuation trustees: in Australia under Section 52(2)(f) of the Superannuation Industry (Supervision) Act 1993 binds trustees to ensure that the investment strategy of the fund pays due regard to: the risk involved; the likely returns; the expected cash flow requirements; the extent to which the investments are diverse or involve the fund being exposed to risks from inadequate diversification; the liquidity of the funds investments having regard to its expected cash flow requirements and the ability of the fund to discharge its existing and prospective liabilities.

10 Linking Screened Investments to Shareholder Value: An Overview of Screened Investments and the Potential for Impact on Shareholder Value. Erik Mather Senior Manager, Screened Investments.

11 Guerard (1997, p11).

12 Lovins and Link (2003).

13 In Australia, The Department of Environment and Heritage has developed a set of environmental management and performance indicators based on the GRI, but modified for the Australian context. These could be used as the basis for mandatory reporting indicators.

14 Berger (2004).

15 Useful summaries of international developments include Emtairah (2002) and Mansley (2003).

16 Commission Recommendation of 30 May 2001 on the recognition, measurement and disclosure of environmental issues in the annual accounts and annual reports of companies (2001/453/EC).

17 MOE (2003) (in Japanese).

18 Mukoyama and Hiroyuki (2002) (in Japanese).

19 *The Economist* (1994) 'After Valdez', 18 June, p20.

20 Department of Environment and Heritage, Australia publication, 'Environmental Management Accounting: An introduction and case studies for Australia.' Professor Craig Deegan FCA of RMIT University, Melbourne. Sponsored by DEH, EPA Victoria, and the Australian Institute of Chartered Accountants.

21 Burritt et al (2002).

22 Schaltegger et al (2000).

23 Chambers (1966, p54); Schaltegger, S, and Burritt (2000, p45).

24 Parker (1999).

25 Schaltegger and Burritt (2000, p58).

26 Schaltegger et al (2000).

27 Schaltegger and Burritt (2000, p59).

28 Ibid, p90.

29 Ibid, pp61–63.

30 Ibid, p261.

31 The Japanese Institute of Certified Public Accountants (JICPA) has released Environmental Report Assurance Guidelines (Interim Report) for third party reviews of environmental information, indicating the close relationship between the accountancy profession and

environmental accounting information in Japan. These guidelines provide a definition of the level of assurance, guidance for the evaluation of information accuracy/completeness and environmental management information systems.

32 Burritt et al (2003).
33 Kokubu and Eliko (2001).
34 Saio et al (2002) (in Japanese).
35 Porter and van der Linde (1995a, 1995b).
36 Australian Government Department of Industry, Tourism and Resources, Energy Efficiency Best Practice: Making a Difference, Working with industry to achieve results; Holliday et al (2002); Paton (2001).
37 Palmer et al (1995).
38 Jaffe and Stavins (1994); DeCanio (1993, 1994b).
39 DeCanio (1998, 1994a).
40 DeCanio (1997).
41 Kreps (1997).
42 Teece (1990).
43 Kahneman et al (1982); Conlisk (1996).
44 Leibenstein (1987).
45 Paton (1994).
46 Ocasio (1997).
47 Nelson and Winter (1982); Nelson (1995).
48 Nelson (1992).
49 Weibull (1995).
50 Howarth et al (2000).
51 For further information on these topics refer to Segerson and Miceli (1998); Segerson (1999).

Chapter 10

1   Endorsement of the ICC Charter is voluntar where the companies that sign it commit themselves to respecting its 16 principles for environmental management. The ICC reviews how companies that have endorsed the Charter are applying the principles.
2   Refer to www.naturaledgeproject.net for further information regarding this initiative.

Chapter 11

1   Weaver et al (2000).
2   Ibid.
3   Not all UK programmes identified in the country report as addressing sustainable development have been included in this table to allow a comparison of the programmes across the seven countries. In fact, in total there are 35 in the UK alone.
4   Dr Steve Dovers' research activities include theoretical and policy dimensions of sustainability, institutional arrangements for resource management, science–policy linkages, and Australian environmental history. Steve is a co-author of the upcoming publication *Institutional change for sustainable development* (Cheltenham: Edward Elgar), which reviews major developments in institutions and sustainability over the last ten years.
5   Government of Western Australia (2003); Armstrong et al (2002).
6   Newman (2003).
7   A subsidy = a policy that ensures that risks, rewards and costs are altered in favour of the actions of a few groups or companies' actions.
8   World Bank (2003, Ch 2, p28).
9   Roodman (1999) (this publication provides a detailed discussion of government subsidies and the environment).
10 Ibid.

11 As opposed to pollution that originates from a specific point (e.g., sulphur dioxide emissions from the chimney stack of a coal-fired power station), non-point source pollution cannot be traced to a single point of origin (e.g., in the case of fertilizers, they seep into rivers and streams from innumerable sections of agricultural land).

12 As highlighted in the 2002 Australian Prime Minister's Science, Engineering & Innovation Council report *Sustaining our Natural Systems and Biodiversity*.

13 World Bank (2003, pp13–37).

14 Australian Treasury Department (2001, p93).

15 Whilst Hardin's paper (Hardin, 1968) provides the catalyst for recent work in this area, for centuries philosophers have commented on it. Even Aristotle wrote that 'What is common to the greatest number has the least care bestowed upon it. Everyone thinks chiefly of their own interest'.

16 Hardin (1998).

17 Arnold and Campbell (1986).

18 Becker and Ostrom (1995); Ostrom (1986).

19 Ostrom et al (2003).

20 Milton et al (1997).

21 Gandy (1997).

22 Ellsworth et al (1997).

23 Ostrom et al (2002).

24 Roodman (1999).

25 Bridgman and Davis (2000).

26 World Bank (1997).

27 The ACT Schools for the 21st Century Program: Assessment by Exhibition, Student Exhibition Teachers' Kit.

28 Felizardo et al (2002).

29 USA National Council for Sustainable Development, 1996–2000 chaired by Molly Harris Olsen.

30 Leadbeter et al (1999) Ch 7, p84.

31 Murtough et al (2002).

32 Sutton (2004). Sutton describes a proposal to mobilize communities to achieve sustainability ... fast. Concern about the environment has been growing for many decades but most communities around the world have yet to achieve a 'take-off' where commitment to sustainability is seen as an urgent priority. Sutton presents a proposal for a Race to Sustainability, a global race against time.

33 Joint Media Release, Minister for the Environment and Heritage, The Hon Dr David Kemp & Federal Minister for Agriculture, Fisheries and Forestry, Warren Truss, AU$360,000 *for Market-based Projects Tackling Dryland Salinity*, 13 June 2003 – K0133/WTJ164.

34 In their report '*Robust Separation: A Search for a Generic Framework to Simplify Registration and Trading of Interests in Natural Resources*', Professor Mike Young and Jim McColl from CSIRO have outlined a detailed, clear national approach to the issue. This will be discussed in detail in Section 4, Chapter 20.

35 Government of Western Australia (2003).

36 Useful summaries of international developments include Emtairah (2002).

37 Putnam et al (1994); Putnam (1995, 2001).

38 OECD (1999b).

39 Andrews (1998).

40 King and Lennox (2000).

41 Maxwell and Lyon (1999).

42 Gunningham and Rees (1997).

43 'Private regulation' as a phrase has multiple meanings in common use. In particular, legal scholars use the phrase to refer to private enforcement of public rights, through tort law and other civil suits, as opposed to protecting them through pre-emptive public policies such as environmental statutes. This study uses the definition from Yilmaz (1998).

44 Yilmaz (1998).

45 Berman (2000).
46 Gunningham and Rees (1997).
47 Gupta and Lad (1983).
48 Bendell (2000).
49 King and Lennox (2000).
50 Gunningham and Rees (1997).
51 Gupta and Lad (1983).
52 Allars (1990)
53 Industry Canada and Treasury Board (1998); Industry Canada (2000).
54 According to Professor Kernaghan Webb (email correspondence 17 May 2000) the *Canadian Voluntary Codes Guide* was one of the products to emerge from a Voluntary Codes Project, which commenced in 1996, and consisted of a research component, a symposium and then the Guide and other products. The research component involved case studies of some 15 different voluntary codes, supplemented by studies looking at the voluntary codes experience in Australia/NZ, and the US, as well as horizontal studies looking at legal, public administration, political economy and economics aspects. Numerous experts and organizations were consulted.
55 Industry Canada and Treasury Board (1998).
56 UNCED (1992a, paras 30(a) and (b)).
57 Industry Canada and Treasury Board (1998).
58 A sub-committee of the Consumer Policy Committee of the International Organization for Standardization (ISO) has made a recommendation to the main committee, the ISO's Committee on Consumer Policy Committee (COPOLCO), that they should recommend to ISO to introduce an international standard on voluntary codes. This would essentially draw on existing voluntary code guides such as the Canadian guide examined above. This recommendation is for the ISO to create a series of criteria concerning the process of code development, the actual terms of codes, and code implementation.
59 OECD (1999b, p113).
60 Ibid, p99.
61 Ibid, p113.
62 European Environment Agency (1997).
63 Porter and van der Linde (1995a).
64 Gunningham et al (2003); Gunningham and Sinclair (2002); Gunningham and Grabosky (1998).
65 Bleishwitz (2002).
66 Porter (1991).
67 Porter and van der Linde (1995a; 1995b, p97).
68 Stocker and Burke (2000, video).
69 Milton et al (1997).
70 Gandy (1997).
71 Ellsworth et al (1997).
72 Porter and van der Linde (1995a).
73 Typical tax rates come from Jarass and Obermair (1997).
74 OECD (1994); Tindale and Holtham (1996); OECD (1997a, 1997b).
75 Famed British economist, Arthur Cecil Pigou, in his classic, *The Economics of Welfare*, in 1920 was the first to point out the hidden costs of externalities.
76 Roodham (1999).
77 In addition to requiring companies to disclose their revenues, Global Witness believes it is important to increase the transparency of government revenue streams from production sharing agreements and state-owned companies. The organization stresses that the EITI reporting principles must be reinforced by the imposition of appropriate conditionality on relevant bilateral and multilateral development assistance, resource-backed loans from banks, and export credit agency funding.
78 In 1958 Edward Banfield published *The Moral Basis of a Backward Society*, a study of underdevelopment in a village at the southern tip of Italy, 'the extreme poverty and

backwardness of which', he wrote, 'is to be explained largely (but not entirely) by the inability of the villagers to act together for their common good'.

79   In the 1970s Putnam began a collaboration with Robert Lonardi and Raffaella Y. Nanetti that nearly 20 years later resulted in the seminal work *Making Democracy Work Civic Traditions in Modern Italy* (1993). Based on a study of Italian politics and, in particular, the experience of the move to regional government post-1970, this book displays a number of the classic Robert Putnam hallmarks. These include: sustained and detailed attention to empirical data; a commitment to producing material that could help with the task of enhancing the quality of social and political discourse; and grounded and accessible writing. The book's concern with civic community and social capital was a direct precursor to 'Bowling Alone' (1995, 2001) – Putnam's very influential study of the decline in civic engagement in the US.

80   OECD (1999a).

81   Patel and Pavitt (1998).

82   Ibid.

83   Interestingly, after 106 years, in 1991 the World Bank would echo these ideas concluding that investment in knowledge accumulation on the part of the state was a more decisive factor in driving growth than physical capital investment. This very much-echoed List's thinking such as 'The present state of the nations is the result of the accumulation of all discoveries, inventions, improvements, perfections and exertions of all generations which have lived before us: they form the intellectual capital of the present human race, and every separate nation is productive only in the proportion in which it has known how to appropriate those attainments of former generations and to increase them by its own acquirements' (List, 1885, p140).

84   Lundvall (2000, p8).

85   Mytelka (2001).

86   Lundvall (2000, p2).

87   Ibid, p24.

88   Niosi (2002, p31).

89   Rothwell (1993).

90   *National Hydrogen Study*, a report prepared by ACIL Tasman and Parsons Brinckerhoff for the Department of Industry, Tourism and Resources.

91   Environment Agency, Japan, The challenge to establish the Recycling-based Society (2000); Environment Agency, Japan, Basic Law for Establishing the Recycling-based Society 2001 (Japan); Law for Promotion of Effective Utilization of Resources 2000 (Japan); Law Concerning the Promotion of Procurement of Eco-friendly Goods and Services by the State and Other Entities (the Green Purchasing Law) 2000 (Japan); Law for Recycling of Specified Kinds of Home Appliances 2001 (Japan).

92   World Bank (1997).

93   A feebate package involves the imposition of charges (fees) on old technology (e.g., low efficiency cars) and the use of the fee revenue to fund subsidies for adopters of new highly efficient technology. It is anticipated, for example, that the introduction of a feebate package would dramatically speed up the transition to hybrid vehicles.

Chapter 12

1   Named after the economist Vilfredo Pareto (1848–1923), who made several important contributions to economics, especially in the study of income distribution and in the analysis of individuals' choices.

2   Smith, A (1999, Book I, Ch vii).

3   Ibid (Book V, Ch i).

4   Arrow and Debreu (1954).

5   Indeed, the conditions are arguably inconsistent: the more we narrow the definition of a particular good, the less likely is competition.

6   For a seminal model of the market for insurance under conditions of imperfect information see Rothschild and Stiglitz (1976).

7   Shapiro and Stiglitz (1984).
8   In fact, informational imperfections form one of the principal reasons that the completeness and competitiveness requirements of the First Fundamental Theorem do not hold in real-world economies. We noted above that completeness requires a complete set of 'risk markets', yet the informational asymmetries outlined above mean that many insurance markets are fragile and prone to collapse. Similarly, perfect competition requires that there is no 'price dispersal': a can of tomatoes in South Sydney on a Tuesday night should cost the same in every shop. But searching the city to find the lowest price for a tin of tomatoes is time-consuming. Some firms capitalize on this by raising prices and marketing to those customers who are 'money-rich and time-poor', whilst others sell themselves as 'no frills' shops. The cost of obtaining information about prices means that these prices are dispersed and competition is imperfect.
9   Greenwald and Stiglitz (1986).
10 In a democracy, the electoral process confers (some degree of) legitimacy upon the government. This in turn enables governments to exercise their power of compulsion: the state, unlike private institutions or individuals, can compel all of its citizens to adhere to its laws, pay it money, and so on. Such compulsion, legitimately exercised, is one of the principal strengths of the government; unlike trades in the private sector, which are conducted only if they are mutually beneficial, the power of coercion relieves the state of the need to make everybody better off all of the time.
11 For a more detailed discussion of the roles and regulation of capital markets, see Stiglitz (1994, Ch 12).
12 An early seminal paper on credit and asymmetric information: Stiglitz and Weiss (1981). The model in this paper predicts that interest rates may not necessarily adjust to equalize the supply and demand for bank loans, explaining the 'credit rationing' observed in real-world economies, but which classical theories of the interest rate cannot explain.
13 For example, suppose I expect that the Thai baht is going to depreciate in the near future, then, as a speculator, I can sell my baht today and buy it back more cheaply after the depreciation. If I buy and sell in very large quantities I can make a very large amount of money.
14 For a very readable account of the pressures applied to developing countries, see Stiglitz (2002, Ch 3).
15 For a statistical study of the relationship between capital market liberalization and economic performance, see Rodrik (1998). Rodrik investigates the relationship between a country's capital account regime and economic performance using data from nearly 100 countries over the period 1975–1989, finding no evidence that countries without capital controls grow faster, invest more or experience lower inflation.
16 For a more detailed account of the Asian crisis and how Malaysia and China were able to weather the crisis whilst other economies in the region floundered, see Wade (2000).
17 Suggestions for further reading: one of the best technical papers on the causes of the Asian crisis is Corbett and Vines (1999). For a more detailed examination of the issues introduced in this chapter, see Stiglitz (1999).
18 Gittens (2003).
19 IMF response to criticism on the issue of its handling of the Asian economic crisis is as follows: 'When the IMF was created in 1944, its founders envisioned a world in which trade was free but in which the restrictions on movement of capital across countries then in place were to be retained. In the jargon, current accounts were to be open, but capital accounts highly regulated. Capital account restrictions were considered necessary to support the "Bretton Woods system", the system of fixed exchange rates then in place. There is no denying the vision of the world being promoted by the IMF in the mid-1990s was different. At the 1997 IMF–World Bank meetings the proposal on the table was to amend the IMF's articles of agreement to give it jurisdiction over the liberalization of capital movements. But while the popular characterization of a greater push toward capital account liberalization is broadly correct, it is inaccurate in many important details. The IMF did not encourage countries to liberalize short-term flows through the banking sector, which is what turned out to be the Achilles Heel during the Asian crisis'.

20   Prasad et al (2003).
21   Dawson (2002).
22   Braithwaite and Drahos (2000, p704). Professor John Braithwaite and Professor Peter Drahos have been awarded the Grawemeyer Award For Ideas Improving World Order. This award is presented annually to the winner of a competition designed to stimulate the recognition, dissemination and critical analysis of outstanding proposals for improving world order.
23   Ibid.
24   Ibid.
25   World Bank (2003, Ch 1, p3).
26   Dovers (1997).
27   Commonwealth of Australia (1992).
28   Stein (2000); Dovers (2002).
29   Connor and Dovers (2004).
30   Goodin (1996).
31   Dovers (2001).
32   This is a central and contested proposal in the sustainability literature, i.e. that environmental protection depends on economic growth. Here, the issue is not belief or disbelief in this proposal, but rather policy and institutional settings aimed at either establishing such a link in practice, or further testing the proposition.
33   Connor and Dovers (2004).
34   For example, local and state government coordinated action on a widely dispersed but nodal economic activity with particular environmental or social implications.
35   This is illustrative and far from a comprehensive listing of either sustainability principles or options.
36   Note that it is argued by some that such reorganization is unnecessary in local government, given the small size and thus non-fragmentary nature of local councils.
37   Dovers and Wild River (2003). This study, and the one reported in Connor and Dovers (see below), were funded by Land & Water Australia, and R&D agency of the Australian Government.
38   Connor and Dovers (2004).
39   Drawing on this idea from North (1993).
40   Filmer (2000).
41   The following piece summarizes an analysis of NCSDs more fully reported in Connor and Dovers (2004, Ch 5).
42   United Nations (1992, Chs 8, 27, 30).
43   This draws on d'Evie and Beeler (2002); d'Evie et al (2000).
44   Boyer (2000).
45   For basic descriptive material, see d'Evie et al (2000); d'Evie and Beeler (2002).
46   d'Evie et al (2000).
47   Basic information and a range of the Council's submissions to governments are available in English on the website for the Belgian Federal Council for Sustainable Development.
48   Doering (1993).
49   NRTEE (2001).
50   Information can be found on the website for the UK Sustainable Development Commission.
51   d'Evie and Beeler (2002).

Chapter 13

1   Funtowicz et al (1998).
2   Weaver (2002a, (2002b, 2003).
3   CLTM (1990), Weaver et al (2000).
4   Funtowicz and Ravetz (2002).
5   Indeed, uncertainty is not just a feature of complex systems, it is the defining feature that distinguishes complex systems from those that are simple or just complicated. A simple

system can be captured in theory and practice by a deterministic, linear causal analysis. Complicated systems require more variables for explanation or for control than can be neatly managed in its theory. With complexity, we are dealing with phenomena of a different sort. In a complex system, elements and subsystems are defined by their relation within hierarchies of inclusion and function. A complicated system can be modelled reliably despite the large number of elements and relationships involved. A complex system, by contrast, is characterized by multiple potential equilibria and cannot be accurately or reliably modelled. Systems that are complex are not merely complicated, by their very nature they imply deep uncertainties and a plurality of legitimate perspectives.

6   Funtowitcz and Ravetz (2002).
7   Weaver (1994).
8   Myers (1990).
9   Walters (1986); Holling (1978).
10 Thus, Holling (1989, pp359–370) argues that in this case, 'the observed and anticipated changes in carbon dioxide concentration alone are so unambiguous, so great and world-wide that we dare not continue as we are. We cannot predict confidently what impacts will flow from these changes, but we cannot continue to play out such a huge experiment on the whole planet'.
11 Ibid.
12 Myers (1990).
13 Weterings and Opschoor (1992).
14 Weaver et al (2000).
15 Ibid.
16 The aim of EET is to create a synthesis between economic growth and a sustainable environment by fostering the development and application of new technologies and related knowledge/know-how. The EET programme has five research themes, four related to technological strategies for decoupling economic growth and environmental stress and one oriented towards the technological restructuring of a pivotal economic sector. The four strategy-based themes are: sustainable products (eco-design and dematerialization), sustainable services (shifts from a product-oriented to a service-oriented economy), renewable energy and renewable materials. The pivotal sector is sustainable transport.
17 NIDO is oriented towards achieving performance 'leaps' towards sustainability through finding effective ways of innovation and transformation. NIDO sets up experiments in system renewal based upon building inclusive multi-actor/multi-stakeholder innovation networks. HABIFORM is aimed at more sustainable space-use through a strategy of multi-functional space-use. On the basis of the concepts and approaches developed within the HABIFORM programme, space management in the Netherlands should lead to more cost effective, efficient, ecologically-sustainable and livable outcomes (Whitelegg et al, 2002).
18 Weaver and Jansen (2002).
19 Jansen et al (2003).
20 Funtowicz et al (2003).

Chapter 14

1   Their second meeting was held in San Sebastian, Spain, in April 2003, with their third conference in Fremantle, Perth, Western Australia, in September 2003. The fourth conference was held in Cardiff, Wales, in March 2004.
2   OECD (2002b).
3   Key Note Opening Address, Governance for Regional Sustainability: The WA Approach, Third Conference of the Network of Regional Governments for Sustainable Development, University of Notre Dame, Fremantle, Western Australia, 2003.
4   OECD (2003).
5   WBCSD (1997).
6   Newman and Kenworthy (1999).

7   Roseland (1998); Suter (1995).
8   The Network of Regional Government for Sustainable Development, nrg4SD, was set up at the WSSD in Johannesburg in 2002 but nations and local governments first began addressing sustainable development at the Earth Summit in Rio in 1992.
9   Healey (1999).
10 Armstrong and Head (2002).

Chapter 15

1   See the website for the International Council for Local Environmental Initiatives – Australia/New Zealand 2003.
2   CCP™ Australia (2003).
3   Sustainability Street has a dedicated website, from which this text has been summarized. (Information is also available through the Environs Australia website.)
4   Additional team members included Victoria Critchley, Judy Lambert, Garry Smith and Jenny Scott at the School of Resources, Environment and Society, Australian National University.
5   UNCED (1992b).
6   UNCED (1993).
7   Whittaker (1995, 1996a, 1996b).
8   ICLEI (2002).
9   Bambridge (2002).
10 Engineers Australia Sustainable Energy Taskforce (2001, p12).

Chapter 16

1   Brain, P. (1999)
2   Ibid
3   *Newsweek* (2003).
4   O'Meara Sheehan (1999, pp14–15); includes updates from UN (2000).
5   Newman and Kenworthy (1999).
6   Newman and Kenworthy (1999).
7   The principle source is a detailed paper on methodology, from which Alan AtKisson has drawn significant portions of the text, but it has also relied on presentation files, statements of design principles and spreadsheets, together with long conversations. From these sources, Alan has endeavoured to distil the most important features of Goa 2100 for general readers, but it is impossible to do this project justice in a text this short. This part serves only as a general introduction; the serious reader or engaged professional is referred to the original documents, and the members of the design team.
8   Alexander et al (1977).

Chapter 17

1   *The Economist* (2003) 'The End of the Oil Age', 25–31 October.
2   Lovins (2004).
3   Ibid.
4   Lovins and Lovins (1982, 1983).
5   Lovins et al (2002).
6   Grove (1999).
7   Sir John Maddox (1999, p362).
8   AGO (2003).
9   UNEP Finance Initiatives CEO Briefing, 2002 states: 'Worldwide economic losses due to natural disasters appear to be doubling every ten years and, if current trends continue, annual losses will come close to US$150 billion in the next decade'.
10 Myers (1993, p758; 1996b).

11 Myers (2001).
12 Figure estimated from Brown (2001, Ch 2, pp9–10).
13 Simpson (2003).
14 Price (2002).
15 Kaufmann and Stern (2002).
16 O'Neill and Oppenheimer (2002).
17 Cox et al (2000).
18 Bacon (1999).
19 For the last five years, a cutting-edge initiative in climate studies has been the search for an understanding of millennial-scale climate instabilities. These rapid, large-amplitude climate fluctuations were first identified in ice cores in Greenland and later in ocean sediment cores around the world. While other researchers have focused on the geologic record of the past 120,000 years, Professor Raymo and a handful of colleagues have undertaken the far more ambitious effort of looking at climate trends as far back as 1.5 million years ago, at the dawn of the human race. Their work has turned up some unexpected results. 'Our results suggest that such millennial-scale climate instability may be a pervasive and long-term characteristic of Earth's climate, rather than just a feature of the strong glacial–interglacial cycles of the past 800,000 years', the authors wrote.
20 Committee on Abrupt Climate Change (2002).
21 Dr David Kemp, Australia's Environment Minister, 2002.
22 Denniss et al (2004).
23 Department of Trade and Industry (2003).
24 Interlaboratory Working Group (1997); Mintzer et al (2003).
25 March 2000 Australian Energy News reported the effect of minimum energy performance standards being estimated at reducing emissions at a cost of negative AU$31 per tonne of CO_2.
26 Riedy (2003).
27 Paton (2001).
28 Pears and Greene (2003).
29 Lovins and Lovins (1997, Ch 17).
30 Northrop (2003).
31 'Intelligent Energy – Europe' (EIE) is the Community's support programme for non-technological actions in the field of energy, precisely in the field of energy efficiency and renewable energy sources. The duration of the programme is from 2003 to 2006. The programme was adopted by the European Parliament and the Council on 26 June 2003. It was published in the Official Journal of the European Union on 15 July 2003 (OJ, L 176, pp29–36) and entered into force on 4 August 2003.
32 Ambassador Harriet C. Babbitt Deputy Administrator US Agency for International Development International Conference on Accelerating Grid-Based Renewable Energy Power Generation for a Clean Environment Lewis Preston Auditorium, The World Bank, March 7, 2000.
33 This quote is from a transcript of a talk by former President Bill Clinton at the University of California, Berkeley, on 29 January 2002. Clinton spoke at Zellerbach Hall, was introduced by Chancellor Robert M. Berdahl, and was subsequently interviewed by Journalism School Dean Orville Schell. California Gov Gray Davis also spoke at this event.
34 Krishnapillai and Boele (2003).
35 Worldwatch Institute (2003, p102).
36 Green (2000, p58).
37 Brown et al (2000).
38 Australian Prime Ministers Science Engineering Innovation Council (2002).
39 Computer giant NEC has announced recently a small fuel cell for laptop computers that could keep running for ten times longer than regular batteries; they say each fuel cell refill will be able to keep a laptop running for 40 consecutive hours.
40 Lovins and Williams (1999).
41 Lovins (2004).

42   Further reading see Denniss et al (2004).
43   von Weizsäcker et al (1997); Hawken et al (1999, Ch 6).
44   Hamilton et al (2002).
45   CADDET (1995).
46   Benders and Biesiot (1996).
47   Hamilton et al (2002).
48   Tuluca (1997).
49   CSIRO Built Environment (2000).
50   Watts (1997).
51   Sathaye and Moyers (1995).
52   US Department of Energy (2002b).
53   AGO (2000).
54   WEC (1998); OITI (1999).
55   McAlpine and Mitchell (1999).
56   Haimson, L. (2002) 'This just in ...', *Toronto Globe and Mail*, 13 February 2002.
57   Kellogg (1977).
58   Ibid.
59   Kvande (1999); Altenpohl (1998); Martchek (2000).
60   International Iron & Steel Institute website 2000 (www.worldsteel.org).
61   Bureau of International Recycling website 2001 (www.bir.org).
62   Martchek (2000).
63   Wavegen Ltd, UK are a world leader in wave energy. They have developed and operate the world's first commercial-scale wave energy device that generates power for the grid.
64   Marine Current Turbines Ltd's technology represents a novel method for generating electricity from a huge energy resource in the sea. Although the relentless energy of marine currents has been obvious from the earliest days of seafaring, it is only now that the development of modern offshore engineering capabilities coinciding with the need to find large new renewable energy resources makes this a technically feasible and economically viable possibility.
65   Jacobson and Masters (2001).
66   High Temperature Superconductors; The World's First Industrial Field Test of a High-Temperature Superconducting Cable System.
67   Taking Australia as an example, the Australian Terrestrial Biodiversity Assessment 2002 has shown that Australia's ecosystems are overall in crisis.
68   Williams (1996).
69   Lovins and Cramer (2004).
70   ACIL Tasman and Parsons Brinckerhoff (2003).
71   Heiman (2002).
72   The Australian COAL21 is a programme aimed at fully realizing the potential of advanced technologies to reduce or eliminate greenhouse gas emissions associated with the use of coal, whilst at the same time maintaining Australia's competitive advantage of low-cost electricity from coal.
73   Cramer and Taggart (2002).
74   Allen Consulting (2003).
75   Allen Consulting (2002).
76   ABS (2002).
77   Ibid.
78   NAEEEC (2001).
79   Commonwealth of Australia, Official Committee Hansard, Senate Environment, Communications, Information Technology and the Arts References Committee, Roundtable Reference: Global warming Wednesday, 16 August 2000 Canberra by Authority of the Senate.
80   Weyant (2000).
81   Pears (1998).
82   Lumb et al (1996).

83 The NSW Wind Atlas was created with WindScape™, a regional wind resource mapping tool produced by the CSIRO. The CSIRO-modelled Victorian Wind Atlas shows that six of the 12 windiest municipalities are in central Victoria and a seventh in the mountainous Baw Baw Shire. Releasing the atlas, acting Premier John Thwaites said inland sites suitable for wind farms would 'relieve pressure on other (coastal) areas'.

84 Lovins and Lovins (1997). Also highly recommended is Lovins and Lovins (1982, Ch 17).

85 ABARE (1997).

86 Allen Consulting (2003).

87 Lovins and Lovins (1997).

88 These recommendations are a summary from Alan Pears, Ch 2 of submission to Federal Government's 2030 sustainable cities enquiry on behalf of the Planning Institute of Australia.

89 DRE (1987).

90 DEFRA (2003) UK *Emissions Trading Scheme off to Flying Start*, Department for Environment, Food and Rural Affairs, News Release 168/03 12 May, Nobel House, London.

91 Allen Consulting (2003).

92 Watt and Outhred (1999).

93 Pears and Greene (2003).

94 Vine et al (2003).

Chapter 18

1 Wilson et al (1998, p6).

2 Ibid, p19.

3 A video summary is available through the PMM website.

4 A range of building schemes are described further in this chapter, under 'Rating Schemes'.

5 Information taken from an article on the building in *Home Power Magazine*, The Hands-on Journal of Home Made Power, Issue 75.

6 Collis (2002, p422).

7 Fletcher (2003).

8 Statistics taken from Roodman and Lenssen (1995).

9 Birkeland (2004) course notes for Greening the Built Environment, a professional development short course available through Australian National University.

10 Over the past decade, the Listed Property Trust (LPT) sector has become an increasingly large component of the broader Australian Stock Exchange (ASX) sharemarket indexes. Market capitalization of the sector has risen from AU$5 billion in 1992 to AU$45 billion in 2002.

11 Mays (2003, p29).

12 Pears (2003, Ch 5).

13 Mendler and Odell (2000).

14 Collis (2002, p411).

15 Price Waterhouse Coopers (2002).

16 Birkeland (2002).

17 Wilson et al (1998, Ch 4).

18 Birkeland (2002).

19 Ibid.

20 AusCID (2003).

21 Ibid.

22 Refer to the proceedings of The DestiNY USA Environmental Design Charrette (April 2002 – Savannah Dhu Conference Center, Savannah, New York, p7).

23 Department of Sustainability and Environment (2003, pii).

24 A number of key resource lists (books and online) are provided as an appendix in Mendler and Odell (2000).

25 More than 150 researchers and an alliance of 18 partner organizations are involved in and support the activities of the CRC for CI.

26   Personal communications with Alan Pears (21 March 2004).
27   The Education Modules are being developed by a team of young engineers and scientists supported by the Institution of Engineers Australia, through The Natural Edge Project.
28   Urban and Regional Land Corporation (URLC) AURORA development in Epping North – a joint initiative of the Centre for Design at RMIT University, Urban and Regional Land Corporation, and the Sustainable Energy Authority of Victoria.
29   Information about accessing the guide is available from the Royal Australian Institute of Architects and through the BDP website.
30   *EcoSpecifier* is a not-for-profit collaboration by RMIT University's Centre for Design, and Natural Integrated Living Inc. The online database provides knowledge and training on best-practice sustainable materials and product specification and design.
31   Mendler and Odell (2000).
32   Ibid, pxiii.
33   Romm and Browning (1994).
34   Wilson et al (1998, p18).
35   Mays (2003, p37). General Property Trust (GPT) is Australia's largest diversified property trust, owning, developing and managing a AU$6.8 billion portfolio of retail, office, hotel and industrial properties throughout Australia.
36   For example direct observation, target market analysis, visual preference surveys, the 'let's talk' approach, focus groups and 'creative feasibility', as described in Wilson et al (1998, p121).
37   Millicer (2003).
38   Information contained in the supplement for Australian Conservation Foundation's *Habitat* magazine (February 2003 edition). See also the Australian Conservation Foundation and 60L building design website.
39   Information obtained from the UK Action Energy group the UK BedZED website, and the Zedfactory's website. Information about other 'ZED projects' can also be found at the Zed Factory's website.
40   Even though most developed countries have had such requirements for many years. A history of rating schemes in Australia can be found in Pears (2003, Ch 5).
41   The Commonwealth Department of Environment and Heritage has produced the National Australian Building Environmental Rating System, described within the department's website.
42   The NSW Department of Infrastructure, Planning and Natural Resources has developed 'BASIX', the Building Sustainability Index, described in the department's website.
43   CSIRO has developed the Life Cycle House Energy Estimator (see CSIRO's website for a summary of the tool).
44   The Green Building Council of Australia has developed the Green Star – Office Design tool to evaluate the environmental potential of the design of commercial office buildings (base building construction or refurbishment). GBCA intends that Green Star will have rating tools for different phases of the building life cycle (design, fit-out and operation) and for different building classes (office, retail, industrial, residential, etc.). See the Council's website for more details.
45   Two examples include the engineering consultancy firm Arup's Sustainable Project Appraisal Routine called SPeAR™ (see the Arup website), and the World Travel & Tourism Council's GREEN GLOBE 21 Design and Construct Standard for benchmarking and certification (see the Greenglobe21 website).
46   ECOS (2004).
47   Mays (2003).
48   Birkeland (2002).
49   Birkeland (2004) course notes for Greening the Built Environment, a professional development short course available through Australian National University.
50   Amory Lovins quoted in Wilson et al (1998, p174).
51   William McDonough, adapted from a speech at the Cathedral of St John the Divine, New York City, February 1993, cited in ibid, p46.

52 Neal Payton, CHK Architects and Planners, from the AIA/ Nathan Cummings Foundation Roundtables, which were held to identify barriers to green architecture, 1992–1993, in ibid, p55.
53 Alexander et al (1977) and Alexander (1979).
54 Alexander et al (1977, pxii).
55 Ibid, pxiii.
56 McDonough and Partners (1992).
57 For a summary of design principles, see Roaf et al (2003). For Australian examples, see Baggs and Baggs (1996). See also Pearson (1998). For retrofits, see Mobbs (1998).
58 Birkeland (1995); Romm (1999).
59 Birkeland (2002).
60 For more information on the solar core concept, see Birkeland's sustainable systems website ('sustainable systems'). This summary of the concept was provided by Dr Birkeland to the editorial team (April 2004).
61 Orr (1994, Ch 2).
62 Koelman (2004). Available through RMI's website.
63 Birkeland (2002).
64 Personal communication with Alan Pears (March 2004).
65 Information obtained from Rocky Mountain Institute – Green Developments 2.0 CD-ROM, produced by Sunnywood Designs (Companion CD to Wilson et al (1998)).
66 Photo courtesy of ZplusPartners – see their website for an article on the development.
67 Information obtained from a review by Lindsay Johnston, available through Melbourne City Council's website.
68 Melbourne City Council (2003) CH2 *Media Release: Council on Track for New Standard in Green D*, Melbourne City Council, August.

Chapter 19

1   Extract from an interview on Australian Radio National Earthbeat with Alexandra de Blas, Saturday 12 September 1998.
2   Newman and Kenworthy (1999)
3   Campbell (1997).
4   AAA (2000).
5   Laird et al (2001).
6   The database contains data on 69 primary variables which, depending on the city and the administrative complexity and multi-modality of its public transport system, can mean up to 175 primary data entries. The methodology of data collection for all the factors was strictly controlled by agreed upon definitions contained in a technical booklet of over 100 pages and data was carefully checked and verified by three parties before being accepted into the database. From this complex range of primary factors, some 230 standardized variables have been calculated. Cities can thus be compared across the areas of urban form, private and public transport performance, overall mobility and modal split, private and public transport infrastructure, the economics of urban transport (operating and investment costs, revenues), passenger transport energy use and environmental factors, including CO_2 emissions. More detail about the database can be found in Kenworthy and Laube (2001).
7   Lave (1992); Kirwan (1992).
8   Refer to the tabulated data in Tables 2 and 4 contained in the source paper Kenworthy (2003).
9   Peden et al (2002).
10 Stephenson et al (2000).
11 AIHW (2003).
12 ABS (2000).
13 Sustainable Development Information Service: Global Trends, *Proceed with Caution: Growth of Global Motor Fleet*, World Resources Institute.

14 Benkhelifa et al (2001).
15 Kemp (2001).
16 WBCSD (2001c).
17 WHO (2000).
18 For more information on the latest developments in China see Kenworthy and Hu (2002).
19 Pucher and Dijkstra (2000).
20 Transport SA (2002).
21 Hass-Klau (1993).
22 ITDP (2002).
23 Road and Traffic Authority (1999).
24 ITDP (2002).
25 UN-HABITAT (2002).
26 Singh (2004).
27 Wright (2002).
28 ITDP (2003a).
29 ITDP (2003b).
30 WBCSD (2001c).
31 Newman and Kenworthy (1999); Kenworthy and Laube (1999); Cervero (1998).
32 Refer to the tabulated data in Tables 2 and 5 contained in the source paper Kenworthy (2003).
33 The New Jersey Smart Growth Gateway is an online resource to provide local government officials, civic leaders, and concerned citizens with the information necessary to begin implementing 'Smart Growth Strategies' in their communities.
34 Refer to the report written by the 1000 Friends of Oregon (1999) *Myths & Facts About Oregon's Urban Growth Boundaries*, available at www.friends.org/resources/myths.html.
35 Herlands (1999).
36 Refer to the Sierra Club campaign on Stopping Sprawl.
37 EPS (2000).
38 Breithaupt (2001).
39 Lim Lan Yuan (1997).
40 Kenworthy (1991).
41 Collaborative Economics (1998).
42 Brog and John (2001).
43 Travel Awareness, Publicity and Education Supporting a Sustainable Transport Strategy in Europe (TAPESTRY) is a research and demonstration project funded by the European Commission (DG Energy and Transport) under the 5th RTD Framework Programme. The project brings together 25 partners from 12 European countries, ranging from local authorities and local public transport operators to national research agencies and leading researchers in the field of travel behaviour (www.eu-tapestry.org).
44 Transport For London (2003).
45 Kingham and Donohoe (2002).
46 Barter (1999).
47 Warren Centre (2002).
48 INRA Europe (1991).
49 Intermodal Surface Transportation Efficiency Act 1991; TEA-21: Transport Equity Act for the 21st century, 1998.
50 Rasagan (1999).
51 Jacobson and Aldana (2001).
52 SAVE (2000).
53 Manchester Airport Plc. is an example of one organization that has introduced an on-site crèche. For more information see the United Kingdom Department for Transport.
54 Pikora and Miller (2001).
55 Warman (2001).

Chapter 20

1   The background to future water problems at the global level is described in such books as Gleick (1993); Postel (1984); Raskin et al (1996).
2   UN/WWAP (2003). Coordinated by the World Water Assessment Programme, the report is the result of the collaboration of 23 UN agencies and convention secretariats.
3   World Commission on Dams (2000).
4   Ibid.
5   The Sydney 'Every Drop Counts' project offers subsidized appliances to householders including not only the expected efficient showerheads but also rainwater tanks and mulchers. Rocky Mountain Institute pioneered many studies on water management issues in the 1980s, material available on the RMI website.
6   Weaver et al (2000, p151).
7   Booker et al (2000).
8   Speers et al (2001).
9   De Blas (2001).
10   Another of the biggest drivers for change this century will come from the need to avoid conflict and ensure water security. There are 261 watersheds that cross the political boundaries of two or more countries. Michael Klare in his classic book *Resource Wars* (2001) outlines this in detail; hence we will not cover it here.
11   Clearly this varies from country to country.
12   Postel (1999).
13   IEA (1998).
14   NSW owns all the Tumut; 50/50, for the Murray between the states of Vic and NSW; the Murrumbidgee passes through both NSW and ACT.
15   Bevitt et al (1998).
16   There have been calls for more dams in Australia. However, since the Snowy scheme already captures 99 per cent of the water in the Snowy catchment, a new dam would actually lose more water through evaporation than it could possibly additionally collect.
17   See www.seawatergreenhouse.com for further information on this topic.
18   Bevitt et al (1998).
19   Ibid.
20   Snowy Water Licence issued Under Part 5 of the Snowy Hydro Corporatisation Act 1997 in New South Wales, Australia.
21   ANCID (2000).
22   Megalogenis (2003).
23   Three of these generators just spin as back up generators so that they can respond to a major failure in the eastern seaboard grid within 28 seconds. The three spinning generators, at 750 tonnes each, also act as the alternators for the grid, ensuring that the frequency stays within a certain margin of cycles per second. As loads go on and off the grid, the voltage changes. In condenser mode those three rotors can either draw power off the grid or add power to the grid to keep the voltage within an acceptable range. These generators can black start the grid of the entire eastern seaboard for 40 hours if they have to.
24   ABC 4 Corners Reporter Ticky Fullerton interviews Professor Mike Young, CSIRO economist and member of the Wentworth Group on 15 June 2003 near Tailem Bend, SA.
25   Ibid.
26   Murray–Darling Basin Ministerial Council (2002).
27   ABC 4 Corners Reporter Ticky Fullerton interviews Professor Mike Young, CSIRO economist and member of the Wentworth Group on 15 June 2003 near Tailem Bend, SA.
28   Young, M et al (2002).
29   ABC Earthbeat interview with Alexandra de Blas (2003) with Professor Mike Young, Director Policy & Economic Research Unit, CSIRO Land & Water, Dr John Langford, Executive Director Water Services Association of Australia, and Dr Poh-Ling Tan, Senior Law Lecturer, Queensland University of Technology.

30 We will provide a succinct overview, but for those interested in the detail, Young and McColl's CSIRO papers will be linked from the companion website to this book (www.thenaturaladvantage.info).
31 This is a transcript from *The World Today*. The programme is broadcast around Australia at 12:10pm on ABC Local Radio.
32 World Bank (2003).
33 ABC 4 Corners Reporter Ticky Fullerton interviews Professor Mike Young, CSIRO economist and member of the Wentworth Group on 15 June 2003 near Tailem Bend, SA.
34 Wentworth Group of Concerned Scientists (2002).
35 Beare et al (1998).
36 Wentworth Group of Concerned Scientists (2002).
37 Young and McColl (2002).
38 ECOS magazine, September 2003.
39 Wentworth Group of Concerned Scientists (2002).
40 NRMMC (2003).

Chapter 21

1 The UNDP 1998 *Human Development Report* stresses the need for sustainable consumption to be defined in ways that avoid ideas of giving up or losing out, emphasizing instead the idea of what could be called low-impact affluence.
2 Thus patterns of consumption may differ between communities or populations because different volumes of goods and services are consumed which are, nevertheless, produced in the same way (i.e. with the same resource/waste impacts per good or service) or because the same volumes of goods and services are consumed in different contexts where their production impact is different.
3 UNDP (1998).
4 For a detailed analysis of this idea see Hawken et al (1999).
5 UNEP (2002b).
6 Fukasaku (1999, p48)
7 See Tables 22.1–22.3 for a summary of the agreement about actions and policies regarding sustainable consumption.
8 UNEP (2000); Bentley (2000).
9 UNEP SCOPE Pilot Workshop in Sofia, Working papers, UNEP DTIE, Paris [AS2] (2001).
10 This approach is evident in UNEP initiatives both planned and underway – see for example the WBCSD Chairman's Paper, WSSD Prep-Com 3.
11 Highlighted in the 'Sustainability through the market' report, World Business Council for Sustainable Development. For a wider view of the global trends shaping business activity, see also UNEP, WBCSD and the WRI (2002).
12 Specific targets for such reductions are being set and are expected to require a reduction of 20 per cent by 2010 and 50 per cent by 2020.
13 Initial experience with such panels has emerged from trials in Denmark.
14 Kerr and Ryan (2001).
15 WBCSD (2001a, 2001b).
16 As an example, see the recent review of current literature in this area: Princen (2001).
17 Even talking of unsustainable consumption is open to a misinterpretation (which may exaggerate the role of consumer behaviour). What such a phrase actually means is: taking the consumption of resources, embodied in goods and services, as a measure of the performance of current systems of production and consumption, and demonstrating that these systems are unsustainable. Of course, as the OECD has emphasized in its own analysis, consumption data can only be interpreted for a particular site, problem and time, and the sustainability or un-sustainability of that data can be interpreted only where specific ecological limits can be established; OECD (2001).
18 For an overview see, for example, the website of Redefining Progress.
19 A point that the industry appears well aware of; see GeSI (2002). This is also the focus of a research project for the Melbourne based Lab 3000 – innovation in digital design. See: Ryan (2004).

20 This is the basis, for example, in UNEP work with youth and activities which focuses on individuals who are sensitive to the 'life behind the product'.

21 Michaelis (2000), for example, proposed a framework consisting of four sets of forces which shape consumption: Demographic, economic and technical changes; Resources, infrastructure and time constraints; Motivations, habits needs and compulsions; Social structures, identities, discourse and symbols. The UNDP *Human Development Report* 1998 examines the history of the idea of consumption and nine hypotheses about consumption from Veblen, through Keynes to Amartya Sen.

22 ACA (2002).

23 The term 'systems of provision' has been used to describe a framework for understanding production, consumption and life styles. It is used here in a closely related, but more narrowly focused, way; Chappells et al (2001).

24 A point made in UNDP (1998), OECD (2001) and the Kabelvåg Workshop (1998).

25 Based around Maslow's hierarchy – see UNDP (1998); OECD (2002a).

26 Spaargaren and van Vliet (2000) describe the ways that consumers and producers are co-actors in the creation and maintenance of systems of provision.

27 See for example, Tischner et al (2000).

28 AdBusters, www.adbusters.org.

29 The development of eco-footprint measurements for some cities is a good indication of future possibilities.

30 Ryan (2002).

31 For a good review of such strategies see: Tischner et al (2000).

32 Studies of new car sharing systems demonstrate this well; Meijkamp (2000).

33 The UNEP DTIE plan to produce a new eco-design support system will thus be an important step in the integration of their production and consumption programmes.

34 McDonough and Braungart (2002).

35 After Manzini (2001).

36 Stated at the International Business Forum on Sustainable Consumption and Production; Creating Opportunities in a Changing World, Berlin, October, 1999.

37 Pine and Gilmore (1998).

38 See UNEP (2001, 2002a) (both available from UNEP DTIE website).

Chapter 22

1   Orr (1994, p27).

2   PCENZ (2004).

3   The Sustainable Schools programme is the integration of existing and fragmented approaches to sustainability education into a holistic programme with measurable environmental, financial and curriculum outcomes. The programme does not seek to replace other environmental education initiatives in schools, rather it links to and complements existing resources such as Energy Smart Schools, WasteWise, Waterwatch, Waterwise and Landcare.

4   UNESCO (1997a, 1997b).

5   Thomas (2004).

6   Hawken et al (1999).

7   Tilbury (2003).

8   Jenni Goricanec and Roger Hadgraft of RMIT University provided this discussion to the Editors.

9   Refer to the RMIT Global Sustainability Institute.

10 Information about this curriculum project is available through the BELL section of the WRI website.

11 This curriculum work is available through the Natural Capitalism Inc website.

12 More information is available at the Presidio world college, San Francisco website.

13 See the Delft University of Technology website for information about the conference.

14 Sudan Virtual Engineering Library – Sustainability Knowledge Network (SudVEL-SKN),

Pilot Project Report: 15 December 2003 to 15 February 2004, Charlie Hargroves, The Natural Edge Project.

15 The Green Chemistry Institute has affiliate organizations in over 20 countries (refer to their website for more details).

16 Contact John Fein through Griffith University, or refer to the UNESCO website.

17 More information about the Institute for Sustainability and Technology Policy is available through Murdoch University's website.

18 The ECOS magazine is published on CSIRO's publishing website.

19 This e-newsletter is coordinated by Dr Elizabeth Heij of CSIRO.

20 The university is based in Canberra, Australia. More information can be found at ANU's website.

21 Those involved with the ANU Green Guide project are keen to network with other local green/sustainability guide teams worldwide to build a central website. More information can be found online through ANU's website.

22 Refer to the ANU website for information on the symposium.

23 'Tela' refers to the Latin word for 'integrated/web' and has been used for the Australian Conservation Foundation (ACF) report. The report is available online, through the ACF website.

Chapter 23

1   Rukato and Osborn (2001, p1).

2   These definitions are taken from Hemmati (2002).

3   Wheeler and Sillanpaa (1997).

4   Zadek and Raynard (2002).

5   Multi-stakeholder Workshop on Partnerships and UN-Civil Society Relationships, 10–12 February 2004, Pocantico, New York.

6   Hemmati (2002).

7   Ibid.

8   Meadows (1998).

9   AtKisson and Hatcher (2001).

10 The Compass is not the only sustainability framework that works with Pyramid; the Triple Bottom Line (TBL), Economy–Environment–Equity (EEE) and other sustainability frameworks can also be used depending on the context of the application.

11 The name 'Magic Eyes' grew from TECDA's popular anti-litter campaign of the early 1990s, which had the slogan 'Magic Eyes are watching you'.

12 Readers can review the documentation for the entire process, as well as the results of the June 2004 summit, online at www.baltic21.org.

13 Please refer to the acknowledgments and further to the website at www.naturaledgeproject.net for further information on our supporters, endorsees and partners.

14 Please refer to the website at www.naturaledgeproject.net for further information on both the Advisory Board and Steering Committee and Working Group under the tab 'Meet the Teams'.

REFERENCES

AAA (Australian Automobile Association) (2000) *Motoring Clubs Combine to Call for Freeze and Reform of Fuel Tax*, AAA (online), 30 October

ABARE (Australian Bureau of Agricultural and Resource Economics) (1997) *Kyoto Report*, ABARE, Canberra

Abramovitz, J. and Dunn, S. (1998) *Record Year for Weather-Related Disasters*, Press Release, 27 November, Worldwatch Institute, Washington, DC

ABS (Australian Bureau of Statistics) (2000) *Household Expenditure Survey Australia: Detailed Expenditure Items*, Cat No 6530, ABS, Canberra

ABS (2002) *Business Operations and Industry Performance Australia*, Cat No 8140.0, ABS, Canberra

ACA (Australian Consumers' Association) (2002) *Green Electricity Watch Report*, ACA, Marrickville, NSW

ACF (Australian Conservation Foundation) (2000) *Natural Advantage: Blueprint for a Sustainable Australia*, ACF, Melbourne

ACF (2004) 'ACF Submission on CLERP (Audit Reform and Corporate Disclosure) Bill 2003', 9 February

ACF/ACTU (Australian Council of Trade Unions) (1994) *Green Jobs in Industry: Research Report*, ACF/ACTU, Melbourne

ACIL Tasman and Parsons Brinckerhoff (2003) *National Hydrogen Study*, A report prepared for the Department of Industry, Tourism and Resources

AGO (Australian Greenhouse Office) (2000) *Impact of Minimum Energy Performance Requirements for Class I Buildings in Victoria*, AGO, Canberra

AGO (2003) *Climate Change An Australian Guide to the Science and Potential Impacts*, AGO, Canberra

AIHW (Australian Institute of Health and Welfare) (2003) *Australia's Young People: Their Health and Wellbeing*, Cat No PHE 50, AIHW, Canberra

Alexander, C. (1979) *The Timeless Way of Building*, Oxford University Press, Oxford

Alexander, C., Ishikawa, S. and Silverstein, M. (1977) *A Pattern Language: Towns, Buildings, Construction*, prepared with Jacobson, M., Fiksdahl-King, I. and Angel, S., Oxford University Press, Oxford

Allars, M. (1990) *Introduction to Australian Administrative Law*, Butterworths, Sydney

Allen Consulting (2000) *Greenhouse Emissions*, Trading Report to Department of Premier and Cabinet, The Allen Consulting Group, Melbourne

Allen Consulting (2002) *Cost Benefit Analysis of New Housing Energy Performance Regulations: Impact of Proposed Regulations Report for Sustainable Energy Authority Victoria and Building Commission*, The Allen Consulting Group, Melbourne

Allen Consulting (2003) *Sustainable Energy Jobs Report: A Report for the Sustainable Energy Development Authority*, The Allen Consulting Group, Sydney

Alley, R. (2000) *The Two Mile Time Machine, Ice Cores, Abrupt Climate Change and our Future*, University Presses of California, Columbia and Princeton

Altenpohl, D. (1998) *Aluminium: Technology, Applications and Environment*, 6th edition, The Aluminium Association, Washington, DC

AMA (American Management Association) (1996) *Survey: Corporate Downsizing, Job Elimination and Job Creation*, AMA, Washington, DC

Anastas, P. and Williamson, T. (1994) *Green Chemistry, Designing Chemistry For the Environment*, American Chemical Series, 208th National Meeting of the American Chemical Society, Washington, DC

Anastas, P. and Williamson, T. (1998) *Green Chemistry, Frontiers in Design Chemical Synthesis and Processes*, Oxford University Press, Oxford

Anastas, P., Heine, L., Williamson, T. and Bartlett, L. (2000) *Green Engineering*, American Chemical Society, November

ANCID (Australian National Committee on Irrigation and Drainage) (2000) *Open Channel Seepage and Control: Current Knowledge of Channel Seepage Issues & Measurement in the Australian Rural Water Industry Goulburn-Murray Water*, ANCID, Victoria

Anderson, R. (1998) *Mid-Course Correction: Toward a Sustainable Enterprise: the Interface Model*, Peregrinzilla Press, Atlanta, GA

Anderson, S. and Cavanagh, J. (1996) *The Top 200, The Rise of Global Corporate Power*, The Institute for Policy Studies, Washington, DC

Andrews, R. (1998) 'Environmental Regulation and Business "Self Regulation"', *Policy Sciences*, vol 31, p177

Angel, J. and Rivoli, P. (1997) 'Does Ethical Investing Impose a Cost Upon the Firm? A Theoretical Examination', *Journal of Investing*, Winter

Annan, K. (1998) 'UN Secretary-General Press Release', SG/SM/6638, 14 July (www.un.org/News/Press/docs/1998/19980714.sgsm6638.html)

Armstrong, R. and Head, G. (2002) 'Liveable Neighbourhoods: Guiding New Development for a More Sustainable Urban Future', in Armstrong, R., Ruane, S. and Newman, P. (eds) (2002) *Case Studies in Sustainability: Hope for the Future in Western Australia*, ISTP Publications, Perth

Armstrong, R., Ruane, S. and Newman, P. (eds) (2002) *Case Studies in Sustainability: Hope for the Future in Western Australia*, ISTP Publications, Perth

Arnold, J. and Campbell, J. (1986) *Collective Management of Hill Forests in Nepal: The Community Forestry Development Project*, National Research Council, Proceedings in the Conference on Common Property Resource Management, National Academy Press, Washington, DC

Arora, S. and Cason, T. (1995) 'An Experiment in Voluntary Environmental Regulation: Participation in EPA's 33/50 Program', *Journal of Environmental Economics & Management*, vol 28, no 3, pp271–286

Arora, S. and Cason, T. (1996) 'Why do Firms Volunteer to Exceed Environmental Regulations? Understanding Participation in EPA's 33/50 Program', *Land Economics* November, pp413–432

Arrow, K. and Debreu, G. (1954) 'Existence of an Equilibrium for a Competitive Economy', *Econometrica*, vol 22, no 3, pp265–290

Arrow, K., Dasgupta, P. and Maler, K. (2003) 'Evaluating Projects and Assessing Sustainable Development in Imperfect Economies', working paper of the Beijer International Institute of Ecological Economics, Stockholm

Atkins, T. (2004) 'Insurer Warns of Global Warming Catastrophe', Reuters, 3 March

AtKisson, A. (1999) *Believing Cassandra, An Optimist looks at a Pessimist's World*, Chelsea Green, Publishing., White River Junction, VT

AtKisson, A. and Hatcher, R. (2001) 'The Compass Index of Sustainability: Prototype for a Comprehensive Sustainability Information System', *Journal of Environmental Assessment Policy and Management*, vol 3, no 4

AusCID (Australian Council for Infrastructure Development) (2003) *Sustainability Framework for the future of Australia's infrastructure*, AusCID

Austin, J. (1990) *Managing in Developing Countries: Strategic Analysis and Operating Techniques*, Free Press, New York

Australian Prime Minister's Science Engineering Innovation Council (2002) *Beyond Kyoto: Innovation and Adaption*, Australian Government, Canberra

Australian Treasury Department (2001) *Public Good Conservation and the Impact of Environmental Measures Imposed on Landholders*, Economic Roundup, Centenary Edition, Australian Treasury Department, Canberra

Bacon, S. (1999) 'Decadal Variability in the Outflow from the Nordic Seas to the Deep Atlantic Ocean', *Nature*, 394, pp871–874

Baggs, S. and Baggs, J. (1996) *The Healthy House: Creating a Safe, Healthy and Environmentally Friendly Home*, HarperCollins, Sydney

Bambridge, P. (2002) *Open Space Educational Technology*, Workshop briefing notes, Murray Darling Basin Commission, Canberra

Banfield, E. (1958) *The Moral Basis of a Backward Society*, Free Press, New York

Barter, P. (1999) *An International Comparative Perspective on Urban Transport and Urban Form in Pacific Asia: The Challenge of Rapid Motorisation in Dense Cities*, PhD, Murdoch University, Perth

Bartolomeo, M., Bennett, M., Bouma, J., Heydkamp, P., James, P. and Wolters, T. (2000) 'Environmental Management in Europe: Current Practice and Further Potential', *The European Accounting Review*, vol 9, no 1, pp31–52

Beare, S., Bell, R. and Fisher, B. (1998) 'Determining the Value of Water: The Role of Risk, Infrastructure Constraints and Ownership', *American Journal of Agricultural Economics*, vol 80, no 5, December

Becker, C. and Ostrom, E. (1995) 'Human Ecology and Resource Sustainability: The Importance of Institutional Diversity', *Annual Review of Ecology and Systematics*, vol 26, pp113–133

Bendell, J. (2000) 'Civil Regulation: A New Form of Democratic Governance for the Global Economy?', in Bendell, J. (ed) *Terms for Endearment: Business, NGOs and Sustainable Development*, published in association with The New Academy of Business, July

Benders, R. and Biesiot, W. (1996) 'Electricity Conservation in OECD Europe: A Scenario Study with the MEED Model', in *Energy Technologies to Reduce CO_2 Emissions in Europe: Prospects, Competition, Synergy*, Conference proceedings, OECD, Paris, pp29–54

Benedick, R. (1991) *Ozone Diplomacy: New Directions in Safeguarding the Planet*, Cambridge University Press, Cambridge

Benkhelifa, F., Cu, T. and Truong, N. (2001) *Air Pollution and Traffic in Ho Chi Minh City: The ETAP Approach*, Transport Planning, Demand Management and Air Quality, Manila, Philippines, 26–27 February

Bentley, M. (2000) 'Global Consumers Have Spoken: An International Study on Consumer Trends and Expectations', *Environment Review*, vol 23, no 4

Benyus, J. (1997) *Biomimicry: Innovations Inspired by Nature*, William Morrow, New York

Berger, C. (2004) *Submission to Treasury on CLERP (Audit Reform and Corporate Disclosure) Bill 2003*, prepared for the ACF by Charles Berger, Law and Corporate Responsibility Coordinator, February

Berman, P. (2000) 'Cyberspace and the State Action Debate: The Cultural Value of Applying Constitutional Norms to "Private" Regulation', *University of Colorado Law Review*, vol 71, no 4, May

Bevitt, R., Erskine, W., Gillespie, G., Harris, J., Lake, P., Miners, B. and Varley, I. (1998) *Expert Panel Environmental Flow Assessment of Various Rivers Affected by the Snowy Mountain Scheme*, Report to the NSW Department of Land and Water Conservation

Birkeland, J. (1995) *Rethinking Pollution, Turning Growth into ESD: Economically*, EIA National Conference, Brisbane, 26–27 October

Birkeland, J. (2002) *Design for Sustainability: A Sourcebook of Integrated Eco-Logical Solutions*, Earthscan, London

Blazejczak, J. and Lubbe, K. (1993) *Environmental Protection and Industrial Location: The Influence of Environmental Location – Specific Factors on Investment Decisions*, Erich Schmidt Verlag, Berlin

Bleishwitz, R. (2002) 'Governance of Eco-Efficiency in Japan, An Institutional Approach', Wuppertal Institute, *International Asienforum/International Quarterly for Asian Studies*, November

Booker, N., Gray, S., Mitchell, G., Priestley, A., Shipton, R., Speers, A., Young, M. and Syme, G. (2000) 'CSIRO Australia Sustainable Alternatives in the Provision of Urban Water Services: An Australian Approach', paper submitted to IWRAs 5th World Water Congress, International Water Resources Association, Melbourne

Boyer, B. (2000) 'Institutional Mechanisms for Sustainable Development: A Look at National Councils for Sustainable Development in Asia', *Global Environmental Change*, vol 10, pp157–160

Brain, P. (1999) *Beyond Meltdown: The Global Battle for Sustained Growth*, Scribe Publishing, Australia

Braithwaite, J. (1980) 'Inegalitarian Consequences of Egalitarian Reforms to Control Corporate Crime', *Temple Law Quarterly*, vol 53, pp1127–1146

Braithwaite, J. and Drahos, P. (2000) *Global Business Regulation*, Cambridge University Press, Cambridge

Breithaupt, M. (2001) *Transport Demand Management: Towards an Integrated Approach to Reducing Pollution from Motor Vehicles*, Transport Planning, Demand Management and Air Quality Seminar, Manila, Philippines, 26–27 February

Brennan, N. (2003) 'Achieving a Sustainable Future: An Architectural Perspective', paper submitted as a representative of the Royal Australian Institute of Architecture to the Young Professions Australia Roundtable, (Council of) Professions Australia

Bridgman, P. and Davis, G. (2000) *The Australian Policy Handbook*, McPherson's Printing Group, Australia

Bright, C. (2000) *State of the World Report, Anticipating Environmental Surprise*, Worldwatch Institute, Washington, DC

Brog, V. and John, G. (2001) 'Individualised Marketing: The Perth Success Story', presented at the Conference of Marketing Public Transport: Challenges, Opportunities and Success Stories, Aotea Centre, Auckland, NZ, August

Brown, L. (2001) *Eco-Economy: Building an Economy for the Earth*, Earth Policy Institute, WW Norton, New York/Earthscan, London

Brown, L., Flavin, C. and French, H. (2000) *State of the World 2000: A Worldwatch Institute Report on Progress Toward a Sustainable Society*, WW Norton, New York/Earthscan, London

Brown, R., O'Leary, H. and Browner, C. (1993) *Environmental Technologies Exports: Strategic Framework for US Leadership*, US Department of Commerce, Washington, DC

Burritt, R. (2002) 'Voluntary Agreements: Effectiveness Analysis – Tools, Guidelines and Checklist', in ten Brink, P. (ed) *Voluntary Environmental Agreements: Process, Practice and Future Use*, Institute for European Environmental Policy (IEEP), Brussels/Greenleaf Publishing, Sheffield, UK

Burritt, R., Hahn, T. and Schaltegger, S. (2002) 'Towards a Comprehensive Framework for Environmental Management Accounting: Links Between Business Actors and EMA Tools', *Australian Accounting Review*, July, vol 12, no 2, pp39–50

Burritt, R., Schaltegger, S., Kokubu, K. and Wagner, M. (2003) 'Corporate Environmental Management Accounting Information and Appraisal of Staff Members: Some Cross Country Evidence', in Bennett, M., Rikhardsson, P. and Schaltegger, S. (eds) *Environmental Management Accounting: Purpose and Progress*, Kluwer Academic, Boston/Dordrecht/London, pp151–188

Business Wire (2000) 'Shell's Commitment to Ethics Includes Hundreds of Millions in Investment, According to Shell Chairman Sir Mark Moody-Stuart, Appearing in World Energy', *Business Wire*, 31 October

Button, K. and Weyman-Jones, T. (1992) 'Ownership Structure, Institutional Organization and Measured X-inefficiency', *American Economic Review*, May, pp439–445

CADDET (Centre for the Analysis and Dissemination of Demonstrated Energy Technologies) (1995) *Saving Energy with Electric Motor and Drive*, CADDET Energy Efficiency, www.caddet.org)

Campbell, C. (1997) *The Coming Oil Crisis*, Multi-Science Publishing, Brentwood

Carson, R. (1962) *Silent Spring* (40th Anniversary Edition published in 2002 by Houghton Mifflin, Boston)

Cascio, W. (1993) *Downsizing What do we know, What have we learned?* Academy of Management Executive 7

Castleman, B. (1979) 'The Export of Hazardous Factories to Developing Nations', *International Journal of Health Services*, vol 9, pp569–606

Castleman, B. (1981) 'More on the International Asbestos Business', *International Journal of Health Services*, vol 11, pp339–340

CCP (Cities for Climate Protection) Australia (2003) *2003 Measures Evaluation Report*, CCP, Australian Government, Australia

Cervero, R. (1998) *The Transit Metropolis*, Island Press, Washington, DC

Chambers, R. (1966) *Accounting, Evaluation and Economic Behaviour*, Scholars Book Co, Houston, Texas

Chappells, H., Klintaman, M., Linden, A., Shove, E., Spaargaren, G. and van Vliet, B. (2001) *Domestic Consumption Utility Services and the Environment*, Final DOMUS report, University of Lancaster, Wageningen and Lund

CLTM (Dutch Committee on Long-term Environmental Policy) (1990) *The Environment: Concepts for the 21st Century*, CLTM, Zeist, Netherlands, Kerkebosch

Coleman, J. S. (1988) 'Social Capital and the Creation of Human Capital', *American Journal of Sociology*, vol 94, Supplement, pp95–120

Collaborative Economics (1998) *Linking the New Economy to the Livable Community*, The James Irvine Foundation, San Francisco

Collins, J. and Porras, J. (1994) *Built to Last: Successful Habits of Visionary Companies*, Century, London

Collis, B. (2002) *Fields of Discovery: Australia's CSIRO*, Allen & Unwin, Sydney

Committee on Abrupt Climate Change, National Research Council (2002) *Abrupt Climate Change: Inevitable Surprises*. National Academies Press, Washington, DC

Commonwealth of Australia (1992) *National Strategy for Ecologically Sustainable Development*, Australian Government Publishing Service, Canberra

Commonwealth of Australia (1997) *Investing for Growth: The Howard Government's Plan for Australian Industry*, Commonwealth of Australia

Conlisk, J. (1996) 'Why Bounded Rationality?', *Journal of Economic Literature*, vol 34, no 2, pp669–700

Connor, R. and Dovers, S. (2004) *Institutional Change for Sustainable Development*, Edward Elgar, Cheltenham

Corbett, J. and Vines, D. (1999) 'The Asian Crisis: Lessons from the Collapse of Financial Systems, Exchange Rates and Macroeconomic Policy', in Agenor, P., Miller, M., Vines, D. and Weber, A. (eds) *The Asian Financial Crisis: Causes, Contagion and Consequences*, Cambridge University Press, Cambridge

Costanza, R., d'Arge, R., de Groot, R., Farber, S., Grasso, M., Hannon, B., Limburg, K., Naeem, S., O'Neill, R. and Paruelo, J. (1997) 'The Value of the World's Ecosystem Services and Natural Capital', *Nature*, 387, 15 May, pp253–260

Cox, P., Betts, R., Jones, C., Spall, S. and Totterdell, I. (2000) 'Acceleration of Global Warming Due to Carbon-Cycle Feedbacks in a Coupled Climate Model', *Nature*, 408, pp184–187

Cramer, D. and Taggart, D. (2002) 'Design and Manufacture of an Affordable Advanced-Composite Automotive Body Structure', Proceedings of The 19th International Battery, Hybrid and Fuel Cell Electric Vehicle Symposium & Exhibition, EVS-19

CSIRO (Commonwealth Scientific and Industrial Research Organisation) (2000) *New Plant for Green Energy and Landcare*, CSIRO Media Release, Ref 2000/333, 13 December

CSIRO (2001) *Water Limit to Australia's Economic Growth*, CSIRO Media Release, Ref 2001/151, 20 June

CSIRO Built Environment (2000) 'Green Campus Design Savings 60% on Energy', *Innovation Online*, no 13, June

d'Evie, F. and Beeler, B. (eds) (2002) *Integrating Global Environmental Conventions at National and Local Levels*: NCSD Report 2001, Earth Council, San Jose, Costa Rica

d'Evie, F., MacDonald, M., Mata, R. and Rodriguez, R. (eds) (2000) *National Experiences of Integrative, Multi-Stakeholder Processes for Sustainable Development*: NCSD Report 2000, Earth Council, San Jose, Costa Rica

Daily, G. and Ellison, K. (2003) *The New Economy of Nature*, Stanford University

Dasgupta, P. and Maler, K. (2001) *Wealth as a Criterion for Sustainable Development*, Beijer Institute Discussion Paper 139, Beijer International Institute of Ecological Economics, Stockholm

Dawson, T. (2002) The IMF's Role in Asia: Part of the Problem or Part of the Solution?, prepared remarks for the Institute of Policy Studies and Singapore Management University Forum, Singapore, 10 July

de Blas, A. (2001) 'Can Adelaide Survive without the Murray', Interview ABC *Earthbeat*, broadcast on Saturday 15 December

de Blas, A. (2003) 'Water: What's a Fair Price to Pay?', Interview ABC *Earthbeat*, broadcast on Saturday 23 August

DeCanio, S. (1993) 'Barriers Within Firms to Energy-efficient Investment', *Energy Policy*, vol 21, no 9, pp906–914

DeCanio, S. (1994a) 'Agency and Control Problems in US Corporations: The Case of Energy-Efficient Investment Projects', *Journal of the Economics of Business*, vol 1, no 1, pp105–123

DeCanio, S. (1994b) 'Why Do Profitable Energy-Saving Investment Projects Languish?', *Journal of General Management*, vol 20, no 1, pp62–71

DeCanio, S. (1997) *The Economics of Climate Change. Background Paper*, Redefining Progress, San Francisco

DeCanio, S. (1998) 'The Efficiency Paradox: Bureaucratic and Organizational Barriers to Profitable Energy-Saving Investments', *Energy Policy*, vol 26, no 5, pp441–454

DeCanio, S. and Watkins, W. (1998) 'Investment in Energy Efficiency: Do the Characteristics of Firms Matter?', *Review of Economics and Statistics* February, pp95–107

Deni Greene Consulting Services (2001) A *Capital Idea: Realising Value from Environmental and Social Performance*, prepared with Standards Australia and Ethical Investment Services for the Australian Department of Environment and Heritage

Denniss, R., Diesendorf, M. and Saddler, H. (2004) A *Clean Energy Future for Australia*, a report by the Clean Energy Group of Australia

Department of Sustainability and Environment (2003) *Sustainability in the Built Environment. Discussion Paper*, Victorian Government, September

Department of Trade and Industry (2003) *Our Energy Future: Creating a Low Carbon Economy, Energy White Paper*, UK Department of Trade and Industry, Version 11

Dickson, B., Yashayaev, I., Melncke, J., Yurrell, B., Dye, S. and Holfort, J. (2002) 'Nature, Rapid Freshening of the Deep North Atlantic Ocean over the Past Four Decades', *Nature*, 25 April, vol 416, no 6883, pp832–837

Dodds, S. (1997) 'Economic Growth and Human Well-Being', in Hamilton, C. and Diesendorf, M. (eds) *Human Ecology, Human Economy: Ideas for an Ecologically Sustainable Future*, Allen & Unwin, Sydney, pp99–124

Doering, R. (1993) *Canadian Round Tables on the Environment and the Economy: Their History, Form and Function*, Working Paper 14, National Round Table on the Environment and the Economy (NRTEE), Ottawa

Dore, J., Woodhill, J., Andrews, K. and Keating, C. (2003) 'Sustainable Regional Development: Lessons from Australian Experiences', in Dovers, S. and Wild River, S. (eds) (2003) *Managing Australia's Environment*, Federation Press, Sydney

Dorfman, J. (1991) 'Stocks of Companies Announcing Layoffs Fire up Investors, but Prices Often Wilt', *The Wall St Journal*, 10 December

Dovers, S. (1997) 'Sustainability: Demands on Policy', *Journal of Public Policy* vol 16, pp303–318

Dovers, S. (2001) *Institutions and Sustainability*, ACF Tela Paper 7, Australian Conservation Foundation, Melbourne

Dovers, S. (2002) 'Sustainability: Reviewing Australia's Progress', *International Journal of Environmental Studies*, vol 59, pp559–571

Dovers, S. and Wild River, S. (eds) (2003) *Managing Australia's Environment*, Federation Press, Sydney

Downes, L. and Mui, C. (1998) *Unleashing the Killer App: Digital Strategies for Market Dominance*, Harvard Business School Press, Boston

DRE (Department of Resources and Energy) (1987) *Energy Demand and Supply Australia 1960–61 to 1984–85*, DRE, Bureau of Resource Economics, AGPS, Canberra

Drozdiak, W. (2000) 'Firms Become "Green" Advocates Global Warming Talks Near End', *Washington Post*

Drucker, P. (2001) 'Will the Corporation Survive?' in A Survey of the Near Future, *The Economist*, 3 November

Dumaresq, D. and Greene, R. (2001) *Soil Structure, Fungi, Fauna & Phosphorus in Sustainable Cropping Systems*, Rural Industries Research and Development Corporation (RIRDC)

Dunphy, D., Benveniste, J., Griffiths, A. and Sutton, P. (eds) (2000) *Sustainability: The Corporate Challenge of the 21st Century*, Allen & Unwin, Sydney

Dunphy, D., Griffiths, A. and Benn, S. (2002) *Organizational Change for Corporate Sustainability*, Routledge, Hove, East Sussex

Dunstan, B. (2003) 'Henderson Top of the Global Pack, in theory', *Australian Financial Review*, 24 October

EcoRecycle (2002) *A Materials Efficient Future for Victoria: Developing a Solid Waste Strategy – A Discussion Paper*, EcoRecycle, Melbourne

ECOS (2004) *Greener Buildings at the Touch of a Button*, CSIRO Publishing, Issue 118, January–March, p6

Ehrenberg, R. (2003) 'Rapidly Multiplying Invasive Species Pose Host of Dangers to US', *The Dallas Morning News*, Friday, 19 December

EIA (Energy Information Administration) (2000) *Annual Energy Review*, EIA, Washington, DC

Ellis, M. and Associates (1999) *Contribution of the Sustainable Energy Industry to the* NSW *Economy*, Sustainable Energy Development Authority (SEDA) Discussion Paper, Sydney

Ellsworth, J., Hildebrand, L. and Glover, E. (1997) 'Canada Atlantic Coastal Action Program: A Community Based Approach to Collective Governance', *Oceans and Coastal Management*, vol 36, nos 1–3, pp121–142

Emtairah, T. (2002) *Corporate Environmental Reporting: Review of Policy Action in Europe*, International Institute for Industrial Environmental Economics, February

Engineers Australia Sustainable Energy Taskforce (2001) *Towards a Sustainable Energy Future: Setting the Directions and Framework for Change*, Institution of Engineers of Australia, Canberra

EPS (2000) *Truckee Meadows Region: Facing the Future*, Economic and Planning Systems Report No 9222, USA

Etheridge, D., Steele, L., Francy, R. and Langenfelds, R. (1998) 'Atmospheric Methane Between 1000 AD and Present: Evidence of Anthropogenic Emissions and Climatic Variability', *Journal of Geophysical Research*, vol103, pp15, 979–15 and 993

Etheridge, D., Steele, L., Langenfelds, R., Francey, R., Barnola, J. and Morgan, V. (1996) 'Natural and Anthropogenic Changes in Atmospheric CO_2 over the Last 1000 Years from Air in Antarctic Ice and Firn', *Journal of Geophysical Research*, vol 101 (D2), pp4115–4128

European Commission (2001) *Commission Issues Guidelines for Environment-Friendly Procurement*, Press Release IP/01/959, Brussels, 5 July

European Environment Agency (1997) *Environmental Agreements: Environmental Effectiveness*, Environmental Issues Series No 3, vols 1 & 2, European Environment Agency, Copenhagen

Fairbanks, M. (2000) Changing The Mind of a Nation: Elements in a Process for Creating Prosperity, in Harrison, L. and Huntington, S. (eds), *Culture Matters: How Values Shape Human Progress*, Basic Books, New York

Fairbanks, M. and Lindsay, S. (1997) *Plowing the Sea: Nurturing the Hidden Sources of Growth in the Developing World*, Harvard Business School Press, Boston, Chs 1–7 (with a Foreword by Michael E. Porter)

Feketekuty, G. (1993) 'The Link between Trade and Environmental Policy', *Minnesota Journal of Global Trade*, vol 2, pp171–205

Feldman, S., Soyka, P. and Ameer, P. (1997) 'Does Improving a Firm's Environmental Management System and Environmental Performance Result in a Higher Stock Price?', ICF Kaiser International, *The Journal of Investing*, Winter, pp87–97

Felizardo, K., Virtucio, Jr, Mayo, G., Amit, C. and Encabo, S. (2002) *From Rio to Manila: Ten Years After – An Assessment of Agenda 21 Implementation in the Philippines*, Philippine Council for Sustainable Development

Filmer, D. (2000) *The Structure of Social Disparities in Education: Gender and Wealth*, World Bank Research Policy Working Paper 2268, World Bank, Washington, DC

Fletcher, K. (2003) 'How Green is thy City', *Business London*, Spring

Florida, R. (2002) The Rise of the Creative Class: And How It is Transforming Work, Leisure, Community and Everyday Life, Basic Books, New York

Forde, H. (2003) *Building an Entrepreneurial Economy Through a Systematically Managed Process of Cluster Driven Innovation*, Industry Cluster Project, Business SA, Australia

Forty, A. (1986) *Objects of Desire: Design and Society Since 1750*, Thames and Hudson, UK

Foss, M., Gonzales, E. and Noyen, H. (1999) 'Ford Motor Company', in Hastings, M. (ed) *Corporate Incentives and Environmental Decision Making*, Houston Advanced Research Center, Houston, TX, pp35–52

Foster, R. and Kaplan, S. (2001) *Creative Destruction: Why Companies that are Built to Last Under-Perform the Market and How to Transform Them*, Doubleday, New York

Fukasaku, Y. (1999) 'Stimulating Environmental Innovation', *The STI Review*, no 25, issue 2, Special Issue on Sustainable Development, OECD, Paris

Fuller, L. (1965) 'A Reply to Professors Cohen and Dworkin', 10 *Villanova Law Review*, pp655, 657

Funtowitz, S. and Ravetz, J. (2002) 'Environmental Policy under Conditions of Complexity', *Post-Normal Science*, EC-JRC/ISIS, Ispra, Italy/RMC Ltd, London

Funtowicz, S., Ravetz, J. and O'Connor, M. (1998) 'Challenges in the Use of Science for Sustainable Development', *International Journal of Sustainable Development*, Inderscience, vol 1, no 1

Funtowicz, S., Guimaraes-Pereira, A., Lonza-Ricci, L. and Wolf, O. (2003) *Recommendations for Sustainability-Oriented European Research Programs*, Deliverable 6, AIRP-SD Project, EC-STRATA Program

Gandy, M. (1997) 'The Making of a Regulatory Crisis, Restructuring New York's Water Supply', *Transactions of the Institute of British Geographers*, New Series vol 22, no 2, pp338–358

Garz, H., Volk, C. and Gilles, M. (2002) *More Gain than Pain, SRI: Sustainability Pays Off*, WestBL Panmure

Geczy, C., Stambaugh, R. and Levin, D. (2003) *Investing in Socially Responsible Mutual Funds*, Research Paper, Finance Department, Wharton School, University of Pennsylvania

GeSI (Global e-Sustainability Initiative) (2002) *Information and Communications Technology*, GeSI/UNEP Division of Technology, Industry and Economics, Paris

Gipe, P. (2002) 'Soaring to New Heights: The World Wind Energy Market', *Renewable Energy World*, July–August

Gittens, R. (2003) 'The Humbled Fund has had to Rethink its Operations', *Sydney Morning Herald* 29 March and 'The International Monetary Fund does a www – we were wrong', *The Age* 29 March

Gleick, P. (1993) *Water in Crisis: A Guide to the World's Fresh Water Resources*, Stockholm Environment Institute, Sweden

Glenn, J. and Gordon, T. (1998) *State of the Future Report: Issues and Opportunities*, American Council for the United Nations University, Millennium Project, Washington, DC

Gliessman, S. (1998) *Agroecology: Ecological Processes in Sustainable Agriculture*, Sleeping Bear Press, Michigan

Gomez-Ibañez, J. (1991) 'A Global View of Automobile Dependence', *Journal of the American Planning Association*, vol 57, no 3, pp376–379

Goodin, R. (1996) 'Institutions and Their Design', in Goodin, R. (ed) *The Theory of Institutional Design*, Cambridge University Press, Cambridge

Government of Western Australia (2002) *Focus on the Future: The Western Australian State Sustainability Strategy: Consultation Draft*, Department of the Premier and Cabinet, Perth

Government of Western Australia (2003) *Hope for the Future: The Western Australian State Sustainability Strategy A Vision For Quality of Life in Western Australia*, Department of the Premier and Cabinet, Perth

Green, M. (2000) *Power to the People: Sunlight to Electricity using Solar Cells*, University of New South Wales

Greenwald, B. and Stiglitz, J. (1986) 'Externalities in Economies with Imperfect Information and Incomplete Markets', *Quarterly Journal of Economics*, vol 101, no 2

Griffin, K. (1989) *Alternative Strategies of Economic Development*, St Martin's Press, New York

Grove, A. (1999) *Only the Paranoid Survive: How to Exploit the Crisis Points that Challenge Every Company and Career*, Bantam Books, New York

Grove-White, R. (1997) 'Brent Spar Rewrote the Rules: Shell Oil Co's Decision to Dispose the Brent Spar Oil Platform in the North Sea', *New Statesman*, 20 June (www.findarticles.com/p/articles/mi_m0FQP/is_n4339_v126/ai_20534418)

Guerard, J. B. Jr. (1997) 'Is There a Cost to being Socially Responsible in Investing? It Costs Nothing to be Good', *Journal of Forecasting*, vol 16, p475 (the 1997 Moskowitz Prize winner concluding: 'no')

Gundling, E. (2000) *The 3M Way to Innovation, Balancing People & Profit*, Kodansha International Ltd, Japan

Gunningham, N. and Grabosky, P. (1998) *Smart Regulation: Designing Environmental Regulation*, Oxford University Press, Oxford

Gunningham, N. and Rees J. (1997) 'Industry Self Regulation: An Institutional Perspective', *Law and Policy*, vol 19, no 4, pp363–414

Gunningham, N. and Sinclair D. (2002) *Leaders and Laggards: Next Generation Environmental Regulation*, Greenleaf Publishing, Sheffield, UK

Gunningham, N., Kagan, R. and Thornton, D. (2003) *Shades of Green: Business, Regulation and Environment*, Stanford University Press, USA

Gupta, A. and Lad, L. (1983) 'Industry Self Regulation: An Economic, Organizational, and Political Analysis', *Academy of Management Review*, vol 8, no 3, pp416–425

Hamilton, C. (1998) 'Measuring Changes in Economic Welfare: The Genuine Progress Indicator for Australia', in Eckersley, R. (ed) *Measuring Progress: Is Life Getting Better?* CSIRO Publishing, Australia

Hamilton, C. and Diesendorf, M. (eds) (1997) *Human Ecology, Human Economy: Ideas for an Ecologically Sustainable Future*, Allen & Unwin, Sydney

Hamilton, C., Pears, A. and Pollard, P. (2001) *Regional Employment and Greenhouse Policies*, Australia Institute

Hamilton, C., Schlegelmilch, K., Hoerner, A., and Milne, J. (2000) *Environmental Tax Reform: Using the Tax System to Protect the Environment and Promote Employment*, Tela series, Australian Conservation Foundation

Hamilton, C., Turton, H., Saddler, H., and Jinlong, M. (2002) *Long Term Greenhouse Gas Scenarios: A Pilot Study of Australian can Achieve Deep Cuts in Emissions*, Discussion Paper 48, The Australia Institute, Canberra

Hamilton, K. and Clemens, M. (1999) 'Genuine Savings Rates in Developing Countries', *World Bank Economic Review*, vol 13, no 2, pp333–356

Hammond, M. (1946) 'Economic Stagnation in the Early Roman Empire', *Journal of Economic History*, Supplement vol 6, pp75–76

Hanley N., Shogren, J. and White, B. (1997) *Environmental Economics in Theory and Practice*, Macmillan, London

Hansen, B., Turrell, W. and Osterhus, S. (2001) 'Nature Decreasing Overflow from Nordic Seas into the Atlantic Ocean through the Faroe Bank Channel Since 1950', *Nature* 411, pp927–930, 21 June

Hardin, G. (1968) 'The Tragedy of the Commons', *Science*, vol 162, issue 3859, 13 December, pp1243–1248

Hardin G. (1998) 'Extensions of "The Tragedy of the Commons"', *Science*, vol 280, issue 5364, 1 May, pp682–683

Hass-Klau, C. (1993) 'Impact of Pedestrianization and Traffic Calming on Retailing: A Review of the Evidence from Germany and the UK', *Transportation Policy*, vol 1, no 1, pp21–31

Hawken, P., Lovins, A. and Lovins, L. H. (1999) *Natural Capitalism: Creating the Next Industrial Revolution*, Earthscan, London

Hayek, F. (1949) 'The Uses of Knowledge in Society', in Hayek, F., *Individualism and Economic Order*, Routledge and Kegan Paul, London

Healey, P. (1999) 'Sites, Jobs and Portfolios: Economic Development and the Planning System', *Policy and Politics*, vol 18, no 1, pp91–103

Healy, J. (2003) *Corporate Governance & Wealth Creation in New Zealand*, Dunmore Press, Palmerston North, New Zealand

Heij, E (2002) CSIRO FutureCorp Forum, CSIRO *Sustainability Newsletter*, no 12, Adelaide (www.bml.csiro.au/susnetnl/netwkl2E.pdf)

Heiman, J. (2002) *Fostering a Green China: RMI's Bill Browning Heads to the Far East's Wild West to Promote Sustainable Development*, Rocky Mountain Institute Newsletter, Colorado

Hemmati, M. (2002) 'Introduction', from *Multi-stakeholder Processes for Governance and Sustainability: Beyond Deadlock and Conflict*, Earthscan, London

Herlands, J. (1999) *The Connection Between Growth Management and Local Economic Development*, News and Views, American Planning Association Economic Development Division

Hildyard, N. and Mansley, M. (2001) *The Campaigners Guide to Financial Markets*, The Corner House, Dorset

Holliday, C.O., Schmidheiny. S. and Watts, P. (2002) *Walking the Talk: The Business Case for Sustainable Development*, World Business Council for Sustainable Development/Greenleaf Publishing, Sheffield, UK

Holling, C. (1978) *Adaptive Environmental Assessment and Management*, John Wiley & Sons, London

Holling, C. (1989) 'Integrating Science for Sustainable Development', in *Sustainable Development, Science and Policy*, Proceedings of the Bergen Conference, 8–12 May, Norwegian Research Council for Science and the Humanities

Holm, H. and Sorensen, G. (1995) *Whose World Order: Uneven Globalization and the End of the Cold War*, Westview Press

Howarth, R., Haddad, B. and Paton, B. (2000) 'The Economics of Energy Efficiency: Insights from Voluntary Participation Programs', *Energy Policy*, vol 28, nos 6–7, pp477–486

Hughes, D. (1975) *Ecology in Ancient Civilizations*, University of New Mexico Press

ICLEI (International Council for Local Environmental Initiatives) (2002) *Local Government and the Johannesburg Summit*, ICLEI

IEA (International Energy Agency) (1998) *Key World Energy Statistics*, IEA

IFC (International Finance Corporation) (2002) *The Business Case for Sustainability In Emerging Economies*, IFC, Ethos Institute, Sustainability Ltd

Industry Canada (2000) *An Evaluative Framework for Voluntary Codes*, Office of Consumer Affairs, Industry Canada, Ottawa

Industry Canada and Treasury Board (1998) *Voluntary Codes: A Guide for Their Development and Use*, Office of Consumer Affairs, Industry Canada and Regulatory Affairs Division at the Treasury Board, Industry Canada, Ottawa

Inglehart, R. (1997) *Modernization and Postmodernization: Cultural, Economic and Political Change in 43 Societies*, Princeton University Press

INRA Europe (1991) *European Attitudes to Traffic Problems and Public Transport*, Survey for ECE and UITP, Institut National de la Recherche Agronomique, Brussels, July

Interlaboratory Working Group (1997) *Scenarios of US Carbon Reductions: Potential Impacts of Energy-Efficient and Low-Carbon Technologies by 2010 and Beyond*, Oak Ridge, TN and Berkeley, Oak Ridge CA

IPCC (Intergovernmental Panel on Climate Change) (1995) *Climate Change 1995: Impacts, Adaptations and Mitigation of Climate Change: Scientific-Technical Analysis*, contribution of working group 2 to the second assessment report of theIPCC, Cambridge University Press, Cambridge

IPCC (2001a) *Climate Change 2000*, IPCC, Cambridge University Press, Cambridge

IPCC (2001b) *Climate Change 2001 Third Assessment Report: The Scientific Basis*, IPCC

ITDP (Institute for Transportation and Development Policy) (2002) *Guangzhou Makes Pedestrian Area Permanent*, Sustainable Transport E-update, ITDP, May–June

ITDP (2003a) *International Bus Rapid Transit Program*, ITDP, Available online

ITDP (2003b) *Seoul to Raze Elevated Freeway, Giving Way to Revitalized City Center*, Sustainable Transport E-update, ITDP, May

Jacobson, B. and Aldana, S. (2001) 'Relationship Between Frequency of Aerobic Activity and Illness-Related Absenteeism in a Large Employee Sample', *Journal of Occupational and Environmental Medicine*, December, vol 43, no 12, p1019

Jacobson, M. and Masters, G. (2001) 'Wind is Competitive with Coal', *Science* 24 August, vol 1438, Department of Civil and Environmental Engineering, Stanford University, Stanford, USA

Jaffe, A. and Stavins, R. (1994) 'The Energy-Efficiency Gap', *Energy Policy*, vol 22, no 10, pp804–810

Jaffe, A., Adam, B., Peterson, S., Portney, P. and Stavins, R. (1995) 'Environmental Regulation and the Competitiveness of US Manufacturing: What does the Evidence Tell Us?', *Journal of Economic Literature*, vol 33, pp132–163

Jansen, J. Bosch, G. and Weaver, P. (2003) 'Research and Technology Development Programs: From the Very Start to the Very Finish', In *Final Report of the* AIRP-SD *Project*, EC-STRATA Program, Vienna, June

Japan NEDO (2003) 'Japan's Hydrogen Vision', Toshiaki ABE, Director General, Hydrogen Energy Systems Technology Development Department of New Energy and Industrial Technology Development Organization (NEDO), Toward Hydrogen IEA Renewable Energy Working Party Seminar, 3 March

Jarass, L. and Obermair, G. (1997) *More Jobs, Less Tax Evasion, Cleaner Environment Options for Compensating Reductions in the Taxation of Labour, Taxation of Other Factors of Production*, European Commission, College of Weisbaden, Germany, August

Jones, A. (1974) *The Roman Economy: Studies in Ancient Economic and Administrative History*, Basil Blackwell, Oxford

Jones, D. (2003) 'Supply Chains of the Future', presentation to the Efficient Consumer Response (ECR) Conference, Berlin, Germany

Jones, R. (2001) *The Big Idea*, Profile Books, London

Kabelvåg Workshop (1998) *Consumption in a Sustainable World*, International Institute for Environment and Development, London

Kahneman, D., Slovic, P. and Tversky, A. (1982) *Judgment Under Uncertainty: Heuristics and Biases*, Cambridge University Press, Cambridge

Kaufmann, R. and Stern, D. (2002) 'Evidence for Human Influence on Climate from Hemisphere Temperature Relations', *Nature*, 3 July

Kellogg, H. (1977) 'Sizing up the Energy Requirements for Producing Primary Metals', *Engineering and Mining Journal*, vol 178, no 4, pp61–65

Kemp, D. (2002) *National Pollution Inventory, 2001–02*, Press Release, Australian Government

Kenworthy, J. (1991) 'The Land Use/Transit Connection in Toronto: Some Lessons for Australian Cities', *Australian Planner*, vol 29, no 3, pp149–154

Kenworthy, J. (2003) *Transport Energy Use and Greenhouse Gases in Urban Passenger Transport Systems: A Study of 84 Global Cities*, as submitted to the International Sustainability Conference: Second Meeting of the Academic Forum of Regional Government for Sustainable Development 2003, Department of the Premier and Cabinet, Perth

Kenworthy, J. and Hu, G. (2002) *Transport and Urban Form in Chinese Cities: An International Comparative and Policy Perspective with Implications for Sustainable Urban Transport in China*, DISP [Zurich], vol 151, pp4–14

Kenworthy, J. and Laube, F. (1999) *An International Sourcebook of Automobile Dependence in Cities, 1960–1990*, University Press of Colorado, Colorado

Kenworthy, J.and Laube.F (2001) 'The Millennium Cities Database for Sustainable Transport', *Soziale Technik* 4, pp17–18

Kerr, W. and Ryan, C. (2001) 'Eco-Efficiency Gains from Remanufacturing', *Journal of Cleaner Production*, vol 9 no 2

Keynes, J. (1936) *The General Theory of Employment and Economics*, Macmillan Cambridge University Press, Cambridge

King, A. and Lennox, M. (2000) 'Industry Self Regulation Without Sanctions: The Chemical Industry's Responsible Care Program', *Academy of Management Journal*, vol 43, no 4, pp698–716

Kingham, S. and Donohoe, S. (2002) 'Children's Perception of Transport', *World Transport Policy and Practice*, vol 8, no 1, pp6–10

Kirwan, R. (1992) 'Urban Form, Energy and Transport: A Note on the Newman-Kenworthy Thesis', –*Urban Policy and Research*, vol 10, no 1, pp6–23

Klare, M. (2001) *Resource Wars: The New Landscape of Global Conflict*, Henry Holt Books, New York

Koelman, O. (2004) *Bio-Inspired Design: Ideas, Wisdom, and Applications from Nature*, RMI Green Development Services publication, Rocky Mountain Institute, Colorado

Kokubu, K. and Eliko, N. (2001) *Environmental Accounting Practices of Listed Companies in Japan*, IGES Discussion Paper No 2

Kreps, D. (1997) 'Economics: The Current Position', *Daedalus*, vol 126, no 1, pp59–85

Krishnapillai, S. and Boele, N. (2003) 'Clean Energy Doesn't Cost the Earth: Putting a Lid on Our Greenhouse Pollution', Australian Conservation Foundation, *Habitat*, August

Krugman, P. (1994) 'Does Third World Growth Hurt First World Prosperity?', *Harvard Business Review*, June–August, pp113–121

Kumarasivam, K. (1996) 'Implementation of EMS in Malaysia', paper to the ISO Conference 14000: Regulatory and Trade Challenges, Canberra

Kuznets, S. (1962) 'How to Judge Quality', *The New Republic*, 20 October, pp29–32

Kvande, H. (1999) 'Environmental Improvements in Aluminium Production Technology', *Light Metal Age*, February, pp44–53

Laird, P., Newman, P., Bachels, M. and Kenworthy, J. (2001) *Back on Track: Rethinking Transport Policy in Australia and New Zealand*, UNSW Press, Sydney

Lajeunesse, R., Lanoie, P. and Patry, M. (2001) *Environmental Regulation and Productivity: New Findings on the Porter Analysis*, CIRANO Working Papers/CIRANO (RePEc:cir:cirwor:2001s-53)

Lave, C. (1992) 'Cars and Demographics', *Access*, 1, pp4–11

Leadbeter, P., Gunningham, N. and Boer, B. (1999) *Environmental Outlook No 3 Law and Policy*, Federation Press

Leibenstein, H. (1987) *Inside the Firm: the Inefficiencies of Hierarchy*, Harvard University Press, Cambridge, MA

Leonard, J. (1988) *Pollution and the Struggle for World Product*, Cambridge University Press

Leone, F., Whitelegg, K. and Weber, M. (2002) *National Research Activities and Sustainable Development: A Survey and Assessment of National Research Initiatives in Support of Sustainable Development*, IPTS Technical Report Series, EUR 20389 EN. Seville, Spain: European Commission Joint Research Centre, Institute for Prospective Technological Studies (IPTS)

Lewis, A. (2002) *Morals, Markets and Money: Ethical, Green and Socially Responsible Investing*, Prentice Hall, London

Lim Lan Yuan (1997) *Case Study on Urban Transportation Development and Management in Singapore*, Second International Expert Panel Meeting on Urban Infrastructure Development, Bangkok, Thailand, 8–9 December

Lindert, P. H. (2004) *Growing Public: Social Spending and Economic Growth Since the Eighteenth Century*, Cambridge University Press, New York

List, F. (1885) *The National System of Political Economy*, translated from German by Sampson S. Lloyd, Longmans, Green and Co, London

Littler, G., Wiesner, R. and Vermeulen, L. (1997) *The Effects of Downsizing Cross-Cultural Data from Three Countries*, Academy of Management Meeting, Boston MA

Lopez-Claros, A. (2003) 'Boom Towns: Is Asia's Urban Explosion A Blessing Or A Curse?', *Newsweek International*, Special issue 37, vol 142, no S (3684) s1, pp10–12

Lovins, A. (2003) *Twenty Hydrogen Myths*, Rocky Mountain Institute, Colorado

Lovins, A. (2004) 'Energy Efficiency, Taxonomic Overview for Earth's Energy Balance', in Cleveland, C. J. (ed) *Encyclopedia of Energy*, Volume 1, Elsevier

Lovins, A. and Cramer, D. (2004) 'Hypercars, Hydrogen and the Automotive Transition', 2004 Future Vehicles Special Edition, *International Journal of Vehicle Design*, 23 March, vol 35, nos 1/2, pp50–85

Lovins, A. and Lovins, L. H. (1982) *Brittle Power*, Brick House

Lovins, A. and Lovins, L. H. (1983) 'The Fragility of Domestic Energy', *The Atlantic Monthly*, November, pp118–126

Lovins, A. and Lovins, L. H. (1997) *Climate: Making Sense and Making Money*, Rocky Mountain Institute, Colorado

Lovins, A. and Williams, B. (1999) *A Strategy for the Hydrogen Transition*, Rocky Mountain Institute, Colorado

Lovins, A., Datta, K., Feiler, T., Rábago, K., Swisher, J., Lehmann, A. and Wicker, K. (2002) *Small Is Profitable: The Hidden Economic Benefits of Making Electrical Resources the Right Size*, Rocky Mountain Institute Publications, Colorado

Lovins, L. H. and Link, W. (2002) *Insurmountable Opportunities?: Steps and Barriers to Implementing Sustainable Development*, Comments to the UN Regional Roundtable for Europe and North America, Vail, Colorado

Lovins, L. H. and Link, W. (2003) *Pension Funds: Key to Capitalizing Natural Capitalism*, Rocky Mountain Institute and Global Academy, Colorado

Lovins, A., Datta, E. K. and others (2004) *Winning the Oil Endgame: Innovation for Profits, Jobs, and Security*, Rocky Mountain Institute, Colorado/Earthscan, London

Lumb, J., Pears, A. and Buckley, K. (1996) *Key Areas for the Review of the National Greenhouse Response Strategy*, Report to ICESD Greenhouse Working Group, Melbourne

Lundvall, B. (2000) 'Introduction', in Edquist, C. and McKelvey, M. (eds) *Systems of Innovation: Growth, Competitiveness and Employment*, An Elgar Reference Collection, Edward Elgar, Cheltenham, UK

Lynch-Stieglitz, J., Curry, W. and Slowey, N. (1999) 'Weaker Gulf Stream in the Florida Straits During the Last Glacial Maximum', *Nature*, 402, p644

Maddox, Sir J. (1999) *What Remains to be Discovered?* Papermac, London

Mansley, M. (2003) *Open Disclosure: Sustainability and the Listing Regime*, Claros Consulting

Manzini, E. (2001) 'Leap-Frog: Short-Term Strategies for Sustainability', in Allen, P. (ed) *Metaphors for Change*, Greenleaf Books, Sheffield

Margolis, J. and Walsh, J. (2001) *People and Profits: The Search between a Company's Social and Financial Performance*, Lawrence Erlbaum, Mahwah, NJ

Martchek, K. (2000) 'The Importance of Recycling to the Environmental Profile of Metal Products', in Proceedings of the Fourth International Symposium on Recycling of Metals and Engineered Materials, The Minerals, Metals & Materials Society, Warrendale, PA

Matos, G. and Wagner, L. (1998) 'Consumption of Materials in the United States, 1900–1995', *Annual Review of Energy and the Environment*, vol 28, pp107–122

Maxwell, J. and Lyon, T. (1999) *What Caused US Voluntary Environmental Agreements?*, European Research Network on Voluntary Approaches (CAVA) Workshop, Copenhagen, Denmark

Mays, S. (2003) *Corporate Sustainability: An Investor Perspective: The Mays Report*, prepared with BT Financial Group for the Department of Environment and Heritage, Australian Government

McAlpine, G. and Mitchell, C. (1999) CSIRO *Solutions for Greenhouse*, based on an overview prepared for the Australian Greenhouse Office (AGO), June

McDonough, W. and Braungart, M. (1998) 'The Next Industrial Revolution', *The Atlantic Monthly*, vol 282, no 4, pp82–92

McDonough, W. and Braungart, M. (2002) *Cradle to Cradle: Remaking the Way We Make Things*, North Point Press, San Francisco

McDonough, W. and Partners (1992) *The Hannover Principles: Design for Sustainability*, Prepared for EXPO 2000, The World's Fair, Hannover, Germany

McMichael, A. (2002) 'The Biosphere, Human Health and Sustainability', *Science*, vol 297, p1063

McMichael, T. (2001) *Human Frontiers, Environments and Disease: Past Patterns, Uncertain Futures*, Cambridge University Press, Cambridge

McNeill, W. (1975) *Plagues and Peoples*, Anchor/Doubleday, Garden City, NY

Meadows, D. (1998) *Indicators and Information Systems for Sustainable Development*, Sustainability Institute, Hartland Four Corners, VT

Megalogenis, G. (2003) 'We Sink or Swim on Liquid Licence', *The Australian*, 10 November

Meijkamp, R. (2000) Changing Consumer Behaviour through Eco-Efficient Services, Thesis, Technical University of Delft , Netherlands

Mendler, F. and Odell, W. (2000) *The HOK Guidebook to Sustainable Design*, John Wiley & Sons, Indianapolis, IN

Michaelis, L. (2000) 'The Drivers of Consumption Patterns', in Heap, B. and Kent, J. (eds) *Towards Sustainable Consumption: A European Perspective*, The Royal Society, London, pp75–84

Millicer, H. (2003) 'Acting Accordingly: Tenants at 60L Have Signed a Most Unusual Occupancy Agreement', an article in a supplement for Australian Conservation Foundation's *Habitat* magazine, ACF, February

Milton, J., Kiker, C. and Lee, D. (1997) 'Adaptive Ecosystem Management and the Florida Everglades: More than Trial-and-Error?', *Journal of Agriculture and Applied Economics*, vol 29, July, pp99–107

Mintzer, I., Leonard, J. and Schwartz, P. (2003) US *Energy Scenarios for the 21st Century*, Pew Center on Global Climate Change, Washington, DC

Misra, M. and Misra, P. (2002) *Best Employers in India 2002 Study*, Hewitt Associates LLC Mumbai

Mobbs, M. (1998) *Sustainable House*, A Choice Book, Marrickvill, NSW

MOE (Ministry of Environment, Japan) (2003) A *Survey of Environmentally Corporate Behaviour*, MOE (in Japanese)

Mukoyama, A. and Hiroyuki, I. (2002) 'Environmental Information and Corporate Evaluation', paper presented to the Japan Accounting Association Annual Meeting

Murray–Darling Basin Ministerial Council (2002) *The Living Murray: A Discussion Paper on Restoring the Health of the River Murray*, Murray-Darling Basin Commission, Canberra

Murtough, G., Aretino, B. and Matysek, A. (2002) *Creating Markets for Ecosystem Services*, Australian Productivity Commission

Myers, M. (1995) 'Environmental Unknowns', *Science*, vol 21, July

Myers, N. (1990) 'Facing up to the Lack of Interface', in *Sustainable Development, Science and Policy*, Proceedings of the Bergen Conference, 8–12 May, Norwegian Research Council for Science and the Humanities, pp513–522

Myers, N. (1993) 'Environmental Refugees in a Globally Warmed World', *BioScience*, vol 43, no 11, December

Myers, N. (1996a) 'Key Challenges for Biodiversity: Discontinuities and Synergisms', *Biodiversity and Conservation*, September

Myers, N. (1996b) *The Ultimate Security: The Environmental Basis of Political Stability*, Island Press, Washington, DC

Myers, N. (2000) *Sustainable Consumption: the Meta-Problem*, The Royal Society, London

Myers, N. (2001) 'Environmental Refugees: a Growing Phenomenon of the 21st Century', *Philosophical Transactions, Biological Sciences*, vol 357, no 1420, pp609–613

Mytelka, L. (2001) 'Promoting Scientific and Technological Knowledge for Sustainable Development', paper for the Third UN Conference on Least Developed Countries, Round Table: Education for All and Sustainable Development in LDCs, May

NAEEEC (National Appliance and Equipment Energy Efficiency Committee) (2001) *National Appliance and Equipment Energy Efficiency Program: Achievements 2001 Report 2002/02*, NAEEEC, Ministerial Council of Energy, Canberra

Nelson, R. (1992) 'The Roles of Firms in Technical Advance: a Perspective from Evolutionary Theory', in Dosi, G., Giannetti, R. and Toninelli, P. (eds) *Technology and Enterprise in a Historical Perspective*, Clarendon Press, Oxford

Nelson, R. (1995) 'Recent Evolutionary Theorizing about Economic Change', *Journal of Economic Literature*, vol 33, no 1, pp48–90

Nelson, R. and Winter, S. (1982) *An Evolutionary Theory of Economic Change*, Belknap Press of Harvard University, Cambridge, MA

New York Times (2004) 'At Shell, New Accounting and Rosier Oil Outlook', *New York Times*, 12 March

Newman, P. (2002) 'Sustainability, Urban Design and Transport', paper submitted to the online conference In Search of Sustainability (www.isosconference.org.au)

Newman, P. (2003) *On Climbing Trees: An Australian Perspective on Sustainability and Political Risk*, Sustainability Policy Unit, Department of the Premier and Cabinet, Government of Western Australia, Perth

Newman, P. and Kenworthy, J. (1999) *Sustainability and Cities*, Island Press, Washington, DC

Niosi, J. (2002) 'National Systems of Innovations are "X-Efficient" (and X-Effective): Why Some are Slow Learners', *Econpapers Research Policy*, vol 31, issue 2, pp291–302

Norgate, T. and Rankin, J. (2002) *Tops at Recycling: Metals in Sustainable Development*, CSIRO, Green Processing 2002 Conference, Cairns

North, D. C. (1990) *Institutions, Institutional Change, and Economic Performance*, Cambridge University Press, New York

North, D. (1993) 'Institutions and Credible Commitment', *The American Economic Review*, vol 84, pp359–368

Northrop, M. (2003) *Cutting Greenhouse Gas Emissions is Possible and Even Profitable*, Institute for International and European Environmental Policy

NRMMC (Natural Resource Management Ministerial Council) (2003) *Report to the Council of Australian Governments*, NRMMC, Chief Executive Officers Group on Water, April

NRTEE (2001) *National Round Table on the Environment and the Economy Annual Report 2000–2001*, NRTEE, Ottawa

NZBCSD (New Zealand Business Council for Sustainable Development) (2002) *Industry Guide to Zero Waste*, NZBCSD, August

O'Meara Sheehan, M. (1999) *Reinventing Cities for People and the Planet*, Worldwatch Paper 147, Worldwatch Institute, Washington, DC

Ocasio, W. (1997) 'Towards an Attention-Based View of the Firm', *Strategic Management Journal*, vol 18, special issue supplement, pp187–206

OECD (Organisation for Economic Co-operation and Development) (1994) *Environment and Taxation: The cases of Netherlands, Sweden and the United States*, OECD, Paris

OECD (1997a) *Environmental Taxes and Green Tax Reform*, OECD, Paris

OECD (1997b) *Evaluating Economic Instruments for Environmental Protection*, OECD, Paris

OECD (1999a) *Managing National Systems of Innovation*, OECD, Paris

OECD (1999b) *Voluntary Approaches for Environmental Policy in OECD Countries: An Assessment*, Working party on Economic and Environmental Policy Integration, Environmental Policy Committee, OECD, Paris, April

OECD (2001) *Policies to Promote Sustainable Consumption: An Overview*, OECD, Paris

OECD (2002a) *Towards Sustainable Household Consumption? Trends and Policies in OECD countries*, OECD, Paris

OECD (2002b) *Governance for Sustainable Development: Five OECD Case Studies*, OECD, Paris

OECD (2003) *Improving Policy Coherence and Integration for Sustainable Development: A Checklist*, OECD, Paris

OITI (Office of Industrial Technologies) (1999) *Review of Combined Heat and Power Technologies*, OITI, US Department of Energy

Olsen, M. and Toyne P. (2000) 'Guiding Principles: the Way Ahead', in Dunphy, D., Benveniste, J., Griffiths, A. and Sutton, P. (eds) (2000) *Sustainability: The Corporate Challenge of the 21st Century*, Allen & Unwin, Sydney

Olson, M. (1982) *The Rise and Decline of Nations: Economic Growth, Stagflation, and Social Rigidities*, Yale University Press, New Haven

O'Neill, B. and Oppenheimer, M. (2002) 'Dangerous Climate Impacts and the Kyoto Protocol', *Science* 296, pp1971–2

Orr, D. (1994) *Earth In Mind*, Island Press, Washington, DC

Ostrom, E. (1986) 'How Inexorable is the "Tragedy of the Commons?" Institutional Arrangements for Changing the Social Structure of Social Dilemmas', presented at a Faculty Research Lecture, Office of Research and Graduate Development, Indiana University, 3 April

Ostrom, E., Burger, J., Field, C., Norgaard, R. and Policansky, D. (2003) 'Revisiting the Commons: Local Lessons, Global Challenges', *Science*, 9 April

Ostrom, E., Dietz, T., Dol_ak, N., Stern, P., Stonich, S. and Weber, E. (eds) (2002) *The Drama of the Commons, Committee on the Human Dimensions of Global Change*, Division of Behavioural and Social Sciences and Education, National Research Council, National Academy Press, Washington, DC

Oxfam (1997) *Growth with Equity: An Agenda for Poverty Reduction: Oxfam International Report*, Oxfam International, London

Palmer, K., Oates, W. and Portney, P. (1995) 'Tightening Environmental Standards: The Benefit-Cost or the No-Cost Paradigm?' *Journal of Economic Perspectives*, vol 9, no 4, pp119–132

Panayotu, T. and Vincent, J. (1997) *Environmental Regulation and Competitiveness*, The Global Competitiveness Report 1997, World Economic Forum, Geneva, Switzerland

Parker, L. (1999) *Environmental Costing: An Exploratory Examination*, Australian Society of Certified Practising Accountants, Melbourne, February

Patel, P. and Pavitt, K. (1998) *National Systems of Innovation Under Strain: The Internationalisation of Corporate R&D*, Science Policy Research Unit, SPRU Electronic Working Paper Series 22, p4

Paton, B. (1994) 'Design for Environment: a Management Perspective', in Socolow, R. (ed) *Industrial Ecology and Global Change*, Cambridge University Press, Cambridge

Paton, B. (2001) 'Efficiency Gains within Firms Under Voluntary Environmental Initiatives', *Journal of Cleaner Production*, vol 9, pp167–178

Paton,B (2004) *Mental Models of Voluntary Environmental Initiatives*, San Francisco State University College of Business, San Francisco

PCENZ (Parliamentary Commissioner for the Environment New Zealand) (2004) *See Change: Learning and Education for Sustainability*, PCENZ, Wellington

Pears, A. (1998) *Strategic Study of Household Energy and Greenhouse Issues* Australian Greenhouse Office, AGO, Canberra

Pears, A. (2000) 'Using Emissions Trading to Create Incentives for Demand-side Management', paper presented at Sustainable Energy Industry Association National Conference, Melbourne, October

Pears, A. (2003) *Planning Institute of Australia's Submission for Federal Government's Sustainable Cities 2025 Enquiry*, Commonwealth of Australia

Pears, A. and Greene, D. (2003) *Policy Options for Energy Efficiency in Australia*, The Australian CRC for Renewable Energy (ACRE), January

Pearson, D. (1998) *The New Natural House Book*, HarperCollins, Sydney

Pearson, L., Harris, M. and Walker, B. (2003) *Measuring and Modelling Sustainable Development in Australia using Inclusive Wealth*, Commonwealth Science Industry Research Organisation

Peck, M. S. (1997) *The Road Less Travelled and Beyond: Spiritual Growth in an Age of Anxiety*, Simon & Schuster, New York

Peden, M., McGee, K. and Krug, E. (eds) (2002) *Injury: A Leading Cause of the Global Burden of Disease*, World Health Organisation, Geneva

Peters, T. (2004) *Re-imagine! Business Excellence in a Disruptive Age*, Dorling Kindersley, New York

Petit, J., Jouzel, J., Raynaud, D., Barkov, N., Barnola, J., Basile, I., Bender, M., Chappellaz, J., Davis, M., Delayque, G., Delmotte, M., Kotlyakov, V., Legrand, M., Lipenkov, V., Lorius, C., Pépin, L., Ritz, C., Saltzman, E. and Stievenard, M. (1999) 'Climate and Atmospheric History of the Past 420,000 years from the Vostok Ice Core, Antarctica', *Nature*, 399, pp429–436

Pfeffer, J. (1998) *The Human Equation: Building Profits by Putting People First*, Harvard Business School Press, Boston

Pigou, A. (1932) *The Economics of Welfare*, 4th Edition, Macmillan, London

Pikora, T. and Miller, M. (2001) *Promoting Active Transport: An Intervention Portfolio to Increase Physical Activity as a Means of Transport*, National Public Health Partnership, Melbourne

Pine, J. and Gilmore, J. (1998) 'Welcome to the Experience Economy', *Harvard Business Review*, July–August

Porter, M. E. (1985) *Competitive Advantage: Creating and Sustaining Superior Performance*, Free Press, New York and London

Porter, M. (1990) *The Competitive Advantage of Nations*, The Free Press, New York (reprinted in 1998)

Porter, M. (1991) 'Green Competitiveness', *Scientific American*, 5 April

Porter, M. (1995) CIO, magazine interview, 1 October (cio.com)

Porter, M. (1996) 'What is Strategy', *Harvard Business Review*, November–December

Porter, M. and van der Linde, C. (1995a) 'Green and Competitive: Ending the Stalemate', *Harvard Business Review*, September–October, pp121–134

Porter, M. and van der Linde, C. (1995b) 'Toward a New Conception of the Environment–Competitiveness Relationship', *Journal of Economic Perspectives*, vol IX-4, Fall, pp97–118

Postel, S. (1984) *Water: Rethinking Management in Age of Scarcity*, Worldwatch Paper 62, Worldwatch Institute, Washington, DC

Postel, S. (1999) *Pillar of Sand: Can the Irrigation Miracle Last?*, Environmental Alert Series, CSIRO, Australian Conservation Foundation

Prasad, E., Rogoff, K. , Wei, S.-J. and Kose, M.A. (2003) *Effects of Financial Globalization on Developing Countries: Some Empirical Evidence*, 17 March, International Monetary Fund, Washington, DC

Price, T. (2002) *The Canary is Drowning: Tiny Tuvalu Fights Back Against Climate Change*, Tom Price CorpWatch, New York

Price Waterhouse Coopers (2002) *Innovation in the Australian Building and Construction Industry: Survey Report*, prepared for the Australian Construction Industry Forum and the Department of Industry, Tourism and Resources, March

Princen, T. (2001) 'Consumer Society Review', *Journal of Industrial Ecology*, vol 5

Pucher, J. and Dijkstra, L. (2000) 'Making Walking and Cycling Safer, Lessons from Europe', *Transportation Quarterly*, vol 54, no 3, pp25–50

Putnam, R. (1995) 'Bowling Alone', *Journal of Democracy*, vol 6, no 1, January, pp65–78

Putnam, R. (2001) *Bowling Alone: The Collapse and Revival of American Community*, Touchstone Books, New York

Putnam, R., Lonardi, R., Raffaella, Y. and Nanetti, R. (1994) *Making Democracy Work: Civic Traditions in Modern Italy*, Princeton University Press

Rappaport, A. (1986) *Creating Shareholder Value: The New Standard for Business Performance*, The Free Press, A Division of Macmillan, New York

Rasagan, G. (1999) 'A "STEP" Towards Sustainable Transport: A Case Study of Penang, Malaysia', *Transport and Communications Bulletin for Asia and the Pacific*, vol 68, pp33–48

Raskin, P., Hansen, E. and Margolis, R. (1996) 'Water and Sustainability, Global Patterns and Long-Range Problems', *Natural Resources Forum*, vol 20, no 1, pp1–17

Raskin, P., Banuri, T., Gallopin, G., Gutman, P., Hammond, A., Kates, R. and Swart, R. (2002) *Great Transition The Promise and Lure of the Times Ahead: A Report of the Global Scenario Group*, Stockholm Environment Institute

Ray, D. (1998) *Development Economics*, Princeton University Press

Riedy, C. (2003) *Subsidies that Encourage Fossil Fuel Use in Australia*, Working Paper CR 2003/01, Institute for Sustainable Futures, UTS, Sydney

Rifkin, J. (2002) *The Hydrogen Economy*, Tarcher/Putnam, New York City

Road and Traffic Authority (1999) *Action for Bikes: Bike Plan 2010*, NSW Government, Sydney

Roaf, S., Fuentes, M. and Thomas, S. (2003) *Ecohouse 2: A Design Guide*, Architectural Press, Elsevier, Oxford UK

Robinson, B. (2002) *Global Oil Vulnerability and the Australian Situation*, Issues and Background Paper for the Western Australia State Sustainability Strategy, Government of Western Australia

Robinson, S. (2001) 'Looking Beyond the Bunker', *Chemistry and Industry Journal*, 5 November, pp688–689

Rodrik, D. (1998) 'Who Needs Capital Account Convertibility?', paper prepared for the 1998 Princeton International Finance Section Symposium

Rogers, E. (1995) *Diffusion of Innovations*, The Free Press, New York

Romer, P. (1993) 'Economic Growth', in Henderson, D. R. (ed) *The Fortune Encyclopedia of Economics*, Warner Books

Romer, P. (1994) 'From Beyond Classical and Keynesian Macroeconomic Policy', *Policy Options*, July–August

Romer, P. (1997) 'Beyond Classical and Keynesian Macroeconomic Policy', from a presentation at the Hotel InterContinental, London

Romm, J. (1999) *Cool Companies: How the Best Businesses Boost Profits and Productivity by Cutting Greenhouse-Gas Emissions*, Island Press, Washington, DC

Romm, R. and Browning, W. (1994) *Greening the Building and the Bottom Line: Increasing Productivity Through Energy-Efficient Design*, Rocky Mountain Institute, Colorado

Roodman, D. (1999) *The Natural Wealth of Nations: Harnessing the Market and the Environment*, Worldwatch Environment Alert Series, WW Norton, New York/Earthscan, London

Roodman, D. and Lenssen, N. (1995) *A Building Revolution: How Ecology and Health Concerns Are Transforming Construction*, Worldwatch Paper 124, Worldwatch Institute, Washington, DC

Roseland, M. (1998) *Toward Sustainable Communities*, New Society Publishers, Gabriola Island, BC, Canada

Rothschild, M. and Stiglitz, J. (1976) 'Equilibrium in Competitive Insurance Markets: An Essay on the Economics of Imperfect Information', *Quarterly Journal of Economics*, vol 90, no 4

Rothwell, R. (1993) 'The Fifth Generation Innovation Process', in Oppenländer, K. and Popp W. (eds) *Privates und Staatliches Innovationsmanagement*, Ifo-Institut für Wirtschaftsforschung, Munich, pp25–42

Rowlands, I. (1995) *The Politics of Global Atmospheric Change*, Manchester University Press

Rudasingwa, T. and Donahue, N. (2004) 'Context and Prospects of Nation Building: How Business Strategy is Transforming Rwanda', *Fletcher Forum of World Affairs*, vol 28, no 1

Rukato, H. and Osborn, D. (2001) 'Count Us In, Count On Us', Co-Chairs Summary, UNED Forum International Workshop on Multi-stakeholder Processes, New York, 28–29 April

Ryan, C. (2002) 'EcoLab: A Jump Towards Sustainability', *Journal of Industrial Ecology*, vol 5, no 3

Ryan, C. (2004) *The Digital and Sustainability: Realising an Innovative Potential*, Lab Report 02, Melbourne

Sachs, J. and Warner, A. (1995) *Natural Resource Abundance and Economic Growth*, National Bureau of Economic Research, Cambridge, MA

Saio, K., Kokubu, K., Nashioka, E. and Imai, S. (2002) *Current Status and Issues of Environmental Accounting Practices*, Institute of Global Environment and Society (IGES) Discussion Paper No 2 (in Japanese), IGES, Japan

Sathaye, J. and Moyers, S. (1995) *Greenhouse Gas Mitigation Assessment: A Guidebook*, Kluwer Academic

SAVE (2000) *Toolbox for Mobility Management in Companies*, European Union, Brussels

Schafer, H. and Stederoth, R. (2002) 'Portfolioselekton und Anlagepolitik mittels Ethikfilters: Ein Uberblick zum Stand der Empirischen Kapitalmarktforschung', *Kredit und Kapital 35*, Jahrgang, Heft 1, S, pp101–148

Schaltegger, S. and Burritt, R. (2000) *Contemporary Environmental Accounting: Issues, Concepts and Practice*, Greenleaf Publishing, Sheffield, UK

Schaltegger, S., Hahn, T. and Burritt, R. (2000) 'Environmental Management Accounting: Overview and Main Approaches', in Bennett, M. and Bouma, J. (eds), *Environmental Management Accounting and the Role of Information Systems*, Kluwer Academic

Schmidheiny, S. (1992) *Changing Course: A Global Perspective on Development and the Environment*, The MIT Press, Boston, MA

Schwartz, P. and Randall, D. (2003) *An Abrupt Climate Change Scenario and Its Implications for United States National Security*, October 2003, a report commissioned by the US Defense Department

Segerson, K. (1999) *The Efficiency of Voluntary Approaches*, Presentation at European Research Network on Voluntary Approaches (CAVA) Workshop, Copenhagen, Denmark

Segerson, K. and Miceli, T. (1998) 'Voluntary Environmental Agreements: Good or Bad News for Environmental Protection?', *Journal of Environmental Economics & Management*, vol 36, no 2, pp109–130

Sen, A. (1996) 'The Concept of Wealth', in Myers, R. (ed) *The Wealth of Nations in the Twentieth Century: The Policies and Institutional Determinants of Economic Development*, Hoover Press, Stanford University Stanford, California

Serageldin, I. and Dasgupta, P. (1997) *Social Capital: Integrating the Economist's and Sociologist's Perspective*, World Bank, New York

Shapiro, C. and Stiglitz, J. (1984) 'Equilibrium Unemployment as a Worker Discipline Device', *American Economic Review*, vol 74, no 3

Sheehy, B. and Dickie, P. (2002) 'Facing the Future', Australian submission to the Report of the Mining Minerals and Sustainable Development (MMSD) Project *Breaking New Ground*, MMSD/Earthscan, London

Shell International (2001) *Energy Needs, Choices and Possibilities, Scenarios to 2050*, Global Business Enviroment

Simpson, V. (2003) *Climate Change and the Pacific*, Australian Conservation Foundation

Sinclair Knight Merz (2001) *Portland Wind Energy Project Environmental Effects Statement and Planning Assessment Report: Summary Document*, Sinclair Knight Merz

Singh, S. (2004) 'Delhi Metro Blazes a Trail of Profit', *India Times*, 4 February

Smith, A. (1999) *An Inquiry into the Nature and Causes of the Wealth of Nations*, Penguin, London

Smith, B. (2003) *Principles of MacroEconomic Analysis*, Australian National University, Australia

Smith, D. (2000) *Asian Development Bank Sustainable Development in Asia Report*, Asia Development Bank, Manila

Solow, R. (1986) 'On the Intergenerational Allocation of Natural Resources', *Scandinavian Journal of Economics*, vol 88, no 1, pp141–149

Solow, R. (1992) *An Almost Practical Step Towards Sustainability*, Invited Lecture, Resources for the Future, Washington, DC

Sonnenfeld, J.A (2004) 'A Return to the Power of Ideas', MIT *Sloan Management Review*, Winter, vol 45, no 2, pp30–33

Sowell, T. (1998) *Conquests and Cultures*, Basic Books, New York

Spaargaren, G. and van Vliet, B. (2000) 'Lifestyles, Consumption and the Environment: The Ecological Modernization of Domestic Consumption', *Environmental Politics*, vol 9, no 1, pp50–76

Speers, A., Booker, N., Burn, S., Gray, S., Priestly, T. and Zappou, C. (2001) *Sustainable Urban Water-Analysis of the Opportunities*, CSIRO, IWRA's 6th National Water Conference, Melbourne, Australia

Stanley, S. (2000) 'The Past Climate Change Heats Up', *National Academies of Science of the USA Editorial*, vol 97, issue 4, 15 February, pp1319–1319

Stein, J. P. (2000) 'Are Decision Makers too Cautious with the Precautionary Principle?', *Environmental and Planning Law Journal*, vol 17, pp3–24

Stephenson, J., Bauman, A., Armstrong, T., Smith, B. and Bellew, B. (2000) *The Cost of Illness Attributable to Physical Inactivity in Australia: A preliminary study*, Commonwealth Department of Health and Aged Care and the Australian Sports Commission, Canberra

Stiglitz, J. (1994) *Whither Socialism?*, MIT Press, Cambridge MA

Stiglitz, J. (1999) *Must Currency Crises be this Frequent and this Painful?* In Agenor, P., Miller, D., Vines and Weber, A. (eds) *The Asian Financial Crisis: Causes, Contagion and Consequences*, Cambridge University Press, Cambridge

Stiglitz, J. (2002) *Globalization and its Discontents*, Allen Lane, London

Stiglitz, J. (2003) *The Roaring Nineties: A New History of the World's Most Prosperous Decade*, Allen Lane, London

Stiglitz, J. and Weiss, A. (1981) 'Credit Rationing in Markets with Imperfect Information', *American Economic Review*, vol 71

Stocker, L. and Burke, G. (2000) *A View from the Bridge* (Video), Production Function, Perth

Suter, K. (1995) *Global Agenda*, Albatross, Sydney

Sutton, P. (2000) 'Is it Possible for a Green Economy to have High Economic Performance?' Green Innovations, Melbourne (www.green-innovations.asn.au/econ-mdl.htm)

Sutton, P. (2004) 'The Race to Sustainability', Green Innovations, Melbourne (www.green-innovations.asn.au/Race-to-Sustainability.htm)

Suzuki, D. and Dressel, H. (2002) *Good News For A Change: Hope For A Troubled Planet*, Allen & Unwin, Sydney

Tainter, J. (1988) *The Collapse of Complex Societies*, Cambridge University Press, Cambridge

Teece, D. (1990) 'Contributions and Impediments of Economic Analysis to the Study of Strategic Management', in Fredrickson, J. (ed) *Perspectives on Strategic Management*, Harper Business, New York

Thailand Environment Institute (1999) *How Can It Benefit Business? A Survey of ISO 14001 Certified Companies in Thailand*, Thailand Environment Institute, Bangkok

Thomas, I. (2004) 'Sustainability in Tertiary Curricula: What is Stopping it Happening?', *International Journal of Sustainability in Higher Education*, vol 5, no 1, 23 January, pp33–47

Tilbury, D. (2003) 'Environmental Education for Sustainability: A Force for Change in Higher Education', in Wals, A. and Cocoran Blaze, P., *Higher Education and the Challenge of Sustainability*, Kluwer, London

Tindale, S. and Holtham, G. (1996) *Green Tax Reform: Pollution Payments and Labor Tax Cuts*, Institute for Public Policy Research, London

Tischner, U., Schmincke E., Rubik, F. and Prösler, M. (2000) *How to do Ecodesign?*, Verlag Form Praxis, Frankfurt

Transport For London (2003) *Congestion Charging 6 Months On*, Transport For London, London

Transport SA (2002) *Adelaide Travel Patterns: An Overview, Research Summary* TP-02/8, Government of South Australia, Adelaide

Tuluca, A. (ed) (1997) *Energy Efficient Design and Construction for Commercial Buildings*, McGraw-Hill, New York

Turton, H., Ma, J., Saddler, H. and Hamilton, C. (2002) *Long-Term Greenhouse Gas Scenarios A Pilot Study of How Australia can Achieve Deep Cuts in Emissions*, The Australia Institute No 48

UN-HABITAT (United Nations Human Settlements Programme) (2002) *Best-practices Database*, UN-HABITAT, Nairobi

UN/WWAP (United Nations/World Water Assessment Programme) (2003) *UN World Water Development Report: Water for People*, UN/WWAP, Water for Life, UNESCO and Berghahn Books, Paris, New York and Oxford

UNCED (United Nations Conference on Environment and Development) (1992a) *Agenda 21: United Nations Conference on the Environment and Development*, UNCED

UNCED (1992b) *Rio Declaration on Environment and Development*, United Nations Conference on Environment and Development – The Earth Summit, Rio de Janeiro, United Nations Environment Programme/Commission for Sustainable Development, New York

UNCED (1992) 'Local Agenda 21', in UNCED *Agenda 21*, UNCED/Commission for Sustainable Development, New York, Chapter 28

UNDP (United Nations Development Programme) (1998) *Human Development Report*, UNDP/Oxford University Press, New York

UNDP (2001) *Human Development Report: Making New Technologies Work For Human Development*, UNDP, New York

UNDP (2003) *Human Development Report: The Millennium Development Goals. A Compact Among Nations to End Human Poverty*, UNDP, New York

UNEP (United Nations Environment Programme) (1998) *Voluntary Industry Codes of Conduct for the Environment*, Technical Report 40, Industry and Environment, UNEP, Paris

UNEP (2000) *Consumer Trends and Expectations: An International Survey Focusing on Environmental Impacts* by Matthew D Bentley, in UNEP, *Industry and Environment Review: Sustainable Mobility*, UNEP, Paris

UNEP (2001) *The Role of Product Service Systems in a Sustainable Society*, UNEP, Paris

UNEP (2002a) *Product Service Systems and Sustainability: Opportunities for Sustainable Solutions*, UNEP, Paris

UNEP (2002b) *Sustainable Consumption: Global Status Report 2002*, UNEP, Paris (report written by Professor Chris Ryan, RMIT University, Melbourne, Australia, and the International Institute for Industrial Environmental Economics (IIIEE), Lund University, Sweden)

UNEP and Consumers International (2001) *Towards Sustainable Consumption in Asia and the Pacific: Background Paper*, Workshop on Sustainable Consumption for Asia & the Pacific, Kuala Lumpur, Malaysia, UNEP

UNEP, WBCSD and the WRI (2002) *Tomorrow's Markets: Global Trends and Their Implications for Business*, Earthprint, Washington, DC

UNESCO (United Nations Educational, Scientific and Cultural Organization) (1997a) *Educating For a Sustainable Future: A Trans-disciplinary Vision For Concerted Action*, UNESCO, International Conference Tessaloniki, 8–12 December

UNESCO (1997b) *Environment and Society: Education and Public Awareness for Sustainability*, November, UNESCO, Paris

United Nations (1992) *Agenda 21: The UN Programme of Action from Rio*, United Nations, New York

United Nations (2000) *World Urbanization Prospects: The 1999 Revision*, UN, New York

US Department of Energy (2002a) *A National Vision of America's Transition to a Hydrogen Economy: To 2030 and Beyond*, US Department of Energy

US Department of Energy (2002b) *Annual Energy Outlook 2002*, US Department of Energy, Washington, DC

US National Academies of Science (2000) *Abrupt Climate Change: Inevitable Surprises*, National Academies Press, Washington, DC

USAID (United States Agency for International Development) (2002) 'Field Report: East Timor – April 2002. Joint Report between Office of Transition Initiatives (OTI) and USAID/East Timor Mission', USAID, Bureau for Democracy, Conflict and Humanitarian Assistance, OTI, Washington, DC (www.usaid.gov/hum_response/oti/country/timor/rpt0400.html)

USGCRP (US Global Change Research Program) (1998) *Origin, Incidence, and Implications of Amazon Fires*, USGCRP Seminar, 30 March

van der Ryn, S. and Cowan, S. (1996) *Ecological Design*, Island Press, Washington, DC

Vine, E., Hamrin, J., Eyre, N., Crossley, D., Maloney, M. and Watt, G. (2003) 'Public Policy Analysis of Energy Efficiency and Load Management in Changing Electricity Businesses', *Energy Policy*, vol 31, pp405–30

Vogel, D. (1995) *Trading Up: Consumer and Environmental Regulation in a Global Economy*, Harvard University Press

von Weizsäcker, E. and Jessinghaus, J. (1992) *Ecological Tax Reform: A Policy Proposal for Sustainable Development*, Zed Books, London

von Weizsäcker, E., Lovins, A. and Lovins, L. H. (1997) *Factor Four: Doubling Wealth, Halving Resource Use*, Earthscan, London

Wackernagel, M. (2000) *Carrying Capacity, Overshoot and the Need to Curb Human Consumption*, Royal Society, London

Wade, R. (2000) *Governing the Market a Decade Later*, London School of Economics Development Studies Institute Working Paper No 00-03, London School of Economics, London

Walters, C. (1986) *Adaptive Management of Renewable Resources*, Macmillan, New York

Warman, B. (2001) *Cars: Where are They Taking Us?* Charter Keck Crammer, Richmond, Victoria

Warren Centre (2002) *Community Values Research Report* (Executive Summary), Sydney University Press, Sydney

Watt, M. and Outhred, H. (1999) *Electricity Industry Sustainability: Policy Options*, Australian Centre for Renewable Energy

Watts, R. (1997) *Engineering Response to Global Climate Change*, Lewis Publishers, New York

WBCSD (World Business Council for Sustainable Development) (1992) *Changing Course: A Global Perspective on Development and the Environment*, MIT Press, Boston

WBCSD (1997) *Exploring Sustainable Development: Global Scenarios 2000–2050*, WBCSD, London

WBCSD (2001a) *Sustainability Through the Market*, WBCSD, Geneva

WBCSD (2001b) *The Business Case for Sustainable Development*, WBCSD, Geneva

WBCSD (2001c) *Sustainable Mobility Project*, WBCSD, Geneva

Weale, A. (1992) *The New Politics of Pollution*, Manchester University Press

Weaver, P. (1994) *Bridging Gaps Among Scientific Disciplines*, CP-94-8, IIASA, Austria

Weaver, P. (2002a) *Defining Science for Sustainable Development*, Deliverable 2, AIRP-SD Project, EC-STRATA Program, also as an Interim Paper, Greenleaf Publishing, Sheffield, UK

Weaver, P. (2002b) *Evaluating Science for Sustainable Development*, Deliverable 3, AIRP-SD Project, EC-STRATA Program, also as an Interim Paper, Greenleaf Publishing, Sheffield, UK

Weaver, P. (2003) 'Defining and Evaluating Sustainability Science', paper prepared for the Easy-Eco Conference, Vienna, May

Weaver, P. and Jansen, J. (2002) *National Research Activities and Sustainable Development: A Survey and Assessment of National Research Initiatives in Support of Sustainable Development – Country Report for the Netherlands*, Report of the European Science and Technology Observatory, Institute for Prospective Technological Studies (IPTS), Seville, Spain

Weaver, P., Jansen, J., van Grootveld, G., van Spiegel, E. and Vergragt, P. (2000) *Sustainable Technology Development*, Greenleaf Publishing, Sheffield, UK

WEC (World Energy Council) (1998) *Industry's Technical Initiatives Towards Climate Change Mitigation*, WEC, London

Weibull, J. W. (1995) *Evolutionary Game Theory*, MIT Press, Cambridge, MA

Wentworth Group of Concerned Scientists (2002) *Blueprint for a Living Continent: A Way Forward*, Wentworth Group of Concerned Scientists, World Wide Fund for Nature

Weterings, R. and Opschoor, J. (1992) *The Eco-Capacity as a Challenge to Technology Development*, Advisory Council on Nature and the Environment (RMNO) Report No 74 A, Rijswijk, Netherlands

Weyant, J. (2000) *An Introduction to the Economics of Climate Change Policy*, prepared for the Pew Center on Global Climate Change, Stanford University, July

Wheeler, D. and Mody, A. (1992) 'International Investment Location Decisions: The Case of US Firms', *Journal of International Economics* August, pp57–76

Wheeler, D. and Sillanpaa, M. (1997) *The Stakeholder Corporation: The Body Shop Blueprint for Maximizing Stakeholder Value*, Pitman Publishing, London

Whitelegg, K., Weber, M. and Leone, F. (2002) 'National Research Activities and Sustainable Development', Research Report EUR 20389 EN, Vienna, Sevilla: ARC/JRC-IPTS

Whittaker, S. (1995) *Case Studies of Local Agenda 21*, Local Government Management Training Board, London

Whittaker, S. (1996a) 'Are Local Councils "Willing and Able" to Implement Local Agenda 21? A Study of Local Government in Australia', keynote paper, Environs Australia National Conference, Sydney, November

Whittaker, S. (1996b) 'Local Agenda 21: The UK Experience', *Local Environs*, vol 7, no 2

WHO (World Health Organisation) (2000) *Fact Sheet No 187: Air Pollution*, Fact Sheets, WHO

Wilkinson, A., Hill, M. and Gollan, P. (2001) 'The Sustainability Debate', *International Journal of Operations and Production Management*, vol 21, no 12, pp1492–1502

Willard, B. (2002) *The Sustainability Advantage: Seven Business Case Benefits of a Triple Bottom Line*, New Society, Gabriola Island, Canada

Williams, R. (1996) *Fuel De-Carbonization for Fuel Cell Applications and Sequestration of the Separated* CO_2, Princeton University Center for Energy and Environmental Studies January, Research Report No 295, Princeton

Wilson, A., Uncapher, J., McManigal, L., Lovins, L. H., Cureton, M. and Browning, W. (1998) *Green Development: Integrating Ecology and Real Estate*, Rocky Mountain Institute/John Wiley & Sons

Womack, J. and Jones, D. (1996) *Lean Thinking: Banish Waste and Create Wealth in Your Corporation*, Touchstone & Design, New York

World Bank (1997) *World Bank Development Report 1997: The State in a Changing World*, Oxford University Press, Oxford

World Bank (2000) *World Bank Development Report 2000: Attacking Poverty*, Oxford University Press, Oxford

World Bank (2003) *World Bank Development Report 2003: Sustainable Development in a Dynamic World*, Oxford University Press, Oxford

World Commission on Dams (2000) *Dams and Development: A New Framework for Decision-making*, The Report of the World Commission on Dams, Earthscan, London

Worldwatch Institute (2003) *State of the World 2003*, WW Norton, New York/Earthscan, London

WRI (World Resources Institute) (2000) *World Resources: People and Ecosystems: The Fraying Web of Life*, WRI, Washington, DC

Wright, L. (2002) *Sustainable Transport: A Sourcebook for Policy-makers in Developing Countries: Module 3b Bus Rapid Transport*, Deutsche Gesellschaft für Technische Zusammenarbeit, Eschborn

WWF (World Wildlife Fund) (1998) *Consumption Pressures*, WWF, Gland, Switzerland

Yashayaev, I. (2004) *Abrupt Climate Change, Inevitable Surprises*, National Research Council, Bedford Institute of Oceanography

Yilmaz, Y. (1998) *Private Regulation, A Real Alternative for Regulatory Reform*, Cato Policy Analysis no 303, 20 April

Young, M. and McColl, J. (2002) *Robust Separation: A Search for a Generic Framework to Simplify Registration and Trading of Interests in Natural Resources*, CSIRO Land and Water, Adelaide

Young, M., Young, D., Hamilton, A. and Bright, M. (2002) *A Preliminary Assessment of the Economic and Social Implications of Environmental Flow Scenarios for the River Murray System*, report prepared for Murray Darling Basin Commission, Policy and Economic Research Unit, Canberra

Zadek, S. and Raynard, P. (2002) 'Stakeholder Engagement: Measuring and Communicating Quality', *Accountability Quarterly*, vol 19, December

INDEX

Page numbers in **bold** refer to Figures and Tables